PATIENT-CENTERED CARE

A MODEL FOR RESTRUCTURING

Mickey L. Parsons, RN, MN, MHA
University Medical Center
Tucson, Arizona

and

Carolyn L. Murdaugh, RN, PhD, FAAN
National Institute of Nursing Research
Bethesda, Maryland

AN ASPEN PUBLICATION®
Aspen Publishers, Inc.
Gaithersburg, Maryland
1994

Library of Congress Cataloging-in-Publication Data

Patient-centered care : a model for restructuring / [edited by] Mickey L. Parsons and Carolyn L. Murdaugh.
p. cm.
Includes bibliographical references and index.
ISBN 0-8342-0573-4
1. Hospitals—Administration. 2. Organizational change. 3. Academic medical centers—Administration—Case studies. I. Parsons, Mickey L. II. Murdaugh, Carolyn L.
[DNLM: 1. Hospital Units—organization & administration. 2. Quality Assurance, Health Care—organization & administration—United States. 3. Nursing Care—organization & administration. 4. Patient Satisfaction. 5. Patient Care Team—organization & administration. 6. Cost Control. 7. Models, Organizational. WX 200 P298 1994]
RA971.P288 1994
362.1'1'068—dc20
DNLM/DLC
for Library of Congress
94-127
CIP

Editorial Resources: Jane Colilla

Library of Congress Catalog Card Number: 94-127
Casebound: ISBN: 0-8342-0573-4
Paperback : ISBN: 0-8342-0983-7

Printed in the United States of America

1 2 3 4 5

To all UMC staff members who
accepted the risks
to implement what,
at first, looked like heresy.

Contents

Contributors

Kathe Barry, BSN, RN
Unit Coordinator, Patient Care Restructuring Project
University Medical Center
Tucson, Arizona

Robert Black, MPA
Vice President, Human Resources
University Medical Center
Tucson, Arizona

Suzan Bohnenkamp, BSN, RN
Nurse Case Manager
University Medical Center
Tucson, Arizona

Joe Bojorquez, BSN, RN
Nurse Manager
University Medical Center
Tucson, Arizona

Denise Dillon Brice, MS
Manager, Research and Evaluation
University Medical Center
Tucson, Arizona

Tim Brown, MBA, RRT
Director, Cardio Pulmonary Services
University Medical Center
Tucson, Arizona

Katherine K. Duncan, MS, RD
Associate Director, Food and Nutrition Services
University Medical Center
Tucson, Arizona

John F. Duval, MBA
Vice President
University Medical Center
Tucson, Arizona

Marty G. Enriquez, MS, RN
Director, Women and Children's Services
University Medical Center
Tucson, Arizona

Alicia Eyherabide, MS, RN, CS, CCRN
Nurse Manager
University Medical Center
Tucson, Arizona

Valerie J. Evans, BS, CLS(NCA), MT(ASCP)SH
Associate Director, Department of Pathology
University Medical Center
Tucson, Arizona

Rose M. Gerber, PhD, RN
Associate Professor
University of Arizona College of Nursing
Tucson, Arizona

Ken Gilbert, BS
Director, Environmental Services
University Medical Center
Tucson, Arizona

Theresa Grzyb-Wysocki, MS, MA, RN
Director, Adult Health Services
University Medical Center
Tucson, Arizona

Stephanie Higie, MS, RN
Director, Emergency Services
University Medical Center
Tucson, Arizona

Sandy Kurtin, MS, RN, OCN
Oncology Clinical Nurse Specialist
University Medical Center
Tucson, Arizona

Betsy Lindsey, BS, PT
Assistant Manager, Physical Therapy Department
University Medical Center
Tucson, Arizona

Michael Lortie, BS, MGA
Director of Materials and Clinical Engineering
University Medical Center
Tucson, Arizona

John C. Mahn
Associate Director, Environmental Services
University Medical Center
Tucson, Arizona

Joseph Maltos
Sterile Processing Supervisor, Materials Management
University Medical Center
Tucson, Arizona

George A. Martinez, BA
Director of Community
Tucson Unified School District
Tucson, Arizona

Juanita McDonough, BSN, RN
Education Coordinator
University Medical Center
Tucson, Arizona

Pat McGee, RNC
Nurse Manager
University Medical Center
Tucson, Arizona

Doris A. Milton, PhD, RN
Director, Nursing Research
Samaritan Health System
Phoenix, Arizona

Kelly Morgan, BA, RN, CEN
Nurse Manager
University Medical Center
Tucson, Arizona

Carolyn L. Murdaugh, PhD, RN, FAAN
Nurse Scientist
National Institute of Nursing Research
National Institutes of Health
Bethesda, Maryland

Lisa Sinclair Olson, BS
Senior Accountant, Financial Services
University Medical Center
Tucson, Arizona

Beth Orenduff, MS, RN
Employment Manager
University Medical Center
Tucson, Arizona

Josephine Sacco Palmer, MS, RN, PNP
Program Manager, Patient Care Restructuring Project
University Medical Center
Tucson, Arizona

Mickey L. Parsons, MN, MHA, RN
Vice President
University Medical Center
Tucson, Arizona

Lora Pirzynski, BS, OTR
Manager, Occupational Therapy Department
University Medical Center
Tucson, Arizona

Alice Pollard, RD, LD, DHCFA
Director, Food and Nutrition Services
University Medical Center
Tucson, Arizona

Sally Poore, MEd
Manager, Human Resource Development
University Medical Center
Tucson, Arizona

Jim Richardson, JD
Assistant Vice President
Legal/Risk Management
University Medical Center
Tucson, Arizona

Pam Sapienza, BSN, MBA
Vice President
University Medical Center
Tucson, Arizona

JoAnne Schnepp, BSN, RN, CNA
Nurse Manager
University Medical Center
Tucson, Arizona

Leigh Shaffer, MS, RN
Director, Nursing Resources
University Medical Center
Tucson, Arizona

J. Verne Singleton, MSPH
Senior Vice President
University Medical Center
Tucson, Arizona

Carol Stumpf, BS, PT
Manager, Physical Therapy Department
University Medical Center
Tucson, Arizona

Joyce A. Verran, PhD, RN, FAAN
Professor and Division Director, Adult Health Nursing
University of Arizona College of Nursing
Tucson, Arizona

Foreword

Patient-Centered Care: A Model for Restructuring deals with a key success factor for all health providers—how to deliver high quality patient care while minimizing expense and maximizing patient satisfaction. Our health care delivery system is seriously flawed, suffering from escalating costs, variable quality, increasing bureaucracy, and a lack of access. Maintaining the status quo is no longer an option and most providers acknowledge that substantial improvement is required in order to provide a viable health care system in the future.

This transformation necessitates fundamental structural change in the mechanisms of delivering health services. We are shifting from managing illness to managing the health status of the patient. The focus of care is shifting from the hospital to primary care and a network of providers. The traditional, episodic, fee-for-service model will not survive. Instead, the new model must be an integrated, price-sensitive system, oriented toward delivering value and maintaining the health of enrolled populations under capitated arrangements.

It is within this new setting that this book takes on significant importance. *Patient-Centered Care: A Model for Restructuring* demonstrates the value large scale institutional change initiatives have on improving patient satisfaction, increasing or maintaining quality, and reducing expenses. Its focus on restructuring patient care is comprehensive, extending from planning through implementation, evaluation, and future planning. It is an application-based book with excellent unit case studies and serves as a comprehensive how-to guide to patient care restructuring.

The authors challenge managers and providers to re-examine how care is delivered. Rules of the past must be reconciled with the emerging needs and requirements of the future. They posit that the key success factors in a restructured environment are interdisciplinary team management and shared values of excellence. They stress the importance of education, communication, management development, and managing the change process.

Academic health centers are uniquely positioned to develop creative approaches to the patient care delivery process. Along with patient care, the education and research missions are fundamental to this environment and support innovation and creativity. This book is an excellent example of the kind of research and evaluation we are seeing in many academic centers across the country. It is efforts such as these that demonstrate the vital role academic centers play in developing new models for the delivery of patient care.

Robert J. Baker
President, University Hospital Consortium
Oak Brook, Illinois

Preface

Operational restructuring is the current topic in hospitals. Information on patient care restructuring is vital to the health care industry, as hospitals are required to provide outstanding quality of care and service while controlling costs. *Patient-Centered Care: A Model for Restructuring*, is one of the first, if not the first, comprehensive book that reports on one hospital's, University Medical Center (UMC), experience in implementing hospital-wide patient care restructuring. This multidisciplinary book describes large scale institutional change that crosses the traditional boundaries of ancillary, support, and nursing functions.

Part 1 of the book describes the planning and implementation process. The need to move away from the traditional bureaucratic, fragmented, and compartmentalized structure of care is discussed. Chapters 1 and 2 outline the rationale for change and describe the patient-centered model at UMC. Chapter 3 provides an overview of the University of Arizona College of Nursing Differentiated Group Professional Practice in Nursing Grant, which served to stimulate new ideas for restructuring. The planning and change process is reported in detail in Chapter 4. The role of the project coordinator for planning and implementing an innovative project is discussed in Chapter 5. Chapters 6 and 7 provide the reader with specific curriculum planning and programs for multipurpose support and technical workers. The educational preparation for registered nurses for professional practice is reported in Chapters 8 and 9. Human resource professionals will be particularly interested in Chapters 10 through 12, as personnel issues in restructuring are discussed, including personnel involvement in the employment process, and the training and developmental issues of team building. The implementation of participative management and group governance is discussed in Chapter 13, and unit management restructuring is described in Chapter 14. The comprehensive recognition and awards program to support the major change is described in Chapter 15. No plan is complete without a viable financial plan, which is detailed in Chapter 16. The communication plan is reported in the last chapter of this section. Communication, both internal and external to the organization, is the most important key to building success by preventing and/or diffusing obstacles to the restructuring process.

Part II provides unit case studies from staff members who have been involved in planning and implementing the restructuring project from the beginning. Pediatric, medical-surgical, medical-surgical intermediate care, postpartum and newborn nursery, and the emergency department staff members share their experiences. These chapters represent true stories from the field.

Part III reports the quality control and operational aspects of the project. Quality control standards for decentralized services are essential for long-term success. Each chapter outlines the requirements for restructuring from ancillary and support service perspectives. Experience with eleven inpatient units restructured to date is reported in Chapter 27.

Part IV narrates the evaluation of the patient-centered model before and after restructuring. The evaluation plan is outlined in Chapter 28. In Chapter 29 the patient satisfaction results are reported. The results of labor cost savings are described in Chapter 30, and staff and physician satisfaction are described in Chapters 31 and 32, respectively. Our initial experience in beginning to evaluate quality of care with outcomes other than patient satisfaction are discussed in Chapter 33.

Part V provides an overview of the next generation of restructuring at UMC. The labor and delivery model is discussed in Chapter 34. Future opportunities in professional ancillary services are described in Chapter 35, while the future is forecast in Chapter 36.

This information is shared so that future pioneers may learn from our positive experiences as well as from our mistakes. Professionals in every practice area—administration, nursing, human resources, rehabilitation, cardiology, respiratory care, dietary, environmental services, materials management, laboratories, finance, and other administrative support services—will be able to utilize this information to plan and implement restructuring projects in their own facilities. Academics involved in health services, administration, and research will be interested in the redesign and evaluation process. Clinical educators will find information to better prepare practitioners for tomorrow's ever changing patient care environment. We wish you the best in your own restructuring endeavors and hope you find the adventure as challenging and rewarding as we have.

Acknowledgments

First and foremost, special thanks to Keith J. Waterbrook, President and CEO of UMC, and the Board of Directors for their support of the restructuring process and of this publication. The hospital and nursing administrative staff members are pathfinders and deserve special recognition. Without all of them, none of this would have been possible.

Special recognition is due Carmen Warner, our special editor and coach. She enabled the dream to become a reality by her publication experience, editorial expertise, and cheerleading. Without her facilitation this book would not have been possible.

Special recognition is also due to Sheila Baker, Executive Secretary, whose organizational skills and able assistance made this book a reality. The forty contributors to the book and their staff members all worked unselfishly both for the restructuring effort and to write their chapters. They are indeed the real pioneers.

The families of all the contributors deserve special thanks for allowing their loved ones the extra time for this project. It has not all been easy, and their understanding and patience made the difference. To Mickey's daughter, Paige, You're the best; thanks for helping!

Mickey L. Parsons
Carolyn L. Murdaugh

PART

I

Planning and Implementation

CHAPTER

1

An Executive Perspective: Strategic Implications

J. Verne Singleton

Chapter Objectives

1. To describe the strategic issues and implications of patient care restructuring.
2. To describe the organizational implications of restructuring.

One constant in health care today is that it is always in a state of flux. Social pressures, technological developments, and government policy all contribute to the feeling that the rules and expectations are continually changing. In spite of the constant change, little change has been observed in the internal organizational structure of hospitals. Patient care and support personnel have remained, for the most part, organized according to their respective clinical fields or functions. As new technologies developed, additional organizational structure was created to support them, particularly in physician-directed services. Although this may have proved successful from a clinical skills and a political perspective, it did little in the way of providing efficient services that truly met the needs of patients and the entire health care team.

STRATEGIC ISSUES

Several issues have been nearly impossible for hospital management to resolve: customer service, cost management, and fragmented care/responsibilities.

Customer Service

Customer service levels have never met expectations. Too often, management and direct care providers do not even know the customer's expectations. For far too long the attitude existed that the clinicians knew best, and everything that was done revolved around the clinicians' expectations and needs. For many years, little attention was paid to the patient's expectations. When competition among providers increased in the 1980s, marketing efforts began to address the patient's perspective. Frequently this attention focused on facility/service location and new programs that the community "could not do without." Rarely did the study of customer expectations focus on basic organizational and patient care delivery models and the impact of these models on customer satisfaction. The services and people closest to the patient were never really considered a solution to meeting the ever increasing service demands. Whole new corporate structures and joint ventures were created to meet the changing marketplace. Seldom did anyone look inside the organization and question the fundamental way in which services were provided to patients.

Physicians' expectations have generally received more attention. Hospital management has always realized that success is directly dependent on physician satisfaction. Too often this focus has been amenities and, more recently, financial joint ventures. Hospital–physician relations have recently begun to change with the greater managed care presence and a more complicated inpatient clinical environment. Information demands alone have created a complexity that is sometimes overwhelming. The internal hospital organizational structure does little to facilitate the physicians' needs.

A more complex clinical environment has led to higher nursing staffing levels and additional ancillary and support personnel. Even with all the additional staffing, no one ever seems to be in the right place at the right time. Health care personnel believe they are working harder, yet they never have the right body in the right place at the right time. Staff are frustrated and think that they are unable to provide the level of care demanded of them.

Consumer expectations, market pressures, and increasing clinical demands have necessitated a rethinking of how services are delivered. Hospital administrators have come to realize that they must be responsive to these demands if they hope to maintain their hospitals as viable entities. Generally management realizes that future success will be dependent on how responsive an institution is to today's service expectations.

Cost Management

A unique health care economic model was created with Medicare's cost-based reimbursement. For almost 20 years financial decisions were made in an entirely different fashion that allowed hospitals to recover their costs. This changed rapidly with the implementation of Medicare's diagnosis-related group reimbursement methodology in the mid-1980s. Cost management emphasis has been increasing ever since. Today the cost pressures are even greater with the proliferation of managed care throughout the country.

For years productivity and efficiency studies have been conducted in the nation's hospitals to get a handle on the cost of care. In spite of this emphasis, costs continue to rise, and clinical demands continue to increase. Until recently cost studies failed to concentrate on the specific way in which hospitals provided patient care and support services. Even when work processes were analyzed, interdepartmental structure and job roles were not routinely considered. Basically, everything was tried within existing organizational boundaries to improve the hospital's efficiency. In general, hospital efficiency has improved, but it has not kept pace with service demand or cost pressures.

Personnel shortages have been a significant cost factor. Wage rates along with recruitment and retention programs for many health professionals have increased the cost of providing care. Escalating labor costs and recruitment difficulties require management to look at the specific job functions that health professionals perform. Even with the increased professionalization of health care personnel, many classifications retain routine functions that are well below their skill level and could often be provided by less skilled and less costly staff.

New models of care have not been considered a solution to providing cost relief. Productivity standards, purchasing consortiums, and joint ventures have all been actively used to pursue cost management. Until recently the idea of modifying our patient care delivery model was not on the list of cost-saving strategies.

Fragmented Care/Responsibilities

Increasing pressure to lower costs, reduce lengths of stay, and retain only the sickest patients in the hospital only further complicated the delivery of services. Severity of illness, increasing technology, and shorter lengths of stay have forced more activity into a shorter time frame.

For many years hospitals were rather simple organizations. Personnel consisted mostly of nurses and a few support personnel. Physicians went to the hospital to treat their patients, as they do today. The rapid development of technology, especially since the inception of Medicare in the mid-1960s, led to a proliferation of additional health professionals. The era of specialization and professionalization has continued, and there is no indication that the trend is about to slow. What has developed is a team of health professionals and supporting staff that is disjointed, uncoordinated, and unempowered to provide the care for which it is responsible.

In the first few hours of a routine hospitalization, a patient may encounter anywhere between 10 and 15 different individuals. Each person has a task to perform that is strange and often fear-provoking to the patient. When this type of encounter is multiplied by three shifts per day plus a few trips out of the nursing unit for diagnostic testing, a patient may encounter 30 to 50 different people in the first day alone. Even when hospital staff do their best to introduce themselves and explain procedures, patient confusion is a certainty.

Physicians have the same difficulty sorting through the multiple people and services interacting with their patients. No service industry would ever subject its customers to the different staff interactions that occur in a hospital on a daily basis. Only a small percentage of these encounters can be justified on the basis of real specialization of technical expertise. For years hospitals have continued to put more and more people and technology into the equation and then struggle like mad to coordinate the various patient services.

The result is a mass of highly trained, highly motivated, and dedicated individuals who are unable to provide services in a manner that is acceptable to the customer, no matter how hard they try. Personnel specialization has decreased the flexibility to respond to patient and physician needs in a timely fashion. There are always competing demands, but no one is in a position to prioritize these demands. The result is frustrated and often acrimonious service delivery. Nurses have generally considered themselves the most responsible for the patient on a moment-to-moment basis. Nursing staff continuously express frustration with the inability to get response to patient care needs. This is not because other staff are unresponsive, uncaring, or even understaffed. More often it is related to the fact that the entire care process is unplanned and uncoordinated. This situation creates patient and physician dissatisfaction. Patient care and support staff frustrations are exacerbated. Costs and even the quality of care can suffer.

STRATEGIC IMPLICATIONS

The preceding issues have been confounding hospital management for years. The only viable alternative is to rethink and redesign the patient care delivery model. The patient care delivery model can be changed in many different ways to meet current demands. No single approach will work for everyone. Anyone who states that he or she has the universal solution is ignoring the complexities and the unique characteristics of health care institutions. Common attributes of any restructured approach should include the following:

- Any approach must be comprehensive in addressing the services being restructured.
- If you are going to restructure, do not hesitate to create a model that is radically different from current practice.
- Be flexible in how far and how rapidly restructuring progresses. Realistically there is only one opportunity to be successful, and success should not be jeopardized by a lack of flexibility.

Hospitals must be willing to challenge the way things have been done over the years. The health care industry is changing rapidly in terms of reimbursement and technology. Reimbursement and technology issues have profound effects on acute care hospitals. Hospital management and the entire staff must recognize that the current delivery model may not be adequate to meet the evolving health care marketplace. The expansion of managed care is placing expectations on service and financial performance that are new to many hospitals. If an institution's organization is unable to evolve to meet these expectations, the institution's long-term viability may be in doubt.

A willingness and a perceived need to introduce change led to the patient care restructuring efforts at University Medical Center. Restructuring patient care delivery models to a more patient-centered approach is essential in the evolving marketplace. Managed care is affecting everyone's financial performance. Historical referral patterns and working relationships are being eroded through new alliances and contracts. There are basically three areas in which hospitals must compete in the coming years. Price is always an issue, but efforts to address price soon become self-defeating as price approaches marginal cost levels. Cost is the real issue, and materially affecting costs will require tearing down organizational barriers and constraints, not just underbidding the competition. Service levels are key to ongoing success. Patients and physicians will need to be satisfied with service levels to ensure an ongoing stream of patients and thus revenue. The last major competitive area is patient outcome. Although there is a lot of work in this area, there is no agreed upon definitive model to compare outcomes objectively. It is not known how cost and clinical outcome should affect decision making. The industry is not even sure just what factors drive quality outcomes. In the long run, clinical outcomes may be the driving force behind patient care decisions; in the meantime cost and service will be the driving forces.

Service and cost expectations demand an organization that presents a more streamlined and cohesive presentation for the patient. Staff must be singularly focused on the total needs of their customers. Personnel must become more versatile in their skill levels and support capabilities. Service organizations must take a value-added approach to the work process. Every function must directly contribute positive value to the care process. The idea of one-stop shopping for the patient must apply to as many personnel interactions as possible. A new encounter with staff to accomplish the next task is no longer a viable option. Patients and physicians must feel that the staff closest to the patient must be able to handle efficiently and effectively the vast majority of the patient's needs. This is not the status quo today but is quickly becoming the expectation.

Decision making needs to be granted to the care providers. They must have the authority and ability to prioritize the routine needs of patient care. Empowerment must be accomplished in conjunction with a real appreciation of customer service expectations. Restructuring will require a new relationship among all the direct care providers, including medical staff. Regardless of all the technology, health care is a service business that is highly dependent on personnel and the teamwork of the personnel involved. Historically teamwork has been confined to a specific task, such as a surgical procedure. Few health care personnel would characterize the entire delivery process as a model of efficient, coordinated teamwork. Expectations must be consistently communicated to the entire health care team. More standardization of clinical management is to be expected. For far too long practitioners argued that every patient encounter was unique and therefore that standardization was not possible. Outcome evaluation studies are proving that standardization is effective. Patients and insurers have begun expecting a more coordinated type of clinical management.

CONCLUSION

It is apparent that the old way of doing things in hospitals is no longer sufficient. The 30-year-old organizational model and specialization no longer seem to meet the expectation of consumers and providers alike.

Change is inevitable. Managed care and regulatory pressures will actually be a great motivator for implementing change in the hospital organization. Those facilities that are able to adapt rapidly will find themselves well situated for the oncoming changes. Those that do not may become health care dinosaurs. Available capacity in the delivery system ensures that there is room for providers to become extinct with no adverse effect on patient care. Patient care restructuring is not the saving grace to hospitals but rather is just one step in ensuring a facility's ongoing success.

CHAPTER

2

The University Medical Center Model of Patient-Centered Care

Mickey L. Parsons

Chapter Objectives

1. To describe the objectives of the University Medical Center (UMC) model of patient-centered care.
2. To describe the components of the UMC model of patient-centered care.

As a university teaching hospital accustomed to rapid change, University Medical Center (UMC) at the University of Arizona Health Sciences Center, Tucson, was uniquely positioned to develop and implement a radically redesigned patient care delivery system. The three primary missions of the institution are patient care, education, and research. The missions directly support a process to improve patient services and to evaluate the results systematically through research. Faculty and staff within each of the multiple components of the Health Sciences Center, the College of Nursing, the College of Medicine, the hospital, the faculty group practice (clinics), and affiliated private and group practices supported the goals of the patient care restructuring project. The multitude of professionals and staff added complexities in the planning and implementation process, but their feedback only strengthened the leadership's conviction that the patient care process must be redesigned.

In the beginning discussions, the two groups that were most positive about restructuring the patient care delivery process were the physicians and the patients. Faculty physicians responded favorably to the ideas for restructuring patient care during presentations and discussions. Several physicians remarked that their clinic needed the same ideas applied in its ambulatory practice. Correspondingly, former patients responded favorably to the restructuring model because of their own experience with inadequate hospital service. They could readily give examples of how their own care could have been better.

The UMC model of patient care delivery as shown in Exhibit 2–1 has been implemented in 10 units, including approximately 200 beds, the emergency department, and labor and delivery. In year 1, phase I was implemented on 2 medical-surgical units, and 2 pediatric units. Phase II

Exhibit 2–1 UMC Model of Patient-Centered Care

	Restructured care delivery
• Unit secretary	• Receptionist, unit clerk
• Patient support attendant	• Patient room cleaning, dietary assistant, transportation, materials management
• Patient care technician	• Nursing assistant, technical procedures including phlebotomy, ECG, selected respiratory care, selected rehabilitation procedures
• Registered nurse case manager	• Planning, coordinating, and implementing the interdisciplinary plan of care
	Interdisciplinary team management
• Unit participative management	• Involvement of all members of the team
• Unit patient care council	• Continuous quality improvement and utilization management
• Career development and career advancement	• Career ladder and internship peer review
	Shared values of excellence in patient care
• Corporate culture of excellence	• Patient-centered quality and service • Support for creativity and innovation • Internal and external recognition

Source: Copyright © 1994 University Medical Center, Tucson, Arizona.

was implemented in year 2; 2 medical-surgical intermediate care units, a postpartum unit, and the newborn nursery unit were restructured. Phase III was implemented in year 2 in the emergency department and labor and delivery. Additional clinical areas are planning for implementation. Patient care restructuring (PCR) unit steering committees are active in 2 adult critical care units and the oncology and bone marrow transplant unit. The introductory process for the pediatric and neonatal critical care units is also being planned.

OBJECTIVES FOR THE UMC MODEL

Four primary objectives were selected for the demonstration project:

1. To maintain and enhance the quality of patient care and service.
2. To address the labor shortage by utilizing personnel more effectively in the delivery of patient care.
3. To address cost containment by reducing the annual rise in the cost of patient care services.
4. To maintain and enhance the satisfaction of all patient care providers in their job roles.

The objectives were tested by appropriate research instruments, and the results are presented in Part IV. Please see Chapters 28 through 33 for specific information.

Quality of Care

The first objective of the UMC model demonstration project was to maintain and enhance the quality of patient care and service. The majority of hospitals in America provide excellent medical-technical care. Meeting patient expectations for customer service, however, has become a requirement to compete in today's health care market.[1] Patients judge the quality of nursing care primarily on the basic service components of human care. Examples such as how quickly their call lights are answered and the attention given to personal requests such as a cup of coffee or an extra blanket represent situations in which care is judged. It is becoming more commonplace for health care consumers to have the knowledge base to judge the medical-technical aspects of care. Nevertheless, consumers continue to base their judgments on the human side of care and caring.

Whiteley reports on the Forum Corporation's research. Results revealed that almost 70 percent of the identifiable reasons why customers left typical companies were not related to the product. Fifteen percent of customers switched to another company because they found a better product, and another 15 percent switched because they found a cheaper product. Twenty percent switched because of lack of personal attention, and another 45 percent switched because of rude or unhelpful service.[2]

If we equate business product quality to technical quality in health care, this study has significant implications for health care providers. The results demonstrate that 65 percent of the reasons why customers switch to another company are primarily related to personal interaction, attention, and being helpful. Similarly, Leebov states emphatically that in the health care industry "The fact is, employee behavior toward customers is the most powerful marketing and customer satisfaction tool an organization has."[3(p.3)]

The price health care providers and institutions pay for dissatisfied customers is large. According to Leebov, about 96 percent of unhappy customers do not complain. Ninety percent of unhappy customers, however, will not choose the same organization the next time they need care. When customers are dissatisfied with service, they tell 20 relatives and friends. When customers are satisfied, they tell only 5. That means four times as many people have to be satisfied as are disappointed just to stay even in terms of public image.[4] The information is startling for health care personnel and has direct implications for work redesign.

According to Steiber and Krowinski, most patients are generally satisfied with their care experience but are not equally satisfied with all aspects of care. They note that "at its fundamental level, satisfaction is a positive evaluation of specific service dimensions based on patient expectations and provider performance."[5(p.23)] A part of customer expectations is to be clear about the plan and process of care. With the explosion of health care technology and a departmentally based functional organization of the delivery of services, the fragmented system is confusing to consumers and providers alike. A newly admitted patient may well come into contact with more than 30 hospital staff in the first 24 hours of care alone, with the right hand not knowing what the left hand is doing.

Health care providers want patients not only to perceive their basic service and complex medical-technical needs being met but also to have them met. Dissatisfaction with basic service, however, negatively affects patients' perception of nursing and the entire hospital experience. The primary contributor to poor service and high costs is viewed by some experts as the compartmentalization of care.[6] A redesign of the patient care delivery process to provide for basic service requires a move away from the functional, department-based organization to a decentralized patient-centered approach to care.

The Labor Shortage

The second objective of the UMC model was to address the labor shortage by utilizing personnel more effectively in the delivery of patient care. A major category of recommendations from the Secretary's Commission on Nursing was the utilization of nursing resources, which called for the provision of adequate support services and the utilization of the appropriate mix of personnel.[7] In many hospitals, however, nursing continues to struggle with the registered nurse (RN) role and professional practice issues. Many different models have been promulgated over the last 30 years, including primary nursing, differentiated practice, care partners, and case management. In today's modern hospital, nursing demonstrates the excellence achieved in technical and task-centered care. The vacillations in the RN shortage have contributed to the development of a care delivery process that continues to be technical and task centered. Although national data indicate that the RN vacancy percentage was down from 11 percent in 1990 to about 9 percent in 1991, the rate is still high.[8] The design of the role has been further complicated by requiring RNs to spend time on tasks, such as removing dirty linen from the unit, that do not require their education and training. Therefore, the care delivery structure has to change to provide the infrastructure to support professional nursing practice. It is hoped that patients will then be provided with the knowledge and skills needed to participate in their care in the hospital and to manage their care at home.

In addition to the RN shortage, there are actual and projected shortages of other health care workers. Other shortages most frequently cited in Arizona are for radiation technicians, radiation therapy technicians, physical therapists, pharmacists, medical technologists, medical record transcriptionists, and respiratory therapists.[9] A UMC human resources strategic plan identified priority positions for recruitment and retention based upon regional shortage data and UMC's projected needs.[10] All information points toward increasing requirements for health care workers depending upon the growth and funding levels in the industry.

Cost Containment

The third objective of the UMC model was to address cost containment by reducing the annual rise in the cost of patient care services. The media is filled with reports about health care costs and the need for reform. All health care providers today are pressured to reduce costs. External factors like declining reimbursement, increasing uncompensated care, and increasing numbers of managed care plans will force hospitals to be cost conscious in order to survive.

Job Satisfaction

The fourth objective of the UMC model was to maintain the job satisfaction of all patient care givers. Nurses' dissatisfaction with the profession has often been cited as a major factor in the nursing shortage. Studies on the nursing shortage, recruitment, and retention issues suggest that dissatisfaction is multifaceted, requiring diverse intervention to address the problem.[11-14] Additionally, many other health care workers have been limited by single-function, dead-end jobs in functional department-based organizations. It was believed that the new roles based on decentralized functions, broadened skills, and increased pay through career ladder advancement would increase the satisfaction of non-RN employees. It was believed that the satisfaction of nurses and other health care workers would increase through the creation of a new interdisciplinary model of patient care delivery.

THE UMC MODEL OF PATIENT CARE DELIVERY

The UMC model has three components:

1. restructured care delivery
2. interdisciplinary team management
3. shared values of excellence in patient care

Aspects of patient care restructuring have been implemented in various hospitals. The uniqueness of the UMC model, however, is in the holistic approach. It was conceptualized as a holistic model rather than as separate parts of a system. Each component of the UMC model is multifaceted and essential to the overall success of patient care restructuring.

Restructured Care Delivery

The traditional nursing unit, consisting primarily of nursing functions, has become known as a patient care unit in the restructuring process.[15] The title reflects the decentralized selected patient care functions of the unit and the restructured roles in the patient care delivery process. A change is made away from department centered to patient centered. This change represents one of the largest innovations in the delivery of care. With the explosion of technology, the number of specialized departments in hospitals and the bureaucratic routines of compartmentalized care grew. Department leaders now ask: What does the patient need?

Three new roles within the UMC model have been developed and implemented. The first two roles provide the infrastructure to support the professional nursing role. The third new role for the RN provides a framework for managing the care process. The three new roles are the patient support attendant (PSA), the patient care technician (PCT), and the RN case manager. These new care providers are accountable to the manager of the unit who is an RN.

PSAs function as multipurpose support workers. They perform the responsibilities of housekeeping, dietary, transportation, and material management on the unit as well as other related duties as assigned. This position offers a career ladder opportunity to employees in the previously centralized departments. Please see Chapter 6 for a full description of the role at UMC, the curriculum plan, and training realities with more than 141 PSAs to date.

PCTs function as multipurpose technical workers. They perform nursing assistant functions, phlebotomies from the laboratory, ECGs from cardiology, selected rehabilitation-related skills, and selected respiratory therapy skills, all based upon state licensure laws. Please see Chapter 7 for a full description of the role at UMC, the curriculum plan, and training realities with more than 182 PCTs to date.

RN case managers plan and coordinate care for a designated group of patients within the unit in conjunction with physicians and other health care professionals. Critical paths developed by all members of the health care team are utilized to manage the care process. Supervision of other members of the team may be provided by case managers or RN case associates. Please see Chapter 9 for more information.

Interdisciplinary Team Management

Moving from traditional management to leadership of groups utilizing participative management was viewed as essential for success in implementing large-scale change (multiple innovations). According to Johnson et al., participative management provides a structure for staff to have a voice in patient care and the work environment, issues of patient care, and unit operations.[16] Kramer and Schmalenberg, in their comparisons of magnet hospitals with the excellent companies noted in *In Search of Excellence* by Peters and Waterman, document the importance of decentralization of decision making as a hallmark of excellence.[17,18] Minnen et al. outline the importance of sustaining work redesign innovations through shared governance.[19] At UMC, as a first step a hospitalwide PCR steering committee and a PCR task force were created as the two key interdisciplinary groups in the medical center. The PCR steering committee, composed of hospital, nursing, and medical staff leadership, serves as the overall policy and approval body for restructuring. The PCR task force, composed of all involved department directors and nurse managers, is the work group responsible for planning and implementation.

On each patient care unit, the first step was to create a unit PCR steering committee and select a unit coordinator who was not the nurse manager. The functions of the unit committee were to guide the development and implementation of restructuring issues on the unit. The unit coordinator facilitated the process in conjunction with the nurse manager. The unit PCR steering committee evolves into the unit patient care council over time. Other members of the health care team become members as critical paths (or interdisciplinary protocols) are developed and as nursing case management is implemented. The emphasis continues on operational improvement at the unit level. It moves more into continuous quality improvement and utilization management with physicians and other members of the team as critical paths or interdisciplinary protocols of care are implemented.

The rapidity with which innovations have been implemented speaks to the importance of active staff involvement from the beginning. For complete information about staff involvement, please see Chapter 4 on the planning and change process. For a detailed description of staff involvement via unit-based steering committees, please see Chapter 13.

A career ladder was developed, and career advancement is encouraged. The first step is entry level in various roles in the remainder of the centralized departments and/or as a PSA. Seventeen percent of PSAs became PCTs in the first 2 years. In the latest class of 28 PCT students, 8 were previously PSAs. Continuing education is supported, as evidenced by the fact that of the latest PCT class, 11 are prenursing students, 2 are in nursing school, 1 is a premedical student, and 1 is a preveterinary student.

The concept of RN peer review was implemented on the three Differentiated Group Professional Practice Grant units, two of which are now restructured. The concept of RN peer review will be incorporated on all units as a regular component of the individual performance evaluation on an annual basis.

Shared Values of Excellence in Patient Care

An organization's culture shapes and guides the behavior of the staff in their work.[20] Therefore, the fact that the concept of corporate culture is a major interest in business organizations is not surprising.[21,22] Kramer and Schmalenberg found that valuing excellence in quality of care and service is a hallmark of magnet hospitals, as it is of excellent companies as described by Peters and Waterman.[23,24] The goal in the UMC model is to promote shared values of excellence in patient care in the redesign of the patient care units and in the ongoing operational process.

Another component of shared values of excellence is support for creativity and innovation. Staff were encouraged to be creative both in planning for the new model and during implementation. An idea that did not work was not a failure. Instead, it was seen as an opportunity to find a better approach. In other words, the process of continuous improvement is valued, as is dissatisfaction with the status quo.

Increasing the staff's level of awareness about the values in action on their work units prompted both individual and group inquiry. A unit cultural assessment was completed before restructuring, and the results were shared with the staff. The information has been utilized by the staff in choosing the content presented in communication and team-building workshops.

Implementation of recognition and award programs was another important approach to support the shaping of the shared values of excellence in patient care. Students who completed educational programs for each of the three new roles, PSA, PCT, and RN case manager, were recognized at special ceremonies that inspired both students and staff. Family members and coworkers were proud of the accomplishments of the students and their unique contribution to a special new program for patient-centered care. Additional formal and informal mechanisms are utilized to recognize excellence. For additional information, please refer to Chapter 15.

CONCLUSION

This chapter has outlined the objectives of and summarized the UMC model of patient-centered care. Each of the chapters that follow provides comprehensive information about all stages of the actual experience at UMC. Lessons learned from the first 2½ years of planning and implementation are shared in the hope that future designers may learn from the UMC experience.

NOTES

1. J. O'Malley and D. Serpico-Thompson, Redesigning Roles for Patient Centered Care: The Hospitality Representative, *Journal of Nursing Administration* 22, no. 7/8 (1992): 30–34.

2. R. Whiteley, *The Customer Driven Company: Moving from Talk to Action* (Reading, Mass.: Addison-Wesley, 1991), 9–10.
3. W. Leebov, *Customer Service in Health Care* (Chicago, Ill.: American Hospital Publishing, 1990), 3.
4. Leebov, *Customer Service,* 3.
5. S. Steiber and W. Krowinski, *Measuring and Managing Patient Satisfaction* (Chicago, Ill.: American Hospital Publishing, 1990), 23.
6. J.P. Lathrop, The Patient-Focused Hospital, *Health Care Forum Journal* (July/August 1991): 17–21.
7. Secretary's Commission on Nursing, *Final Report of Commission of Nursing* (Washington, D.C.: Department of Health and Human Services, 1988).
8. W. Erwin, AHA Survey: Nursing Shortage Eases Dramatically, *Hospitals* (February 1993): 52.
9. Arizona Hospital Association, *Arizona Hospital Association Manpower Study* (Phoenix, Ariz.: Arizona Hospital Association, 1990).
10. University Medical Center, *University Medical Center Human Resources Strategic Plan* (Tucson, Ariz.: University Medical Center, 1990).
11. M. McMure, et al., *Magnet Hospitals: Attraction and Retention of Professional Nurses* (Kansas City, Mo.: American Academy of Nursing, 1983).
12. M. Kramer and C. Schmalenberg, Magnet Hospitals: Part I—Institutions of Excellence, *Journal of Nursing Administration)*18, no. 1 (1988): 13–24.
13. M. Kramer and C. Schmalenberg, Magnet Hospitals: Part II—Institutions of Excellence, *Journal of Nursing Administration* 18, no. 2 (1988): 11–19.
14. Secretary's Commission on Nursing, *Final Report.*
15. R. Spitzer-Lehman and K.J. Yahn, Patient Needs Drive on Integrated Approach to Care, *Nursing Management* 23, no. 8 (1992): 30–32.
16. L.M. Johnson, et al., A Model of Participatory Management with Decentralized Authority, *Nursing Administration* Quarterly 8 (1983): 30–36.
17. Kramer and Schmalenberg, *Magnet Hospitals: Part II.*
18. T.J. Peters and R.H. Waterman, Jr., *In Search of Excellence* (New York, N.Y.: Harper & Row, 1982).
19. T.G. Minnen, et al., Sustaining Work Redesign Innovations through Shared Governance, *Journal of Nursing Administration* 23, no. 7/8 (1993): 35–40.
20. L. Smircich, Concepts of Culture and Organizational Analysis, *Administration Science Quarterly* 28 (1983): 339–58.
21. T.E. Deal and A.A. Kenneday, *Corporate Cultures* (Reading, Mass.: Addison-Wesley, 1982).
22. E.H. Schein, *Organizational Culture and Leadership* (San Francisco, Calif.: Jossey-Bass, 1985).
23. Kramer and Schmalenberg, *Magnet Hospitals: Part II.*
24. Peters and Waterman, *In Search of Excellence.*

SUGGESTED READINGS

Corporate Culture

Alexander, G.R. 1990. Management styles and corporate culture. *Nurse Manager's Bookshelf* 2:1–127.

Bettinger, C. 1989. Use corporate culture to trigger high performance. *Journal of Business Strategy* 10:38–42.

Bice, M. 1990. Corporate culture must foster innovation. *Hospitals* 64:58.

Clifton, R. 1986. Corporate culture and the healing mission. *Health Progress.* 67:49–50.

Conner, D. 1990. Corporate culture: Healthcare's change master. *Healthcare Executives* 5:28–29.

Consultant describes corporate culture pyramid. 1988. *Hospital Guest Relations Report* 3:6–7.

Curran, C.R., and N. Miller. 1990. The impact of corporate culture on nurse retention. *Nursing Clinics of North America* 25:537–49.

Denison, D.R. 1984. Bringing corporate culture to the bottom line. *Organizational Dynamics* 13:4–22.

Eubanks, P. 1991. Acclimating the new exec should be first goal. *Hospitals* 65:50.

Eubanks, P. 1991. Identifying your hospital's corporate culture. *Hospitals* 65:46.

Eubanks, P. 1991. Retreats advance the corporate culture. *Hospitals* 65:58.

Evans, S.A. 1991. Conflict resolution: A strategy for growth. *Heart and Lung* 20:20A, 22A, 24A.

Johnson, J.E. 1991. Corporate culture in the year 2000: A barometer for nursing. *Nursing Connections* 4:1–3.

Johnson, J.E. 1991. Corporate culture in the year 2000: Follow the Yellow Brick Road. *Aspen's Advisor for Nurse Executives* 6:7–8.

Jorgensen, A. 1991. Creating changes in the corporate culture: Case study. *American Association of Occupational Health Nurses* 39:319–21.

Kramer, M., and L.P. Hafner. 1989. Shared values: Impact on staff nurse job satisfaction and perceived productivity. *Nursing Research* 38:172–77.

Miyake, S., and R.J. Trostler. 1987. Introducing the concept of a corporate culture to the hospital setting. *American Journal of Occupational Therapy* 41:310–14.

Moore, W.W. 1991. Corporate culture: Modern day rites and rituals. *Healthcare Trends in Transition* 2:8–10, 12–13, 32–33.

O'Donnell, K.P. 1989. Shared values, corporate culture foster good hiring. *Modern Healthcare* 19:44.

Petrock, F. 1990. Corporate culture enhances profits. *HR Magazine* 35:64–66.

Redeker, J.R. 1990. Code of conduct as corporate culture. *HR Magazine* 35:83–84, 86–87.

Rustige, R.F., et al. 1987. Value-based leadership: Are Catholic hospitals a step ahead? *Health Progress* 68:62–65.

Scandiffio, A.L. 1990. Group dynamics. *Nurse Manager's Bookshelf* 2:77–109.

Shortell, S.M. 1984, Fall. Can corporate culture enhance productivity? *Health Management Quarterly*, pp. 10–14.

Smith, M.M. 1987. Getting ahead in the corporate culture. *American Journal of Nursing* 87:513–14.

Smith, R.E. 1988. Corporate culture: A forgotten impact on success. *Topics in Hospital Pharmacy Management* 8:62–77.

Patient Care Restructuring

Anderson, H.J. 1993. Patient-centered care changes focus of materials management. *Materials Management in Health Care* 2:12–15.

Bolster, C.J. 1991. Work redesign: More than rearranging furniture on the Titanic! *Aspen's Advisor for Nurse Executives* 6:4–7.

Burns, J. 1992. Patient-centered care plan sets departments working together. *Modern Healthcare* 22:65.

Coelins, H.V., and L.M. Simms. 1993. Facilitating innovation at the unit level through cultural assessment, part 2: Adapting managerial ideas to the unit work group. *Journal of Nursing Administration* 23:13–20.

Coile, R.C. Jr. 1992. Patient-centered care: Reinventing the hospital for the 21st century. *Hospital Strategy Report* 4:1–8.

Curran, C. 1993. Work redesign means major changes for hospitals, ORs. *OR Manager* 9:1, 6–7.

DeBack, V. 1991. The National Commission on Nursing Implementation Project. *Nursing Outlook* 39:124–27.

Eubanks, P. 1990. Nursing restructuring renews focus on patient-centered care. *Hospitals* 64:60, 62.

Eubanks, P., et al. 1991. Restructuring care: Patient focus is key to innovation. *Hospitals* 65:26–33.

Farris, B.J. 1993. Converting a unit to patient-focused care. *Health Progress* 74:22–25.

Hanrahan, T.F. 1991. New approaches to caregiving. *Healthcare Forum Journal* 34:33–37.

Henderson, J.L. 1991. Operational restructuring: The people side of patient care redesign. *Healthcare Forum Journal* 34:33–44.

Henderson, J.L., and J.B. Williams. 1991. Ten steps for restructuring patient care. *Healthcare Forum Journal* 34:50–54.

Jenkins, J.E. 1992. Work redesign: Ensuring success. *Aspen's Advisor for Nurse Executives* 7:4–6.

Lathrop, J.P. 1991. The patient-focused hospital. *Healthcare Forum Journal* 34:16–21.

Lee, H.J., et al. 1993. Physicians can benefit from a patient-focused hospital. *Physician Executives* 19:36–38.

McQueen, J. 1993. Overcoming the barriers to implementing patient-focused care. *Healthcare Information Management* 7:17–21.

O'Malley, J., and T.D. Serpico. 1992. Redesigning roles for patient-centered care. *Hospitality Representative* 22:30–34.

Porter-O'Grady, T. 1993. Patient-focused care service models and nursing: Perils and possibilities (editorial). *Journal of Nursing Administration* 23:7–8, 15.

Ritter, J., and M.C. Tonges. 1991. Work redesign in high-intensity environments. ProACT for critical care. *Journal of Nursing Administration* 21:26–35.

Robinson, N.C. 1991. A patient-centered framework for restructuring care. *Journal of Nursing Administration* 34:29–34.

Scahill, M. 1992. CARE 2000 program refocuses on patients at Mercy in San Diego. *Computers in Healthcare* 13:30–32.

Schartner, C. 1993. Principles of patient-focused care. *Healthcare Information Management* 7:11–5.

Sherer, J.L., et al. 1993. Putting patients first. Hospitals work to define patient-centered care. *Hospitals* 67:14–24.

Shortell, S. 1988. Management partnerships: Improving patient care in healthcare organizations of the future. *Healthcare Management Forum* 1:17–20.

Tarte, J.P. 1992. Patient-centered care delivery and the role of information systems. *Computers in Healthcare* 13:44–46.

Troup, N. 1992. Patient-focused care. A macro approach to productivity and quality improvement. *Healthcare Executive* 7:24–25.

Watson, P.M., et al. 1991. Operational restructuring: A patient-focused approach. *Nursing Administration Quarterly* 16:45–52.

Weber, D.O. 1991, July/August. Six models of patient-focused care. *Healthcare Forum Journal*, pp. 23–31.

Zander, K. 1988. Nursing case management. Resolving the DRG paradox. *Nursing Clinics of North America* 23:503–20.

Shared Governance

Anderson, B. 1992. Voyage to shared governance. *Nurse Manager* 23:65–67.

Baker, J., et al. 1991. Discharge planning: Shared-governance model. *Discharge Planning Update* 11:3–5.

Biltz, J., and L. Mild. 1992. A hospital's teamwork and CQI advance shared vision, interdependence among top managers (interview). *Hospitals* 66:57–58.

Boissoneau, R., and B.M. Shwahn. 1989. Participatory management. Its evolution, current usage. *Association of Operating Room Nurses Journal* 50:1079, 1082–24, 1086.

Brodbeck, K. 1992. Professional practice actualized through an integrated shared governance and quality assurance model. *Journal of Nursing Care Quarterly* 6:20–31.

Burnell, L. 1992. Striving for balance in a shared governance environment. *Critical Care Nursing Quarterly* 15:44–50.

Callahan, C.B., and L.L. Wall. 1987. Participative management: A contingency approach. *Journal of Nursing Administration* 17:9–15.

Caramanica, L. 1991. A pilot unit approach to shared governance. *Nursing Management* 22:46–48.

Counte, M.A., et al. 1987. Participative management among staff nurses. *Hospital Health Services Administration* 32:97–108.

Craig, C. 1989. Shared governance. *Journal of Nursing Administration* 19:15, 42.

Davis, P.A. 1992. Unit-based shared governance. Nurturing the vision. *Journal of Nursing Administration* 22:46–50.

Felder, B.J. 1992. Using a game format to improve compliance with required review of hospital standards and policies. *Journal of Continuing Education in Nursing* 23:209–11.

Flarey, D.L. 1991. Quality circles: The nurse executive as mentor. *Health Care Supervisor* 10:2–61.

Goodykoontz, L., and M.H. Miller. 1990. Does participatory management make a difference? *Journal of Nursing Administration* 20:7, 29.

Guinn, J. 1989. Shared governance. *Today's OR Nurse* 11:10–12.

Gyongyos, D.G. 1988. Shared governance: A human resources viewpoint. *Aspen's Advisory for Nurse Executives* 4:1, 6–7.

Hawthorne, J., et al. 1989. The professional practice climate and peer review. *Nursing Connections* 2:47–54.

Hendrich, A.L., and T.C. Smith. 1991. A shared governance model. *Journal of Nursing Quality Assurance* 5:75–76.

Hibberd, J.M., et al. 1992. Implementing shared governance: A false start. *Nursing Clinics of North America* 27:11–22.

Hospers, C.J. 1989. The middle manager in shared governance. *Aspen's Advisory for Nurse Executives* 4:4–5.

Johnson, L.M. 1987. Self-governance: Treatment for an unhealthy nursing culture. *Health Progress* 68:41–43.

Jones, L.S., and M.E. Ortiz. 1989. Increasing nursing autonomy and recognition through shared governance. *Nursing Administration Quarterly* 13:11–16.

Kerfoot, K.M. 1991. An interview with Karlene M. Kerfoot. *Nursing Economics* 9:141–47.

Kerfoot, K.M. 1991. Developing self-governed teams: The nurse manager's goal in shared governance. *Nursing Economics* 9:121,125.

Kerfoot, K.M. 1991. From shared governance in nursing to integrated patient care teams. *Aspen's Advisor for Nurse Executives* 7:4–6.

Lockwood, B.J. 1990. Shared governance in a union environment. *Aspen's Advisor for Nurse Executives* 5:1, 3, 6–7.

Ludemann, R.S., and C. Brown. 1989. Staff perceptions of shared governance. *Nursing Administration Quarterly* 13:49–56.

Matlosz, D.L. 1986. Participatory management in hospitals—Myth or reality? *Hospital Topics* 64:18–19.

McDonagh, K.J., et al. 1989. Shared governance at Saint Joseph's Hospital of Atlanta: A mature professional practice model. *Nursing Administration Quarterly* 13:17–28.

McMahon, J.M. 1992. Shared governance: The leadership challenge. *Nursing Administration Quarterly* 17:55–59.

Nowell, A.H., and G. Nowell. 1986. Participation management as a strategy for nurse adaptation to hospital unit management systems. *Hospital Topics* 64:28–31, 42.

O'Malley, J. 1992. Organizational empowerment: Moving shared governance beyond nursing. *Aspen's Advisor for Nurse Executives* 7:1, 4–5.

Ortiz, M.E., et al. 1987. Moving to shared governance. *American Journal of Nursing* 87:23–26.

Patterson, P. 1988. Magnet hospitals. Shared governance, salaried status help to retain nurses. *OR Manager* 4:1, 4–6.

Peterson, M.E., and D.G. Allen. 1986. Shared governance: A strategy for transforming organizations. Part I. *Journal of Nursing Administration* 16, no. 1:9–12.

Peterson, M.E., and D.G. Allen. 1986. Shared governance: A strategy for transforming organizations. Part 2. *Journal of Nursing Administration* 16, no. 2:11–16.

Pinkerton, S.E., et al. 1989. St. Michael Hospital: A shared governance model. *Nursing Administration Quarterly* 13:35–47.

Porter-O'Grady, T. 1985. Credentialing, privileging, and nursing bylaws. Assuring accountability. *Journal of Nursing Administration* 15:23–27.

Porter-O'Grady, T. 1987. Participatory management: The critical care nurse's role in the 21st century. *Dimensions in Critical Care Nursing* 6:131–33.

Porter-O'Grady, T. 1987. Shared governance and new organizational models. *Nursing Economics* 5:281–86.

Porter-O'Grady, T. 1989. Shared governance: Reality or sham? *American Journal of Nursing* 89:350–51.

Porter-O'Grady, T. 1991. Shared governance for nursing. Part I: Creating the new organization. *Association of Operating Room Nurses Journal* 53:458–59, 461–67, 464–66.

Porter-O'Grady, T. 1991. Shared governance for nursing. Part II: Putting the organization into action. *Association of Operating Room Nurses Journal* 53:694–703.

Porter-O'Grady, T. 1992. Of quorums and quality: Integrating shared governance and continuous quality improvement. *Aspen's Advisor for Nurse Executives.* 7:6–8.

Puckett, F. 1991. The project shift: A form of participative management and staffing. *Hospital Pharmacy* 26:960–65.

Rabkin, M.T., and L. Avakian. 1992. Participatory management at Boston's Beth Israel Hospital. *Academic Medicine* 67:289–94.

Rauer, R. 1990. Practicing participative management. *Nurse Manager* 21:48A–48B, 48F, 48H.

Shidler, H., et al. 1989. Professional nursing staff: A model of self-governance for nursing. *Nursing Administration Quarterly* 13:1–9.

Smith, S. 1990. Evaluating a shared governance model. *Aspen's Advisor for Nurse Executives* 5:4–5, 7.

Stanfill, P.H., and P. Herring. 1987. Participative management becomes shared management. *Nurse Manager* 18:69–70.

Stichler, J.F. 1989. Shared governance: What it means to those involved. *Aspen's Advisor for Nurse Executives* 4:1, 3, 6–8.

Strifler, S.V. 1993. Shared governance: Participatory management. *Florida Nurse* 41:1, 10.

Sullivan, M.F., and J. Guntzelman. 1991. The grieving process in cultural change. *Healthcare Supervisor* 10:28–33.

Taylor, C.M. 1990. Shared governance: A three-year perspective. *Aspen's Advisor for Nurse Executives* 5:4–6.

Thrasher, T., et al. 1992. Empowering the clinical nurse through quality assurance in a shared governance setting. *Journal of Nursing Care Quality* 6:20–31.

Totten, N.W., and V.L. Scott. 1993. Who's on first? Shared governance in the role of nurse executive. *Journal of Nursing Administration* 23:28–32.

Twomey, W.E. Jr. 1991. Negotiating a shared governance program in a unionized hospital—a road less traveled. *Aspen's Advisor for Nurse Executives* 6:1, 3–5.

Ulz, L. 1989. Leadership via participatory management. *Nursing Connections* 2:62–65.

Wake, M.M., et al. 1992. Classroom shared governance. *Nurse Educator* 17:19–22.

Wilson, C.K. 1989. Shared governance: The challenge of change in the early phases of implementation. *Nursing Administration Quarterly* 13:29–33.

Wilson, D. 1992. Paradigms and nursing management, analysis of the current organizational structure in a large hospital. *Healthcare Management Forum* 5:4–16.

CHAPTER

3

Differentiated Group Professional Practice in Nursing Project: Pathfinder for Patient Care Restructuring

Joyce A. Verran, Rose M. Gerber, Doris A. Milton, and Carolyn L. Murdaugh

Chapter Objectives

1. To examine the differentiated group professional practice (DGPP) model as a pathfinder for the patient care restructuring project.
2. To gain an understanding of the processes and unit-based structures used to implement DGPP within three nursing units.
3. To review the staff nurse outcomes as a result of DGPP implementation.

The Differentiated Group Professional Practice (DGPP) in Nursing grant was a cooperative agreement between the University of Arizona College of Nursing and the two funding agencies of the National Center for Nursing Research, National Institutes of Health and the Division of Nursing, Public Health Service (U01 NR02153). The 5-year project was a

The authors acknowledge the efforts of Julie Fluery, Ph.D., R.N., research specialist for the DGPP grant at UMC, and the two UMC program coordinators Sandra Kurtin, M.S., R.N., and Josephine Palmer, M.S., R.N.

response to a request for application for research and demonstration models. The purpose was to change the work environment for registered nurses (RNs) and to improve retention in hospitals, especially in medical-surgical and critical care areas. One of the many unique aspects of the project was the combination of a demonstration (implementation of the innovative practice model) in conjunction with a strong evaluative research design. Both the demonstration and the research models were grounded in previous literature.[1]

Each of the four demonstration sites selected two general medical-surgical patient care units and one critical care unit to participate in the DGPP project. At University Medical Center (UMC), the demonstration units included a 29-bed general surgery/trauma unit (unit 1), a 16-bed step-down cardiac monitoring unit (unit 2), and a 16-bed intensive care unit with trauma, neurological, neurosurgical, general surgery, and internal medicine subspecialties (unit 3). Unit level leadership was provided by a nurse manager on all three units, and staffing patterns varied from unit to unit.

In terms of the timeline for the project, after being funded the remainder of the year (4 months) was used to develop plans with the four demonstration hospitals whose administrative staff had agreed to participate in the project. Baseline staff nurse data were collected during the first quarter of the following year with subsequent data collection times in each October of the next 4 years. Unit level information about retention variables, fiscal outcomes, and quality outcomes was also collected throughout the project. The unit level data are currently under analysis, and results are not reported in this chapter. Implementation activities for the DGPP model began in the eighth month after funding began and officially ended 42 months later. At UMC, little additional implementation occurred during the last 12 months of implementation with the exception of some synthesis of component parts into a total practice model. In other words, model implementation at UMC was essentially completed in 30 months.

The purpose of this chapter is to provide an overview of the DGPP demonstration model, the processes for implementation at UMC, and the results in terms of change in indices of professional practice (control over nursing practice, group cohesion, work autonomy, and organizational commitment) and job satisfaction. Two points are critical to understanding the DGPP project. First, the demonstration model was directed at improving the professional work environment for RNs. No other nursing staff or staff from other departments were included in the processes for implementation or evaluation. Second, the project was truly unit based. Although some coordination occurred across units, the focus was the environment and culture of the individual nursing units involved in the project. At UMC, these demonstration units were only three of several nursing units in the hospital.

THE DEMONSTRATION MODEL

The DGPP demonstration model was designed with three components: group governance, differentiated care delivery, and shared values in a culture of excellence. It is the combination and synthesis of these components that makes the DGPP model unique. The three components and their subcomponents as separate entities are presented in the following overview (Figure 3–1). A more complete review of the model is provided by Milton et al.[2]

Group Governance

The group governance component of the DGPP model was envisioned as a participatory nursing group practice at the unit level that would facilitate control over nursing practice, working conditions, and professional affairs.[3] The group governance framework provided the structure for RNs to make decisions concerning patient care and unit operations. Subcomponents of group governance included participatory unit management, shared decision making through staff bylaws, peer review, and a professional salary structure.

Participative Unit Management

Participative unit management provided a unit-based structure for nursing staff and managers jointly to make decisions that affect care delivery and unit operations, allowing staff to have a voice in patient care and the work environment.[4] Management's major role became obtaining appropriate resources for the work to be accomplished. Decisions about resources needed and resource allocation became a shared responsibility of management and staff.[5]

Shared Decision Making through Staff Bylaws

Bylaws were developed to guide the actions of nurses in the group practice. These written guidelines provided a structure that delineated how decision making was to be shared between management and staff. Christman states that bylaws, "when well constructed, can instill a sense of professional dignity; a heightened awareness of professional obligation, responsibility and accountability; a mechanism for enhancing cohesion and organized purpose; and a device for sensitizing the membership to patient welfare in a persistent and sustained fashion."[6(p.4)]

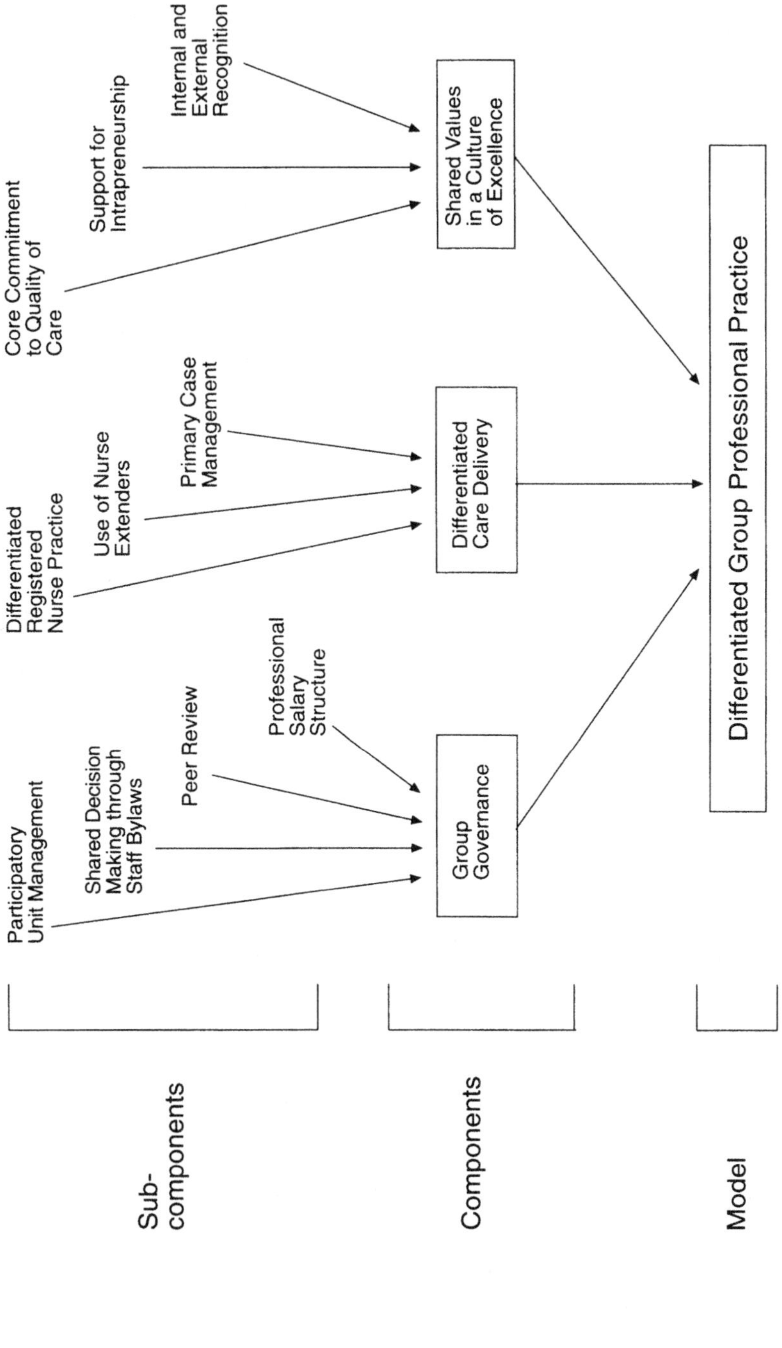

Figure 3–1 DGPP components and subcomponents.

Peer Review

Peer review provided a process for evaluation of credentials and performance by colleagues. Criteria for peer evaluation for employment and performance review fostered staff accountability and responsibility for care provided by others. Peers influenced the quality of nursing providers and, in turn, the quality of care provided.

Professional Salary Structure

A professional salary structure was proposed as part of the group governance component to compensate professionals for the entire job performed, not specific tasks within the job, as is often inherent in an hourly wage. A professional salary method of compensation was viewed as reflective of professional practice responsibilities. Kramer and Schmalenberg describe a professional salary structure as the difference between being compensated to perform highly professional work and being paid to put in hours.[7]

Differentiated Care Delivery

The second component of the DGPP model to be reviewed is differentiated care delivery. This component was incorporated in the model to allow nurses with various educational preparation and work experiences to use their knowledge and skills efficiently. The subcomponents of differentiated care delivery include differentiated RN practice, use of nurse extenders, and primary care management.

Differentiated RN Practice

Differentiated RN practice was designed to distinguish professional and technical nursing roles from the single composite role of the RN. Two RN staff roles were developed based on competencies expected of future graduates of associate degree and baccalaureate degree nursing education programs. Differentiated RN practice incorporated the three components of the practice role: provision of direct care, communication with and on behalf of patients, and management of patient care.[8] The differences between the two roles centered on complexity of decision making, timeline of care, and the structure of the situation and setting.

Nurse Extenders

Nurse extenders were assistive personnel who were trained to perform patient care or unit management tasks delegated by RNs. RNs would remain responsible for planning patient care and appropriate delegation of activities. Nurse extenders within the DGPP model would perform tasks that had been delegated to nursing but were determined by unit group practices not to require performance by an RN in either the professional or the technical role. The nurse extender role was in operation on the nursing units before DGPP implementation. The plan was to facilitate the RN role by delegating appropriate tasks to the nurse extender, however.

Primary Case Management

Primary case management provided a framework for describing, monitoring, and tracking patient care and care outcomes during an episode of hospitalization. Nurses who participated in the case management process had the authority, responsibility, and accountability for cost efficiency and quality of patient outcomes.[9] Case management would provide a systematic approach of providing quality, cost-effective care for high-risk, high-volume patients who consume a large proportion of resources.

Shared Values in a Culture of Excellence

The final component of the DGPP model was shared values in a culture of excellence. Shared values referred to the adoption of homogenous attitudes and beliefs by people in an organization, forming a culture to help guide and shape behavior in the system.[10] A mark of excellence in organizations is the extent to which a system of common and shared core values is in place. The three subcomponents of the shared values component were a core commitment to quality of care, support for intrapreneurship, and internal and external recognition.

Quality of Care

A characteristic common to magnet hospitals is a culture that places emphasis on the quality of care that is provided.[11] In institutions of excellence, decisions related to resource use are made in terms of the contribution those resources make to improving the quality of care provided. Thus the DGPP demonstration model included plans to alter or enhance core values of quality.

Support for Intrapreneurship

Intrapreneuring uses the entrepreneurial spirit within an institution.[12] Support for intrapreneurship was designed to foster creativity and innovation by people in an organization. The goal was to encourage nurses to develop alternative strategies for improving the quality of care. A commitment to creating a climate supporting the intrapreneurial spirit facilitated innovation within group practices.

Internal and External Recognition

Development of systems for recognition within and outside an institution to provide a sound foundation for recognizing excellence was an integral part of the DGPP model. Once values are internalized, formal and informal mechanisms can reward behaviors consistent with quality practice. Visibility in internal publications or submission for external awards are examples of recognition promoted on the demonstration units to recognize excellence.

Summary of the Model

In the integrated DGPP professional practice model, RNs were expected to participate in management of their unit, to share in making decisions that affect their practice, to participate in review of their peers, and to be compensated in accordance with a professional salary structure. They were to perform nursing functions commensurate with their knowledge and skill base, to use assistive personnel employed on the nursing unit to perform nonnursing tasks related to patient care and unit operations, and to participate in a case management system. Behaviors that reflect the value of excellence in providing quality care were supported, innovation and intrapreneurship were facilitated, and efforts as well as achievements were recognized.

MODEL IMPLEMENTATION

A co–principal investigator for the DGPP project worked primarily with the chief nurse executive and other administrators at UMC. The investigator assumed major responsibility for implementation of the practice model in the clinical setting. A half-time program coordinator was also employed within the DGPP project to assist the investigator with implementation of the DGPP model on the patient care units. All other staff and manager participation in implementation activities occurred as part of usual unit operations. Six key aspects of model implementation are reviewed in this section:

1. implementation change strategy
2. necessary system supports
3. program coordinator role
4. communication networks
5. unit level work groups
6. sequence of implementing activities

The section concludes with the results of measuring the level of implementation on the three demonstration units.

Change Strategy

Adoption of the DGPP model required acceptance of new ideas and changes in individual behavior by both staff nurses and unit managers. Although each component of the DGPP model was viewed as a single innovation, each component contributed to the wholeness of the model. Adoption of the DGPP model as an integrated totality involved a paradigm shift by those involved in the project. Implementation of the new model required a shift from practicing within a traditional institutional model of care delivery to practicing within a new system. Staff nurses were increasingly empowered to control their practice. Role enrichment was facilitated for those expert practitioners interested in becoming nurse case managers. Innovativeness was encouraged among staff and patient care units. High quality care was valued and rewarded. Adoption of the DGPP model necessitated many changes in the thinking and behavior of staff nurses and managers. These changes required considerable time and effort on the part of staff, managers, and the DGPP project team.

The conceptual approach to the adoption of new ideas and new practices was based on the diffusion of innovation as described by Rogers.[13] As an intentional and rational process, the diffusion of an innovative model embodies decision making and active participation of those most affected by the innovation. The five steps as described by Rogers are shown in Exhibit 3–1. The decision making units for planning and applying the DGPP model to practice were the three demonstration units. Staff nurse involvement in planning the details of model implementation was conceptually and philosophically consistent with the practice model, which sought to legitimize the authority of staff nurses to influence their work and work setting.

Exhibit 3–1 Steps in Diffusion of Innovation Model

- Introduction of the decision-making unit to the innovation
- Persuasion toward the innovation
- Adoption or rejection of the innovation
- Actual implementation of the innovation
- Confirmation that the decision was correct

Rogers and Agarwala-Rogers point out that innovativeness can be measured in two different ways: earliness of adoption of a new idea or practice, and the number of innovations adopted.[14] Earliness of adoption is usually used to index the adoption of a single innovation. When multiple innovations are underway, progress or success is generally measured as the total number of innovations adopted at any point in time. As might be expected, innovativeness varied somewhat among the three demonstration units at UMC. Within any given demonstration unit, the extent of adoption of each component of the DGPP model also varied.

System Supports

According to Rogers, two important aspects of successful planned change are key people and policymakers.[13] They must both be interested in the innovation and committed to making it happen.

Based on the findings of a case study conducted at UMC by Geller et al., near the end of implementation activities two important factors that related to successful implementation of DGPP were a core group of committed people to attend meetings and to see the implementation through and, most important, the level of unit managerial commitment to the process.[15] A core group of people dedicated to the concept of professional nursing practice was present on each of the three units. Without a supportive nurse manager who acted as a strong group leader, it was difficult to motivate people to make change and to keep adoption of the innovation moving.

Rogers and Agarwala-Rogers identify slack resources as another factor that affects the nature and direction of the process of innovation.[14] Staff nurse time was a resource that was critical to the adoption of the DGPP model at UMC. Staff nurses who chose to become actively involved in the DGPP project were relieved of direct caregiving responsibilities at times so that they could participate in educational activities and work on committees. If DGPP work had not been valued by management or the nurses, implementation of the DGPP model would have been extremely difficult if not impossible.

Role of the Program Coordinator

Another key factor in the implementation of this particular innovative practice model was utilization of a program coordinator. The half-time program coordinator had three major responsibilities: facilitation and coordination of project work on the three demonstration units, collection of data for evaluation purposes, and communication with staff, managers, administrators, and investigators. Although the program coordinator was employed through the externally funded grant and reported directly to the investigative team, the office was located at UMC, and the majority of the coordinator's time was spent in the practice setting.

Familiarity with hospital policies and procedures and credibility among staff and managers were considered prerequisite conditions for employment as a program coordinator. Internal applicants were sought for the position. The minimal educational preparation required for the position was the baccalaureate degree in nursing, although graduate preparation in nursing was preferred. Basic computer skills were desired for using electronic mail and computer conferencing. Evidence of commitment to professional nursing practice and the ability to work effectively with people were considered essential characteristics for appointment as a program coordinator.

Staff nurse involvement was extensive throughout the adoption of the new model of practice; therefore, the ability of the program coordinator to create and build teams was critical to the success of the innovation. Competence in obtaining voluntary staff participation and then keeping staff members goal oriented and committed was indispensable. Because multiple components of the model were being implemented simultaneously, the program coordinator also needed to possess expert organizational abilities. Heating one iron in the fire of change can be difficult; heating multiple irons simultaneously can easily become impossible. Needless to say, the role of the program coordinator was extremely vital and needed to be performed well.

Communication and Information Sharing

Multiple communication networks were established to meet different needs for information sharing during implementation of the DGPP model. Because of the use of a team approach throughout the project, a circle or all-channel network with a give-and-take flow of information was used most frequently. Committees and work groups were used to gain consensus and to enhance consistency in model adoption. Developmental workshops involving staff nurses and nurse managers were held. For example, a special workshop was held to develop staff nurse knowledge and skill in writing bylaws relative to the group governance structure. Other workshops were held to learn about differentiated practice and case management. The usual method of dissemination of information to larger numbers of people, especially to staff nurses, included the use of unit bulletin boards, notebooks, and newsletters. The open forum technique was particularly useful to disseminate information as well as to receive feedback from staff members. In general, the open forum was similar to usual staff meetings but was called and conducted by nursing staff rather than the nurse manager. A report from the manager was often included in the forum, but the more typical pattern involved the manager as facilitator rather than chair.

At all times, information sharing with staff nurses was an essential aspect of model implementation. The program coordinator played a pivotal role in keeping the communication networks operational and open to the flow of information.

Committees As Work Groups

The basic work groups for the implementation of the DGPP model were called the unit-based DGPP project committees. These ad hoc committees were composed primarily of staff nurses who either had a vision for a change in the way they practiced nursing or just wanted to help influence their work and work setting. Each demonstration unit formed four DGPP project committees—a bylaws committee, a participative management committee, a differentiated practice committee, and a peer review committee—reflective of various components of the practice model. Meetings were scheduled on a monthly basis.

As might be expected, multiple committees working simultaneously resulted in a need for a formal mechanism to enhance communication and integration of committee efforts. Early in the project, unit-based steering committees were established to coordinate implementation activities at the unit level of the organization. Membership of the steering committee included the nurse manager, DGPP project committee members, the program coordinator, and anyone else who was interested in planning the details of model implementation.

Similarly, communication and collaboration among all three demonstration units were also needed. A professional practice project team (affectionately referred to as the P-3 team) was formed to maintain fundamental consistency among the three patient care units. In addition to representation by each of the three demonstration units and the program coordinator, membership of the P-3 team included the co–principal investigator and the chief nurse executive. The P-3 committee guided the operationalization of the project at UMC.

As the DGPP model evolved at UMC, the DGPP practice committees were dissolved when they had achieved their purpose. For example, once the UMC Professional Nursing Congress Bylaws were written, approved, and ratified, the ad hoc committee established for the purpose of writing bylaws was no longer needed. As an evolutionary process, the movement to group governance was fairly subtle. The functions of the unit-based steering committees were incorporated into the newer nursing care committees (NCCs), which were also unit based. With time, the P-3 team was replaced by the nursing care coordinating committee that provided for coordination of nursing activities across units.

Sequence of Implementing Activities

Although the DGPP model was conceptualized as a single, unitary phenomenon, it became increasingly apparent that the existence of some components would support the development of other components. The presence of group governance, which formalized participatory unit management and shared decision making, facilitated the adoption of other components of the new practice model. The bylaws provided for several unit level practice committees and an NCC. The NCC committee coordinated the activities that related to maximizing the effectiveness of the practice of nursing at the nursing unit level in the areas of nursing care standards, quality assurance, employee recognition, credentialing, education, research, and collaborative practice. Early adoption of group governance was important to adoption of other aspects of the DGPP model.

A professional salary structure (as opposed to hourly wages) is intended to reflect professionalism and the practice of professional nursing. It would be inappropriate to salary staff nurses until warranted by a sufficient change in practice. Forcing such a change prematurely could have produced undesirable outcomes in those directly affected by the change. Adoption of a professional salary structure did not occur within the time frame of the DGPP project.

On the other hand, facilitating shared values of excellence occurred throughout the project. Unit specific programs of activity were ongoing to encourage and recognize excellence in practice. Celebration of achievement and excellence also was an ongoing activity.

Rogers recognized that the decision-making unit may actually reject adoption of an innovation.[13] Differentiated RN practice as specified in the model was passively rejected by all three demonstration units for the time being. Instead, differentiated care delivery was implemented through nursing case management. Interested staff nurses self-selected the role of nurse case manager and had the initiative to develop the knowledge and skills needed to perform the role.

Level of Implementation

During the course of the DGPP project, it became increasingly apparent that full implementation of all model subcomponents would not be achieved in any of the demonstration hospitals. Therefore, a scale was developed to measure the degree of implementation across components.[16] The scale was completed for the three units at UMC at the end of implementation in August 1992, as shown in Table 3-1. Evidence indicated that the subcomponents' professional salary structure (group governance) and differentiated RN practice (differentiated care delivery) had not been implemented to any extent. Other aspects of group governance were highly implemented. The most difference across the three units occurred with the subcomponents of differentiated care delivery and shared values, with unit 3 scoring in the low to moderate range on primary case management, the shared value of quality of care, and processes for internal and external recognition.

RESEARCH RESULTS

The DGPP project incorporated formal research methodology to test the effect of the innovative practice model on staff nurse perceptions of professional practice and job satisfaction. Data were collected from all RN staff members on the demonstration units at five times during the course of the project. The survey design provided data for a cross-sectional analysis of cohorts. No attempt was made to ensure paired or longitudinal data. Because the innovative practice model was unit based, it was believed that change in staff perceptions as a group was a more valuable approach to analysis than change in the same individual's perceptions over time.

Respondents were assured of the confidentiality of information submitted. Response rates for all five data collections on all three units were above the 60% deemed to be representative of the work group.

Table 3–1 DGPP Level of Implementation

Components	*Unit 1 (%)*	*Unit 2 (%)*	*Unit 3 (%)*
Group governance	65.0	68.7	68.7
Differentiated care delivery	62.0	62.0	50.0
Shared values in a culture of excellence	91.6	91.6	58.3
Total	71.0	72.0	58.0

Staff nurse perceptions were collected using established instrumentation. The instruments used to index the professional practice variables included a group cohesion scale, a control over nursing practice scale, an organizational commitment questionnaire, and an autonomy in professional practice scale, which was adapted from Sims et al. and Quinn and Staines.[17–21] Job satisfaction was measured with the Index of Work Satisfaction.[22] Instrument revision resulted in eliminating items to improve construct validity as examined with factor analysis. After these revisions, instruments evidenced adequate reliability (Cronbach $\alpha > .75$) at all testing times.

Although data are available from UMC for all five data collection times, the most appropriate analyses are comparisons of baseline data for time 1 to time 4. As mentioned, little DGPP implementation was initiated after time 4 data collection, and no changes related to patient care restructuring had as yet been initiated on the demonstration units. At the time 5 data collection, patient care restructuring innovations had been implemented on the demonstration units; thus these results may be more reflective of the disequilibrium caused by a record set of innovations rather than of the presence of an established practice model.

Variability across units negated an examination of changes across time without consideration of the degree to which the DGPP model had been implemented on each unit. Therefore, the analysis strategy involved the use of analysis of covariance for the difference between time 1 (n=62) and time 4 (n=66) responses, controlling for the effect of level of implementation. For all analyses, item means are reported. Mean scores could range from a low of 1.0 to a high of 7.0. Level of significance was set at $P \leq .05$.

Changes in Professional Practice Indices

The professional practice indices were group cohesion, control over nursing practice, organizational commitment, and work autonomy. Table 3–2 shows the increase in professional practice indice means from time 1 to time 4.

Analysis of covariance indicated that, for all four variables, both the covariate of level of implementation and the main effects of the difference between time 1 and time 4 were statistically significant. These results suggest that the greater the level of model implementation, the greater the change in scores from baseline levels in 1989 to postimplementation responses in 1991. Furthermore, findings suggest that even with the degree of implementation controlled there were significant positive changes in staff perceptions of professional practice indices over time.

Table 3–2 Changes in Professional Practice Indices and Satisfaction from Time 1 to Time 4

Variable	*Time 1 Mean (S.D.)**	*Time 4 Mean (S.D.)**
Group cohesion	5.18 (.93)	5.42 (.92)
Control over nursing practice	5.16 (.65)	5.37 (.79)
Organizational commitment	4.93 (.85)	5.16 (.98)
Work autonomy	5.01 (.64)	5.32 (.74)
Satisfaction	3.93 (.66)	4.18 (.73)

*S.D., standard deviation.

Changes in Satisfaction

Scores for job satisfaction changed from time 1 to time 4, as shown in Table 3–2. Only one covariate, level of implementation, was statistically significant for job satisfaction, indicating that only the degree of implementation had an effect on changes in satisfaction over time.

Six subscales of the Index of Work Satisfaction were also analyzed. Those subscales that evidenced the greatest positive degree of change over time were Satisfaction with Task Requirements, Satisfaction with Interaction with Nurses, and Satisfaction with Organizational Policies.

CONCLUSION

The DGPP in Nursing project was designed to improve the work environment for RNs to increase professional practice, nurse satisfaction and resources, quality of care, and fiscal outcomes. The demonstration model aimed to enhance professional nursing practice and was developed before patient care restructuring. The model therefore served as a foundation for later efforts that crossed several units or departments. Although limited to the department of nursing, the DGPP project can be considered the pathfinder for UMC patient care restructuring efforts.

Changes in professional practice and work satisfaction variables were noted between the beginning and the end of DGPP implementation. Increases in these outcomes were largest on unit 1, the unit that began with fewer model implementation supports in place. In contrast, unit 2 did not demonstrate a similar gain in outcome measures, partly because more implementation supports preexisted. Implementation was less rapid on unit 3 (critical care unit) because of factors such as an early skepticism among some staff that was enhanced by the absence of a permanent nurse manager for 1 year of the project.

The DGPP project provided an essential base for more broad-based restructuring efforts. By focusing on redesigning the practice of RNs and examining the degree to which the professional practice model met desired quality and fiscal outcomes, the implementation stimulated thoughts about wider organizational implementation. In addition, the DGPP model components complemented the patient care restructuring efforts that had begun to be developed at UMC. The patient care restructuring project has expanded beyond professional nursing practice, but the DGPP model subcomponents have been useful throughout the restructuring process.

NOTES

1. J. Verran, et al., Differentiated Group Professional Practice in Nursing, the University of Arizona College of Nursing: Tucson *(Cooperative agreement award U01-NR02153 funded by the National Center for Nursing Research, National Institutes of Health and the Division of Nursing, Department of Health and Human Services*, 1988–1993).
2. D. Milton, et al., Differentiated Group Professional Practice in Nursing: A Demonstration Model. *Nursing Clinics of North America* 27 (1992): 23–30.
3. M.K. Aydelotte, Governance, Education Are Watchwords for the 80s. *American Nurse* 12 (1980): 18.
4. L.M. Johnson, et al., A Model of Participatory Management with Decentralized Authority. *Nursing Administration Quarterly* 8 (1983): 30–36.
5. T. Porter-O'Grady, Credentialing, Privileging, and Nursing Bylaws: Assuring Accountability. *Journal of Nursing Administration* 15 (1986): 23–27.
6. L. Christman, Bylaws by Themselves May not Be Sufficient (*Paper presented at the meeting, Self-Governance: A Climate for Professional Practice*, Rose Medical Center, Denver, Colo., 1982).
7. M. Kramer and C. Schmalenberg, Magnet Hospitals: Institutions of Excellence. *Journal of Nursing Administration* 18 (1988): 13–24.
8. P.L. Primm, Entry into Practice: Competency Statements for BSNs and ADNs. *Nursing Outlook* 34 (1986):135–37.
9. J. O'Malley and S.H. Cummings, Nursing Case Management III: Implementing Case Management: Operational Model. *Aspen's Advisor for Nurse Executives* 3 (1988): 7–8.
10. L. Smircich, Concepts of Culture and Organizational Analysis. *Administration Science Quarterly* 28 (1983): 339–58.
11. M. McClure, et al., *Magnet Hospitals: Attraction and Retention of Professional Nurses* (Kansas City, Mo.: American Academy of Nursing, 1983).
12. K.K. Rauen, et al., *The Nurse Intrapreneur: Opportunities and Benefits from Nursing* (Philadelphia, Pa.: Lippincott, 1988).
13. E. Rogers, ed., *Diffusion of innovation* (New York, N.Y.: Free Press, 1983).

14. E. Rogers and R. Agarwala-Rogers, *Communication in Organizations* (New York, N.Y.: Free Press, 1984).

15. S. Geller, et al., *Case Study Evaluations: Differentiated Group Professional Practice* (Unpublished manuscript, University of Arizona, Tucson, 1992).

16. D. Milton, et al., *Development of a Scaling Methodology to Examine Implementation and Synthesis of a Professional Practice Model* (Unpublished manuscript, University of Arizona, Tucson, 1992).

17. L.R. Good and O. Nelson, Effects of Person–Group and Intragroup Attitude Similarity on Perceived Group Attractiveness and Cohesiveness, *Psychological Reports* 15 (1973): 551–60.

18. R. Gerber, *Control over Nursing Practice Scale: Psychometric Analysis* (Poster presented at the National Conference on Instrumentation in Nursing, Tucson, Ariz., September 1990).

19. R.T. Mowday, et al., The Measurement of Organizational Commitment, *Journal of Vocational Behavior* 14 (1979): 224–47.

20. H.P. Sims, et al., The Measurement of Job Characteristics. *Academy of Management Journal* 19 (1976): 195–212.

21. R.P. Quinn and G.L. Staines, *The 1977 Quality of Employment Survey: Descriptive Statistics with Comparison Data from 1969–70 and 1972–73* (Ann Arbor, Mich.: Institute of Social Research, University of Michigan, 1979), 195–212.

22. L.P. Stamps and E.B. Piedmonte, *Nurses and Work Satisfaction: An Index for Measurement* (Ann Arbor, Mich.: Health Administration Press Perspectives, 1986).

CHAPTER

4

The Planning and Change Process

Mickey L. Parsons

Chapter Objectives

1. To describe the planning process and organizational infrastructure created to implement the model.
2. To describe the implementation timeline to restructure an individual unit.
3. To describe the approach utilized to manage the process of change.

Effective management of the planning and change process is necessary for the successful implementation of any new innovation. If the idea is perceived to be controversial and radical, as in restructuring of the patient care delivery system, recognition of the importance of planning and constant attention to the management of the change process are both critical and essential. The purpose of this chapter is to outline the specific details utilized at University Medical Center (UMC) to plan and implement the new model of care discussed in Chapter 2. The rational approach to large-scale organizational change and the organizational infrastructure utilized are outlined. The implementation process is described, and a sample timeline to restructure an individual unit is presented. The philosophical and practical approach to support and facilitate individuals and groups through the process of change is addressed.

PLANNING PROCESS

The planning process utilized can best be described as a rational, logical, analytical approach. It begins with preparation of the leader and hospital leadership and proceeds with a building-block approach to solidify involvement and support at each stage of the change effort. Common sense and basic problem-solving skills are integral to each stage. All eight planning phases and steps are listed in Exhibit 4–1.

Phase 1: Leader's Preparatory Phase—"Do Your Homework"

The most important beginning work for administrative change agents is to do their homework. Doing the homework is defined as completing a review of the literature and determining nationally how other organizations are approaching the restructuring of patient care. When staff at UMC began to plan for a change, essentially no literature was published on the ideas that were under discussion. The next option available is to attend meetings, network with colleagues, and utilize telecommunications to

Exhibit 4–1 The Planning Process

Phase 1: Leader's preparatory phase—"Do Your Homework"
Phase 2: Prepare the Leadership

- Step 1—Grow the idea
- Step 2—Decide the restructuring objectives
- Step 3—Provide top leadership information and obtain support
- Step 4—Build momentum
- Step 5—Provide key physician leaders information

Phase 3: Create the organizational infrastructure
Phase 4: Prepare the staff
Phase 5: Involve the staff
Phase 6: Address liability concerns
Phase 7: Decide final role definitions of new workers
Phase 8: Prepare implementation time line

learn from others in the field. Sharing on the telephone with other professionals or networking via computer conferencing systems are primary methods available today to acquire the latest information about innovative ideas and their implementation.

The second part of the preparatory phase is to recognize the context of the environment that is to undergo massive change. At UMC the entire planning and implementation schedule was based on the philosophy, accomplishments, and capabilities of the hospital administrative staff and senior leaders at the department director level. The hospital administrative staff are highly motivated, committed, and fast paced with a track record of significant accomplishments in program growth and new program implementation. The nursing administrative team demonstrated these same attributes. Therefore, an innovative and aggressive new approach to patient care delivery was not only conceivable but perceived as possible to accomplish.

Phase 2: Prepare the Leadership

There are five key steps in preparing the hospital leadership for major organizational change:

1. Grow the idea
2. Decide the restructuring objectives
3. Provide top leadership information and obtain support
4. Build momentum
5. Provide key physician leaders information

Each step builds upon the preceding one. The series of building blocks forms the foundation upon which it is possible to move to the next major phase of preparing the staff.

Step 1: Grow the Idea

At UMC two senior hospital administrative staff were committed to the need for restructuring based upon the stimulants for change as discussed in Chapters 1 and 2. There was a full discussion of issues and a mini-retreat for operational hospital administrative staff, including the chief operating officer, vice presidents for nursing and patient care services, ancillary and support services, and human resources. This meeting was 6 months before the organizational structure was initiated to plan to implement a new model, and it resulted in agreement on key concepts for improvement in the patient care delivery process. The mini-retreat was the most important step in growing the idea and obtaining operational administrative staff concurrence. The hospital administrator who was selected to lead the hospitalwide restructuring effort was the vice president for nursing and patient care services.

These agreements led to presentations (for the hospital, medical, and nursing administrative staff) on restructuring initiatives or pilot projects at other facilities, such as Vanderbilt University Hospital,[1] Georgetown University Hospital,[2] and University of Indiana Hospitals[3] and in the University of Arizona College of Nursing grant described in Chapter 3. Pilot unit successes from the St. Joseph's System in Orange, California were shared from another conference that same year.[4] This information and discussion led to full hospital administrative, hospital medical director, and nursing administrative staff agreement to pursue patient care restructuring.

Step 2: Decide the Restructuring Objectives

The specific objectives for the restructuring effort will determine the process and issues to be addressed in the planning and implementation process. As outlined in Chapter 2, at UMC the number 1 objective was to improve patient satisfaction and service. If the number 1 objective is to reduce expenses, another approach is needed. Finance continued to be an important objective at UMC but in the context of cost containment by reducing the annual rise in the cost of care. This fundamental difference determines the significant barriers and problems encountered in the restructuring process. If staff believe that the only reason for restructuring is to decrease costs, the implementation of a new model of care could be quite problematic. A large-scale institutional change is difficult enough without having to contend with cost as the number 1 goal.

Step 3: Provide Top Leadership Information and Obtain Support

The chief operating officer and vice president for nursing and patient care services met with the hospital chief executive officer and the dean of the College of Medicine to present information and obtain concurrence to proceed. Because UMC is an academic medical center, it is essential that the hospital administrative staff collaborate with the medical school leadership in all major endeavors. Both leaders were totally supportive, and the restructuring effort was approved. Additionally, the vice president for nursing and patient care services met the dean of the College of Nursing to provide information and to encourage the involvement of interested faculty.

Step 4: Build Momentum

A primary strategy to build momentum for a hospital change effort is to provide information. This step included detailed presentations to hospital department directors and nurse managers and educators. The response from the nursing leadership was positive; some managers requested to participate as a pilot unit immediately. Some ancillary department directors were not as positive. For a further description of their concerns and needs, please see Chapters 24 through 26. One nurse manager who had been requesting several new registered nurse (RN) positions changed the request after hearing the presentation and ideas for restructuring.

Step 5: Provide Key Physician Leaders Information

In the interest of collaboration in an academic medical center, numerous meetings with physician leaders were held to provide information and obtain support to participate in the project or support it indirectly. Over a period of 6 weeks, the chief operating officer and the vice president of nursing and patient care services met with the ancillary department medical directors and/or department chairs. The adult and pediatric respiratory and cardiology section heads, pathology department chair and medical director, and the physician leader of the rehabilitation medical staff committee were all considered priority for involvement because their departments were potential areas for restructuring and decentralization of functions to new workers on the patient care units. All were open to change and involvement; some were actively supportive and shared that support within their departments. Other key leaders, such as the incoming and outgoing elected chief of the medical staff and the medical staff executive committee, were priority for information sharing. Again, most were supportive, and none was opposed to the restructuring ideas and project .

Sharing information with physicians continued over the next 5 months as the vice president of nursing and patient care services met with the chairs of the departments of surgery, pediatrics, neurology, and family practice and the section chiefs for neurosurgery, gynecology, and urology. This process created a large group of physician leaders who were interested in and supportive of implementing a restructured model of patient care.

With the completion of these five steps and the support of the hospital, nursing, and medical leadership, it is possible to address the next stages of the planning and change process. In the next major phase the infrastructure is created to plan, implement, and operate (maintain) a restructured environment.

Phase 3: Create the Organizational Infrastructure

Infrastructure To Plan

Three essential groups from different parts of the organization and three essential support structures are necessary to plan a new model of patient care delivery. The three essential groups are the patient care restructuring (PCR) steering committee, the PCR task force with multiple ad hoc work groups, and the unit PCR steering committees (see Figure 4–1). The three essential support structures are administrative support, educational support, and evaluation (research) support. The purpose and organization of each group and support structure are described later in this chapter.

PCR steering committee. The PCR steering committee functions as the policy and advisory body with final approval of the project. It is composed of members of the hospital administrative staff; vice presidents for ancillary, support, human resources, planning, and marketing departments; finance; the hospital medical director; and the chief of staff. It is led by the vice president for nursing and patient care services. Monthly review meetings have continued since the project's inception.

PCR task force. The PCR task force serves as the functional group to plan and operate the entire restructuring process. It is composed of department directors from materials management, food services, cardiology/respiratory, laboratory, social services, rehabilitation services, environmental services, and nursing. Managers and specialists from finance, human resources, food services, materials management, nursing, physical and occupational therapy, and transportation also participate on a regular basis. The task force is led by the vice president for nursing and patient care services. Two additional administrators participate: a vice president for selected ancillary/support departments, and the vice president of human resources. For the first 2 years the group met every 2 weeks. Currently the

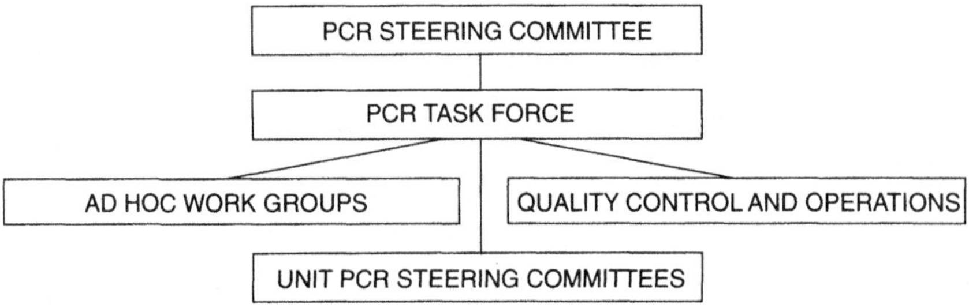

Figure 4-1 Organizational infrastructure.

group meets monthly. Two new positions, PCR program manager and PCR education coordinator, were created and are essential to the entire restructuring process.

The PCR task force created ad hoc work groups to plan components of the project. They are listed in Exhibit 4–2. These groups met intensively over a period of approximately 3 months in the beginning of the project. New minigroups are formed to address issues that require problem solving and recommendations to the task force, and are then disbanded.

The most challenging tasks were for the three work groups, which were to define the roles of the RN case manager and associate, patient care technician (PCT), and patient support attendant (PSA). These groups met the most frequently and had the longest meetings. It was here that the struggles of turf and opposition to change were most often played out, both inside nursing and in the ancillary and support departments.

The RN case manager and associate work group was cochaired by an area nursing director and program manager for PCR. Clinical nurses, nurse managers, and representatives from social services and human resources participated in the work group. Staff nurses who had participated in the University of Arizona College of Nursing Differentiated Group Professional Practice (DGPP) grant as described in Chapter 3 shared their experience with case management, and the conceptual program was built from that beginning foundation. Please see Chapter 9 for a full description of the implementation of case management.

Exhibit 4–2 Organizational Infrastructure

PCR task force ad hoc work groups

1. RN case manager and case associate role
2. Patient care technician (PCT) role
3. Patient support attendant (PSA) role
4. Unit manager role
5. Staffing plans, all roles
6. Comprehensive education plan
7. Communication plan, internal and external
8. Implementation of interdisciplinary management (introduced via creating the unit PCR steering committee)
9. Implementation of shared values of excellence in patient care (introduced via recognition and awards programs)
10. Evaluation criteria
11. Cost and billing implications, including information systems
12. Quality control and operations

The PCT work group was cochaired by an area nursing director and the director of the cardiorespiratory department. Clinical nurses, managers, and specialists from laboratory, physical and occupational therapy, respiratory therapy, and social work participated in the group. This group's function was to define the role, outline the tasks to be performed, draft the job description, and design an initial training program. Time was spent discussing positive and negative reasons for restructuring as well as fears and concerns. Discussions of issues enabled the group to complete its tasks in a timely manner. Please refer to Chapter 7 for a full description of this role and training realities.

The PSA work group was cochaired by an area nursing director and the director of the environmental services department. Clinical nurses, managers, and specialists from environmental services, food services, materials management, and transportation participated in the work group. This group's function was to define the role, outline the tasks to be performed, draft the job description, and design an initial training program. This group also spent considerable time discussing the restructuring issues as well as concerns about major full-time equivalent (FTE) transfers to nursing for the project. Please refer to Chapter 6 for a full discussion of this role and the training program.

The unit manager role work group was cochaired by an area nursing director and the director of human resources. Clinical nurses, nurse managers, directors, and human resource professionals served on this work group. Their function was to redefine the role of the nurse manager in a restructured environment and to draft the job description and performance standards for performance appraisals. The most difficult part of restructuring the unit manager's role was determining the title. At UMC the managers of nursing units are nurse managers, and consensus could not be reached on a new title. Therefore, their title continues to be nurse manager primarily because of the managers' feedback. There is strong support for the restructuring effort but an equally strong preference to continue to be called nurse manager. For a full discussion of this role, please refer to Chapter 14.

The staffing plans work group was led by the two area nursing directors in conjunction with the nurse managers of the first four pilot units and the staff. Their function was to develop staffing patterns for all roles, 24 hours a day and the FTE budget required to support those patterns. The unit PCR steering committees with their nurse managers drafted staffing options based upon the roles defined, the FTEs to be transferred from the ancillary and support departments, and the unit FTEs. Staff reported that this process was effective in two of the four units. Therefore, significant efforts have been made to be certain that unit staff are involved in drafting staffing options as new units have been restructured.

The comprehensive education plan work group was led by the vice president for nursing and patient care services. The purpose of this effort was to ensure the development of a comprehensive plan to educate new workers and staff on the units for the restructuring process. The curriculum and training program for the PCTs and PSAs were developed by a new position, the PCR education coordinator. These training programs were designed with all departments based on the draft job descriptions and training programs from each work group. The RN educational component, communication and team building, supervision and delegation, and the process of change management with selected technical skill training were developed by the vice president, PCR program manager, and human resources training specialist with input from the entire task force and unit PCR steering committees. Please refer to Chapters 8 and 12 for more information about RN education and building the team.

The communication plan work group was led by the vice president for nursing and patient care services. The PCR program manager, vice president for planning and marketing, and director and staff from the news and communication department participated in this effort. The task was to define and implement a comprehensive communication plan both internal to the Medical Center and Health Sciences Center and also for the professional community and lay community in the state. Please see Chapter 17 for a full description of this component of the project.

The implementation of interdisciplinary team management work group consisted of the vice president for nursing and patient care services, the program manager for PCR, and the former DGPP Grant principal investigator at UMC. The beginning implementation of these concepts was in the introduction of unit PCR steering committees. The group recognized that this was the infancy of implementing group governance on the units and that it would be necessary to follow a building-block approach to ensure success over the next several years. The hope was that, as the unit steering committees developed and as the nurses fully implemented case management, participatory involvement with all professionals would evolve. Please see more information in this chapter and in Chapter 13.

The implementation of shared values of excellence in patient care work group consisted of the vice president for nursing and patient care services, the program manager for PCR, and the former DGPP Grant investigator at UMC. Implementation of this concept began on the grant research units and was strongly supported by the vice president and program manager because of the success seen both on the grant units and in the military with recognition and award programs. The development and implementation of a comprehensive recognition and awards program became a cornerstone of the entire restructuring effort. For a full description of this intensive program, please refer to Chapter 15.

The evaluation criteria work group was led by the vice president for nursing and patient care services. The goal was to develop and implement in an extremely short time frame a comprehensive evaluation program for the restructuring process. The vice president for planning and marketing, the manager of the planning department, the planning analyst, the PCR program manager, and a manager from the information systems department all participated in this work group. Two nurse investigators from the DGPP Grant provided assistance in determining evaluation instruments to utilize and ideas for organizing the unit data collection efforts. Please refer to Chapters 28 through 33 for more information.

The cost and billing implications work group, including information systems, was cochaired by the vice president for nursing and patient care services and the assistant controller of the finance department. The purpose of the work group was to evaluate and plan for systems to support the restructuring process. A financial analyst, a planning analyst, an area nursing director, the assistant director for information systems, and an information systems analyst participated in the work group. Please see Chapter 16 on the financial planning process. The group faced insurmountable barriers in information systems that are currently being documented in the literature and will play a major role in the future success of restructuring nationally. The issue is lack of comparable database systems to evaluate productivity and costs due to restructuring.

The quality control and operations work group became an ongoing group as each unit was restructured. It was led by the vice president of nursing and patient care services with one participant from each department and unit involved in restructuring. The purpose was to develop, implement, and utilize quality control standards for functions being decentralized to the patient care units. Please see the next section of this chapter and refer to Chapters 24 through 27 for more information.

Unit PCR steering committee. The unit PCR steering committee is critical to the success of the restructuring process on an individual unit. It is led by a clinical nurse leader on the unit who is not the nurse manager, and is composed of staff nurses and representatives from other work roles on the unit. The committee functions are to participate in the following key functions:

- defining roles for new workers in their units
- planning educational and training programs

- planning for the change process
- determining criteria for hiring new workers
- hiring and selection processes
- preparing RN preceptors for the PCTs
- developing unit workflow plans
- evaluating operations and problem solving

This group of unit leaders significantly influences overall staff participation, involvement, planning, and success on the unit. If the unit steering committee, in conjunction with the nurse manager, effectively involves and communicates with all staff, the problems encountered in the change process are more manageable. For a full discussion of the role of the unit coordinator and the impact of the unit steering committee, please refer to Chapter 13.

Support Structures

Administrative support structure. The office of patient care restructuring and a program manager position were created. The program manager reports to the administrator of the project, who also serves as the vice president for nursing and patient care services. The program manager serves as a special assistant to the administrator of the project to plan, implement, and evaluate the project. A highly visible component of the program manager role is the official liaison role with all unit PCR steering committees and with each unit coordinator. Each unit coordinator is provided initial training in the project and in leading groups and meetings. Unit-specific restructuring time lines are planned with the nurse manager, unit steering committee, and program manager. The program manager assists the nurse manager with each step of the implementation time line and involves the vice president and/or appropriate others if problems arise. A particularly enjoyable part of the role has been the development and implementation of the recognition and awards program. The PCR office is staffed by a full-time secretary and a periodic data entry clerk for assistance in the management of data collection and data entry. For more specific information about the role of the program manager, please see Chapter 5.

Educational support structure. A second new position, the PCR education coordinator, was created. The education coordinator's initial responsibility was to complete the development of the training program for the PCTs and PSAs. The work groups' first drafts were utilized, and each ancillary, support, and nursing area finalized its particular areas of expertise with the education coordinator. The second primary function was to coordinate and teach in the PCT and PSA training programs. The education coordinator with preceptors in each area determines whether a trainee has met the requirements from both the didactic classroom instruction and the clinical skill training instruction and return demonstration. The new area that has evolved after eight units have been restructured is the need for continuing education updates for both the PCTs and the PSAs. Coordination of this effort has become the responsibility of the education coordinator as well. The coordinator is a member of the nursing staff development department and reports to the director of nursing resources. In Chapters 6 through 8 more specific information concerning the training programs for PCTs, PSAs, and RNs may be found that provides more insight into the complexities of the PCR education coordinator's role.The expertise of this individual enabled the project to expand rapidly to more than eight units in less than 2 years.

Evaluation (research) support structure. The rapidity with which the entire evaluation scheme had to be planned and organized necessitated that the vice president for nursing and patient care services lead this effort. Research design was facilitated by the director of nursing research, who was on leave from the UMC position, with the assistance of a College of Nursing faculty member. Instrument selection was completed by the vice president, the director of nursing research, and the evaluation work group. Organization of the survey instruments and staff data collection were managed by the PCR program manager. The survey instruments for patient and physician satisfaction were designed, managed, and analyzed by the UMC planning department. The analysis of the staff satisfaction data was also completed by the planning department. From an overall organizational perspective, this infrastructure could have been better supported. In an effort to contain overhead expenses, additional FTEs were not added to support this function. The result was tremendous stress on a number of staff. In retrospect, this effort should have been planned differently.

Infrastructure To Implement and Manage

The PCR task force continues to be the primary group to implement the restructuring process. The ad hoc work group on quality control and operations, however, has become an ongoing subgroup. Initially, quality control and operations met weekly when the first four pilot units implemented the new PCT and PSA roles. With experience, quality control and operations now meets only when new units are implementing restructuring, and for the postrestructuring units this function is addressed at regular task force meetings. For further discussion, please see more information in this chapter and in Chapters 24 through 27.

Phase 4: Prepare the Staff

There are two related steps in preparing the hospital staff for major organizational change. As with the hospital leadership, these steps form the foundation upon which it is possible to move to the next major phases of planning and implementation.

Step 1: Introductory Presentations for Nursing Units

Four pilot units were selected as the first units to restructure. Two were medical-surgical units that had not had the opportunity to participate in the DGPP Grant described in Chapter 3, and two were pediatric units. The pediatric director of nursing requested that the pediatric units participate in the initial project for special considerations in pediatrics to be addressed from the beginning. The recommendations were accepted because it was logical to avoid creating an adult model and later superimposing it on a pediatric area.

Each unit's staff were invited to attend one of three special presentations for their individual unit, which included the service of breakfast, luncheon, or light dinner meals. The vice president for nursing and patient care services' slide presentation included information about current health care trends nationally and regionally with the stimulants for change, objectives for restructuring, status of pilot restructuring efforts across the nation, and the goals and general approach for UMC's planning. Each unit's nurse manager and staff were requested to organize their unit PCR steering committee and to designate a unit PCR coordinator after the 12 presentations. These 12 meetings required a tremendous commitment on the part of nursing directors, nurse managers, the PCR program manager, and administration. Each nursing director personally attended all 6 repeat meetings for his or her area, and each nurse manager personally attended all 3 repeat meetings for his or her unit. The vice president for nursing and patient care services presented the repeat session 12 times, and the PCR program manager attended each time. This demonstration of commitment was meant to provide consistent information for the staff, to provide ample opportunity for discussion, and to begin to establish the unit structure to plan and implement the new model of care.

Step 2: Introductory Presentations for Ancillary and Support Departments

Almost concurrently, ancillary and support departments were invited to introductory presentations identical to the nursing unit meetings. The area of greatest staff interest was the ancillary professional area of rehabilitation services, social services, ECG, quality assurance and utilization management, risk management, laboratory, and respiratory therapy. Managers and supervisors from support/technical departments, materials management, transportation, environmental services, and cardiology–ECG also attended. These presentations were also made by the vice president for nursing and patient care services, and each vice president for the respective department attended his or her area's meetings. This afforded the opportunity to demonstrate administration's commitment to restructuring and to provide information and a communication forum for the staff. Each department involved in restructuring had at least one representative on each restructuring task force or work group, and this participation was shared with the staff to assure them that their concerns would be addressed.

Phase 5: Involve the Staff

Two primary methods are utilized to involve the staff. The first is the creation of a unit PCR steering committee. The function and composition of this group is discussed in the section on infrastructure in this chapter; for further information please see Chapter 13. This step cannot be overemphasized. For the first four pilot units, this meant that one committee for each unit had to be developed, nurtured, and guided by the PCR program manager, unit nurse manager, and director of nursing for the area. This effort requires tremendous support from these individuals and from the PCR program secretary. It is commonplace for the unit PCR coordinators to share information with the program secretary. The secretary facilitates communication and meetings, prepares minutes, and sometimes provides that listening ear for human support.

The second approach to involving staff is in the PCR task force ad hoc work groups. Staff served on the initial work groups to define the roles of PCT, PSA, RN case manager and associate, and nurse manager. As new problem-solving minigroups are formed either by the task force or via a unit, staff from the unit and other involved restructured departments are involved. This may sound like a simple concept. The reality is that it is challenging to implement regularly and consistently. For ongoing success in continuous quality improvement initiatives, however, it is imperative that staff involvement be planned as an integral component of the change process.

Phase 6: Address Liability Concerns

The immediate initial concern of the nursing staff was liability and licensure issues. The concern was their legal liability in working with assistive personnel. In each of the 33 introductory meetings during the past 2 years with staff across 11 units, it has been imperative to provide information about legal issues from the beginning.

The hospital and nursing leadership staff were struck by the lack of information the staff had about the legal areas of professional practice. This was particularly surprising because all units had at least one assistive personnel role on their units as well as unit secretaries, licensed practical nurses (LPNs), and/or nursing assistants (NAs). Therefore, informal and formal educational approaches were selected to address the needs.

The assistant vice president for risk management and legal affairs was consulted, and a short briefing paper was written for the management staff (see Exhibit 4–3). This information and opinions were utilized by the vice president and directors of nursing to discuss the practical issues of concern to the staff in future introductory meetings and by the PCR program manager and education coordinator in educational sessions and workshops for the staff. The hospital attorney also provided presentations for the staff.

Basically, there were two real-world situations that needed clarification for the staff RNs. It was important to discuss that their legal liability, according to their license, was not new as a result of restructuring. Legal terminology can quickly frustrate and frighten the staff. Because restructuring can become an emotional issue, a practical approach in nursing language was taken.

The first area for clarification is when the RN is personally liable for another worker's mistake. It was discussed that, if an LPN or NA today or a PCT or PSA in the future performed a procedure incorrectly or performed a procedure that was not part of his or her approved role and for which he or she was not qualified, the individual LPN/NA/PCT/PSA and the hospital would be held responsible. The RN would be responsible (and liable) for his or her actions from the moment of learning of the situation and for the actions that he or she took as a result. In the discussions, staff were able to recognize that the legal liability is indeed not new. This decreased some of the emotionality of the liability issue. The hospital attorney assisted by explaining the difference between vicarious liability

Exhibit 4–3 Liability of Nurses for Supervising Others

Insurance Coverage

All UMC employees, including nurses, are covered by the UMC professional liability insurance program for negligence they may commit in the course and scope of their employment.

Therefore, if for example an RN patient care manager and/or a patient care nurse were found to be negligent in the supervision of a PCT, the nurse would be protected by the UMC insurance program.

Nursing License

The Nurse Practice Act, at ARS 32-1663D4, says that the State Board of Nursing may revoke or suspend a nursing license if a nurse is found to be guilty of unprofessional conduct or to be unfit or incompetent by reason of negligence, habits, or other causes.

Liability of Nurses

State Board of Nursing Rule R4-19-402C states:

> The registered nurse shall be held accountable for the quality and quantity of nursing care given to patients rendered by self or others who are under his or her supervision.

State Board of Nursing Rule R4-19-403.9 defines unprofessional conduct, unfitness, or incompetency by reasons of negligent habits to include:

> Failure to supervise persons to whom nursing functions have been delegated or assigning unqualified persons to perform functions of licensed nurses.

There are two legal situations in which a nurse might be held responsible for the acts of another:

1. possibly by virtue of the fact that the nurse was the person's supervisor, even if the nurse was not guilty of any negligence himself or herself; this would be called vicarious liability
2. where the nurse actually was guilty of negligent supervision; this might be called actual negligence

Question: Can a nurse's license be affected by negligence committed by someone he or she supervises?

Answer: Yes, but in my opinion action could only be taken if the nurse was guilty of actual negligence rather than vicarious liability. Also, it would appear that there would have to be a pattern of negligence (more than one incident) to establish a habit unless the negligence was so gross as to indicate that the nurse was incompetent.

Conclusion: This is really nothing new. Nurses have always been accountable for the people they supervise. Under the PCR concept, there may be more people for the nurse to supervise, which may increase the chances of liability arising.

Prepared by Jim Richardson, Esq., Assistant Vice President, Risk Management and Legal Affairs, University Medical Center, Tucson, Arizona.

and actual negligence. The legal opinion was that it was remote for nurses to have vicarious liability for another worker's performance if they had not been actually negligent themselves.

The second area requiring clarification was actual negligence. Discussion centered on the fact that it would be considered actual negligence if an RN instructed any employee, for example an LPN, NA, PCT, or PSA, to perform a patient care function outside his or her approved scope of role and training. The area was not such a concern for the staff because they did not perceive this to be a potential problem. The administration and management staff's goal, however, was to share the information to avoid ever having the problem of employees, particularly PCTs, requesting to function outside the boundaries of their role.

Phase 7: Decide Final Role Definitions of New Workers

The PCR task force ad hoc work groups that are responsible for drafting the role and task lists for the PCTs and PSAs reported to the PCR task force at a special day-long planning retreat 3 months after beginning their work. There was substantial agreement on the roles but significant reluctance on the part of some ancillary and support departments. The PCR steering committee made the final decision on the task lists and roles and convened a special meeting with the involved vice presidents and department directors. The special meeting clarified issues and administration's commitment to restructuring the care delivery process.

The RN roles were less of an issue in the overall hospital. Inside the clinical nursing units, however, the definition of the RN case manager and case associate role was important. It was decided to implement the support and technical worker roles first to build the infrastructure to support the professional nursing role. Without the new roles, there was concern that it would only frustrate the nurses to try to change from task-centered nursing to case management.

Phase 8: Prepare the Implementation Time Line

A rudimentary implementation time line had been prepared from the beginning by the vice president. As each step of the planning proceeded, additional issues to be addressed were added to the list. A sequential approach for the entire implementation process was utilized in terms of what tasks needed to be completed before the next step. The categories that influence the implementation time line the most are the dates for the PCR introductory meetings, human resource coordination for hiring and selection, and educational coordination for training all new workers and current staff. With all the complexities, the PCR task force and unit steering committees spent considerable time developing and revising the time line.

UNIT IMPLEMENTATION TIME LINE

The time frame that has developed to be the most viable for restructuring a unit after the roles have been defined is approximately a 34-week schedule. Table 4–1 lists specifically the dates from kickoff and the major

Table 4–1 Unit Implementation Time Line

Date from Kickoff	*Activity*
34 weeks	Baseline data: Patient satisfaction
28 weeks	Baseline data: Staff satisfaction
25 weeks	Staff PCR introductory presentations
24 weeks	Unit PCR coordinator designated Unit PCR steering committee begins PCT and PSA skill inventory Evaluation for specific unit
23 weeks	RN interview committee selected
22 weeks	Unit budget coordination: ancillary, finance, nurse manager, and director
21 weeks	Administration review/approval of restructured area budgets Skills inventory and interviewing plan complete
20 weeks	PCT position request to human resources (HR) Interview skill training by HR
19 weeks	HR posting of PCT and PSA positions and advertising
18 and 17 weeks	HR screening of PCT applicants
16 and 15 weeks	Unit interviews of PCT applicants
14 weeks	Nurse manager interviews of PCT applicants
13 weeks	PCT positions offered

continues

Table 4–1 continued

Date from Kickoff	*Activity*
12 weeks	PCT positions offered Unit interviews for PSA applicants
11 weeks	PCT employment physicals Nurse manager interviews of PSA applicants
10 weeks	PCT training begins PSA positions offered
9 weeks	PCT training RN preceptorship workshop
8 weeks	PCT training RN selected skill training RN delegation and supervision workshop
7 weeks	PCT training PSA training begins
6 weeks	PCT training PSA training completed recognition ceremony
5 weeks	PSAs begin on units PCTs begin 4-week supervised clinical practicum
4 to 2 weeks	PCT supervised clinical practicum Unit staff communication workshop
1 week	Special PCT review Program completion ceremony
Kickoff	PCTs join PSAs on the units
4 weeks after kickoff	Unit team-building workshops
2 months after kickoff	Identification of unit case managers
3 months after kickoff	Case manager educational program begins
4 to 6 months after kickoff	Transition: Working out the kinks
5 months after kickoff	Case manager educational program completion ceremony
12 to 18 months after kickoff	Transition team building, and operational refinement

activities necessary to process and complete for implementation. Kickoff is defined as the date on which both the PSA and PCT new workers have completed their training programs and are officially new employees on the units. It is the day on the individual unit that the change to the PCR model of care officially begins and the transition is started.

To have an evaluation of the outcomes of the new model, it is important to complete baseline (prechange) data collection. Coordination with the planning department was necessary because the planning department ensured the collection of patient and physician satisfaction data. The PCR program manager and secretary organized the collection of staff satisfaction data several weeks before the vice president gave the introductory PCR presentations. The remainder of the evaluation data did not have to be collected at a specific interval of time because they were already available. Please see Chapters 28 through 33 for more information.

As previously discussed in this chapter, the development and implementation of the unit PCR steering committee is essential to the process. The unit committee is developed after the initial PCR presentations. Typically a small subgroup of the steering committee is appointed as the RN interview committee, and a subgroup works with the nurse manager to develop staffing pattern options after the roles are defined. With the area director of nursing's approval, the budget request would be submitted to administration for final approval, and the FTE requests would be forwarded to human resources.

Human resource coordination for hiring and selection requires extensive time and effort and is a critical area for success in the new model of care. Please see Chapter 11 as well as the unit case studies for detailed information. For the initial restructuring effort, the nurse managers found the hiring process time consuming because of the massive numbers of applicants and extensive involvement of the staff. The RN interviewing committee receives training from human resources and interviews and recommends all PCT and PSA applicants for hire to the nurse manager. This proved to be a valuable process because it gave the nurses increased confidence in the caliber of the new people who would be working with them.

For others contemplating restructuring, it is important to prepare staff and managers for an extensive hiring process. The reality is that it is only a problem during the initial restructuring effort, when all positions are open and need to be filled. Thereafter, it is much less of a consumer of time when one replacement position is being filled at a time.

After the hiring process is completed, coordination of the educational training programs for PCTs and PSAs becomes the major activity. The PCR education coordinator is responsible for these programs. Typically the PCTs require a 10-week training program, and the PSAs require a 2-week training program. The PCR education coordinator, the PCR program manager together with the human resources manager, and the nurse manager coordinate the RN educational programs and the unit communication and team-building workshops. Please refer to Chapters 6 through 8 and 12 for more information.

After completion of the training programs and the recognition ceremonies (program completion ceremonies), Kickoff Day is a focal point for the change. The entire hospital recognizes the change by banners and decorations, including balloons. The PCR slogan, "PCR Is Teamwork" is made highly visible on the decorations. In reality, Kickoff Day is when the next level of important work must begin. It is the transition process after the actual change has been implemented. A beginning workshop for the entire unit staff on building the team is held, and more follow-up is required. Additionally, the entire professional nursing role for unit-based case management officially begins after the support and technical worker roles. Approximately 5 months after the new workers have become a part of the unit to provide the infrastructure for the new nursing role, case management is implemented.

MANAGEMENT OF THE CHANGE PROCESS

There is probably no more challenging area in organizational management than managing the process of change. Change is talked about so much but understood so little. The literature abounds with theories and information about the management of the process of change. The human side of change, however, seems to be given lip service by middle and senior management in organizations. Historically, managers have not been comfortable with the softer side of managing people and dealing with feelings. It has been almost taboo. The process of change will be even more difficult if this is not recognized by the administrative change agents.

Hospital senior leadership, however, must pave the way for middle level managers to facilitate their staff in managing effectively the process of change. Particularly in a hospitalwide patient care restructuring process, both manager and staff responses to change in every department must not be underestimated. Working with staff to understand and manage the personal and emotional impact that change can have on individuals and groups makes the difference between success and failure. The UMC staff approach to the grief aspect of change was from the model developed by Elizabeth Kuebler-Ross.[5] Perlman and Takacs have labeled 10 phases of the emotional voyage of the change process.[6] Their proposed interventions were helpful in the process of change at UMC. Please see Table 4–2 for a full listing of these phases of change, characteristics/symptoms of each phase, and interventions.

Imagine the departments of pathology (laboratory), respiratory therapy, cardiology, physical and occupational therapy, environmental services, food services, transportation, materials management, and nursing on multiple units in various phases of the change process. The best strategy utilized was to conduct workshops and seminars on the change process and its management for all levels of personnel, including hospital administration. The leadership group, the PCR steering committee, must stay focused, persistent, goal directed, and patient with individuals and groups. Active listening and facilitating the staff in expressing their anger, frustration, and feelings in general prove to be helpful. Team-building workshops for staff both during restructuring and a year later are important. Too often leaders are uncomfortable expressing anger and conflict. This is essential to the process of change, however, and needs to be recognized as such. Additionally, attention must be placed on the group process and managing the group by clarifying where we are, where we need to go, and what we need to do to get there. This is an integral part of the human resources training component of team building and learning to work together in new ways. For a full description of the change process and building the team, please see Chapter 12.

An important lesson learned for the administrative leader of the restructuring effort was not to underestimate the follow-up needed after the change itself occurs. The managers and staff might have been spared additional frustration if the postimplementation transition had been better addressed. Every manager, including the chief executive officer and the board of directors, however, needs to be aware of the turmoil, both predictable and unpredictable, that a hospital will undergo during massive, facilitywide change during the actual change and during the transition process for at least a year afterward.

CONCLUSION

This chapter has described the planning process utilized in the PCR process. The organizational infrastructure created to implement the model is described. The implementation process and sample time line to restructure an individual unit are outlined. The approach utilized to facilitate the staff in the management of the process of change is described, and the most useful strategies are discussed.

Table 4–2 Growing with the Change: The Emotional Voyage of the Change Process

Charted Summary

Phase	*Characteristics/Symptoms*	*Interventions*
1. Equilibrium	High energy level. State of emotional and intellectual balance. Sense of inner peace with personal and professional goals in sync.	Make employees aware of changes in the environment which will have impact on the status quo.
2. Denial	Energy is drained by the defense mechanism of rationalizing a denial of the reality of the change. Employees experience negative changes in physical health, emotional balance, logical thinking patterns, and normal behavior patterns.	Employ active listening skills: e.g., be empathetic, nonjudgmental. Use reflective listening techniques. Nurturing behavior, avoiding isolation, and offering stress management workshops also will help.
3. Anger	Energy is used to ward off and actively resist the change by blaming others. Frustration, anger, rage, envy, and resentment become visible.	Recognize the symptoms, legitimize employees' feelings and verbal expressions of anger, rage, envy, and resentment. Active listening, assertiveness, and problem-solving skills needed by managers. Employees need to probe within for the source of their anger.
4. Bargaining	Energy is used in an attempt to eliminate the change. Talk is about "if only." Others try to solve the problem. "Bargains" are unrealistic and designed to compromise the change out of existence.	Search for real needs/problems and bring them into the open. Explore ways of achieving desired changes through conflict management skills and win-win negotiation skills.
5. Chaos	Diffused energy, feeling of powerlessness, insecurity, sense of disorientation. Loss of identity and direction. No sense of grounding or meaning. Breakdown of value system and belief. Defense mechanisms begin to lose usefulness and meaning.	Quiet time for reflection. Listening skills. Inner search for both employee and organization identity and meaning. Approval for being in state of flux.

continues

Table 4–2 continued

Charted Summary		
Phase	*Characteristics/Symptoms*	*Interventions*
6. Depression	No energy left to produce results. Former defense mechanisms no longer operable. Self-pity, remembering past, expressions of sorrow, feeling nothingness and emptiness.	Provide necessary information in a timely fashion. Allow sorrow and pain to be expressed openly. Long-term patience, take one step at a time as employees learn to let go.
7. Resignation	Energy expended in passively accepting change. Lack of enthusiasm.	Expect employees to be accountable for reactions to behavior. Allow them to move at their own pace.
8. Openness	Availability to renewed energy. Willingness to expend energy on what has been assigned to individual.	Patiently explain again, in detail, the desired change.
9. Readiness	Willingness to expend energy in exploring new events. Reunification of intellect and emotions begins.	Assume a directive management style: assign tasks, monitor tasks and results so as to provide direction and guidelines.
10. Re-emergence	Rechanneled energy produces feelings of empowerment, and employees become more proactive. Rebirth of growth and commitment. Employees initiate projects and ideas. Career questions answered.	Mutual answering of questions. Redefinition of career, mission and culture. Mutual understanding of role and identity. Employees will take action based on own decisions.

Source: Exhibit 1 from "The 10 Stages of Change," by Dottie Perlman and George J. Takacs. Reprinted with permission from *Nursing Management*, Vol. 21, No. 4 ©April 1990.

NOTES

1. J. Spinella, Vanderbilt University Hospital, Operations Restructuring (Presentation at the meeting of the University Hospital Consortium Nurse Executive Council, San Francisco, July 1990).
2. C. O'Brien and S. Costello, Georgetown University Hospital: A Patient Centered Health

Care Delivery System (Presentation at the meeting of the University Hospital Consortium Nurse Executive Council, San Francisco, July 1990).

3. S. Erlich. University of Indiana Hospital, Interdepartmental Work Redesign Project (Presentation at the meeting of the University Hospital Consortium Nurse Executive Council, San Francisco, July 1990).
4. R. Spitzer-Lehman, St. Joseph's Health System Work Redesign (Presentation at the meeting of the Arizona Organization of Nurse Executives, Sedona, Ariz., September 1990).
5. E. Kuebler-Ross, *On Death and Dying* (New York: Macmillan, 1969).
6. D. Perlman and G. Takacs, The 10 Stages of Change, *Nursing Management* 21, no. 4 (1990): 34.

CHAPTER

5

Role of the Program Manager

Josephine Sacco Palmer

Chapter Objectives

1. To identify characteristics needed in a successful program manager.
2. To describe the program manager's role in the patient care restructuring process.

The role of the program manager is new in hospitals. Operational restructuring in health care organizations is a relatively new concept, and guidelines for the role of program manager had not been developed when University Medical Center (UMC) began the process.

Weiss describes the program manager as one whose work involves multiple priorities, deadlines, complex and numerous tasks, limited resources, and constant communication across organizational boundaries. All these activities are often performed with little, if any, precedents or guidelines.[1] This is especially true for a new project that has never been attempted before. The implementation of patient care restructuring (PCR) at UMC presented a challenging opportunity to create a program manager role and to adapt industry's approach to the health care organization.

ROLE OF THE PROGRAM MANAGER AS DESCRIBED IN THE LITERATURE

The program manager must be 200% committed to the success of the project and totally supportive of the administrative project leader. Program managers must possess a strong sense of mission, have excellent communication and people skills, and have a good sense of humor while remaining enthusiastic and self-confident. The role demands great dedication and considerable expenditure of energy. Strengths include someone who thrives on challenges, likes to solve problems creatively, and enjoys creating order out of chaos. A high tolerance for frustration is helpful.

Stallworthy and Kharbanda discuss qualifications of a project manager. They cataloged a list of desirable qualities from A to Z and qualified it by stating, "this may be light hearted in its approach to the subject, but it is not intended to be frivolous. Have no doubt about it: a successful project manager must have all these qualities and many more."[2(p.72)] The list cataloged includes the following characteristics:

- Adaptable
- Benefactor
- Communicator
- Delegates
- Enthusiast
- Flexible
- Go-getter
- Handler of people
- Initiative
- Jovial
- Keen
- Listener
- Motivator
- No-nonsense
- Organizer
- Persuasive
- Quiet
- Reliable
- Sensitive
- Team builder

- Understanding
- Versatile
- Winsome
- X-Ray view
- Yearns
- Zestful

The authors stress that, above all else, the program manager must be adaptable.[2]

In addition to being adaptable, a program manager has the role of integrator. Koontz and O'Donnell state that systems integration is related to the essence of management coordination. In other words, the purpose of the program manager is to achieve harmony of individual efforts toward the accomplishment of group goals.[3(p.46)]

Struckenbruck describes integration as the process of ensuring that all elements of the project—the tasks, components, organizational units, and people—fit together to function according to plan. All levels of management participate in integration. Project managers, however, must make a concerted effort and take specific actions to ensure that integration occurs.[4]

Roseneau also agrees that the program manager's interaction with the project support teams is a key to the people management phase.[5] Roseneau examines the overriding importance of the program manager's ability to influence other team members and further states that leadership ability depends on motivational skills rather than authority. Influence rather than authority is the approach that must be taken because many people working on the project do not report directly to the program manager. Therefore, program managers must operate by winning the respect of team members.

Silverman has described the key components for the ideal flow of power within an organization. These key components are authority, responsibility, and accountability. Authority is defined as the power to make final decisions. Responsibility is defined as the obligation to perform assigned tasks effectively.[6] Administration starts with the delegation of responsibility, which is generally accompanied by the authority to accomplish the job. The authority from administration or top management may be direct or implied. An inappropriate balance of responsibility and authority results in difficulty in achieving project objectives and goals.

Silverman defined accountability as being answerable for satisfactory completion of specified tasks.[6] Responsibility may be delegated downward, but accountability cannot be delegated downward. Final accountability rests with top administration and/or management. An important factor for the program manager is the knowledge that the authority that has been assigned will be supported by the authority in administration. In complex projects, the formal appointment of the program manager to the position implies direct authority. Silverman also explains, "Because authority is based partly on the particular manager's reputation for sound and consistently correct decisions, that reputation should be a major goal."[6(p.23)] Figure 5–1 illustrates the ideal flow of authority, responsibility, and accountability.

An effective program manager must have excellent communication skills and be persuasive to be effective. The program manager spends the majority of his or her time working with people.

Roseneau states that program managers need to be people oriented.[5] The most challenging aspect of the role is the management of human resources. Energies must be focused on the people involved in the project. Program managers spend an inordinate amount of time with people, so they should be chosen because of their interest and skill in human relations.

The program manager must also cope with conflict. Projects, especially new ones that require major change, are bound to have conflict. Because conflicts are to be expected, the program manager should have the skills and tolerance to cope adequately. Skills for conflict reduction and conflict resolution are required. Conflicts inevitably arise because projects are tem-

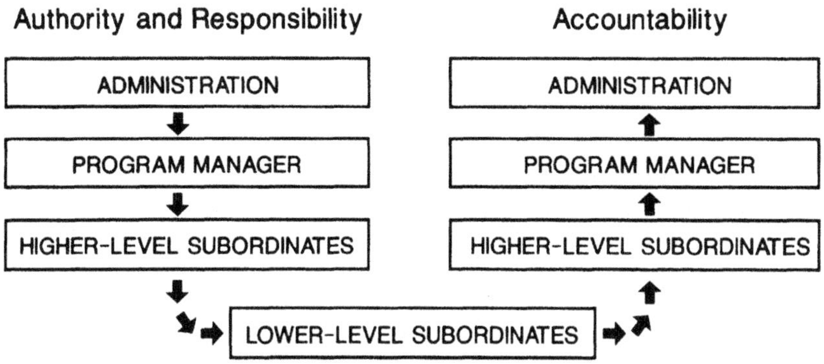

Figure 5–1 Power flow in program management: Ideal flow of authority, responsibility, and accountability. *Source:* Adapted from *Project Management, A Short Course for Professionals* by M. Silverman, p. 19, with permission of John Wiley & Sons, Inc., © 1976.

porary entities within a permanent organization.[5] Recommendations to reduce the occurrence of conflicts include frequent and thorough communication. Program managers must continually expedite communications throughout the course of the project.

The program manager needs to be alert to identify quickly and avoid possible common pitfalls that are likely to be encountered in managing the project. It should be expected that problems will arise, however. Slevin and Pinto identified 10 critical factors in effective project implementation. One factor reported was troubleshooting.[7] Troubleshooting was defined as the ability to handle unexpected crises and deviations from the plan. It is impossible to foresee every problem that can possibly arise, no matter how well the project is initially planned. As a result, the project manager must make adequate initial plans for troubleshooting operations to be included in the implementation plan.[8]

One of the keys to success as a program manager is being able to maintain a global picture of the status of the project. A common problem is getting so caught up in the helter-skelter of putting out fires and focusing on minutiae that program managers lose the big-picture perspective.[9] When multiple issues and circumstances that require immediate attention are happening all around them, it is difficult for program managers to step back and view the project from a distance.

Another key to success in the role is efficient use of time. Roseneau states that the overriding issue in time management is doing first things first. The project manager must be able to prioritize tasks that need to be accomplished daily as well as long term.[5]

THE PROGRAM MANAGER ROLE AT UMC

The program manager may be described as an individual who is operationally responsible for implementation of the patient care restructuring (PCR) project within predetermined time lines and budgetary constraints. A clear understanding of the project goals and objectives is necessary from the beginning, as is a solid belief in the potential for project success. The program manager reports directly to the vice president, who provides authority, direction, and support (Figure 5–2). The program manager's primary mission is ultimately to implement the vice president's plan and goals for PCR.[5] The degree of visible support form the vice president can affect the amount of acceptance the project receives. Identification of essential supports and their availability is necessary at the beginning of the project. These supports include allocation of sufficient resources, including funds, time, office space, staffpower, and equipment.

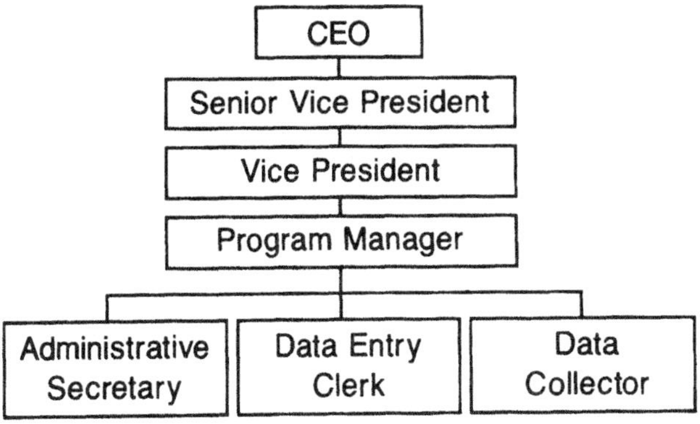

Figure 5–2 Reporting flow in the PCR project.

At UMC, assurances were made from the outset that these necessary resources would be forthcoming.

Establish a Formal PCR Office

Determining the number of individuals and skill mix needed to operate the PCR office was one of the first priorities. The project was also going to expand hospitalwide, and the scope of future requirements needed to be determined as well. It was essential to select a top-notch administrative secretary for this role because this individual would be the key to the efficient and smooth flow of implementation. Because of the broad scope of data collection requirements, it was important to select a master's-prepared registered nurse to perform this important role. The volume of data being collected would be enormous, requiring a data entry operator. The final key role was the education coordinator. A registered nurse with previous teaching experience as college faculty was selected. This individual needed to possess high-level skills to develop a curriculum and needed to be a self-starter. The education coordinator formally reports to the staff development coordinator for nursing and works closely with the PCR program manager.

Develop the PCR Office Budget

One of the first requirements was drafting an operating budget to set up the PCR office. Actually detailing all the anticipated material requirements and their cost and compiling this into a projected budget for the coming year needed to be as accurate as possible. A new project that has never been implemented cannot be estimated easily. A great deal of time and energy was needed to identify all the detailed aspects that would be required during the first year, such as computer hardware and software programs, filing system needs, communication system needs, reference and support material, and staffpower.

Determine a Time Line

When drafting the initial time frame, one must be prepared for flexibility the first few weeks and months. In the planning phase, underestimating the length of time certain tasks would require was common. An example was how quickly baseline data could be collected. Developing an instrument required much more time than initially estimated. Data collection dates had to be rescheduled several times.

Coordinate Data Collection

Baseline data needed to be collected before the project was implemented. Data were collected on patient satisfaction, physician satisfaction, and staff satisfaction. In addition, data related to fiscal and quality of care outcomes were obtained. Strategies to maximize data collection returns were implemented. For example, management's support for data collection was elicited, a publicity blitz was implemented for staff before collection, incentives for staff were identified, and personal communication occurred with staff. In addition, brightly colored envelopes were used for questionnaires placed on the units, and brightly colored collection boxes that were easily noticed were constructed. Frequent feedback was provided to staff on return rates, and celebrations were planned when staff achieved an 80% rate of return. Computer software programs for data entry needed to be identified. A data entry operator also needed to be hired and trained.

All fiscal, quality, and risk management data needed to be defined and sources identified for data collection to begin. Forms needed to be designed to record the data. Time is required to identify the data collection needs of the project.

Facilitate Communication Channels

The program manager needs to identify all channels of communication that must be maintained. Program managers are required to interact with many different people at various levels and in a wide range of departments (Figure 5–3). General communication problems should be antici-

Figure 5–3 Program manager's realm of interaction. The program manager interacts with a wide range of departments and individuals at various levels.

---

pated. Not all the staff with whom the program manager communicates will necessarily perceive messages the same way. People hear the message they expect or want to hear, especially those who are going through the process of change. When staff are in the denial or anger phase, the message perceived is not always the message delivered. The program manager must be prepared to repeat the same message many times.

Strategies to solve anticipated problems in communication include using multiple methods to deliver a message, such as memos, telephone conversations, and face-to-face meetings.

The program manager must determine which sequence or combination of methods will be most effective and must use language that is clear and simple. In addition, one must plan in advance what is to be communicated. Follow-up on communications is critical.

A major information blitz regarding the PCR project was prepared at UMC for staff and physicians. Visual graphics were prepared for top administrative leaders' presentations to introduce the project to staff. It was important to convey the significance of restructuring to staff working on the baseline units. Unit staff were treated in the fashion usually reserved for physician meetings. Three presentation meetings were scheduled for each of the four baseline units to enable all staff to attend. A full meal was served each time (breakfast, lunch, or dinner). The meetings provided staff an opportunity to ask questions and to clear misinformation that was churning through the rumor mill.

The program manager must identify all committee meetings, coordinate meeting schedules and rooms, and prepare a calendar. The calendar facilitates coordination and communication. The program manager is also responsible for scheduling and planning retreats, including selecting the location, menu, agenda, and visual aids; preparing educational material; and distributing notification to participants with follow-up.

Promote Staff Participation

Unit-based steering committees were formed at UMC to increase unit staff involvement. The committee meetings were open to all unit staff members. Unit-based steering committees represented the beginning groundwork for group governance on the PCR demonstration units. Please see Chapters 2, 3, and 13 for a discussion of group governance.

In the early phases, staff may be negative and lack motivation. The program manager helps staff see why their participation is important. If they clearly understand their role in the project on their unit, they will be much more enthusiastic. Involving staff from the beginning and spending time communicating with them are critical. Learning how the staff feel and identifying issues important to them provide valuable information about which plan to support throughout the change process.

A first step in staff participation is the selection of a unit coordinator. A unit coordinator is a nonmanagerial staff member responsible for coordinating and chairing the unit-based steering committee meetings. The program manager assists the nurse manager in identifying important qualities needed in a unit coordinator. Important qualities include an individual who is an informal leader with good communication skills, has a positive attitude, and is well organized. The program manager prepares the unit coordinators for the role by sharing the vision and goals of the project, coaching them on effective conduct of meetings, providing informative literature, and providing organizational assistance in getting started with coordinating unit-based steering committee meetings. The PCR office also provides clerical support for typing meeting minutes, providing a calendar of events for meetings, and making signs or notices that post announcements for staff communication.

Facilitate Meetings

Project meetings consume the greatest amount of staff time. Therefore, managing effective meetings is essential. The program manager's role is to facilitate the most effective/efficient conduct of meetings. Attempts are made always to begin meetings on time. Rooms are arranged to enhance communication; a circular arrangement with all parties facing each other is preferred. Agendas are always printed (Exhibit 5–1). An action items form is completed, and minutes are recorded (Exhibit 5–2).

The program manager attends all committee meetings to maintain a global perspective of the progress of the project. Major meetings include the major steering committee with administrators and major task forces, consisting of all department directors and managers involved in PCR. Subcommittee meetings include ad hoc groups to define roles, such as the PSA committee, PCT committee, nurse manager committee, and nurse case manager committees. Ad hoc committees include the internal/external communication committee, the research/evaluation committee, the comprehensive education planning committee, and the cost and billing committee.

Operations and quality control meetings were also determined to be of major importance at UMC. Working with the ancillary and support department directors and managers to identify and solve operational issues during implementation was important. Quality control and operations meetings were scheduled frequently when the units were first going up with the patient support attendant and patient care technician roles. Operations and quality control meetings continue to be valuable. In addition, the program manager meets regularly with the administrative leader of the project to evaluate progress continually and to plan for implementation.

Exhibit 5–1 PCR Project Task Force Committee Meeting Agenda

I.	Action items
II.	Continuing education—JM
III.	Policy: Wheelchair/stretcher maintenance/storage—JM
IV.	Policy: IV pump, storage & cleaning—MR
V.	Phase I update—JB, RH, ME
VI.	Phase II update—AE, JS
VII.	Phase III update—ME
VIII.	Phase IV update—KM
IX.	Phase V Update—PM
X.	Other

Exhibit 5–2 Project Task Force Meeting: Action Items

Action Item	*Person Responsible*	*Status*	*Date Received*
Continuous improvement team for hiring process	LB, team leader	Ongoing	
Laboratory quality control issues	VE and nurse managers	Ongoing	
PT/OT data on unnecessary requests	RK	Report in May	
Ancillary ad hoc coordinating committee	JB, Chair, JM, TB, JD, KM, JP	Report in May	
PCR policy and procedure manual	LS	Review in May—Manual due in June	
Master memo on lab accreditation	LS, VE, CH	Report in May	

Coordinate the Recognition Program

The program manager plans and implements the formal and informal recognition program for staff. The program manager is also responsible for planning and conducting formal completion ceremonies for patient support attendants, patient care technicians, and nurse care managers. All informal appreciation and recognition events are planned and operationalized by the program manager. See Chapter 15 for details.

Plan Change Process Workshops

The program manager at UMC assisted in guiding staff through the change process and in identifying their educational needs. Preparation for the major change was accomplished in workshops on communication, team building, and delegation. See Chapter 12 for details.

Staff had not previously participated in the hiring process. Thus arrangements needed to be made for the staff and members of the unit-based steering committees to work with persons in the human resources department to facilitate the interview screening and hiring process of new multi-

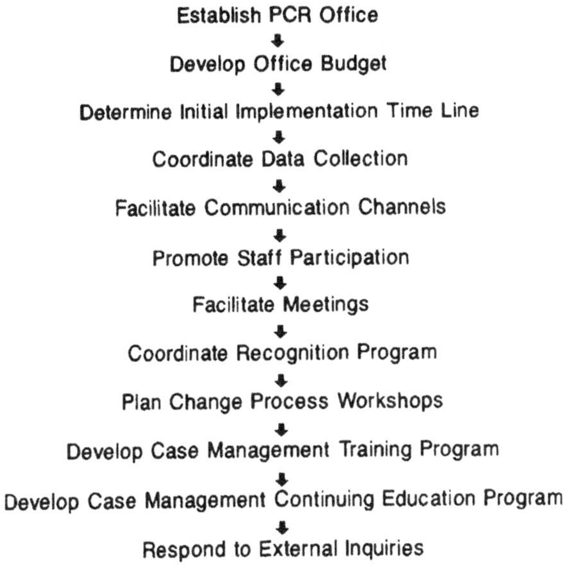

Figure 5–4 Program manager role at UMC.

purpose ancillary and support workers. A collaborative working relationship between the unit nurse managers and the manager of human resources was crucial, and the program manager facilitated the relationship.

Respond to External Inquiries

The program manager initially responds to external inquiries for information regarding the operational aspects of PCR. At UMC, a deluge of phone inquiries followed the appearance in a national publication of an article describing the PCR project. Educational handouts were designed to meet the multitude of requests for information nationwide. In addition, the program manager planned all-day site visits from external groups from around the state, such as the Arizona Hospital Association staff, Arizona Nurse Executives, and Arizona Nurse Leaders in Education. The program manager also prepared presentations for selected external groups, such as the University of Arizona College of Nursing and the State Board of Nursing.

Preparation included contacting individuals interested in a site visit, issuing invitations, and doing follow-up on RSVPs. Planning an agenda and coordinating room reservations, staff for panel presentation, and unit tours are initial responsibilities. Furnishing name tags, preparing handouts, and selecting a luncheon menu for the visitors is essential to make visitors feel welcome. Evaluation forms are designed to record responses for the critique session at the end of the day. A slide presentation needs to be prepared as well as arrangements for audiovisual equipment. A successful site visit is a result of extensive coordination and careful planning.

CONCLUSION

Because a project can be full of surprises, the program manager must be as flexible as possible. A tremendous amount of time needs to be spent listening. One must listen not only to the words that are stated but also for emotions expressed. The program manager must continually assess the current situation and ask, "Where are we now, where are we going, and what do we need to do to get there?" In other words, the program manager must coordinate the day-to-day operations of the project while keeping the overall goals in perspective (Figure 5–4).

NOTES

1. J.W. Weiss, 5-Phase Project Management, *A Practical Planning and Implementation Guide* (Reading, Mass.: Addison-Wesley, 1992).
2. E.A. Stallworthy and O.P. Kharbanda, *Total Project Management from Concept to Completion* (Aldershot, England: Gower, 1983).
3. H. Koontz and C. O'Donnell, *Principles of Management: An Analysis of Managerial Functions* (New York, N.Y.: McGraw-Hill, 1972).
4. L.C. Struckenbruck, *"Integration: The Essential Function of Project Management,"* in Project Management Handbook, ed. D.I. Cleland and W.R. King (New York, N.Y.: Van Nostrand Reinhold, 1988).
5. M.D. Roseneau, Jr., *Successful Project Management, A Step-by-Step Approach with Practical Examples* (New York, N.Y.: Van Nostrand Reinhold, 1992).
6. M. Silverman, *Project Management, A Short Course for Professionals* (New York, N.Y.: Wiley, 1976).
7. D.P. Slevin and J.K. Pinto, The Project Implementation Profile: New Tool for Project Managers. *Project Management Journal* 9 (1986): 57–58.
8. J.K. Pinto and D.P. Slevin, *"Critical Success Factors in Effective Project Implementation,"* in Project Management Handbook, ed. D.I. Cleland and W.R. King (New York, N.Y.: Van Nostrand Reinhold, 1988).
9. J.D. Frame, *Managing Projects in Organizations, How To Make the Best Use of Time, Techniques and People* (San Francisco, Calif.: Jossey-Bass, 1987).

CHAPTER

6

Patient Support Attendant Training

Juanita McDonough and Leigh Shaffer

Chapter Objectives

1. To describe the role of the patient support attendant (PSA).
2. To describe the process of curriculum development for the training program.
3. To describe the development and implementation of the PSA role.
4. To discuss ongoing evaluation and refinement of the training program.

The role of the patient support attendant (PSA) includes duties traditionally performed by staff from several different departments. The PSA is a multipurpose support person with primary responsibility for environmental services duties as well as other maintenance functions. The role is designed to facilitate and streamline basic aspects of the patient care unit functions and to enhance patient satisfaction.

ROLE OF THE PSA

The PSA is a multipurpose worker providing support to the professional nursing staff as well as attending to the needs of the patient. The

PSA performs basic environmental services, dietary, transportation, and materials management duties. The role includes the following:

- cleaning patient rooms and bathrooms
- cleaning the nursing unit
- serving meal trays
- assisting the patient with setting up for meals and snacks
- transporting patients for procedures and at discharge
- transporting supplies and specimens
- performing materials management inventory
- ordering supplies
- replacing the inventory after delivery from the warehouse

The materials management functions are completed during the night shift, when discharges and transfers are at a minimum. The remainder of the duties are performed during all shifts, depending upon the specific unit demands.

QUALIFICATIONS NEEDED TO BE A PSA

The PSA role is an entry level position. The qualifications include an ability to follow English written and verbal instructions. The preferred candidates are those who have experience performing multiple tasks that require the ability to take directions from others. Effective interpersonal skills and a strong work ethic are preferred attributes. The PSA reports to the nurse manager but is directly supervised by the charge nurse.

PLANNING AND DEVELOPING THE TRAINING PROGRAM

The planning and development of the PSA role and training program involve several steps and include the active participation of many departments:

- define the respective roles of the nursing and ancillary departments
- develop a job description
- develop a detailed skills list
- develop the curriculum and training program
- identify nonclinical training issues and expectations
- establish time frames for training
- maintain ongoing communication

Defining Departmental Roles

The initial step in creating the PSA role is to determine the general scope of the role. As stated above, the PSA role involves services that had been provided by various departments. The ancillary departments that affect the PSA role include environmental services, dietary, transportation, and materials management. The development process brings together departments that are accustomed to working independently. Therefore, clarification of the role of the various departments in defining the PSA job description, creating a curriculum, and planning and implementing training is necessary to ensure a collaborative, multidisciplinary approach.

The role of the ancillary department is to provide the expertise needed to define the role and to provide training. The departments remain current on the changing regulations in their specific areas and therefore can provide ongoing support to ensure compliance.

Ancillary department staff are included in each part of the program development process. The following are the main areas of involvement:

- defining the specific duties of the role
- providing the performance expectation for the duties
- providing the learning objective for the curriculum
- developing the department-specific content for the training
- providing the didactic and preceptor content of the training program
- providing ongoing evaluation and feedback

The importance of including affected departments in defining the role and training cannot be underestimated. The restructuring process can be threatening to ancillary departments, which may lose staff and perceive a loss of status and value within the organization. This threat may lead to an undermining of the PSA role and the project as a whole. By involving department members, staff have a greater commitment to the success of the role and feel that the individual department's standards of quality are being maintained in the face of such great change.

It is often the education coordinator who directly encounters the resistance to change from other departments and individual staff. Therefore, it is necessary for the education coordinator to have highly developed interpersonal skills. Each department has its own unique character and culture. The coordinator must develop an understanding of and appreciation for these characteristics to work effectively. If there is a particular department or staff member who has shown resistance or difficulty in dealing with the changes, the coordinator can provide closer support and supervision in training.

Developing the Job Description

Before the development of a PSA job description, the scope of the role must be defined. Each department provides suggestions for appropriate tasks for the PSA to perform, considering the scope and complexity appropriateness of the duty. For example, at University Medical Center (UMC) environmental services identified that the PSAs should clean patient rooms and the patient care units but that the areas beyond the patient care units (the corridors and offices) should be maintained by the environmental services staff. After the list of duties is finalized, a job description can be developed (Exhibit 6–1).

The job description may be drawn from the job descriptions and the detailed standards of performance used in the ancillary departments. By using existing standards of performance, there is less confusion regarding expectations during the training and evaluation periods.

Developing a Detailed Skills List

The next step in developing a PSA training program is to define a specific skills list. As the job description is being finalized, each department compiles a list of skills needed for its area of the PSA role (Exhibit 6–2). Detailed skills lists outlining steps involved in performing each task are developed to guide training and for ongoing competency testing as required by regulatory agencies.

The patient care units may expand the skills list to provide additional services. For example, at UMC PSAs now clean the staff microwave and refrigerator. In addition, the PSAs transport bagged linen to the linen chute. Some units have expanded the skills of the PSA. For example, the intensive care units and the emergency department have the PSAs restock the supply carts in the patient rooms, tasks formerly performed by registered nurses. PSAs may serve as sitters for patients who are confused or need constant observation.

Any expansion of skills on a unit basis should be done in collaboration with the education coordinator. It is important to include any new information in the training sessions and to ensure some consistency in how the role is structured. PSAs should be able to work on a variety of units to meet staffing needs. If the roles differ too widely from unit to unit, staffing flexibility is lost.

Exhibit 6–1 UMC Job Description: PSA

EFFECTIVE DATE:	October 14, 1991
APPROVED BY:	______________________
HUMAN RESOURCES:	______________________
FLSA:	Nonexempt
JOB CODE:	9D01
BBF RISK CLASSIFICATION:	High

POSITION SUMMARY: Facilitates the efficient functioning of the patient care unit by performing housekeeping, dietary, and materials management duties and transporting patients, specimens, and medications.

ESSENTIAL FUNCTIONS:

STATED CRITERIA REFLECT TRAITS NECESSARY TO ACHIEVE A SCORE OF 1.0

I. INTERPERSONAL SKILLS/TEAM WORK—Demonstrates a positive attitude and willingness to facilitate unit functioning.

II. PRODUCTIVITY—Is a productive member of the patient care unit team.

III. SAFETY—Maintains a safe working environment.

IV. ENVIRONMENTAL SERVICES—Performs housekeeping functions properly.

V. TRANSPORTATION—Transports patients, specimens, and medications in a safe and efficient manner.

VI. MATERIALS MANAGEMENT—Maintains adequate floor stock on a daily basis.

VII. DIETARY—Distributes and assists patients with meals and nourishments.

VIII. PROFESSIONAL GROWTH/GOAL SETTING—Establishes and accomplishes goals jointly set with the immediate supervisor.

IX. COMPLIES with departmental and/or hospital rules and regulations regarding absenteeism, tardiness, dress code, etc.

WORKING CONDITIONS:	Comfortable, air-conditioned work areas with rotation of weekends. Possible exposure to burns, bruises, cuts, and minor injury.
REPORTING RELATIONSHIP:	Reports directly to the supervising RN and the charge nurse under the supervision of the nurse manager.
QUALIFICATIONS:	Ability to follow English written and verbal instructions.

Exhibit 6–2 PSA Skills Check-off List

SKILL	SUCCESSFULLY DEMONSTRATED	OBSERVER'S SIGNATURE AND DATE	COMMENTS
I. DIETARY A. Tray Passing			
—Completes within 40 min. of cart arriving on floor.			
—PCU patient diet census report completed and returned to Food Svcs. within time guideline.			
—Appropriate techniques utilized when interrupted with other procedures (e.g., handling dirty linen, patient transfer, handling urinals or specimens, etc.).			
—Communication of problems (e.g., patient dissatisfaction with tray selection, etc.) to appropriate personnel. Provides exact patient comment.			
—Time/temperature guidelines adhered to.			
—Each tray checked to ensure proper retherm temperature.			
B. Tray Retrieval			
—Soiled trays and carts returned within established time guidelines in appropriate manner to the appropriate location.			
—Intake recorded for patient on calorie count.			
—*Intake recorded on I&O sheet for fluid intake. (*Nurse educator to teach)			

continues

Exhibit 6–2 continued

SKILL	SUCCESSFULLY DEMONSTRATED	OBSERVER'S SIGNATURE AND DATE	COMMENTS
—Trays not left with patient beyond established holding guidelines.			
—Inappropriate items (medical supplies, pharmaceuticals, body fluids) are not to be left on meal trays.			
C. Floor Stock			
—Inventories taken and forwarded to Food Svcs. within designated time guidelines.			
—Inventories are accurate.			
—Outdated items are removed.			
—Food rotation follows FIFO rule.			
—Refrigerator temperature documented twice daily.			
D. Diet Orders			
—Diet orders sent to diet office within time guidelines, including NPOs, holds, and changes.			
—All foods served to patient in accordance with diet order.			
E. Nourishments			
—Appropriate nourishment delivered to patient at appropriate times.			
—Communication of nourishment problems.			

continues

Exhibit 6–2 continued

SKILL	SUCCESSFULLY DEMONSTRATED	OBSERVER'S SIGNATURE AND DATE	COMMENTS
—Snacks and nourishments unable to be served are placed in refrigerator as appropriate for later. Distribution not to exceed 12 hours.			
II. GENERAL			
Demonstrates working knowledge of the following:			
—Hand washing technique.			
—Universal precautions.			
—General abbreviations.			
—CPR.			
III. HOUSEKEEPING			
—Linen change, unoccupied bed.			
—Soiled linen collection and proper disposition.			
—Complete cleaning of room using eight-step cleaning procedure.			
—Proper handling and disposal of trash.			
—Weekly cleaning of unit microwave.			
—Monthly cleaning and defrosting of refrigerator.			
—Chemical use/dilution.			
IV. TRANSPORTATION			
–Proper body mechanics with patient transfers.			
—Wheelchair transfer/ transport.			

continues

Exhibit 6–2 continued

SKILL	SUCCESSFULLY DEMONSTRATED	OBSERVER'S SIGNATURE AND DATE	COMMENTS
—Stretcher transfer/ transports.			
—Introduce yourself to the patient and explain where you will be taking him/her.			
—Check patient's name band to ensure the proper patient is being transported.			
—Notify appropriate staff of the patient's departure from the nursing unit or department.			
—Secure proper transport equipment and obtain assistance if necessary to transport patient (e.g., lock brakes on transport equipment).			
—While transporting patient, make sure all IV/O_2 lines are free and clear from wheelchair or stretcher wheels.			
—Notify appropriate staff of patient's arrival.			
—Assist in taking patient off transport equipment if necessary.			
—Identify proper pick-up/ drop-off points for diagnostic departments (e.g., X-Ray, echo lab, EKG, cath lab, etc.).			
—Identify proper pick-up point for pharmaceuticals.			

continues

Exhibit 6–2 continued

SKILL	SUCCESSFULLY DEMONSTRATED	OBSERVER'S SIGNATURE AND DATE	COMMENTS
—Obtain signatures on appropriate pharmaceuticals.			
—Identify proper pick-up points for materials management supplies.			
—Identify proper drop-off points for lab specimens.			
—Identify proper methods for exchanging O_2 regulators.			
—Proper storage areas for O_2 tanks (never leave O_2 tanks in alcoves of floors).			
V. MATERIALS MANAGEMENT Adequately performs the following tasks:			
—Sticker charge system.			
—Inventory-specified supply by item number and par level.			
—Proficiently enter cart list into computer and print at the warehouse for pulling.			
—Receive carts of supplies that were ordered and deliver to appropriate area.			
—Pick up CS supply list, pull and deliver to area.			
—Pick up credits from area and fill out appropriate form. Send back credits to materials management warehouse.			

Developing the Curriculum and Training Program

Each of the ancillary departments provides the learning objectives and content for the curriculum. The education coordinator, who has an understanding of adult education principles and how to integrate them into a training program, works with the appropriate ancillary department staff to create lesson plans and a comprehensive curriculum for the PSA training.

Each department also provides the staff support for the didactic portion of the training. Often, a manager or a supervisor is the designated educator. Initially at UMC, the department also provided on-unit preceptor support. As more units have been restructured, however, a greater portion of supervised clinical training is provided by the PSAs on the units. This training is under the direction of the ancillary departments. A train-the-trainer format is used to educate the PSA trainer to provide the supervised clinical portion of the training.

All departments use internal resources, however, to keep a portion of the training within their respective departments. Transportation does the training for body mechanics and patient transfers. The patient tray services manager conducts a 1-day training session to cover appropriate dietary services content. Materials management conducts a 1-day training session on computerized ordering and the process for stocking carts. Another day is spent with the PSA trainee shadowing an experienced PSA on the unit. Environmental services offers didactic training, and, as with materials management, there is a 1-day shadowing experience with an experienced PSA.

The educational contact person from the department develops handouts for the new PSA trainees. He or she also develops a trainer manual for the PSAs and assists with supervised clinical training when applicable.

Identifying Nonclinical Training Issues and Expectations

Education for the PSA also should address nonclinical issues and expectations such as work ethic, punctuality, and accountability. Trainees have various degrees of work experience and may have had little formal training in such issues. Time spent reviewing the absenteeism/tardiness policy is essential. The trainees may not fully understand the need to call in sick or to be on time. If a trainee has previously had experience in positions that have tolerated such behavior, he or she may not understand the significance of such infractions in a hospital setting. Lack of punctuality, sleeping on the job, leaving the work area for an extended time, or failing to inform the supervisor before leaving the work area are not acceptable behaviors in health care settings. At times, managers may encounter these behaviors in professional staff, but such behaviors are more prevalent with the nonprofessional staff.

Accountability for one's actions and a clear understanding of reporting responsibility need to be emphasized. Again, these are concepts that entry-level, nonprofessional staff may not have had stressed in prior experiences.

Establishing Time Frames

The ancillary departments in collaboration with the education coordinator define the learning objectives for PSA skills and set appropriate time frames for training. The 10-day PSA training session is as follows:

- Day 1: hospital orientation
- Day 2: customer service excellence/general didactic presentations
- Days 3 to 4: materials management
- Days 5 to 6: dietary
- Days 7 to 8: environmental services
- Day 9: transportation
- Day 10: supervised training and CPR

Day 10, which is a supervised training experience on a restructured unit, is used to help the new PSA experience how the various duties fit together into one role. PSAs who are assigned to the in-house supplemental staffing pool (float pool) get additional cross-training to multiple units.

Maintaining Ongoing Communication

The education coordinator and the managers/directors for the ancillary departments are members of the patient care restructuring task force. Key developments such as the skills list and the training program need to be presented to the task force for input before implementation. Various departments represented on the task force are then able to voice questions and concerns.

IMPLEMENTATION OF THE TRAINING PROGRAM

Implementation involves coordinating the flow of candidates through the 2-week training program with optimal utilization of available resources. The hospital orientation and customer service content is provided by human resources. General didactic information such as behavioral expectations is provided by the education coordinator.

Each department supervises or directly provides the relevant training for the PSAs. The education coordinator works with each department to facilitate the training schedules. It is important to consider each department's special needs in scheduling the training sessions. For example, dietary and materials management training is best limited to two trainees at a time. Unit training with a PSA trainer is best when done on a one-to-one level.

The education coordinator should know the number of trainees 1 week before initiating the training. The time frame enables the coordinator to facilitate the flow of students through the various areas of training. In addition, at UMC managers and supervisors of the ancillary departments are notified of training times that may affect their schedules. All departments have key individuals who provide the PSA training. A back-up system is in place, however, to support the continuation of training in the absence of the key contact person. Once the training schedules are set, the education coordinator develops a calendar for each PSA, which is also given to the nurse manager and the appropriate ancillary departments.

Supervision during Implementation

Supervision of training is conducted through daily rounds of the various areas by the education coordinator. The rounds provide the coordinator with an opportunity to address issues immediately and offer an opportunity for students, staff, and trainers to ask questions. The coordinator is also able to evaluate training informally on an ongoing basis.

At times, the ancillary department managers will make rounds to check on training and offer additional support. For example, during phase I implementation at UMC the dietary manager and her staff were available on the newly restructured units during meal times to assist the PSAs and help troubleshoot problems.

Completion Ceremonies

It is important to celebrate the completion of training for the PSA candidate with a formal completion ceremony. The ceremony is held just before implementation of the PSA role on the newly restructured units. If a PSA is hired for a unit that has already been restructured, the candidate participates in the next completion ceremony. The ceremony provides an opportunity for the friends, families, and coworkers of the PSAs to celebrate their new role. Hospital administrators as well as the involved department personnel participate in the program.

EVALUATION AND REFINEMENT OF THE TRAINING PROGRAM

Formal evaluation of lecturers and trainers is accomplished through written evaluations by the PSA candidates. The evaluation forms are distributed, collected, and tallied by the education coordinator. The results are then shared with the appropriate persons or departments. The purpose of the written evaluation is to identify areas for improvement in the training program. If improvements or changes are needed, the coordinator and the department staff work together to propose new strategies.

Maintaining Quality

Evaluation of the effectiveness of training is based on criteria developed by the ancillary departments and the patient care units. The ancillary departments use similar tools developed before restructuring to ensure continuity in evaluating the quality of services provided. For example, dietary supervisors continue to monitor tray pick-up and retrieval times, and materials management staff inventory overstocked items that have been sent back to the warehouse for credit. Environmental services supervisors perform routine housekeeping inspections.

The patient care units have developed an evaluation tool that includes both performance and quality issues related to all areas of the PSA role (Exhibit 6–3). General evaluation results are presented at the task force meetings. Appropriate ancillary department staff notify nurse managers of any problems/concerns if needed. If additional training is warranted, the education coordinator facilitates the training needs.

At times problems are identified that require the collaboration of two or more departments. These problems may be of a system nature (i.e., related to how a task or operation is designed to be accomplished). The appropriate staff will work together under the authority of the task force to resolve the problem. The continuous improvement process can be of value in such instances.

Ongoing Competency Maintenance

An efficient mechanism for maintaining competency and providing continuing education for PSAs is an important aspect of restructuring. Be-

Exhibit 6–3 Quality Control and Performance Tool for PSAs

NAME: ______________________ DATE: ______________

1. Housekeeping:

A. Room cleaning:	Satisfactory	Unsatisfactory
Night stand	____	____
Bathroom	____	____
Floor	____	____
Bed	____	____
Closet	____	____
Garbage cans	____	____
Overbed lights	____	____
Walls (if needed)	____	____
Curtains changed	____	____
Corners	____	____
B. Nurses station:		
High dusting	____	____
Cleaning behind rolling carts	____	____
Sweep and mop	____	____
Garbage cans	____	____
Refrigerator cleaned	____	____
C. Assignment completed by end of shift	yes ____	no ____

COMMENTS: ______________________________

____

____

2. Transportation

A. Patient transfers done safely	yes ____	no ____
B. Transports occur within 20 minutes	yes ____	no ____

COMMENTS: ______________________________

____

continues

Exhibit 6–3 continued

3. I&Os

A. Meal intake added properly to I&O	yes ____	no ____
B. Water pitchers changed at end of shift	yes ____	no ____

COMMENTS: ______________________________

4. Dietary:

A. Meals delivered on time	yes ____	no ____
B. Proper documentation after trays	yes ____	no ____
C. Bulk stock ordered correctly	yes ____	no ____
D. Restocking done in timely manner	yes ____	no ____

COMMENTS: ______________________________

____

5. Materials management:

A. Inventory done accurately	yes ____	no ____
B. Restocking done in timely fashion	yes ____	no ____
C. Credits sent to materials management	yes ____	no ____

COMMENTS: ______________________________

6. Dress code

A. Follows dress code established for PCR	yes ____	no ____

COMMENTS: ______________________________

7. Interpersonal skills:

A. Is courteous to patients	yes ____	no ____
B. Is courteous to ancillary personnel	yes ____	no ____
C. Responds appropriately to nursing	yes ____	no ____
D. Is courteous to coworkers	yes ____	no ____
E. Is open to constructive criticism	yes ____	no ____
F. Offers assistance to others	yes ____	no ____

COMMENTS: ______________________________

____

fore restructuring, each department at UMC had a system developed for the staff to receive ongoing educational and institutional updates. As the department functions became decentralized, it was necessary to look for creative ways to maintain communications with staff.

Ancillary departments have responsibility for maintaining expertise in their relative areas of specialty. For example, nurse managers cannot be expected to keep up on which new cleaners are being recommended. The environmental services department must continue to provide the hospital with this kind of support.

One possible format to provide ongoing inservices is an annual 4-hour continuing education workshop. These workshops are costly, however. The workshop also creates staffing problems because units attempt to avoid overtime by scheduling PSAs to cover one another as they attend the workshop.

A more efficient option for providing continuing education is to assign a PSA representative from each unit to attend the update sessions and to serve as a resource person to other persons on the unit. The update meetings are held at the same time each month in the same location to facilitate scheduling of the unit representatives. The ancillary departments meet with the representatives, review new information or changes, and provide written handouts. Additionally, an update book is kept on each unit with handouts and information for each PSA. A copy of the new information is kept on the unit for reference. The update meeting format gives the PSA an opportunity to voice any questions or concerns and serves to maintain communication between the PSAs and the ancillary staff.

CONCLUSION

The development and maintenance of the PSA role is a multidisciplinary effort requiring cooperation and collaboration among a variety of departments and services. The creation of the role and the implementation of the training program require separate departments to alter old ways of providing services and to create new ways of perceiving their value to the institution. Each department now serves as the quality expert and the specialty content expert, providing guidance and support for the maintenance of quality and institutional expertise in its individual area.

Training is no longer provided on a departmental basis but can be supported through an education coordinator. A benefit from these changes is consistency in the training and evaluation process.

CHAPTER

7

Patient Care Technician Training

Leigh Shaffer and Juanita McDonough

Chapter Objectives

1. To describe the role of the patient care technician (PCT).
2. To describe the process of curriculum development.
3. To describe the development and implementation of the PCT training program.
4. To discuss ongoing evaluation and refinement of the training program.

The role of the patient care technician (PCT) includes duties traditionally performed by the staff from several different departments. The PCT is a multidisciplinary technical worker trained to provide basic nursing assistant care as well as other skilled functions. The role is designed to facilitate the efficient delivery of care, support the professional role of the registered nurse, and to enhance patient satisfaction.

ROLE OF THE PCT

The PCT is a multidisciplinary technical worker providing support to the professional nursing staff and delivering direct care to the patient. The

PCT performs traditional basic nursing assistant skills and additional selected skills appropriate to the nonlicensed care provider. The role includes the following:

- providing basic nursing assistant skills
- performing phlebotomy
- performing 12-lead ECGs
- assisting patients with incentive spirometry
- assisting patients with selected rehabilitation-related duties
- documenting observations and care provided

In accordance with licensure laws for each of the involved disciplines, the duties within the PCT role are performed under the supervision of the licensed care provider and are within the scope of the technician role for the discipline. The PCT reports directly to the nurse manager but is supervised on a daily basis by the registered nurse (Exhibit 7–1).

It is important to frame the PCT role in the context of the nursing assistant so that staff are clear about what can and cannot be expected of the PCT. The registered nurse is responsible, as with any unlicensed or nonprofessional caregiver, for the assessment and planning of care. PCTs charting must be limited to observations. PCTs can chart patient care provided on a daily flow record or note brief observations in a progress note, but they may not chart information based on assessments.

QUALIFICATIONS NEEDED TO BE A PCT

The PCT is required to have excellent English verbal and written skills. A high school education with 1 year of higher education or the equivalent is required. Health-related experience is strongly preferred. This experience may be as a ward secretary, nursing assistant, phlebotomist, other technician, or as a patient support attendant (PSA).

Applicants are screened for the ability to handle multiple tasks and to take directions from others. As with the PSA, good interpersonal skills and a strong work ethic are preferred attributes. The PCT interacts frequently with patients and must be able to demonstrate a mature, professional demeanor.

PLANNING AND DEVELOPING THE TRAINING PROGRAM

The planning and development of the PCT role and the training program, as for the PSA role, involve multiple stages and require the collabo-

Exhibit 7–1 University Medical Center Job Description: PCT

EFFECTIVE DATE:	November 1, 1991
APPROVED BY:	______________________
HUMAN RESOURCES:	______________________
FLSA:	Nonexempt
JOB CODE:	3A01
BBF RISK CLASSIFICATION:	High

POSITION SUMMARY: Facilitates the provision of patient care by performing specific nursing tasks and support functions as delegated by a registered nurse.

ESSENTIAL FUNCTIONS:

I. PATIENT CARE SKILLS—Provides basic age-appropriate nursing care to patient under the direct supervision of a registered nurse.

II. REHABILITATION-RELATED DUTIES—Performs nonskilled nursing duties that may relate to rehabilitation to carry out the multidisciplinary care plan for each patient.

III. PHLEBOTOMY AND CLINICAL LABORATORY—Obtains and maintains integrity of specimens in accordance with University Medical Center (UMC) policies and procedures and physician orders.

IV. RESPIRATORY THERAPY—Provides selected respiratory care to patients following accepted respiratory care practices, UMC policies and procedures, and physician orders.

V. ECG—Performs ECGs following UMC policies and procedures.

VI. DOCUMENTATION/REPORTING—Documents and reports care delivered under the direct supervision of a registered nurse.

VII. INTERPERSONAL SKILLS/TEAMWORK—Demonstrates a positive attitude and willingness to facilitate unit functioning.

VIII. PRODUCTIVITY—Is a productive member of the patient care unit team.

IX. SAFETY—Maintains a safe environment for patients and coworkers.

X. PROFESSIONAL GROWTH/GOAL SETTING—Establishes and accomplishes goals jointly set with the immediate supervisor.

XI. COMPLIES with departmental and/or hospital rules and regulations regarding absenteeism, tardiness, dress code, etc. (Reference H.R. Policy 302, paragraphs 3.0 and 6.b).

WORKING CONDITIONS: Air-controlled, moderately warm area subject to occasional temperature changes. Some noise disturbance with increased exposure to disease, radiation, chemicals, and patient behavior with danger of more serious injury.

continues

Exhibit 7–1 continued

REPORTING RELATIONSHIP:	Reports directly to the supervising registered nurse and the charge nurse under the supervision of the nurse manager.
QUALIFICATIONS:	Excellent verbal and written skills in English. High school diploma or GED required. One year of higher education or equivalent required. Health-related experience strongly preferred.

Reviewed/Revised Date ______________ Initial __________

Reviewed/Revised Date ______________ Initial __________

Reviewed/Revised Date ______________ Initial __________

ration of many departments:

- define the respective roles of nursing and other departments
- develop a job description and detailed skills list
- develop the curriculum and training program
- identify nonclinical training issues and expectations
- establish time frames for training
- maintain ongoing communication

Defining Departmental Roles

The initial step in developing the PCT role is to determine which technical skills from the various departments would be appropriate to include. The departments affected by the PCT role are as follows:

- rehabilitation services
- clinical pathology (laboratory)
- cardiopulmonary services (respiratory therapy and ECG)
- nursing services

The role of the involved departments is to provide the guidelines for basic quality assurance and expertise needed for effective training. Members of these departments are continuously updated on the regulations in their specific areas. In addition, they are required to maintain the level of expertise needed to provide effective training and follow-up. The affected departments are involved in the following activities:

- defining the specific duties of the role
- providing performance expectations
- providing the learning objectives for the curriculum
- supporting the development of the department-specific didactic and preceptor content for the training
- providing ongoing evaluation and feedback

The development process requires the various departmental staff to collaborate closely on this project. In large institutions such as hospitals, the tendency is to compartmentalize work, creating a sense of competition among departments. The restructuring effort spurs the various departments to break down traditional barriers and to cooperate to meet a common goal.

The need to clarify the role of the involved departments in training also aids the development of a multidisciplinary curriculum. Staff members learn about the other departments and their interrelated functions. Interdepartmental teamwork is a valuable byproduct of the restructuring process and lays the groundwork for further continuous improvement efforts.

The departments are asked to envision a role and to develop a program that is quite different from established patterns. For example, clinical pathology staff train phlebotomists, who will report to patient care services. What was once a department-specific role totally under departmental control is now decentralized to the patient care units. Yet the responsibility for training and maintenance of expertise remains with the former department. The effective management of such arrangements requires a willingness to share authority and to demonstrate interdepartmental teamwork.

Some department members may be reluctant to collaborate in the patient care restructuring project. They may verbalize support for the project, but their behaviors indicate that they are resistant to change. Effective strategies should be used to handle this resistance to change to get the work of defining the roles and planning the training accomplished. The strategies should incorporate the concept of maintaining the self-esteem of individuals and maintaining a good working relationship. This is done through a respect for the values and the culture of each department and its individuals. For example, the education coordinator may interface with six or more departments in developing the PCT training. One department may have a participative, relaxed culture, whereas another department may have a more structured, autocratic environment. The coordinator must respect and appreciate that the departments function well within their various cultures and values and must learn to work effectively in a variety of settings.

Developing the Job Description and Skills List

The involved departments assess their services performed by both professional and technical staff to identify appropriate tasks for the PCT role. The development process for the PCT role requires careful consideration of state licensure laws to ensure the appropriateness of the duties assigned (see Exhibit 7–1).

At University Medical Center (UMC), the nursing assistant skills come from a skills list formerly used for the nurse assistant I and II roles. The identified tasks are based on the Arizona State Board of Nursing's Validated Competencies for Nursing Assistants (Appendix 7–A).

The rehabilitation skills (physical and occupational therapy) derive from some of the basic skills formerly performed by the physical and occupational therapy technicians. These duties include monitoring continuous passive motion treatments, assisting with gait activities, and assisting with activities of daily living.

The duties drawn from the cardiopulmonary services areas (respiratory therapy and ECG) are assisting with incentive spirometry and performing 12-lead ECGs. Phlebotomy duties are moved from clinical pathology into the PCT role.

As with the PSA role, the PCT job description and detailed standards of performance are drawn from the documents used in the originating department whenever possible. Some aspects of the tasks may change, but the basic expectations are similar. By using existing standards of performance, there is less confusion regarding expectations during the training period.

Developing the Curriculum and Training Program

The development process of the PCT curriculum and training program is similar to that for the PSA role but differs somewhat because of the more complex nature of the PCT role and the longer training required.

The PCT training is 10 weeks. The first 3 weeks include the nursing assistant component and general hospital orientation. The next week includes the rehabilitation-related, 12-lead ECG, respiratory therapy, and phlebotomy didactic components. Two weeks are spent on practicing phlebotomy skills, and the final 4 weeks are spent in the clinical setting with a preceptor.

The nursing training is provided by the education coordinator. The nursing assistant portion of the training includes classroom lectures and use of a video skills series, manikins for labs, and practice supplies to enhance the learning of new skills.

Each of the departments provides the trainers for its specific section of the PCT program. Some departments, such as phlebotomy and respiratory, have lead trainers or educators, who assume the training position for the PCT program. Cardiology and rehabilitation departments utilize core staff members to do the training. Each department maintains the same format for education and training that was utilized before restructuring. The education coordinator seeks out the appropriate resources from each unit and develops a communication network to ensure effective collaboration in the development and implementation of the educational program.

Trainers and educators from the departments develop their lecture outlines, handouts, and exams. Each major area of training provides a written exam at the completion of training. In addition, phlebotomy, nursing assistant training, and 12-lead ECG have competency-based evaluations of appropriate skills. The education coordinator provides copying services, makes room reservations, and arranges for equipment and supplies when needed. The coordinator may also assist in the development of objectives, outlines, tools, and other teaching materials for trainers who are less familiar with the education process.

If a department does not have a designated skilled educator or trainer, the education coordinator provides additional support for the staff person selected to provide the PCT training for his or her department. The train-the-trainer approach used by the education coordinator includes ensuring that the skills and qualifications of the trainer are adequate. The coordinator provides assistance with organization and preparation of the curriculum components and gives the training educator support on how to communicate and work with a technical level candidate.

The education coordinator also offers guidelines and assists the departments to set realistic expectations for training. For example, the phlebotomy department may be accustomed to training two to three candidates at a time for 6 weeks. This is not realistic for PCT training when there are 30 PCTs who need to be fully trained in 10 weeks.

It is important that departments work with the education coordinator and identify a key individual to serve as the contact person for training issues. The contact person can provide consistency in training and help in the development of a smooth working relationship with the education coordinator and other departments.

Identifying Nonclinical Training Issues and Expectations

As with the PSAs, important nonclinical issues and expectations need to be addressed in the training program. Work ethic, timeliness and accountability, and personal appearance/uniform are included in the basic training program. Time spent reviewing the absenteeism/tardiness policy clarifies expectations and responsibilities. Also, accountability for one's actions and a clear understanding of reporting responsibility are stressed throughout the entire training (see Chapter 6 for more about nonclinical issues).

Objectives and Time Frame for Training

Each department defines the learning objectives and time required for mastering the skills. The time frame for the 10-week PCT program is as follows:

- weeks 1 to 3: nursing assistant/hospital orientation/unit-specific skills training (e.g., basic ECG monitoring)
- week 4: ancillary didactic—physical therapy, occupational therapy, respiratory, 12-lead ECG, phlebotomy
- weeks 5 and 6: phlebotomy clinical experience
- weeks 7 to 10: supervised clinical with a preceptor (see Appendix 7–B; perceptors are discussed in detail in Chapter 6)

Training may not be limited to 10 weeks. Occasionally, a candidate needs additional training in one of the tasks, such as phlebotomy, or supervised clinical experience to meet the objectives. The education coordinator and the trainer or preceptor will discuss the need for additional training. Together with the PCT and the nurse manager, a decision may be made to extend training.

Training may also be extended if the PCT requires additional training and the staff on the units request it. Cross-training for the PSA role or cross-training in unit secretary skills are some instances where additional training is needed.

Maintaining Ongoing Communication

The education coordinator and the contact persons from the involved departments are members of the patient care restructuring task force. Key components of the curriculum such as the skills list and scheduling time frames need to be discussed by the task force for input before implementation. Information sharing at the task force meetings provides an opportunity for departments represented to voice questions and concerns. Additionally, individuals who are responsible for curriculum development are provided an opportunity to share their successes.

IMPLEMENTATION OF THE TRAINING PROGRAM

Implementation involves coordinating the flow of candidates through the 10-week training program with optimal utilization of available resources. For example, nursing assistant skills labs are limited to 12 participants, phlebotomy clinicals are limited to 6 participants, and so forth. The education coordinator knows the total number of potential participants 2 weeks before initiating the training program to schedule the program. The time frame enables the trainer to facilitate the flow of students through the various areas of training. The education coordinator develops a training calendar for each student and provides a copy of the calendar to the nurse manager and the appropriate departmental staff (Figures 7–1 to 7–3).

Supervision

Supervision of training is best accomplished through daily rounds of the various clinical areas by the education coordinator. Students are in a variety of settings at any given point in the training program. Some students may be in the classroom while others are in phlebotomy clinical and others are on the patient care units for the supervised portion of the training. Daily rounds give the education coordinator an opportunity to address issues as they arise and offer an opportunity for students, staff, trainers, and preceptors to raise questions and to evaluate closely the training process.

Completion Ceremonies

It is important to celebrate the successes of the program with a completion ceremony just before implementation of the PCT role on the units. The ceremony enables the PCTs to invite their friends, families, preceptors, and coworkers to share in the celebration. Administrators as well as the involved department personnel participate in the program. A slide show of pictures of the PCTs in the various stages of training is a nice touch. Pictures give the families and coworkers an opportunity to see the various stages of training from the first day of orientation to the final weeks of supervised clinical.

EVALUATION AND REFINEMENT OF THE TRAINING PROGRAM

Evaluation of the Training Program

Formal evaluation of trainers, lectures, and clinical experience is accomplished through written evaluations by the PCT candidates. These are is-

SUNDAY	MONDAY	TUESDAY	WEDNESDAY	THURSDAY	FRIDAY	SATURDAY
				1	2	3
4	5 New Empl Orientation 08-1630 Room 5403	6 H.R. Presentation Room 5403 08-1630	7 Lecture Staff Dev. Classroom 08-1630	8 Lecture Staff Dev. Classroom 08-1630	9 Units 07-1530	10
11	12 Lecture Staff Dev. Classroom 08-1630	13 Lecture Staff Dev. Classroom 08-1630	14 Lecture Staff Dev. Classroom 08-1630	15 Units 07-1530	16 Lecture Staff Dev. Classroom 08-1630	17
18	19 Units 07-1530	20 (Nursing Exam) Lecture Staff Dev. Classroom 08-1630	21 Lecture Staff Dev. Classroom 08-1603	22 Ortho Skills Lab Room 0523 08-1200 Lecture Room 4120 1230-1630	23 Lecture Staff Dev. Classroom 08-1630	24
25	26 Lecture Staff Dev. Classroom 08-1630	27 Physical Therapy W/S (exam) Room 0430 08-1630	28 Occupational Therapy W/S Room 0430 (exam) 08-1630	29 Resp. 12-Lead ECG (exam) Staff Dev. Classroom 08-1630	30 Phlebotomy Didactic Staff Dev. Classroom 08-1630	31

Figure 7–1 PCT training calendar, July.

SUNDAY	MONDAY	TUESDAY	WEDNESDAY	THURSDAY	FRIDAY	SATURDAY
1	2 Phlebotomy Clinical Day 1 06-1430 1st Floor Lab	3 Phlebotomy Clinical Day 2 06-1430	4 Phlebotomy Clinical Day 3 06-1430	5 Phlebotomy Clinical Day 4 06-1430	6 Phlebotomy Clinical Day 5 (midway eval) 06-1430	7
8	9 Phlebotomy Clinical Day 6 06-1430	10 Phlebotomy Clinical Day 7 06-1430	11 Phlebotomy Clinical Day 8 (exam) 06-1430	12 Phlebotomy Clinical Day 9 06-1430	13 Phlebotomy Clinical Day 10 (final eval) 06-1430	14
15	16 Supervised Clinical with Preceptor	17 Supervised Clinical with Preceptor	18 Supervised Clinical with Preceptor	19 Supervised Clinical with Preceptor	20 Supervised Clinical with Preceptor	21
22	23 Supervised Clinical with Preceptor	24 Supervised Clinical with Preceptor	25 Supervised Clinical with Preceptor	26 Supervised Clinical with Preceptor	27 Supervised Clinical with Preceptor	28
29	30 Supervised Clinical with Preceptor	31 Supervised Clinical with Preceptor				

Figure 7–2 PCT training calendar, August.

SUNDAY	MONDAY	TUESDAY	WEDNESDAY	THURSDAY	FRIDAY	SATURDAY
			1 Supervised Clinical with Preceptor	2 Supervised Clinical with Preceptor	3 Supervised Clinical with Preceptor	4
5	6 Supervised Clinical with Preceptor	7 Supervised Clinical with Preceptor	8 Supervised Clinical with Preceptor	9 Supervised Clinical with Preceptor	10 Supervised Clinical with Preceptor	11 Training Complete
12	13	14	15	16	17	18
19	20	21	22	23	24	25
26	27	28	29	30		

Figure 7–3 PCT training calendar, September.

sued, collected, and tallied by the education coordinator. The results are shared with the appropriate persons or departments. The purpose of the written evaluations is to identify areas for improvement in curriculum and training. When improvements or changes are needed, the coordinator and the department work together to propose solutions. An education coordinator with strong interpersonal skills is essential to effective, ongoing evaluation and improvement of the training program. As mentioned above, daily rounds by the education coordinator are another valuable evaluation mechanism.

Hospitalwide restructuring results in shrinking of the resources of the ancillary departments. At UMC, areas such as phlebotomy have become limited to the outpatient lab as the only unrestructured training site. It is important to retain the ancillary department staff as the experts in training and evaluation in their respective fields. Training may place a strain on limited resources, and it may be necessary to seek creative alternatives. One example of this occurred with the limited number of phlebotomy draws available for PCTs in the outpatient setting. The manager of pathology contacted nurse managers from two of the restructured inpatient units, offering to perform the early morning phlebotomy draws for those units on training days. She was able to utilize these resources to add dozens of training phlebotomy draws for the PCT trainees.

Once housewide restructuring is accomplished, a mechanism for periodic training must be established. The education coordinator can schedule PSA and PCT training on a regular basis. The mechanism must also permit nonscheduled classes to be organized if mandated by staff turnover.

Maintaining Quality

Evaluation of the effectiveness of training is based on criteria developed by the ancillary departments and the patient care units (Exhibits 7–2 and 7–3, Table 7–1). At UMC, the departments use similar tools developed before restructuring to ensure continuity in evaluating the quality of services provided. The patient care units developed a tool to evaluate performance and quality issues in all areas of the PCT role. All results are presented at the task force meetings. When necessary, however, ancillary departments notify a nurse manager of any problems/concerns as they arise. If additional training is needed, the education coordinator facilitates it.

Ongoing Competency Maintenance

An important aspect of maintaining quality of services is ongoing competency training and testing of all levels of staff, including PCTs. The de-

Exhibit 7–2 Performance Tools for PCTs

NAME: ______________________ DATE: ____________

1. Phlebotomy draws:	Patient complaints:	yes	no		
	Comments: ______________________				
	______________________				
2. Activity records:	# assigned ____	# done ____	# missed ____		
3. HS/PM care	# assigned ____	# done ____	# missed ____		
4. Bed and bath:	# assigned ____	# done ____	# missed ____		
5. Vitals:	# done ____	# within range ____	# out of range ____		
6. Room neatness:	# acceptable ____	# unacceptable ____			
7. Physical therapy:	# assigned ____	# done ____			
	proper technique:			yes	no
	proper charting:			yes	no
8. Sterile technique/follows hospital policy:					
	blood draws:			yes	no
	intermittent caths:			yes	no
	dressing changes:			yes	no
9. Incentive spirometry:	adequate documentation:			yes	no
10. Fingersticks:	utilizes proper technique:			yes	no
	proper documentation:			yes	no
11. Interpersonal skills:					
A. Is courteous to patients				yes	no
B. Is courteous to ancillary personnel				yes	no
C. Is courteous to coworkers				yes	no
D. Offers assistance to others				yes	no

Skills/activities performed well: ______________________

____

Areas needing improvement: ______________________

____

____

centralization of such skills as phlebotomy presents challenges to providing ongoing competency testing.

One option is to conduct monthly PCT update meetings. Each patient care unit assigns a representative to attend the updates and to serve as a resource person upon return to the unit. The update meetings are held at the same time each month in the same location to facilitate scheduling of the unit representatives. For example, meetings at UMC are held the third

Exhibit 7–3 PCT Internal Quality Assurance—Rehabilitation Related

Observed by: ______________________

Random samples will be directly observed over the next 4-month period to check compliance and quality care.

	Compliant	Noncompliant
Referral follow-through		
Safe transfers		
Knowledge of total joint precautions		
Proper documentation		
Good communication		
Good communication between therapist and PCT		
CPM follow-up		

Comments:

Thursday of each month at 1:00 P.M. The ancillary departments meet with the representatives, outline any updates or changes, and supply necessary handouts or information. Additionally, each unit has an update book with reference handouts and information for each PCT. Videotapes distributed to each unit are also helpful to include in the update meetings. The meeting format gives the PCTs an opportunity to voice any questions or concerns. In addition, the meeting serves to maintain contact between the PCTs and the ancillary staff.

New information is also shared by the nurse manager at the unit staff meetings. If needed, a staff liaison from the nursing staff development department or a representative from the ancillary departments may attend the staff meeting or present additional unit-based updates. Competency testing for selected skills is done with PCTs before the annual review.

Table 7–1 Quality Assurance Indicators for PCT Respiratory/ECG Procedures

Indicators	*Assessment*	*Action*
Uninterpretable ECG due to poor technique	Physician will identify ECG that cannot be interpreted due to poor technique	1. ECG supervisor will review ECG to determine cause 2. Each ECG will be retained to help identify patterns 3. Reeducation/inservicing will be provided if problem appears chronic 4. Nurse manager will be informed of chronic problem
Incentive spirometry patient requiring more intensive respiratory modalities	Any patient previously receiving incentive spirometry is changed to additional respiratory therapy intervention after initial RT/IS assessment	1. Charts will be reviewed to determine cause of patient deterioration; if patient deterioration is caused by lack of incentive spirometry therapy (e.g., less than frequency ordered), PCT will be reeducated/reinserviced 2. Nurse manager will be informed of any patterns

CONCLUSION

Implementing the PCT role provides the professional nursing staff with support in providing patient care. The PCT is able to perform those tasks that are more efficiently performed by nonlicensed staff while allowing the registered nurse to focus on the professional aspect of the nursing role, such as the planning of care.

As with the PSA role, interdepartmental teamwork is fostered through the common goal of creating a well-trained multidisciplinary worker.

Appendix 7–A

PCT General Patient Care Skills List

Name: ______________________ Unit: ______________

Skill	Instructed Didactic/ Skills Lab	Performs w/ Assistance	Performs Independently
I. PHLEBOTOMY A. Venipuncture technique 1. Vacutainer collection			
2. Syringe collection			
3. Two-syringe technique			
B. Microcollection technique 1. Fingersticks			
2. Heelsticks			
3. Microtainers			
4. Unopettes			
C. Special collection procedures 1. Blood bank banding			
2. Blood culture			
3. Specimen labeling			
II. REHABILITATION RELATED, PT A. Cold pack application			
B. Hot pack application			

continues

Skill	Instructed Didactic/ Skills Lab	Performs w/ Assistance	Performs Independently
C. Use of assistive devices 1. Walker			
2. Axillary crutches			
3. Forearm crutches			
4. Cane			
5. Level surfaces			
6. Stairs			
D. Exercise 1. Planes of motion, lower extremity			
2. Planes of motion, upper extremity			
3. Passive ROM			
4. Active-assistive ROM			
5. Active ROM			
6. Stretching			
7. Resistive exercise			
8. Isometrics			
9. Postoperative precautions for total knee patients			
10. Postoperative precautions for total hip patients			
E. Transfers 1. Proper body mechanics			
2. Using draw sheet			
3. Using slide board			
4. Standing pivot transfer			
5. Lateral transfers (two persons)			

continues

Skill	Instructed Didactic/ Skills Lab	Performs w/ Assistance	Performs Independently
III. REHABILITATION RELATED, OT A. Feeding/swallowing precautions 1. Set-up for specific disorders (left neglect)			
2. Use of adaptive equipment (dycem, roller knife)			
3. Monitoring for safety			
4. Infant feeding			
B. ADL adaptive equipment 1. Use of adaptive equipment a. Sock aid b. Dressing stick c. Long shoehorn and elastic shoelaces			
2. Safety issues (bedside, balance, pacing)			
C. Positioning 1. Bed			
2. Chair			
D. Exercise programs 1. Theraputty			
2. Hand helper			
3. Towel–dowel exercises			
4. Theraband			
E. Shoulder CPM monitoring			
F. Splinting 1. Check for pressure areas			
2. Position appropriately for edema			
G. Edema 1. Retrograde massage			

continues

Skill	Instructed Didactic/ Skills Lab	Performs w/ Assistance	Performs Independently
2. Coban wrap			
3. Positioning			
H. Pediatrics 1. Infant massage			
2. ROM			
3. Oral–motor stimulation			
IV. RESPIRATORY CARE A. Demonstrates intervention for use of: 1. Incentive spirometry			
2. Positioning			
3. Pulse oximeter			
B. Manual resuscitator/masks 1. Adult			
2. Pediatric, self-inflating			
3. Infant, PEEP bag			
V. PERFORMS 12-LEAD ECG			
VI. NURSING ASSISTANT SKILLS A. Turning a conscious patient			
B. Turning an unconscious patient			
C. Basic hygiene 1. Reports condition of skin			
2. Partial bed bath			
3. Complete bed bath			
4. Linen change, unoccupied bed			
5. Linen change, occupied bed			
6. Shave a male patient			
7. Oral hygiene/denture care/ use of Water Pik for patients with wired jaws			

continues

Skill	Instructed Didactic/ Skills Lab	Performs w/ Assistance	Performs Independently
8. Shampoo			
9. Place patient on bedpan/ urinal, empty bedpan			
D. CPR			
E. I&O 1. Calculating intake			
2. Measuring outputs a. Urinary b. Hemovacs c. JPs d. NG cannisters e. Ostomy bags			
F. Vital signs 1. Adult			
2. Child			
3. Infant (to include weight, length, head circumf.)			
4. Orthostatic BP			
G. Safety 1. Universal precautions			
2. Proper handling of syringes or sharp instruments			
3. Use of soft restraints/poseys			
4. Proper use of side rails when appropriate a. Crib b. Confused patient c. Sedated patient			
5. Climber crib with toddlers			
6. ID bands, allergy bands			
7. Handling contaminated linen/trash			
8. Seizure precautions			

continues

Skill	Instructed Didactic/ Skills Lab	Performs w/ Assistance	Performs Independently
H. Weights 1. Standing scale			
2. Bed scale			
3. Infant scale			
I. Urological nursing 1. Observe and report urine for color/character			
2. Specific gravity			
3. Straight catheterization			
4. Foley catheterization			
5. Foley care on a male patient			
6. Foley care on a female patient			
7. Obtaining a urine specimen from a Foley			
8. 24-hour urine specimen collection			
J. Wound care 1. Observation of an incision and drainage			
2. Simple and brief dressing changes			
K. Admit patient			
L. Patient discharge			
M. Documentation: Recording of patient data onto flowsheets			
N. Mixing and replenishing existing tube feedings (pediatrics assisted with GT tube feeds)			
O. Demonstrates use of Kangaroo feeding pump			
P. Preop procedures: checklist/ forms in order			

continues

Skill	Instructed Didactic/ Skills Lab	Performs w/ Assistance	Performs Independently
Q. Postop care 1. Frequent vital signs/ observations			
2. TC & DB			
R. Enemas 1. Cleansing			
2. Fleets			
3. Oil retention			
4. Tidal wave			
S. Additional equipment 1. Cooling blanket			
2. PAS stockings			
3. Intermittent suction			
4. Continuous suction			
5. Pediatrics: CR monitors, set alarms, collect data			
6. Doppler			
7. Regular TED hose			
8. Dinamap			
9. First-step bed			
10. Kenair bed			
T. Orthopedic nursing 1. Pin care for skeletal traction			
2. Pressure ulcer prevention			
3. Skin care protocol			
4. Proper body alignment			
5. Skin protector appliances			
6. Neurovascular checks a. Color b. Temperature			

continues

Skill	Instructed Didactic/ Skills Lab	Performs w/ Assistance	Performs Independently
c. Movement d. Sensation e. Capillary refill f. Pedal pulse			
7. Plantar/dorsiflexion			
U. Ortho skills lab 1. Assembly of over-bed trapezes, Hillrom, Simmons			
2. Bucks traction			
3. Total hip precaution, abduction wedge			
4. Bulky Jones dressing			
5. Log rolling			
V. Change ostomy and ileostomy appliances			
W. Ancillary testing 1. Obtain urine specific gravity (using refractometer)			
2. Obtain fingerstick blood glucose using visual testing			
3. Obtain fingerstick blood glucose using Accucheck			
4. Urine dipstick (may be unit specific)			
5. Hemocult (SKI) for fecal occult blood (may be unit specific)			
X. Basic ECG interpretation (monitor units only)			

Appendix 7–B

PCT General Orientation Program

Weeks 1–3

Day 1: Hospital orientation (new employee orientation)

Day 2: Customer service excellence
Infection control
Universal precautions/OSHA blood-borne pathogens
Fire safety
Hazardous materials

Nursing

Day 3: Introduction/greeting
Program overview

- Patient care restructuring
- Job description
- Standards of performance
- Skills list
- Orientation schedule
- Program objectives
- Modes of health care delivery
- Unit structure
- Time sheets

PCT guidelines

- Absenteeism policy and procedure
- Personal/career growth and development

Billing

- Nursing/equipment charge voucher
- Sticker charge system

CPR/basic first aid

Day 4: Integumentary system
Patient care and hygiene
Postmortem care
Bed making
Cardiovascular system
Vital signs
Flowsheets/Kardex

Day 5: PCT to follow an RN/LPN on patient care units; focus is beds, baths, vital signs

Day 6: Safety

- Restraints
- Side rails
- Seizure precautions
- Environmental safety
- Suicide precautions
- Machine alarms
- IV site observations
- Chest tube precautions

Common abbreviations/medical terminology
Introduction to the Vax system
Admissions/discharge
Assisting the physician with simple diagnostic procedures
Age-appropriate behavior/special care and consideration of the elderly patient
Communication skills

- Verbal
- Nonverbal
- Interacting with the patient with visual, hearing, or speech impairment

Day 7: The nervous system
Preop checklist/postop care
Accuchek
The art of skilled observation and reporting
Child abuse/elderly abuse/domestic violence

Day 8: Renal system
GI system
Tube feedings
Enemas and drainage system
I&O

Day 9: PCT to follow an RN/LPN on patient care units; focus is beds, baths, vital signs, admissions/discharges, tube feedings, enemas, I&O

Day 10: Medical asepsis
Aseptic technique
Pin care
Gastrostomy tube care
Sterile dressing change
Urinary catheterization

Day 11: PCT to follow an RN/LPN on patient care units; focus is tube feedings, enemas, I&O, pin care, gastrostomy care, sterile dressing change, urinary catheterization as patient census/acuity permit

Day 12: Care and consideration of the pediatric patient
Care of the postpartum patient
Stress management
Review session

Day 13: Stoma care
Hospital beds
Customer service
Question and answer period with panel of experienced PCTs
Nursing exam

SPECIALTY BREAK-OUT SESSION:

- Care of the postpartum patient for postpartum PCTs

- Care of the newborn for newborn nursery PCTs
- Basic ECG monitoring (monitored units only)
- Orthopedic skills lab

Week 4

Ancillary didactic

Occupational therapy
12-lead ECG
Physical therapy
Respiratory
Phlebotomy

Weeks 5 and 6

Phlebotomy clinical

Weeks 7–10

Supervised clinical with an RN/LPN preceptor

CHAPTER

8

Registered Nurse Preparation

Leigh Shaffer and Juanita McDonough

Chapter Objectives

1. To describe the rationale for formally preparing licensed staff to work with new health care workers.
2. To delineate specific components of the training program and the rationale for inclusion.
3. To discuss the content and sequence of training used in preparing the licensed staff for restructuring.
4. To identify ongoing educational needs to support staff.

It is essential to provide adequate preparation of the licensed staff for functioning in a restructured environment. The registered nurses (RNs) need education and training in delegation, supervision, and precepting. They also need to be trained in the aspects of ancillary duties and policies and procedures, for which they will be supervising the patient care technicians (PCTs) and patient support attendants (PSAs).

PREPARING THE RN FOR RESTRUCTURING

Creating a Need To Know

The RN is key to the success of patient care restructuring (PCR). The RN is crucial to the smooth transition from a primary nursing model to a patient-focused model, incorporating new levels of multipurpose staff. Adequate time is allocated to prepare the RNs because the role of the RN in a restructured environment is fundamentally altered. The RN is given time to practice new behaviors and to verbalize concerns so that he or she can fully incorporate the new ways of thinking and acting. The educational preparation provides the RN with the skills needed to work effectively with the unlicensed technical worker.

Adult learning principles stress the need for the learner to have a significant need to know. The adult learner wants to know how training will be useful and immediately applicable. The immediacy of implementation creates a strong need to know within the staff.

At University Medical Center (UMC), the initial educational efforts involved 8 hours of team building and 4 hours of communication classes. In addition, an all-day delegation workshop was held 2 months after implementation of PCR. These classes were helpful, but the experience indicated that the greatest effort needs to be focused on the issues of delegation and supervision of the technical worker before implementation. A positive approach is stressed in the educational programs to set the stage for restructuring and thereby to avoid a negative beginning.

Unit Cultural Assessment

Another important component to initiate before restructuring is evaluation of the unit environment. A culture assessment instrument that assesses unit culture was used to obtain information about the unit culture before implementation and 10 months after implementation. The preimplementation information gives baseline data that allow the managers and educators to have insight into the values and beliefs of the staff. Information obtained describes the following:

- how unit members work together
- what the staff value
- who fits in
- the underlying work ethic of the unit

The cultural data provide guidance for allocation of training and support resources. If the data show that one unit is having difficulty with teamwork, then additional efforts can be directed toward enhancing the unit's functioning and ensuring the success of the restructuring effort. Data collected after restructuring provide information about changes in the cultural norms over time.

COMPONENTS OF EDUCATIONAL PREPARATION

Delegation and Supervision

Delegation of tasks to an unlicensed health care provider is both challenging and frightening to RNs who have not worked with technicians before. Often, RNs are concerned about the legal implications of delegation. A common question that arises is: "Is my license on the line every time I delegate a task to a PCT?" In addition, some nurses are comfortable with delegation but are uncertain about their responsibilities in supervising the PCT. Therefore, a delegation and supervision workshop is provided to RNs and includes the following content:

- the changing health care environment
- licensure and liability
- barriers to delegation
- building trust
- delegation skills, evaluation, and feedback

In the recent past, many RNs' educational backgrounds and clinical experiences focused on a type of primary nursing care where RNs provided total direct patient care (also referred to as all-RN staffing). This type of primary nursing calls for the RN to perform all the skilled and nonskilled activities within the nursing scope to the patient. The RN performs the following duties:

- assesses and reassesses the patient on an ongoing basis
- develops and revises the plan of care
- coordinates discharge planning
- delivers medications
- provides all appropriate treatments
- provides for activities of daily living
- assists with feeding, if necessary
- changes linen and perhaps restocks rooms

Restructuring separates out the nonlicensed aspects of care and allocates those duties to trained support staff under the supervision of and as delegated by the RN. Therefore, it is essential to provide education and support for the RN in the areas of supervision and delegation.

The major content areas of the delegation and supervision workshops are discussed in the following sections.

The Changing Health Care Environment

Increasing patient acuity coupled with decreasing reimbursements is forcing hospitals and clinics to explore new ways to increase productivity with shrinking resources. This trend, matched with the shortage of workers and an aging population, sends the clear message that hospitals need to respond by developing creative approaches to providing care. PCR is a strategic response to the national health care dilemma. Nursing as a profession must recognize the inevitable changes and join forces to help navigate the trends affecting health care and the profession.

Licensure and Liability

No topic surrounding delegation is more significant to an RN than the relationship of delegation to licensure. The RN's responsibility is twofold when delegating tasks to a PCT. First, the task must fall within appropriate practice limits for the PCT role. Second, the PCT must work under the supervision of the RN.

The Rules and Regulations of the State Board of Nursing addresses the use of assistants in the delivery of patient care. Under Section R4-19-402, "Functions of the Registered Nurse," the Act reads, "Giving direct nursing care to each patient according to the needs or assigning these functions to assistants in accordance with the preparation and competency of the available staff."[1(p.15)] Therefore, RNs need to be familiar with the role, the training, and the competencies of the PCT as stated on the skills list and job description.

The RN is responsible for the direct supervision of the PCT who has been delegated a task. RN responsibility includes acquiring a baseline assessment of the patient as well as periodic assessments during the shift as needed to plan, implement, and evaluate effectively the patient's care.

An RN's license is not in jeopardy when he or she has delegated a task within the scope and role of the PCT and has supervised the individual. If a PCT makes an error when performing a task, the RN's responsibility begins when he or she has been notified of the incident. At the point of notification, the RN is responsible for appropriate reporting and follow-up.

Barriers to Delegation

When asked about delegation, RNs respond with a variety of concerns. Taking risks, trusting, letting go, and a sense of loss of achievement and control are some of the concerns verbalized by RNs. These concerns represent potential barriers to delegation. Identifying such barriers is an initial step toward overcoming some of the fears and losses commonly associated with change as a whole and with delegation specifically.

During the workshop, the nurses are asked to state some of their personal barriers to delegation. Their answers often reflect a lack of knowledge and experience concerning delegation. Discussions with the RNs also highlight that there are few role models available because so many RNs have only practiced within an all-RN model. At UMC, many nurses said, "I know that I can do it better and quicker myself than when I have to take time to teach someone, and I know it is done the right way." This theme is common among RNs who have become accustomed to providing total patient care.

Overcoming the barriers to delegation involves stressing the benefits of the appropriate allocation of duties. Nurses readily admit that they are often frustrated with the frantic pace of the current system. They are burdened with multiple tasks that keep them from performing the type of nursing role for which they were educated. This role includes providing patient and family education, implementing case management, and maintaining communication with other health care team members. Open discussion of the purpose of delegation enables nurses to appreciate that many tasks can be delegated to an unlicensed health care provider. The RN is then free to focus on the rewarding, professional aspects of the role.[2]

Nurses identify other benefits of overcoming personal barriers to delegation. For example, pride in preceptoring a PCT and seeing the individual grow and develop is a commonly stated benefit. Increased efficiency and effectiveness of the nurse and the potential for better patient care are other benefits they identify.

Building Trust

Trust is an essential component of effective delegation. RNs new to the art of delegation often have a skeptical attitude toward the PCT. The attitude is described by the statement, "I'll feel comfortable delegating when you prove you are worthy of my trust." The RN is responsible to know the competencies and abilities of individuals to whom they delegate tasks, but a cautious approach should not interfere with the RN's willingness to work with the PCT. The need for the RN to work together with the PCT to identify strengths and weaknesses is stressed. Over time, the RN will learn who is conscientious and responsible and who needs closer supervision with clearer guidelines.

Trust in the PCT training process is as important as developing trust in individual PCTs. Staff need to be able to trust that the training program for which they are preceptors provides a solid basis for the PCTs as a whole.

It is important for the RN to discern educational weaknesses from other types of deficiencies on the part of the PCT. If the PCT has a weak knowledge base, the staff nurse can utilize the resources of the nursing staff development department, the education coordinator, and other team members to support the PCT. Other weaknesses, such as an inability to prioritize, may require additional precepting and closer supervision.

Delegation Skills, Evaluation, and Feedback

Clear, concise communication is a key to effective delegation. The workshop stresses the need for the RN to make expectations clear. Telling the PCT to get started on his or her morning tasks and that the RN will check in later gives the PCT little of the RN's expectations. Clear instructions with time lines for reporting, however, help the PCT understand the RN's expectations. For example, the RN tells the PCT to start with vital signs at 8:00 A.M. and, when finished, to start beds and baths for Mrs. Smith and Mr. Moore. The RN will discuss the status of duties with the PCT at 9:00 A.M. If the PCT gets pulled away for other tasks and cannot complete the assignment, he or she should let the RN know as soon as possible.

The RN is also responsible for giving feedback and evaluating the performance of the PCT. The skills needed for effective evaluation and feedback include the following:

- initiate open discussion of problems
- seek specific input from the PCT
- recognize individual effort
- maintain the self-esteem of individual PCTs
- explore possible solutions
- agree on potential actions

PCTs may require different levels of supervision. The situational leadership model of Blanchard et al. is helpful in teaching which is the best choice of leadership style for the type of employee.[3]

Successful delegation leads to a sense of trust and respect among the team members. RNs may not find that they are less busy, but they will discover that they are busy accomplishing the professional aspects of the

RN role, including both supervision and delegation. As Barnum notes, effective delegators "recognize that being at the head of a work group instead of being the work group may not be all that great a loss."[4(p.395)]

Workshop on Precepting the PCT

The final 4 weeks of PCT training is a supervised clinical experience. The PCT is assigned to an RN preceptor. Specific content on how to be an effective preceptor for a PCT is provided to the RN preceptors before the clinical experience (Exhibit 8–1). The PCT is also given a list of expectations for

Exhibit 8–1 PCT Preceptor Qualifications

1. One year of experience as an RN or LPN.
2. Six months of experience on designated nursing unit.
3. Nursing unit competencies completed.

Preceptor Expectations

1. Meet with PCT before starting the supervised clinical training.
   - Set up and clarify the supervised clinical training schedule.
   - Review skills list with the PCT at the onset of supervised clinical training.
2. Review the progress/orientation needs of the PCT with any staff members also working with the PCT during the supervised clinical training.
3. Perform weekly evaluations of the PCT: Put the evaluation forms in the education coordinator's mailbox. Adapt the supervised clinical training for the individual's experience and rate of progress.
4. Give weekly updates of the PCT's progress to the nurse manager.
5. Give prompt notification of any problems or concerns to the education coordinator.
6. Formally release the PCT from orientation when appropriate:
   - evaluation forms are complete and given to the education coordinator
   - conference with preceptor and PCT
   - decision to prolong or end supervised clinical training
   - complete skills list given to nurse manager
7. Perform skills update at 6 months:
   - review skills list
   - nurse manager/preceptor/PCT conference

being precepted (Exhibit 8–2). The preceptor's schedule is paired with that of the PCT's as much as possible, allowing for continuity of training and mentoring. This scheduling arrangement is designed to avoid duplications and omissions in training.

In addition to being a mentor, the preceptor serves as the contact person for the education coordinator and the nurse manager. The preceptor communicates with the coordinator through weekly evaluation forms and the final release from orientation form (Exhibits 8–3 and 8–4). In addition, telephone conferences as well as meetings with the PCT, the nurse manager, and the education coordinator are mechanisms used by the preceptor to communicate the progress and needs of the PCT. The PCT has an opportunity to evaluate his or her preceptor at the end of the clinical training experience (Exhibit 8–5).

Timing of Supervision, Delegation, and PCT Preceptor Training

The delegation and supervision workshop and the PCT preceptor workshop are generally presented as a combined 3-hour program. For newly restructured units, the delegation, supervision, and advanced preceptor content is provided to RNs during the first 3 weeks of PCT training. The training is done just before initiation of supervised clinical precepting of

Exhibit 8–2 Expectations of the PCT

1. Meet with preceptor before start date to review supervised clinical training schedule and general guidelines.
2. Meet with preceptor on a weekly basis to evaluate progress and needs.
3. Obtain release from orientation:
   - evaluation forms complete
   - conference with nurse manager and preceptor
   - informal self-evaluation as to decision to prolong or end orientation
   - completed skills list given to nurse manager
4. Skills update at 6 months:
   - review skills list
   - PCT/nurse manager/preceptor conference
5. General expectations:
   - attend unit workshops and meetings
   - complete competencies

Exhibit 8–3 Evaluation of the PCT

PCT: ______________________ Unit: ______________

Preceptor: ______________________

Date of evaluation: ______________ Dates of OJT: __________

	AGREE				DISAGREE
1. Shows ability to set own learning objectives.	5	4	3	2	1
2. Takes initiative to achieve objectives.	5	4	3	2	1
3. Delivers safe patient care utilizing knowledge of basic and unit-specific skills.	5	4	3	2	1
4. Incorporates infection control principles in patient care.	5	4	3	2	1
5. Exhibits effective time management skills to complete assignment.	5	4	3	2	1
6. Has ability to set priorities in caring for a group of patients.	5	4	3	2	1
7. Communicates effectively with staff and ancillary department personnel to meet patient needs and to solve problems.	5	4	3	2	1
8. Displays professionalism in appearance and manner.	5	4	3	2	1
9. Has areas for further growth/goals.	5	4	3	2	1

Please return this promptly to the education coordinator.

the PCTs by the RNs. The delegation and supervision content is included in the nursing orientation for newly hired RNs. The PCT preceptor content is provided to new RNs when they are assigned to precept a PCT.

Initially at UMC, delegation and supervision classes were provided to RNs several weeks after the program was implemented because it was thought that staff would benefit after working with PCTs and therefore would have a greater understanding of the issues. The benefits of delaying the training were far outweighed by the need to introduce the skills of delegation and supervision before implementation. The precepting and supervising skills are needed throughout implementation and are best introduced during the unit orientation period. Only licensed staff attend this workshop.

Exhibit 8–4 PCT Release from Orientation Form

Name:______________________________ Date: __________________

Title: ______________________________ DOH: __________________

_______ Skills list signed off for completed tasks.

_______ Skills list turned in to nurse manager.

_______ Completion of ________ hours of clinical orientation.

_______ Attended all mandatory education programs: PCR, fire/safety, infection control, electrical safety

Any deficiencies are indicated on the back with an action plan.

____

PCT

____

Primary Preceptor

Please return to education coordinator

The timing of other educational programs is also important. Human resources offers programs on team building, communication, the change process, and interview techniques (see Chapters 11 and 12). The change process programs are offered during the initial orientation phase. Early discussions of PCR prompted various reactions to change. An understanding of the change process is needed to recognize normal responses and to identify where persons are in the process.

Team building and communication workshops are held within 1 month to 6 weeks of implementation. This time frame has proven to be effective because the staff have identified issues and are motivated to work together to create solutions. All levels of staff are included.

Educational Support for Supervision of Ancillary Roles

RNs supervise PCTs and PSAs as they perform duties previously done by ancillary department staff, such as environmental services and clinical

Exhibit 8–5 Evaluation of the Preceptor

PCT: ______________________________ Unit: ______________

Preceptor: ______________________________

Date of evaluation: ____________________ Dates of OJT: __________

	AGREE				DISAGREE
The preceptor was able to:					
1. explain information clearly (comments)	5	4	3	2	1
2. be flexible in individualizing the orientation plan based on your learning needs	5	4	3	2	1
3. provide adequate feedback during your orientation	5	4	3	2	1
4. serve as a clinical resource using an advanced knowledge base	5	4	3	2	1
5. offer support in a consistent manner	5	4	3	2	1
6. demonstrate consistency in the approach to patient care	5	4	3	2	1

laboratory. The staff receive education from the various ancillary departments to provide the basic knowledge needed to supervise the staff appropriately. The information can be provided in workshops or during staff meetings, depending on the amount of time needed and the content.

THE ROLE OF THE RN IN ORIENTING THE PCT

Role of the Nurse Manager

The nurse manager hires the PCTs and selects the appropriate preceptor for the new PCT before the clinical training experience (Exhibit 8–6). The nurse manager may choose to involve staff in the hiring process (see Chapter 10). A mismatch of personalities can make supervised clinical training stressful for the PCT trainee and frustrating for the preceptor. When a mismatch has occurred, the nurse manager reassigns the PCT to another staff member who is better suited for the trainee.

During weekly updates, the nurse manager tracks the progress of both the preceptor and the PCT. These updates are usually informal unless

Exhibit 8–6 Expectations of the Nurse Manager in Orientation of the PCT

1. Weekly update with preceptor to track progress of PCT.
2. Check with PCT at least every other week as to progress on orientation and skills list.
3. Conduct release from orientation meeting; PCT, preceptor, and nurse manager to be present.
4. Conduct 3-month probationary review meeting with PCT to set goals for remainder of probationary period.
5. Evaluate appropriateness of match of PCT and preceptor.
6. Evaluate preceptor for effectiveness.

problems have occurred. Three-month and 6-month probationary review meetings between the nurse manager and the PCT evaluate the ongoing progress of the new employee.

Expectations of the RN Preceptor

At the onset of the supervised clinical training experience, the RN preceptor and the PCT meet and review the skills list. The list reflects the didactic and clinical content of PCT training and provides the nurse a baseline assessment of the educational needs of the PCT.

The preceptor and new employee need to review any issues concerning the scope of the PCT role. Such a review is especially important with student nurses, medics, and other PCT trainees who previously have had jobs in the medical field. For example, while in the Army a medic may have been allowed to start IVs, but as a PCT she may not do this. The role of the PCT is limited to the role of a nursing assistant. Likewise, the student nurse may have been taught to administer medications. In fact, candidates may have worked as student nurses on the very unit where they are now PCTs. Nevertheless, when working as a PCT students must understand that they are to work within the limits of the PCT role.

Also, the preceptor emphasizes the role of the RN as the individual who directly supervises the PCT. The trainees need to understand from the onset what the PCT reporting responsibilities entail. The RN reviews with the PCT when to notify the RN and gives guidelines for what is to be reported to the preceptor.

During the first week of clinical training, the PCT closely shadows the preceptor. The close contact enables the preceptor to get to know the trainee and gives the PCT a chance to feel comfortable on the unit. During this time, the PCT learns both the physical environment and the culture of the unit. The preceptor introduces the new PCT to unit members and to other staff who play a significant role on the unit.

Throughout the supervised clinicals, the preceptor observes and documents the progress of the PCT. New skills are observed by the preceptor until the candidate is able to perform them without assistance. The preceptor documents the completion of competencies with the skills list and the overall progress of the PCT with the weekly evaluation forms. The expectations of the RN preceptor detailed here are explained to the preceptors during the PCT preceptor workshop.

DETERMINING ONGOING EDUCATION NEEDS OF SUPPORT STAFF

As PCR implementation progresses, it is important to revisit the educational needs of staff. Each unit is unique and requires individual assessment of ongoing learning needs. Topics such as communication, delegation, and principles of teamwork may need to be reviewed. For example, at UMC one unit began PCR with minimal problems, but after a year of implementation the issues of delegation and supervision needed to be readdressed. The scope of practice of the nonlicensed worker needed to be reviewed, and the importance of direct RN supervision needed to be reemphasized.

ORIENTATION OF NEW STAFF

Nursing orientation at UMC includes an introduction to the UMC model of patient-centered care to ensure successful integration of new staff into restructured units. PCT and PSA roles are discussed with a brief overview of the care delivery method. Delegation and supervision of the unlicensed technical worker are also reviewed.

CONCLUSION

The training and educational needs of the RN in implementing restructuring are complex. Restructuring places a new emphasis on delegation and supervision of the unlicensed worker coupled with a need to refocus away from the task-oriented components and toward the more complex professional aspects of the RN role. The RN must learn new skills and develop new behavior patterns for an effective transition into the professional practice model inherent in a restructured environment.

NOTES

1. Arizona State Board of Nursing, *Rules and Regulations of the State Board of Nursing* (Phoenix, Ariz.: State Board of Nursing, 1987).
2. R. Hasten and M. Washburn, Delegation: How To Deliver Care through Others, *American Journal of Nursing* 92 (1992): 87–90.
3. K. Blanchard, et al., A Situational Approach to Supervision: Leadership Theory and the Supervising Nurse, *Supervisor Nurse* 7 (1976): 17–20.
4. B.J. Barnum, Cycles of Nursing, *Nursing Health Care* (1990): 395.

CHAPTER

9

Professional Nursing Practice

Sandy Kurtin, Suzan Bohnenkamp, and Josephine Sacco Palmer

Chapter Objectives

1. To describe elements of professional nursing practice.
2. To describe the pilot of a unit-based case management model.
3. To describe the unit-based nurse case manager role.
4. To describe the pilot educational program preparing nurse case managers.
5. To identify strategies to integrate changes in delivery systems into the pilot of nurse case management.

With the increasing percentage of the Gross National Product being allocated to health care and the sense of urgency to reduce the national budget deficit, the health care delivery system is under close scrutiny. The introduction of diagnosis-related groups (DRGs) to regulate reimbursement for Medicare recipients was an initial attempt to set guidelines for allocation of health care resources by the federal government. The impact on health care agencies, organizations, and professionals as well as on the health care consumer has been dramatic.

Because of the high cost of care in the acute care setting, access to services was restricted, and the term *average length of stay* became associated with a predetermined level of financial reimbursement. Acute care agencies were pushed to create cost-effective means of delivering care that achieved similar outcomes with reduced periods of hospitalization. The 24-hour hospital stay for an uncomplicated vaginal delivery of a healthy newborn has become a standard.

The challenge for nursing professionals has been to meet the needs of patients and families within a shortened hospitalization and to prepare them to assume continuing care needs after discharge. Health care consumers are expected to participate actively in every phase of their care, including management of medications, use of medical equipment, and seeking additional care based on identified physical and/or emotional symptoms.[1] Early discharge from the acute care setting has increased the demand for alternative health care delivery systems that are responsive to the needs of the consumer and the mandate to decrease cost. Professional nurses as case managers are key to the effective integration of these changes. This chapter describes the rationale and process for implementation of nurse case management as a professional practice model at University Medical Center (UMC).

RATIONALE FOR PROFESSIONAL NURSE CASE MANAGEMENT

The shift in emphasis to patient-centered health care and the expectation that patients and families will take responsibility for self-care require both clear communication between patients and health care providers and clear identification of desired patient outcomes based on approved standards of care. Several factors support the professional nurse as the primary coordinator for management of efficient and effective care, or case management.

The professional nurse is the health care provider with the greatest amount of patient and family contact. Professional nurses are able to provide the vital communication link that allows efficient implementation of care and promotes patient and family involvement. The educational background of the professional nurse emphasizes a holistic approach to assessment, planning, implementation, and evaluation of care based on desired patient outcomes and standards of care. This background enables the professional nurse effectively to integrate ongoing and timely consultation with collaborating professionals.

The delivery of care in the acute care setting involves staff at many levels and represents several departments. Professional nurses who function as case managers have identified key contacts and effective procedures for getting things accomplished in the institution. The professional nurse case manager has the ability to navigate the patient through the system, to prioritize patient needs, to delegate appropriate tasks to ancillary staff, and to serve as the primary communication link for the patient and family. These attributes increase the autonomy and accountability the professional nurse has in the planning and delivery of quality, cost-effective patient care. Nurse case management promotes the following:

- collaborative practice
- continuity of care
- use of appropriate or reduced resources
- increased professional development
- increased nurse satisfaction
- increased patient satisfaction

NURSE CASE MANAGEMENT AS A PROFESSIONAL PRACTICE MODEL

Numerous nurse case management models are currently in place in a variety of settings. Most models are defined by the characteristics of the institution or setting, the scope of services provided, and the primary population served. Several definitions exist for case management, and several titles are used, including case manager, nurse case manager, and registered nurse (RN) case manager.

The Differentiated Group Professional Practice Project defined case management as a patient care delivery system that focuses on the defined achievement of patient outcomes within effective timeframes and with appropriate use of resources.[2] The American Nurses Association identifies key components of case management described as a process of assessing a person's physical, mental, and functional level; determining what services are needed; planning for these services; locating, developing, arranging, and coordinating those services; and monitoring changes in recipients' conditions and adjusting the service plan model.[3]

The New England Medical Center (NEMC) defines case management as comprising a primary nurse who works with the patient and health care team to coordinate patient care in the hospital and after discharge. The case manager is a member of a collaborative practice that includes the physician and selected inpatient and outpatient nurses.[4] The NEMC model has been adopted and modified by many institutions based on their individual needs. The NEMC model is a hospital-based model that presumes a primary nursing care delivery system targeted at high-risk and high-cost DRGs. The case manager is at the staff nurse unit-based level and provides direct care. Criteria for case managers include the following:

- interest
- clinical maturity or expertise
- skill with the nursing process
- skill with assessment follow-up and problem solving
- demonstration of initiative
- willingness to be a team player

The NEMC model has been in practice longer than other formally identified hospital-based case management models. The major results achieved are quality and decreased cost of care, improved retention of nurses, decreased length of stay, and increased patient satisfaction.

Various institutions have expanded the NEMC model to encompass health care delivery in the community and acute care settings. The Carondolet St. Mary's nursing network model utilizes a nurse case manager who coordinates care for a group of patients in the inpatient, outpatient, and extended care settings.[5] The nurse case managers do not provide direct care to the patient. Regardless of the definition or model employed, the implementation of nursing case management as a means to provide cost-effective, quality care that is responsive to ongoing health care reform is a rapidly growing trend.

UMC NURSE CASE MANAGEMENT MODEL

Nursing case management is an integral part of the UMC model for patient care restructuring (PCR). Case management is defined as a system of patient care delivery that focuses on achievement of outcomes within effective time frames and with appropriate use of resources. The model is based on collaborative involvement by all team members in the development of clinical protocols, also called critical pathways. The clinical protocols or critical pathways serve as guidelines by which to anticipate and standardize the course of treatment according to the patient's diagnosis and identified needs.

The primary goals for the UMC case management model include the following:

- decreased length of stay through providing quality, coordinated care to achieve desired patient outcomes effectively and efficiently

- decreased incidence of preventable patient readmissions through effective patient and family teaching and planning for continuing care needs
- increased patient, physician, and nurse satisfaction through consistent integration of multidisciplinary communication, planning, and evaluation of care delivery

Development of the Nurse Case Manager Pilot Project

Operationalizing of goals began with identifying a process for planning and implementing case management. According to Zander, anyone embarking on case management should be able to work interdependently in at times high ambiguous situations. Potential case manages should be interested in the model and ready to make a new level of commitment to patients, colleagues, and the well-being of the institution. Greater emotional energy is required because people must be open, take more risks, and work at developing trust and trusting each other.[6]

The initial phase of development for the UMC case management model involved convening a role identification task force. The group included the following:

- interested RNs from the units that were initially implementing PCR
- a representative from the hospital human resources department
- a clinical nurse specialist
- a clinical director from patient care services

Each task force member received literature describing various case management models, copies of current job descriptions for RNs, and additional information describing each component of the PCR project. Initial meetings focused on discussion of the literature with particular emphasis on hospital-based models that presume a staff nurse case manager. The objectives of the task force were as follows:

- Define the process for case manager application.
- Describe the role of case manager, including duties and responsibilities.
- Describe the role of the case associate, including duties and responsibilities.
- Discuss the integration of the case manager role into the PCR project and the existing nursing care delivery system.

Eligibility criteria for the case manager position were selected based on the characteristics of the hospital and individual pilot units, including the patient population. Anticipated changes that might result from the overall PCR project were also considered. The pilot units included two adult care units and two pediatric care units. RNs applied for the case manager's position through normal hiring mechanisms established in the human resources department. All RNs who met the following criteria were eligible to apply:

- interest in the position
- RN in a core or per diem position on the pilot unit
- B.S.N. preferred, or 4 years of experience as an RN
- a minimum of 1 year of experience as an RN at UMC
- employed a minimum of 0.8 full-time equivalent (FTE; 32 hours/week); a job share between two 0.4 to 0.5 FTE staff with the same skill level on the same shift could substitute for 0.8 FTE

Criteria selected reflect the emphasis on interest, clinical expertise or maturity, familiarity with and commitment to the institution and unit, and facilitation of continuity of care. The position is clinical in nature but also incorporates management responsibility. The nurse case manager coordinates care of a given caseload of patients on a 24-hour basis in addition to managing a group of patient care providers. Primary responsibilities of the nurse case manager include the following:

- assessing patient/family needs
- formulating the plan of care
- managing/delegating interventions
- collaborating with physicians and other professionals
- thoroughly documenting all aspects of care delivery
- supervising patient care staff
- evaluating patient outcomes
- consulting with specialists

Initial role descriptions were adapted from the NEMC model by the task force to describe the role to interested staff. The existing job description for RNs was retained for the case associate role description and the definitions of duties and responsibilities. The case management role description (Exhibit 9–1) was refined through a series of meetings after the nurse case

Exhibit 9–1 Role Description for Case Manager

1. Establishes a mechanism for notification when a new patient enters the caseload (this includes determining which patients he or she will case manage).
2. Introduces self to patient or family and explains the role of case manager and case associate.
3. Contacts physician(s) to begin sharing assessments, goals, and plans for the duration of the patient's hospital stay.
4. Knows the anticipated DRG, length of stay, and transfer or discharge dates for assigned caseload.
5. Discusses ongoing and future care with the other nursing and ancillary inpatient unit staff.
6. Negotiates work schedule with the nurse manager and/or assistant nurse manager to attend weekly case management meetings.
7. Identifies a critical path for the patient and places it in the nursing Kardex.
8. Compares the standard critical path against the patient's individual needs in such areas as social and economic data, family resources, functional abilities, knowledge needs, potential risk factors and complications, and special issues.
9. Reviews and revises the individual critical path with the physician(s) within 24 hours of admission.
10. Contacts other key members of the patient's team (e.g., social worker, dietitian, physical therapist, community resource personnel, and others) as needed.
11. Gives and monitors the delivery of care and the patient's responses to care every day that the patient is on the case manager's unit.
12. Arranges with the case associate RN continuity of plan and provides coverage during short, long, and unexpected absences.
13. Gives the patient and family a time schedule and tells them who to contact during the case manager's absence.
14. Documents the achievements of intermediate goals and clinical outcomes as they occur.
15. Integrates case management information and revised interventions (processes) into intershift report and case management meetings.
16. Plans, participates in, and follows through with health care team meetings as needed.
17. Manages the patient's transition through the system and transfers accountability to the appropriate person or agency upon discharge.
18. Completes a follow-up evaluation.

Source: Adapted with permission from *Collaborative Care: Nursing Case Management*, published by American Hospital Publishing, ©1989.

managers were hired and the responsibilities of the patient care technician and patient support attendant were identified.

Pilot Educational Plan for Nurse Case Manager Preparation

Content critical to integration of the case manager role was identified through literature review and discussions with staff who were participating in the PCR pilot project. A training program for case managers and case associates that incorporated this information was then developed. Case managers were scheduled to attend a series of eight 2-hour sessions. Case associates were invited to participate in selected sessions to encourage collaboration and understanding of the case manager role. Notebooks were distributed to case managers that contained session orientation materials, objectives and outlines, selected articles, and additional information about the PCR project. Case associates also received relevant information for sessions they attended. Each session included a lecture and discussion to encourage the exchange of information, the solicitation of ideas, and the opportunity to clarify content. Four case managers were selected to attend a national conference before the training program was implemented. Thus they added a valuable contribution to the discussion within each training session. Each session was videotaped to accommodate those unable to attend. Specific learning objectives for each session are included in Exhibit 9–2.

Case managers at UMC participated in a final discussion session after session 8. Among topics discussed were the titles to be used for case managers and clinical protocols. The group decided to use the title *nurse case manager* and completed a form to obtain new name badges with that title. The term *critical path* was selected to identify clinical protocols. Monthly meetings were selected as the mechanism to continue discussion, to allow planning for work assignments, and to provide continuing education. All nurse case managers were invited to attend a completion ceremony.

Continuing education planning included identification of local, regional, and national workshops or conferences that focused on nursing case management. Twenty nurse case managers attended a regional workshop after completion of the training program.

Nurse case manager meetings were planned twice a month to discuss issues and to brainstorm as well as to provide ongoing education. Nurse case managers were asked to attend at least one lecture session and one discussion session monthly. Initial topics included the following:

- continuous quality improvement
- social services and home health

Exhibit 9–2 Educational Program for Nurse Case Managers

Session 1: Case Management Overview—Case Manager and Case Associate Attendance

Learning Objectives

1. Examine and discuss the various models of case management and how nurses may want to incorporate ideas into their own model.
2. List the steps involved in gaining support for case management at UMC.
3. Identify the skills required to be a case manager.
4. Discuss the collaboration that will be needed and the departments that will need to be involved.
5. Define in 25 words or fewer what case management is to a physician on their nursing unit with whom they want to collaborate.

Session 2: Review of Roles (Duties and Responsibilities)—Case Manager Attendance

Learning Objectives

1. List the various skills that the Case Manager will need.
2. Describe how you conduct an admission assessment.
3. Describe the components of the plan of care and documentation required for the case manager.
4. Identify resources available for patient care, how to access them, and the skills needed for collaboration with various resources.
5. Discuss and describe what aspects of patient care you would delegate and how you might do this.
6. Examine the similarities and differences in the duties and responsibilities of the case manager and case associate.
7. Describe how you personally would work with a case associate.

Session 3: Empowerment of Nurses—Case Managers and Case Associates Attendance

Learning Objectives

1. Define empowerment.
2. Examine own attitudes about power and its relevance to solving nursing care delivery problems.
3. Discuss the interaction of individual and social factors as it relates to empowerment efforts in clinical settings.
4. List the structural conditions that may impede nurses' empowerment in clinical settings.
5. Identify two resources that may promote nurses' empowerment in practice settings.
6. Discuss the role of colleague relationships in the empowerment efforts of nurses.
7. Describe the relationship of effort and persistence to empowerment efforts of nurses.
8. Define a clinical practice outcome that would represent personal success in a self-empowerment process.

continues

Exhibit 9–2 continued

Session 4: Critical Pathways—Case Manager Attendance

Learning Objectives

1. Examine the five critical paths used in other facilities.
2. Discuss the concerns one might have as a case manager in relation to developing and implementing critical paths on your unit.
3. List the components of the critical path.
4. Identify a physician with whom one would like to collaborate to work on a critical path.
5. Describe the difference between a critical path and a care plan.
6. Define the purpose of a critical path.

Session 5: Conflict Resolution—Case Manager and Case Associate Attendance

Learning Objectives

1. List common conflicts encountered in the case manager role.
2. Discuss the value of conflict resolution in effective case management.
3. Describe the effects of conflict avoidance on patient care outcomes.
4. Identify several strategies for dealing with conflict.
5. Examine the pros and cons of each strategy.
6. Recognize the strategy one might use most often in patient care situations.
7. Explore the skills necessary to employ alternative strategies.
8. Assess own readiness to practice at least two skills necessary for effective conflict resolution in patient care situations.

Session 6: Time Management and Delegation—Case Manager and Case Associate Attendance

Learning Objectives

1. Identify personal factors that affect skills development in time management and delegation.
2. List time-consuming role functions of the nurse case manager.
3. Plan a time management strategy incorporating the role functions.
4. Describe the rationale for delegation in case management.
5. Differentiate delegation from dumping.
6. List skills necessary for effective delegation.
7. Plan own skills practice necessary for case manager role development.

Session 7: Team Building—Case Manager Attendance

Learning Objectives

1. Examine one's own unit and where to start in team building.
2. Discuss what skills are needed to be a team leader.
3. List the qualities of a good team member and team leader.
4. Identify the differences between a group and a team.
5. Discuss the effect that case management will have on building a team.

continues

Exhibit 9–2 continued

Session 8: Reimbursement Realities and Responsibilities—Case Manager and Case Associate Attendance

Learning Objectives

1. Identify current difficulties with reimbursement.
2. Describe various methods of reimbursement.
3. Examine strategies used in utilization management.
4. Discuss effective utilization management strategies.
5. Describe the process of commercial insurance audit.

- documentation
- management information systems and chart access
- overview of the physician relations program

One session included a visiting case manager from a local institution who described role implementation and participated in discussion with the nurse case managers. These monthly meetings and discussion sessions provided the opportunity to mold the nurse case manager role based on the individual unit needs and allowed effective identification and understanding of hospital resources. The meetings were also used to continue to develop tools and systems necessary to implement the nurse case manager role, including critical path development.

The initial phase of critical path development involved reviewing critical path models used in other institutions and published in the literature. High-volume or high-risk DRGs were selected as the initial focus for critical path development. Common DRGs by unit were identified, and the case managers selected populations seen as high risk. The key components of the critical path included teaching, consults, tests and labs, activity, medication, treatment, diet, discharge plan, and assessment and evaluation. Sources of information for critical path development that were identified included chart review, clinical experience, physician expectations, insurance guidelines, literature on treatment, and DRG information. Key questions were outlined to guide the framework for mapping the course of hospitalization for a given case type. The purpose of the questions was to identify factors that significantly influence the length of stay. Initial questions included the following:

- When does the admission diagnostic work-up occur, day 1 or day 2 of admission?

- What is included in the admission diagnostic work-up?
- When do key consultations occur?
- When must tests be ordered so that they are completed in a timely fashion?
- When do postsurgical patients begin to ambulate?
- When is a full diet resumed?
- When should teaching be initiated so that effective learning occurs before discharge?

Nurse case managers were given blank worksheets adapted from the NEMC model to begin to map the course of hospitalization for the DRG they had selected to develop. An example of the completed critical path for transurethral prostatectomy is included in Exhibit 9–3. The nurse case managers contacted the key physician to schedule meetings to discuss the content identified in the draft of the critical path. Interdisciplinary collaboration provided additional input and promoted a broader understanding of both the case manager role and the critical path. The vice president of patient care services held initial information sessions with medical department heads to define nurse case management and discuss implementation strategies. Letters were distributed to all other physicians and department heads to provide them with information about nurse case management and critical pathways. A multidisciplinary conference was held to evaluate each critical pathway and to make final revisions before implementation.

UNIT-BASED CASE MANAGEMENT IMPLEMENTATION

Four case managers on each of the pilot units participated in the pilot program for unit-based nurse case management. RNs from all shifts were eligible to apply for the positions. A caseload of six patients was considered maximum by the group, with input from the nurse manager, clinical director, and PCR program coordinator. If necessary, case managers would be assigned an additional two patients for direct care plus their case management load. Based on previously established criteria, the nurse-to-patient ratio remained the same for all nurses. Therefore, the case manager did not always provide direct care to the entire caseload. On one unit the nurse case manager chose to continue to provide direct patient care to five patients and to case manage one to six patients inclusive of those being case managed. The decision was made as a result of three factors: increased patient load of case associates, increased knowledge of the patient

Exhibit 9–3 Critical Path for Transurethral Prostatectomy

Unit 4 East ___ Critical Path Turp ___ Patient ___ Case Manager ___ DRG 337 ___ Physician ___

Date Reviewed ___ Expected LOS 3.7 ___ Admission Date ___ Discharge Date ___ Discharge Time ___

Date	Day 1	Day 2	Day 3	Day 4	Day 5	Day 6	Day 7
Consults							
	SS ------------------------------→						
Tests							
		H & H Lytes					
Lab							
Activity							
	BR turn --------→	00B ------------→	↑ ambulation ----→				
	q 2° --------------	amb tid					
Treatments							
	VS q 4° --------------------→		VS q shift -------------→				
	I & O ---------	Encourage fluids ------------------------→					
	TCDB ---→						
	Foley care ---------------------------------			DC foley at 0400 Rack and record urine			
	CBI ------------------------------		DC CBI per MD orders ----------→ Hand irrigate foley prn until clear				
	Traction on ---	Release traction					
Diet							
	DAT -------→	Encourage fluids ---------------------------------→					

continues

Exhibit 9–3 continued

Date	Day 1	Day 2	Day 3	Day 4	Day 5	Day 6	Day 7
Discharge Planning Teaching:							
	Assess home situation Make referrals		Place DC instruction on chart, reinforce teaching, watch urine output, problem with blood in urine.	Give pt./S.O. D/C form.			
			Give DC summary, teach on rack and record urine.	DC Teaching, reinforced refer to home instructions after a TURP.			
	Assess previous learning. Instruct on IV pain meds. CBI meatal care, need for I & O and IV antibiotics.	Increase activity. Instruct pt./S.O. on any *new* meds and usual meds that will be taken at home.		Instruct on what to do if unable to urinate. Instruct on follow-up visit. Instruct on meds., activity and diet. Reinforce teaching regarding what to do if unable to urinate.			

Source: Copyright © 1993 University Medical Center, Tucson, Arizona.

when the nurse case manager provided direct care, and improved communication with the physicians regarding the patients' progress and needs.

Case managers continued to function under the job description for RNs with the additional responsibilities outlined in the role description. Various work schedules were piloted to allow time for planning and critical path development. One nurse case manager initially worked 10-hour shifts and then went to 9-hour shifts to facilitate development of critical pathways. Eight hours were spent providing direct patient care, and the remaining hour was utilized for rounds, consultations and follow-up, documentation of critical paths, and educational sessions with patients and families. Case managers were not expected to float or have charge responsibilities unless they did not have a caseload.

The nurse case managers provided inservices on each of the pilot units to describe their role and responsibilities. Staff participating in the inservice had the opportunity to ask questions or make suggestions. Training sessions offered case managers additional strategies to market their role in each of the units with staff, physicians, and ancillary personnel. Questions and concerns raised during implementation of the role were then discussed at the monthly meetings. Ongoing communication provided the opportunity continually to adapt the program to meet the needs of individual units.

Patients were selected for case management by the physician, the case manager, or the charge nurse or by collaboration with a case associate. The case managers also served as key resource people for nurses or patients in other departments. Several tools assisted the case managers in organizing their workload and addressing individual aspects of their role. A checklist was distributed to case managers that identified a step-by-step approach to case managing a patient (Exhibit 9–4). The primary tool that guided implementation was the critical path and associated standards of care and protocols. The critical path was used to describe the plan of care for individual patients to other members of the health care team.

The case managers developed additional tools as the process became more defined, including "to do" lists that provided informal communication between case managers and case associates. Contacts needed or discharge items to be ordered were frequently communicated on the lists. Monthly reports (Exhibit 9–5) were completed by the case managers on the pilot units to accomplish the following:

- document the number and type of patients case managed
- document the number of referrals made

Exhibit 9–4 Case Manager Checklist

1.	Choose to case manage the patient. Sources to identify patient: admit list, schedule, M.D., nurse specialist, AHN, charge nurse.	______
2.	List case managed patients on board.	______
3.	List name of case manager on board.	______
	List name on chart.	______
	List name on Kardex.	______
4.	Identify self and case manager role to patient/family.	______
	Give patient case manager business card.	______
5.	Explain the team approach and role of case associate.	______
6.	Admit patient and assess needs.	______
7.	Initiate and follow up all consults. Use resource book to assist with identification of consultants.	______
8.	Establish working relationship with M.D., communicating daily.	______
9.	Initiate, individualize, and follow critical path. Place critical path in Kardex.	______
10.	Discuss critical path variances in shift report.	______
11.	Document critical path variances in progress notes.	______
12.	Initiate the "to do" list for follow-up of consults, etc.	______
13.	Discuss "to do" list in shift report.	______
14.	Initiate and follow up discharge planning and patient teaching.	______
15.	Provide direct care to case managed patients unless plan of care is well established.	______

- support evaluation of nurse case manager role performance
- identify specific issues that need to be addressed

A patient satisfaction survey was developed as a result of feedback obtained in the monthly reports (Exhibit 9–6). The satisfaction surveys were distributed by the case managers to the patients being managed to obtain additional feedback.

Interdisciplinary communication was facilitated by patient care conferences, patient rounds with physicians and other staff, multidisciplinary discharge rounds, informal meetings with staff from ancillary departments, lecture/discussion sessions conducted at the monthly case management meetings, and professional practice committees on each unit. The monthly case manager meetings allowed the nurse case managers to share opinions and ideas, to discuss the future of the role, and to assist in mutual development of the program. In addition, case managers served as key

Exhibit 9–5 Case Manager Monthly Report

Case manager: ________________ Date: ________________ Unit: ______________

1. Service: Names of patients:

2. Phone calls ______________________________
3. No. of visits ______________________________
4. Letters ______________________________
5. No. of critical paths instituted ______________________________
6. No. of critical paths reviewed with M.D.s in 24 hours of accepting patients ______________________________
7. No. of readmits ______________________________
8. No. of patients referred to:
   Social services ______________________________
   Home health ______________________________
   Nutrition ______________________________
   Home IV ______________________________
   Ostomy ______________________________
   Other ______________________________
9. No. of patients discharged ______________________________
   No. of teaching materials distributed ______________________________
10. No. of patients discharged within LOS ______________________________
11. No. of meetings attended ______________________________
12. No. of critical paths developed ______________________________
13. No. of rounds made with M.D. ______________________________
   Structured C.P. Shift Report: Always _____ Most of the time _____ Sometimes _____ Never _____

continues

Exhibit 9–5 continued

14. What is the level of collaboration with M.D.s?

    High ____ Medium ____ Low ____

15. Response of M.D. ____

    ____

    ____

16. List which goals were achieved and how ______________________________

    ____

    ____

17. New goals for managing care ______________________________________

    ____

    ____

18. Comments ____

    ____

    ____

members on hospital committees, including standards of care, protocols and procedures, documentation, patient education, and continuous quality improvement. This committee participation was vital to integrating the case management component of the PCR model into the infrastructure for the patient care services department.

The case management program continues to be effective on the units involved in the initial phases of the PCR project. Several issues have been identified that are currently under consideration to continue to adapt the model to meet the needs of the patients and the institution in response to the recent and dramatic shifts in health care policy.

EVALUATION AND CONTINUING DEVELOPMENT OF NURSE CASE MANAGEMENT

Many agencies and institutions are changing their delivery systems in anticipation of significant health care reform. The UMC PCR model has improved patient satisfaction. Several positive outcomes have been observed in relation to the nurse case manager role. Patient teaching has been implemented sooner and has been provided in greater detail, nurse–physician collaboration has been enhanced, physicians have requested case

Exhibit 9–6 Questionnaire for Nurse Case Managed Patients

Please circle appropriate response. You may explain your responses or add specific comments. The questionnaire will be used to evaluate the nurse case management program. Thank you for your time.

1. How do you feel about the care you received?

   RESPONSE:

1 Very Dissatisfied	2	3	4	5 Very Satisfied

   COMMENTS:

2. How do you feel about the case management program?

   RESPONSE:

1 Very Dissatisfied	2	3	4	5 Very Satisfied

   COMMENTS:

3. What **DID** you like about the case management program?

   COMMENTS:

4. What **DIDN'T** you like about the case management program?

   COMMENTS:

5. How do you feel about the care provided by the case manager?

   RESPONSE:

1 Very Dissatisfied	2	3	4	5 Very Satisfied

   COMMENTS:

continues

Exhibit 9–6 continued

6. How did you feel about the teaching received from the case manager?

RESPONSE:

1	2	3	4	5
Very Dissatisfied				Very Satisfied

COMMENTS:

7. Did you feel more comfortable being made aware of future events during your stay? For example, what happens on day 1? (Ambulate three times a day.)

_____ YES _____ NO

Please explain:

8. Any other comments on the case management program?

management for some of their patients, and patient responses to the satisfaction survey have been positive.

The majority of case management models are implemented in institutions that support primarily private physicians or physician groups. The challenge at UMC has been to integrate case management into a tertiary care academic setting with acutely ill patients with multiple, complex problems and unpredictable underlying illnesses. In addition, the need to enculture interns and residents to this system of care delivery presents a challenge. Nurse–physician consultation effectively communicates the role of the case manager. As the case management model expands to all patient care units, however, education of the role must be included in the training of all staff members of the health care team.

Regulatory agencies including Medicare and the Joint Commission on Accreditation of Healthcare Organizations have dramatically changed accreditation criteria for hospitals, stressing outcome evaluation. As the primary coordinators of care, nurse case managers will be integral to the effective ongoing evaluation and continuous improvement of patient care delivery systems. UMC medical director William Scott, M.D., has stated,

"The RN case manager will take the place of what we had 40 years ago—the family doctor, the one person who coordinates care and looks out for the well-being of the whole patient."[7]

As the UMC PCR model expands to all patient care units, nurse case management as the professional practice component will continue to be refined. The challenge will be continually to integrate changes generated by health care reform while effectively meeting the health care needs of patients and families.

NOTES

1. Joint Commission on Accreditation of Healthcare Organizations, *1993 JCAHO Criteria for Hospital Accreditation* (Oakbrook, Ill.: JCAHO, 1992).
2. J. Veran, et al., *Differentiated Group Professional Practice in Nursing Grant,* National Center for Nursing Research, 1 UO1 NR02153, 1989.
3. *Report on Case Management by Nurses* (Kansas City, Mo.: American Nurses Association, Congress of Nursing Practice, 1991), 1–63.
4. K. Zander, Managed Care within Acute Care Settings: Design and Implementation via Nursing Case Management, *Health Care Supervisor* 6, no. 2 (1988): 27–43.
5. C. Michaels, A Nursing HMO—10 Months with Carondolet St. Mary's Hospital Based Nurse Case Management. *Aspen's Advisor for Nurse Executives* 6 (1991): 1, 3–4.
6. K. Zander, personal communication.
7. W. Scott, personal communication.

CHAPTER

10

Patient Care Restructuring and Human Resources

Robert Black

Chapter Objectives

1. To describe human resource issues related to restructuring.
2. To report lessons learned to date.

"Restructuring is 90 percent human resources issues," stated John Mote, former University Medical Center (UMC) Vice President for Human Resources as he retired in the fall of 1991. Although the exact percentage of restructuring issues related to human resources has not been quantified, certainly the people issues should be of utmost concern in any major organizational change.

UMC employs 2,600 people, or 2,150 full-time equivalent (FTE) employees. This number of FTEs is high for a 312-bed community hospital but not out of line for a university-affiliated teaching facility. The employee population has increased by more than 1,000 from 1985 to 1993, largely as a result of new programs and additional services. Some of the larger departments and associated FTEs are as follows: clinical pathology (180), emergency services (62), environmental services (70), food and nutrition services (85), home health (59), information systems (51), materials management (63), medical information services (70), nursing adult intensive care units (172), nursing adult health (183), obstetrics and gynecology (103), operating room (80), patient financial services (93), pediatrics (162), pharmacy (61), radiology (103), and respiratory (45). The human resources staff consists of the vice president (also responsible for the security department), executive secretary, employee relations manager, compensation manager, development manager, benefits manager, employment manager, special projects manager, three coordinators, two senior human resources representatives, and two human resources representatives. None of the hospital's employees is unionized. Arizona is a right-to-work state with unions in mining, government, and education but not typically in other employment sectors.

Before restructuring, UMC's organizational structure was typical of hospitals with centralized support departments. All responsibility and authority for housekeeping throughout the hospital, for example, resided in the centralized environmental services department. If immediate housekeeping assistance was needed on a nursing unit, it was necessary to request the assistance formally from the central department and hope that the request was given suitable priority by those in authority to assign such assistance. Although interdepartmental support was relatively good, time constraints and competing priorities determined service levels more than any sense of internal customer service.

A June 1991 employee opinion survey showed that 71 percent of the employees felt that cooperation between departments within UMC was average or poor and that 65 percent felt that communications between departments within UMC was average or poor. Interdepartmental cooperation was identified in the survey summary as one of five major opportunities for improvement.

UMC employs minorities in percentages roughly equivalent to the workforce population. Minorities are concentrated in the lower-paying jobs, where limited opportunity has existed for career advancement. This problem is compounded by the fact that many employees of Hispanic origin have limited ability to speak, read, or write in English. How to provide hospital services and employment opportunities to an increasingly greater Spanish-speaking population is of major concern at UMC. UMC faces the same problem of educating underrepresented populations regarding the advantages of health care careers as all hospitals. Although some minorities have been able to succeed at UMC, there is a lack of excitement and hope about the possibility of health care careers among the general population in Tucson. Much needs to be done to develop opportunities for members of underrepresented populations to build careers in the health care field.

Turnover among all staff during 1992 was 19 percent. Among full-time employees the turnover rate was 14 percent, among part-time employees the rate was 22 percent, and among per diem employees the rate was 41 percent. The unemployment rate in Tucson has been consistently below the state and national average. With relatively good pay and an excellent benefits program, UMC is one of the more desirable employers in the area.

HUMAN RESOURCES PHILOSOPHIES RELATING TO PATIENT CARE RESTRUCTURING

Relevant philosophies that guided the hospital's actions need to be discussed to convey better the human resources decisions related to patient care restructuring (PCR).

First, UMC uses a typical market-based compensation system (Exhibit 10–1). In addition to the principles in the philosophy statement, it is the general belief that doing more of the same level of work does not justify an increase in pay. For example, at UMC the pay grades of the unit secretary

Exhibit 10–1 UMC Organizational Philosophy on Compensation

- Compensation is based foremost on the hospital's financial ability to pay.
- Compensation will be determined primarily on the relevant competitive market. In addition, to the extent feasible relative internal equity between positions will be maintained.
- The objective of the compensation plan is to recruit and retain quality employees and to support organizational goals and strategies.
- Special pay practices may be implemented as needed to ensure that the objectives of the compensation plan are achieved.
- Incentive programs appropriately structured to assist in achieving the objectives of the compensation plan may supplement or replace traditional methods of compensation.
- The hospital supports career ladders that compensate skills and/or scope of responsibilities instead of career ladders based on longevity and/or those that serve only as a method of recognition.
- Pyramiding of pay (such as paying standby pay and call-back pay simultaneously) is not a valid compensation practice.
- In determining appropriate compensation, all aspects of compensation, including base pay, differentials, special pay practices, and benefit costs, will be considered.

and nursing assistant are equal. If a nursing assistant were to be assigned to work as a unit secretary as part of his or her duties, there would not be a pay increase because the responsibility levels of both jobs are equal. A pay increase might be considered if it were determined that nursing assistants with secretarial skills are scarce. The market-based compensation program would then allow a higher pay level to compete for such scarce workers.

A second issue is the lack of enthusiasm among the administrative staff and the human resources staff for artificial career ladders. Examples of artificial career ladders include six levels of secretary, four levels of nursing assistant, or three levels of supervisor. Too often levels of positions are created when employees reach the top of a pay range, when they demand the right of advancement when no openings exist in which to be promoted, or when an influential manager or physician exerts pressure to create a new level. Definable differences are needed in the qualifications, duties, and responsibilities of positions to warrant creating career ladders. Opportunities for continued learning and professional advancement are essential to recruiting and retaining staff. Career ladders that support continued learning and professional advancement receive full organizational support at UMC. Career ladders also should not be limited to vertical movement within the organization but should provide for easy lateral mobility.

HUMAN RESOURCES STRATEGIC PLAN

A final element to consider when discussing restructuring at UMC is the human resources strategic plan dated June 1990. Five key findings and recommendations that relate to PCR include the following:

1. In the next 10 years, health care will be one of the leading industries in the creation of new jobs (i.e., demand for health care professionals will rise dramatically).
2. Shortages of certain health care workers already exist and are expected to worsen in the near future. Many allied health educational programs are facing decreased enrollments and are therefore not expanding in a way that would allow them to meet demand projections.
3. UMC's success in the 1990s will largely depend on how well it addresses the shortage of health care workers considering its projected growth, bed count, and continued introduction of new services.

4. Certain trends will greatly affect the number and composition of the health care worker supply, including the following three areas:
   - *population*: the aging of the workforce; the rising numbers of women, minorities, and immigrants with different needs; and a lower education level of entry workers
   - *financial and regulatory*: the continued emphasis on efficiency and productivity, a shift to more outpatient procedures, and the possibility of greater federal involvement in health care financing
   - *technological*: increased automation, rapid evolution of new imaging techniques and drug therapies, new developments in surgical techniques and transplantation, and a growing understanding of genetics
5. Recommendations of the UMC human resources task force to meet the hospital's future staffpower needs include two considerations:
   - Enhance and expand techniques to utilize and retain current UMC employees by restructuring job responsibilities; dedicate space for education for additional activities; enhance in-house training; and establish career ladders to allow mobility.
   - Increase the supply of health care workers by implementing the following changes: working with existing facilities to expand programs and to develop faculty; developing a consortium of health care providers to expand training programs in selected occupations; creating health care career awareness programs for elementary and secondary school students; and developing an internal career advancement program for UMC employees.

JOB DESCRIPTIONS AND COMPENSATION ISSUES

Human resources representatives were involved throughout the development and implementation of PCR. The vice president of human resources was a member of both the PCR steering committee and the PCR task force. The employment manager, human resources development manager, and compensation manager were members of the PCR task force. The employee relations manager also served on an ad hoc subcommittee regarding dress standards on the restructured units.

One of the first specific projects undertaken by the PCR task force was to develop job descriptions for four new roles: patient support attendant (PSA), patient care technician (PCT), and registered nurse (RN) case manager and case associate.

Representatives from environmental services, nursing, food services, transportation, and materials management met as a subcommittee to develop the PSA job description and performance standards (Exhibits 10–2 and 10–3). Once the basic draft was completed by the subcommittee, the

Exhibit 10–2 UMC Job Description: PSA

EFFECTIVE DATE:	October 14, 1991
APPROVED BY:	______________________
HUMAN RESOURCES:	______________________
FLSA:	Nonexempt
JOB CODE:	9D01
BBF RISK CLASSIFICATION:	High

POSITION SUMMARY: Facilitates the efficient functioning of the patient care unit by performing housekeeping, dietary, and materials management duties and transporting patients, specimens, and medications.

ESSENTIAL FUNCTIONS:

I. INTERPERSONAL SKILLS/TEAMWORK—Demonstrates a positive attitude and willingness to facilitate functioning.
II. PRODUCTIVITY—Is a productive member of the patient care unit team.
III. SAFETY—Maintains a safe working environment.
IV. ENVIRONMENTAL SERVICES—Performs housekeeping functions properly.
V. TRANSPORTATION—Transports patients, specimens, and medications in a safe and efficient manner.
VI. MATERIALS MANAGEMENT—Maintains adequate floor stock on a daily basis.
VII. DIETARY—Distributes and assists patients with meals and nourishments.
VIII. PROFESSIONAL GROWTH/GOAL SETTING—Establishes and accomplishes goals jointly set with the immediate supervisor.
IX. COMPLIES with departmental and/or hospital rules and regulations regarding absenteeism, tardiness, dress code, etc.

WORKING CONDITIONS: May occasionally be exposed to one or more disagreeable elements (dust, oil, fumes, grease, water, vibration, heat, cold, noise, and dirt) but not to the extent of being considered excessive. Possible exposure to burns, cuts, bruises, and minor injury.

REPORTING RELATIONSHIP: Reports directly to the supervising RN and the charge nurse under the supervision of the nurse manager.

QUALIFICATIONS: Ability to follow English written and verbal instructions.

Exhibit 10–3 UMC Performance Standards: PSA

EFFECTIVE DATE:	October 14, 1991
APPROVED BY:	______________________
HUMAN RESOURCES:	______________________
FLSA:	Nonexempt
JOB CODE:	9D01
BBF RISK CLASSIFICATION:	High

POSITION SUMMARY: Facilitates the efficient functioning of the patient care unit by performing housekeeping, dietary, and materials management duties and transporting patients, specimens, and medications.

REQUIRED PERFORMANCE STANDARDS:

I. Employee complies with employee health policies on a timely basis.

II. Employee attends CPR, fire and safety, and infection control update courses annually.

ESSENTIAL FUNCTIONS:

STATED CRITERIA REFLECT TRAITS NECESSARY TO ACHIEVE A SCORE OF 1.0: The following criteria will be documented and/or evaluated by the nurse manager and supervisory personnel to whom the PSA reports.

I. Interpersonal Skills/Teamwork—demonstrates a positive attitude and willingness to facilitate unit functioning. (PV 150) (PL 0, .5, 1.0, 1.5, 2.0)
   A. Demonstrates a willingness to assist when asked.
   B. Demonstrates flexibility in responding to patient/unit needs.
   C. Demonstrates a respectful manner with patients.
   D. Respects and maintains patient confidentiality.

II. Productivity—Is a productive member of the patient care unit team. (PV 100) (PL 0, .5, 1.0, 1.5, 2.0)
   A. Shows independence by completing duties with minimal supervision.
   B. Utilizes time in an efficient manner, completing duties in a timely fashion.
   C. Shows initiative in seeking out appropriate additional duties.

III. Safety—Maintains a safe working environment. (PV 100) (PL 0, .5, 1.0, 1.5, 2.0)
   A. Recognizes unsafe conditions and takes action or reports conditions to supervisor immediately.
   B. Turns in broken or damaged equipment for repairs immediately.
   C. Operates all types of transport and cleaning equipment, both mechanical and electrical, in a safe and conscientious manner at all times.
   D. Checks in and checks out all necessary keys.
   E. Uses *Wet Floor* signs at all times when working with solutions on floors or carpets.

IV. Environmental Services—Performs housekeeping functions properly (PV 150) (PL 0, .5, 1.0, 1.5, 2.0)
   A. Sweeps and mops floor areas, vacuums and spot cleans carpets, arranges furniture and equipment in an orderly fashion after cleaning assigned area.

continues

Exhibit 10–3 continued

B. Returns unused supplies to supply room; places soiled trash (and linens as required) in designated areas; thoroughly cleans cart and equipment.
C. Demonstrates thoroughness in cleaning assigned area by following established daily cleaning procedures and reporting specials situations/needs to supervisor.
D. Moves and arranges furniture as assigned.
E. Thoroughly washes walls, ceilings, and inside windows and changes curtains as required.
F. Accurately selects cleaning materials and equipment needed in advance; obtains and sets up equipment in a timely manner.
G. Ensures that all solutions and chemicals are properly stored in clearly and correctly labeled containers.
H. Notifies housekeeping when supplies are low; requests special chemicals and instructions where appropriate.
I. Requests special equipment and chemicals when necessary; asks pertinent questions concerning usage and procedures as needed.

V. Transportation—transports patients, specimens and medications in a safe and efficient manner. (PV 150) (PL 0, .5, 1.0, 1.5, 2.0)
A. Transports patients in a safe manner on the proper transportation device.
B. Checks patient identification and band to ensure transport of the correct patient.
C. Demonstrates use of proper transfer techniques when moving patients.
D. Adheres to universal precautions while delivering specimens and cultures.
E. Reports discrepancies on order of specimens, cultures, and nonnarcotic medication to proper personnel.
F. Is able to set priority requests according to criteria (STATS).
G. Complies with laboratory protocol when filling out log sheet, being sure to enter all pertinent information.
H. Notifies patient care unit in a timely manner of any delays that may occur during transports.
I. Observes patient condition and notifies appropriate personnel of any change in status.

VI. Materials Management—Maintains adequate floor stock on a daily basis. (PV 100) (PL 0, .5, 1.0, 1.5, 2.0)
A. Inventory of patient care unit done by item number and par level.
B. Enters exchange cart list into computer and prints at warehouse for pulling.
C. Delivers carts of supplies from warehouse to appropriate areas.
D. Pulls any sterile specimens from central service area and delivers to appropriate area.
E. Picks up credits from patient care unit, fills out credit log with correct information, and sends items back to warehouse via carts.

VII. Dietary—Distributes and assists patients with meals and nourishments. (PV 150) (PL 0, .5, 1.0, 1.5, 2.0)
A. Delivers trays and ordered snacks and collects soiled trays on patient care unit after verifying menu and current recorded diet.

continues

Exhibit 10–3 continued

B. Recognizes age-related and special group needs and reports them to supervisor.
C. Tray distribution is on time and accurate.
D. Restocks food and nonfood supplies to patient care units.

VIII. Professional Growth/Goal Setting—Establishes and accomplishes goals jointly set with the immediate supervisor. (PV 75) (PL 0, .5., 1.0, 1.5, 2.0)
A. Goals for year are discussed between employee and supervisor, agreed to, and recorded at the evaluation meeting.
B. Goals for this evaluation were consistently worked on throughout the evaluation period.
C. Goals were satisfactorily accomplished within the evaluation period.

IX. Complies with hospital and department policies, procedures, rules, etc. (reference H.R. policy 302, paragraphs 3.0 and 6.b). (PV 25) (PL 0, .5, 1.0, 1.5, 2.0)

Performance Level:
0.0 = Employee is not meeting performance standards
0.5 = Employee needs continued growth to meet performance standards
1.0 = Employee consistently meets acceptable performance standards
1.5 = Employee consistently meets and occasionally exceeds acceptable performance standards
2.0 = Employee consistently exceeds performance standards

compensation manager finalized the wording and format, which then went to all members of the PCR task force for review and input. The purpose of the PSA role was relatively easy to define by concentrating on indirect patient care tasks such as housekeeping, food tray service, transportation, and supplies. The only requirement established to qualify as a PSA was the ability to follow written and verbal instructions in English. Most of the entry level positions in the centralized departments contained similar limited qualifications. The most significant aspect of the PSA job description was that the PSA would report to a patient care nurse on the unit. This change alone could have caused major disruption and created significant resistance from centralized departments in most hospitals. At UMC concerns and resistance were overcome by a common vision and an assumption that the new reporting structure could and would work.

Significant issues have needed to be addressed by making the PSA responsible and accountable to the nursing structure on the patient care unit. Major concerns about quality assurance and continuing education are addressed elsewhere. The biggest issue faced by human resources at UMC was the lack of supervisory skills among the nurses. The basic educational curriculum of nurses does not include delegation skills, hiring of employees, or day-to-day supervision of employees. Much of the PCR training support provided by the human resources department focused on these critical areas.

Determining an appropriate compensation level was not an easy task. Using UMC's market-based approach to setting compensation, other facilities throughout the country were contacted to see how they had set compensation for their indirect patient care positions in relation to positions such as housekeeper and transporter. There was no consensus. Some were setting the PSA-like position at the same level as housekeepers, and others had decided to pay PSAs as much as 6 percent more than the housekeeper level. Based on UMC's compensation philosophy of not paying more for additional duties at the same level, the compensation level for PSA should have been set at the same level as housekeeper. The decision was made, however, to pay PSAs 5 percent more than housekeepers, transporters, food service workers, and the like. This decision was based on the desire to recruit PSAs from within the organization. Internal candidates with UMC experience in one of the centralized departments could bring knowledge of the organization and expertise in particular duties to the new role. Many dedicated employees in entry level positions have the potential to contribute much more to the organization if given an opportunity and incentive to do so. Many of these employees did take advantage of the opportunity and are now serving as excellent PSAs.

The PSA training course, discussed elsewhere, takes 10 days to complete. The decision was made to pay the PSAs the higher rate beginning the first day of the training course.

Developing the PCT job description, performance standards, and compensation level was more complex (Exhibits 10–4 and 10–5). As with the PSA, a subcommittee developed the basic job description and performance standards for the PCT, and human resources personnel were responsible for final wording and format. The PCT subcommittee consisted of representatives from nursing, respiratory, rehabilitation, clinical pathology, and pharmacy. The approach was to develop a nursing assistant position that could perform ECGs, phlebotomies, and basic rehabilitation duties. Because of Arizona state scope of practice regulations, respiratory care duties that could be performed by PCTs were extremely limited, so that the PCT role has minimal respiratory care components. Pharmacy technician duties were also not included because of some internal process issues.

The same decision process used for the PSA position was used to determine PCT compensation levels. One significant difference was the timing of the pay increase because of the length of the PCT training program. The pay rate for an entry level PCT was set at the base of a pay grade. A rate

Exhibit 10–4 UMC Job Description: PCT

EFFECTIVE DATE:	November 1, 1991
APPROVED BY:	____________________
HUMAN RESOURCES:	____________________
FLSA:	Nonexempt
JOB CODE:	3A01
BBF RISK CLASSIFICATION:	High

<u>POSITION SUMMARY</u>: Facilitates the provision of patient care by performing specific nursing tasks and support functions as delegated by an RN.

<u>ESSENTIAL FUNCTIONS</u>:

I. PATIENT CARE SKILLS—Provides basic, age-appropriate nursing care to patients under the direct supervision of an RN.
II. REHABILITATION—Performs nonskilled nursing duties that may relate to rehabilitation to carry out the multidisciplinary care plan for each patient.
III. PHLEBOTOMY AND CLINICAL LABORATORY—Obtains and maintains integrity of specimens in accordance with UMC policies and procedures and physician orders.
IV. RESPIRATORY THERAPY—Provides selected respiratory care to patients following accepted respiratory care practices, UMC policy and procedures, and physician orders.
V. ECG—Performs ECGs following UMC policy and procedures.
VI. DOCUMENTATION/REPORTING—Documents and reports care delivered under the direct supervision of an RN.
VII. INTERPERSONAL SKILLS/TEAMWORK—Demonstrates a positive attitude and willingness to facilitate unit functioning.
VIII. PRODUCTIVITY—Is a productive member of the patient care unit team.
IX. SAFETY—Maintains a safe environment for patients and coworkers.
X. PROFESSIONAL GROWTH/GOAL SETTING—Establishes and accomplishes goals jointly set with the immediate supervisor.
XI. COMPLIES with departmental and/or hospital rules and regulations regarding absenteeism, tardiness, dress code, etc. (reference H.R. policy 302, paragraphs 3.0 and 6.b).

<u>WORKING CONDITIONS</u>: Air-controlled, moderately warm area subject to occasional temperature changes. Some noise disturbance with increased exposure to disease, radiation, chemicals, and patient behavior with danger of more serious injury.

<u>REPORTING RELATIONSHIP</u>: Reports directly to the supervising RN and the charge nurse under the supervision of the nurse manager.

<u>QUALIFICATIONS</u>: Excellent verbal and written skills in English. High school diploma or GED required. One year of higher education or equivalent required. Health-related experience strongly preferred.

Exhibit 10–5 UMC Performance Standards: PCT

EFFECTIVE DATE:	November 1, 1991
APPROVED BY:	____________________
HUMAN RESOURCES:	____________________
FLSA:	Nonexempt
JOB CODE:	3A01
BBF RISK CLASSIFICATION:	High

POSITION SUMMARY: Facilitates the provision of patient care by performing specific nursing tasks and support functions as delegated by an RN.

REQUIRED PERFORMANCE STANDARDS:

I. Employee complies with Employee Health policies on timely basis.
II. Employee attends CPR, fire and safety, and infection control update course annually.

ESSENTIAL FUNCTIONS:

STATED CRITERIA REFLECT TRAITS NECESSARY TO ACHIEVE A SCORE OF 1.0: The following criteria will be documented and/or evaluated by the nurse manager and supervisory personnel to whom the PCT reports.

I. Patient Care Skills—Provides basic, age-appropriate nursing care to patients under the direct supervision of an RN (PV 150) (PL 0, .5, 1.0, 1.5, 2.0)
   A. Delivers physical care and comfort measures to assigned patients in a safe and efficient manner.
   B. Demonstrates competence in performing technical procedures.
   C. Provides emotional support and considers patient and family needs.
   D. Organizes and prioritizes workload to complete assignments during the shift.
II. Rehabilitation—Performs nonskilled nursing duties that may relate to rehabilitation to carry out the multidisciplinary care plan for each patient. (PV 100) (PL 0, .5, 1.0, 1.5, 2.0)
   A. Appropriately assists patients at the bedside with their individualized exercise/activity program.
   B. Safely assists and guards patients during ambulation and ADLs.
   C. Monitors patient safety and compliance with established CPM and splinting programs.
   D. Demonstrates good observation and communication skills to enhance interdisciplinary approach.
III. Phlebotomy and Clinical Laboratory—Obtains and maintains integrity of specimens in accordance with UMC policies and procedures and physician orders. (PV 100) (PL 0, .5, 1.0, 1.5, 2.0)
   A. Maintains rigid accuracy in the identification of all patients, including armbanding procedures for blood bank.
   B. Demonstrates knowledge of specimen labeling procedures, including blood bank banding procedures, and applies this knowledge by correctly and accurately labeling all specimens.

continues

Exhibit 10–5 continued

- C. Demonstrates ability correctly to perform venipuncture and capillary drawing techniques as assessed by the supervisor and maintains a minimum repeat draw and unsuccessful draw rate.
- D. Demonstrates an understanding of specimen suitability for testing by awareness of proper anticoagulation and special handling techniques as designated in the laboratory handbook and procedure manual.
- E. Notifies supervisor in a timely manner of all problems with phlebotomy duties.
- F. Demonstrates ability to read and review physician orders such that tests are not missed and samples do not have to be redrawn.
- G. Demonstrates ability to prioritize tasks with particular emphasis on response to STATS, ASAPS, timed draws, and the like. Arranges for timely delivery of specimens to laboratory.
- H. Skills list: venipuncture technique, capillary puncture technique, timed draws, blood culture collection, blood banking procedures.

IV. Respiratory Therapy—Provides selected respiratory care to patients of all ages following accepted respiratory care practices, UMC policies and procedures, and physician orders. (PV 25) (PL 0, .5, 1.0, 1.5, 2.0)
- A. Demonstrates basic understanding of respiratory anatomy and physiology as trained.
- B. Demonstrates proper technique for use of incentive spirometry.

V. ECG—Performs ECGs following UMC policies and procedures. (PV 50) (PL 0, .5, 1.0, 1.5, 2.0)
- A. Successfully completes technician check-off sheet.
- B. Demonstrates knowledge of appropriate lead placement.
- C. Completes ECG within 10 minutes of order.
- D. Demonstrates troubleshooting skill with equipment.

VI. Documentation/Reporting—Documents and reports care delivered under the direct supervision of an RN. (PV 125) (PL 0, .5, 1.0, 1.5, 2.0)
- A. Recognizes changes in patient status and reports appropriate information to the RN and/or therapist in a timely manner.
- B. Accurately and appropriately documents patient's treatment and observation of progress and response to treatment.
- C. Documents care in the medical record in a manner that enhances the legal protection of the institution.

VII. Interpersonal Skills/Teamwork—Demonstrates a positive attitude and willingness to facilitate unit functioning. (PV 150) (PL 0, .5, 1.0, 1.5, 2.0)
- A. Demonstrates a willingness to assist when asked.
- B. Demonstrates flexibility in responding to patient/unit needs.
- C. Demonstrates a respectful manner toward patients.
- D. Willingly floats to other unit/shifts when necessary to provide for patient care needs.

VIII. Productivity/Professional Behavior—Is a productive/professional member of the patient care unit team. (PV 100) (PL 0, .5, 1.0, 1.5, 2.0)
- A. Shows independence by completing duties with appropriate supervision.
- B. Utilizes time in an efficient manner, completing duties in a timely fashion.

continues

Exhibit 10–5 continued

C. Shows initiative in seeking out appropriate additional duties.
D. Respects and maintains patient confidentiality.
E. Attends department meetings and inservices regularly.

IX. Safety—Maintains a safe environment for patients and coworkers. (PV 100) (PL 0, .5, 1.0, 1.5, 2.0)
A. Recognizes unsafe conditions and takes action or reports conditions to supervisor immediately.
B. Adheres to universal precautions and principles of asepsis.
C. Demonstrates awareness of and concern for patient safety.
D. Assists patients in transfer using proper body mechanics and transfer techniques.

X. Professional Growth/Goal Setting—Establishes and accomplishes goals jointly set with the immediate supervisor. (PV 75) (PL 0, .5, 1.0, 1.5, 2.0)
A. Goals for the year are discussed between employee and supervisor, agreed to, and recorded at the evaluation meeting.
B. Goals for this evaluation were consistently worked on throughout the evaluation period.
C. Goals were satisfactorily accomplished within the evaluation period.

XI. Complies with hospital and department policies, procedures, rules, etc. (reference H.R. policy 302, paragraphs 3.0 and 6.b). (PV 25) (PL 0, .5, 1.0, 1.5, 2.0)

Performance Level:
0.0 = Employee is not meeting performance standards
0.5 = Employee needs continued growth to meet performance standards
1.0 = Employee consistently meets acceptable performance standards
1.5 = Employee consistently meets and occasionally exceeds acceptable performance standards
2.0 = Employee consistently exceeds performance standards

during the training program that was 5 percent lower than the pay grade base, however, was also established. At the end of the training period the PCTs were moved to the base of the PCT pay grade. Not only was paying a lower rate during training a minor cost savings, but the pay increase at the completion of training was an important recognition of a milestone. The graduation ceremonies, certificate of completion, and pay increase all established the employees as official PCTs.

The RN case manager and case associate job descriptions and compensation took an entirely different track. Initially a subcommittee composed primarily of nurses with human resources and finance representatives attempted to develop case manager and case associate job descriptions. Using a similar approach to that used in developing PSA and PCT job descriptions, the committee began drafting the duties and responsibilities of the two new positions. Much discussion revolved around what, if any, additional compensation would be paid to assume case manager and case associate responsibilities, especially because nurses would be shifting between the two roles on a daily or patient-by-patient basis. Compensation options reviewed included the following:

- promotion to the new positions with a 5 percent pay increase
- not paying any extra on a trial basis until the roles were fully developed on the patient care units
- paying an hourly differential when performing the new duties

None of the options seemed to fit any established internal compensation strategies. The answer to the dilemma came from within the ranks of the staff nurses. The staff nurses perceived the case manager and case associate duties to be part of the expectations of a professional RN, and they also saw no particular reason to pay extra for those duties. Therefore, separate job descriptions for the case manager and case associate were not developed. A list of specific responsibilities within the already defined job description of staff nurse was developed instead (Exhibit 10–6).

Once compensation levels were determined, estimating labor costs on restructured units became the next priority. The clinical directors of nursing and nurse managers developed tentative staffing plans for the restructured units. Each centralized department estimated the amount of time (FTE) spent by its particular positions on the units to be restructured. Comparing the existing costs of supporting the units using centralized services with the costs of using PSAs and PCTs on restructured units indicated that the project would be cost neutral. Because PSAs and PCTs would be performing the nonprofessional duties historically performed by the nurses, the staffing plans included some reduction in the number of RNs needed. FTEs increased on the restructured units, but costs remained fairly equal because of the reduced hourly expense for the FTEs. If training costs were also factored into the payroll costs, initial restructuring was more expensive than maintaining historic staffing patterns.

EMPLOYMENT PROCESS ISSUES

The most significant impact of restructuring on the human resources department was the employment process, described in Chapter 11.

Serious issues evolved as a result of the need to move internal staff into the new roles. By reducing the FTEs in the centralized departments, there was a potential for layoffs if the staff did not apply for PSA and PCT openings. At that time UMC was under the administrative direction that no layoffs would occur as a result of restructuring. This put tremendous pres-

Exhibit 10–6 Role Description for Case Manager

1. Establishes a mechanism for notification when a new patient enters the caseload (this includes determining which patients he or she will case manage).
2. Introduces self to patient or family and explains the role of case manager and case associate.
3. Contacts physician(s) to begin sharing assessments, goals, and plans for the duration of the patient's hospital stay.
4. Knows the anticipated DRG, length of stay, and transfer or discharge dates for assigned caseload.
5. Discusses ongoing and future care with the other nursing and ancillary inpatient unit staff.
6. Negotiates work schedule with the nurse manager and/or assistant nurse manager to attend weekly case management meetings.
7. Identifies a critical path for the patient and places it in the nursing Kardex.
8. Compares the standard critical path against the patient's individual needs in such areas as social and economic data, family resources, functional abilities, knowledge needs, potential risk factors and complications, and special issues.
9. Reviews and revises the individual critical path with the physician(s) within 24 hours of admission.
10. Contacts other key members of the patient's team (e.g., social worker, dietitian, physical therapist, community resource personnel, and others) as needed.
11. Gives and monitors the delivery of care and the patient's responses to care every day that the patient is on the case manager's unit.
12. Arranges with the case associate RN continuity of plan and provides coverage during short, long, and unexpected absences.
13. Gives the patient and family a time schedule and tells them who to contact during the case manager's absence.
14. Documents the achievements of intermediate goals and clinical outcomes as they occur.
15. Integrates case management information and revised interventions (processes) into intershift report and case management meetings.
16. Plans, participates in, and follows through with health care team meetings as needed.
17. Manages the patient's transition through the system and transfers accountability to the appropriate person or agency upon discharge.
18. Completes a follow-up evaluation.

Source: Adapted with permission from *Collaborative Care: Nursing Case Management*, published by American Hospital Publishing, ©1989.

sure on everyone to find ways to encourage internal candidates to apply for the new positions. Knowledge of a no-layoff policy caused some employees to take a wait-and-see attitude before committing to changing positions, even though compensation would be greater in the new positions. Furthermore, nursing staff did not want to hire internal candidates who were already known as less than desirable workers, and some potential candidates did not want to, or were not suited to, accept new responsibilities. For example, environmental service workers who had been assigned to particular nursing units in the past were potentially ideal candidates for PSA roles on the new restructured patient care units. In instances where the nurses did not want to hire the housekeeper or the housekeeper did not want any patient contact as required by the PSA role, it was hoped that other internal candidates would apply and be accepted, thus leaving a transfer opportunity for the housekeeper within environmental services. Fortunately, between normal attrition and the number of internal candidates who applied and were hired as PSAs and PCTs, the problem of overstaffed central departments in a no-layoff environment did not materialize. Since the inception of the new roles, there have been layoffs not related to PCR, and policies for involuntary transfer have been developed that address overstaffing.

Another issue not yet addressed is the limited ability of many employees qualified to become PSAs who are unable to speak, read, or write English fluently. Various options have been discussed to assist employees with their English abilities. The problem has not been resolved, however, and the increasing number of non–English-speaking employees in the workplace will require a successful solution.

CAREER LADDER IN PCR

Perhaps the most exciting PCR result from a human resources perspective is the creation of a true career ladder. It is now possible to move from entry level housekeeper or food service worker to RN at UMC. Housekeepers and food service workers can easily become PSAs. This transition has occurred. PSAs can become PCTs. This promotion has also occurred. PCTs can become LPNs or RNs. Some of the PCTs and LPNs are currently taking appropriate courses for the promotion.

A career advancement loan program was implemented as part of the human resources strategic plan. Employees or their dependents who want to become educated for careers in positions determined to be in short supply by the hospital can receive up to $5,000 in career advancement loans. The loan is repaid at $1 per hour forgiven for each hour worked in the position. For example, there is presently a PCT who is studying to become an RN who has been supported with a $5,000 career advancement loan. When the employee becomes an RN, he will repay the loan by working 5,000 hours, or approximately 30 months at full-time employment.

With the career ladder in place and funding available, the next step is to reach underrepresented populations that have traditionally been stuck in low-paying positions.

LABOR ORGANIZATIONS AND PCR: POTENTIAL ISSUES

The major concern of some facilities interested in restructuring will be the reaction of labor organizations. Although UMC is a nonunion environment, the following suggestions are offered.

Communication before, during, and after restructuring will increase the chances for success in both union and nonunion environments. The need for communication cannot be overstressed. Major efforts to communicate with employees at UMC have occurred, and ongoing efforts are needed. Communication is especially important once a unit has been restructured. Communication has occurred on the restructured units both from presentations on each unit by the vice president for patient services and by involving as many staff as possible in planning, developing, implementing, and managing PCR on their units.

Some of the restructured units had been part of a group governance pilot study before restructuring. These units had already developed ways of involving staff in unit management decisions. These group governance units were far more successful than those restructured under traditional hierarchical governance structures.

Labor organizations might derive advantages from PCR through the following: expanded membership opportunities among nonlicensed personnel now assigned to patient care units; greater operational input on restructured units, where more of the work performed on the unit is reported to unit management; involvement in developing facility-specific restructuring plans; and increased professionalism of licensed personnel who no longer are required to perform nonprofessional work.

Threats to labor organizations of PCR might include the following: perceived loss of power and numbers, more diverse needs to represent, more difficulty with control issues in multidisciplinary team management, and unfamiliar change. Many reports in recent health care and nursing journals have suggested that using nurse extenders such as PCTs is a threat to the safety of patients. At UMC, all the PCT duties were performed by nonlicensed personnel even before restructuring. If, as some in the nursing profession have claimed, 52 percent of a typical staff nurse's duties involve nonnursing tasks, why should there be an outcry when these tasks are assigned to others at lesser pay and lower skill levels? Has not the goal of nursing appropriately been to achieve the professional recognition long overdue? Allowing staff nurses the opportunity to use their professional skills more than 48 percent of the day, even if some are comfortable with the status quo, could be the most significant accomplishment of PCR at UMC.

LESSONS LEARNED

Some of the human resource–related lessons learned in restructuring at UMC are the following:

1. Restructuring can be accomplished.
2. Restructuring can be done without using consultants.
3. Involving representatives from all affected departments is critical to establishing a common vision and to maintaining momentum.
4. The restructuring process assists with breaking down communication barriers between departments.
5. Opportunities for underrepresented populations to develop careers in health care are greater in restructured organizations.
6. A legitimate career ladder can be established in restructured organizations.
7. Restructured organizations will be better able to use the skills of the future workforce, where availability of specialists will decrease and the need for generalist workers will increase.
8. Restructured organizations will be better able to adapt to technological change because of their less specialized workforce.
9. RNs are not adequately prepared to assume supervisory responsibilities for nonlicensed personnel and need much education on recruiting, interviewing, hiring, and supervising nonlicensed personnel.
10. Job satisfaction can be increased by expanding the scope of duties and responsibilities.
11. RNs can utilize their professional expertise to a greater extent.
12. Labor costs on restructured units are no greater than on nonrestructured units.
13. Training in communication skills, assertiveness, delegation, and team building is an ongoing need in restructured units.

14. Hiring a large number of new workers (PCTs and PSAs) in a short time frame places tremendous pressure on the human resources employment function.

CONTINUED SUPPORT FOR PCR

As restructuring moves forward, some specific actions are needed to continue to support PCR. Educating nurses on delegation, supervision, and team building is an ongoing activity. Chapter 12 discusses some of the continuing training before, during, and after restructuring a unit.

The culture of individual units needs to be assessed continually because the changes brought about through PCR are not always universally accepted. Opportunities to meet with the units in a training setting have brought out frustrations and concerns not expressed through normal channels. The training function needs to be intimately involved at all stages of the restructuring process to ensure that all training is allied with the individual unit needs at the time.

The hiring process will develop as nurses become more familiar with the principles involved in effective selection. Many improvements have already occurred as the nurses and employment personnel work closely together.

Training PCTs should occur outside UMC as other local hospitals begin using multiskilled workers. UMC has joined with all the other Tucson hospitals in forming a consortium for health care training. The consortium is in the process of developing a PCT training curriculum to submit to local educational facilities. The educational facilities have agreed on the need for training multiskilled health care workers. The consortium and one local educational facility already successfully collaborated on a medical transcriptionist training program.

CONCLUSION

PCR has been a difficult process and has placed tremendous pressure on the human resources department, especially the employment and training sections. UMC is committed to restructuring. Many of our strategic human resources goals are being achieved through PCR. Human resources support is essential to the success of any restructuring project.

CHAPTER

11

Human Resources' Role in Implementation: Employment's Contributions

Beth Orenduff

Chapter Objectives

1. To describe the employment department's role in the hiring process of multipurpose workers.
2. To describe the process of registered nurse staff involvement in hiring.

By the 1990s there was an abundance of job openings for registered nurses in Tucson, Arizona. Certified nursing assistant and medical assistant programs were plentiful. The supply of graduates from these two programs was greater than the area demand. The technical problems for utilizing these people were as follows:

- limited hands-on experience
- graduate's knowledge confined to long-term care or physician offices
- University Medical Center's (UMC's) limited experience with paraprofessionals

The situation in Tucson reflected what was happening in the rest of the country. Although there was a shortage of nurses in the Tucson area, there remained an untapped abundance of paraprofessionals unable to secure employment in an acute care setting. The patient care restructuring (PCR) project led to programs to utilize this large group of people in an acute care setting.

Human resource expertise bridges the gap between the conceptualization and implementation of a new program that introduces new classifications of workers into a facility. This chapter provides a practical explanation of the steps to help implement the first phases of restructuring. Several improvements in the process are included to help prevent other health care institutions from repeating detours taken by UMC.

PLANNING

The employment process begins with a needs assessment that finalizes as a job description. A hiring department and human resources will usually work closely together to create a job description. In the development of the patient care technician (PCT) and the patient support attendant (PSA) job descriptions, multiple departments participated through PCR ad hoc work groups. Each of the affected departments developed the essential functions of the job that would be pertinent to its particular area. The employment manager met with the four pilot units to see how closely their needs matched the newly created job descriptions. Nursing and the ancillary departments quickly identified the essential functions of the jobs. Interestingly, it was a much slower process to identify the minimum requirements of the job. The fear in the nursing areas that there would not be enough qualified people hindered defining the minimum requirements. Human resources was aware of the availability of many paraprofessionals in the Tucson area. These people were waiting for employment in an acute care setting that offered benefits and opportunities for advancement.

The PCR task force developed the minimum requirements for each new job classification. The essential functions of the job are the daily tasks of the role. The PCT and PSA position skills and tasks are identified in Exhibits 11–1 and 11–2.

All the tasks are objectively described in measurable criteria that human resources can use to screen applications. Identification of the minimum requirements for the job was illusive at best. The premise was to find persons who had the potential to complete UMC's education program. The minimum requirements for the PCT became the following: excellent verbal and written skills in English, high school diploma or GED required, and health-related experience preferred.

Exhibit 11–1 PCT Skills under the Supervision of a Registered Nurse

Nursing assistant functions
Physical therapy: Performs specific rehabilitation-related duties to carry out the patient's therapeutic plan of care
Occupational therapy: Performs specific rehabilitation-related duties to carry out the patient's therapeutic plan of care
Phlebotomy and clinical laboratory: Obtains and maintains integrity of specimens in accordance with UMC policies and procedures and physician orders
Respiratory therapy: Provides selected respiratory care to patients following accepted respiratory care practices, UMC policies and procedures, and physician orders
ECG: Performs ECGs following UMC policies and procedures and physician orders
Documentation/reporting: Documents and reports care delivered under the direct supervision of a registered nurse

The PSA is the first step in a career ladder for UMC's employees to enter and advance to registered nurse. The new consolidated PSA job consisted of areas that were entry level with minimum educational requirements. Many of UMC's environmental services employees did not have a high school education or a GED, yet they would be competing with people who wanted to become a PSA to enter the career ladder leading to registered nurse. The PCR task force was faced with a dilemma. Did the assigned minimum requirements reflect the emphasis on housekeeping, or were they written to allow for persons who desired to enter the career ladder into nursing? In the end, the minimum requirements became the ability to follow both written and verbal instruction in English, experience with performing multiple tasks, and experience in taking direction from others. The PCR task force knew that a good portion of the time a PSA spent would be committed to housekeeping tasks, but no one anticipated how extensive the housekeeping emphasis would be. After phase II was completed, the standard job posting for the PSA position included a statement that the job consisted of approximately 75 percent housekeeping tasks.

Exhibit 11–2 PSA Tasks

Environmental services: Performs housekeeping functions properly
Transportation: Transports patients, specimens, and medications in a safe and efficient manner
Materials management: Maintains adequate floor stock on a daily basis
Dietary: Distributes and assists patients with meals and nutrition

The employment section at UMC is responsible for the hiring process from recruitment to scheduling the new hire physical for all positions. Everyone in the employment section was familiar with hiring paraprofessionals. Nurse managers and nursing staff, however, were not familiar with the hiring process and needed support. Nurse managers had experience hiring nurses and experienced unit clerks. Hiring a unit clerk periodically is a relatively simple process for the nurse manager. The nurse managers were about to begin hiring large numbers of people for the new support roles. They did not have experience with the extensive timeframe needed to hire these types of positions, nor had they experienced hundreds of people applying for a single position. How could there be hundreds of qualified people when hundreds of unit clerks or nurses were never available? A broad collection of minimum requirements was established based on nursing's experience of dealing with a limited applicant pool. Human resources sought minimum requirements that would limit the number of applicants, and nurse managers were concerned about not having enough qualified applicants. Human resource's role is to advise, recommend, support, and facilitate the hiring process. In this situation, that meant accepting and working with a much broader set of minimum requirements while having full knowledge of the large number of applicants who would apply for the position.

Part of the planning process was to determine the full-time equivalents (FTEs) for each of the new positions and then to translate that into the total number of people that needed to be hired. It is important to remember that FTEs are not equal to the number of people that will be needed to meet staffing requirements. The bottom line for human resources to begin the hiring process is to know from each unit the number of people it plans to hire. Included in this information should be the mix of full-time and part-time employees, the number of people per shift, and the shift hours.

SELECTION PROCESS

Employment Policy

The employment procedure at UMC includes the following steps. The hiring authority completes and submits an employee requisition for department and administrative signatures. The form includes classification, pay grade, salary range, FTEs, interviewer, and the number of days to accept applications. The request form also includes information that will define the objective qualifications the ideal candidate will possess at the time of hire.

At UMC, applications are only accepted for a position where a requisition form has been received by the employment section. Any testing done at the department's request is developed and administered by the employment section of human resources.

Development of Selection Tools for Application Screening

The employment section, with the above information in mind, had several areas needing to be addressed to institute successfully the hiring of the new roles. The first issue to address was the nursing staff's limited experience with paraprofessionals. The second and greater issue was the potential in Tucson for hundreds of applicants to apply for the PSA and PCT openings.

Human resources approached the pilot unit PCR steering committee with the idea of developing tools for screening applicants. Using a written screening test had not been considered in the original plans because testing is not common at UMC. Some of the concern over testing was related to the fact that it is uncommon. Testing also represented the possibility of eliminating potentially good applicants. The nurse managers were concerned that Tucson could not provide the necessary number of applicants for the four pilot units and that testing could be a barrier to both external and internal candidates. The ancillary departments that were part of the PCR task force helped present the concept of testing. These areas had years of experience working with many applicants for open positions in their department. The ancillary departments became strong supporters of the need to develop a testing tool to screen applicants.

A team of subject matter experts from pediatric and adult nursing, pathology, food services, environmental services, materials management, transportation, and human resources designed the original screening tools. It may appear that each area could easily define the skills necessary to accomplish the job in its department. Each area knew exactly what its needs were, but identifying qualities or characteristics to transfer into PSA and PCT positions was difficult. The nurses knew that tasks such as keeping the work area clean and stocking the unit were done every day, but trying to choose the qualities that made individuals successful and that would also fit with the personality of their unit was not an easy task. Nurses also would be giving up some of the tasks they performed for their patients to people whose qualifications were questionable in the minds of the nurses. The new caregivers did not come equipped with preapproved education, certification, or licensure. The lack of tangible evidence that these new workers could provide basic care for a nurse's patients added to the confusion of identifying qualities and characteristics that could be used by human resources in developing screening tools.

The concept of testing entered close to the time designated to open the positions for the first four pilot units. The short timeframe to design the tool added stress to the process. Applications could not be accepted without the completion of the written screening test, and yet there was not enough time for human resources to complete all the testing of the instrument before its use. A considerable amount of concern was also expressed about test anxiety for the applicants. The first group included many internal candidates, who were already performing jobs that were incorporated in the PCT roles.

The skills inventories for PSAs and PCTs were developed simultaneously. In retrospect, the process would have flowed better if the less complicated PSA skills inventory had been developed first and those data used to complete the PCT skills inventory. Designing the tools simultaneously made the role separation less well defined. Extremely tight time constraints necessitated the development in tandem.

The following PSA job skills were identified as essential for success: read labels, mix chemicals, stock equipment and supplies, read patient trays, identify dietary needs, assist with menus, and lift heavy objects repeatedly. Several identified subjective areas were dependability, flexibility, neatness, and orderliness.

The PCT essential job duties were nursing assistant duties, phlebotomy, ECGs, rehabilitation-related technician duties, basic math skills, reading orders, writing in charts, and simple sterile procedures. The skills inventory tool also identified subjective qualities of reliability, team player, good verbal communications skills, ability to prioritize, and desire to learn.

It quickly became apparent to the group that some qualities are appropriate for testing and that others may be appropriate for the interview. Another development from this process was that each unit differs in both objective and subjective desired qualities. For example, adult medicine needs workers who can physically move and then transport people, and the pediatric staff expressed the need for a person with an outgoing personality. The adult units seek people who can physically handle the amount of work that is required. One of the units has 50 to 75 phlebotomies every morning and many patient transfers. The employees of these units need to communicate as adults to adult patients. They need to provide courteous, professional care and appear professional in appearance. On the pediatric units, the worker needs to demonstrate patience and the ability to communicate with children. There are only 5 or 10 phlebotomies in the pediatric unit in the morning, and no one is transferred to other units. The pediatric worker may need to cuddle a frightened child before a phlebotomy. The needs of each unit are unique and must be recognized to provide applicants who can fill these special needs.

Reliability and validity must be taken into consideration when administering any test. Validity is assessed by determining whether the test is relevant to the specific functions of the job, and reliability is evidenced when the test results remain consistent over time. It is more difficult to test for subjective, personal information. Restructured units incorporated subjective behaviors into the interview format. Because the interview is another form of testing, the same questions needed to be asked to each candidate. Consistency helps guarantee an equal opportunity for all the candidates.

PSA Skills Inventory

The original PSA skills inventory contained three sections. The first section was a self-assessment tool containing a list of procedures. Interestingly, people who gave themselves the highest rating on the assessment section usually did not do well on the remainder of the test. People who rated themselves with a mixed response or in the middle range did well in the actual testing. This finding held true for both PSA and PCT skills self-evaluation. Exhibit 11–3 provides the legend format used in the PSA self-evaluation. The second section contained a list of 20 words to alphabetize. The words were randomly chosen from a dictionary. The third section contained eight mathematical questions to answer without using a calculator. The questions are shown in Exhibit 11–4.

The purpose of the self-assessment tool is to enable individuals to assess the level of expertise they possess in the skills necessary to do the job. The PSA is responsible for stocking and using the computer for order entry. PSAs also need to be able to read labels and mix chemicals. Therefore, alphabetizing complex words should demonstrate the ability to recognize

Exhibit 11–3 Scale for Candidate Proficiency (Rate 1–5 on 16 procedures)

1 = Procedure never done before
2 = Procedure done a few times
3 = Feel comfortable doing procedure
4 = Feel very comfortable doing procedure
5 = Expert

Exhibit 11–4 PSA Math Skills Inventory

1. 417 +231	4. 786 −459	7. 100/20 = ____
2. 573 + 57	5. 56 ×21	8. 144/12 = ____
3. 921 − 87	6. 98 × 9	

English and read words. The mathematical section tests the ability to mix simple amounts and order the correct number of stock items.

The applicants also take a writing test. The candidates write why they want to be a PSA. Alphabetizing is helpful in determining the ability to stock but does not adequately reflect an ability to read labels or input data. The writing test validates an applicant's ability to read and write. Sentence structure, paragraphs, spelling, and grammar are then evaluated.

PCT Skills Inventory

The original skills inventory for the PCT contained five sections. The first section was a self-assessment tool containing a list of procedures. Successful PCTs have consistently scored themselves either in a generalized mix or in midrange. The self-assessment tool enables applicants to determine whether they possess the skills necessary to do the job. The results also identify educational needs of the applicants. Exhibit 11–5 describes the legend used for section 1 of the skills inventory. During phases I, II, and III of restructuring, the second section was a list of 10 true or false questions. These questions are now asked in a multiple choice format. The third section contained standard medical abbreviations to translate into medical terms. The fourth section consisted of a mathematical test (Exhibit 11–6). The fifth section contained a writing test as described in Exhibit 11–7.

Exhibit 11–5 Scale for Candidate Proficiency (Rate 1–5 on 61 Procedures)

1 = Procedure never done before
2 = Procedure done several times
3 = Procedure done enough times to feel competent
4 = Procedure done many times
5 = Expert and could instruct others

The writing test was more difficult to score. The following steps were to be included: introduce themselves, tell the patient what they will do, have the patient decide the level of help they will need with breakfast and bath, report drainage or any other unusual findings to the nurse, change the dressing, and assess whether assistance will be needed moving the patient to a chair. Everyone scoring the writing test must have a clear understanding of the correct answer. A copy of a test with the correct steps identified was available to help evaluate the applicants.

Internal and External Applicant Flow

The application form provides the prospective employee ample space to describe his or her qualifications. The information requested on UMC's

Exhibit 11–6 PCT Math Skills Inventory

1. 178 563 36 337 + 85	2. 10.3 23.9 3.6 + 2.1
3. 456 −437	4. 13.5 −6.9
5. 853/21= _____	

Exhibit 11–7 Written Test

Please take a few minutes and read the description of a patient and the care given to this patient. Then write a summary of the events.

Nancy Smith is a 75-year-old woman and has been in the hospital for 3 days. She had surgery yesterday for gallbladder disease. This morning you are going to:

- help Nancy with breakfast
- do a partial bed bath
- change linen
- get Nancy into a chair for the first time

Some of the things you should know are the following: Nancy lived on her own without help before surgery; her dressing has a little drainage on it; Nancy wears glasses; Nancy has no periods of confusion.*

*The writing test changes to the specific needs of the unit. This is the test used for the medical-surgical unit. There are tests for postpartum, labor and delivery, and newborn nursery.

internal transfer form was too brief to determine the qualifications of internal applicants. Therefore, both internal and external candidates completed a new application.

When the first units were restructured, nursing assistants were employed on some units. Confusion arose among the nursing assistants as to who needed to apply for the new roles. All internal applicants were asked to apply to be consistent in the application process and to seek the most qualified candidates.

Advertising

Flyers were sent to each address at the Arizona Health Sciences Center, which includes the University of Arizona colleges of medicine, nursing, pharmacy, and health-related professions; the university physicians' outpatient clinics; and UMC. A display advertisement that highlighted the new program and the training program was placed in the local newspaper. The position was posted on the internal job posting list and placed on the job line.

In the first two phases of restructuring, the PCT position was posted first. Several weeks later, the PSA position was announced using the same protocol. The advertisements ran separately and coincided with the internal job posting. One problem encountered was that approximately 25 percent of the PCT candidates wanted to apply for both the PSA and PCT positions. Collecting the applications at two different times meant that applicants repeated the process or that the employment section was called upon to locate the PCT application, make a photocopy, and have it ready for the applicant to take the PSA test.

Applicant Flow

The lobby of the human resources department has six available seats. Frequently 20 or more people were waiting to complete an application. The testing was difficult to monitor. The human resources conference room became a second site for applicants. Applicants had to walk through the back areas of the department to get to the conference room. Slightly more than 200 candidates applied for PCT positions, and close to that number applied for PSA positions.

Recruiting and screening such a large number of candidates represented a new experience for UMC. By using a flyer and other communication methods, it was explained that internal applicants would need to complete the entire application. Some employees who worked on the units to be restructured thought their jobs would just become the new positions. This group included housekeepers, who may have been assigned to the unit for years, and phlebotomists, who were routinely assigned to the unit. Because of these and other technical problems, applications were accepted by human resources until positions were filled. Employees who did not know that they needed to apply were allowed to complete their applications late. This extended the application process by several weeks, which in turn increased the number of applicants and the time it took to process the applications.

INTERVIEWING

During phases I and II of restructuring, the tests were scored immediately. A combined average score greater than 50 percent was needed to be interviewed by human resources representatives. There were more than 30 openings for PCTs and nearly that number for PSAs. Applicants who met the testing criteria and the minimum job requirements were first interviewed in human resources. The interview lasted 30 minutes. Human resources conducted more than 125 interviews for PCT positions and nearly 100 interviews for PSA positions.

The patient care units were anxiously waiting for the applicants to begin interviews at the units. Each day human resources would score the interviews and send copies of the applications of those with an average on the interview of 2.5 or higher (of a possible 5.0) to the units. The application, skills inventory, and human resources interview were included in the information sent to the units. Staff nurses conducted the second round of interviews. Few of these nurses had ever been involved in interviewing candidates for employment, especially paraprofessionals. Human resources recommended two-person panel interviews, which resulted in the need to produce two interview packages per applicant. The units in phase I conducted unit-specific interviews. During the human resources interview, candidates were asked their units of choice. Every applicant stated at least two and frequently all four pilot units. Copying eight sets of the application package (two for each unit) delayed getting the human resources interview package to the units.

The interview questions used in human resources were based on information gathered by the subject matter experts when they defined the screening tool. The objective criteria in the skills inventory became technical interview questions, and scenarios became a method to evaluate the subjective qualities. In the first phases, half the questions were technical and half were scenarios. Exhibit 11–8 contains several of the original questions.

Interview questions changed with each restructured unit. Currently interview questions contain one or two technical questions and the same number of scenarios. The majority of the questions are now behaviorally based. Examples of questions are found in Exhibit 11–9.

The current scoring method is a 0 to 5-point scale. Zero represents a wrong answer, and 5 represents a perfect answer. Because more than one person interviews, all interviewers need to know the correct answers through the use of a written key.

Exhibit 11–8 Skills Questions

1. What are universal precautions, and when do you use them?
2. You are in Mr. Smith's room. He is an 80-year-old, confused patient in a Posey and wrist restraints. While giving him a complete bed bath, you hear a crash in the next room. What are you going to do?
3. Tell me how you would transfer an unresponsive male patient from the bed to the gurney.
4. Your friend calls you up and says he read in the local paper that a famous movie star is a patient at UMC, and he wants to know everything you know about this person. As it turns out, this person is one of your patients. What will you tell your friend?
5. How would you make an occupied bed?

Exhibit 11–9 Behaviorally Based Questions

1. Tell me an experience you have had on a team and what your role was on the team.
2. All jobs have stress. Give an example of a time when you were proud of your ability to cope.
3. Tell me the worst experience you have had dealing with an angry family member.
4. Tell me the most stressful experience you have had working with an infant.
5. In your current/recent position, explain a work situation that required you to have schedule flexibility to meet job expectations. How often did this situation come up?

Each applicant is told the job expectations at the beginning of the interview. The interviewer provides compensation and benefits information. The list of available shifts and the hours needed on the unit are also part of the start of the interview. The interviewer tells the applicant the number of questions that he or she will be asked to answer and that the interviewer will be writing responses to the questions (because writing the responses can increase the anxiety of an applicant). The interviewer adds that many interviews are being conducted and that writing the answers enables the interviewer to remember what was said. One applicant asked the interviewer if he or she needed to talk slower so that the interviewer could get all the information.

Human resources has always completed a scoring grid (see Table 11–1). During the first two phases of restructuring, the grids were primarily a method to keep track of where each applicant was referred. It soon became evident that this method was not efficient, so that human resources created a new grid that gave more pertinent information (see Table 11–2).

Changes in the Application Process

The new screening grid includes 12 experience areas and the 5 individual test scores. Interviews now begin after the posting has ended, and applications are no longer accepted. The quality of the process has increased by reviewing individual applicants in relationship to all the applicants. Applicants who score more than seventy-five percent and have at least 1 year of relevant experience interview for PCT positions. The PSA candidates need to score greater than 75 percent and have at least 6 months of relevant experience. By reviewing all the applicants at one time, the time required for human resources screening interviews has decreased by 30 percent.

Human resources also completes all the interviews before referring any applicants to the units. In the first two phases, human resources sent every-

Table 11–1 UMC PCT Scoring Sheet: Original Version

Name	*UMC**	*Interview Date*	*Score*	*Referral Date*	*Ped Score*	*Peds*	*M/S*	*M/S Score*	*Hire*
	Yes, N	7/23	4.4	7/23	59	Yes	Yes		4w
	Yes, T	7/22	3.0	7/23	63	Yes			4w
	Yes, L	7/22	4.1	7/23	59	Yes			No
		7/23	3.0	7/23			Yes	3.7	4e
	Yes, T	7/22	4.0	7/23	66	Yes	Yes		Pca
	Yes, T	7/22	2.7	7/23	63	Yes			3w
		7/22	4.4	7/23	62	Yes	Yes	4.5	3e
		7/22	2.7	7/23	63	Yes	Yes	4.0	
	Yes, N	7/22	4.7	7/23	57	Yes	Yes	4.4	4e
		7/22	3.0	7/23	50	Yes	Yes	4.0	4e
		7/22	4.7	7/23			Yes		4w
	Yes, N	7/24	2.9	7/25	59	Yes			3e
		7/24	3.8	7/25		Yes	Yes	3.2	4e
		7/24	3.3	7/25	66	Yes			3w
		7/24	4.1	7/25	53	Yes	Yes	3.8	No
		7/24	3.3	7/25	69	Yes			3e
		7/24	3.8	7/25	56	Yes	Yes		3e
		7/22	3.0	7/25		Yes	Yes		Flo
		7/22	2.9	7/25	50	Yes	Yes		Pca
	Yes, T	7/22	3.8	7/25	58	Yes	Yes	4.5	3e
	Yes, N	7/22	4.5	7/25	47	Yes	Yes		4w
	Yes, L	7/24	3.0	7/26	47	Yes			No

*Yes = internal candidate; N = candidate from Nursing; T = candidate from Transportation; L = candidate from Laboratory one who scored above 2.5. In phase III, human resources recommended that the total number of unit interviews be equal to three times the total number needed to fill all the vacant positions. For example, if a unit had 20 openings, then 60 people needed to be interviewed. Human resources then worked down the list of scores of candidates and selected an appropriate number to send to the units. In phase III, units received candidates with a score 3.5 or higher to interview. In phase IV the cut-off point was 4.1.

In the last three units to be restructured, human resources moved the application process out of the building into a College of Medicine classroom. Applications were accepted for 6 hours per day for 3 days. All the advertisements and flyers provided the room, dates, and times for the application process. A human resources representative monitored the testing process. Also, a laptop computer was used to input the scores and information on the grid while applications were being completed. Immediate input of data shortened the application process by several days.

Approximately 100 people applied for PCT positions and 80 for PSA positions. Moving the application process to the College of Medicine decreased the confusion caused by processing several hundred people in the small human resources reception area. In addition, the test could be monitored more effectively.

Registered Nurse Involvement in the Hiring

Training for the nursing staff in interviewing skills was conducted by the employment section. The training was required for anyone who would be interviewing PSAs and PCTs. The interview skills inservice was an afterthought for the pilot groups. Because of short timeframes, trainings occurred during multiple time slots of 20 to 30 minutes. An enormous amount of material was presented in a short timeframe. A fun title emerged to describe the purpose of the training: "Employment Doesn't Want To Go to Court." The brief inservice described the legal aspects of interviewing. The most important aspects of these inservices were as follows: do not ask personal questions, human resources needs to approve all interview questions, and be sure to call human resources if you have any questions about interviewing. For the first four pilot units, all the nurses completed a 2-hour session in basic interviewing skills. The program is outlined in Exhibit 11–10.

Registered nurse interview training sessions occur two or three times per restructured unit. The sessions are scheduled to meet the needs of the staff nurses. Training groups usually range from 4 to 10 nurses. The small size of the group is conducive to a relaxed atmosphere and facilitates dis-

Table 11–2 UMC PCT Scoring Sheet: Revised Version

PCT positions for labor and delivery posted 4/9/93; ran single column ad 4/11/93; position closed 4/14/93. Requisition 3378 for 12 positions at .9, 2 positions at .6, total of 14 PCT openings.

Name/Phone #	UMC Employee	Education Nursing	CNA/PCT/MA Experience	NA/Acute	NA/HH/LTC Experience	OB/GYN Experience
		Health Occupations Education				
	no		MA			
	no 1+ yr/OR Attd. 5 mos	Red Cross Vol. 2 yrs in surgery/ maternity ward at Yokota Base Hospital				Currently works in L&D as a UA/ Runner
		2nd yr pima				
	no	Medical College Pakistan Certified				
	no		EMT			

Med-Surg Experience	ER EMT	Phlebotomy Experience	Skills	Multi %	Med. %	Math %	Writing %	Referred Y/N	Interview Time
		Was phlebot-omist at Humana Hospital for 1 yr	1, 2	90	60	100	100		
	1 yr	1 yr	1, 2	90	60	100	100		
			mixed	60	65	53	100		
			mixed	70	60	76.8	100		
			4, 5	70	25	100	25		
			1, 5	60	60	76.9	75		

Exhibit 11–10 Interviewing for Best Results

1. Introduction
2. Objectives, definition, purpose
3. Steps in the hiring process
4. Setting the stage
5. Interview structure
6. Behavior vs. gut feelings
7. "Guess your trainer"
8. Rating system

cussion between the trainer and the group. The introduction includes a brief overview of the reasons for teaching what might appear to be a simple process and the definition of an interview. Interviews are defined as a gathering of information, not a method for choosing the best candidate. The purpose of interviewing is to provide enough information to ask questions that will obtain data to determine the most qualified candidates.

The format used for training in legal issues is a description of the law, whom it protects, and what regulatory agencies enforce that particular law. The discussion centers around equal employment opportunity, affirmative action, and the Americans with Disabilities Act. A flowchart is used to demonstrate the 54 steps it takes from employee requisition to the employee's start date.

The nurses learn how to structure the interview and design questions in a manner that will ease the anxieties of both the interviewer and the candidate. The more structure that the interview has, the easier it will flow. There is a definite beginning, middle, and end to the interview. Each interview lasts only 30 minutes, so that each minute must count. Structure and preparedness are essential for the successful interview.

Most people rely on their gut feeling when interviewing, which does not necessarily result in choosing the most qualified person. A film titled *More than a Gut Feeling II* is shown, which emphasizes the use of behaviorally based questions.[1]

"Guess your trainer" is a quick group activity to help participants grasp the concept of stereotyping. Most of the nurses have had little to no contact with the trainer before the inservice. An overhead projector is used to show four pictures: a television, a radio, a clock, and a cooking pot. The participants are asked to guess quickly the favorite television show, favorite radio station, favorite pastime, and favorite food of the trainer. The results are based on what the participants think about the trainer in the short time they have been together. Rarely does anyone guess anything correctly. The issue of stereotyping people by first impressions is driven home, however. The exercise is also a lot of fun during an inservice devoted to much legal information.

The program ends with a discussion of rating systems. Any rating system can work if it is used correctly. The simple rating system used by human resources is discussed along with a more complex rating system. Each group develops a rating system that will be used to obtain uniform results on the unit.

Human resources introduces and recommends panel interviewing. Each of the restructured units performs panel interviews with two nurses per panel. The team then averages the rating scores. Some units use the average method, and others keep individual scores. The type of method is not critical; what is important is consistency.

Evolution

During phase IV a staff position developed on the unit-based steering committee for a human resources representative. The role began when the PCR unit steering committee and human resources agreed on a proposed time line for restructuring a unit.

The employment section dedicated one FTE for the entire week in which applications are received. Although both PCT and PSA candidates submitted applications, only PCT applications were entered into the computer. The following week, two employment FTEs scheduled and conducted interviews and completed the paperwork needed to refer PCT applications to the nursing unit. In week 3, one FTE repeated the process of scoring and entering the PSA applications into the computer. In week 4, the interview stage was repeated for PSAs using two employment FTEs.

After the timeframe was established, a meeting was scheduled that included the PCR program manager, nurse manager, employment manager, and employment point person. An overview of the employment department's involvement was discussed, and follow-up meetings were scheduled. The purpose of the first meeting was to introduce all the players and to begin developing a relationship that would enable the patient care unit to complete the hiring process successfully.

The role for the employment manager on the unit-specific restructuring steering committee was exciting. Before the employment manager role on the committee, last-minute problems occurred between the unit and employment. The presence of an employment representative as a member of the unit steering committee enabled the nurses and employment to become allies in the hiring process. Attending committee meetings promoted cooperation in discovering qualities and characteristics that are unit specific. These qualities and characteristics became the basis for interview question development. The employment manager and the steering committee created the broader screening interview questions that human resources used, as well as the questions for the registered nurse unit-based interviews.

The interview training sessions took place during question development. The meetings were held off the unit to create a conducive atmosphere for training. It is important to remember that training must meet the needs of the department requesting the training to be successful.

CONCLUSION

The recruitment, screening, interviewing, referral, selection and hiring process has evolved significantly over the course of restructuring. Concerns about using screening tools and involving staff nurses in the selection process have been addressed. The ethnic, age, and gender breakdown of PSAs and PCTs shows that a diverse group of applicants has been employed. The ability of underrepresented populations to enter career ladders in health care has improved greatly using the new PSA and PCT roles.

The employment section plays an active and enthusiastic role in PCR. Development of new roles with their job descriptions, screening tools, interview questions and training is an element to which human resources has made major contributions. Human resources also is the catalyst in breaking down the barriers between staff who occupy traditional roles and those who become multifunctional team members. The human resources professional is familiar with all the aspects of these new roles and provides the expertise to teach others the skills needed to select appropriate candidates to fill the new roles.

NOTE

1. P.C. Green, *More than a Gut Feeling II* (Des Moines, Iowa: American Media, Inc., 1991).

CHAPTER

12

Human Resource Issues: Team Building

Sally Poore

Chapter Objectives

1. To describe the training support provided to unit patient care restructuring steering committees.
2. To describe the conceptual approach to building the team.
3. To describe the components of team building/communication training sessions and retreats.
4. To describe lessons learned from the training sessions and retreats.

A key element in the management of the change process in patient care restructuring (PCR) at University Medical Center (UMC) was the training provided by human resource development (HRD) professionals. The focus of the training was twofold: to support the registered nurses (RNs) on each unit, and to help build the team through all-unit sessions. The trainer worked with the RNs and unit steering committees in three separate sessions: managing change, role clarification, and leadership/delegation. Team-building sessions were held with all staff. A model guiding the content of these sessions was drawn from Drury, whose foundations of an outstanding team are as follows:

1. *Alignment*: Everyone is pulling in the same direction and sharing the same vision and goals.
2. *Clear communication:* An effective team has planned channels of communication, its members demonstrate the ability to listen and assert, and members are comfortable sharing across roles.
3. *Mutual respect:* Teams that demonstrate mutual respect have ground rules or group norms, their members frequently share positive feedback, and they give and receive criticism gracefully.
4. *Effective problem solving:* After thorough exploration of the situation and root cause, teams brainstorm multiple solutions and then agree on a course of action.
5. *Management of conflict and disruption:* Healthy conflict is encouraged, members know their conflict styles and "hot buttons," and silent conflict is brought into the open.[1]

The team-building workshops, which included the separately titled communication workshops, focused mainly on the first four aspects of the Drury model. Time constraints restricted the inclusion of conflict resolution. Please see Exhibit 12–1 for a complete description of the HRD training modules.

Team-building training is not an isolated event that will provide a permanent quick fix. Rather, it is part of a process of transition. It allows members of the team to come together to learn how to build a team and to share feelings and thoughts about the transition. The process of truly building the team happens in the everyday interactions among team members and through the support of leadership. For example, if the team decides on a group norm of no backstabbing, then individuals need to take responsibility to refrain from backstabbing and to discourage others who do it. Also, managers need to tie team-enhancing and team-detracting behaviors to job standards and performance evaluations, taking corrective action when appropriate.

Team building during a time of change must take into account the team's ability to function before the change and other institutional changes. A team that was dysfunctional before restructuring will continue in, and perhaps will exacerbate, their patterns. It cannot be assumed that problems will suddenly be erased with the introduction of this change. In UMC's case, other institutional changes added layers of stress. In fact, unit managers did slow down the introduction of new changes, such as a new documentation system, to lessen the stress felt by employees.

Exhibit 12–1 HRD Training Modules

All-unit RN and unit PCR steering Committee

Session Title	*Length*	*Time Line*
Managing change	1 hour	Early in committee's formation
Role clarification	1 hour	1 month later
Leadership/delegation	1 hour	1 month later

All-unit employees (RNs, patient support attendants, patient care technicians, unit secretaries)

Session Title	*Length*	*Time Line*
Communication workshop	4 hours	1 month either side of implementation date
Team building	4 or 8 hours	1–3 months after communications workshop
Retreat	4 or 8 hours	1 year after implementation date

Embedded in all the change taking place in the units was a change in personnel in the HRD position. The original trainer resigned from the corporation a year after the first units restructured. A training consultant was utilized to bridge the interim until the current HRD manager was in a position to assume the training responsibilities. As one could expect, each facilitator stamped the workshops with his or her preferred teaching style and workshop design.

LOGISTICS

Scheduling roughly followed the time line noted in Exhibit 12–1 but was flexible to accommodate different needs. For instance, when one unit put all its nurses through phlebotomy training, the communication skills module was delayed in an attempt not to create too much stress on the system. Responsibilities for tasks are listed in Table 12–1.

Sessions were designed for an average of 20 participants. Therefore, a unit with 60 employees would hold three sessions so that all could attend. An effort was made by unit managers to include a mix of all job categories in the team-building sessions.

Table 12–1 Team-Building Module Responsibilities

Tasks	*Position*
Decide training dates	HRD manager, PCR coordinator, and unit manager
Schedule training rooms	PCR secretary
Order audiovisual, catering	PCR secretary
Schedule participants	Unit management
Provide handouts	HRD manager
Tabulate evaluations	HRD volunteer
Send evaluations and rosters to unit manager	HRD volunteer

Workshops were held in a variety of rooms, depending upon availability. The best case scenario was off site at a hotel, where participants could focus more fully on the task at hand in clean, well-lighted surroundings. Next best were two rooms in the neighboring College of Nursing, where the rooms were large enough (25 by 30 ft) to accommodate up to 24 people around tables arranged in a U.

NEEDS ASSESSMENT AND EVALUATIONS

Because PCR was in progress when this author joined the team, an early task was to learn as much as possible about PCR. This was accomplished in a threefold manner: in meetings with the PCR coordinator to get an overview of the project; in meetings with the education coordinator to get her impressions of issues encountered by her students [patient care technicians (PCTs), patient support attendants (PSAs), and preceptors], and through input from the previous trainers. For an understanding of the rhythm of a restructured unit, the author shadowed an RN on a restructured unit for 4 hours starting at shift change. Also, the author facilitated a retreat for one unit at its 1-year restructuring anniversary before becoming involved in any of the new units and so gained a long-term perspective of issues raised by restructuring.

In addition to the aforementioned orientation, the major sources of information were the unit managers, the chair of the PCR steering committee, and committee members. Also, issues raised in one session along with the formal evaluations were used to plan future sessions for that particular unit.

Workshop evaluation instruments were included in workshop packets (Exhibit 12–2). Results were tabulated and shared with both unit management and the PCR coordinator. Evaluations provided valuable information for revisions and refinements to the training. Informal evaluation was also provided by unit management in discussions with the trainer.

Alternatives to the formal evaluation instrument were used at retreats. At the end of one, the trainer drew a large target on a flipchart. Participants were given half sheets of paper with the instructions to write a few sentences regarding what they liked about the retreat and what could have been improved. Then, as they left the session, they were asked to mark an X with a marking pen on the target to indicate how close to the

Exhibit 12–2 UMC Workshop Evaluation

Speaker: ______________________________ Date: ____________

Topic: ______________________________

Your feedback will help us provide the quality and variety of programs that will assist you in your continued growth and development.
[For questions 1 and 2, please circle the number that approximates the value you assign to each statement. On a scale of 1 to 5, 1 equals POOR and 5 equals EXCELLENT.]

1. Overall rating of the speaker: 1 2 3 4 5
2. Overall rating of the content: 1 2 3 4 5
3. How will this workshop help you in your job?
4. Comments regarding the speaker.

   What I liked was:

   Suggestions for improvement:
5. Comments regarding the content.

   What I liked was:

   Suggestions for improvement:
6. What other training would be useful to you and/or your employees?

Please turn in at the end of the workshop or mail to Sally Poore, UMC Human Resources.

Thank you!

bull's eye the training was for them. Finally, they were to leave their half sheet of comments on the floor beneath the flipchart. The other method used at a retreat was for participants to verbalize what they liked about the day and what could have been improved. One participant recorded the comments.

RN AND STEERING COMMITTEE TRAINING

Typically, three modules were presented to the unit steering committees 1 month apart (Table 12–2).

Methodology

In the module on managing change, discussion was based on Perlman and Takacs 10 stages of change.[2] Participants were asked for examples of what behaviors they might typically notice for each of the stages of change. Steering committee members were additionally asked to consider where they were, what their end goal was, and what steps it would take to get there.

The role clarification module was presented using flipchart pages and brightly colored markers. The steering committee was asked to choose which role it wanted to address first. The trainer wrote that role on a flipchart page and then headed two columns *What Is Clear/Working* and *What Is Not Clear/Working*. The trainer simply recorded group discussion.

Table 12–2 RN and Unit PCR Steering Committee Training

Module	*Purpose*
Managing change	Help committee recognize emotional aspects of change so that it can help other unit members through acceptance rather than condemnation of different ways of dealing with loss.
Role clarification	Help committee pinpoint where it was clear on the roles and responsibilities of each position and where it still needs to make decisions or get answers from the PCR task force.
Leadership/delegation	Help RNs become comfortable with delegating to nonnursing personnel.

The process was repeated for each job title on the unit. Then discussion focused on where to begin based on what still needed to be clarified.

The leadership/delegation module presented a delegation model based on situational leadership ideas (please refer to Chapter 8 for more information). Discussion focused on what it would take for nurses to become comfortable delegating to nonnursing personnel and how to delegate to people with various levels of willingness and ability. Learning curves of new workers were also discussed as a factor to consider when delegating.

GROUP NORMS

All 4- and 8-hour training modules included establishing group norms at the beginning of the session. Group norms are statements of what the group members will and will not accept in terms of behavior from each other during the session. The facilitator may initiate the following: Use a flipchart page with only *Ground Rules* or *Group Norms* at the top and write participants' ideas in their own words; present two or three norms and then ask for suggestions from the group; or present a fairly complete list and ask for agreement. One way to prime the pump for discussion is to ask participants to discuss in pairs what behaviors they liked or did not like at other workshops. When their list is complete, the facilitator needs to ask for group members' acceptance, or buy-in, of their norms. Another way to phrase acceptance is to ask: "Does anyone disagree with this list?"

Whether the facilitator is using overhead transparencies or flipcharts, the group norms are best put on a flipchart page and taped on a wall for continuous viewing. A desirable alternative to the flipchart sheets are the plastic sheets that cling to walls by static electricity. Examples of typical group norms and their discussion points are shown in Table 12–3.

COMMUNICATION SKILLS MODULE

The goal of the 4-hour communication sessions (Exhibit 12–3) was to focus on key interpersonal skills that would engender team building. Session objectives were:

- to enable participants to communicate thoughts and feelings regarding the change to PCR
- to help participants clarify the new roles
- to increase participants' abilities to delegate and receive assignments
- to practice listening skills

Table 12–3 Group Norms Using a Flip Chart

Flip Chart	*Trainer/Facilitator Responses*
Confidentiality	What is said in this room stays in this room. When discussing another person, do not use his or her name. Although the rule is always in effect, participants are encouraged to bring it up again when they are about to say something they want to remain confidential: "Please keep this confidential."
Everyone participates	If all participants have introduced themselves, you could say that this norm has been fulfilled and they don't need to talk anymore today! Invite people who notice that they talk a lot in a group to practice a new behavior: listening. Invite those who are normally quiet in a session to take a risk by speaking up. It is through putting yourself out there that you learn.
One conversation at a time	Mention how distracting it can be when a few people are having a side conversation. Also, those doing the whispering miss out on the main conversation. This is the most frequently violated norm. The trainer either may ask "May we have one conversation at a time?" or simply motion to that norm on the chart.
No interruptions	This means two things: not interrupting other people while they speak, and making a decision as to whether beepers will be permitted.
Teacher and learner	Everyone is both a teacher and a learner. The instructor is not the expert. Everyone in the room has expertise to share.
Okay to make mistakes	The trainer encourages people to risk trying on new behaviors or expressing ideas without trying to be right or perfect.
Okay to ask questions	There is no such thing as a dumb question! Usually you are not the only one with the question, just the only one willing to speak up and ask it.
Take care of yourself	This means that if you need to get coffee or use the restroom when it is not break time, feel free. Also, people with back problems may want to stand up and move around. Acknowledge that if someone does not have a desk job it may be difficult to sit for so long.
Be flexible	This is good, too, from the trainer's perspective because there may be some flexibility needed in the agenda.
No "hitting," or no "ouch"	We tell children not to hit. Likewise, we don't want people verbally hitting each other with put downs. When someone feels that he or she has been "hit," he or she can say "ouch."

continues

Table 12–3 continued

Flip Chart	*Trainer/Facilitator Responses*
Zapp, not sap	This is similar to the no-hitting norm but from another angle. Taken from the book *ZAPP!: The Lightning of Empowerment*, empower each other by maintaining or enhancing self-esteem, listening and responding with empathy, and asking for help. The opposite is to sap with a put down. People's energy is increased with a zapp and drained with a sap.[3]
Respect diversity	First state that it is important to respect diversity. Then ask the class to state some examples of diversity.
Have fun!	Have fun! Use your sense of humor!

Exhibit 12–3 Communications Workshop Agenda

08:00	Gather; sign in; agenda; introductions; group norms	
08:30	Communicating the change	
	Exercise:	Where are we now?
		Groping, Griping, Grasping, Grouping
09:00	Communicating our new roles	
	Discussion:	What is clear; what is not clear
09:45	Break	
10:00	Communicating assignments	
	Exercise:	Barriers/benefits to delegating
	Exercise:	Assertive delegation
		What delegators need to do
		What delegatees need to do
10:40	Communicating by listening	
	Exercise:	30 seconds: listening/nonlistening
	Discussion:	Keys to active listening
11:00	Communicating criticism or requesting a change in behavior	
	Exercise:	Productive and destruction criticism
	Lecture:	How to give criticism
	Exercise:	Practice giving criticism using three models
		Practice receiving criticism
11:35	Communicating positive feedback	
	Discussion:	To whom, where, when, how, how often?
	Exercise:	Share appreciations
11:50	Commitment to action	
	Workshop evaluation	

- to learn positive ways to give and receive criticism
- to be able to communicate positive feedback to others

Communications Skills Objectives 1 and 2: Communicate Thoughts and Feelings Regarding the Change to PCR and Clarify the New Roles

The agenda items communicating the change and communicating our new roles were designed to facilitate the first two workshop objectives. Although listed separately, in practice these exercises melded together.

The trainer briefly introduced the change model "Groping, Griping, Grasping, Grouping." Groping was likened to turning off the lights (in training rooms that could be fully darkened, the trainer actually turned off the lights). When groping, a person must feel his or her way around. Things that were familiar and easy are now strange and difficult. Griping was easily identified with; participants chuckled that they understood what was meant by griping. Grasping was explained as coming to more clarity about the vision of how things will eventually be when homeostasis is reached again. The point made here was that clear visions help people move through the change process more quickly. Grouping was explained as the group coming together again to work as a team with a shared sense of unity.

The trainer then posted signs marked *Groping* on one wall, *Griping* on the adjacent wall, *Grasping* on the third wall, and *Grouping* on the fourth. Participants were asked to stand next to the sign that best represented where they were right now, recognizing that they could be in more than one place or would, of course, go through all four phases. The direction was given to stand by the sign you most strongly resonate with right now.

After participants sorted themselves, the four groups were given flipchart pages, colored markers, and instructions to complete the following statements for their specific group:

- *Groping*: "I still need to know . . . I'm not clear about . . . "
- *Griping*: "I don't like . . . My problem is . . . "
- *Grasping:* "I'm starting to see . . . What's starting to work is . . . "
- *Grouping*: "I feel . . . I sense . . . "

Each group discussed its thoughts and feelings, wrote them on the flipchart, and then reported to the large group. Members in other groups could ask for clarification or add to their report. After all reports were made, the trainer went back and asked each group, "What would it take for these people to move to the next phase?" Group answers were recorded in a different colored marker on each flipchart page. This exercise was repeated in the 8-hour team building sessions as a way to mark progress.

Communication Skills Objective 3: Be Able To Delegate and Receive Assignments

Two exercises were used to help participants become more comfortable with delegation. First, barriers to and benefits of delegation were explored. The large group was divided into four small groups of four to five people. Two teams were instructed to list barriers, internal and external, to delegation and the other two to list benefits to the delegator, delegatee, and organization. The small groups presented to the large group, with the barriers stated first. The trainer noted that, just as a clear vision pulls a person toward a change, a clear understanding of benefits will pull a person toward a change in behavior.

The second exercise was based on a handout that listed six steps of assertive supervision/delegation (Exhibit 12–4). Again, four small groups worked on the assignment. Two groups studied the handout to discern what delegators need to do to create a successful delegation; two groups looked for factors that delegatees need to do. The group's answers were then flipcharted by the trainer. Key points for both delegators and delegatees were to clarify the assignment by giving specific instructions or asking questions, to be open to alternative ways, and to agree on a time to follow up.

Communication Skills Objective 4: Listening Skills

Nonverbal listening skills were demonstrated by an exercise in which participants were paired. Each pair decided who would be A and B. Person A was instructed to tell a story about anything in his or her life, something as simple as what happened today on the way to work. Person B was instructed to practice his or her best listening behavior. At "Go," Person A started talking. After 30 seconds, the trainer said "Stop" and then instructed person B to put on his or her worst listening behaviors when person A started to talk again. Person A was instructed to pick up the story where interrupted at the signal "Go." Again, after 30 seconds the trainer said "Stop." Processing of the activity was as follows:

- What behaviors did you notice people doing when they weren't listening?

Exhibit 12–4 Assertive Supervision/Delegation

1. Assess the situation
   - Look at employees' capabilities. Give them as much control over their own work and work environment as possible.
   - Look at your part. Are you treating your staff consistently (not playing favorites)? Are you letting your mood affect your behavior?
2. Decide what you want
   - Have a clear idea of what you want before you approach the other person(s).
   - If you aren't clear, invite their input and reach agreement on the outcome.
3. Create a picture
   - Let others know exactly what you expect of them.
   - Don't assume they know what you want. Don't make them guess.
   - Give clear and concise instructions. Demonstrate when useful. Ask questions to make sure you understand each other.
   - Give as much background information as possible. Let others know why things need to get done and how their jobs fit into the overall picture.
4. Get their input
   - Involve others in problem solving and decision making whenever their input might be useful, and especially when the decisions concern their work.
   - Don't ask for an opinion unless you are ready to listen and change.
5. Allow time for the work to be accomplished or changes made
   - Establish clear and realistic time frames.
   - Be available when needed. Give new employees extra support.
6. Follow through: Reward or give corrective feedback
   - Provide positive and useful feedback.
   - Celebrate successes.
   - Give others room to grow. As they are ready for more responsibility, back off and give them space.
   - If they persist in undesirable behavior, persist in telling them about it. Work at uncovering the underlying problem.
   - If it becomes evident that the employee can't or won't perform to agreed standards, use disciplinary action.

- What did you think and feel when your partner wasn't listening to you?
- What behaviors did you notice people doing when they were doing their best listening behaviors?
- What did you think and feel when your partner was listening?

The main point from this exercise was that people felt frustrated when others did not listen and had difficulty finishing their stories, but they felt valued and cared for when others listened. Participants were astounded that they could have such strong feelings in just 30 seconds. The point was well made that team members can affect each other quickly just by their nonverbal behaviors.

The second part of this section was a handout on active listening (Exhibit 12–5). Participants were asked to read the list and then mark one item they were particularly good at and one item where they would like to improve. If time permitted, they were asked to share in pairs.

Exhibit 12–5 Active Listening

1. Limit your own talking. You cannot talk and listen at the same time.
2. Think like the other person. Focus on the other person's problems and needs. You will understand and retain needs better if you use his or her point of view.
3. Ask questions. Clarify points you don't understand.
4. Don't interrupt. Allow the other person to finish a thought, even if he or she is taking a long pause.
5. Don't jump to conclusions. Avoid making assumptions or mentally completing the other's thoughts.
6. Concentrate. Focus on what the other person is saying. Practice shutting out outside distractions. Likewise, practice shutting out your own internal monologue.
7. Take notes. As a memory jogger, you may want to jot down key points.
8. Listen for ideas, not just words. Get the whole picture, not just bits and pieces.
9. Listen for intent, not just words. What does the other person really want or hope?
10. Prepare in advance. When appropriate, have remarks and questions prepared in advance to free your mind for better listening.
11. React to ideas, not the person. Focus on the content of the message, not personal characteristics or behavior that you find irritating or distracting.
12. Listen for overtones. Observe the way things are said and how the other person reacts to what you say.
13. Allow anger to be vented. Realize that anger is a symptom of a problem. Anger is usually legitimate and not directed at you.
14. Use encouraging statements. When you want the other person to continue to clarify thoughts or feelings, invite him or her to say more by saying, "Tell me more," "Say more about that," "I see," "Uh-huh," "Yes," "Then," "So," or "Because."
15. Use encouraging nonverbal messages. Use appropriate head nods, leaning forward, and eye contact.
16. Paraphrase. Summarize the other person's concerns, ideas, and feelings. This allows him or her to feel heard. Example: "So what you're saying is that you felt ________ because . . . ." Or use metaphors: "You felt as if you were walking on eggshells," "That must have felt as if the wind was knocked out of you," "That wasn't a pretty picture."

Communication Skills Objectives 5 and 6: Give and Receive Criticism and Give Positive Feedback to Others

The teamwork in a unit can benefit from employees who know how to give and receive criticism and who support each other with positive feedback. To set the framework for criticism, participants were asked to describe productive and destructive criticism, which the trainer recorded on a sheet of newsprint. Several models for giving criticism were presented; participants then formed triads with instructions for each person to practice one of the models. For each practice there was one speaker, one listener, and one observer, with everyone rotating through all three roles.

The final exercise was a brief discussion on the need always to nurture each other in the workforce through positive feedback but in particular during times of change, when stress levels are increased. As the trainer stood behind each participant, other members of the class were invited to state positive feedback to that person. Statements were "I appreciate you for . . . ," "Thank you for . . . ," and the like.

The session closed with participants filling out commitment to action and evaluation forms. The commitment page asked participants: "Please review today's agenda and workshop materials. Pick one new behavior or technique that you will practice for the next month. As a result of this workshop, I commit to: . . . " There was a line on the page for the participant's signature along with a request for the participant to tell one person about the commitment.

TEAM-BUILDING MODULES

The content of the sessions varied from trainer to trainer and from unit to unit because sessions were tailored to specific needs for time (4 or 8 hours) and content. In general, session goals focused on the importance for employees in each unit to grasp the vision of the new organizational structure, to socialize the new team members well, to clarify the new roles, to redefine the old roles, and to let go of what was.

The following is a collection of information and activities that were drawn from but not necessarily included in every training session. Therefore, agendas and learning objectives are not listed because they varied from unit to unit. Once designed, however, every session for a particular patient care unit was the same.

Didactic

Lecture material included definitions, stages of team development, trust building, and factors that help and hinder team development.

Definitions of a group, team, and teamwork were presented in a handout (Exhibit 12–6). The trainer summarized a group as a collection of people or things. For the definition of team, another Webster's definition was stated: "Two or more draft animals harnessed to the same vehicle." It was noted that the root of the word *team* means "to draw or pull." The point was made that a team must pull together in the same direction, going toward a mutual vision. The notion of teamwork was also explored in the context of a continuous quality improvement (CQI) environment.[4]

The stages of team development—forming, storming, norming, and performing—were presented as a conversational lecture (Exhibit 12–7).[4] It was explained that the stages are more clear with a team, such as a CQI/total quality management team, that is starting to work together for the first time. The trainer pointed out the four stages and noted the chart read from bottom to top. Under each stage, the question to participants was; "What jumps out at you about this stage? What are you noticing in your unit?" The trainer affirmed the normalcy of each stage because part of the task of team building is to understand a team from a systems approach rather than assign blame to individual members.

A lecture on team building was based on the handout "Factors That Help and Hinder Team Development" (Table 12–4). Key points included the importance of group norms, the need to socialize new members well, a sense of status equality across roles, and clarity of roles.[5]

Exhibit 12–6 Definitions

Group:	A number of individuals assembled together or having some unifying relationship (*Webster's*)
Team:	A number of persons associated together in work or activity (*Webster's*)
Teamwork:	Work done by several associates with each doing a part but all subordinating personal prominence to the efficiency of the whole (*Webster's*)
Teamwork:	Where once there may have been barriers, rivalries, and distrust, the quality company fosters teamwork and partnerships with the workforce and their representatives. This partnership is not a pretense, a new look to an old battle. It is a common struggle for the customers, not separate struggles for power. The notion of a common struggle for quality also applies to relationships with suppliers, regulating agencies, and local communities.[4(pp.1-13)]

Exhibit 12–7 Stages of Team Development

4. Performing
   - Team can diagnose and solve problems
   - Members accept each others' strengths and weaknesses
   - Members are satisfied with team progress and feel close attachment

3. Norming
   - Members accept team norms
   - Members know their own roles
   - Members are willing to help each other
   - May achieve harmony by avoiding conflict
   - Members share personal and professional problems

2. Storming
   - Usually the most difficult stage
   - Members are impatient about lack of progress
   - Members may realize the task is more difficult than they originally thought
   - Members argue, may not agree on real issue
   - Members choose sides
   - Some members doubt the team's chance of success

1. Forming
   - People transition from individual to group member
   - People may feel excitement and optimism or suspicion and anxiety
   - People usually feel pride
   - Group attempts to define the task
   - Group may discuss concerns that are not relevant to the task
   - Group attempts to set norms
   - There may be complaints about organizational barriers to the task
   - Little is accomplished

Source: From *The Team Handbook.* Copyright © 1988, Joiner Associates, Inc. All rights reserved. Reprinted with permission.

Group Exercises and Activities

Balloon Game

Participants were divided into groups of six to eight. The trainer gave each group a fully blown-up, 10-inch balloon and announced that the object of the balloon game was to keep the balloon in the air. After a minute or two, when teams had settled on patterns, the trainer gave each team a second balloon to keep in the air. After 30 seconds or so, the trainer gave

Table 12–4 Factors That Help and Hinder Team Development

Factors That Pull Teams Apart	*Factors That Bring Teams Together*
Group norms allow: backbiting gossip whining shirking of responsibility	Group norms encourage: positive reinforcement sending "mail to right address" sharing solutions to problems
New members not socialized well	New members socialized well
Unrealistic expectations	Realistic expectations
Status incongruence	Status congruence
Ambiguous roles	Clear roles
Role conflict (multiple demands)	Lack of role conflict
Disagreement on group goals	Agreement on group goals
Infrequent interaction	Frequent interaction
Low personal attractiveness	High personal attractiveness
Low intergroup competition	High intergroup competition
Lack of or unfavorable public evaluation	Favorable public evaluation
Personality traits	Personality traits
Abilities and intelligence	Abilities and intelligence
Low trust	High trust

each team a third balloon that was inflated to less than half size. Then a fourth balloon, also only partially inflated, was added. The small balloons were difficult to keep in the air, resulting in much scurried activity to keep them afloat. After another 20 or 30 seconds, the game was halted.

Participants were then asked how what they just did was related to their jobs. The lesson learned from the exercise is that everyone knows what to do before a change but then stress increases and accuracy decreases after a change until a team figures out its new way of working together.

Change: Friend or Foe?

Participants discussed the following in pairs or small groups: In what ways do individuals experience change as foe and as friend? In what ways do teams experience change as foe and as friend? The large group then discussed the issues. Answers were flipcharted or recorded on an overhead transparency as they were brought up. The key lesson was for participants to examine how they view change and to recognize that people who welcome change will have an easier time in life than people who fear and avoid change.

Worst of the Worst/Best of the Best

Participants were asked to imagine that a hospital exists somewhere that has the worst possible teamwork and another that has the best possible teamwork. The large group was split into four small groups of four to five each. Two small groups printed with markers on flipchart paper what they imagined they would observe in the worst of the worst, and two groups recorded the best of the best. They observed what people would do, say, think, and feel in each scenario. Each group reported to the large group, and large group discussion followed.

Group Vision of Teamwork

Everyone was instructed to draw his or her vision of teamwork on his or her unit in 1 year. They could not use numbers or words. In small groups, participants explained their drawings. Then their group merged the individual visions into a group vision, drawing it with colored markers on newsprint. Each group then explained its picture to the large group. Pictures were taped to the wall for the duration of the training session and then were posted in the unit's staff room.

Group Norms

A group norm is described as a standard of behavior or performance that is established by group members (as opposed to being set by management). The trainer explained that every group establishes norms, some of which help and some of which hinder teamwork. The goal was to make the covert norms overt. In small groups, participants listed on newsprint what they agreed would be good group norms for their unit. They were referred to the workshop group norms for ideas. Each team reported to the large group. Because the participants for 1 day could not set the norms for the entire unit, the newsprint pages were collected and then later merged by a small committee from the unit. The idea was for each unit to make its desired group norms public as a way to shape team behavior of present and future members.

Reward and Recognition

This exercise was usually conducted toward the end of the module. Participants were asked how they would like to be rewarded and recognized for being team players by management, by coworkers, and by themselves. Management was defined to include anyone to whom another person reports. The trainer recorded their answers on an overhead transparency or flipchart. Emphasis was put on what coworkers can do for each other and how a person can nurture himself or herself.

Individual Contributions: What I Bring the Team

This activity worked well at the end of the session. Participants were asked to list 10 skills, abilities, or traits that they bring to the team. Then they were asked to share 1 or 2 with the large group. A fake gift box was tossed from person to person; the person with the box spoke. The box was tossed until everyone had a chance to speak.

Problem Solving

This module was included only in the day-long team-building modules or retreats because of the 2-hour time requirement. The trainer flipcharted all the opportunities for improvement mentioned by participants. The number of issues (from 8 to 30) was narrowed to 3 or 4 through weighted voting. People selected an issue to work on, and the teams worked from a problem-solving model for 1 hour. The trainer requested that teams spend the first half hour on problem definition, emphasizing the importance of getting to the root cause (otherwise the solution developed might not solve the problem). The second half hour was to be spent on solution decision with plans to continue work if the problem was too big to pinpoint and solve in one session. Members recognized that they could lay the groundwork to be turned over to a CQI committee.

Teams chose a facilitator, recorder, and reporter. The facilitator role was to keep the team on track through the problem-solving steps and to ensure that every member felt comfortable to participate. The facilitator also gave the team the rules for brainstorming. The recorder took notes on the handout, summarized the brainstorming activity on flipchart paper, and then at the end flipcharted key points describing the problem and outlining the action plan. The reporter presented the problem description and the action plan. The large group asked questions for clarification and added ideas and suggestions. The trainer helped clarify who was going to do what by when. Usually, a member of unit management was asked to take responsibility for follow-up after the workshop to ensure that the hard work was more than a mere exercise.

Commitment to Action

At the end of a team-building session, participants were asked to make a commitment to change. The commitment to action page in the handouts stated four items:

1. To improve teamwork on my unit, one thing I will *start* doing or doing more of is:
2. To improve teamwork on my unit, one thing I will *stop* doing is:

3. The benefits of making the above changes are:
4. I will reward my success by:

As with the communication module commitment, participants were asked to sign the document, but not to turn it in.

RETREATS

From empirical observation, the more the unit takes ownership of the retreat, the higher chance for success. One successful retreat at UMC was prepared by one person from each role (RN, licensed practical nurse, case manager, assistant nurse manager, nurse manager, unit assistant, PCT, and PSA) in a 2-hour brainstorming session with a trainer. Using information from a recent staff satisfaction survey and their own observations, the assembled group members first stated successes and problems on the unit and then agreed on a general outline for the agenda. The trainer was responsible for compiling the final agenda, facilitating the sessions, and providing flipcharts, markers, and tape. The planning committee was responsible for arranging a site and refreshments for 2 days, scheduling the employees (arranging to have half of each job role at each session), and working with each job role ahead of time on role clarification presentations and tips of the trade. The role clarification exercise had a spokesperson for each job role describe a typical "day in the life" and then state what he or she liked about his or her job and what some frustrations were.

Another successful retreat was prepared mainly by unit management. The trainer was asked only to do two half-hour energizers (one in the morning and one in the afternoon) and to facilitate several small group discussions. The morning energizer had two parts. First, the group was told to imagine that the space outlined represented a map of the United States. Participants were invited to go to the spot on the map where they were born. People born outside the continental United States stood at the edge in the direction of their birthplace (this usually evoked laughter). Everyone introduced himself or herself from that spot, giving his or her name, job position, shift, and birth town. The second part of the energizer was the setting of group norms (see above). The energizer helped make the transition from the lecture by nurse management to group sharing, which occurred the rest of the day.

The afternoon energizer was "A Pat on the Back." The planning committee had prepared the outline of hands drawn on construction paper. Each participant then attached a sheet on his or her back with masking tape. The instructions were to write affirmations on each others' sheets: "What I like about you is . . . ," "I appreciate you for . . . ," and the like. This was a fun exercise because the group, on its own, formed long trains of people. After each person had about eight statements on his or her sheet, the instructor called time (sometimes the group members will want to write on everyone's sheet). The game players took the sheets from their backs and read them, feeling appreciated and supported, of course!

LESSONS LEARNED/ACTIONS UNDERWAY

The role of the PCR unit steering committee is under revision. The steering committees have done an excellent job of managing the tasks to accomplish change but have given less attention to managing the transition. According to Bridges, "It isn't the changes that do you in, it's the transitions."[6(p.3)] In PCR terms, the change is the redesign of the patient care delivery system, and the transition is the psychological process of moving from an ending (the way things were) by letting go and experiencing the losses to a new beginning. Moving toward an increased leadership role, the steering committees would decide how they wanted to observe, report, and manage the transition and for what duration. The steering committees of the past have expected to have their work done shortly after "Balloon Day" (the author's term for the kick-off day on which a formal ceremony marks the rite of passage to a restructured unit). In the future, their role is expected to continue until the unit has developed its new homeostasis.

Another area for exploration would be training for the unit steering committees. Using a modified meeting observation tool with one steering committee, it was discovered that the committee members came to agreement amicably on many issues.[4] Their meetings could have been enhanced with some basic meeting management training, however, including agenda building and setting their own group norms for meetings.

Judging from the situation 1 year after the retreats, a major issue for PCR is the acceptance by RNs. Although the original conceptualization was for RNs to receive training on managing change and leadership, the training evolved, perhaps for scheduling reasons, to presentations at the unit steering committees with all other unit employees welcome. By holding sessions for RNs only, they would be able to pinpoint their losses. They might even hold a "funeral" or a "burial" of the past to facilitate the letting go process. Then they would turn to the tasks of stating what elements would not change and what would be new, reframing the change as an opportunity for growth. The RN role is moving from task-centered care provider to planner and coordinator of care and from total direct care provider to manager of assistive personnel.

During team-building sessions, issues were raised that participants expressed a desire for higher-ups to hear. Therefore, another piece to consider adding is a separate administration/management feedback session so that employees will feel that their issues are being heard and addressed (please see Chapter 17). A suggestion for future sessions to allow venting and to develop a sense of safety would be to get attendees into small groups to discuss issues and then have small groups make presentations, perhaps using flipcharts. Factors at times inhibiting the expression of negative opinions to management include lack of trust to follow through and fear of retribution.

Because of time considerations, we were unable to devote time to one of the building blocks of an outstanding team, namely conflict resolution.[1] It would be a logical next step for a training topic as a unit settles into restructuring.

A sharp lesson learned by the author was the perception of loss of neutrality in one training session, where remarks by the trainer were seen as proemployee and antimanagement. The trainer must not have a hidden agenda and must support both management's and employees' rights to express their viewpoints. If the trainer were perceived as the hand of management, conditions for resistance by employees would be inherent. On the other hand, if the trainer were perceived to be antimanagement, management would seek to replace the trainer because of fear of the trainer stirring up the employees. It is key for the trainer to maintain a balance and to serve as a conduit of information from and to both management and employees.

A final lesson learned is to include the trainer in the initial contact with the unit. For instance, it was successful to have the trainer attend the administrative orientation. The trainer was able to hear the unit's comments and questions and to begin the assessment necessary to tailor programs to the unit's specific needs. One director recently held a meeting with the managers of two units slated for restructuring in 11 months. At the same table were the PCR coordinator, the PCR education coordinator, the human resources employment manager, and the author. It is anticipated that the coordinated effort will enhance a smooth implementation.

Most of the lessons learned also point to a personpower issue that is due to other organizational demands on the human resources trainer's time. In the ideal of ideal worlds, the trainer would be more actively involved with each unit steering committee and would attend more of its meetings, even when he or she is not presenting. The role would include an organizational development specialist as well as a training specialist. Finally, training sessions would become even more tailored, and other modules, such as conflict resolution, might be added.

CONCLUSION

The team-building portion of PCR is one of the critical components of successful implementation. If, as they restructure, unit employees accept, orient, and mentor the new employees into their team, the results are high productivity and high morale. Working together, administrators, managers, unit steering committees, unit staff, the education coordinator, and the HRD trainer support all unit staff as they make the transition to the new work design and structure.

NOTES

1. S. Drury, Notes from a presentation on team-building training sessions (Tucson, Ariz., December 1992).
2. D. Perlman and G. Takacs, The 10 Stages of Change, *Nursing Management* 21 (1990): 33–38.
3. W. Byham and J. Cox, *ZAPP!: The Lightning of Empowerment* (Pittsburgh, Pa.: Development Dimensions International Press, 1988).
4. P. Scholtes, *The Team Handbook: How To Use Teams To Improve Quality* (Madison, Wis.: Joiner Associates, 1988).
5. A. Szilagyi and M. Wallace, *Organizational Behavior and Performance* (New York: HarperCollins, 1990).
6. W. Bridges, *Managing Transitions: Making the Most of Change* (Reading, Mass.: Addison-Wesley,1991).

CHAPTER

13

Group Governance and the Role of the Unit Patient Care Restructuring Coordinator

JoAnne Schnepp, Kathe Barry, and Kelly Morgan

Chapter Objectives

- To describe how group governance facilitates the patient care restructuring change on a patient care unit.
- To describe the role of the unit coordinator in the change process.
- To discuss the relationship of the unit patient care restructuring committee to the change process.

This chapter describes how to introduce group governance to facilitate the implementation of patient care restructuring (PCR). The promotion and support of a staff registered nurse (RN) as unit coordinator for the restructuring process are key to accepting the group governance concept. The role this RN plays as the chair of the group governance unit PCR steering committee is also described. The impact of the PCR unit-based steering committee on the change process is discussed, and the change that occurs in formal unit management structure after restructuring is fully implemented is described as well.

Introduction of a group governance model at University Medical Center (UMC) was an important part of the PCR project from the start. Several units in the hospital had various degrees of experience with group governance through a previous research project that was in its final stages of implementation. The purpose of the previous research project, entitled differentiated group professional practice (DGPP), was to evaluate the effects of implementing a professional practice model on both nurse and patient outcomes (see Chapter 3). The DGPP model included group governance, peer review, and case management. Five East participated in this 5-year project. A review of the literature indicated that group governance had a positive effect on RN job satisfaction and patient care productivity. In addition, positive effects had been observed on the units that had implemented group governance. Therefore, it was important to include this concept in the PCR planning process. The governance model could be introduced into new units by forming a PCR unit steering committee to assist in implementing the project and to introduce the change process. The benefits of utilizing a group governance model within a major change process such as this one are twofold. First, change is accepted more readily at the staff level if staff have some control and input into how that change occurs. Second, change can occur more rapidly and with fewer revisions if the staff directly involved help create the how-to's of implementation.

Therefore, the unit steering committee should primarily consist of staff members. This committee must be able to make recommendations, and most important it is vital that committee recommendations be taken seriously by both the nurse manager and administration. The nurse manager, with support from administration, must implement as many of the staff's recommendations as are pertinent and possible to reinforce the significance of staff having their issues heard and being able to implement change. To ensure that staff would have the opportunity to implement group governance with positive outcomes, the UMC PCR model utilized a unit steering committee chaired by a unit coordinator. Setting up the committee to comprise primarily staff members and having the committee chaired by a staff RN coordinator gave staff a clear message that administration strongly welcomed the staff's input into the change process.

THE ROLE OF THE UNIT COORDINATOR

The unit coordinator is a key person in the restructuring project. The person must be an RN with leadership skills who is viewed with credibility and respect by the staff. It is most helpful if this person volunteers, but if no appropriate person volunteers the nurse manager may decide to meet with a staff member who has the qualifications and to solicit the person to volunteer. Qualified staff members may not want to volunteer because the prospect of coordinating a project of this magnitude is just plain scary. The person selected may be someone who has ambivalent or negative feelings about the proposed change. The person must be able to verbalize an intent to remain open minded, however, and must contribute to making the project work on the unit.

The unit coordinator will act as the chair of the steering committee for the duration of the restructuring project. Therefore, the nurse manager must negotiate the limitation of membership on other committees or projects during the duration of this project. The unit coordinator should also be offered financial compensation for work involved in the project. This is important because there will be much more work than just attending a meeting once or twice a month. The coordinator needs skills to network with staff, including receiving and giving feedback about the project. The coordinator also solicits committee members or additional members at key discussion times so that they have an opportunity to voice concerns formally that may have been expressed informally on the unit. The unit coordinator may also have to act as cheerleader while the project moves forward. Change is difficult for all, but some people have greater difficulty adjusting than others. In addition, people react to change at different times. Many people resist the project until the change is actually affecting them. The coordinator works one on one with staff to ease the process. Another major part of the coordinator's role is to communicate information, issues, concerns, and suggestions among the staff, the nurse manager, and at times the PCR task force.

THE IMPACT OF THE UNIT STEERING COMMITTEE ON THE CHANGE PROCESS

The unit steering committee consists of the group of staff who actually begin the process of change on the unit. Therefore, volunteers who are interested in the project need to make up the membership of the committee. At UMC, the steering committee was formed during discussions and educational sessions about the PCR project at staff meetings. Discussions began a couple of months before the project was to start. Staff were informed that steering committee membership meant that they would have input into major decisions as they occurred, such as staffing ratios, job descriptions, project time lines, feedback, and making revisions to the overall model for the unit.

These reasons for involvement were readily understood and appreciated on the units that had previous experience with group governance. Other units had more difficulties getting the committee functioning without active participation from the nurse manager and assistant nurse managers. The difficulty in the second example is that staff may have perceptions that the project belongs to and is being managed by administration. Ideally, therefore, the project should not begin until the committee has a number of staff people who are willing to participate over the long time span of implementation.

Once the group of staff volunteers exists, it is important to reach consensus on the idea that committee membership should be open and fluid. This means that all meetings are open to all interested staff members. Agendas and discussion topics need to be posted in advance. Some staff members have a strong interest in providing input, asking questions, and assisting with staff decisions on selected topics but not all topics. Also, a strong possibility exists that covert power and control issues on a unit may surface with this committee. If a unit has strong informal leaders who have exerted a lot of control over other staff members, there is increased likelihood that these same people will be interested in joining this committee or even becoming the chairperson. Generally, these informal leaders are not as interested in creating a group governance model because this reduces the power base they have on the unit. Therefore, they may get involved in the project and then attempt to maintain power by maintaining control rather than encouraging and allowing all staff members to participate.

After implementation, the staff in the new roles need to be included in steering committee meetings so that they feel welcomed to the unit and can provide feedback where necessary. The current management team for the unit needs to be involved, but in the background during the change process. This committee not only will actually initiate the change process but also will set the tone and the speed of the change. It will be informally and formally relaying thoughts and feelings about the project to all the other staff members. It will be either selling the project or destroying others' views of it. A group that works positively together is crucial. Staff members who are ambivalent or negative about either change in general or the project in particular need to be on the committee because the critics often have valid points to make and because, if a few critics are converted to a positive outlook, they will become the biggest salespersons of the project.

COMMITTEE MEETINGS

The unit-based committee represents a long-term commitment for the members. A 6-month timeframe is necessary for implementation, and then another 3 to 6 months is needed to revise and work out details after the new roles are in place and the staff are working together as a team. During the 12 months, there must be a centralized method of bringing issues forward for discussion. Staff may need to be compensated for the time spent in committee work to maintain the active participation necessary on a long-term basis. The committee may meet biweekly for the first month or so, until some implementation begins, and then may move to a monthly meeting. Eventually, as revision times come around, the group can meet only as needed.

There may be other short-term task forces or other committees that evolve from the work of the steering committee. Several units developed staff interviewing committees when the time came to hire staff for the new roles of patient care technician and patient support attendant. A case management committee may be formed as more RNs become case managers. Eventually, there may be several key ongoing committees on the unit. Some examples are a clinical practice committee, a professional practice committee, and a continuous improvement committee. The chairs from each of these committees have membership on the unit steering committee. The unit steering committee may eventually replace any organized management team meetings that existed before on the unit, indicating full inception of the group governance model. At this point, the unit would be managed by a committee that had both staff and management membership providing equal input. This also would indicate full inception of a group governance model.

THE 5 EAST UNIT COORDINATOR'S PERSONAL EXPERIENCE

The 5 East unit coordinator accepted this project and the ensuing role with some concrete plans in mind. She found it helpful that she personally had some ambivalent feelings about the entire change because, by not being totally and overly positive about the impending change and by sharing her own concerns, she was able to hear others' feelings of concern and then keep the focus on actions rather than simply complaining. She verbalized that, had she been overly positive in her own feelings, she would not have had the energy over the long term of the project to continue hearing other staff members' issues and concerns. She did think that she was able to remain open minded about the change, and this was well demonstrated in her well-designed plans for implementation and in the outcomes that occurred.

As the unit coordinator, her first consideration was how she would personally introduce the change on the unit. She was not threatened by change. However, she knew that some staff would be resistant to change because it is always easier to continue the current routine than to change it. She first reviewed all staff members and made concrete decisions as to which ones she would attempt to recruit initially. She considered that she would need to have at least one person from each current job category, that she would need to bring in those who might be most resistive as well as those who would be more positive, and that her key people would all need to be positive role models for their job categories. She recognized that after implementation the two new categories of workers would need to be included as well.

Her next decision was to determine how and when to have regular meetings and what topics would be planned for the agendas. She felt that attendance would be increased if there was a sense of normalcy to the meetings in that they would always occur on the same day, at the same time, and in the same place. She also implemented and encouraged the nurse manager to post a long-term schedule that stated meeting dates for the first 6 months of the implementation phase. About a week before each meeting, a reminder notice was posted with an agenda if there was a planned topic for that meeting.

The unit coordinator was well aware that before the change she would focus on two groups of staff: those who were resistant to any change at all, and those who were willing to become involved in the process. She needed to relate to both groups equally. Over time, she developed a consistent method of listening to those in the first group complain about what was happening or being planned, and always after listening she encouraged them to come to a steering committee meeting and voice their concerns directly and formally. She spent a lot of time with this group, assuring these people that they would not be disciplined or viewed negatively if they were vocal about their issues. She also had to spend a lot of time with this group explaining what was occurring in steering committee meetings and clarifying the rumor mill. Over time, she was instrumental in getting these staff members either to begin attending meetings or to attend when the topic was of great concern to them. With the second group, she provided information, clarification, and encouragement also to work with the first group. The second group was more consistent in attending meetings and assisted with actual decision making.

Once implementation occurred, the unit coordinator sometimes needed to make strong statements to the more resistant people to stop complaining and start showing support because they had been given the opportunity to take part and had chosen not to do so. She felt strongly that the new staff needed support from everyone, including the more resistant staff, once they joined the unit. She consistently provided the message throughout the process that the change was inevitable and that the ability of staff to participate in the planning and implementation process made the change controllable. Many of the more resistive staff believed that if they complained long and hard enough, management and administration would terminate the project.

Soon after full implementation, the unit coordinator became involved in issues related to role clarification for the new staff. The nonprofessional staff needed more clearly defined information about their day-to-day functioning. The unit was evolving from a mostly professional and licensed staff with experience functioning in more of a group governance model, so that explicit directions had not been necessary. As the staff spent more time verbalizing what was not working with the new roles, the coordinator's role became one of facilitator to encourage them to identify clearly in a formal way what worked and what did not. She then moved the staff toward identifying what would work and encouraged them to become part of the solution rather than continue their complaining.

The staff in the second, more positive group began to be helpful after implementation. They were always able to provide assistance and to role model the concept of identifying solutions and trying them. Because they were more positive, they always believed that a solution was possible and that the issues were temporary.

In summary, the unit coordinator believed that, if the person in the role anticipates that he or she might become a scapegoat for the negative feelings of others and if the person takes things personally, the role can become uncomfortable. She found it helpful to think this through and to design a clear plan to use when the going got tough. Rather than take comments personally, she continually refocused and encouraged persons who complained to verbalize their concerns. She encouraged the persons with negative attitudes to attend meetings and formally express their views. She did not get drawn into the complaining but always reminded staff members that changing course was not a negotiable option. She also shared with them that she, too, initially had ambivalent feelings about different components of the project. She stressed, however, that staff had control over creating the plan that would make the change work for them in the best way possible if they became involved in the restructuring process.

CONCLUSION

Introducing group governance in accordance with the UMC model provided a structured mechanism for staff to begin functioning in a group governance mode. This long-term project allowed sufficient time for most staff to work through change and to experience the results of group governance.

Once the model is in place, it can be reactivated for any other type of future changes for which a unit may plan. Examples might include implementing a new clinical program, implementing a new patient assignment method, and planning a major unit remodeling or a move to a new location. The nurse manager will never again feel entirely alone when a major project is introduced. One simply activates a special unit steering committee with a unit coordinator.

CHAPTER

14

Restructured Unit Management

Theresa Grzyb-Wysocki and JoAnne Schnepp

Chapter Objectives

1. To describe the new nurse manager role in a restructured unit.
2. To describe the new reporting relationships.
3. To describe new roles created by restructuring unit management.

Restructuring the patient care delivery system has served as a vehicle to redesign traditional management roles and to introduce group governance concepts into unit management. The planning and implementation process is structured to involve staff and unit management in decision making. Staff members actively participate in creating new roles, altering existing systems, and problem solving operational issues that arise in response to the changes made in the unit's patient care delivery system.

NURSE MANAGER'S ROLE CHANGES WHEN A UNIT RESTRUCTURES

When a unit restructures, nurse managers are finding that their role is changing from a traditional manager to a facilitator and resource to staff.

Nurse managers are becoming aware that, to lead staff successfully in restructuring, they must change. This change process requires nurse managers to:

- assess their personal management style
- become more committed to nurturing a unit culture that promotes decentralized decision making and the empowerment of staff
- seek educational opportunities to acquire new management/leadership skills

Personal Management Style

Traditionally, managers influence others as a result of their position power. The organization gives nurse managers formal authority to plan, organize, lead, and control. Managers who have relied more heavily on formal power find the restructuring process at University Medical Center (UMC) more threatening than those who have already developed a more participatory style.

In adult health services, two nurse managers who participated in the Differentiated Group Professional Practice Research Project introduced group governance concepts over a 5-year period. These nurse managers had already successfully worked through the process of changing from a traditional to a more participatory management style. In contrast, two other nurse managers of restructured units were more traditional. They had not been involved in the development of unit group governance. One of the nurse managers was new to the organization. This manager did not have an opportunity to develop a relationship with the work group before the implementation of restructuring but was hired at the completion of the planning phase.

It is not surprising that observable differences were found between the two groups of nurse managers. The two with more participatory managers approached committee participation with less anxiety. They were able to organize groups and to facilitate group process with greater skill. One nurse manager utilized the existing unit committee structure to plan new staffing patterns, specify work flow, and prepare for staff participation in new employee selection. The more traditional managers did not have an existing framework established for group decision making. They also had staffs with limited experience in group problem solving and minimal skill in utilizing a group interactive format for resolving unit problems. Staff on these units were less empowered and did not view the planning process as an opportunity to redesign the care delivery system and to improve the quality of patient care.

New Management Skills

Nurse managers may need to learn new skills to be successful in restructuring. In planning an educational program for nurse managers, one should consider including skill training in consensus building, conflict resolution through mediation, and facilitation strategies to work with task forces and committee structures.

Consensus Building

Restructuring the patient care delivery system requires many decisions. These decisions can be made solely by nurse managers. The nurse manager can seek input from the staff for him or her to make the decision, or the manager can set up a committee or a task force that is delegated with the authority to make decisions. If decision making is to be done by committee, the nurse manager will need to learn facilitation skills to assist group leaders and committees with consensus-based decision making.

As a group, nurse managers at UMC were not skilled in making consensus-based decisions. Because this type of decision making has not been the dominant style for the division of patient care services, it is not surprising that many nurse managers have not developed these skills. However, as more directors and nurse managers model these behaviors, there is growing awareness by the leadership group that education is needed in this area.

Conflict Resolution through Mediation

Nurse managers also need to develop basic mediation skills to be able effectively to work with groups and to coach group leaders in handling controversial issues. In mediation, the mediator usually does not make the decision; rather, the mediator facilitates the identification of interests, the formulation of compromises, and the evolution of a mutual agreement.

In general, most nurse managers do not possess sophisticated mediation skills. They need to participate in a practical training program that provides simulated learning through role playing in a small group context. Unfortunately, it is not easy to find training programs that meet these objectives. Most programs focus on providing experience in resolving simple two person conflict situations. Therefore, the nursing leadership team may need to work closely with the educator who is responsible for developing the training program to ensure that the conflict simulations used in the program are more representative of real-world situations.

Creating a Climate for Nurse Management Sharing

Nurse managers can learn from each other. Managers who are more participatory and have been working with staff to develop a committee structure for decision making should be encouraged to share experiences and strategies with the other managers. At first, the more traditional and controlling managers may be reticent to ask their colleagues specific questions. Although they may possess knowledge of group dynamics, they may not know how to translate this theory into practice. Gradually, if time is provided for sharing and if their colleagues are encouraged to describe in detail how they approach group process and committee participation, many of the how to questions will be answered. In addition, the group can be supportive of the more traditional nurse manager who makes attempts to use group decision making. Group members can listen to strategy, offer suggestions, and provide encouragement and support. Nurse managers who are more participatory know that it is not easy to change one's personal management style. At the same time, however, they are able to acknowledge that they have reaped great benefits from expending energy to change their own management style. They have had the vision to develop the skills to lead the way.

COPING WITH RADICAL CHANGE

Restructuring introduced new roles into the patient care delivery system. As each unit adjusted to the role changes, it did not take long for responsibility and accountability issues to surface. A lack of role clarity and poorly defined lines for communication resulted in confusion, the development of turf battles, and poor morale.

The staff of a newly restructured unit need time to come to grips with the fact that restructuring is here to stay. They have to work through the process of releasing the old pattern of patient care delivery before they are able to take ownership for making restructuring work.

Unit Retreats

Two of the four medical-surgical units at UMC that have been restructured organized unit retreats to focus on delegation issues, strategies to improve assignment making, and the clarification of role relationships among the registered nurses (RNs), licensed practical nurses (LPNs), and patient care technicians (PCTs). It was inspiring to observe participatory management in operation as the nurse manager, assistant nurse managers, clinical specialists, human resource educator, and staff planned retreat activities. The retreat was held on 2 days. Half the staff were assigned to attend the first session and the other half attended the second session to provide for maximum staff participation while still caring for patients.

Staffing was indeed a challenge considering that on retreat days occupancy was high. Part-time staff volunteered to work extra time, and the float pool helped supplement a minimum number of core staff scheduled on retreat days. Nurse managers were motivated to make time for team building and group problem solving; therefore, they were quite persuasive and successful in securing supplemental staff. Feedback from unit staff and management indicates that these retreats were significant turning points in restructuring for their units. Both work groups appear to be communicating more effectively and resolving unit operational problems.

Scope of Practice

Once RNs resolve their initial concerns about the adequacy of PCT training and have an opportunity to work side by side with PCTs to assess individual competency, mutual trust and respect begin to emerge. As the PCTs gain experience, they become more confident. It is at this stage that management should anticipate the emergence of scope of practice issues. One may find RNs allowing PCTs to perform tasks that they were not taught in the formal training program. An RN may demonstrate to a PCT how to do a new procedure and then may allow the PCT to perform the procedure independently or under his or her supervision. Physicians may also direct PCTs to perform tasks or procedures that are within the scope of practice of an RN or LPN but not within the scope of practice of a technical worker. Occasionally, managers may find PCTs independently performing tasks that are the responsibility of RNs, emergency medical technicians, and/or respiratory therapists.

In response to questions from PCTs, charge nurses, and nurse managers, a task force was formed to assess the situation and develop a statement on PCT scope of practice (Exhibit 14–1). This statement was designed to clarify scope of practice and to give notice to health care providers that they will be disciplined for violations of scope of practice.

The task force also provided a description of situations that are prone to cause role confusion and scope of practice problems. Health care workers frequently are not knowledgeable about the tasks within the scope of practice of these new multiskilled technical workers. In addition, a university setting has faculty and staff who are recruited from other parts of the country. They are not always familiar with the licensing laws for other health care workers in the state in which they are now working.

Exhibit 14–1 PCT Scope of Practice

> The purpose of this statement is to clarify both the PCT role and the relationship between licensed care providers (RNs, LPNs, physicians, respiratory therapists, etc.) and PCTs. PCTs are to deliver care in accordance with their PCT training. They may not perform skills, tasks, or duties that are not within the specific scope as detailed in the job description and the skills list. A skill learned during the performance of another role or in other educational training programs that is not in the PCT role may not be performed by a PCT. For example, an emergency medical technician performing as a PCT may have experience at bagging patients receiving supplemental oxygen, but he or she may not do so as a PCT because the PCT scope of practice does not permit administration of any medications such as oxygen.
>
> If a physician, nurse, or other health care provider requests a PCT to perform a skill, task, or duty outside the specific PCT role, the PCT must decline to perform the duty. The PCT must report any such instance to his or her immediate supervisor so that there can be follow-up clarification of the PCT role with the provider. If the PCT performs outside the role even if under the order and supervision of a licensed care provider, disciplinary action will occur. Disciplinary actions can affect both the delegating care provider and the PCT.

New Reporting Relationships

Restructuring not only introduced new roles into the existing patient care delivery system, but also altered traditional reporting relationships. Before restructuring, the housekeeper reported to an environmental services supervisor, the transporter reported to a supervisor in transportation, and so on. After restructuring, the functions of a group of workers from several different departments were combined to create a new multipurpose worker who now reports to the nurse manager. The day-to-day supervision and monitoring of work performance is delegated by the nurse manager to a shift charge nurse.

Changes in the Charge Nurse Role

The charge nurse role significantly changed when patient support attendants (PSAs) and PCTs started working on the units. In retrospect, the magnitude of this change was seriously underestimated. Insufficient time had been given to preparing this important group for the major changes in their role. Therefore, charge nurses were inadequately prepared to cope with new staffing issues, to modify routine assignment patterns, to assist the new multiservice workers with priority setting, or to monitor the quality of work performance.

Staffing

One of the first signs indicating that the charge nurses were not adequately prepared for the new roles occurred when a PSA called in sick and the staffing office clerk was not able to replace the PSA with float pool staff. The charge nurse simply accepted this information. Off-duty PSAs were not called to determine whether they would come in to work an additional shift. Neither the unit's nurse manager nor the clinical supervisor was called to help solve the problem. The problem was ignored, and this resulted in the patients not receiving housekeeping services for a 24-hour period.

On some units, charge nurses had to be reminded to check on the adequacy of PSA staffing. They were accustomed to someone else being responsible to ensure that there was a sufficient number of support workers to provide services to patients.

Assignment Making

PSA assignment making also proved to be a new challenge for charge nurses. Even though the unit's patient care restructuring (PCR) steering committees developed unit-specific work flow plans for the PSA and PCT duties, some unanticipated lessons were learned when problems in the quality of housekeeping services began to surface in the first few months after restructuring.

The first lesson learned illustrates the importance of the charge nurse checking to ensure that each PSA rotates periodically between performing the housekeeping services and the dietary and transportation activities. If staff do not rotate, they will not maintain their competence in performing all aspects of their role. This happened to PSA staff on one unit because the PSAs were allowed to choose which duties they would perform each day. In this particular case, the PSA who originally came from the environmental services department selected the housekeeping duties; the other PSA who routinely worked the day shift came from the transportation department and performed the dietary and transporting activities. Quality problems frequently arose when the PSA who was most experienced in housekeeping had a day off. The other PSAs were then responsible for doing housekeeping. They lacked experience and were not skilled in performing these duties.

The second unanticipated negative learning situation illustrates the impact of interruptions on the quality of work performance. In this situation, transportation was an underlying factor. Units with a high volume of transportation requests may not have sufficient staffpower to meet these requests if the requests occur simultaneously. At these peak workload times, the charge nurse may need to direct the PSA assigned to housekeeping to perform a transport. These interruptions may result in delays in cleaning patient rooms; but they also may cause the PSA to forget to complete essential steps in the cleaning process. After several patient complaints about the quality of housekeeping services in which interruptions were found to be a contributing factor, charge nurses have been encouraged to communicate clearly to unit staff that they should not ask the PSA assigned to housekeeping to perform other tasks. It is essential for the charge nurse to provide staff assistance in setting priorities and to explore other options for accomplishing the work.

Priority Setting

Charge nurses also were not prepared for the degree of assistance that they would have to provide to PCTs and PSAs in setting priorities. Although the roles of these new workers were described as multiskilled, unit management did not anticipate the potential for simultaneous demands for different services. Initially, charge nurses did not see the need to monitor the work flow of PCTs and PSAs. However, when they observed that these new employees were becoming stressed and frustrated, they became more aware that they needed to intervene and play an active role in assisting these new workers in sorting out what to do first.

For example, when a PCT was bathing a patient and the unit assistant informed the PCT that there was an order for blood work, the PCT frequently stopped giving the bath and went to draw the blood on another patient. To the PCT, drawing blood obviously was a higher priority than completing the patient's bath. Phlebotomy is a highly technical skill, and the PCTs have had a tendency to view this task as the most important aspect of their role. Therefore, it is not surprising that they would choose blood drawing as the greatest priority in these situations. They need the assistance of an RN or the charge nurse to help them learn when the blood work is a priority and when the procedure could wait until the bath is completed.

Similar problems occurred with PSAs. Because many PSAs did not have hospital housekeeping experience before being employed as PSAs, they had difficulty making decisions between continuing routine cleaning versus stopping to clean vacated rooms when there were few empty beds to receive admissions. The concept of a stat clean was not clearly understood by some of the new support workers. They had difficulty understanding that the dirty room needed to be cleaned right away because a patient needed to be transferred out of the post anesthesia recovery unit (PACU).

Even though this concept had been explained in the training program, they were unable to see why the PACU could not wait until the routine cleaning was completed before they cleaned the vacated rooms.

Charge nurses played an important role in helping PSAs see the larger picture and gain awareness that the decisions made regarding cleaning rooms can create bottlenecks in other departments (e.g., PACU, emergency departments, and special procedure rooms). PSAs have been able to become more flexible in adjusting their work plans to meet the changing demands for patient bed placement.

Monitoring the Quality of Work Performances

In the planning phase of restructuring, the process for monitoring the quality of work performance was not as clearly defined as it should have been. When the first units were restructured, systems had not been well developed to monitor all aspects of job responsibilities. In general, the development of quality monitoring has been an evolutionary process. Nurse managers and managers from the ancillary departments have had to work together to define interdisciplinary standards to assess staff performance. They also had to develop mechanisms for data collection and review of findings.

Charge nurses did not expect to be involved in the actual monitoring of how these new workers performed their tasks. The charge nurses thought that the other departments would continue to monitor quality as they did before restructuring. Even though other departments were still involved in quality monitoring, the degree of involvement and how it was to occur would change.

Some charge nurses were not enthusiastic about having the assistant director of environmental services come to their unit to teach them informally the key areas to examine to evaluate the quality of PSA work performance in cleaning a patient room. For example, they were instructed to check the vents for dust, the draperies for missing hanging pins, the toilet plumbing for lime build-up, and so forth. Although in the past they had been making personal judgments about the adequacy of housekeeping services, now they were being told that it was their responsibility to ensure that specific standards of work performance are achieved. It was no longer someone else's problem. It was their problem to solve.

Many charge nurses have not positively accepted these new responsibilities. Some have verbalized that they were already overworked and that now administration was asking them to take on even more. Over time, however, there have been signs that they are adjusting and are more involved in monitoring quality.

Impact on Supplemental Staffing

Charge nurses were not the only group to be significantly affected by restructuring. Initially, the staffing clerks would suggest replacing a PSA with a PCT, or vice versa. Although the staffing office staff had attended the general orientation on restructuring, their behavior indicated that they did not understand the significant differences between the two new roles. They needed some reeducation on which aspects of each role overlap and which aspects are unique to each role. The most important thing that they needed to understand, however, was that when a charge nurse indicates that a PSA is needed, a PSA is indeed needed, and the staffing clerk cannot substitute another type of worker for the multiple-skilled worker.

Supplemental staffing is critical to the success of restructuring. Renting an agency PSA or PCT for a shift is not an option. Because these workers are multiskilled, there are several functions that may not be done if they are replaced by the wrong category of worker.

In addition, as restructuring progresses in an institution, it may not always be possible to ask laboratory to provide back-up assistance with phlebotomy or to call environmental services for the names of per diem housekeepers who may be willing to pick up an extra shift. Ancillary departments have decreased the number of employees in their departments, and the extra personnel are just not there to help in an emergency.

Nurse managers and directors also have been reluctant to ask for assistance. They have developed a sense of pride in what they have been able to achieve by taking on these additional support and technical functions. All internal options are explored before a call is placed to another department for assistance. In planning for restructuring, however, it is important to discuss options for assistance from other departments when internal resources are exhausted. Patient care cannot be jeopardized.

Determining the right number of PSAs and PCTs for the float pool has continued to be an elusive estimation dilemma at UMC. As more units are restructured, the demand for replacement and augmentation increases. Employees initially employed in the float pool frequently request transfer to unit positions when new units open or when vacancies occur. There has also been a fairly high turnover rate in these two groups of workers as a result of absenteeism. Careful study and analysis of supplemental staffing needs are essential to ensure a sufficient number of trained, supplemental staff for all shifts and on weekends.

RESTRUCTURING UNIT MANAGEMENT

Staff at UMC have been challenged with radical change in the patient care delivery system. They have demonstrated that they are adaptable, resilient, and innovative in coping with change. However, restructuring is an ongoing process, so that most recently the leadership team in patient care services made the decision to restructure unit management.

Before Restructuring

Before restructuring, unit management consisted of a nurse manager, three to four assistant nurse managers for the different shifts, and charge nurses. The nurse manager has 24-hour responsibility for providing patient care services and managing unit personnel. Nurse managers delegated selected personnel management functions to the shift assistant nurse manager (e.g., counseling/discipline and performance evaluation). On some units, assistant nurse managers are responsible for developing the schedule, whereas on other units there are scheduling committees that prepare the schedule for nurse manager approval. Frequently, assistant nurse managers have been delegated responsibility for coordinating the continuous improvement activities. On all units, however, they carry out the charge nurse functions on a routine basis. Experienced RNs usually only assume the charge nurse functions in the absence of an assistant nurse manager.

Beliefs As the Foundation for Restructuring Unit Management

Restructuring unit management at UMC was strongly influenced by an evolving vision of patient care services. The first belief in this vision is the desire to redirect all division energies to becoming more patient centered. Therefore, in restructuring unit management roles the concept of patient-centered care is an underlying driving force.

Another belief or principle that influenced the direction in restructuring was the desire to create a management structure to empower staff through participation in unit group governance. A traditional bureaucratic structure is not conducive to promoting the development of autonomy, commitment, and involvement of the staff.

The third principle is closely related to the second but is slightly different. This belief is based on the assumption that simple is better and that it is desirable to reduce the multiple layers within unit decision making. The model of nurse manager through assistant nurse manager to staff may actually be a barrier to the further development of group governance. Group governance models are based upon the use of committee structures for decision making with delegated authority from the nurse manager.

The final belief that influenced unit management restructuring was the belief that care must be cost effective. Therefore, the challenge in redesign was to create a new, more effective management structure but at the same time to reduce or minimize the rise in the indirect cost of unit management.

Redesign of the Assistant Nurse Manager Role

After much discussion and debate at a retreat, the patient care leadership group (nurse managers, educational coordinator, directors, and vice president) made the decision to restructure the assistant nurse manager role. The decision had significant role change implications for assistant nurse managers, nurse managers, and staff. To facilitate implementation of the change, three task forces were established.

The first task force was charged with developing a job description and performance standards for a new unit leadership role that focused more upon the clinical management of patient care. Volunteers were solicited from the assistant nurse managers. The director of nursing resources coordinated the group process. Drafts were presented to the patient care leadership group for input and final approval.

Exhibit 14–2 is a summary of the essential functions for the new clinical nurse leader role. It is important to note that, when the task force of assistant nurse managers began working on the new job description, they initially had difficulty in envisioning a role without traditional personnel management functions. Like nurse managers who are more controlling in their management style, some assistant nurse managers verbalized great concern that they would be losing power. Some questioned whether they would be effective in working with staff without formal position power. Others seemed less threatened and appeared relieved that they would no longer be responsible for counseling/discipline and performance evaluation.

Performance Evaluation Support

The second task force was established to revise the Clinical Nurse I and II performance standards and to develop tools to support the nurse manager in the evaluation process. This task force was also interested in promoting some form of peer review to further the development of unit group

Exhibit 14–2 Clinical Nurse Leader Job Responsibilities

Essential functions

1. Uses effective communication skills to facilitate the delivery of patient care and to enhance customer satisfaction.
2. Consistently performs nursing process according to patient age and unit standards. Assessments include biophysical, psychosocial, environmental, self-care, and educational needs.
3. Consistently documents all aspects of care on appropriate documentation forms.
4. Demonstrates effective team-building/leadership skills.
5. Demonstrates fiscal responsibility in decision making.
6. Effectively fulfills the charge nurse role when assigned.
7. Participates in evaluation of current nursing practice to improve quality and appropriateness of patient care.
8. Involves patient/family in development of the plan of care, including discharge planning and education, and documents appropriately.
9. Manages care and promotes customer satisfaction.
10. Coordinates unit functions and resources.
11. Promotes professional development and continuous improvement.
12. Performs unit-specific roles/duties.
13. Establishes and achieves professional goals jointly set with supervisor.
14. Complies with departmental and/or hospital rules and regulations regarding absenteeism, tardiness, dress code, and the like.

governance as well as to provide nurse managers with input on staff performance from all shifts. A staff feedback tool (Exhibit 14–3) was developed by the task force for nurse managers to use to gather input from staff for performance evaluations.

Because there are only three units at UMC that have had experience with some form of peer review, nurse managers will be able to phase in the use of staff input into the evaluation process. The concept of peer review can be threatening to staff. They need time to discuss the issue and to develop unit-specific standards to regulate the process. Once the peer review process is operationalized on each unit, a performance standard will be added to the performance evaluation to hold staff accountable for providing staff input.

In the near future, all RNs and clinical nurse leaders will be expected to provide the nurse manager with feedback on staff performance. This information plus chart audits and a self-evaluation will assist nurse managers in determining ratings on criteria. Individual scores will then be entered into a new computer program that was developed with the assistance of information systems services staff to generate a composite score.

Exhibit 14–3 Staff Feedback Tool

Your feedback is very important to a fair and equitable performance evaluation for your peers. Participation in this process is an expectation of your role and a standard of performance. (VII,3)

INSTRUCTIONS:

- PLEASE COMPLETE AND RETURN TO NURSE MANAGER BY ______________
- DO NOT FILL IN SHADED AREAS. PLACE A CHECK MARK IN THE MOST APPROPRIATE BOX FOR EACH CRITERION.
- SECTION VI IS ONLY FOR CN IIs WHO ARE IN CHARGE.

THIS INFORMATION AND RESPONSES ARE CONFIDENTIAL FOR USE BY NURSE MANAGER ONLY. NOT TO BE VIEWED BY EMPLOYEE BEING EVALUATED.

I. USES EFFECTIVE COMMUNICATION SKILLS TO FACILITATE THE DELIVERY OF PATIENT CARE AND ENHANCE CUSTOMER SATISFACTION.	Not Applicable	Not consistent in this area, needs growth	Consistently does this, meets standards	Is very good, a resource for staff	Is excellent, leads unit in this area
1. Delivers care in a manner that supports excellence in customer satisfaction.					
2. Deals with interpersonal problems directly and in private.					
3. Provides care while respecting patient's dignity and providing for their safety and rights to privacy.					
4. Demonstrates positive communication/problem solving skills.					

II. CONSISTENTLY PERFORMS NURSING PROCESS ACCORDING TO PATIENT AGE AND UNIT STANDARDS. ASSESSMENTS INCLUDE BIOPHYSICAL, PSYCHOSOCIAL, ENVIRONMENTAL, SELF-CARE, AND EDUCATIONAL NEEDS.

1. Assesses and reassesses patient as indicated by unit standards and patient conditions.					
2. Recognizes and anticipates changes in patient status based on interpretation of assessment findings and diagnostic findings.					

continues

Exhibit 14–3 continued

	Not Applicable	Not consistent in this area, needs growth	Consistently does this, meets standards	Is very good, a resource for staff	Is excellent, leads unit in this area
3. Plans care for patients based on assessments, standards of care, and patient/family educational needs and by incorporating interdisciplinary information.					
4. Initiates, implements, and revises applicable critical pathways, standards of care, protocols, and procedures within guidelines.					
5. Implements care based on established interdisciplinary plan of care.					
6. Demonstrates expertise in performing technical nursing skills following established protocols and plans of care.					
7. Evaluates and revises plan of care/discharge plan based on patient condition and progress toward desired patient outcomes.					

IV. DEMONSTRATES EFFECTIVE TEAM-BUILDING/LEADERSHIP SKILLS.

1. Effectively delegates to all levels of staff based on their scope of practice, job description, abilities, and patient/unit needs.					
2. Participates in the orientation of new staff/students. (FOR CN IIs ONLY)					
3. Willingly acts as a resource for coworkers.					
4. Actively supports and participates in planned change.					
5. Is effective in setting priorities and organizing care to support unit functioning.					
6. Actively participates in the accomplishment of unit and hospital goals in a positive, professional manner.					

continues

Exhibit 14–3 continued

V. DEMONSTRATES FISCAL RESPONSIBILITY IN DECISION MAKING.	Not Applicable	Not consistent in this area, needs growth	Consistently does this, meets standards	Is very good, a resource for staff	Is excellent, leads unit in this area
1. Supports budgeted staffing guidelines while supporting patient safety.					
2. Delivers care in a manner that appropriately conserves resources (i.e., linen and supplies).					
3. Organizes care to complete duties within designated shift time.					

VI. EFFECTIVELY FULFILLS THE CHARGE NURSE ROLE WHEN ASSIGNED.

THIS SECTION FOR CN IIs ONLY. DO NOT USE FOR CN Is.

1. Demonstrates effective decision-making and organizational skills in response to changes in unit operations and emergency situations.					
2. Communicates effectively with other charge nurses and ancillary staff to facilitate patient care.					
3. Keeps nurse manager informed of relevant patient care and staffing issues.					
4. Staffs according to budgeted staffing guidelines.					
5. Prioritizes, monitors, and delegates tasks to all staff.					

continues

Exhibit 14–3 continued

VII. PARTICIPATES IN THE EVALUATION OF CURRENT NURSING PRACTICE TO IMPROVE QUALITY AND APPROPRIATENESS OF PATIENT CARE.	Not Applicable	Not consistent in this area, needs growth	Consistently does this, meets standards	Is very good, a resource for staff	Is excellent, leads unit in this area
1. Actively supports the development, evaluation, and revision of standards of care, critical pathways, and protocols.					
2. Is actively involved in data collection for the CI process.					
3. Participates in the staff feedback process.					
4. Actively supports in interdisciplinary approach to the planning and provision of care.					
5. Protects professional practice and the patient's safety by recognizing and reporting substandard or unsafe practice to nurse manager/charge nurse.					

NAME OF STAFF MEMBER BEING REVIEWED: ______________________

NAME OF STAFF MEMBER FILLING OUT FORM:

____

Administrative Secretarial Support

As the other task forces at UMC were working on their projects, a third group was organized to write duties and responsibilities for a new secretarial support role (Exhibit 14–4). With the change in the assistant nurse manager position, which previously provided administrative support to the nurse manager, it was decided to replace this administrative assistance with nonnursing personnel.

Nurse managers in adult health and women and children's services were motivated to secure the additional secretarial support because they have the majority of full-time equivalent (FTE) in the division of patient care services. They were able to fund four new positions (two for adult health and two for women and children's services) by contributing salary dollars from proposed unit budgets.

In the department of adult health services, it was decided that there would be a critical care secretary who would work for three nurse managers and a general medical-surgical care secretary who would work for four nurse managers. This method for dividing the workload was based on the number of FTEs and the assumption that these subdivisions may have similar issues and systems.

The administrative coordinator for each department will be responsible for the direct supervision of these secretaries. It is essential that communication and feedback between the nurse managers and the administrative coordinator occur frequently and openly to ensure timely feedback on performance to these new employees. Evaluation tools will be developed for this purpose.

The new secretaries will be responsible for cross-coverage. It is also anticipated that they will be working closely with each other to develop systems and to streamline the current practices. For these reasons, it will be advantageous to standardize unit systems.

It has been interesting to observe nurse managers and the administrative coordinator making preparations for the introduction of this new secretarial support worker. In the past, nurse manager support has been limited to typing; therefore, many managers have difficulty envisioning how to use a secretary. To remedy this problem, several administrative secretaries were asked to make a presentation to nurse managers. All found the class helpful. Some nurse managers have already incorporated some of the important tips on organizing and setting up filing systems into their daily routines.

In addition to office organization, nurse managers have also started to examine clinical and administrative systems. Because the evaluation pro-

Exhibit 14–4 Administrative Secretary Duties and Responsibilities

Purpose of Job: To provide secretarial support to assigned nursing areas.

Duties and Responsibilities:

1. Complies with departmental and/or hospital rules and regulations regarding absenteeism, tardiness, confidentiality, dress code, and the like.
2. Tabulates attendance records of staff for assigned areas. Tracks compliance with attendance policies and provides nurse manager with appropriate disciplinary forms when required (i.e., verbal, written, or final warning).
3. Collects or compiles preliminary copies of the unit's schedules, assembles and writes them into final form for approval by the nurse manager, and distributes them to the staff as required.
4. Develops tracking tools to monitor evaluation records for assigned areas. Notifies appropriate peers, charge nurses, and clinical supervisors that evaluations are approaching, supplies them with appropriate forms to submit their input, and assembles information and appropriate forms for the nurse manager in a timely fashion. Schedules employee and nurse manager appointments to go over the final evaluation.
5. • Maintains employee files (commendations, personnel action forms, disciplinary actions and evaluations, etc.) in the department and forwards appropriate documentation to human resources, nurse recruiting, and nursing information services.
   • Tracks individual use of education allowances and education leave days.
   • Verifies overtime log against time sheets and prepares time sheets for nurse manager's signature.
   • Maintains other unit logs. Collects and tabulates other data as required.
6. Provides support for unit meetings, including preparing agendas, posting notices, securing room schedules, and typing and distributing minutes.
7. Maintains an up-to-date mail distribution system of assigned units. Sorts and distributes mail for the staff.
8. Updates and distributes unit disaster call list quarterly and as needed.
9. Maintains bulletin boards for the nursing staff, presenting material in an organized style and updating with current information as appropriate.
10. Maintains schedule of reports that the nurse manager is responsible for preparing. Issues reminders and appropriate forms to facilitate the completion of each required report.
11. Provides general secretarial support, including photocopying, filing, and general typing as needed by the nurse manager.
12. Establishes and accomplishes goals jointly set with the immediate supervisor.
13. Maintains an organized, efficient work area, including computerized records. Exhibits a working knowledge of hospital routines and carries out duties in a manner that is perceived by others as pleasant, positive, professional, and in support of UMC's client relations program.
14. Carries out other secretarial duties as assigned.

cess is an area of major change and concern, nurse managers and the administrative coordinator have been spending time to identify key activities in the unit evaluation process that could be delegated to the new secretaries. In the past, assistant nurse managers distributed paperwork, monitored staff response, scheduled performance review conferences, and completed the necessary paperwork. Now nurse managers are developing a system in which the administrative secretary will be responsible for initiating the paperwork, organizing the feedback from staff for peer review, and scheduling performance review conferences.

In summary, the evaluation process is just one example of how nurse managers are planning to use their new administrative support workers. These workers have expertise in office organization and the development of administrative systems. It is anticipated that they can significantly reduce the amount of time that nurse managers devote to these activities.

CONCLUSION

Restructuring the patient care delivery system and unit management has been a challenge. All the upfront planning cannot prepare unit staff for the magnitude of change that they experience when the new system is operationalized.

The UMC experience has shown that nurse managers' management style influenced the restructuring process. Nurse managers who were more participatory and who had previously set up a committee structure for decision making were better prepared to redesign the delivery system. They were more skilled in facilitating group process and decision making by consensus. They also were more adept at mediating conflict situations that arose and required problem solving during implementation.

The leadership role of the charge nurse was also significantly changed as a result of restructuring. Although charge nurses were included in the planning process, there were some charge nurses who were not adequately prepared to cope with the day-to-day problems. They did not anticipate the scope of practice issues. On occasion, some were not proactive in assessing staffing needs and ensuring that there were sufficient staff to meet workload requirements. They learned the pitfalls of substituting other workers for the new multiskilled workers. Finally, charge nurses have had to revise their concept of monitoring the quality of work performance to include the monitoring of functions that have traditionally been the responsibility of ancillary departments.

Other patient care support systems have also been affected by PCR. The staffing office has expanded the float pool to include new multiskilled workers. Although it has been extremely difficult to predict the number of staff needed to fill the ever expanding demand, the staffing office continues to explore new approaches to meet supplemental needs.

Finally, because restructuring is ongoing, it was also important to examine the unit management structure to determine whether there were opportunities for redesign to promote the development of a professional practice model. After much discussion and debate, the patient care leadership group made the decision to eliminate the assistant nurse manager role. A new leadership role, called the clinical nurse leader, was created to enhance the management of patient care and to promote greater staff involvement in unit-based decision making. In addition, because assistant nurse managers had provided administrative support for nurse managers in personnel management, a second new role was created. The administrative secretary role was designed to assist the nurse managers with the paperwork associated with unit management. In the future, nonnurses will be used to provide administrative support to nurse managers.

CHAPTER

15

Comprehensive Recognition and Awards Program

Josephine Sacco Palmer

Chapter Objectives

1. To describe the significance of a comprehensive recognition and awards program.
2. To outline the benefits of reward programs to the health care facility and the employee.
3. To discuss strategies for recognition and methods to celebrate accomplishments.

INTRODUCTION

A comprehensive recognition and awards program was established early in the restructuring process to recognize contributions, celebrate accomplishments, and link rewards with performance.

SIGNIFICANCE OF RECOGNITION

Recognition promotes a positive environment in the work setting. Successful leaders in any profession or occupation have mastered, consciously or unconsciously, the art and techniques of motivating their people. They all hold a strong belief in recognition programs and techniques. Such programs are designed to foster morale, incentive, and esprit de corps through prompt, public recognition of the individual's achievements and acts of service. Research by management scholars and behavioral scientists, such as Herzberg and White, has substantiated the relationship among recognition, motivation, and job satisfaction. Herzberg's studies indicate that the factor with the highest percentage rate and frequency of response as a motivator is achievement.[1,2] Motivational factors most often lead to positive feelings. Failure to receive recognition has been associated with negative feelings.

Celebrations provide an opportunity to recognize achievements that are valued in the organizational culture. These events reinforce corporate commitment and can have an impact on employee behavior. Deal and Kennedy, addressing rites and rituals, stated, "Strong culture companies create a great deal of hoopla when someone does well and exemplifies the values the company seeks to preserve. The best-run firms always make certain that everyone understands why someone gets a reward, whether it's trivial or grand ceremony."[3(p.72)] As Peters and Waterman describe, "The systems in the excellent companies are not only designed to produce lots of winners, they are constructed to celebrate the winning once it occurs. Their systems make extraordinary use of non-monetary incentives. They are full of hoopla."[4(p.58)] These celebrations can be formal or informal.

Just as national celebrations are important reminders of sacrifices and struggles, organizations celebrate for a variety of reasons. Reasons for organizational celebrations at University Medical Center (UMC) during patient care restructuring (PCR) were the following:

- accomplishments of organizational change
- recognition of people
    1. teamwork
    2. team successes
    3. individual achievements
- acknowledgment of special events (e.g., the kickoff date)

Administrative leaders at UMC establish the corporate culture and set the stage for what is valued. They model their commitment to the success of the project and of UMC to employees through their sincere and enthusiastic participation in completion ceremonies and through the awarding of certificates of recognition to staff. This involvement and visibility is an opportunity to provide personal encouragement and attention to staff—

focusing energies and driving on UMC's visions and goals for PCR. When leaders say thank you, as UMC's senior vice president and vice president do at the completion ceremonies, they establish a human connection with hospital staff.

Cheerleading is a major part of a leader's function. As Kouzes and Posner state: "After all, leaders can't get extraordinary things done in organizations alone—they need the help of their teams. . . . Encouraging the heart is not only the process of recognizing individual achievements; it also includes celebrating the efforts of the entire group."[5(p.260)]

UMC'S PROGRAM FOR RECOGNITION

The Process

Strategies to consider when planning recognition events include the following:

- identification of occasions to celebrate, formally or informally
- selection of meaningful tokens of recognition
- recognition by the public
- selection of the time for greatest effect
- definition of ceremony program details
- selection of meaningful presenters

Identifying occasions to celebrate was considered early in the project. Change is difficult at best, and many staff members were not happy or enthusiastic about the idea. It was especially important to recognize staff members who from the beginning were willing to participate and go that extra mile. Both formal and informal occasions were needed to recognize accomplishments publicly. Occasions selected included completion ceremonies for PSAs, PCTs, and nurse case managers, and a variety of recognition events for task force members and administrators such as a Thanks-for-Giving brunch, a Groundbreakers Appreciation dinner, and a Patient Care Services banquet.

Completion Ceremonies

Well-known locations, established for presentations, were selected in which to conduct these ceremonies. Certificates of completion were designed and printed on parchment paper with the UMC gold-embossed seal signed by administration (Figure 15–1).

Figure 15–1 Certificate of completion. Courtesy of University Medical Center, Tucson, Arizona.

All the details for the ceremony were planned well in advance. This planning included date, time, program design and printing, room scheduling, photographer scheduling, and scheduling of caterers to provide refreshments for the reception after the ceremony. At UMC, the stage or room was set with flags of the United States and the state of Arizona, printed banners, and skirted tables. For the PCT ceremony, a special slide presentation was prepared to highlight the experiences of each class. The slide presentation was coordinated with music and required considerable advance preparation and scheduling with an audiovisual technician. Volunteers were identified to assist with distributing programs and serving refreshments. Before the ceremony, a class picture was taken. During the hour before the ceremony, the candidates were briefed on the conduct of the ceremony. Careful advanced planning minimizes unexpected problems and contributes to a smooth-flowing ceremony.

Timeliness is of the essence to achieve the greatest positive effect. The PSA completion ceremonies are normally scheduled on the last day of their 10-day training period, and the PCT completion ceremony is scheduled at the end of their 10-week training program. Four o'clock in the afternoon was selected by the students as the best time for most relatives and friends to attend. Family attendance was the most important factor in determining the best time of day. Typically the ceremonies were held at the end of the week, which lends a more festive atmosphere.

A typical completion ceremony agenda includes the following:

- welcome and introduction by program manager
- opening remarks by vice president
- congratulatory remarks by senior vice president
- recognition and awards
- congratulatory remarks by PCR educator
- closing remarks by program manager
- refreshments and socializing

These ceremonies have generated spectator interest from coworkers, staff members from ancillary and support departments, and nursing staff in patient care units. Celebrations empower those who attend and bond PCTs and PSAs with staff members of the health care teams they are joining. Families and friends of the PSAs and PCTs attend the completion ceremony and reception amid pictures, cheers, and tears. Some family and friends travel long distances to share in this proud moment, and they bestow hugs, kisses, and flowers to show their pride. There is a definite cordial and close feeling to the ceremonies. Proud staff RN preceptors, nurse managers, and department directors attend. The PCR educator often receives a standing ovation after her congratulatory comments. Candidates, families, and friends enjoy the opportunity to socialize with administration and staff. The ceremony promotes both group interaction and communication.

The nurse case managers' completion ceremony is held at the end of their 9-week education program. Each graduating individual is presented with a certificate of completion, an engraved pin (Figure 15–2), and a flower. The event is followed by group photographs and a reception. Members of their families and other staff also attend along with administration and management.

Employee Recognition Events

The task force Thanks-for-Giving brunch, conducted just before the Thanksgiving holiday, provides a formal method for top administration to recognize the contributions of all members of the PCR task force. The brunch consists of a full breakfast served on an elegantly decorated table complete with floral arrangements and candles. In the first year of the

Figure 15–2 Nurse case manager pin. Courtesy of University Medical Center, Tucson, Arizona.

project, the vice president who headed PCR presented each member with a humorous certificate of appreciation followed by a more formal certificate emphasizing each individual's contribution toward the project's success. In the second year the banquet was even more lavish, and each member was presented with a gift of an engraved desk clock wrapped in gold foil and embossed with words, *Thanks for your time.* This form of recognition has proven to be meaningful to all members of the task force, who put in both extra effort and many hours to ensure the success of the project.

Another formal event was designed to recognize patient care unit managers from the four demonstration units in phase I of PCR. The celebration was sponsored by the senior vice president and attended by all other vice presidents and directors in nursing administration. Formal invitations were issued to the Groundbreakers Appreciation dinner, which was held 7 months after implementation kickoff. A formal dinner preceded by a cocktail party was held at a country club. Spouses were also invited. After congratulations by the senior vice president, each assistant nurse manager received a certificate of appreciation. The nurse managers also received a special engraved plaque on which a gold shovel was affixed with the words *The Groundbreaker Award* (Figure 15–3). Photographs of all awardees were taken with the senior vice president. The senior vice president and vice president who were the administrative leaders of the project were in turn presented with a framed picture titled *PCR is Teamwork,* which was affixed to the engraved plaque, for their outstanding leadership (Figure 15–4).

UMC already had established an annual nurse awards ceremony during National Nurses Week, during which each unit selected nominees for nurse of the year awards in their specialty. This ceremony was expanded as a result of PCR and renamed the Patient Care Services banquet. The ancillary and support department directors were also recognized at this event for their support of the PCR project. Additionally, awards were established for PSA, PCT, and nurse case manager of the year.

Figure 15–3 Groundbreaker Award plaque. Courtesy of University Medical Center, Tucson, Arizona.

Figure 15–4 Award plaque for PCR administrative leaders. Courtesy of University Medical Center, Tucson, Arizona.

Informal Awards

Informal awards are numerous. For example, certificates of appreciation were presented to staff members who participated in the PCT and

PSA training. These staff members included staff nurse preceptors, staff nurse educators, and ancillary and support department training staff.

A key factor in the success of the PCR project has been the in-house training program for PCTs, in which staff RNs serve as lab instructors for various skill training. Four weeks of the 10-week training program are spent in on-the-job-training. Staff RNs serve as preceptors for each PCT during the 4-week period. The RNs participate in a special preceptorship training workshop before participating in the training activity. The RNs generally volunteer for preceptorship. They must go the extra mile, ensuring that the PCT training and skill levels meet all competency requirements while incorporating the PCT as a new team member on the unit. Certificates of appreciation (Figures 15–5 and 15–6) signed by the vice president and PCR program manager are presented to RNs who serve as skills label instructors and preceptors. The certificates are received in front of peers and are presented by the vice president or program manager.

Project Celebrations

Many celebrations are planned throughout the project. For example, the four demonstration units celebrated the 1-year postimplementation anniversary. The celebration was marked by a banner on each unit with the words *Congratulations, you made it happen!*, and pizza and soda for all staff members were served on all shifts. This informal party was provided to ensure that the staff realized that administration recognized all their efforts during the preceding 12 months to make PCR a success.

An institutionwide celebration was conducted on the kickoff date for each fully implemented unit. The celebration was intended to demonstrate to both the unit staff and the entire hospital that administration recognized their hard work and accomplishments. On these days, colored balloons were delivered to each unit undergoing restructuring. Colored balloons were also placed at the main lobby of the hospital and in the hospital cafeteria. Free popcorn was available for everyone in the cafeteria that day. Even members of the cafeteria staff wore the PCR celebration buttons. All PCTs and PSAs received a $1 gift certificate good for use at either the cafeteria or the night vending cart. Large, colorful posters on which *PCR is Teamwork* was written were placed on easels in strategic locations around the hospital. A banner with the words *Congratulations, you made it happen!* was hung on each patient care unit that had completed implementation. All members on the unit received a colorful "PCR is Teamwork" button (Figure 15–7) to include them in the celebration.

Being included leads to a sense of belonging and promotes team building and the sharing of common goals. Staff members who share the same

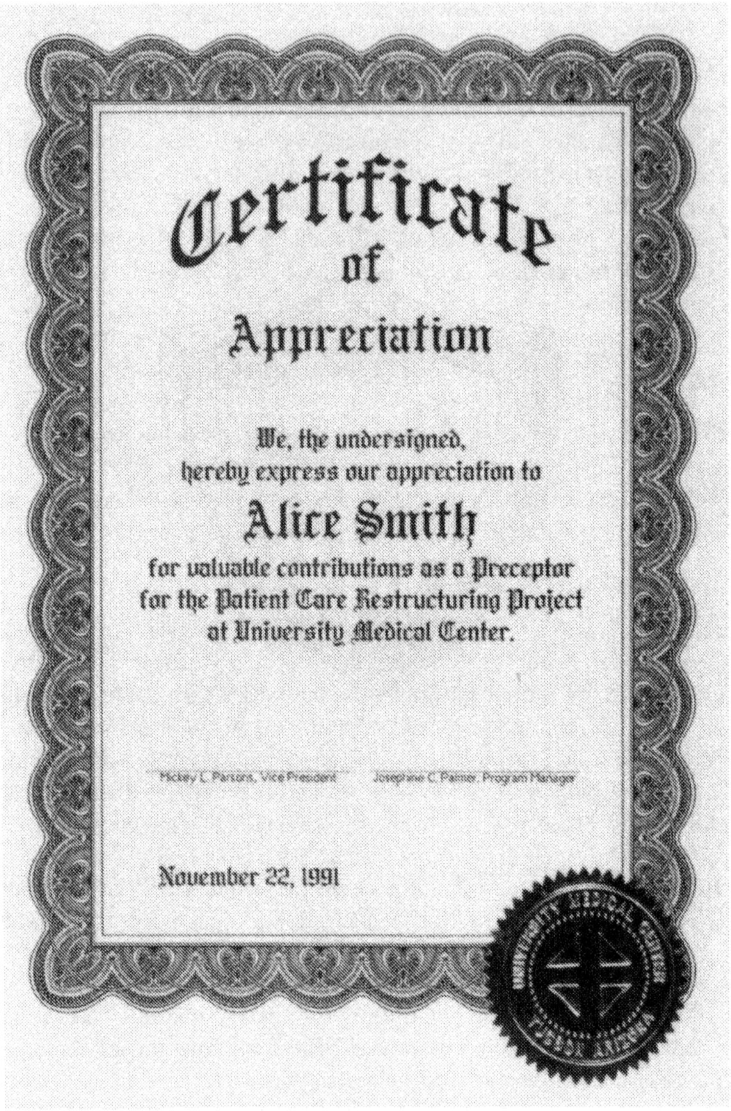

Figure 15–5 Certificate of appreciation for RNs serving as preceptors. Courtesy of University Medical Center, Tucson, Arizona.

---

goals are more likely to be supportive of one another. The decorations (balloons and posters) in the public areas of the hospital called attention to the unit's achievement and everyone was aware that something special had occurred in the hospital that day.

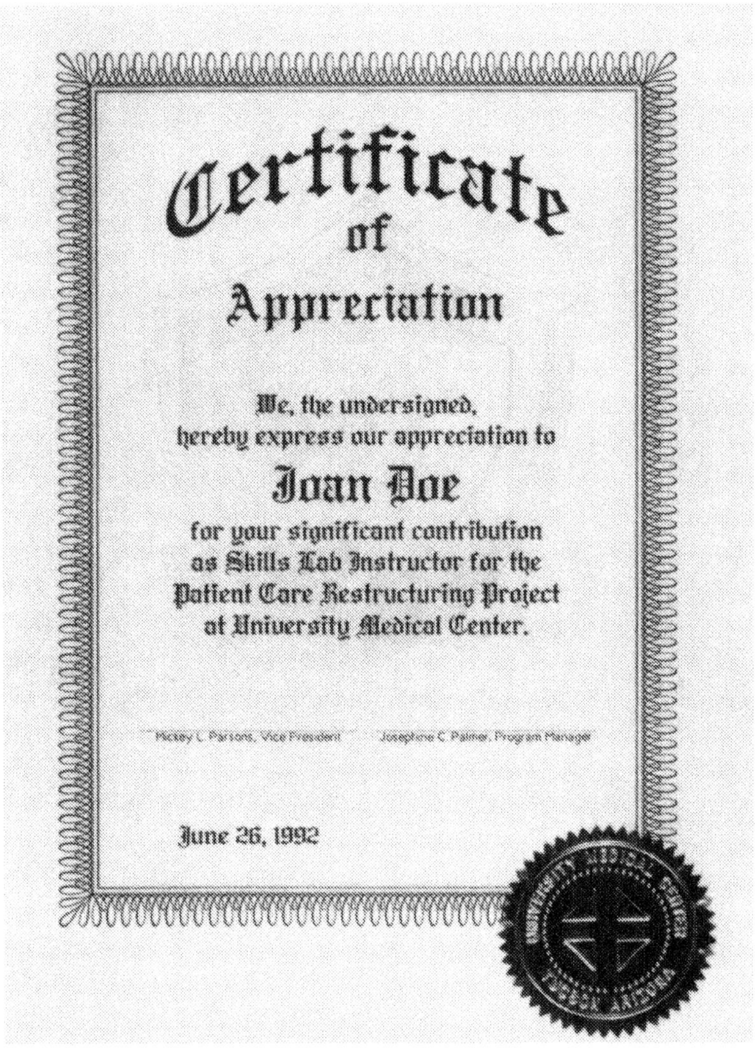

Figure 15–6 Certificate of appreciation for RNs serving as skills lab instructors. Courtesy of University Medical Center, Tucson, Arizona.

The very first kickoff celebration day was marked by task force members wearing the same "PCR is Teamwork" button with a blue ribbon attached with the words *Task Force*. All members of the task force received T-shirts that matched the buttons. The T-shirts were also worn the day of the first kickoff celebration. Members of the task force assisted in prepar-

Figure 15–7 "PCR is Teamwork" button. Courtesy of University Medical Center, Tucson, Arizona.

ing and delivering all the balloons that day. The day provided an opportunity for administration to demonstrate its appreciation, pride, and delight to the staff. The support resulted in an upbeat atmosphere on what might have otherwise been a stressful day for staff members as they formally transitioned into a new process.

BENEFITS TO THE HEALTH CARE FACILITY AND THE EMPLOYEE

A Focus on Key Values

UMC, as a teaching institution, places a high value on education. This emphasis is apparent in the large number of existing training and continuing education programs. Recognition and celebration ceremonies highlight the value UMC places on individuals taking the initiative to increase their personal education and attain new and varied skills. Key institutional values such as a strong customer service focus in the patient-centered care model are promoted at these times.

Promotion of Two-Way Communication

The completion ceremony provides an opportunity for trainees to speak directly to administration and peers alike. The initial contact promotes open communication from the beginning of employment and demonstrates that management wants to hear from these workers and be available to them. As PCR has evolved, many good ideas for improving operations have come directly from PSAs and PCTs. This process is a critical first step in promoting continued two-way communication and alleviates employee anxiety over sharing information and offering ideas for improvement.

Motivation toward Excellence

When the culture of an institution promotes and values excellence, a new employee will be motivated to meet those expectations. Team members are made to feel important through the recognition of accomplishments. They feel like winners. They also increase their self-esteem through this positive reinforcement. The training and completion ceremonies are mechanisms to stress that their best efforts are essential to meet the high standards expected of all health care team members. They are told that both their caring and their concern can make a major difference for a patient in the hospital. The PSAs and PCTs need to know that they, as individuals, can be successful within the institution. It is not unusual at the reception after a ceremony to hear comments such as, "We are going to do our very best for you" or "We are really going to work hard to make PCR a success for you." The incentive to continue to achieve is deeply rooted in the desire to make a difference. Knowing that there is meaning and purpose in one's work is important. Personal satisfaction is derived from our work. When we communicate the significance and meaning of organizational work, the team members can understand their importance and contribution. An attitude of commitment to excellence is what UMC administration strives to achieve, and that attitude is facilitated through recognition.

Increased Employee Commitment, Loyalty, and Retention

When an employee's actions and achievements are public, employees are more likely to become committed to a course of action that leads to positive behavior. According to Kouzes and Posner, "The small win process makes people feel like winners. In turn, people who feel like winners have a heightened interest in continuing with the journey."[5(p.226)] Public ceremony and presentations are tangible, undeniable forms of evidence of the institution's belief in the value of employee accomplishments.

Employee commitment cannot be bought with certificates, uniform emblems, and pins, but the psychological benefits of these tangible rewards make employees feel like winners. Winners will contribute in important ways to the success of this project. One PSA stated, "I know we are the first [class] so we are going to try hard so this [project] will work." The statement is a good example of an employee's personal dedication and sense of responsibility. Other PSAs were heard to say, "I am so proud. This is the first time I've ever graduated from anything and I'll really try hard to make this a success." People are willing to work hard when they are motivated and feel like winners.

During the formal awards and recognition ceremonies, PSAs and PCTs are awarded special uniform emblems with the job title (Figure 15–8). When anyone, staff or visitor, sees PSAs and PCTs wearing this emblem, the success in meeting the course requirements for that position is reinforced. An additional recognition for PSAs is a blue pouch designed to be worn around the waist (a fanny pack) imprinted with the title and the name of the hospital, which was also presented at the completion of their training. Through this token of recognition, the PSA and PCT affiliation with UMC is made visible. This visible identification with UMC serves to strengthen and build PSA and PCT personal commitment.

CONCLUSION

Kouzes and Posner state, "Making people's actions visible by publicizing and recognizing their work, strengthens others in two ways. First, it opens doors to potential new relationships because people are more aware of one another's contributions. Success is an attractive magnet for pulling people together and increasing their attachment to the project. Second, publicity calls attention to the significance of people's actions, creating both internal and external expectations that an action is worthy of their own and others' time and energy."[5(p.231)]

Figure 15–8 PSA and PCT uniform emblems. Courtesy of University Medical Center, Tucson, Arizona.

Recognition by the public is vanity, but it is also a deep desire of everyone. McCormick said, "How important to the human being is the eagle on the colonel's shoulder, the broad stripe of the admiral on his sleeve, and the pins worn by men on their lapels? Why not use these forces to advantage."[6(p.8)]

It is important to link recognition and celebration to accomplishments as both employer and employee benefit. Celebrating accomplishments together strengthens the feeling of belonging and increases commitment, loyalty, and retention. Celebrations also promote endurance during times of change and stress.

In health care, improving human relations with patients is stressed. It is imperative to show the same consideration for staff through recognition of their accomplishments.

NOTES

1. F. Herzberg, *The Managerial Choice: To Be Efficient and To Be Human* (Salt Lake City, Utah: Olympus, 1982).
2. B.L. White, *The Origins of Human Competence: The Final Report of the Harvard Preschool Project* (Lexington, Mass.: Lexington, 1979).
3. T.E. Deal and A.A. Kennedy, *Corporate Cultures, the Rites and Rituals of Corporate Life* (Reading, Mass.: Addison-Wesley, 1982).

4. T.J. Peters and R.H. Waterman, *In Search of Excellence, Lessons from America's Best-Run Companies* (New York, N.Y.: Warner, 1982).
5. J.M. Kouzes and B.Z. Posner, *The Leadership Challenge, How To Get Extraordinary Things Done in Organizations* (San Francisco, Calif.: Jossey-Bass, 1987).
6. C.P. McCormick, *The Power of People* (New York, N.Y.: Penguin, 1973).

CHAPTER

16

The Financial Planning Process

Lisa Sinclair Olson

Chapter Objectives

1. To describe the financial services department involvement in patient care restructuring and the structure of the program.
2. To analyze and report the process of full-time equivalent and dollar reallocation and analysis.
3. To illustrate the budget development process.
4. To recount the finance components of training for charging patients for restructured services.
5. To report on the development of the charging hierarchy.
6. To share the model for monitoring change on an ongoing basis.

Over the past decade, political philosophy regarding health care has resulted in increased competition, strained resources, and inadequate profits. As a result, the most complex and nationally challenging task is complete health care reform. For hospitals to remain viable within the industry, it is critical that new processes that secure or improve productivity be developed and implemented from within. Hospital administrators seek innovative approaches to cost containment. One of the most auspicious topics today among leaders in the health care industry is patient-centered care and work redesign. To date, University Medical Center (UMC) has restructured nine nursing units with more than 200 beds. The goals of this project are as follows: to maintain or enhance the quality of patient care and services, to address the labor shortage, to address cost containment and the annual rise in the cost of patient care services, and to maintain or enhance the satisfaction of all patient care providers in their job roles.

Throughout the planning, implementation, and evaluation phases, teamwork and excellent analytical skills are of paramount importance. Critical to the success of any such program is the financial management team. This chapter is designed to share information about the financial planning process as it relates to the work redesign of the first units restructured under the UMC model of patient care restructuring (PCR).

Restructured care delivery is accomplished when the nursing unit becomes patient centered. Three new roles are implemented. These are new care providers who report directly to the nurse manager. The patient support attendant (PSA) assumes the responsibilities of housekeeping, dietary, transportation, materials management, and other related duties as assigned. The other paraprofessional position created is the patient care technician (PCT). PCTs perform as multipurpose technical workers. Based upon licensure laws, the following ancillary services are provided:

- phlebotomies
- ECGs
- selected rehabilitation related skills
- selected respiratory therapy skills
- other nursing assistant functions as assigned

Registered nurse (RN) case managers plan and coordinate care for a designated group of patients in conjunction with physicians and other health care professionals.

The organizational culture changed as UMC departed from traditional management philosophy in the health care industry. Communication and education throughout the process aided in the success of this program.

STRUCTURE AND FINANCIAL ANALYST INVOLVEMENT

In year 1/phase I, two medical-surgical units and two pediatric units were restructured. Year 2/phase II restructuring consisted of two intermediate units, the postpartum unit, and the newborn nursery. Phase III implemented restructuring in the emergency services department. Additional clinical service areas scheduled for restructuring are labor and delivery, an additional adult medical-surgical unit, the bone marrow unit, two intensive care units, and the neonatal intensive care unit.

To facilitate continued discussion of the entire financial planning process, it is advantageous to begin with an overview of the key individuals and work groups involved in the overall restructuring process. The vice president of nursing and patient care services initiated and is responsible for directing the entire process. Overall goals and objectives are developed by the PCR steering committee. The steering committee consists of the following key individuals: the chief operating officer, the vice president of nursing and patient care services, the vice president of human resources, the vice president of financial services, and selected department directors. Status meetings are currently scheduled on a monthly basis but were more frequent in the early stages. From the steering committee, the PCR task force was developed. The task force meets semimonthly and includes the department directors listed above, nurse managers from departments to be restructured, managerial accounting staff, and other key employees from related areas. The task force is chaired by the vice president of nursing and patient care services. Functions include planning and implementation of the entire restructuring process. Individual work groups are organized as needed to address specific issues when they arise.

In conjunction with the above mentioned groups, a temporary department of PCR was established to meet the operational and training needs of the program. This department is separate from the staff development office and consists of two full-time equivalents (FTEs) as follows: the director, who has a nursing administration and education background; and an administrative assistant. Time requirements of the finance department increase as patient care units are about to enter the restructuring process. Generally speaking, one senior managerial accountant spends an average of 20 to 30 hours per month to complete the tasks required for the restructuring process.

FINANCIAL ANALYSIS FOR FTE REALLOCATION

Many systems and key personnel are involved during the financial planning process. Based on licensure restrictions, individual procedures and tasks are defined for reclassification to the patient care unit, and the process of FTE and dollar reallocation begins. Careful attention must be paid to the quantification of time necessary to complete procedures because it becomes the basis for staffing.

Labor standards are universally expressed in the total direct minutes needed to complete the task. Included in the equation are prep time and any other administrative duties, such as labeling a blood draw or entering the specimen details into the system. Excluded is travel time from the lab to the bedside. UMC utilizes a personal computer–based cost accounting software that by industry standards is fairly sophisticated. Each year standards are reviewed and revised as necessary. For nursing services, labor standards are impossible to evaluate by task because most services are rolled into the daily room charges. Estimates for reclassifying nursing services must be acceptable. Ancillary services, however, are well defined and are driven by the need for such detail because it is required for outpatient reimbursement. For example, spirometry is a reclassifiable procedure and has always been charged separately by the respiratory therapy ancillary department. Whenever possible, hospital labor standards should be reviewed against industry standard time worked units. This provides a good check to see if the hospital labor standards fall in line with the average time expected to complete the task. Once the amount of time is estimated for each of the procedures that will be allocated to the three new staff classifications, estimated volume for each procedure must be determined.

UMC's information systems department and the mainframe software vendor do not provide standard summary reports by nurse station or patient care unit that show the volume of ancillary services patients receive during their stay. Two options are available, however: the hospital case mix system, which is minimainframe based and has a flexible report writer; and the actual mainframe tables. Information about case mix is received from the mainframe and other sources but is not extracted from the nurse station field that is critical to the analysis. Structured query language is available through the mainframe software. Structured query language allows for great flexibility because all internal tables are then accessible. The query is designed to pull data by nurse station and ancillary department, the two departments that are currently performing the procedures. Fields that must be extracted to complete the analysis are: procedure code, procedure code description, date of service, nurse station or location, ancillary department number, volume of charges, and gross revenue. Care should be taken to analyze enough data to eliminate any seasonality. Once volume is determined, the applicable labor standard is multiplied and translated into FTEs.

Table 16–1 illustrates the calculation for the following two ancillary procedures: venipuncture and ECG. The FTEs are the number necessary to reclassify from the ancillary service areas to the new patient care unit. Because selected ancillary departments are giving up FTEs, extreme care must be taken to ensure accuracy in the above numbers. For instance, overstating the numbers may cause a shortage in FTEs to cover the remaining inpatient and all outpatient volume. Completion of the above process for each of the designated procedures determines the total ancillary contribution of FTEs. The addition of the nursing assistant duties assigned will determine how many FTEs are required to fill the PCT role in the restructured environment.

Estimating the time necessary to complete designated nursing duties is much less demanding. The patient mix and average daily census may be used to determine each unit's requirements. For instance, PCTs may permanently substitute for nursing assistants who serve as monitor technicians. The nurse manager, with the assistance of finance, estimates the amount of time spent on the unit performing this task. As mentioned earlier, UMC bundles nursing duties together into the daily room rate. Therefore, task-by-task information is currently unavailable.

FTEs allocated from ancillary areas that are not direct care in nature (e.g., materials management) are estimated by the ancillary department that currently performs the work. For example, the materials management department restocks each nurse station with supplies on a daily basis. Food services provides meal trays to the patients three times a day, and environmental services cleans the patients' rooms. The directors of these areas can provide accurate estimates of the number of hours required to perform these indirect services. Depending on the nature of the patient care unit, the numbers may vary widely even if the units have the same or similar number of beds.

Table 16–1 Sample Ancillary FTE Determination Process

Procedure Description	*Labor Standard Minutes*	*Total Annual Volume*	*Total Annual FTEs*
Venipuncture	19	25,894	3.94
ECG	25	2,986	0.37

Note: Determine labor standard from costing system and annual volume by nurse station in revenue system.

Figure 16–1 illustrates the actual FTE allocation by department for the first six restructured units at UMC. Seventy-five percent of the FTEs contributed to the patient care units was allocated from the indirect care ancillary service areas to cover the new PSA role. Twenty-five percent of the FTEs contributed to the patient care units came from the direct care ancillary areas, with additional nursing time donated.

THE RESTRUCTURED UNIT BUDGET

To plan conservatively for the actual impact on salaries and wages for the hospital, the assumption is that expenses are budget neutral. The starting rates for the PCT and PSA positions, as multipurpose positions, are set slightly higher than for specialized compartmentalized positions like phlebotomist. Instead of forcing a layoff in the ancillary areas, UMC actively recruited employees from within the affected ancillary areas and then relied upon attrition to make up any difference. The historical data indicate a 50 percent rate of hire from within the hospital. This percentage is greater than originally anticipated, and those who transferred from within are earning a greater hourly rate. A weighted average hourly wage rate is calculated for the budget revision.

UMC calculates employee-related expenses as a percentage of total salaries and wages for each of the patient care units. These expenses must be

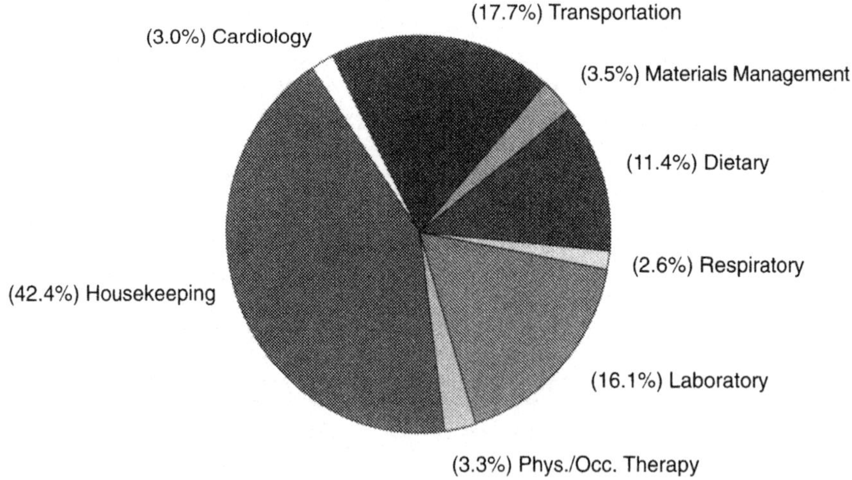

Figure 16–1 FTE allocation. Each piece is the percentage of total FTEs contributed by the ancillaries for the new PSA and PCT positions.

reclassified and accounted for in the new total salary and wage expenses for each unit.

Unfortunately for the managerial accounting department, restructuring of units almost never occurs at the beginning of the fiscal year. UMC does not currently utilize a flexible budgeting process. Therefore, the hospital must revise the budget upon implementation. It is critical that revisions occur because productivity is evaluated on an ongoing basis by flexing budgeted volume to actual volume. The nurse managers must revise the budget detail within their salary and wage budget templates. The template is a common spreadsheet file accessible through the VAX mainframe system. These files are easily converted to the personal computer version of the software, which makes the process of budgeting salary and wage for nursing efficient.

UMC uses staffing patterns as the basis for the salary and wage budgets. The average daily census provides half the equation, and the predetermined staffing ratios provide the other half. Pay differentials and overtime are added as necessary based upon assumptions about seasonality and/or other volume fluctuations. Table 16–2 illustrates the change in staffing patterns before and after restructuring. See Chapters 18 and 19 for unit-specific examples. In this particular example the PCT and the PSA FTEs replace some of the RN, unit assistant, and nursing assistant FTEs. The net result is an overall increase to the total number of FTEs budgeted for a patient care unit due to the addition of ancillary services. The budget is then revised with the new staffing pattern results to reflect the date of implementation.

The second and third objectives of the UMC model of PCR are accomplished by changing the skill mix within each patient care unit. These objectives again are to address the labor shortage by utilizing personnel more effectively in the delivery of patient care and to address cost containment by reducing the annual rise in the cost of patient care services. Before restructuring, UMC was experiencing an overall shortage of professional staff, including RNs and physical therapists. The PCT role has diminished shortages in staffing while maintaining a high level of care. Patient and physician satisfaction have increased by conversion of the unit into a patient-centered comprehensive care unit.

Restructuring the phase I units resulted in a net increase of 17 FTEs overall because of the new staffing patterns and changes in skill mix with coincidentally a net decrease in RN FTEs of 17. Table 16–3 indicates the actual change in skill mix by quantifying the percentage of RN FTEs before and after restructuring. Within the first two phases of the project, the skill mix changed up to 28 percent for the RN staff classes. These figures are

Table 16–2 Staffing Patterns before and after Restructuring

Before PCR

Staff Nurse/Staffing Pattern

Shift	*Sun*	*Mon*	*Tue*	*Wed*	*Thu*	*Fri*	*Sat*	*Total People*	*Total FTEs (Regular)*	*Benefit Relief FTEs (Paid Time Off)*	*Total FTEs with Benefit Relief*
DAY—Shift 1	5.00	5.00	5.00	5.00	5.00	6.00	6.00	37.00	7.40	0.74	8.14
EVE—Shift 2	6.00	6.00	6.00	6.00	6.00	6.00	6.00	42.00	8.40	0.84	9.24
NIGHT—Shift 3	7.00	7.00	6.00	6.00	6.00	6.00	6.00	44.00	8.80	0.88	9.68
Totals	18.00	18.00	17.00	17.00	17.00	18.00	18.00	123.00	24.60	2.46	27.06

Nursing Assistant/Staffing Pattern

Shift	*Sun*	*Mon*	*Tue*	*Wed*	*Thu*	*Fri*	*Sat*	*Total People*	*Total FTEs (Regular)*	*Benefit Relief FTEs (Paid Time Off)*	*Total FTEs with Benefit Relief*
DAY—Shift 1	3.00	3.50	4.00	3.50	3.50	4.00	3.00	24.50	4.90	0.49	5.39
EVE—Shift 2	3.00	3.00	3.00	3.00	3.00	3.00	3.00	21.00	4.20	0.42	4.62
NIGHT—Shift 3	1.00	1.00	1.00	1.00	1.00	1.00	1.00	7.00	1.40	0.14	1.54
Totals	7.00	7.50	8.00	7.50	7.50	8.00	7.00	52.50	10.50	1.05	11.55

continues

Table 16–2 continued

After PCR

Staff Nurse/Staffing Pattern

Shift	*Sun*	*Mon*	*Tue*	*Wed*	*Thu*	*Fri*	*Sat*	*Total People*	*Total FTEs (Regular)*	*Benefit Relief FTEs (Paid Time Off)*	*Total FTEs with Benefit Relief*
DAY—Shift 1	4.00	4.00	4.00	4.00	4.00	5.00	5.00	30.00	6.00	0.60	6.60
EVE—Shift 2	5.00	5.00	5.00	5.00	5.00	5.00	5.00	35.00	7.00	0.70	7.70
NIGHT—Shift 3	6.00	6.00	5.00	5.00	5.00	5.00	5.00	37.00	7.40	0.74	8.14
Totals	15.00	15.00	14.00	14.00	14.00	15.00	15.00	102.00	20.40	2.04	22.44

PCT Staffing Pattern

Shift	*Sun*	*Mon*	*Tue*	*Wed*	*Thu*	*Fri*	*Sat*	*Total People*	*Total FTEs (Regular)*	*Benefit Relief FTEs (Paid Time Off)*	*Total FTEs with Benefit Relief*
DAY—Shift 1	4.00	4.50	5.00	4.50	4.50	5.00	4.00	31.50	6.30	0.63	6.93
EVE—Shift 2	4.00	4.00	4.00	4.00	4.00	4.00	4.00	28.00	5.60	0.56	6.16
NIGHT—Shift 3	2.00	2.00	2.00	2.00	2.00	2.00	2.00	14.00	2.80	0.28	3.08
Totals	10.00	10.50	11.00	10.50	10.50	11.00	10.00	73.50	14.70	1.47	16.17

PSA/Staffing Pattern

Shift	*Sun*	*Mon*	*Tue*	*Wed*	*Thu*	*Fri*	*Sat*	*Total People*	*Total FTEs (Regular)*	*Benefit Relief FTEs (Paid Time Off)*	*Total FTEs with Benefit Relief*
DAY—Shift 1	2.00	3.00	3.00	3.00	3.00	3.00	2.00	19.00	3.80	0.38	4.18
EVE—Shift 2	2.00	2.00	2.00	2.00	2.00	2.00	2.00	14.00	2.80	0.28	3.08
NIGHT—Shift 3	0.50	0.50	0.50	0.50	0.50	0.50	0.50	3.50	0.70	0.07	0.77
Totals	4.50	5.50	5.50	5.50	5.50	5.50	4.50	36.50	7.30	0.73	8.03

Table 16–3 Percentage Change in Actual RN Skill Mix by Unit

Unit	*% RN FTEs before Restructuring*	*% RN FTEs after Restructuring*
3 East Pediatrics	74	57
3 West Pediatrics	75	47
4 East Med-Surg	74	47
4 West Med-Surg	57	44
5 East Med-Surg	56	45
6 East Med-Surg	61	43

based on the payroll systems' labor cost distribution report. Hours by staff class were segregated and compared with total hours for the applicable time periods. Reclassifying certain duties and responsibilities of the RNs to the PCTs resulted in lower RN vacancy rates and changes in the skill mix. These outcomes in turn resulted in lower agency and overtime expense and in lowering the increase in salaries and wage costs on an ongoing basis.

TRAINING

As mentioned earlier, a new department was established to train the employees in the newly created roles. Training sessions for the existing staff were also required to reeducate everyone to both the new philosophy of restructured care delivery and the interdisciplinary team management. Although training is the main mission, the PCR department has many other educational, research, and operational functions. Because of the newness of the redesign concept, the requirements for specialized training necessitated the development of courses tailored to the unique functions of each of the two new paraprofessional positions. UMC has mainstreamed the training for the PCT position. Phase I PCTs were trained within 14 weeks. Phase II and III PCTs completed training within 10 weeks. The current format for training is as follows: 2 weeks nursing, 4 weeks ancillary/support, and 4 weeks on-the-job training. Trainees who have had previous experience are fast-tracked through the process in as little as 6 weeks. Upon implementation of restructuring, all staff attend team-building workshops. The number of trainees depends on the previous analysis plus an amount determined by human resources to cover any turnover during training. Managerial accounting is involved in the training process in the context of charging for the new services.

CHARGE STRUCTURE

UMC, like most hospitals, has developed a series of inpatient room rates that relate to the level of care delivered to the patient. These rates have remained unchanged throughout restructuring and are consistent throughout the hospital. For example, a semiprivate rate charged on a nonrestructured unit is the same amount charged on a unit that has been restructured. The room rates are automatically charged to the patient's bill each night at midnight along with a daily supply charge. The only items that have been individually charged by nursing are uncommon services over and above usual duties required and pharmaceuticals that are charged by the sticker method. Therefore, nursing staff are not necessarily used to filling out charge sheets on a daily basis.

Specially designed training packages were developed and are presented to each new group of PCT trainees during the 10-week process. The actual billing training manual was developed by the senior managerial accountant. Approximately 1 hour is set aside for the senior managerial accountant to present the billing information to each group of trainees. As stated earlier, the number of trainees may vary, but overall time required is not affected greatly by fluctuating numbers of trainees. Charges for procedures performed by the PCTs are the same as those used to quantify FTEs donated by the direct care ancillary areas, specifically physical therapy, occupational therapy, cardiology, respiratory care, and laboratory.

At least 90 percent of the hospital's inpatient reimbursement is diagnosis related. A predetermined amount is paid no matter what additional services are provided. It has been proposed that a set amount be added to the room rate that would alleviate any distortion in gross revenue due to lost charges. Prior year comparisons would not be distorted. It may seem like a non–value-added process to have the PCTs charge patients for individual procedures performed. However, individual charges must exist in the system to provide a means for tracking. The actual volume of charges compared with the original budget may be used as justification for some of the total FTEs that are PCTs on any given patient care unit. It is critical that all PCTs understand the philosophy of charging and the methodology to follow for each of the direct care ancillary services they will provide.

TRAINING FOR PCT BILLING

The initial PCT training package for billing was developed by the senior managerial accountant (Exhibit 16–1). Once the initial draft was complete, copies were sent to the directors of all departments involved. Reviews and

Exhibit 16–1 PCT Training Information

Physical/Occupational Therapy

Procedures:

- You will receive instructions from the rehabilitation department as needed based upon the circumstances for each patient.
- Once the procedure(s) are completed, use tick marks to complete the number of times charged.
- Remember that most rehabilitation charges are listed in 15-minute increments. For instance, if the patient is undergoing supervised exercise for 25 minutes, you would enter two tick marks on the encounter form under the number of times charged column.
- CPM charges are daily, and hot/cold pack, one area, should be multiplied by the number of areas treated (e.g., the neck and lower back would be two).

Cardiology

Procedures:

- You will receive a diagnostic cardiology UPI encounter form from the unit coordinator for each patient scheduled to have an ECG.
- To avoid double charging the patient, *keep only the white UPI copy*. Rip up and toss away the other two copies (yellow, UMC; pink, cardiology).
- Check the appropriate box on the UPI copy: ECG (standard 12 lead) or ECG rhythm strip. Once you have transmitted the ECG, check the box and deliver the UPI form to the cardiology department.
- Fill in the number of times ordered column each morning for those patients requiring an ECG (see your PCT encounter form).
- Once the procedure(s) are completed, use tick marks to complete the number of times charged.

Pathology

Procedures:

- Orders from the lab to draw blood will come up regularly throughout the day or night.
- Once the procedure(s) are completed, use tick marks to complete the number of times charged.

Respiratory Therapy

Procedures:

- You will receive orders from respiratory therapy for each patient scheduled to have continued spirometry.
- Each time a patient is treated, you will charge for both spirometry procedures.
- Once the procedure(s) are completed, use tick marks to complete the number of times charged.

revisions were executed until a final version was decided. The protocol to determine how to charge varies greatly depending upon the skill, yet the final result is a quantity figure listed on the charge voucher.

The training sessions begin with an overview of the history and philosophy behind the UMC model of PCR. The goals are highlighted, the strengths of the program are discussed, and any future plans for restructuring other patient areas are mentioned. The class topic then turns to billing procedures and the implications of lost charges. The importance of the role of PCT is reinforced as it relates to the success of this program. Billing not only maintains the hospital's level of gross inpatient revenue but also provides a means of tracking the procedures reclassified into the redesigned patient care units. Unique ancillary services require unique billing procedures.

Patients who require physical/occupational therapy will initially be seen by a licensed physical therapist. Once it is determined that procedures will be referred to the PCT, the therapist informs the PCT of the plans. Physical therapy procedures are generally charged for by modality or in increments of time. The physical therapy procedures that have been reclassified are hot/cold pack, massage, ambulation with assistance, supervised ambulation, bedside assistance, and CPM/Jobst monitoring. Occupational therapy procedures are charged exactly like physical therapy procedures. All the above procedures are accounted for by the time increment except for hot/cold pack, which is location driven. For instance, a patient may require a hot pack on one arm and one leg. The PCT would make two tick marks or enter the number 2 on the charge sheet. One charge sheet is used for each patient on each of the shifts. Therefore, there are usually three sheets per patient for each patient day based on 8-hour shifts.

Charging for cardiology procedures is unique because of the direct involvement of the physician. ECGs are performed by the PCTs. A physician's order form is received by the patient care unit. The order is then assigned to the PCT. Once the test is completed, the quantity column is filled in on the charge form.

Respiratory therapists will refer patients to the PCTs for the following procedures: incentive spirometry set-up and incentive spirometry procedure. The set-up charge is a one-time charge, but the spirometry procedure is charged each time the PCT performs the procedure. If the patient is able to do the procedure, no charge is submitted.

Orders from the laboratory are sent to the patient care units regularly throughout the day and night. The PCT will perform the phlebotomy and charge the patient. Patients are charged for venipuncture or withdraws from catheters. Exhibit 16–2 is an example of an actual charge voucher used by all nursing staff within the department of adult services. A similar form is used by the department of women's and children's services. The internal billing form contains all other nursing services, including PCT charges. The two types of charges are differentiated by the code number.

Exhibit 16–2 Charge Voucher

4 EAST 6122				4 WEST 6123	
CODE	QTY	DESCRIPTION	UNIT OF MEASURE	QTY	CODE
725299		NURSE ASSIST 1ST 30 MIN	HALF HOUR		725319
725309		NURSE ASSIST ADDL. 15 MIN	QTR. HOUR		725329
936549		SPECIAL PROCEDURE HOURLY	HOUR		
936889		MIDLINE CATHETER KIT	KIT		936909
936899		MIDLINE CATHETER INSERTION	INSERTION		936919
1040039		ELECTROCARDIOGRAM	TEST		1040049
1055059		INC SPIRO TREATMENT	EACH		1055079
1055069		INC SPIRO SETUP	EACH		1055089
1070039		VENIPUNCTURE	PROCEDURE		1070049
993349		NON-INVASIVE BP MONITOR/DAY	24 HOURS		996769
991699		PATIENT CARE ASSIST.(SITTER)	HOUR		992839
993329		CVP	24 HOURS		996749
993339		LACTATION BRIEF	QTR. HOUR		996759
993359		RECOVERY CHARGE I	4 HOURS		993849
993369		ACCU-CHECK	TEST		936559
993379		CNS CONSULT FEE BASE	HALF HOUR		936569
993669		CNS CONSULT ADDL. 15 MIN	QTR. HOUR		996739
	PHYSICAL THERAPY:				
1010129		HOT/COLD PACK 1 AREA	EACH		1010189
1010139		MASSAGE	15 MINUTES		1010199
1010149		AMBULATION W/ASSISTANCE	15 MINUTES		1010209
1010159		SUPERVISED AMBULATION	15 MINUTES		1010219
1010169		BEDSIDE ASSISTANCE	15 MINUTES		1010229
1010179		CPM/JOBST MONITORING	8 HOURS		1010239
	OCCUPATIONAL THERAPY:				
1025079		HOT/COLD PACK 1 AREA	EACH		1025109
1025089		BEDSIDE ASSISTANCE	15 MINUTES		1025119
1025099		CPM/JOBST MONITORING	DAY		1025129

continues

Courtesy of University Medical Center, Tucson, Arizona.

Exhibit 16–2 continued

5 EAST 6124				7 WEST 6113		BMT 6126	
CODE	QTY	DESCRIPTION	UNIT OF MEASURE	QTY	CODE	QTY	CODE
725339		NURSE ASSIST 1ST 30 MIN	HALF HOUR		725259		725979
725349		NURSE ASSIST ADDL. 15 MIN	QTR. HOUR		725269		725389
996819		CNS CONSULT FEE BASE	HALF HOUR		936509		936769
936579		CNS CONSULT ADDL. 15 MIN	QTR. HOUR		936519		936659
936589		CVP	24 HOURS				
936599		RECOVERY CHARGE I	4 HOURS		936529		
936759		NON-INVASIVE BP MONITOR/DAY	24 HOURS		606839		936669
936929		MIDLINE CATHETER KIT	KIT		936849		
936939		MIDLINE CATHETER INSERTION	INSERTION		936859		
1040059		ELECTROCARDIOGRAM	TEST		1040079		1040089
1055099		INC SPIRO TREATMENT	EACH		1055139		1055159
1055109		INC SPIRO SETUP	EACH		1055149		1055169
1070059		VENIPUNCTURE	PROCEDURE		1070079		1070089
936949		HEMOCULT	TEST		609759		606919
991839		PATIENT CARE ASSIST.(SITTER)	HOUR		991689		936679
996799		ACCU-CHECK	TEST		996909		606899
996809		CARDIAC MONITOR/DAY	24 HOURS				606909
	PHYSICAL THERAPY:				1010369		1010429
1010249		HOT/COLD PACK 1 AREA	EACH		1010379		1010439
1010259		MASSAGE	15 MINUTES		1010389		1010449
1010269		AMBULATION W/ASSISTANCE	15 MINUTES		1010399		1010459
1010279		SUPERVISED AMBULATION	15 MINUTES		1010409		1010469
1010289		BEDSIDE ASSISTANCE	15 MINUTES		1010419		1010599
1010299		CPM/JOBST MONITORING	8 HOURS				
	OCCUPATIONAL THERAPY:				1025199		1025229
1025139		HOT/COLD PACK 1 AREA	EACH		1025209		1025239
1025149		BEDSIDE ASSISTANCE	15 MINUTES		1025219		1025249
1025159		CPM/JOBST MONITORING	DAY				

PCR charge codes are seven digits long. All charge vouchers must be dated and have the patient name addressographed in the upper right corner of the form, or the billing department cannot charge.

After each shift, the PCTs send the charge vouchers to the billing department to be added to the patient's bill, as is done for other nursing services. Of course, the unit has the option to formalize and centralize the batching process by placing the unit assistant in charge of submitting the charge sheets to the billing department. At the conclusion of the training session, a short quiz is helpful if time permits.

In addition to the information provided by the finance department, ancillary areas also stress the importance of billing. During the on-the-job training period, personnel from the ancillary departments demonstrate the billing of patients as they guide the PCTs through the procedures. Charging is presented as an integral part of the procedure performed. The training philosophy is to teach about the charging mechanism from a finance perspective with reinforcement from the clinical areas on the job. Once again, the desired result is to maintain gross revenue and to provide data for program analysis.

INITIAL FTE MONITORING

During the initial planning phases of PCR, the steering committee provided direction to develop methodologies for tracking the success of the program from a financial perspective. For the first 6 to 12 months after implementation of the phase I restructuring plan, the senior managerial accountant closely monitored any changes in FTEs. The analysis encompassed both the ancillary areas affected by restructuring and the actual restructured units. A detailed report was developed that enabled administration to evaluate additional approved FTEs and dollars by department (Table 16–4). A report titled "Approved FTEs for Departments Affected by PCR" is prepared on a pay period basis and contains three sections: FTEs by department, salary and wage dollars, and FTEs by job classification.

Table 16–4 shows the detail for section I, FTEs by department. Section I lists the department name and the prerestructuring budgeted FTEs. The budgeted FTE number before PCR contains the total number of FTEs for each department. The PCR change column is applied to the original budget to get the budget after PCR or the current budgeted FTE column. These numbers should be readily available from the initial planning process and original budget revisions. Additional approved FTE information is provided by the departments backed up by formal requests for FTEs, which have to be approved by administration. No additional FTEs have been

Table 16–4 Monitoring Changes in FTEs: UMC Approved FTEs for Departments Affected by PCR

Department Name	*Original Budgeted FTEs*	*FTE Change with PCR*	*Current Budgeted FTEs*	*Additional Approved FTEs**	*Current Approved FTEs*	*Actual Paid FTEs*	*Variance Favorable (Unfavorable)*
Materials management	64.41	(0.43)	63.98	0.00	63.98	62.91	1.07 F
Diagnostic cardiology	16.49	0.00	16.49	2.00	18.49	16.44	2.05 F
3 West	22.86	3.96	26.82	0.00	26.82	25.12	1.70 F
4 West	38.91	(0.07)	38.84	0.00	38.84	39.10	(0.26) UNF

*Per information provided by departments.

approved because of the inability to perform at the current level of services provided. Additional FTEs may be approved through increased volume or an actual change in the nature of the service provided in the department or on the unit, but approval is not limited to this factor. Current approved FTEs are simply the sum of the two previous columns. The approved FTEs report can easily be developed in spreadsheet format. The report is necessary to identify potential problem areas on a semimonthly basis.

ONGOING FTE MONITORING

UMC utilizes a report generated from the payroll system, called the labor cost distribution report (Table 16–5), to quantify types of hours and dollars charged to the various departments.

There are three components to the report: productive dollars and hours, supplemental dollars and hours, and nonproductive dollars and hours. The actual paid FTEs are calculated by summing the two types of hours and then dividing by the number of hours in the pay period.

ONGOING GROSS REVENUE MONITORING

Tracking charging and gross revenue is sometimes tedious. The budget has been established, which provides ease in comparing actual with budget on a monthly basis. Pinpointing individual departments that missed charges throughout the month requires a detailed list of the actual patients

Table 16–5 Labor Cost Distribution Analysis: UMC Current Period Analysis for 2-Week Pay Period Ended 06/19

Department:	Pediatrics 3 East	Department:	Pediatrics 3 East
Total Worked FTEs:	28.56	Regular FTEs:	28.05
Total Paid FTEs:	33.68	Agency FTEs:	0.00
Budgeted FTEs:	37.16	Overtime FTEs:	0.20
Paid FTEs (Over)/ Underbudgeted FTEs:	3.48	Call-Back FTEs:	0.31
Actual Dollars:	39,846	Total Worked FTEs:	28.56
Agency Dollars:	0	Paid Time Off/Extended Illness Bank FTEs:	4.20
Budgeted Dollars:	41,494	Paid Out FTEs:	0.00
Dollars (Over)/Under Budget:	1,648	Orient FTEs:	0.92
		Other Nonprod FTEs:	0.00
		Total Nonprod FTEs:	5.12
		Nonprod as % of Paid FTEs:	15.21%
		Total Paid FTEs:	33.68

who were supposed to receive treatments from PCTs. ECGs are easy to track because they are sent over a dataline to cardiology's main office. Physical and occupational therapy services are tracked based upon handwritten lists kept by the physical or occupational therapist. Venipunctures are also fairly easy to track through the main laboratory system. Respiratory therapy charges are also tracked through a manual system prepared by the referring therapists. Once it is known exactly what should have been charged and which patients should have been charged, the patient's bill provides a means for comparison. Lost charges have occurred in all areas as a result of PCR, and efforts are underway to extend the education process to ensure that the gross revenue is captured on an ongoing basis.

CONCLUSION

Health care reform is not the sole responsibility of elected officials. Administrators and especially financial managers must be proactive in their approaches to reducing inefficiencies. Innovative processes can be developed from within that address the annual rise in cost of services while maintaining the quality of care, patient satisfaction, and employee satisfaction. Information must be shared with other hospitals to identify industry's best practices. The financial department's role in implementation of the UMC model of PCR is thorough and perpetual, from involvement on the steering committee and the task force during the planning process to the monitoring skills provided after implementation.

CHAPTER

17

Comprehensive Communication Plan

Mickey L. Parsons

Chapter Objectives

1. To describe the internal and external communication plan before the initial restructuring process on the first four units.
2. To describe the internal and external communication plan after restructuring.
3. To summarize the communication plan to expand the restructuring process to eight additional areas.
4. To report lessons learned in the communication process.

A rational planning process requires that a communication plan be developed and implemented. The patient care restructuring (PCR) process changes people and their work. Therefore, an essential component for success is an effective and extensive communication program for all the people affected by the changes directly and indirectly. As human beings, people need information that provides them with a sense of importance, partnership, and involvement in the organization. Too often employees develop negative attitudes because of lack of information and fear of the unknown. The negativity can become fertile breeding ground for just the opposite of what is needed for effective facilitywide change. The goal at University Medical Center (UMC) was to maximize communication flow within the Health Sciences Center to have informed and involved staff and physicians.

When the initial PCR process ideas were in their infancy, they were perceived to be radical by some and innovative by others. Therefore, it was important to have informed outside constituencies. Whenever significant areas of potential professional and/or lay community controversy exists, the leadership must be informed. This chapter discusses the individuals and groups who were incorporated into the internal and external communication plan, the extension of the restructuring process to additional units, and the lessons learned.

INTERNAL AND EXTERNAL COMMUNICATION BEFORE RESTRUCTURING

Internal Communication

The communication of information is essential in the overall planning, implementation, and change process. As described in Chapter 4, the phase of preparing the leadership is critical because, without leadership buy-in and support, no new project is possible. The steps of growing the idea, obtaining top leadership approval, building momentum, and providing key physician leaders information all require communication. The planning phase of preparing the staff is the next most important communication component in the beginning of the process. Table 17–1 lists and summarizes all internal communication meetings that were held by the administrative leader of the project before implementation. The information reflects five intense months of communication meetings in the beginning phases to prepare the hospital and medical staff leadership and the staff. This effort is believed to be a significant contributor to the success of the restructuring effort.

Early in the process, the board of directors needs to be informed about the restructuring program. At UMC the board members are knowledgeable about health care trends, and they were supportive of a radical restructuring of the care delivery process. They were particularly pleased with the objectives of the project because of their belief in and desire for UMC constantly to provide excellent patient care and services. The board members also needed to understand the potential controversy that might

Table 17–1 Summary of Administrative Internal Communication Meetings before Restructuring the First Four Units*

Date from Kickoff	*Individuals and/or Groups (number of meetings)*
13 months	Administration operations (1)
12 months	Chief executive officer and dean, College of Medicine (1)
12 months	Dean, College of Nursing (1)
12 months	Administrative staff (1)
12 months	Incoming and outgoing chiefs of the medical staff (2)
12 months	Hospital department directors (1)
12 months	Nurse managers (1)
11 months	Chair, departments of surgery, pediatrics, neurology (3)
11 months	Section chiefs, cardiology and respiratory, adult and pediatrics (2)
11 months	Chair and medical director, pathology (1)
11 months	Medical director and committee chair, physical and occupational therapy (2)
11 months	Senior leaders, College of Nursing (2)
11 months	Medical staff executive committee (1)
10 months	Section chiefs, neurosurgery, urology, gynecology, general pediatrics (3)
10 months	Thomas Davis gynecology physician group (1)
10 months	Hospital managers and supervisors (1)
9 months	Ancillary departments and support departments introductory meetings (6)
9 months	Four pilot units, two med-surg and 2 pediatric, introductory meetings (12)
8 months	Pilot units nurse manager and assistant nurse manager coordination meetings initiated (one monthly for 8 months)
7 months	Administration, department director, manager, and supervisor updates (3)
7 months	Unit steering committees (4)
7 months	UMC board of directors presentation (1)
7 months	Chair, family practice; pediatric faculty; urology faculty section (3)
6 months	Neurology faculty, cardiology faculty section (2)
5 months	Pilot unit updates (4)
5 months	Hospitalwide support (secretarial) staff briefing (1)
4 months	Emergency services, perioperative services, surgical units, all staff briefings (3)
4 months	Pilot unit updates (2)
3 months	Perinatal services, medical units, all staff briefings (2)
3 months	Thomas Davis pediatric physician group (1)
2 months	Laboratory physician leaders update (1)
2 months	Clinical services (professional ancillary) updates (2)
2 months	Dean, College of Medicine; chair, pediatrics updates; chair, ophthalmology briefing (3)
1 month	Medical staff executive committee (1)
1 month	Pilot unit updates (4)
2 weeks	Hospital medical director case manager planning (1)
1 week	Medical directors, pilot units (2)

*Communication meetings held in addition to PCR steering committee, task force, and ad hoc work group meetings.

arise as a result of the change process and the turmoil that hospital staff might experience. The board's strong expression of support, in spite of the potential for conflict, was appreciated by the PCR steering committee members and the task force.

After the leader and pilot unit planning and implementation are well underway, information needs to be provided to the employees in all the other departments. Although all hospital directors, managers, and supervisors had participated in briefing sessions, direct opportunities for information flow from administration to employee groups was considered important. Beginning 5 months before implementation, forums for employee groups that were not directly affected were held. Groups from support staff, clinical services, emergency services, perioperative services, and all other nursing units had the opportunity to participate. Good attendance was commonplace at all informational meetings on PCR.

During the month before the kickoff date, updates for the hospital and medical staff leadership are important. These serve as final reminders that the project phases are beginning to be implemented and provide another opportunity for questions, comments, and concerns to be discussed. In addition to verbal communication, a special briefing paper (fact sheet) with questions and answers was prepared with the public affairs department. The fact sheet was distributed to all members of the medical staff executive committee, hospital leaders, and selected others. Please see Exhibit 17–1 for more detail. One week before kickoff, PCR was a routine announcement at hospital administrative and department director meetings.

External Communication

Because restructuring roles is a radical departure from the traditional hospital bureaucracy, a priority was to communicate and inform primary professional colleagues, organizations, and purchasers of care outside the organization. The objectives of the restructuring project would probably be acceptable to all, but the strategies chosen to reach the goals had the potential to be controversial. Therefore, full briefings were held with senior leadership at the state Health Department, board of nursing, state nursing and hospital associations, and Tucson hospitals. Executives and medical directors, who represented purchasers of care, and academic leaders in health administration and nursing in the state were also briefed. For a full listing of the external communication meetings, please see Table 17–2. This component of the communication plan must not be forgotten.

Exhibit 17–1 UMC PCR, October 1991

PCR at UMC is an innovative new approach to delivering the highest quality of care to patients in the hospital. The new system, to be implemented in December 1991 on four pilot units, aims to improve the quality of care and service to patients and to address the escalating labor shortages in the health care industry. The pilot units will be 3 East and 3 West (both pediatric units) and 4 East and 4 West (medical-surgical and orthopedics units). Based on our evaluation of the results, plans call for a phased implementation throughout all patient care units within approximately 3 years.

The Patient Care Team

The key to PCR is a redefinition of the roles and responsibilities of the hospital workers who interact with patients. The design of hospital jobs frequently has not matched the education and training of employees or maximized efficiency of patient care. For example, a registered nurse (RN) is not needed to stock supplies, transport patients, or remove dirty laundry. Frequently, jobs have been designed around a single function that does not allow for flexibility or efficiency. Examples of single function jobs include phlebotomists and ECG technicians. The new approach at UMC is to create multipurpose workers for basic health care support and technical functions. The RN role will be restructured to include those functions that require a nurse's education for direct patient care. These are the responsibilities of the restructured roles:

- *RN case manager*—Manages the care of the patient in collaboration with physicians and the patient care nurse by developing and implementing the plan of care for a designated group of patients. This includes nursing assessment and evaluation, response to medical/nursing treatment, patient and family education, and supervising patient support attendants (PSAs) and patient care technicians (PCTs).
- *Patient care nurse*—Performs patient assessment during the assigned work shift, participates in the development and implementation of the plan of care with the patient care team, administers medication and IV therapy and prescribed treatments, evaluates and documents outcomes, and conducts patient and family education.
- *PCT*—Performs nursing assistant skills, including basic hygiene care for patients; performs technical procedures such as phlebotomy (drawing blood) and ECGs; performs selected physical and occupational therapy skills as determined by the physical or occupational therapist; performs minimal, selected respiratory therapy assistance as determined by the respiratory therapist.
- *PSA*—Cleans patient rooms; transports patients, such as to and from radiology or other UMC patient care areas; provides dietary assistance; manages materials and supplies; and completes other tasks.

PCR would benefit UMC in the following ways:

- by reducing the number of hospital workers who deal with any given patient, thereby ensuring greater continuity in patient care. For example, a cancer patient or an orthopedics patient may see as many as 15 different hospital employees in a day. Currently, ECG technicians, housekeepers, food service employees, pa-

continues

Exhibit 17–1 continued

thology employees, and many others serve patients each day. As a result, some patients have expressed dissatisfaction and concern regarding the number of different people who enter their room throughout the day.

- by addressing inevitable shifts in the workforce. The nursing shortage is expected to continue indefinitely, and hospitals nationwide will need to take creative steps to maintain the current level of service to patients. The labor shortage also is growing in other health care fields. For example, shortages exist in medical technology, physical therapy, respiratory therapy, pharmacy, and other support positions. PCR ensures that all health care employees' unique abilities are used as efficiently as possible, resulting not only in better patient care but also in greater employment satisfaction for all staff.
- by allowing nurses to perform nursing care in the truest sense by overall case management with physicians, development of plans of care, patient and family education, administration of medication, and the like. Nurses spend a great amount of time performing tasks that do not require RN skills, such as making beds, transporting patients, and stocking supplies. These types of activities place greater burdens on nurses and take time away from patient care.
- by reducing costs. Overall, patient care costs will not change. Start-up costs for training and evaluation have been held to the minimum. Savings are anticipated as the project is implemented hospitalwide.
- by promoting interdisciplinary team management. Everyone on the patient care team—physicians, nurses, PCTs, PSAs, clinical pharmacists, housestaff (residents and interns), physical therapists, and others—will work together to manage the activity of hospital units. As a result, UMC will be recognized as a model of excellence for hospitals nationwide.

The objectives of PCR are as follows:

- to maintain and enhance the quality of patient care and service
- to address the labor shortage by utilizing personnel more effectively in the delivery of patient care
- to address cost containment by reducing the annual rise of the cost of patient care services
- to maintain and enhance the satisfaction of patients, physicians, and caregivers

Training the Patient Care Staff

A comprehensive training program is being implemented to ensure that patient care nurses, PCTs, and PSAs perform at the highest level. Numerous UMC departments (clinical pathology, physical therapy, respiratory therapy, nursing, housekeeping, food services, and materials management) are providing this extensive hands-on training. All new employees will undergo a specialized training program to prepare them for their role.

Society's Need for PCR: The Demands of Demographics

Without question, PCR is at the forefront of a growing national trend toward streamlining the use of hospital personnel and empowerment of nurses. The United

continues

Exhibit 17–1 continued

States is at a crossroads in which millions of Americans are entering retirement years and leaving the workforce. At the same time, the elderly increasingly need hospital services. By recognizing this inevitability and acting now to address it, UMC will be among the pioneers in revolutionizing patient care in the United States.

The Precedent of PCR

Although the concept of PCR is quite new, variations on restructuring have been implemented successfully at Vanderbilt University Medical Center in Nashville, Tennessee; Mercy Hospital and Medical Center in Chicago, Illinois; Lakeland Regional Hospital in Lakeland, Florida; Bishop Clarkson Hospital in Omaha, Nebraska; St. Vincent's Hospital in Indianapolis, Indiana; and Georgetown University Hospital in Washington, D.C. These restructured hospitals have reported an increase in patient and physician satisfaction, and their employees have reported excitement in learning new job skills.

Questions and Answers about PCR

Q: Will PCR result in layoffs of any UMC employees?

A: Employees will not be laid off. All employees whose individual positions will be affected will be offered an opportunity to train for an alternative position.

Q: How many PCTs and PSAs will be hired?

A: Approximately 40 PCTs and 20 PSAs will be hired for the four pilot units.

Q: Is PCR just a way for the hospital to reduce its own costs?

A: No. The driving force for the PCR project is to improve quality of care and service and to address the serious labor shortages in health care.

Q: Will nurses lose authority to the PCTs and PSAs?

A: RNs will direct and prioritize the activities of the PCTs and PSAs.

Q: Will nurses have career opportunities to move up within this new system?

A: Nurses will continue to have numerous career opportunities in today's complex hospital. This system of care offers the RN improved job satisfaction by allowing for more time to devote to direct patient care. The RN's caseload will change as the job duties and functions change. The RN will have the PCT to assist in providing care and service to patients, allowing RNs to focus on those patients requiring more complex care. The RN also will have the PSAs' assistance to provide needed care responsibilities such as bed changes, transportation, dietary needs, and the like.

Q: How can one person be trained to do such a wide range of tasks, such as skills from physical and respiratory therapy, ECGs, and so forth?

A: The PCT's job is designed to include basic technical procedures from various clinical disciplines. The PCT will receive 14 weeks of extensive clinical and didactic

continues

Exhibit 17–1 continued

training and follow-up to do the job. In each case, the RN, the physical therapist, the respiratory therapist, and others will be completing the patient care assessment and treatment plan and determining what technical skill the patient's care may demand. Ongoing supervision of those activities will occur.

Q: Why does UMC administration expect PCR to work?

A: In view of the serious need for innovative approaches to health care to address better the needs of our patients, UMC administration has taken many months to communicate the direction in which health care is going and the changes this will bring. The PCR project is now at the stage to pilot those plans by hiring the best applicants and training them to meet the needs of our patients. Maintaining a system of care for a growing number of patients while having fewer workers in the health care industry is a serious challenge. We are committed to trying alternative approaches to address our patients' needs.

Note: Prepared by George Martinez, Former Associate Director, University of Arizona Public Affairs; Josephine Palmer, PCR Program Manager; and Mickey L. Parsons.

Courtesy of University Medical Center, Tucson, Arizona.

INTERNAL AND EXTERNAL COMMUNICATION AFTER RESTRUCTURING

Internal Communication

Completion of planning and coordination for nursing case management with the physicians was the primary communication effort at UMC immediately after implementation of the support roles. Pilot unit meetings with the administrator for the project, nursing director, program manager, nurse manager, and staff began early, 2 months after implementation, and continued over the next year. On a regular basis, each unit had meetings to problem solve operational issues.

Informational meetings for all hospital employees and the University Physicians Clinic staff were held early in the postimplementation phase. Communication occurred 3 months after implementation with the clinical supervisors, who led the units on the off hours and weekends; the staffing clerks; and the float pool staff. The time delay proved to be a significant oversight; events should have occurred earlier. Operational issues of unit coordination and staffing of off hours would have been avoided if this support area had been oriented earlier.

One of the most important follow-up meetings was the presentation of the patient satisfaction results to the staff on the four pilot units. The patient satisfaction results compared baseline (prerestructuring) data with

Table 17–2 Administrative External Communication Meetings before Restructuring the First Four Units

Date from Kickoff	*Individuals and/or Groups*
4 months–1 month	Chief, Arizona Department of Health Services Licensing Division
	Executive director, Arizona State Board of Nursing
	President, Arizona Hospital Association
	Executive director, Arizona Nurses Association
	President and chief executive officer, Intergroup of Arizona, Inc. (health maintenance organization)
	Executive director and medical director, Cigna Health Plan of Arizona (health maintenance organization)
	Medical director, Thomas Davis Medical Center (affiliation with Intergroup)
	Area vice presidents, nursing
	Dean, College of Nursing, Arizona State University
	Head, graduate program, health administration, Arizona State University

the first postimplementation data. Although dramatic differences were not seen, there were some noticeable positive changes. The reaction of staff demonstrated the importance of providing feedback. The meeting also served as a forum for staff who were involved in a major change project.

Although the pilot unit reviews were held in the following months, there were fewer communication meetings held subsequently. The priority was completion of the evaluation of the project. At 18 months after implementation, the results of patient satisfaction, staff satisfaction, physician satisfaction, and cost savings studies were shared with all hospital staff, including those on the pilot units, and a full report was made to the board of directors. For more detailed information, please see Table 17–3, which lists the administrative internal communication meetings after restructuring of the first four units.

External Communication

Plans were made to inform key leaders about the status and initial results of the project after restructuring of the first four units. The executive director of the Arizona Hospital Association requested a site visit for all the association executive staff, which was held 10 months after implementation. Two invitational site visits were also held. The vice presidents for nursing at several large hospitals in the state were invited to participate in a site visit to learn about the project and to provide critiques. All deans and

Table 17–3 Administrative Internal Communication Meetings after Restructuring the First Four Units

Date after Kickoff	*Individuals and/or Groups (number of meetings)*
3 weeks	Physician leaders, case management coordination (1)
2 months	Pilot units review (2)
2 months	Faculty clinic staff briefing (1)
2 months	All hospital employee update (1)
3 months	Clinical supervisors, float pool staff briefing (3)
6 months	Pilot unit update "Your Patient Speaks" (results of patient satisfaction data) (3)
10–12 months	Pilot units review (4)
15 months	Pilot units review (2)
18 months	Hospital directors, managers, supervisors (results of patient, staff, and physician satisfaction surveys, cost savings, and the future) (1)
18 months	Board of directors report (1)
18 months	All hospital employee forums, PCR results, and the future (1)

*Communication meetings held in addition to PCR steering committee and PCR task force meetings.

directors of schools of nursing in the state were also invited to a program for educators. The representatives of the educational programs were encouraged to incorporate the new roles and the corresponding requirements for the education of nurses into their curricula. Please refer to Table 17–4, which lists the administrative external communication meetings after restructuring of the first four pilot units.

EXPANSION OF THE RESTRUCTURING PROCESS TO NEW UNITS

A request from nursing units to be restructured was not anticipated. Two units, medical intermediate care and surgical intermediate care, had been participants in the Differentiated Group Professional Practice Grant described in Chapter 3, and staff on these units were most anxious to begin. Therefore, with PCR steering committee and task force approval, within 1 month after implementation of the first pilot units, planning with the managers and staff began for the new units. Concomitantly, the nursing director of women's and children's services requested that postpartum and newborn nursery also begin planning for restructuring. The PCR steering committee and task force approved the request, and planning and introductory processes began. The decisions to continue restructuring were based on positive early experience with training and implementa-

Table 17–4 Administrative External Communication Meetings after Restructuring the First Four Pilot Units

Date after Kickoff	*Individuals and/or Groups*
10 months	Arizona Hospital Association all executive staff site visit (requested by the Association)
11 months	Arizona nursing leaders, vice presidents site visit (invitational)
13 months	Arizona deans and directors of schools of nursing site visit (invitational)
Ongoing	Individual group requests for information, presentations, and site visits (as possible)

tion. The leadership at UMC believed that the delivery system was proceeding to meet the project goals. The adaptations to the implementation process can most readily be learned by reviewing the case studies on these four units. Please see Chapters 20 to 22 for more information.

After the first official patient satisfaction evaluation results at 3 months after restructuring and additional experience planning for four additional units, emergency services and labor and delivery requested to begin planning. The request was approved. For more information, please see Chapters 23 and 34. The communication process for the initial implementation was adapted as each successive area was restructured. The adult critical areas, which have begun their planning, continue to adapt the beginning approach as the staff struggle to develop a new model. Please refer to Table 17–5 for a summary of administrative meetings to restructure additional units.

LESSONS LEARNED

The most important communication process lesson learned was the need to provide structure to the follow-up process after kickoff. An extensive administrative prerestructuring communication process was planned and implemented. Although follow-up meetings occurred for the first four pilot units during the first year and a half, greater communication of administrative support might have facilitated the process.

The second lesson learned was the need to provide introductory information to the nursing support staff before restructuring. The clinical supervisors, staffing clerks, and staff in the float pool were not prepared, and predictable operational problems resulted. For example, a staffing clerk tried to substitute a PSA for a PCT while trying to replace a staff person who was ill. The clinical supervisors were predictably angry at having to manage a new situation that they could have been better prepared to

Table 17–5 Summary of Administrative Meetings for New Units to Restructure*

Date after Kickoff of First Pilot Units	*Individuals and/or Groups (number of meetings)*
1 month	Administration, directors, nurse managers (next four inpatient units to restructure) (1)
2 months	Medical and surgical intermediate care unit introductory presentations (4)
2 months	Emergency services, planning and physician introduction (1)
3 months	Medical director briefings (obstetrics, newborn nursery, medical and surgical intermediate care, oncology/bone marrow transplant) (2)
3 months	Postpartum and newborn nursery introductory presentations (3)
11 months	Emergency services introductory staff presentations (3)
11 months	Labor and delivery planning (1)
13 months	Chairs, departments of medicine and surgery critical care discussion (2)
14 months	Labor and delivery introductory staff presentations (3)
16 months	Medicine (oncology) and bone marrow transplant unit staff presentations (3)
18 months	Cardiothoracic and medical-surgical intensive care unit introductory presentations (4)
21 months	Surgical section chiefs update and critical care discussion (1)

*Communication meetings held in addition to PCR steering committee and PCR task force meetings.

handle. The situation was resolvable, but it could have been prevented. Enough stressors occur in a new delivery system change, so that manageable ones need to be avoided whenever possible.

CONCLUSION

The requirements for an extensive communication plan for large-scale institutional change have been outlined. A summary of prerestructuring and postrestructuring communication meetings has been discussed. The most significant lessons learned are described in the hope that future change agents will not repeat UMC's mistakes.

PART

II

Unit Case Studies

CHAPTER

18

Pediatrics Case Study

Marty G. Enriquez

Chapter Objectives

1. To describe the pediatric units, including staff mix, patient population, and delivery systems, before restructuring.
2. To describe the staffing plan and patient care assignments before and after restructuring for each pediatric unit.
3. To describe the specific pediatric skills list developed for the patient care technicians for each of the pediatric units.
4. To discuss the full-time equivalent allocations after restructuring for each pediatric unit.
5. To describe the barriers to implementation of restructured care in the pediatric setting.
6. To discuss special considerations for pediatrics in restructuring.

Patient care restructuring (PCR) is a new and innovative approach to delivering the highest quality of care to pediatric patients while they are hospitalized. This approach aims to improve the quality of care and service to patients and to address labor shortages in various health care occupations. This chapter discusses the process for restructuring patient care in the pediatric areas. A description of the service areas involved is included. The chapter addresses the introduction of the concept to the staff and physicians, describes their involvement via committees and open forums, and discusses barriers to implementation. Specific information about full-time equivalent (FTEs) before and after restructuring as well as staffing plans is also provided.

GENERAL SERVICE DESCRIPTION

The pediatric department at University Medical Center (UMC) offers the following specialized children's programs:

- level I trauma center
- AirCare (rotor and fixed-wing) air transport
- heart transplant
- kidney transplant
- liver transplant
- bone marrow transplant
- comprehensive epilepsy monitoring program
- orthopedic illizarov program
- pediatric cardiology
- pediatric hematology/oncology
- pediatric respiratory
- pediatric critical care medicine
- neonatology

These specialized programs bring many patients from all over Arizona to UMC. Some of the specialty programs have been identified as the best or only one of that nature, so that most of the diagnoses related to these specialized programs are referred to UMC. The majority of the pediatric inpatients are provided care and are followed by the attending physicians, who belong to University Physicians, Inc., and by pediatric residents. Other patients are private patients of two major health maintenance organizations that contract with UMC to bring obstetrical and pediatric patients to UMC.

The pediatric department at UMC had never really experienced a nursing shortage. Excellent programs have always aimed at recruiting and retaining nurses. However, as UMC looked at the larger picture and identified housewide shortages in nursing in other departments and in other health care occupations, it was clear that pediatrics needed to be part of PCR. Everyone was in agreement that the main goal of PCR was to improve patient satisfaction, to increase nurse and physician satisfaction, and to decrease overall costs of care at a time when reimbursement was continuing to decline. The pediatric department wanted to be part of this new and exciting change, especially because PCR had not occurred with pediatrics.

Many special mandatory meetings were held with the nursing staff to discuss PCR, to identify why it was necessary, and to clarify why UMC was choosing to embark on what at the time appeared to be a radical change. The staff were clearly told that their role was an important one within the overall plan for PCR. They were told that they needed to direct this change and to identify how PCR could be implemented on their unit. Most important, they would be the ones to develop the new roles and to determine the staffing plan under PCR. Staff were given ample opportunity to ask questions and address concerns. The major concern noted was the fear of what this major change would mean as well as its impact on job security. If new, nonprofessional roles were being introduced, the staff were concerned that registered nurse (RN) roles would be affected by the change. Because both pediatric units were primarily staffed by RNs, the staff were not initially convinced that a nonnurse could do anything else for their patients. Even the identified nonnursing tasks were thought to be tasks that nurses needed to do to provide appropriate care. Obviously, the ongoing meetings were held with the staff for the following reasons: to discuss PCR with a focus on addressing concerns, to maintain open lines of communication that would prevent unnecessary and incorrect information from being disseminated, to allay anxieties about job security, and to reinforce that the staff would be instrumental in directing this change.

Introductory PCR meetings were also held with both the pediatricians and the residents. Overall they did not object to the change and just wanted reassurance that their patients would be taken care of and that their orders would continue to be followed. It was agreed at these initial meetings that the progress of the PCR project would be followed closely and reported at the monthly pediatric faculty meetings. Any concerns or questions could also be informally addressed to either the nurse managers of the units or the director of the area.

Once the introductory meetings were held for the staff and physicians, specific task forces were established to begin the work of identifying generic job descriptions for the two multipurpose roles that were being created. The work of the various task forces was followed by the development of a unit-specific steering committee for each unit. Each steering committee was composed of nursing staff volunteers from each of the pediatric units. These volunteers played a critical role in PCR in that their purpose was to develop further the generic job descriptions of the two multipurpose workers to meet the specific needs of the pediatric patients. In addition, the steering committee members helped develop the educational and communication plan for PCR as well as the skills list specific to pediatrics. The steering committees also served as the interviewing committees, which screened applications for the new roles and conducted the first level of interviews. Members of these committees were also instrumental in serving a liaison role between the staff of a particular unit and the main PCR task force that was leading the project. It was through the unit-specific steering committees that staff were able to verbalize issues of concern as well as present new ideas for the implementation of the PCR project. The unit steering committees also had a problem-solving role in that, by the time the issues were presented to the main PCR task force, possible solutions for those issues were also presented. Because membership on the steering committees was voluntary, most members were supportive of the PCR project, and their biggest challenge was to educate the staff who were ambivalent and thus resistant to change. Again, ongoing education and communication were critical to this process.

There are five pediatric inpatient units, representing a total of 113 beds, at UMC:

1. a 33-bed neonatal intensive care unit (NICU)
2. an 8- to 12-bed pediatric intensive care unit (PICU)
3. a 30-bed newborn nursery
4. an 18-bed infant to toddler medical-surgical unit (3 West)
5. a 24-bed toddler to young adult medical-surgical unit (3 East)

At the time of this writing, three of the five pediatric units had undergone PCR. Plans are underway to restructure the remaining two units, NICU and PICU, by the end of 1994. The restructuring of the two general pediatric units, 3 East and 3 West, is discussed in this chapter. The restructuring of the newborn nursery is discussed in Chapter 20 under the postpartum and newborn nursery case study.

PEDIATRIC UNIT DESCRIPTIONS: BEFORE RESTRUCTURING

3 West Description and Roles

The infant to toddler unit, known as 3 West, is an 18-bed medical-surgical pediatric unit. The ages of the patients on this unit range from 1 day to

2.5 years. Only under triage situations when there is a bed shortage are older children (up to age 7) placed on 3 West. The restriction is due to the bathrooms on 3 West being limited to toilets and sinks. No showers or bathtubs are available. Children are usually taken to a unit tub room if they need to be bathed.

The patient population on 3 West includes patients from the following pediatric services: cardiology, gastroenterology, pulmonary, orthopedics, hematology/oncology, and general medical-surgical. The top three diagnosis-related groups (DRGs), by number of cases, that are seen on this unit are 98 (bronchitis and asthma), 422 (viral illness), and 298 (nutritional/miscellaneous metabolic disorders). The average daily census for the past few years has consistently been at about 12 patients. The census varies year round, with the busy season being from November to March of each year.

The staff delivering direct patient care before restructuring were primarily RNs except for one part-time licensed practical nurse (LPN), who worked nights. Four of the RN positions are utilized for unit management, with a clinical nurse leader (CNL) overseeing each shift. In the absence of a CNL there is always a designated charge nurse. Before restructuring, these CNLs were called assistant nurse managers (ANMs). ANMs spent 90 percent of their work time (FTEs) doing direct patient care and overseeing the shift. The remaining 10 percent of their time was considered management time, time away from the unit to work on special unit projects, to attend certain committee meetings, and to conduct staff evaluations. Currently, the CNLs spend 100 percent of their time doing clinical care and clinical management of a particular shift. The only additional staff under nursing were unit assistants, who provided clerical support to the unit on a 24-hour basis. Other staff involved with the patients were from a variety of ancillary departments and did not report to nursing. These staff included housekeepers, dietary aides, phlebotomists, transportation aides, materials management personnel, and therapists and aides from respiratory and physical and occupational therapy.

3 East Description and Roles

The toddler to young adult unit, known as 3 East, is a 24-bed medical-surgical pediatric unit. The ages of the patients on this unit range mainly from 2.5 years to 21 years. Infants as young as 7 months of age are also placed on this unit under triage and/or bed shortage situations. However, this particular unit is unique in that it also houses adult patients with cystic fibrosis and some adult patients with cardiac disease who are still under the care of a pediatric pulmonologist or a pediatric cardiologist. These adult patients are usually between 21 and 40 years of age, but the oldest patient with cystic fibrosis has been in the mid-50s. These patients enjoy being on this pediatric unit, and previous attempts to hospitalize them on an adult unit have been unsuccessful. In addition, 3 East is the designated overflow unit for routine postpartum care and for the general adult medical-surgical areas when pediatric volume is down. This overflow situation occurs most frequently between March and November, when pediatric admissions decrease.

Aside from the adult patients mentioned previously, the main patient population on 3 East comes from the following pediatric services: hematology/oncology, cardiology, pulmonary, neurology, orthopedics, and general medical-surgical, including gastroenterology. The top three DRGs, by the number of cases, that are seen on this unit are 98 (bronchitis and asthma), 410 (chemotherapy), and 184 (esophagitis/gastritis). The average daily census on this unit, based on historical data, has been 16 patients. This represents a 66 percent occupancy rate. As with 3 West, the census varies on 3 East, with the highest pediatric volume being between November and March.

The staff delivering direct patient care before restructuring were all RNs except for one full-time LPN, who started on 3 East more than 20 years ago, when the unit first opened. This particular LPN was so skilled and experienced that many of the staff and physicians often thought of this person as an RN. Thus from its own perspective, before restructuring, 3 East had an all-RN staff. Three of the RN positions are utilized for unit management, with a CNL overseeing each shift. Before restructuring, these CNLs were called ANMs. As ANMs, the CNLs spent 90 percent of their time performing clinical work and 10 percent involved in management time. Again, this 10 percent was spent on unit-specific projects, committee work, and evaluations of the staff. Currently, the CNLs spend 100 percent of their time on the unit in a clinical leadership role. In the absence of a CNL, a charge nurse manages a particular shift. As with 3 West, the only additional personnel reporting to nursing before restructuring were unit assistants, who provided 24-hour clerical coverage.

Unit-Specific Skills List for Patient Care Technicians

The job description that was initially developed by the task force for the patient care technicians (PCTs) was finalized approximately 1 month before the start of the PCR project in pediatrics. The role of the PCT was to facilitate the provision of patient care by performing specific nursing tasks and support functions as delegated by an RN. The areas of focus were patient care skills, selected physical therapy and occupational therapy, phlebotomy and clinical laboratory, respiratory therapy, and ECG skills. This generic housewide job description was maintained in pediatrics. However, when the generic skills list for the PCT was finalized, the task of the unit-specific steering committee was to individualize the skills list further to meet the specific needs of the pediatric patients on 3 West and 3 East. Appendixes 18–A and 18–B are the unit-specific skills lists for each of the pediatric units. The PCTs are required to have these skills mastered during their training. The training for the first PCTs (pediatrics was included in this group) was 14 weeks total, primarily because lab required 4 weeks for phlebotomy, which has now been changed with experience. Currently the training is 10 weeks. This period includes training in each area of focus. The generic PCT skills list appears in Chapter 7 and can be referenced for comparison with the pediatric-specific skills list.

The success of the PCT role in pediatrics is highly dependent on the appropriate utilization of the PCT by the RN. If the RN truly delegates all his or her nonnursing tasks to the PCT, then the RN can be freed to complete the tasks that only nurses can perform. This includes ample time for further development of the professional practice of nursing (see Chapter 9). If the RN does not use PCTs to their full potential, however, the RN will have to pick up the extra nonnursing tasks because the PCTs are included in the direct hours for patient care. The successful completion and the future maintenance of the PCT skills list are also dependent on the RN's willingness to serve as a preceptor to the PCTs.

The generic job description that was developed for the patient support attendant (PSA) was adopted without modification for the PSA role in pediatrics. The PSA role was designed to facilitate the efficient functioning of the patient care unit by indirect patient care tasks. The responsibilities of the PSA include the following: all housekeeping and materials management duties; transportation services of patients, specimens, and medication; assistance of patients and/or their parents with menu selection, maintaining the unit's dietary bulk supplies, and providing patient tray distribution and retrieval. The training for the PSAs was 10 days and it focused on the areas where they had to learn new skills. The PSA role was highly supported by the nursing staff. The value of having this multipurpose ancillary worker as part of the patient care team was quickly evident. This role, compared to the PCT role, never threatened anyone and was well received from the start. The main challenge with this role has been minimizing turnover rates since the largest percentage of the role is housekeeping and many of the PSAs originally hired were overqualified. As

UMC has gained more experience with the screening of these applicants, the PSA turnover rate has decreased.

STAFFING PLANS BEFORE AND AFTER RESTRUCTURING

Before restructuring there were two identified levels of care for the pediatric patients on both 3 West and 3 East. The first level of care is the standard for most medical-surgical pediatric units across the country and it is a 1:4 nurse-to-patient ratio. The second level of care is an intermediate level requiring a 1:3 nurse-to-patient ratio. Since the standard care is 1:4, criteria is developed to specifically identify the 1:3 level of care. Children requiring more than a 1:3 ratio of care are usually placed in the PICU in one of four different levels of care that can be provided in the PICU. There is no pre-established acuity system utilized for pediatrics at UMC, aside from the criteria just mentioned. Exhibit 18–1 indicates the criteria for the 1:3 level of care.

Both 3 West and 3 East were budgeted for 1:4 care, but 1:3 care was more the norm on 3 West. The staffing guidelines for each of the units before restructuring reflected budgeted nursing hours per patient day (NHPPD) for direct care of 7.39 for 3 West and 7.30 for 3 East. These direct hours included only the nurses and LPNs giving direct care. Hours of the nurse

Exhibit 18–1 Recommended Criteria for 1:3 RN/Patient Care Ratios on 3 East and 3 West (High Acuity Patients)

1. "Every 2 hour" procedures: feeds, Chemstrips, vital signs, irrigations/flushes, etc.
2. Frequent/unstable respiratory diagnosis patients requiring frequent aerosols (2–3 hours) or aminophylline drips, patients with history of apnea
3. Observation for heart dysrhythmias/CHF patients requiring digitalization/diuresis
4. Patients receiving chemotherapy/blood product transfusions/TPN
5. Patients with tracheostomies or patients requiring frequent suctioning; patients weaning off oxygen/requiring pulse oximetry and CR monitor
6. First 4 hours:
   - after surgery/catheterization
   - after transfer from PICU
   - after admission for R/O sepsis patients
   - after admission for dehydration
7. Difficult social situations/complicated discharges
8. Procedures requiring nurse to accompany patient

manager and unit assistants and management time of the ANMs were all part of the indirect hours.

After restructuring, the levels of care for 3 West and 3 East remained the same: 1:3 and 1:4. In fact, the PCT was added to the RN 1:3 or 1:4 ratio. Restructuring occurred in December of fiscal year (FY) 1991–92. The direct NHPPD for each of the units was changed at the time of the restructuring to reflect the addition of the PCT role to direct care. The staffing guidelines for each of the units after restructuring reflected budgeted NHPPD for direct care of 7.65 for 3 West and 7.56 for 3 East for FY 1992–93. There was an increase in NHPPD from 1991–92.

Table 18–1 illustrates the total FTEs by job classification before and after restructuring for 3 West and 3 East. Note the decrease in the RN FTEs for each of the units. These FTEs were eliminated through attrition and vacancies; not one RN lost his or her position as a result of PCR. Also note the addition of the PCT and PSA FTEs. The PCT FTEs are added to the direct hours of care, and the PSA FTEs are added to indirect care. In the first year of restructuring, the LPN FTEs were increased from 0.5 to 2.2 on 3 West in an attempt to maintain more licensed but less expensive personnel. This proved to be a problem as a result of the Arizona State Board of Nursing not allowing LPNs to perform phlebotomy in pediatrics. In addition, it was often difficult to maintain two RNs for safety purposes on 3 West when almost a third of the licensed staff were LPNs. As planning began for

Table 18–1 Specific Unit Job Classifications and Budgeted FTEs

		Budgeted FTEs	
Unit	*Job Classification*	*Before Restructuring*	*After Restructuring*
3 West	RN	12.8	6.2
	ANM/CNL	3.0	4.0
	LPN	0.5	2.2
	PCT	0	4.2
	PSA	0	4.9
	Unit assistant	4.4	4.4
	Nurse manager*	1.0	1.0
3 East	RN	17.7	12.8
	ANM/CNL	3.0	3.0
	LPN	1.0	1.0
	PCT	0	7.0
	PSA	0	5.6
	Unit assistant	4.1	4.2

*Nurse manager is responsible for both 3 West and 3 East but charges hours to 3 West cost center.

FY 1993–94, all LPN positions in pediatrics were eliminated. PCTs proved to be more flexible when it came to the multipurpose training they had received, which included phlebotomy skills. Tables 18–2 and 18–3 illustrate the staffing guidelines for the new budget year. Table 18–4 shows the FTEs by job classification that were submitted after restructuring for FY 1993–94.

These FTEs reflect the elimination of the LPNs and the subsequent increase of RN FTEs on both 3 West and 3 East. In addition, the direct NHPPD for 3 West was increased from 7.65 to 9.57 for FY 1993–94 to reflect the level of care the staff provide, which is 1:3 versus 1:4. There is also a decrease in unit assistant FTEs as a result of some budgetary cutbacks related to a decrease in volume but not related to PCR.

Because the goal of the PCR project was to be budget dollar neutral, the additional FTEs added to 3 West and 3 East in FY 1992–93 and FY 1993–94 were part of FTE reallocations from the affected ancillary departments (i.e., housekeeping, dietary, laboratory, transportation, materials management, and some occupational/physical therapy and respiratory therapy).

Table 18–2 Staffing Guidelines after Restructuring, 3 West

	Days		*Nights*		
Total Patients	*RN*	*PCT*	*RN*	*PCT*	*Direct HPPD*
3–6	2	0	2	0	N/A
7	2	1	2	0	8.6
8	2	1	2	1	9.0
9	3	1	2	1	9.3
10*	3	1	2.5	1	9.0
11	3	1	3	1	8.7
12	4	1	3	1	9.0
13	4	1	4	1	9.2
14	4	2	4	1	9.4
15	4	2	4	1	8.8
16	4	2	4	2	9.0
17	5	2	4	2	9.2
18	5	2	5	2	9.3

PSA: days 2 (if census 7 and up)
evenings 1 (if census 7 and up)
nights 1

* Budgeted average daily census: 10
Budgeted NHPPD: 9.57

Table 18–3 Staffing Guidelines after Restructuring, 3 East

	Required Staff						
	Days		*Evenings*		*Nights*		
Total Patients	*RN*	*PCT*	*RN*	*PCT*	*RN*	*PCT*	*Direct HPPD*
8	2	1	2	0	2	0	7.0
9	3	0	3	0	2	0	7.11
10	3	0	3	0	2	1	7.2
11	3	1	3	0	2	1	7.27
12	3	1	3	1	2	1	7.33
13	3	1	3	1	2.5	1	7.08
14	3.5	1	3	1	3	1	7.14
15	4	1	3.5	1	3	1	7.2
16*	4	1	4	1	3.5	1	7.25
17	4	2	4	1	3.5	1	7.29
18	4	2	4	2	3.5	1	7.34
19	5	2	4	2	3.5	1	7.37
20	5	2	4	2	4	1	7.2
21	5	2	5	2	4	1	7.24
22	5	2	5	2	4	1	6.89
23	6	2	5	2	5	1	7.3
24	6	2	6	2	5	1	7.33

PSA: days 2 — * Budgeted average daily census: 16

evenings 1–2 — Budgeted NHPPD: 7.37

nights 1

BARRIERS TO PCT IMPLEMENTATION IN PEDIATRICS

As mentioned previously, a major change in delivery of care can be viewed negatively by the staff who are affected, and the first reaction is often resistance to change. It is of the utmost importance to keep lines of communication open with both staff and physicians to answer questions and address any and all of their concerns. Understanding the process of change that groups and individuals must go through to reach acceptance is critical in recognizing the appropriate corrective action required to assist those groups and/or individuals in moving through the process. Restructuring was viewed as such a radical change with so many unknowns that it created a fear of the unknown, leading to resistance. The resistance was exhibited in many forms. Rumors circulated concerning the actual

Table 18–4 Specific Unit Job Classifications and Budgeted FTEs after Restructuring

Unit FY 1993–94	*Job Classification*	*Budgeted FTEs*
3 West	RN	8.8
	ANM/CNL	3.8
	PCT	4.2
	PSA	4.2
	Unit assistant	3.5
	Nurse manager	1.0
3 East	RN	13.10
	ANM/CNL	3.0
	PCT	4.58
	PSA	5.6
	Unit assistant	3.5

role of the PCTs and the possibility of UMC cutting costs by eliminating RN positions. During the training period, some RNs did not welcome the PCTs to their units. A few RNs even did things to let the PCTs know they were not going to be supported. Other nurses refused to utilize the PCTs and then complained that the PCTs were "sitting around" while the RNs were working hard and feeling overwhelmed.

Scope of practice issues for the RNs were identified, and all of a sudden the same nurses who had worked side by side with an LPN (and, in reality, thought of the LPN as an RN) were now raising concerns about the PCT role and their own liability as RNs. Most of the RNs in pediatrics had never worked with unlicensed personnel and really did not know what or how to delegate appropriately. Although it was clear from the beginning of the PCR project that the PCT was no more and no less than a nurse's aide with additional skills (i.e., phlebotomy, ECG, some occupational/physical therapy, and some minimal respiratory therapy), some RNs still had difficulty understanding the difference between observation and assessment.

Another barrier identified in pediatrics involved staff mix issues. Regulations placed by the Arizona State Board of Nursing on the LPN scope of practice did not allow the LPNs to perform phlebotomy in pediatrics, so that the PCT role was viewed as more flexible. In addition, particularly on 3 West (which is a smaller unit), it was often difficult for the sole RN to supervise both the LPNs and the PCTs, provide patient care, and perform all patient admissions. These issues led to the elimination of the LPN positions in pediatrics when some downsizing had to occur as a result of decreased volume on both 3 West and 3 East. This change did improve the RN FTEs on both units because 3 West had 2.2 LPN FTEs eliminated and 3

East had 1.0 LPN FTE eliminated. Although this reduction in force, driven by a decrease in patient days and staffing mix issues, was difficult for the staff and physicians, the nurse-to-patient ratio and the direct NHPPD were not decreased on either of the pediatric units.

SPECIAL CONSIDERATIONS FOR PEDIATRICS IN RESTRUCTURING

The main basis for PCR, improvement of patient and family (parent) satisfaction, had to be a strongly identified need in pediatrics because a discernible nursing shortage had never occurred. The needs of pediatric patients are different from those of adults, so that it was important for pediatrics to be part of the initial PCR project to develop its own model rather than try later to fit into the adult health model for PCR. Staff education had to focus both on the overall picture and on the unique opportunity that the pediatric staff had to be in the driver's seat of this major change. Education needed to be ongoing in an attempt to prepare the pediatric staff for the issues they were going to face, such as working with unlicensed personnel, supervising unlicensed personnel, delegating to unlicensed personnel, and being part of a team with unlicensed personnel. These issues were unique to pediatrics because, unlike their adult health colleagues, many of the RNs in pediatrics had never worked with unlicensed personnel.

The PCT role in pediatrics was clearly going to be on trial, and a trusting working relationship between the PCT and the RN had to develop quickly to ensure its success. It was initially difficult for the RNs to visualize giving up the feedings, the bed baths, the bed changes, or the vital signs to the PCTs, especially on the infant unit (3 West); the RNs believed that valuable infant assessment occurred during these functions. Time and ongoing development of the PCT role has demonstrated that the PCT is able to perform these tasks and that the nurse can obtain assessments during other quality time spent with the patients. The ongoing education of the PCT will continue to develop the PCTs as PCT utilization is maximized by the RNs. The PCT and the RN continue as partners in this major change of the health care delivery system.

CURRENT PCR STATUS

PCR in pediatrics has been challenging, exciting, and at times even frustrating. The failure to recognize that resistance to change varies with each group and/or individual and that the duration of resistance cannot be predicted led to early frustration when the staff of 3 West and 3 East were not moving along as had been planned. One year into the PCR project, some of the PCTs were still feeling as if they were not being used effectively by some RNs. Also, some RNs were still not happy with PCR and kept making erroneous assumptions that, if they as RNs said it didn't work, it would go away. Ongoing evaluation of the project with patient, staff, and physician questionnaires has helped the staff recognize that the change is positive and that the goal of improved patient outcome is being met. Problem solving at the unit level with immediate corrective action on many issues has led to staff awareness that they are empowered to make changes and that administration is hearing their concerns.

Currently, the majority of the staff would agree that PCR is working well in pediatrics. They feel that the patients have benefitted from the change, and they are comfortable delegating and supervising the PCTs. For the most part, the staff know that PCR is occurring across the country and that, with all the changes developing in health care today, PCR is one way of ensuring improved patient outcomes and ongoing delivery of quality patient care.

CONCLUSION

The process for planning and implementing PCR in the pediatric areas has been discussed. The new approach to health care delivery is a major change and requires education, clarification, communication, and most definitely staff involvement. This chapter has reviewed the importance of initial informational meetings required to identify the need for PCR and the importance of staff involvement and participation early in the process as well as ongoing. Specific FTE information before and after restructuring has been provided, and information about PCT skills lists and unit staffing plans has been outlined.

Any further changes involving PCR will need to include staff who will be affected by the change. The staff need to move toward shared governance and be empowered to continue to direct the change. In today's health care world, change appears to be the only constant. Ongoing education and open communication are critical. Most important, if professionals are to succeed as quality health care providers, it must never be forgotten that the patient is and must continue to be the main focus that drives any change.

Appendix 18–A

PCT Skills List, 3 West

PCTs will be observed performing each skill at least three times, with the supervisory RN dating and initialing each column. When the PCT demonstrates proficiency, the final column should be dated and initialed. If the RN feels that the PCT requires further observation after the third performance of the skill, the proficient column will not be completed.

Skill Performed	*× 1*	*× 2*	*Proficient*
1. Vital signs Temperature Axillary			
Tympanic			
Rectal			
Apical pulse (60 seconds)			
Respiratory rate (60 seconds)			
Height			
Weight			
Head circumference			
2. I & Os, recorded every 2 hours			

Skill Performed	*× 1*	*× 2*	*Proficient*
3. Admissions Set up room (linens, diapers, equip.)			
Perform vital signs			
Orient family to room			
4. CR monitors Set up and placement of electrodes			
Set alarms			
Collect data every 2 hours			
5. Basic hygiene/skin care Diaper changes			
Observation of skin for signs of breakdown—notify nurse			
Application of nonprescription ointments			
6. Ambulation and transfers Safety measures—side rails, climber cribs (toddlers)			
In attendance if child is in highchair, swing, walker, stroller			
Assess for inappropriate objects/ toys in crib			
Observation of gait (toddlers)			

Skill Performed	*× 1*	*× 2*	*Proficient*
7. Feedings Age-appropriate foods			
Observation for swallowing difficulties			
Stable GT feeds Record aspirates			
Gravity feeds			
Continual feeds (enteral pump) Kangaroo pump set up			
No more than 4 hours volume in bag			
Change bag and tubing every 24 hours			
8. Basic CPR Certified every 2 years (write date)			
Attend mock Code inservice yearly (write date)			
9. Universal precautions Gloves when in contact with all body fluids			
Reverse isolation			
Respiratory isolation			
Proper disposal of contaminated objects			

Skill Performed	*× 1*	*× 2*	*Proficient*
Preoperative preps (scrubs, aseptic technique)			
10. Urine collection—bag system Proper technique Single collection			
24-hour collection			
11. Urinary catheterization (children 6 months and older) Collecting supplies			
Sterile technique			
12. Priming IV tubing New IV bag, Buretrol, IMED tubing, extension tubing			
Sterile technique			
Labels on Buretrol and tubing to change in 72 hours			
13. Sterile/aseptic dressing changes Sterile excepting central line dressings			
Aseptic technique Pacer care			
GT site			

Skill Performed	*× 1*	*× 2*	*Proficient*
Urologic stints			
Other:			
Observation for infection/ discharge/dehiscence— notify RN			
14. Stoma care Observation of stoma and skin surrounding site—record			
Application of stoma collection bag			
Application of skin preps			
15. Tracheostomy care Observation of respiratory effort, secretions—record			
Notify nurse if requires suctioning			
Dressing change with assistance			
16. Assist nurse with: NG tube insertion			
IV insertion			
Tracheostomy care—suctioning, cleaning, changing cannula			
Dressing changes			
Urinary catheterization			

Skill Performed	*× 1*	*× 2*	*Proficient*
Collecting supplies			
Maintaining sterile/aseptic technique			
17. Oral hygiene Nasal/oral bulb suctioning			
Toothette swabs if NPO			
Observation of mouth cavity for signs of thrush/breakdown—record and notify RN			
18. Pulse oximetry Set alarms			
Record data every 2 hours			
Record rate of oxygen administration and method			
19. Oxygen/suction set-ups Collect equipment			
Assist with set-up			
20. ECGs Perform using proper technique			
Properly label ECG strips			
Complete charge slip			
21. Rehab-related/physical therapy Proper body alignment/positioning of patient			

Skill Performed	*× 1*	*× 2*	*Proficient*
Assist in change of position every 2 hours			
Infants unable to turn over to be placed on stomach or side with blanket roll behind back			
Observation of proper traction set-up			
Range of motion/massage therapy			
Assist with activity			
22. Rehab-related occupational therapy Assist with ADL program			
Apply splints, monitor adherence to schedule, assess for skin breakdown, record observations			
Oral-motor-tactile stimulation as ordered			
23. Lab procedures Appropriate collection methodology—venipuncture			
Heelstick/fingerstick			
Collect and accurately label specimens			
Place specimens in proper collecting tubes/cups Blood			

Skill Performed	*× 1*	*× 2*	*Proficient*
Stool			
Urine			
Sputum			
Wound			
Viral/*Mycoplasma*/*Chlamydia*			
Attend lab inservice for viral culture collection and QA			
Perform on-unit testing and QA accurately, record: Specific gravity			
Hemoccults			
Accucheck glucose testing			
Proper technique for collecting and processing lab for blood bank			
Sterile technique when collecting blood cultures			
24. Charting/reporting Observation/recording on flowsheets Vital signs			
Breath sounds			
Abdominal appearance/bowel sounds			
Perfusion of lower extremities			

Skill Performed	*× 1*	*× 2*	*Proficient*
Neuro signs Level of consciousness Pupil reaction Anterior fontanelle palpation Movement of extremities			
I & O			
Wound appearance			
IV site appearance			
Drainage sites, appearance of site, discharge qualities			
Parental/family visits			
Parental/family interactions			
Apnea, cyanosis, swallowing/ breathing difficulties			
Equipment used (check off)			
Immediate notification of nurse of changes/abnormal findings			
Subjective/objective progress note on each patient assigned within 2 hours of the end of shift			
Formal verbal report to supervising RN on patients assigned 2 hours before end of shift			

RN initials/signature

____________________ ____________________

____________________ ____________________

____________________ ____________________

Appendix 18–B

PCT Skills List, 3 East

PCTs will be observed performing each skill at least three times, with the supervisory RN dating and initialing each column. When the PCT demonstrates proficiency, the final column should be dated and initialed. If the RN feels that the PCT requires further observation after the third performance of the skill, the proficient column will not be completed.

Skill Performed	*× 1*	*× 2*	*Proficient*
1. Lab procedures Venipuncture technique Vacutainer collection			
Syringe collection			
Two-syringe technique			
Microcollection technique Fingersticks			
Heelsticks			
Unopettes			
Special collection procedures Blood bank banding			
Blood cultures			

Skill Performed	*× 1*	*× 2*	*Proficient*
Specimen labeling			
Urine collection Catheter specimen			
Straight cath specimen			
Bagged specimen			
24-hour collection			
Viral collections Nasopharyngeal specimen			
Rectal specimen			
Throat culture			
Cultures Stool			
Sputum			
Wound			
Lab quality control Urine specific gravity			
Accucheck blood glucose testing			
Stool hemoccult			
Urine dipstick testing			
Patient charging Charge slips initiated and processed			

Skill Performed	*× 1*	*× 2*	*Proficient*
2. Rehab-related/physical therapy Use of assistive devices Walker			
Axillary crutches			
Forearm crutches			
Canes			
Hoyer lift			
Devices, dressings Overbed trapeze			
CPM machine			
Ace Wraps			
TED hose			
Pneumatic stockings			
Hemovac, Vacutainer, Jackson Pratt suction			
Jones dressing			
Knee immobilizer/bunny splint			
Arm sling			
Cast care			
Traction—rewrap, proper alignment, weights			
Transfers Standing pivot transfer—dependent, assisted			

Skill Performed	*× 1*	*× 2*	*Proficient*
Lateral transfer			
Transfer of patient with spica cast			
3. Respiratory care Demonstrates and documents: Breath sounds			
Pulse oximetry—check and document oxygen			
Pulse oximetry—alarm setting			
Incentive spirometry—instruct and charge set-up			
Portable oxygen			
Oxygen—record rate and delivery method			
4. ECG Demonstrates proper technique			
Completes proper paperwork			
Transmits properly			
5. General patient care skills Basic hygiene Bed bath			
Foley care			
Linen change			

Skill Performed	× *1*	× *2*	*Proficient*
Oral care			
Shampoo			
Bedpan and urinal use and care			
I&O Calculating intake			
Measure urine output (BS commode, ostomy bag)			
Measuring hemovac/JP output			
Measuring suction canister output			
Accurate I&O			
Calorie counts			
Fluid restrictions			
Vital signs Oral temperature			
Axillary temperature			
Rectal temperature			
Tympanic temperature			
Apical pulse			
Peripheral pulse			
Respiratory rate			
Blood pressure			

Skill Performed	*× 1*	*× 2*	*Proficient*
Height measurement			
Weight measurement			
Head circumference measurement			
Infant scale weight measurement			
6. Nutrition Correct diet order			
Fluid restriction			
Stable GT feeds—check aspirates			
Gravity feeds			
Continual feeds			
Kangaroo pump set-up			
Feeding tubing change every 24 hours			
Feeding bag volume 4-hour maximum			
7. Safety Universal precautions			
Gowns when holding infants			
Gloves when in contact with all body fluids			
Respiratory precautions			
Proper handling of sharps			

Skill Performed	*× 1*	*× 2*	*Proficient*
Use of restraints/Poseys			
Proper use of side rails (crib, confused or sedated patient)			
Climber crib (toddlers)			
Heat lamps			
ID bands			
Seizure precautions			
Handling contaminated supplies			
CPR, certified every 2 years			
Mock Code—attends inservice yearly			
8. Wound care Sterile dressing change			
Observe and document wound characteristics			
Pacer wire care			
9. Admit patient Obtain appropriate vital signs			
Set up room			
Call light within reach			
Condition of admit form signed			
Visitation rules			
Patient/family oriented to room and unit			

Skill Performed	*× 1*	*× 2*	*Proficient*
10. Patient discharge Necessary RN instructions completed			
Patient has received DC meds			
Patient has all personal belongings			
11. Pre-op procedures Instructions			
Checklist/forms in order			
Current labs on chart			
Necessary equipment available at time of transport			
12. Post-op care Frequent vital signs			
Necessary equipment available at time of return			
Respiratory care			
Progressive activity			
NPO status, advance slowly			
Intravenous—set up IMED tubing			
CR monitor—set up and set alarms			
13. Orthopedic care Pin care for skeletal traction			

Skill Performed	*× 1*	*× 2*	*Proficient*
Traction—rewrapping, proper alignment, weights			
Pressure ulcer prevention			
Proper body alignment			
Neurovascular checks and documentation			
Peripheral pulses			
Plantar/dorsiflexion			
14. Charting and reporting Documenting on flowsheets			
Immediately inform RN of changes/abnormal findings			
S/O progress note on each patient assigned within 2 hours of end of shift			
Formal verbal report to supervising RN on patients assigned 2 hours before shift end			

RN initials/signature

____________________ ____________________

____________________ ____________________

____________________ ____________________

CHAPTER

19

Medical-Surgical Case Study

Joe Bojorquez

Chapter Objectives

- To describe the unit, staffing patterns, and nursing delivery system before and after restructuring.
- To describe the planning process for preparation and implementation of major change.
- To discuss the impact of quality on ancillary departments.
- To describe some of the positives and negatives for staff and patients.
- To describe some of the difficulties encountered with managing nonprofessional workers.
- To share special considerations and lessons learned.

With time being one of the more critical assets, wastage should be kept to a minimum. The nursing profession is frequently asked to hurry up and wait, a phenomenon associated with spinning wheels and efforts in futility. Nursing personnel strive to meet the needs of patients but frequently encounter frustrations related to the delivery of services from centralized support systems as well as barriers associated with the nursing care delivery system. Issues identified within the system at University Medical Center prompted the question of how to better meet the needs of clientele. The climate was right to examine alternative care delivery styles, and fortunately a concept was being formulated and presented to hospital administration. The introduction of unit-based multipurpose workers accompanying changes in the care delivery style was determined to be the answer. Pioneer units were identified, and the voyage into the unknown began. In an effort to identify the changes that occurred with restructuring, it is important to look at the unit before and after implementation.

UNIT DESCRIPTION

The medical-surgical unit is a 31-bed unit for patients with orthopedic diagnoses, neurological disorders, and neurosurgical interventions. The unit also houses the Arizona Comprehensive Epilepsy Program, providing 24-hour inpatient seizure monitoring for patients throughout the Southwest. In addition, patients with hyperthermal bead placement and posttraumatic injuries requiring rehabilitation services are cared for on the unit. The average length of stay for this varied patient population is maintained between 4 and 7 days.

The staffing mix includes the utilization of registered nurses (RNs), licensed practical nurses (LPNs), nursing assistants (NAs), and the unit secretary. An assistant nurse manager (ANM) is also present on each shift. This individual is responsible for addressing any clinical issues on the unit as well as overseeing any management issues related to budget, quality control, patient concerns, or staff problems. Each RN is responsible for a core group of patients and oversees patients who are assigned to an LPN. NAs are utilized as extra pairs of hands on the unit. They are given tasks to accomplish during a given shift and are utilized as clinical support workers for the nurses. An NA II position was also introduced. This person has been trained in specific skills to assist the nursing staff. These skills include dressing changes, catheterization, and simple tube feedings. The unit secretary (ward clerk) performs in the traditional role of clerical support for the unit.

The staffing guidelines for the unit are based on a direct hours per patient day (HPPD) of 6.48. Two separate staffing guidelines were established to reflect the acuity involved with epilepsy patients. The nurse caring for the patients with epilepsy needs to take a smaller patient load because of the care demands. For the purposes of staffing guidelines, the NAs are counted as 0.5 HPPD. This was done in an effort to balance any replacement factors (e.g., two NAs to replace one licensed person). Many times staffing clerks attempt to substitute an NA for licensed staff (Table 19–1). Therefore, on a given day shift with two epilepsy patients and a census of 25, the unit is staffed with seven persons, typically five RNs, one LPN, and two NAs:

- one RN assigned to the epilepsy patients
- two RNs given four patients each (one being the charge nurse)
- two RNs given five patients each
- one LPN taking five patients
- two NAs being given five to six beds and baths to do as well as specific tasks to accomplish during that shift

Table 19–1 4 West Staffing Guidelines by Census (6.48 HPPD)*

	7 A.M.–3 P.M.						3 P.M.–11 P.M.						11 P.M.–7 A.M.					
	*Without***			*With*			*Without*			*With*			*Without*			*With*		
Census	*RN*	*LPN*	*NA*	*RN*	*LPN*	*NA*	*RN*	*LPN*	*NA*	*RN*	*LPN*	*NA*	*RN*	*LPN*	*NA*	*RN*	*LPN*	*NA*
29	5	1	3	5	2	2	4	2	1	4	2	2	4	0	2	4	1	1
28	5	1	2	5	2	1	4	2	0	4	2	1	4	1	0	4	1	0
27	5	1	2	5	1	3	4	1	2	4	1	2	3	1	1	4	1	0
26	5	1	2	5	1	3	4	1	2	4	1	2	3	1	1	3	1	1
25	5	1	1	5	1	2	4	1	1	4	1	2	3	1	0	3	1	1
24	5	1	1	5	1	2	4	1	1	4	1	2	3	1	0	3	1	1
23	4	1	2	4	1	3	3	1	2	3	1	3	3	1	0	3	1	0
22	4	1	2	4	1	3	3	1	2	3	1	3	2	1	1	3	1	0
21	4	1	1	4	1	2	3	1	2	3	1	2	2	1	1	3	1	0
20	4	1	0	4	1	1	3	1	1	3	1	2	2	1	1	3	1	0
19	3	1	2	4	1	1	3	1	1	3	1	2	2	1	0	2	1	1
18	3	1	1	3	1	2	3	1	0	3	1	1	2	1	0	2	1	1
17	3	1	1	3	1	2	3	1	0	3	1	1	2	1	0	2	1	1
16	2	1	2	3	1	1	3	0	1	3	0	2	2	1	0	2	1	1
15	2	1	2	3	1	1	3	0	1	3	0	2	2	0	1	2	1	0
14	2	1	1	2	1	2	2	1	0	2	1	1	2	0	1	2	0	1
13	2	1	1	2	1	2	2	0	2	2	1	1	2	0	1	2	0	1
12	2	1	0	2	1	1	2	0	2	2	0	2	2	0	0	2	0	1
11	2	0	2	2	1	1	2	0	1	2	0	2	2	0	0	2	0	1
10	2	0	2	2	0	2	2	0	1	2	0	2	2	0	0	2	0	1

*These numbers vary depending on the number of epilepsy patients on the unit and/or patient acuity. Nurses assigned to the epilepsy program take two to three patients on days, three to four patients on evenings, and four patients on nights.

** Without or with epilepsy patients.

All staff would have direct line reporting to the ANM for that given shift. The ANMs would report to the nurse manager, and each nurse manager would report directly to the director. All new nursing personnel are given orientation time based on their previous work history and experience. A typical new RN graduate would be given 6 weeks in which to orient with an assigned preceptor. An experienced nurse would be granted 4 weeks, and NAs would be given 2 weeks.

The relationships with ancillary departments were different on each unit. On one unit, the physical therapy and occupational services departments provided care directly to the patients. Therefore, supplies were housed near the unit, and the therapists worked directly on the floor. This provided a well-needed service to the patient population. The patients appreciated the fact that they need not spend a great deal of transit time to and from each department. Other ancillary services were provided by employees who commuted to the unit and were supervised by their own departmental personnel. Centralized services created a great deal of communication delays, such as calling dispatchers for requests and problem solving. It also alienated the nursing staff from workers from other departments because of the infrequency of working together. An exception to this was the environmental services worker (housekeeper), who was assigned to a given area. She provided some continuity of service and was more comfortable with the nursing staff.

PLANNING FOR PATIENT CARE RESTRUCTURING

Patient care restructuring (PCR) was first introduced to provide better support for the nursing units while continuing to provide quality care for the patients. Restructuring was to be a pilot on four units, with the only stipulation being that it remain budget neutral.

Several issues were identified as needing to be addressed before restructuring. It was also determined that a minimum of five steps would be essential before the implementation of change:

1. resource identification
2. staff communication
3. staff education
4. hiring new workers
5. training

Resource Identification

The first step involved the identification of resources to be incorporated on the unit. Time-motion studies were completed in an effort to establish the number of services and full-time equivalents (FTEs) provided to the area from the ancillary departments. The number of identified FTEs was then thrown into an imaginary resource pot. The FTEs were multiplied by the average wage, in accordance with the job classification, and converted into a dollar amount. The established dollars from the studies were then distributed equally among the four pioneer areas. This distribution, combined with the nursing unit's budget, was totaled and provided the resource from which to begin.

Given the dollars and FTEs as a guide, the mix and number of individuals for each category of worker could then be estimated. After deciding the services that needed to be provided, it was determined that two additional workers would need to be introduced. One was an indirect caregiver able to provide services such as housekeeping, transportation, materials management, and dietary responsibilities. The other worker was to provide direct care services relating to NA, phlebotomy, physical therapy, occupational therapy, and some respiratory therapy duties. These workers were identified as patient support attendants (PSAs) and patient care technicians (PCTs). The job descriptions for these workers would later be developed and modified to meet the needs and demands of each unit.

Staff Communication

When things are going well, it is difficult to convince staff that a change is necessary. This was the next step that needed to be addressed. A series of meetings was conducted to educate staff regarding both the new ideas and the introduction of a new classification of workers. The majority of staff resisted change initially but later approved the concept once they realized it was inevitable. Education about the present status of the health care system in the United States and the reimbursement issues relating to the same prompted a change in their way of thinking. Given factual information backed by statistical data, many staff members were more willing to explore other methods of delivering care. A steering committee was formed in an effort to elicit information from the staff themselves and to encourage a sense of participation and worth. The members of this committee were to be a resource to the unit staff, helping communicate information and assisting in diffusing any issues that might surface as a result of misinterpretation or anger. It was extremely important to involve influential, open-minded individuals in an effort to assist in the buffering and introduction of new concepts. A chairperson was also selected in an effort to maintain leadership within the group.

Staff Education

Many subsequent workshops were held to prepare the core staff for major change. First, a team-building workshop was conducted so that the staff would build a more effective working relationship among themselves and the different classifications of workers. The workshop included some group participation with different exercises, in which a mutual outcome would be realized using various talents within the group. These exercises were helpful with informal communication and assisted with realizing who the informal leaders were and looking at different styles of delegation. Next, a communication workshop was held to expand communication styles and techniques. It was feared that the different communication styles of individuals would be detrimental to the working relationships of multiple work groups. During the communication workshop, individuals became more aware of their own communication styles as well as the diversity and variety that existed. Many participants were not aware of these differences and realized that communication styles are not always reflective of the message being delivered. Poor communication may just be a misinterpretation of one's communication delivery style.

Delegation workshops for the RNs were also conducted. Because it was known that delegation would be an integral part of the puzzle, coordinators believed that this workshop was greatly needed. Many of the nursing staff felt uncomfortable in delegating tasks to others because the unit had various degrees of experience within the nursing staff. Half the staff had more than 7 years of experience, and the other half had less than 5 years of experience. It was observed that the nurses with more experience felt more strongly against delegating tasks to others. The feeling was that the quality of nursing care would diminish if they did not administer care themselves. Quality through delegation was an obvious issue that needed to be addressed if the project was going to be successful. Also, it was expressed that patient contact during activities of daily living, such as baths, was utilized as a means of assessing the patient in terms of systems, skin, and so forth. The delegation workshop is addressed in greater detail in Chapter 8.

Hiring New Workers

After staff preparation had begun to be addressed, the new workers were hired. Initial screening was conducted by personnel in the human resources department. They developed minimal work experience criteria as well as a screening tool for potential applicants. It was believed that staggering the introduction of the new workers would be valuable. Consequently it was decided first to introduce the indirect care workers or PSAs. The application process was first available to individuals from whom FTEs were to be reassigned. Applications were then opened to the general public. The general public included housekeeping, transportation, dietary, and materials management personnel. From these applicants the more qualified candidates were screened through a testing process and forwarded to the nurse managers.

The unit's steering committee developed an ad hoc interview panel to screen these applicants. Interview questions were then developed, and the process was completed. This process enabled staff to feel more involved with the project and thus able to provide input regarding who their co-workers would be. From the interview panel, the stronger applicants were then forwarded to the nurse manager. The manager would then hire from this pool. This same process was established and completed for the PCTs, using a different pool from which to draw and with the addition of outside applicants. An attempt was made to design the PSA entry level as a means of furthering workers' careers within the nursing services department. This process was appealing to many of the applicants interviewed.

Training

Once the employees were hired, they participated in an intensive orientation/education program. The PSAs required a 2-week orientation schedule, and the PCTs were placed on a 14-week orientation schedule. Both programs were developed by the PCR education coordinator and supervised by staff from ancillary departments to utilize the expertise from the other areas (see Chapters 6 and 7).

After completion of orientation, a graduation ceremony was held for the new workers. Graduation was conducted complete with the presentation of a certificate and the accompanying fanfare in an effort to instill pride and a sense of accomplishment in the employees. All staff members were encouraged to attend this important function as a means of establishing a sense of teamwork on the entire unit.

Before the implementation of the PSAs, a group of supervisory personnel including representation from nursing, environmental services, transportation, materials management, dietary, and administration met in an effort to determine the workflow for the indirect caregivers. This workflow was developed in an effort to map out the workday for the multipurpose worker (Exhibit 19–1). It was believed that a nonprofessional worker would perform better with stronger direction, and thus a workflow was established for each of the three shifts.

To develop these workflows, it was essential that strong working relationships be established with the ancillary departments. Nursing was not always attuned to the intricacies of everyday work life for the ancillary workers (e.g., what the dietary workflow looked like). It was therefore essential to develop a close working relationship with the departmental supervisors to acquire the information necessary to establish the workflow

Exhibit 19–1 4 West PSA Workflow

Day Shift

0600–0615	Food service floor stock inventory completed and sent to nutrition services by 0615 (tube 19). Linen pick-up if necessary.
0615–0715	Pass out fresh water. Deliver warm washcloths and prepare overbed tables for breakfast trays.
0715–0745	ALL TRAYS MUST BE DELIVERED. All PSAs assist.
0745–0815	Post–tray delivery paperwork to nutrition services by 0815.
0830–0845	Break.
0845–0900	Pick up dirty trays.
0915–0930	Deliver patient nourishments. Put away food service floor stock.
0930–1000	General unit tidy-up; dirty equipment to utility room, etc.
1000–1030	Linen pick-up.
1100–1130	Lunch.
1130–1200	Prepare overbed tables for lunch.
1210–1230	ALL TRAYS MUST BE DELIVERED. All PSAs assist.
1230–1245	Post–tray delivery paperwork to nutrition services by 1245.
1300–1320	Pick up dirty trays. Deliver menus to patients.
1330–1345	Break.
1400–1410	Deliver nourishments to patients.
1410–1430	Wrap up any duties needed. Pass out fresh water.

Note: One PSA on day shift will be assigned PRIMARY housekeeping responsibilities on 4 West. Discharge rooms will be handled by the secondary PSA. Materials management and transportation issues will be handled by the 1000–1830 PSA or other PSAs as necessary. Dietary tray delivery will be a joint effort by the PSAs and available PCTs. Assistance with menu selection should occur as time is available. All selected menus should be returned to nutrition services by the end of the shift and remaining menus communicated to the evening shift.

for the PSAs. Every department had its own order of priorities, making this a difficult issue to overcome.

The workflow of the PCTs changed as the acuity of the patients varied and the census fluctuated. Because the PCT job description was designed as a multipurpose worker, the workflow was adjusted according to the events occurring on the unit (Exhibit 19–2). There would be shifts when a PCT would spend a majority of his or her time with phlebotomy duties, physical therapy, occupational therapy, or assisting the nursing staff with NA skills. As a model for the steering committee, the following is an example of how specific assignments could be developed for each shift. An example of a typical day shift assignment for a PCT would include:

- vital signs for a maximum of 10 patients
- beds and baths for 4 to 5 patients, depending on their acuity
- simple charting of daily activities for these assigned patients, such as vitals, morning care, diet
- division of the unit to deliver specific services as ordered (e.g., blood work, ECGs, incentive spirometry supervision, physical therapy, occupational therapy, simple dressing changes, catheterization)

The PCTs would be responsible to a designated RN, depending on the patient assigned, to communicate observations made during a given shift. In addition, PCTs would be available to assist with any functions requiring multiple staff (e.g., lifts and turns). In the event that the PCTs were not busy, they were also oriented to some PSA duties. Because teamwork was encouraged, if time allowed or if the PSAs were involved with other duties, efforts were supported with assisting in simple tasks such as transporting or tray delivery.

With the development of both new and experienced staff, a date was set for implementation. It was time to make the big jump into a different type of delivery system. It was decided to introduce the PSAs a couple of weeks before the PCTs. The opportunity for staff to adjust to one type of worker instead of two was believed to be beneficial depending on the mentality and the readiness of any given staff to adjust to change.

Naturally, neither the types of patients on the unit nor the needs of particular patient types changed after PCR. What did change were the types of workers who were providing the services for the patients. The staff mix basically remained the same, with two exceptions: There was no longer a need for the services of an NA and the services of the PSAs and PCTs were deemed useful. With these new acquisitions, there was a need to adjust staffing guidelines accordingly.

Exhibit 19–2 4 West PCT Workflow

Day Shift

0700–0730	1. Receive patient assignment and report, special assignments, and break times.
	2. Review Kardexes on assigned patients.
0730–0830	1. Finish any lab draws.
	2. Take vitals and do observations on assigned patients.
	3. Assist with patient feeding.
	4. Turn all every 2 hour patients assigned.
0830–1100	1. Morning care (e.g., baths, linen changes, dressing changes, treatments, preparation for tests and procedures).
	2. Assist with patient mobility (e.g., sitting in chair, ambulation, physical therapy, occupational therapy).
	3. Do 1000 lab draws.
	4. Encourage patients needing incentive spirometry.
1100–1300	1. Take every 4 hour vital signs.
	2. Cover others for lunch, each taking 30 minutes according to assigned lunch times.
	3. Assist with tray passing and feeding.
	4. Do fingersticks on patients requiring this.
	5. Begin chart documentation as time allows.
1300–1430	1. Total shift I&Os.
	2. Give verbal report to nurse who assigned patients.
	3. Finish treatments, dressing changes, special assignments, etc.
	4. Complete any charting needed.
	5. Do 1400 lab draws.
1430–1530	1. Clean patient rooms for oncoming shift.
	2. Complete tasks before going home.

Note: Physical and occupational therapy will be an ongoing priority with respect to the population on 4 West. Patient call lights MUST be answered promptly on the unit. Teamwork is an essential component on our unit. Seek out and help your coworkers.

Because this was a pioneer unit, the focus of PCR was to improve patient services without increasing costs. Financial issues would be explored at a future date. The need to examine restructuring with given resources was the issue now at hand.

UNIT OVERVIEW AFTER RESTRUCTURING

The development of a restructured budget increased the FTEs from 38.99 to 44.98. It changed the direct care HPPD from 6.48 to 6.84 because historically PCTs were not a part of the hours of care and now signified direct caregivers. This change allowed the unit to maintain six licensed personnel and two PCTs for a total census of 25. Remember, with the nonrestructured guidelines, six licensed personnel and two NAs were being used. What is different, however, is that no longer were the services of the ancillary support divisions, including physical therapy, occupational therapy, and phlebotomy, maintained. In essence, more services were provided to the clientele using the same number of staff but in a different capacity. The guidelines for numbers of PCTs on a given shift with a given census were developed by a collaborative effort of management and the steering committee on the unit (Table 19–2).

The PSA staffing guidelines were developed by trial and error. Initially, it was believed that there were sufficient numbers to handle the activity level. With two PSAs on a given day shift, one on the evening shift, and one half on the night shift, it was thought that sufficient coverage was planned. In this situation, it was necessary to designate one of the PSAs to focus almost all his or her attention on the housekeeping aspect of the job during the day shift only. A clean room was one of the key patient satisfiers (as noted in the satisfaction survey). While one of the PSAs concentrated on the housekeeping, the other was designated for other duties, such as dietary, transportation, linen pick-up, and other tasks as needed.

Understandably, this proved to be a hardship on the PSAs. The amount of work to be accomplished had been underestimated. As data were gathered and analyzed, it became evident that there was a need to provide additional coverage at peak hours during the shift. Therefore, additional support was made available between 10:00 A.M. to 6:30 P.M. The day shift PSA normally worked from 6:00 A.M. to 2:30 P.M. The additional help was provided only if the census was greater than 20 patients because two PSAs were found to be adequate for fewer than 20.

With the implementation of PCR came a different philosophy in training new staff. As new employees, especially licensed personnel, came on board, the focus switched from a skill perspective to delegation, accountability, multipurpose workers, and teamwork. What this meant was that the nurse would need to look at a more global picture. The RN would be able to assess the patient and develop a plan of care but then would need to delegate tasks to others capable of competent skill performance. Delegation was definitely a change from the total patient care concept that was

Table 19–2 4 West Staffing Guidelines by Census (6.87 HPPD)

	7 A.M.–3 P.M.				3 P.M.–11 P.M.				11 P.M.–7 A.M.			
Census	*RN*	*LPN*	*PCT*	*PSA**	*RN*	*LPN*	*PCT*	*PSA*	*RN*	*LPN*	*PCT*	*PSA*
31	5	2	3	2+1	4	2	2	1	3	2	2	0.5
30	5	2	3	2+1	4	2	2	1	3	2	2	0.5
29	5	2	3	2+1	4	2	2	1	3	2	2	0.5
28	5	2	2	2+1	4	2	2	1	3	2	1	0.5
27	5	2	2	2+1	4	2	1	1	3	2	1	0.5
26	4	2	3	2+1	4	2	1	1	2	2	2	0.5
25	4	2	2	2+1	3	2	2	1	2	2	2	0.5
24	4	2	2	2+1	3	2	1	1	2	2	2	0.5
23	4	2	2	2+1	3	2	1	1	2	2	2	0.5
22	3	2	2	2+1	3	2	1	1	2	2	2	0.5
21	3	2	2	2+1	3	2	1	1	2	2	1	0.5
20	3	2	1	2+1	2	2	2	1	2	2	1	0.5
19	3	2	1	2	2	2	1	1	2	2	1	0.5
18	3	1	2	2	2	2	1	1	2	1	1	0.5
17	3	1	1	2	2	2	1	1	2	1	1	0.5
16	3	1	1	2	2	1	1	1	2	1	1	0.5
15	3	1	1	2	2	1	1	1	2	1	1	0.5
14	2	1	1	2	2	1	1	1	2	1	1	0.5
13	2	1	1	2	2	1	1	1	2	1	1	0.5
12	2	1	1	2	2	1	1	1	2	0	1	0.5
11	2	1	1	2	2	0	1	1	2	0	1	0.5
10	2	0	1	2	2	0	1	1	2	0	1	0.5

*+1 indicates the 10 P.M.–6:30 A.M. PSA.

previously practiced. It seemed that the greatest concern for the RNs revolved around the competence factor of others and how that factor could potentially affect licensure. Despite the reassurance of the risk management department related to the accountability of RNs and appropriately delegated tasks, there was an obvious resistance to conform. Nurses were not willing to risk their livelihood on verbal reassurance. As the nurses became more familiar and comfortable with the skills of their coworkers, they began to relax, and barriers began to dissolve. Nurses were more willing to relinquish some of the tasks to others.

The training process of the PCTs also evolved as their skills were recognized and the nurses became more comfortable with the role. The established PCTs on the unit were being utilized as preceptors for certain skills, and a train-the-trainer program was developed. Some of the more technical skill training (e.g., phlebotomy) continued under the supervision of the ancillary department. This was done to maintain the supervisory level required by the regulatory agencies. A key point in this training, however, was that the time needed was reduced to 8 weeks. This was a cost savings to the institution.

The PSA role continued to require 2 weeks of training and orientation. Portions of the training were also conducted by established PSAs on the unit because someone in the same role was best suited for that task. The more technical aspects of the various support areas were retrained by the staff employed in that area. This did not affect the orientation cost or time involved with the process. It did provide a more accurate picture of the job for the PSAs.

With the introduction of the two new classes of workers, it was noted that a void would be present if the unit needs increased as a result of census fluctuations or if illness intervened. After discussion in the task force, a supplemental pool was developed. This was handled in the same manner as the licensed float pool, with staff being able to function on multiple units during various hours depending on need. The training and orientation times were the same for the float pool as they were for the unit.

The role of the ANM was most affected by the introduction of the PSA and PCT. In addition to being the overseer of all clinical functions of the unit, ANMs were now needed to manage, staff, schedule, evaluate, and discipline (if necessary) 17 new employees. Their workload increased drastically because they were still expected to perform all prior duties as well. Staff nurses were not exempt from change, either. The expectation of the nurses was that they now would focus more closely on the support services given the patient. They were being asked to view nursing from a customer service perspective.

The reporting relationship of the ANMs and nurse managers remained constant after the implementation of change. One of the changes brought about with restructuring was related to the mindset of charging for services delivered. Historically within the organization, nurses did not concern themselves with this important issue. Revenue relating to the services of ancillary departments was reflected by the charges generated by their own personnel. Documentation of the service rendered was always needed to support this charge. Nursing staff needed to learn how to establish this mindset as well.

With assistance from the finance department, a system was developed from which to begin. This was a simple process, with the services rendered being indicated by a check mark. Examples of this included phlebotomy, Accucheck, and the like, and a cost was associated with the task performed. A cost for multiple tasks was established, and the process began.

For some unexplainable reason, nurses and PCTs found it difficult to charge (or perhaps to remember to charge) for services rendered. This was met with great concern from administration because the amount of revenue being lost was great in relation to the work performed, depending upon the payer. Repetition is one of the best ways to learn a new process or procedure. With continuous reinforcement, the numbers of missed charges appeared to diminish, but this continues as a problematic area. It is tedious work to track charges based on services, to verify charges through finance, and to determine which employees had forgotten to charge appropriately (Exhibit 19–3).

QUALITY CONTROL

Work performance of the PSAs and PCTs needed to be maintained after the roles were implemented. The job description was already developed and in place with workflows established and functioning. The next step was to establish a quality control/performance tool with which to evaluate the employee (Exhibit 19–4). The quality of work needed to be maintained in all the support areas for which nursing was now responsible. The tool was developed by the author and was utilized to assist with staff evaluations. A random staff member would be selected to inspect the work of another and then offered feedback to that individual.

The process worked well because each staff member would then know what to expect. Evaluations were easily done for the PSAs because their functions were better defined and the workflow remained rather constant (e.g., housekeeping functions). Because the expertise remained in the support area departments, the housekeeping supervisory staff would be invited to perform periodic inspections (once a month) and to offer feedback in problem areas and management perspectives. Outside expertise was helpful because we were not always up to speed on the newer techniques and products in specific areas.

The evaluation tool utilized for the PCTs was similar to that of the PSAs (Exhibit 19–5). The form was developed using the job performance standards and formatted to reflect PCT responsibilities. Actual performance was monitored by the nursing staff because they were the ones who had an accurate view of their work performance. Again, the ancillary department supervisors were invited to offer feedback with respect to problematic areas encountered, observed, or anticipated.

A quality control and operations committee was established to address performance concerns and feedback from the ancillary departments. Although the committee did serve an important purpose, with respect to

Exhibit 19–3 Charge Voucher

4 EAST 6122				4 WEST 6123	
CODE	QTY	DESCRIPTION	UNIT OF MEASURE	QTY	CODE
725299		NURSE ASSIST 1ST 30 MIN	HALF HOUR		725319
725309		NURSE ASSIST ADDL. 15 MIN	QTR. HOUR		725329
936549		SPECIAL PROCEDURE HOURLY	HOUR		
936889		MIDLINE CATHETER KIT	KIT		936909
936899		MIDLINE CATHETER INSERTION	INSERTION		936919
1040039		ELECTROCARDIOGRAM	TEST		1040049
1055059		INC SPIRO TREATMENT	EACH		1055079
1055069		INC SPIRO SETUP	EACH		1055089
1070039		VENIPUNCTURE	PROCEDURE		1070049
993349		NON-INVASIVE BP MONITOR/DAY	24 HOURS		996769
991699		PATIENT CARE ASSIST.(SITTER)	HOUR		992839
993329		CVP	24 HOURS		996749
993339		LACTATION BRIEF	QTR. HOUR		996759
993359		RECOVERY CHARGE I	4 HOURS		993849
993369		ACCU-CHECK TEST	EACH		936559
993379		CNS CONSULT FEE BASE	HALF HOUR		936569
993669		CNS CONSULT ADDL. 15 MIN	QTR. HOUR		996739
609529		PULSE OXIMETER CHECK	EACH		609549
609539		METERED DOSE INHALER	EACH		609559
	PHYSICAL THERAPY:				
1010129		HOT/COLD PACK 1 AREA	EACH		1010189
1010139		MASSAGE	15 MINUTES		1010199
1010149		AMBULATION W/ASSISTANCE	15 MINUTES		1010209
1010159		SUPERVISED AMBULATION	15 MINUTES		1010219
1010169		BEDSIDE ASSISTANCE	15 MINUTES		1010229
1010179		CPM/JOBST MONITORING	8 HOURS		1010239
	OCCUPATIONAL THERAPY:				
1025079		HOT/COLD PACK 1 AREA	EACH		1025109
1025089		BEDSIDE ASSISTANCE	15 MINUTES		1025119
1025099		CPM/JOBST MONITORING	DAY		1025129

Courtesy of University Medical Center, Tucson, Arizona.

continues

Exhibit 19–3 continued

5 EAST 6124				7 WEST 6113		BMT 6126	
CODE	QTY	DESCRIPTION	UNIT OF MEASURE	QTY	CODE	QTY	CODE
725339		NURSE ASSIST 1ST 30 MIN	HALF HOUR		725259		725979
725349		NURSE ASSIST ADDL. 15 MIN	QTR. HOUR		725269		725389
996819		CNS CONSULT FEE BASE	HALF HOUR		936509		936769
936579		CNS CONSULT ADDL. 15 MIN	QTR. HOUR		936519		936659
936589		CVP	24 HOURS				
936599		RECOVERY CHARGE I	4 HOURS		936529		
936759		NON-INVASIVE BP MONITOR/DAY	24 HOURS		606839		936669
936929		MIDLINE CATHETER KIT	KIT		936849		
936939		MIDLINE CATHETER INSERTION	INSERTION		936859		
1040059		ELECTROCARDIOGRAM	TEST		1040079		1040089
1055099		INC SPIRO TREATMENT	EACH		1055139		1055159
1055109		INC SPIRO SETUP	EACH		1055149		1055169
1070059		VENIPUNCTURE	PROCEDURE		1070079		1070089
936949		HEMOCULT	TEST		609759		606919
991839		PATIENT CARE ASSIST.(SITTER)	HOUR		991689		936679
996799		ACCU-CHECK TEST	EACH		996909		606899
996809		CARDIAC MONITOR/DAY	24 HOURS				606909
609569		PULSE OXIMETER CHECK	EACH		609489		609589
609579		METERED DOSE INHALER	EACH		609499		609599
	PHYSICAL THERAPY:				1010369		1010429
1010249		HOT/COLD PACK 1 AREA	EACH		1010379		1010439
1010259		MASSAGE	15 MINUTES		1010389		1010449
1010269		AMBULATION W/ASSISTANCE	15 MINUTES		1010399		1010459
1010279		SUPERVISED AMBULATION	15 MINUTES		1010409		1010469
1010289		BEDSIDE ASSISTANCE	15 MINUTES		1010419		1010599
1010299		CPM/JOBST MONITORING	8 HOURS				
	OCCUPATIONAL THERAPY:				1025199		1025229
1025139		HOT/COLD PACK 1 AREA	EACH		1025209		1025239
1025149		BEDSIDE ASSISTANCE	15 MINUTES		1025219		1025249
1025159		CPM/JOBST MONITORING	DAY				

quality control, the nurse managers of the restructured unit were placed in a unique position. The nurse managers had undertaken the responsibilities of a multitude of jobs, so that there was a feeling by some that they were in the spotlight for these meetings. Representatives from the ancil-

Exhibit 19–4 Quality Control and Performance Tool for PSAs, 4 West

NAME: ______________________ DATE: __________

1. HOUSEKEEPING

a. Room cleaning	Satisfactory	Unsatisfactory
night stand	___	___
bathroom	___	___
floor	___	___
bed	___	___
closet	___	___
garbage cans	___	___
overbed lights	___	___
walls (if needed)	___	___
curtains changed	___	___
corners	___	___
b. Nurses station		
high dusting	___	___
cleaning behind rolling carts	___	___
sweep and mop	___	___
garbage cans	___	___
refrigerator cleaned	___	___
c. Assignment completed by end of shift:	yes	no

COMMENTS ______________________________

____

2. TRANSPORTATION

a. Patient transfers done safely	yes	no
b. Transports occur within 20 minutes	yes	no

COMMENTS ______________________________

____

3. I&Os

a. Meal intake added properly to I&O	yes	no
b. Water pitchers changed at end of shift	yes	no

COMMENTS ______________________________

____

4. DIETARY

a. Meals delivered on time	yes	no
b. Proper documentation after trays	yes	no
c. Bulk stock ordered correctly	yes	no
d. Restocking done in timely manner	yes	no

COMMENTS ______________________________

____

continues

Exhibit 19–4 continued

5. MATERIALS MANAGEMENT		
a. Inventory done accurately	yes	no
b. Restocking done in timely fashion	yes	no
c. Credits sent to materials management	yes	no
COMMENTS ______________________________		
6. DRESS CODE		
a. Follows dress code established for PCR	yes	no
COMMENTS ______________________________		
7. INTERPERSONAL SKILLS		
a. Is courteous to patients	yes	no
b. Is courteous to ancillary personnel	yes	no
c. Responds appropriately to nurses	yes	no
d. Is courteous to coworkers	yes	no
e. Is open to constructive criticism	yes	no
f. Offers assistance to others	yes	no
COMMENTS ______________________________		

This tool is to be used to evaluate the performance of PSAs. It will be completed by the nurse manager or designee. This tool may be applied at any time without prior notification of personnel involved.

Completed by: ______________________ Date: __________

lary departments would take their turn in communicating what was going wrong with the restructured unit's performance from their departmental perspectives. The information was vital to the improved performance, but a constant bombardment of negative criticism did not contribute to a positive self-esteem or promote a sense of pride in the unit. A different approach to offering negative feedback seriously needs to be considered. Perhaps working with these departments on a more one-to-one basis would be less threatening to those involved.

Once some of the problematic issues were identified, a need to address them became evident. Working with other departmental supervisors enhanced the realization that the nursing world is just a small piece of the

Exhibit 19–5 Quality Control and Performance Tool for PCTs, 4 West

NAME: ______________________ DATE: ____________

1. Phlebotomy		
a. Performs phlebotomy in a timely fashion	yes	no
b. Utilizes universal precautions	yes	no
c. Explains procedure to patient	yes	no
d. Verifies patient using armband	yes	no
e. Correctly labels specimens	yes	no
f. Documents fingersticks correctly	yes	no
2. ECG		
a. Performs ECG in a timely fashion	yes	no
b. Completes documentation as needed	yes	no
c. Charges for services rendered	yes	no
3. Physical Therapy		
a. Practices proper technique	yes	no
b. Completes documentation appropriately	yes	no
c. Properly charges for services	yes	no
4. Patient Care		
a. Vital signs		
Reports to RN if out of range	yes	no
Properly charts vitals	yes	no
b. Safety		
Side rails up as ordered	yes	no
Call light within reach	yes	no
c. Sterile technique maintained		
Dressing changes	yes	no
Catheterizations	yes	no
d. Incentive spirometry		
Proper teaching documentation	yes	no
e. Morning/evening care		
Sensitive to patient privacy	yes	no
Performs care efficiently	yes	no
Leaves room neat	yes	no
5. Dress Code		
a. Follows dress code	yes	no
6. Interpersonal Skills		
a. Is courteous to patients	yes	no
b. Is courteous to hospital personnel	yes	no
c. Is courteous to coworkers	yes	no
d. Is open to constructive criticism	yes	no
e. Offers assistance to others	yes	no
f. Performs duties without being asked	yes	no
g. Conducts self in a professional manner	yes	no

continues

Exhibit 19–5 continued

Skills/activities performed well: ______________________________

____

____

____

____

Areas needing improvement: ______________________________

____

____

____

____

____

This tool is to be used to evaluate the performance of PCTs. It will be completed by the nurse manager or designee. This tool may be applied at any time without prior notification of personnel involved.

Completed by: ______________________________ Date: ______________

hospital environment and workflow. The influence of one department on another is greater than one imagines. Priorities for each department are essential but differ in the various departments. An example is the simple act of retrieving dirty trays. On the nursing unit, tray retrieval is a low priority for the PSAs. If a patient or a specimen needs to be transported or a discharge bed needs cleaning because of a new admission, the trays become a low priority. From the dietary perspective, however, if the trays are not retrieved on a timely basis the dishroom has a number of employees sitting and waiting for the cart of trays. The delay creates an overtime issue for the dishwashers because they need to remain late so clean dishes are available for the next meal. Only establishing a collaborative relationship with other department supervisors allowed this problem to become evident. In an effort to problem solve issues, flowcharts were developed so that workflow in specific departments could be understood by all (Figure 19–1). The flowchart proved to be beneficial in that responsibilities and workload were redistributed accordingly so that neither patients nor employees suffered.

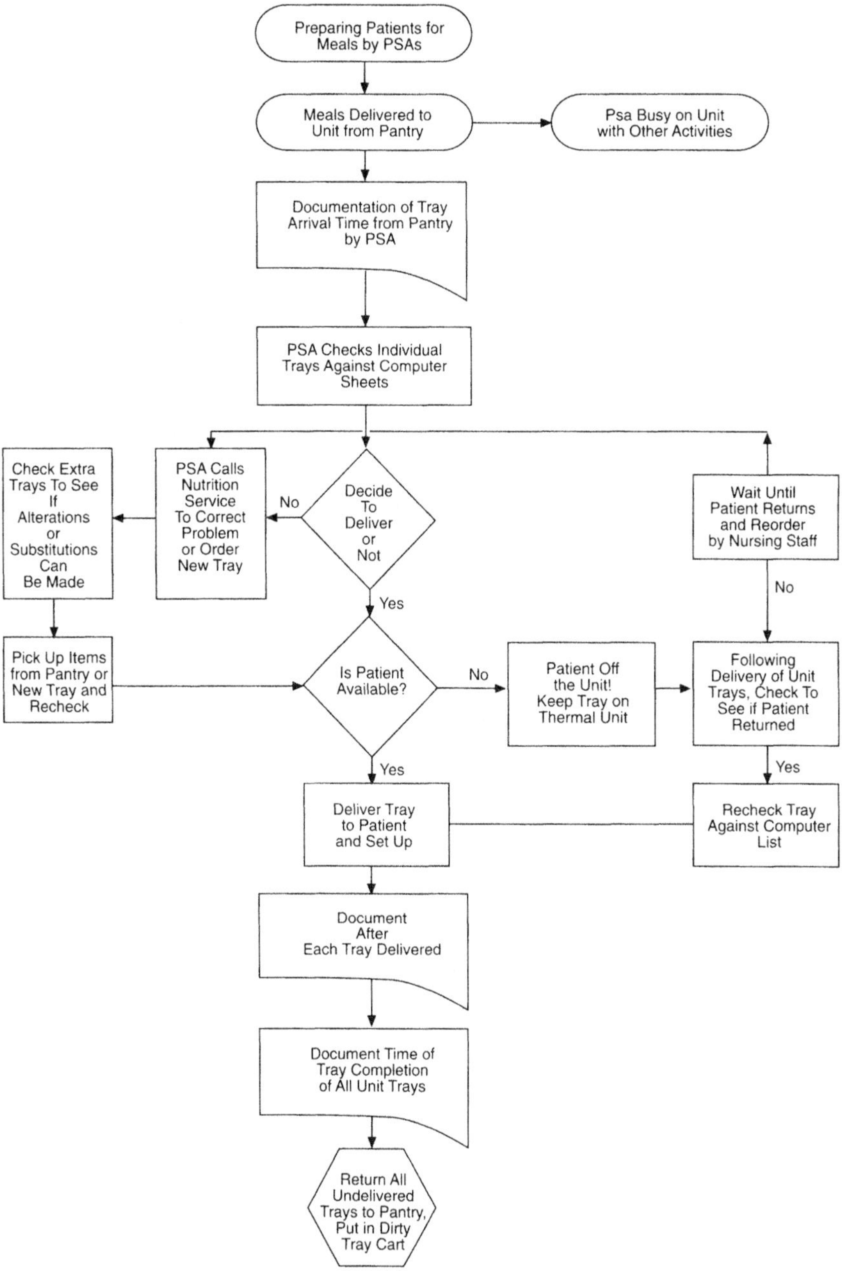

Figure 19–1 Flowchart for tray retrieval.

Naturally, issues were identified in every department that needed to be addressed. For example, in the laboratory a problem occurred when a PCT failed to draw a specimen. The PCT used phlebotomy as a back-up whenever a difficult stick presented itself. Initially, failure to draw was not a big issue, but the problem would escalate when more units became restructured. Therefore, a protocol was established if a PCT was unable to draw a specimen.

An example from the housekeeping department was the utilization of products. It was interesting to see that the amount of products used (toilet paper, towels, cleansers, brushes, etc.) increased dramatically with the introduction of PSAs. Fortunately this was an easy issue to address. Simple educational inservices helped the employees understand the proper methods of using products effectively and productively.

Transportation services are a vital service provided by the unit. It was remarkable to see the number of transports performed during the course of a shift. In the first month after restructuring, an average of 35 transports occurred during the day shift. Because of this activity level, the PSAs were being tremendously overworked. It was important that historical data were looked at with the previous transportation department in an effort to establish guidelines for this area. The initial standard was to transport patients as soon as the request was received. This was not the norm for the institution. A need to follow the policies already established for the hospital became evident. This allowed for more freedom with timeframes and a reprieve for the employees.

The issues concerning physical therapy, occupational therapy, ECG, and respiratory care services did not reflect technique or performance per se. Instead, the issues revolved around the charging process and revenue generation. PCTs were performing the new functions accurately and in a timely fashion, but they were not charging for their services. This was being observed by the other departments because the reports they received indicated the numbers of tests performed and the revenue generated. This feedback allowed us to address this issue in a timely fashion and to retrieve some of the potential lost revenue.

In summary, issues were identified and addressed using a collaborative effort between departments. It is difficult to understand completely the impact of the restructuring project in other areas, but communication enabled the nursing department to understand some of the issues and address them.

An issue that is not yet significant but could escalate is related to the infection control department. The effect of the PSA on the incidence of nosocomial infection is unknown and not easily measured. However, the training program does address this possibility in detail. The issue must be monitored closely as a preventive measure and for continuous quality improvement.

SATISFACTION

One objective of restructuring was to provide quality service to the clientele. Various criteria are used to measure quality, but to the patient quality care is service in a timely fashion. With the implementation of restructuring, the ability to provide immediate access to services previously requiring a waiting period was noted.

With the PSA role, a simple example of this is transportation. In the previous system, a patient would have to wait 30 to 40 minutes to be discharged from the hospital because of calling, availability of transport, and priority of personnel. On the restructured unit, the transporter is available on the unit along with equipment, and the patient is normally out the door in 10 minutes or less. The transporters are usually recognized by the patient, and a comfortable relationship normally had already been established. The patient does not need to encounter another stranger within the system, and is more satisfied with the process.

An example for the PCTs is similar. Functions that previously required phone communication and schedule coordination are now self-contained on the unit. Examples are phlebotomy, ECG, physical therapy, and occupational therapy. The patient is more comfortable with someone who is familiar, which allows the encounter to be a much more pleasant one from everyone's point of view. Additional staff on the unit enable call lights to be answered more timely as well. By sheer numbers alone, the availability of staff allowed the needs of the patients to be met more easily.

Staff satisfaction was initially mixed. The licensed staff were split into two groups: those who were comfortable with delegation and those who were not. The nurses who were comfortable with delegation had less of a workload, whereas the others were overwhelmed by the whole process. Everyone became comfortable with the role over time, however, and delegation was not an issue. Naturally, the PSAs and PCTs were ecstatic over their new jobs. Multipurpose workers were not common within the system, and the idea of not having to be repetitious in their duties excited many of them. The PCTs used the role to test the waters for a nursing career or perhaps another potential career within the health care profession.

Physicians were ambivalent. Those who were aware of the new structure reserved judgment until they had concrete data on which to comment. Others were not even aware of the project and did not care as long as their needs were met. To date, however, no physicians have been encountered who have been unhappy with the concept or the services provided by the new personnel.

Managing Nonprofessionals

The introduction of a nonprofessional worker brought about a concept new to the nursing management staff: how to manage them. Nonprofessional workers have a different type of work ethic and mindset. Examples include dress code, attendance, scope of practice, turnover, priority setting, and chain of command. Difficulties were encountered with dress code development. Nursing management believed that uniformity was needed to avoid confusion from the hospital's perspective as well as from the patients' perspective. Patients needed to be able to differentiate nurses from PSAs and PCTs. A committee was established to develop a dress code that would be acceptable to all. This process was completed after numerous meetings and much discussion for the PSA and PCT groups. One would think that the issue would end there, but it did not. A discipline issue now arose for those who did not conform to or follow the established dress code. When working with employees of a different economic status, the fact that they cannot always afford to buy multiple uniforms must be acknowledged. Naturally, employees would not want to come to work dirty. If they looked presentable, then why not allow them to work?

Attendance was another issue. It appears that some entry level workers do not hesitate to take sick leave. Regardless of the ramifications, employees at this level have a tendency to call in sick. This issue also creates problems for management. Not only does a replacement worker need to be found, but the discipline process is initiated again for absenteeism. Once management weeds these employees out of the system, a vacancy is created and the turnover rate increases. This requires a great deal of paperwork and is time consuming because now there is a need to begin all over again, with interviews, hiring, orientation, and even more paperwork. It begins to look like a vicious cycle after a time.

Once a stable staff is employed, other issues begin to surface. PCTs start to feel more comfortable in their roles and begin to test the waters. What are the fine lines between their job descriptions and those of others? Why can't they start an IV if they can draw blood from the same vein? Why can't they chart lung sounds? What's the difference between an observation and an assessment? Strict guidelines need to be established before the introduction of any new position and must be closely monitored.

PSAs have more difficulty in learning to establish priorities than PCTs. It is important to use the charge nurse as a resource for priority setting for this work group. The PSA is able to focus on the task at hand rather than think about what to accomplish next.

Priorities for the PCT group are usually controlled by functions as they are ordered. Fortunately, tasks are not usually ordered all at once, and the PCT can prioritize much easier. Stats, ASAPs, routines, and the like are normal operating commands for the PCTs and help with some of the prioritizing issues.

Interpersonal conflicts are handled differently with the nonprofessional worker. In this unit's experience, the chain of command was being followed much more closely by the professional than the nonprofessional staff. PSAs and PCTs have a tendency to ignore obvious problems with other staff, especially the licensed personnel. Nonprofessional staff might prefer to ignore a problem than speak to their line supervisor, perhaps because of fear or low self-esteem. These workers would supersede their line supervisor and speak directly to the manager. Perhaps a tolerance level was surpassed, or maybe the working relationships were not optimal among staff.

Special Considerations

Unusual considerations were few and far between on the unit. The epilepsy program did present a few issues that needed to be addressed. Established protocols for patients who had seizures made it necessary to limit the amount of contact the PCT had with the patient until a comfort level was established through the education process. Special inservices needed to be attended by the PCTs on the unit to develop some of their observation skills and strategies on how to interact with this patient population. Different safety measures and documentation procedures also needed to be learned.

Self-scheduling is an issue that was attempted by the new multipurpose workers. Because the regard for their own schedules greatly outweighed the needs of others, this was something that needed to remain with the supervisory staff. Perhaps in time the PCTs and PSAs will be able to handle this task.

The thought of peer review was also discussed for trial by PCTs and PSAs. Issues related to biases and subjective feedback prompted the decision to relinquish this idea and to leave the majority of responsibility for evaluations to the supervisory staff. Feedback was elicited from the licensed staff with respect to evaluations and work performance. The only exception was the tools utilized when performing the quality control issues. This was incorporated into the final evaluation of these employees.

LESSONS LEARNED

Although the effects of the total PCR process have yet to be realized, the entire project has been a great learning experience for all involved. Some of the lessons learned that could have been addressed before implementation and would have improved outcomes include the following:

- Hire the PSAs from a pool of candidates already comfortable with housekeeping responsibilities. They do a better job and do not view cleaning as a menial chore. Good housekeeping services are also a strong satisfier for the patients.
- Hire PCTs with previous NA experience. NAs have better organizational skills and work easier with the nursing staff in terms of delegation and clinical skills.
- Create a supplemental staffing system before implementation. Back-up staff must be available for the unforeseen problems.
- Recognize and address interdepartmental barriers.
- Involve the informal leaders on the unit in communication and troubleshooting.
- Facilitate total staff involvement and address personal biases and attitudes before implementation.
- Provide ongoing education and support.
- Provide sufficient management support time and supervisory personnel to oversee performance and to recognize areas needing improvement and education.

Addressing the above recommendations will be helpful in getting started, but the most important issue continues to be the preparation of nurses for a new patient care delivery system. Delegation skills remain the key to being successful when implementing skilled, task-oriented workers.

In spite of the success in unit restructuring, nurse managers will still encounter a percentage of staff who are unwilling to change and relocate to other positions. Although the number will vary across units, even the loss of one experienced nurse is difficult to accept. Changing something that does not appear to be flawed is a difficult concept to sell. A change of this magnitude affects an entire unit, and everyone must ultimately decide to support the change or move to other areas. Only those who are able to adapt to change are able to endure and flourish.

CONCLUSION

The need to carefully select PSAs and PCTs based on previous work history has become quite evident. PSAs who have had experience with housekeeping duties have greater success in the PSA role. They express greater job satisfaction and show greater longevity in the position.

PCTs who have had experience with the NA role tend to have a higher level of job satisfaction than those who have not. Whether the role descriptors, at the outset of the position, influenced this is hard to measure. Technical skills always appear to be more glorified than the basic personal hygiene needs of patients. However, the NA skills were an essential component in being successful and functioning as a PCT.

Even if the correct personnel were hired for these important new roles, the delegation skills of the RNs remain the key. Without adequate training and/or competence in this area, the ability of the project to flourish is impossible.

CHAPTER

20

Intermediate Care/Telemetry Case Study

Alicia Eyherabide

Chapter Objectives

1. To describe briefly the unit and delivery system before restructuring.
2. To describe the staffing plan before and after restructuring.
3. To describe assignments before and after restructuring.
4. To describe special considerations for intermediate care/telemetry in restructuring.

UNIT OVERVIEW BEFORE RESTRUCTURING

Patient care restructuring began on the intermediate care telemetry unit at University Medical Center (UMC) 4 years after the unit opened. The eight-bed unit was established in October 1988. As a result of demand, the unit quickly expanded to include eight additional beds. From the start, the unit had a mix of staff: registered nurses (RNs), licensed practical nurses (LPNs), nursing assistants (NAs), and unit assistants (UAs). During interviews for unit positions, applicants were told that if they were selected to take a unit position they would need to be prepared to work with multiple levels of staff. The opportunity to select staff who were aware of the staff mix increased the chances for team and staff satisfaction.

The intermediate care unit primarily admits cardiac patients from the cardiovascular intensive care unit, although patients with noncardiac problems may be admitted. Diagnoses of 90 percent of the patients include status post–myocardial infarction, rule out myocardial infarction, unstable angina, dysrhythmias, cardiomyopathy, and status post–heart transplant. Occasional other admissions include patients who need artificial ventilation but no longer require intensive care and patients whose acuity requires a greater nurse–patient ratio than is available on general care units. The beds are regularly in high demand, and the unit is on triage most of the time. The high demand and short supply of beds is one reason why the average patient length of stay is short: 2 days.

The unit is also a site for medical education. Patients are managed by teams of physicians. The team includes the attending physician, resident, intern, and medical student. These teams direct patient care while providing the medical student the opportunity to witness medical and/or surgical practice. The environment allows the intern and resident an opportunity to grow in their medical acumen under the direction of an experienced teacher and practitioner.

Unit Organization and Roles

Before restructuring, the staff mix consisted of the nurse manager, assistant nurse managers, RNs, LPNs, NAs, and UAs. The nurse manager functioned in a traditional management role. Management responsibilities included standards of care, continuous improvement activities, and personnel management. The nurse manager role also included fiscal responsibilities and the formulation of the unit budget.

The assistant nurse manager had a direct care position with some indirect care responsibilities, including direct supervision of the patient care staff, performance evaluations, counseling, and guidance. The assistant nurse manager was authorized to use 8 hours every 2 weeks to handle the indirect care responsibilities. The remainder of the assistant nurse manager's time was spent in direct patient care. When on the unit, the assistant nurse manager usually fulfilled the charge nurse role. He or she is a resource person for the staff. Physicians, social workers, coordinators, and staff from other clinical areas looked to the assistant nurse manager to provide leadership and assistance in handling patient care issues.

The RN provided direct care and supervised other patient care staff. In the role of direct caregiver, the RN frequently delegated to the NA the following types of tasks: taking and documenting vital signs, giving bed baths, changing linen, assisting with activities of daily living, assisting with ambulation, and transporting patients. Because the unit provides telemetry services, the NAs have been trained as monitor technicians. Most NAs who were hired to work on the unit before restructuring did not have monitor technician experience. Nursing assistants attended a training program designed specifically for the nonprofessional worker.

The RN also supervised the LPN in direct care. Each patient was assigned to an RN for assessment, plan of care, and IV medications. RNs worked closely with LPNs in the provision of patient care. The budgeted RN–LPN ratio was 80 percent–20 percent.

Last, the UA served in an indirect role. The UA answered phones, transcribed orders, ordered unit supplies, and managed information flow on the unit.

Unit Orientation and Training

The majority of the nursing staff hired on 6 East have a background in medical-surgical nursing. They possess a good basic knowledge of medical disorders, postsurgical care skills, and hospital routines, and they have organizational skills and experience with commonly used medical equipment. The training needed to bring the nurses to the point of readiness to care safely for the patients requires that they attend UMC's critical care course. The course is 40 hours long and provides the opportunity to review the most commonly seen disorders in the adult critical care units. The unit preceptor's assessment of the newly hired nurse's progress in completing unit competencies and performance in managing patient care determines the length of the nurse's orientation. The clinical orientation varies from approximately 3 weeks for LPNs and experienced RNs to 11 weeks for new graduate RNs. RNs and LPNs are required to complete the basic knowledge assessment tool with a score of 80 percent or higher. It is also mandatory that they complete a cardiovascular rhythms examination with a passing grade of at least 80 percent.

The NAs generally take the same cardiovascular rhythms examinations as the RNs and LPNs. However, they are not required to know interventions with medications or advanced cardiac life support recommendations. NAs are oriented in a departmentwide 8-hour orientation class. This is followed by 2 weeks of precepted unit orientation.

Unit Staffing

When the unit began to accept patients, RNs were routinely assigned to care for four patients. In addition, some RNs were responsible for three additional patients with the assistance of an LPN. For the first few months the nurse–patient ratio was acceptable. However, the acuity level of the patients quickly increased as physicians became acquainted with the unit and staff and their confidence increased in the ability of the nursing staff. Soon the physicians expanded the admissions to include patients with the following: elective cardioversions, antidysrhythmic drips, temporary pacemakers, vasoactive drips, ventilator support, and the like. Changes in the patient population resulted in an increase in the nurse–patient ratio to its present level: 1:3 or 1:4. In addition, as the number of unit beds increased, there was an increasing need to take the charge RN out of the direct patient care ratio to allow for active participation in triage issues. The usual LPN–patient ratio is 1:4 because LPNs do not usually care for patients who are receiving vasoactive infusions or patients who require significant numbers of IV medications. NAs assist with the care of four to five patients. In addition, NAs staff the telemetry monitors, usually in alternating 4-hour blocks of time. Staffing guidelines before restructuring are shown in Table 20–1.

Table 20–1 6 East Staffing Guidelines before Restructuring

Shift	*Patients*	*RNs*	*LPNs*	*NAs*
0700–1530*	25–28	9	0	3
and		9	0	4
1500–2330		8	2	3
		8	1	4
	20–24	8	1	1
		8	0	2
		7	2	1
		7	1	2
		7	0	3
	17–20	7	1	1
		7	0	2
		6	2	1
		6	1	2
		6	0	3
	14–16	6	1	1
		6	0	2
		5	2	1
		5	1	2
		5	0	3
	11–13	5	1	1
		5	0	2
		4	2	1
		4	1	2
		4	0	3
	9–10	3	1	1
		3	0	2
		2	2	1
		2	1	2
	4–8	2	1	1
		2	0	2
2300–0730	25–28	7	0	1
		6	1	1
		5	2	1
	20–24	6	0	1
		5	1	1
		4	2	1
	17–20	5	0	1
		4	1	1
		3	2	1
	13–16	4	0	1
		3	1	1
		2	2	1
	9–12	3	0	1

*These guidelines are increased by one NA/monitor technician Monday through Friday.

Another aspect of patient care that significantly influenced the staffing pattern was the need to monitor patients when they were required to go to other departments for procedures. Although the institution had a transportation department, the transportation staff were not adequately trained to monitor the patients. Therefore, monitored patients needed to be accompanied by a unit staff member. This requirement reduced the number of staff available on the unit by one to two people between 8:00 A.M. and 7:00 P.M.

PLANNING FOR CHANGE

The 6 East staff had informally obtained information from staff employed on the restructured units. The communication resulted in two positive outcomes. The NAs wanted to expand their role to that of patient care technician (PCT), and the RNs and LPNs were eager to employ patient support attendants (PSAs) on the units. Patients changed frequently, and timely response by housekeeping services was an important factor in preparing rooms for new patients. The general feeling on the unit at that time was that the housekeeping services did not meet unit expectations. For these reasons, the 6 East staff approached the nurse manager and requested that the unit be restructured. The nurse manager then forwarded the request to the vice president for patient care services.

Once the decision was made to restructure 6 East, the nurse manager planned for general decision making to occur in staff meetings. All staff were strongly encouraged to attend and participate. Staff participation was a result of the group governance process already established through the Differentiated Group Professional Practice grant. Unit committees were already in existence as a result of the grant. These unit-based committees addressed ongoing unit issues after the initial planning for restructuring was completed.

Staffing Plan

The plan to restructure patient care delivery included the directive to keep the process cost neutral. The staffing plan to add additional technical and support staff at the unit level needed to be equal to or not exceed the previous level of ancillary staffing. For instance, the PCTs would perform some of the tasks previously conducted by phlebotomists, ECG technicians, and physical therapy technicians. These tasks were in addition to the NA and monitor technician work currently being performed. Therefore, in planning for the appropriate number of additional PCTs, the number of procedures performed by the ancillary technicians for patients on the unit over a period of several months was tabulated. The amount of additional staff time required to allow PCTs to perform their job duties was determined by multiplying the number of procedures by the length of time needed to perform each type of procedure. This same process was used to determine the number of both PCTs and PSAs. Unit RN staffing was reviewed, but no reductions were made. The high proportion of LPNs in the staffing mix resulted in a lower number of proposed PCT positions than on other restructured units. In addition, for this staffing pattern to be successful, the LPN role needed to be restructured to include phlebotomy.

The full-time equivalent (FTE) allocation from laboratory, physical therapy, and cardiology for PCTs was 2.2. The FTE allocation from transportation, environmental services, and materials management was 3.5. As a result of an increase in budgeted patient days for the upcoming fiscal year, FTEs were also increased to provide appropriate staff–patient ratios.

Staff Preparation

Initially, staff members were invited to attend a communication session with the vice president for patient care services. In this session, an overview of the model of patient-centered care was shared. Staff members were encouraged to voice their perspectives and concerns at this meeting. Additional follow-up discussions about restructuring occurred at staff meetings. Proposed staffing plans were reviewed, and suggestions from staff were requested. Initial staffing plans were modified in response to staff input. General questions, issues, and staff concerns were discussed. Unresolved issues were referred to unit committees for follow-up.

Previously established unit committees on clinical practice and ancillary department issues each addressed the new issues generated by restructuring. Issues discussed in committee included:

- supervision of additional staff by RNs and LPNs
- scope of practice
- delegation and distribution of workload
- time management
- communication issues with nonprofessional staff
- space problems due to restructuring

Because group governance was established on the unit, each committee was empowered to bring recommendations to staff. Ballots were distributed for voting on decisions that required subsequent staff input. Staff responsibility for determining the environment on the unit and addressing unit problems contributed to a relatively smooth transition in implementing restructured care through group governance.

Staff Training

During the planning process, team-building and communication workshops were conducted. Staff members were scheduled to attend the workshops; attendance was encouraged but not required. The 4-hour workshops were facilitated by a human relations trainer. Several sessions for each workshop were offered to allow for individual scheduling needs. Group activities were a critical component of each session, and active participation of the staff was encouraged. See Chapter 12 for details on the workshops.

Training in the new roles of PCT and PSA was coordinated by a full-time restructuring education coordinator, who had participated in the training of both PCTs and PSAs for units that had been restructured. The education coordinator streamlined the PCT training for 6 East. Training for the PCTs was offered for three distinct groups. Group 1 received 10 weeks of training including the following areas: cardiovascular rhythms, physical therapy, occupational therapy, phlebotomy, respiratory, universal precautions, CPR, and basic patient care. Individuals given the group 1 training had little to no previous NA experience and no previous experience as a monitor technician. Group 2 received 6 weeks of training after successfully performing general NA skills. Group 2 consisted mainly of staff with previous work experience as an NA but no previous training as a monitor technician. Group 3 received 4 weeks of training after completing tests for identification of cardiovascular rhythms as well as general NA skills. This group comprised NAs who were employed on the unit and were trained and functioning as monitor technicians.

Training for the PSAs lasted 2 weeks regardless of previous experience. Training included presentations and demonstrations of housekeeping procedures, patient transportation, inventory, and stocking of unit supplies. Training included both classroom presentation and on-unit demonstration followed by orientee practice. This design allowed for adequate PSA training within the 2-week period.

Hiring Process

A group of six staff RNs and LPNs volunteered for the interviewing committee for PCTs and PSAs. The committee met with the employment manager from the human resources department to learn proper interviewing techniques and tips on ranking candidates. The employment manager reviewed the interview questions developed by human resources for PCTs and PSAs. Committee members formulated their interview questions and scoring criteria. Candidates who successfully interviewed with the unit committee were next referred to the nurse manager. The final candidates were selected through joint decision making by the nurse manager and the unit interview committee.

The unit committee interviewed approximately 45 individuals to recruit 13.1 PCT FTEs. Twenty-three individuals were referred to the nurse manager for interviews. The final 18 candidates were reviewed by both the unit committee and the nurse manager. Fifteen candidates were offered positions. Some of the criteria used to rank candidates included previous direct patient care experience, previous experience at UMC, and previous experience with monitors and cardiac rhythms. Additional areas assessed in the interviews included judgment, delegation, resourcefulness, and interpersonal skills.

A similar process was used to interview PSAs. Ten PSA candidates were referred to the unit by human resources. Seven candidates were offered positions. Based on information provided by units with previous restructuring experience at UMC, preference was given to candidates with experience in housekeeping. Additionally, the employment history was reviewed and information solicited about communication and prioritization skills, attendance, and reliability.

UNIT OVERVIEW AFTER RESTRUCTURING

Unit Organization and Roles

After restructuring, the staff mix consists of the nurse manager, assistant nurse manager, RNs, LPNs, PCTs, PSAs, and UAs. Restructuring has brought changes to each role. The nurse manager and assistant nurse manager now have new supervisory responsibilities. These include phlebotomy, technical issues with ECGs, physical therapy and occupational therapy, patient transportation, tray delivery, inventory and stocking, and housekeeping.

The assistant nurse manager in the direct care role, along with RN staff, has new responsibilities to ensure that patient requests about food service, housekeeping services, and transportation are met. Physician orders for laboratory tests are the responsibility of the patient's nurse. Most staff RNs choose to leave the phlebotomy duties to the PCT assigned to that patient. However, RNs frequently draw blood specimens when placing an IV line. Since restructuring, LPNs have received phlebotomy training and may perform phlebotomies on patients. RNs must oversee and coordinate care activities with LPNs, PCTs, and PSAs in addition to providing daily direct patient care.

The role of the PCT is a new one. The PCTs perform tasks previously performed by NAs on the unit and in addition have phlebotomy, ECG, and transportation skills. Because of the type of patients seen on 6 East, the PCTs are seldom called on to assist with either physical therapy or occupational therapy. However, there is a significant volume of ECGs, phlebotomies, and patient transports on the unit. Before restructuring, NAs routinely assisted in the daily care of four to five patients. Since restructuring, PCTs have been too busy to assist with four to five patients. Therefore, the PCT patient care assignment has been reduced to two to three patients.

Duties of the PSA were incorporated from departments that previously provided food services, environmental services, materials management, and transportation. The new PSA role required a change in the communication of information at the unit level. The accessibility of the PSA simplified communication about housekeeping, dietary, supply, and transportation needs.

UAs no longer call other departments for assistance with housekeeping, supplies, or transportation. Less UA time is spent interacting with other departments, and more time is spent communicating with unit staff. All staff now focus on optimal unit functioning in the delivery of safe and effective patient care.

One issue with restructuring is the ongoing training and updating of staff. A certain amount of training existed before restructuring, but the activity has grown exponentially since restructuring. The most significant increase in the need for ongoing training is in the area of phlebotomy. Changes in procedures occur when new equipment is acquired, necessitating changes in how blood is obtained for certain tests. The information must be communicated rapidly to all RNs, LPNs, and PCTs on the unit. Usually, the phlebotomy procedure must be changed completely by a given date and time. Currently, the laboratory provides monthly updates on changes in procedure or problems with procedures. One representative from the unit attends the session and then follows through with unit PCTs on an individual basis. The written information is also placed in a notebook and kept on the unit. All direct care staff are required to review the notebook regularly.

Staffing Guidelines

Staffing guidelines after restructuring are provided in Table 20–2. Patient assignments have not changed for RNs and LPNs. Because 20 percent

Table 20–2 6 East Staffing Guidelines after Restructuring, Fiscal Year 1992–93

Census	*0700–1530*	*1500–1900*	*1900–2330*	*2300–0730*
30	8–2–3+	8–2–3+	8–2–2+	8–2–1+
29	8–2–3+	8–2–2+	7–2–2+	7–2–1+
28	7–2–3+	7–2–3+	7–2–2+	7–2–1+
27	7–2–3+	7–2–2+	7–2–2+	7–2–1+
26	7–2–3+	7–2–2+	7–2–2+	6–2–1+
25	6–2–3+	6–2–3+	6–2–2+	6–2–1+
24	6–2–3+	6–2–2+	6–2–2+	6–1–1+
23	6–2–3+	6–2–2+	6–2–1+	6–1–1+
22	5–2–3+	5–2–2+	6–1–2+	6–1–1+
21	5–2–3+	5–2–2+	6–1–1+	6–1–1+
20	5–2–2+	5–2–1+	5–2–1+	5–1–1+
19	5–2–1+	5–2–1+	5–2–1+	5–1–1+
18	5–2–1+	5–2–1+	5–2–1+	5–1–1+
17	5–2–1+	5–2–1+	5–2–1+	5–1–1+
16	4–2–1+	4–2–1+	4–2–1+	4–1–1+
15	4–2–1+	4–2–1+	4–1–1+	4–1–1+
14	4–1–1+	4–1–1+	4–1–1+	4–1–1+
13	4–1–1+	4–1–1+	4–1–1+	4–1–1+
(charge out ratio at 13 and over)				
12	3–1–1+	3–1–1+	3–1–1+	3–1–1+
(charge in ratio at 12 and under)				
11	3–1–1+	3–1–1+	3–1–1+	3–0–1+
10	3–0–1+	3–0–1+	3–0–1+	3–0–1+
9	3–0–1+	3–0–1+	3–0–1+	3–0–1+
8	3–0–1+	3–0–1+	3–0–1+	2–0–1+
7	2–0–1+	2–0–1+	2–0–1+	2–0–1+

+, monitor technician.

1. The Monitor technician PCT is not included in these numbers, so you need to remember to add them in when you fill out your staffing request. However, you do not add them in when you do the productivity monitoring form. For example, if your census is 30 on day shift 0700–1530, the staffing guidelines would call for 8–2–3+. On your staffing request sheet you should ask for 8–2–4.
2. These are guidelines for staff mix. The number of RNs and LPNs may vary somewhat, as long as their total does not change. For example, for 30 patients at 0700–1530, the guideline would be 8–2–3+. The total number of nurses is 10. Instead of 8 RNs and 2 LPNs, you could use 9 RNs and 1 LPN or 7 RNs and 3 LPNs.
3. Minimum staffing, regardless of how low the census is, is 2 RNs.

of the unit nurses are LPNs, RNs who supervise an LPN will have more PCT assistance than RNs who are not providing coverage for LPNs. During the day shift, PCTs receive a direct care assignment of 2 to 3 patients and are expected to assist those patients with baths, to change the sheets, and to assist with ambulation and other activities. During the night shift, the PCT staffing is reduced such that the RNs, with the assistance of LPN staff, are expected to provide total care to their patients. The two PCTs on the night shift perform monitor technician and UA duties until approximately 5:00 A.M. At that time, the PCT who has been cross-trained to perform UA duties is expected to assist in patient care tasks, including vital signs, daily weights, ECGs, and lab specimens. Two additional PCTs routinely arrive for duty at 5:00 A.M. to assist with these tasks. The day shift PCTs are also assigned 9 to 10 patients for phlebotomy, transportation, and ECGs.

Supplemental Staffing

The UMC float pool was modified to provide replacement PCTs and PSAs to meet the staffing needs created by sick calls, turnover, and promotions. The need for float pool support has intensified after restructuring because agency staff are no longer available who are adequately trained to function in the new specialized roles. In addition, the RN, LPN, and PCT staff must be familiar with the PSA role because these staff may need to fulfill some of the PSA tasks at times. New graduate RNs and some LPNs have had little to no experience in phlebotomy and need training. As a general rule, however, experienced RNs and LPNs have an easier transition in performing PCT tasks because these have traditionally been part of the nurse's role in many settings.

Charging for Services

As the patient care units assumed the additional responsibilities of ECG and phlebotomy, the unit needed to develop a mechanism to charge for services. The system for charging had already been established by the previously restructured units. However, unit staff needed to be trained in the appropriate charging procedure. Because many nursing staff previously had not been concerned with the financial aspects of care, management had to reinforce continually the necessity of charging for services.

The importance of charging is periodically reviewed at unit meetings. The vouchers are placed on clipboards at the patient's bedside daily to encourage staff to keep the charge vouchers current. An example of a charge voucher is found in Exhibit 20–1.

Quality Control

The nurse managers of restructured units were oriented to housekeeping inspection standards by the environmental services supervisory staff.

Exhibit 20–1 Charge Voucher

CODE	QTY	DESCRIPTION	UNIT OF MEASURE
		6 WEST 6125	
725369		NURSE ASSIST 1ST 30 MIN	HALF HOUR
725379		NURSE ASSIST ADDL 15 MIN	QTR. HOUR
936609		RECOVERY CHARGE I	4 HOURS
936619		RECOVERY CHARGE II MAJOR	8 HOURS
936629		CNS CONSULT FEE BASE	HALF HOUR
936639		CNS CONSULT ADDL 15 MIN	QTR. HOUR
991039		ICP/DAY	24 HOURS
991049		SWAN GANZ/DAY	24 HOURS
991059		A-LINE/DAY	24 HOURS
991069		CARDIAC OUTPUT COMP/DAY	24 HOURS
991089		IABP/NURSING TIME/DAY	24 HOURS
991659		NON-INVASIVE BP MONITOR/DAY	24 HOURS
991669		TEMP MONITOR/DAY	24 HOURS
996409		ACCU-CHECK	TEST
996389		CENTRAL LINE MONITORING	24 HOURS
991079		VAD/NURSING TIME/DAY	24 HOURS
607879		NON-INVASIVE PACING	HOURLY
609649		NON-INVASIVE PACING	SET-UP
		5 WEST 6103	
725239		NURSE ASSIST 1ST 30 MIN	HALF HOUR
725249		NURSE ASSIST ADDL. 15 MIN	QTR. HOUR
990799		CVP	24 HOURS
990929		ICP/DAY	24 HOURS
990939		SWAN GANZ/DAY	24 HOURS
990949		A-LINE/DAY	24 HOURS
990959		CARDIAC OUTPUT COMP/DAY	24 HOURS
990979		IABP/NURSING TIME/DAY	24 HOURS
991119		NON-INVASIVE BP MONITOR/DAY	24 HOURS
991619		TEMP MONITOR/DAY	24 HOURS

continues

Courtesy of University Medical Center, Tucson, Arizona.

Exhibit 20–1 continued

CODE	QTY	DESCRIPTION	UNIT OF MEASURE
996619		ACCU-CHECK	TEST
996639		CENTRAL LINE MONITORING	24 HOURS
996649		CNS CONSULT FEE BASE	HALF HOUR
996659		CNS CONSULT FEE ADDL. 15 MIN	QTR. HOUR
996709		RECOVERY CHARGE 1	4 HOURS
996719		RECOVERY CHARGE II MAJOR	8 HOURS
609469		NON-INVASIVE PACING	HOURLY
609629		NON-INVASIVE PACING	SET-UP
		6 EAST 6117	
725279		NURSE ASSIST 1ST 30 MIN	HALF HOUR
725289		NURSE ASSIST ADDL 15 MIN	QTR. HOUR
936869		MIDLINE CATHETER KIT	KIT
936879		MIDLINE CATHETER INSERTION	INSERTION
1040069		ELECTROCARDIOGRAM	TEST
1055119		INC SPIRO TREATMENT	EACH
1055129		INC SPIRO SETUP	EACH
1070069		VENIPUNCTURE	PROCEDURE
991529		NON-INVASIVE BP MONITOR/DAY	24 HOURS
991539		CARDIAC MONITOR/DAY	24 HOURS
991719		PATIENT CARE ASSIST.(SITTER)	HOUR
993769		RECOVERY CHARGE I	4 HOURS
993779		RECOVERY CHARGE II MAJOR	8 HOURS
993789		ACCU-CHECK TEST	EACH
993809		CENTRAL LINE MONITORING	24 HOURS
993739		CNS CONSULT ADDL. 15 MIN	QTR. HOUR
993819		CNS CONSULT FEE BASE	HALF HOUR
993749		CVP	24 HOURS
606869		VAD/NURSING TIME	24 HOURS
609509		PULSE OXIMETER CHECK	EACH
609519		METERED DOSE INHALER	EACH

continues

Exhibit 20–1 continued

CODE	QTY	DESCRIPTION	UNIT OF MEASURE
609479		NON-INVASIVE PACING	HOURLY
609639		NON-INVASIVE PACING	SET-UP
609669		SWAN GANZ/DAY	24 HOURS
609679		A-LINE/DAY	24 HOURS
609689		CARDIAC OUTPUT COMP/DAY	24 HOURS
	PHYSICAL THERAPY:		
1010309		HOT/COLD PACK 1 AREA	EACH
1010319		MASSAGE	15 MINUTES
1010329		AMBULATION W/ASSISTANCE	15 MINUTES
1010339		SUPERVISED AMBULATION	15 MINUTES
1010349		BEDSIDE ASSISTANCE	15 MINUTES
1010359		CPM/JOBST MONITORING	8 HOURS
	OCCUPATIONAL THERAPY:		
1025169		HOT/COLD PACK 1 AREA	EACH
1025179		BEDSIDE ASSISTANCE	15 MINUTES
1025189		CPM/JOBST MONITORING	DAY

A simple audit tool was devised to assess individual PSA performance (Exhibit 20–2). Peer review had been ongoing for the 4 years before restructuring. Therefore, 6 East staff members were acquainted with participating in the review and feedback process. An audit tool to assess PCT performance was also designed.

Communication with other departments became the key to optimizing functioning after restructuring. For instance, delivery times for patient trays became important in light of other PSA duties. Negotiation with food services on meal times was required to enable the PSAs to complete multiple tasks.

Initially, 6 East staff members were responsible only for routine specimen collection. Later, procedures such as timed draws were added to the unit phlebotomy responsibilities. During the first 6 months after restruc-

Exhibit 20–2 6 East Performance Tool for PSAs

NAME: ________________________ DATE: __________

Please complete by checking or circling appropriate response. If no is circled, briefly explain why in Comments section.

1. HOUSEKEEPING

	Satisfactory	Unsatisfactory
a. Room cleaning		
night stand	___	___
bathroom	___	___
floor	___	___
bed	___	___
closet	___	___
garbage cans	___	___
overbed lights	___	___
walls (if needed)	___	___
curtains changed	___	___
corners	___	___
b. Nurses station		
high dusting	___	___
cleaning behind rolling carts	___	___
sweep and mop	___	___
garbage cans	___	___
refrigerator cleaned	___	___
c. Assignment completed by end of shift	yes	no

COMMENTS ________________________

2. TRANSPORTATION

a. Patient transfers done safely	yes	no
b. Transports occur within 20 minutes	yes	no
c. Observes patient condition and reports changes to nursing staff	yes	no

COMMENTS ________________________

3. I&Os

a. Meal intake added properly to I&O	yes	no
b. Water pitchers changed at end of shift	yes	no

COMMENTS ________________________

continues

Exhibit 20–2 continued

4. DIETARY

a. Meals delivered on time	yes	no
b. Proper documentation after trays	yes	no
c. Menus completed on time	yes	no
d. Bulk stock ordered correctly	yes	no
e. Restocking done in timely manner	yes	no

COMMENTS ______________________________

____

5. MATERIALS MANAGEMENT

a. Inventory done accurately	yes	no
b. Restocking done in timely fashion	yes	no
c. Credits sent to materials management	yes	no

COMMENTS ______________________________

____

6. DRESS CODE

a. Follows dress code established for PCR	yes	no

COMMENTS ______________________________

____

7. INTERPERSONAL SKILLS

a. Is courteous and respectful to patients	yes	no
b. Is courteous to ancillary personnel	yes	no
c. Is courteous to coworkers	yes	no
d. Is open to constructive criticism	yes	no
e. Offers assistance to others	yes	no
f. Demonstrates flexibility in responding to patient/unit needs	yes	no
g. Respects and maintains patient confidentiality	yes	no

COMMENTS ______________________________

____

8. PRODUCTIVITY

a. Completes duties with minimal supervision	yes	no
b. Completes duties in a timely fashion	yes	no
c. Seeks out additional duties when appropriate	yes	no

COMMENTS ______________________________

____

continues

Exhibit 20–2 continued

9. SAFETY

a. Recognizes unsafe conditions and takes action or reports to supervisor immediately	yes	no
b. Turns in broken/damaged equipment for repairs immediately	yes	no
c. Operates cleaning and transport equipment in a safe and conscientious manner	yes	no

COMMENTS ______________________________

____

Completed by: ______________________ Date: __________

turing, laboratory department phlebotomists were occasionally requested to perform phlebotomies on the unit. In each case, the patient had been hospitalized previously at UMC and had experienced difficulty. The patients believed that the laboratory phlebotomists would have greater success with less difficulty, so that the patients' requests were honored. Such requests are now rare and have almost disappeared 6 months after restructuring.

Communication with environmental services continues to be important. The environmental services department continues to strip and wax floors in patient rooms and deep cleans the carpeting in other areas. It also coordinates the changing of cubicle curtains.

The need to communicate with the transportation department was less than on other restructured units because most patients have always been transported by unit staff. Transportation services for the unit require significant periods of time between 8:00 A.M. and 7:00 P.M. on weekdays. An average of one to two staff members are off the unit for either patient transport or patient procedures during this period of time. The addition of the PSA role has not changed the transport function significantly because PCTs, LPNs, and RNs transport all monitored patients. The main transportation issue is an adequate supply of readily accessible transport equipment, such as wheelchairs, gurneys, and oxygen tanks. Lack of storage space on the unit contributes to this ongoing problem.

Daily ECGs were scheduled to be performed in the early evening in the original plans for restructuring. The evening plan allowed for an even distribution of PCT tasks throughout the day. The proposal was well received by the unit medical director. However, in the first 2 days of restructured care delivery, the cardiology group requested that daily ECGs be done at 6:00 A.M., as they had previously. To meet the physicians' request, the staffing plan was altered to provide for routine morning ECGs. More thorough early communication with all the cardiologists may have averted the need for the rapid change in plans that ensued.

Infection is another dimension of quality control that remains a priority. New personnel (PCTs and PSAs) received training in infection control. Unit management continues to monitor the unit nosocomial infection rates. To date, no significant changes have been observed in the rate since restructuring.

Patient, Physician, and Staff Outcomes

Another aspect of quality control that has been monitored is patient, physician, and staff outcomes. Patient satisfaction data have demonstrated improvement in patient perception of nursing response to patient requests for assistance. There has been no reduction in patient satisfaction noted (see Chapter 28).

The medical staff had many questions and concerns about the new staff and the adequacy of their preparation and training. Some physicians continued to seek the RN staff for assistance. Over the first 6 months after restructuring, many physicians began to accept and interact with the PCTs and, to a certain extent, with the PSAs as well. Physician satisfaction has not been directly measured for the unit, but the number of physician complaints has not increased.

Staff outcomes also have not been directly measured for the unit. Staff turnover rates have remained stable and are actually lower in the RN and LPN categories. Some turnover occurs as staff choose to transfer to the intensive care unit. Additional turnover results from relocation. The only significant turnover experienced with restructuring has occurred at the PSA level.

Managing Nonlicensed Staff

The staff readily accepted the PSAs, but they were not prepared to delegate tasks to these staff members. Nursing staff have not traditionally paid attention to the activities of either environmental service or food service staff. A PSA daily schedule was formulated to help provide direction for the PSAs and guidance to the staff about expectations of PSA duties (Exhibit 20–3).

Before restructuring, the following problems had been noted with the NAs: inappropriate scrub attire, attendance problems, and turnover. The

Exhibit 20–3 6 East PSA Daily Schedule

DAY SHIFT:

0600–0720	Collect housekeeping cart; linen pick-up. Transport any stat lab specimens, begin transport of patients for procedures and retrieval of stat supplies from materials management and pharmacy.
0720–0800	Prepare overbed tables and assist patients to wash up. Deliver trays to patients.
0800–0815	Return tray cart to pantry. Serving forms and diet order forms returned to food services by 0815.
0815–0830	Break.
0830–1130	Begin general unit cleaning—admissions and discharges; dirty/used equipment to dirty utility room, etc. Transport patients for procedures; transport of stat lab specimens and retrieval of stat supplies from materials management and pharmacy. Clean nurses station and nursing circle; linen pick-up.
0900	Obtain tray retrieval cart from pantry, pick up all trays, return cart to pantry. Send calorie counts to food services.
0915	Put bulk stock and labeled morning patient nourishments into unit refrigerator or cupboard.
1130–1200	Lunch.
1200–1250	Prepare patients by helping them wash up, and prepare overbed tables for meal service. Delivery of patient trays (1235–1255).
1250–1305	Return tray cart to pantry. Serving forms and dietary order forms returned to food services by 1305.
1305–1330	Distribute preheaded menus for next day; menus to patients and their families. Assist completion as needed. Place afternoon labeled patient nourishments in unit refrigerator.
1330–1345	Obtain tray retrieval cart from pantry, pick up all trays, and return cart to pantry. Send calorie counts to food services.
1345–1400	Break.
1400–1500	Wrap up any duties as needed.
1445	Report to oncoming PSAs.
1500	Home.

Note: Materials management and transportation issues will be handled by the charge nurse as they arise, and the two PSAs will assist each other.

EVENING SHIFT:

1430–1600	General unit cleaning—admissions and discharges; dirty/used equipment to dirty utility room, etc. Transporting patients for procedures; transport of stat lab specimens and retrieval of stat supplies from materials management and pharmacy. Clean nurses station and nursing circle; linen pick-up.
1600–1630	Floor stock inventory taken (must be received by food services by 1630). Remove outdated material, document refrigerator temperature.
1630–1645	Break.

continues

Exhibit 20–3 continued

1645–2030	Continue general unit cleaning. Assist patients in washing up, and prepare overbed tables for dinner.
1730–1755	Deliver trays to patients.
1755	Return tray cart to pantry. Serving forms and diet order forms to food services by 1810.
1830	Obtain tray retrieval cart from pantry, pick up all trays, return cart to pantry. Send calorie count to food services (all patients' menus to food services by 1900 for next day's meals).
1845–1915	Dinner.
1915–1930	Deliver labeled evening patient nourishments. Put bulk floor stock into refrigerator or cupboard.
1930–2030	Check all rooms for leftover trays, tidy bedside tables, check room for space IV pole, remove dirty IMEDS and deliver to dirty utility room.
2200	Clean dirty utility room, taking back items to materials management; transport of stat labs, etc. Miscellaneous cleaning (IV poles, refrigerators, report room, etc.). Clean nurses station and nursing circle. Finish up loose ends, return housekeeping cart for restocking.
2300	Home.
NIGHT SHIFT:	
2200–0630	Take materials management inventory by specified item numbers and par level. Enter exchange cart list into computer and print at warehouse for pulling. Print CS supply list, pull and deliver to appropriate area. Pick up credits from nursing area and fill out appropriate form, send back credits to Materials Management warehouse. Clean nurses report room and nurses station.

Note: Materials management and transportation issues will be handled by the charge nurse as they arise, and the PSAs will assist each other. On the 2200–0630 shift, the PSA is shared with 5 East.

introduction of the PSA role increased these problems. Dress code issues with this group resulted in the selection of standard attire for PSAs: a blue polo shirt and dark blue slacks. The institution has chosen to purchase the first shirt for each PSA. Additional shirts are purchased by the individual PSAs. Since this policy has been in place, dress code issues have diminished significantly.

Attendance and turnover among the PSA group continue to be problems. One explanation is that the PSA role is an entry level position. Some of the turnover is due to PSAs being promoted to PCT positions. UMC has encouraged the process to promote a career ladder for PSAs.

In addition to dress code and turnover problems, RNs have noted that PSAs have difficulty setting priorities. Many PSAs share prioritizing issues with the RN. The unit RNs were not prepared for this behavior. The RN staff needed to learn to assist PSAs in prioritizing care activities. As a result of additional group work, the PSAs are more adept at prioritizing, and both groups are less frustrated.

Last, one problem for which unit management was not prepared occurred when the PSAs left the unit for undetermined periods of time without permission. The PSAs had been instructed that the charge RN on the unit was the person with whom they were to check in before taking a break or from whom to obtain information regarding patient flow. The significance of this point was not demonstrated by the PSA behavior, however. A special PSA meeting was called to address the issue, and the problem was resolved. As new PSAs join the staff, the importance of communication and direction is stressed by the charge RN and monitored closely.

SPECIAL CONSIDERATIONS

Peer Review

Each unit in any hospital has special concerns that are specific to that unit. Issues specific to 6 East included peer review, staff self-scheduling, and case management. Since the unit opening in October 1988, the unit staff have actively participated in peer review. Introducing peer review to the PCT group was a natural extension of the peer review process started with the NA group. In fact, the majority of the PCTs had previously been NAs on the unit. The PSA group also readily accepted peer review as well, possibly because it was simply one more new aspect of a new role.

Self-Scheduling

PCTs and PSAs were also introduced to self-scheduling. Self-scheduling had initially been implemented as a retention mechanism to provide staff with greater flexibility in their work schedule. New staff as well as RNs and LPNs recognize self-scheduling as a satisfier.

Case Management

Case management had initially been implemented on the unit under the auspices of the Differentiated Group Professional Practice grant. Several staff RNs have been case managing patients on an as-needed basis. The opportunity to become case managers was open to all RNs on staff. As additional RNs demonstrated interest in case managing patients, an RN experienced in case management would co–case manage a patient together with the interested nurse. This process continued until the RN new to case management was comfortable with the role.

A key aspect of the RN role within patient care restructuring is case management. Patient care restructuring has provided additional multiskilled workers to relieve the RN of tasks that can be delegated to a nonprofessional worker. The RN has more time to focus on the professional aspects of the role, including case management. Since restructuring, the quality of case management has improved, and many more patients have been case managed. Therefore, case management will continue to be stressed as a critical part of the RN role on the unit.

LESSONS LEARNED

The need to select PSAs carefully has become evident based on unit experience and recommendations from other restructured units. PSAs who have previous working experience with housekeeping duties, either in hospitals or in the hotel industry, have greater success in the PSA role. PSAs report greater job satisfaction as they assist patients in transportation or with their meals. PSAs who are able to commit verbally to the PSA role for a minimum of 1 year are also more likely to adjust well to the PSA role. Those who are not able to make such a commitment usually desire a role beyond the PSA level. These PSAs find the job expectations frustrating on a day-to-day basis and often leave the role as soon as any other positions become available. This factor contributes to the PSA turnover problem.

In contrast, successful PCTs have the capacity to master cardiac monitoring. Because cardiac monitoring is a required competency for the PCT role, PCTs participate in a monitor training program. Before restructuring, several NAs were unable to demonstrate competency with cardiac rhythm monitoring. The NAs transferred to other NA positions within the institution. To date, no PCT has been unable to meet this requirement.

Finally, the impact of patient care restructuring on physician practice must be considered. Although the medical director was consulted about changing the time for obtaining daily ECGs, other members of the cardiology group had not been consulted. It should not have been surprising, then, that when this change was implemented there was little physician support. The lesson learned was that one physician, even in a medical director position, may not be representative of a physician group.

CONCLUSION

Restructuring patient care delivery on the intermediate care telemetry unit has been a challenging and exciting project. Thorough planning by a multidisciplinary team and adequate staff preparation were essential factors in determining a successful outcome. Previously established unit group governance also contributed to our success.

Other areas of importance in planning the restructuring of care delivery include: clearly defined expectations of new roles, including basic expectations with regard to attire and attendance; careful staff selection into new roles; staff training in areas of team building and delegation; RN training with regard to the supervision of nonprofessional staff; and ongoing communication between all ancillary departments, physicians, and nursing.

SUGGESTED READINGS

Allen, D., et al. 1988. Making shared governance work: A conceptual model. *Journal of Nursing Administration* 18:37–44.

Batey, M.V., and F.M. Lewis. 1982. Clarifying autonomy and accountability in nursing service: Part 1. *Journal of Nursing Administration* 12:13–17.

Birkholz, G. 1989. Technicians in critical care: Training, supervisory, and legal aspects. *Dimensions of Critical Care Nursing* 8:113–18.

Burkhart, E., and L. Skaggs, eds. 1993. *Nursing Leadership: Preparing for the 21st Century*. Chicago: American Hospital Publishing.

Clark, K.H., et al. 1991. Turning the organization upside down: Creating a culture for innovation and creativity. *Nursing Administration Quarterly* 16:7–14.

Clifford, P.G. 1992. The myth of empowerment. *Nursing Administration Quarterly* 16:1–5.

Edwards, D. 1988. Increasing staff nurse autonomy: A key to nurse retention. *Journal of Pediatric Nursing* 3:265–68.

Hospers, C.J. 1989. The middle manager in shared governance. *Aspen's Advisor for Nurse Executives* 4:4–5.

Kramer, M. 1990. The magnet hospitals excellence revisited. *Journal of Nursing Administration* 20:35–44.

Kramer, M., and C. Schmalenbert. 1988. Magnet hospitals: Part II. Institutions of excellence. *Journal of Nursing Administration* 18:11–19.

CHAPTER

21

Surgical Intermediate Care/ Telemetry Unit Case Study: Implementing Restructuring and Intermediate Care in the Same Year

JoAnne Schnepp and Theresa Grzyb-Wysocki

Chapter Objectives

1. To give an overview of the unit before patient care restructuring.
2. To describe the planning process for the restructuring change.
3. To give an overview of the unit after patient care restructuring.
4. To discuss the quality control aspects of restructuring.
5. To discuss changes in satisfaction levels of both staff and patients after restructuring.
6. To discuss various issues that arise out of managing more of a nonprofessional work team.
7. To describe the special considerations surrounding restructuring for this particular patient care unit.
8. To report the lessons learned as a result of being among the first units to restructure.

UNIT OVERVIEW BEFORE PATIENT CARE RESTRUCTURING

5 East is a surgical intermediate care unit without any telemetry beds. Patient diagnoses include general surgery, trauma, vascular and cardiothoracic surgery (including heart transplants), and kidney/liver transplants. The average length of stay is 4.5 days. The unit contains 31 beds and five different teaching teams of attendings, chief residents, first- and third-year residents, and medical students.

The staff mix for the unit consisted of one nurse manager, three assistant nurse managers, and a ratio of 88 percent registered nurses (RNs) and 22 percent licensed practical nurses (LPNs), plus nursing assistants and unit assistants. In the fiscal year before restructuring, the unit was budgeted for an average daily census of 26 patients. In addition to the nurse manager and assistant nurse managers, the unit was budgeted for 22.8 full-time equivalents (FTEs) of RNs, 5.6 FTEs of LPNs, 4.2 FTEs of nursing assistants, and 4.9 FTEs of unit assistants. The budgeted hours per patient day (HPPD) of direct care were 6.91. Staff members were distributed according to the staffing guidelines in Table 21–1.

At the time of restructuring, RNs oriented on the unit for 4 to 6 weeks, LPNs for 2 to 4 weeks, and nursing assistants for 2 weeks. All training consisted of 3 days of hospital/nursing department orientation followed by the on-unit clinical orientation. Additional training and education on the unit was arranged through the staff development department and was based on an annual needs survey that involved staff and management.

Assignment methods on 5 East were different from those on other units in the hospital. At a census of 26 patients, for example, the 7:00 A.M. shift was staffed with five RNs, three LPNs, and one nursing assistant, and the 7:00 P.M. shift was staffed with four RNs, one LPN, and one nursing assistant. The LPNs always worked in a dyad partnership with an experienced RN. New graduates and less experienced RNs worked alone with a less acute patient assignment.

PLANNING FOR THE CHANGE

The 5 East unit was among the second group of units to restructure. Planning occurred at the beginning of the usual budgetary process for the upcoming fiscal year. Because a separate budget for restructuring had not yet been formulated, 5 East followed the same fiscal constraints as all other departments of the hospital in that fiscal year. Specifically, 5 East had to plan a restructuring budget that contained a 2 percent budget cut. FTEs for the new positions of patient care technician (PCT) and patient support at-

Table 21–1 5 East Staffing Guidelines before Restructuring, Fiscal Year 1991–92

RN 4.15
LPN 1.85
NA 0.91
6.91 HPPD (with no intermediate care patients)

Census	*7:00 A.M.*	*7:00 P.M.*	*HPPD*
31	6 RN–3 LPN–1 NA	5 RN–2 LPN–1 NA	6.96
30	6–2–1	5–2–1	6.80
29	6–2–1	5–1–1	6.62
28	6–2–1	5–0–1	6.85
27	5–3–1	4–1–1	6.67
26 (budget baseline)	5–3–1	4–1–1	6.92
25	5–2–1	4–1–1	6.72
24	5–2–1	4–1–1	7.00
23	5–2–1	4–0–1	6.78
22	4–2–1	3–1–1	6.55
21	4–2–1	3–1–1	6.85
20	4–2–1	3–1–0	6.60
19	4–1–1	3–1–0	6.31
18	3–2–1	3–1–0	6.67
17	3–2–1	3–0–0	6.35
16	3–2–1	3–0–0	6.75
15	3–1–1	3–0–0	6.40

Note: If there are three intermediate care patients, the 7:00 A.M. shift staffs up one RN and down one LPN, and the 7:00 P.M. shift staffs up one RN (generally speaking). For numbers of immediate care patients other than three, charge RNs will need to determine staffing.

tendant (PSA) were based on data related to usage from the departments that had previously provided the services, namely phlebotomy and cardiology for the PCT position and environmental services, dietary, transportation, and materials management for the PSA position. These departments transferred FTEs from their areas to the units being restructured based on services provided historically. The 5 East unit was allotted 4.2 FTEs for PCTs and 7.0 FTEs for PSAs. It also added an additional 4.2 FTEs for PCTs because the unit was going to add a new telemetry program during the fiscal year and needed to hire and train the new PCTs as monitor technicians. To meet the required 2 percent budget cut and not experience a reduction in licensed staff, vacant RN FTEs were eliminated. Meetings were held with LPNs to determine whether they were willing to expand their role to include phlebotomy and 12-lead ECG skills. If the LPNs agreed, then fewer PCT FTEs would be needed and fewer RN FTEs would be eliminated from the budget. When the process was completed, the LPNs agreed to expand roles, and 4.6 RN FTEs were eliminated. Based on small changes in the budget, the 2 percent cut was achieved, and the patient care restructuring budget was created (Table 21–2).

Once a budget existed for this project, staff preparation began. The 5 East staff had participated in a 5-year research project to introduce group governance. Therefore, the staff had some experience with both the change process and the project interactions as a group. Thus, the new project was much easier to implement. In fact, nursing staff on the unit had officially requested that their unit be among the first to restructure. However, earlier participation may have jeopardized the final data collection needed for the previous research project. The staff had agreed not only to begin this project but also to commit to following the restructuring with implementation of telemetry within the same year. Project preparation began with the introduction of the project at open meetings for all staff. The vice president for nursing also met with the assistant nurse managers and nurse managers. The nurse manager solicited a patient care restructuring unit coordinator after explaining the role to that staff nurse. Within 6 weeks, the unit coordinator scheduled the first meeting of the unit steering committee.

The unit coordinator's role is crucial to the success of the project. The staff nurse must be someone whom the staff views with respect and credibility. The person should feel confident in handling committees and be willing to interact, both informally and formally, as a leader in promoting the project and motivating other staff to become involved in the change. The unit coordinator also functions as a mediator between the staff and the management team in relaying information between the two groups and clarifying each other's issues and concerns. The unit coordinator chairs the unit steering committee, plans the agenda, and keeps the communication lines opened.

The steering committee for 5 East was a fluid committee. Specifically, staff moved on and off the committee according to their interests in the agenda topics and the available time they could offer to committee work. A core group of about six developed and attended most of the meetings. Participation on the steering committee was open to all staff, including unit assistants and nursing assistants. Several nursing assistants participated because they planned to apply for the new PCT positions and because they wanted to participate in the planning. The human resources trainer provided two planned education sessions for the steering committee: one on change theory and one on communications.

Table 21–2 5 East Staffing Ratios after Restructuring (without Direct Care Telemetry FTEs), Fiscal Year 1992–93

RN 4.38
LPN 1.74
PCT 0.87
6.99 HPPD

			Total Hours	
Census	*7:00 A.M.*	*7:00 P.M.*	*Budgeted*	*Actual*
31	7 RN–2 LPN–1 PCT	4 RN–3 LPN–1 PCT	216	216
30	7–2–1	4–2–1	210	204
29	7–2–1	4–2–1	203	204
28	6–2–1	4–2–1	196	192
27	6–2–1	4–2–1	189	192
26	6–2–1	4–1–1	182	180
25	5–2–1	4–1–1	175	168
24	5–2–1	4–1–1	168	168
23	5–2–1	3–1–1	161	156
22	5–2–1	3–1–1	154	156
21	5–1–1	3–2–0	147	144
20	4–2–1	3–1–0	140	132
19	4–2–1	3–1–0	133	132
18	4–1–1	3–1–0	126	120
17	3–2–1	3–1–0	119	120
16	3–2–1	3–0–0	112	108
15	3–1–1	2–1–0	105	96
14	3–1–1	2–1–0	98	96
13	3–1–0	2–1–0	91	84
12	3–1–0	2–1–0	84	84
11	3–1–0	2–1–0	77	72
10	2–1–0	2–0–0	70	60
9	2–1–0	2–0–0	63	60
8	2–1–0	2–0–0	56	60
7	2–1–0	2–0–0	56	60
6	2–1–0	2–0–0	56	60
5	2–1–0	2–0–0	56	60
4	2–1–0	2–0–0	56	60
3	2–1–0	2–0–0	56	60
2	2–1–0	2–0–0	56	60
1	2–1–0	2–0–0	56	60

An additional component of staff preparation included planned training in team building, delegation techniques, communication, and case management (for selected RNs). All training sessions began a few months after the unit's restructuring process was fully in place. This was important for the new team members to be able to join in the training.

One of the first big projects the unit steering committee found was the issue of interviewing staff. Group governance was one of the concepts introduced with patient care restructuring, so that staff needed to assist with the interviewing process for PSAs and PCTs. On 5 East, the staff was more experienced with the group governance process. They asked to interview all the applicants and then send finalists to the nurse manager for selection. An interviewing committee was formed consisting of two RNs, one LPN, and one unit assistant. This committee received an inservice from human resources on proper and legal interviewing techniques so that all legal requirements would be met. It then generated interview questions for both positions and planned a numerical rating system that would ensure equality for all applicants. Questions and interview plans were reviewed and approved by the human resources representative.

The interviewing process required that the committee set up interviews for more than 50 applicants, interview and rate all interviewees, and recommend finalists for the nurse manager to interview and select as new staff. The committee members interviewed in teams of two, with one member always being an RN. Paid time was allotted for the interview time, and sometimes schedules had to be rearranged to accommodate meeting times. The committee received previously screened applications from human resources. Applicants were rated on various attributes, from basic math to decision-making ability, by human resources personnel. Only the applicants who passed the initial screening were forwarded to the units for additional consideration.

The number of qualified applicants for these positions was much larger than anticipated. Many people were interested because of the potential for career advancement. A person with no previous patient care experience could be hired as a PSA and eventually be promoted to a PCT; later, this person could receive assistance from the hospital to move on in his or her education. The interviewing committee expressed amazement at the quality of the applicants who were interviewed.

Fifteen new people and five current nursing assistants were hired for the new positions. Interviewing began first for the PCTs. This position required 10 to 14 weeks of training. As the PCTs began their training program, interviewing began for the PSA positions in the same manner as described above. Within 5 months, the PSA position was fully operational on 5 East. The PCT position was fully operational 1 month later. A housewide celebration occurred during the first week of total restructuring and was immensely enjoyed by all staff.

As patient care restructuring was implemented, it became apparent that the staff in the two new job categories would need more structure. The steering committee recommended that weekly meetings be established for the PSAs and PCTs separately to have them develop written workflows for their jobs. These weekly meetings were held for the first few months until the details were completed. The PSAs needed to work out details of assignments. One of the new PSAs developed a shift assignment sheet to identify who was going to assume first responsibility for dietary, transportation, and housekeeping. This form was shared in the housewide patient care restructuring task force so that other units might also make use of it. Another PSA workflow issue dealt with multiple demands and how to confront them simultaneously. This occurred most frequently in the early morning, when breakfast trays were ready for delivery, multiple patients needed to be transported off the unit for various tests, and rooms required cleaning for those patients who had gone to surgery and were being transferred to the intensive care unit.

5 East historically runs a high census. Therefore, there are usually admissions planned for patients leaving the unit early in the morning. If the unit cannot be responsive to this situation, it affects the workflow of the admitting department. The unit was staffed with a maximum of three PSAs during weekdays on the day shift. One of them was assigned an overlap shift of 9:00 A.M. to 9:30 P.M. Therefore, they were frequently overloaded in this manner. Some decisions that the PSAs worked out regarding their shift routines included the following:

- The PSA who was assigned to housekeeping would not leave the unit to transport but would perform breakfast dietary duties as a first option.
- The PSA who was assigned to transport primarily would be the first one to leave the unit for any reason and would function as a back-up for housekeeping duties.
- The overlap PSA would take over dietary duties and assist with housekeeping when arriving at 9:00 A.M.

Even with the new plan, overload still occurred. Therefore, the issue was discussed at the monthly staff meetings to obtain input from other staff members. The staff as a whole solved the problem by deciding that anyone available could assist with dietary and that PCTs who were available could help with transportation in an overload situation.

The major workflow issue that occurred for the PCTs dealt with the early morning phlebotomies, which occurred between 5:00 and 7:00 A.M. The PCT group suggested changing its work hours to accommodate this high volume of phlebotomies. Rather than adhering to the usual 7:00 start time, PCT hours shifted to begin at 6:00. This allowed the two night PCTs the benefit of two day PCTs arriving at 6:00 to assist with phlebotomy. The work during this busy time flowed more efficiently.

Another major item that became evident and required troubleshooting was capturing revenue charges for procedures performed by the staff that had previously been performed and charged by other departments. A charge form was created and approved by the finance department. Unit staff members were then oriented to the proper use of the form. Three months of consistent discussion with the staff concerning charges was necessary before audits indicated that the majority of predicted charges were actually being captured. Because of the experience with group governance, 5 East again placed responsibility for the project with one of the PCTs on the night shift because all the old charge forms for the previous 24 hours were removed and new ones were placed in patients' rooms by the PCTs. Open meetings for all staff were also scheduled to discuss topics related to charges, revenues, and budgets. These discussion periods gave staff a chance to ask questions and verbalize ambivalent feelings regarding nursing charging for services. The clinical director and nurse managers for the area attended the sessions and provided a panel discussion on the topic.

UNIT OVERVIEW AFTER PATIENT CARE RESTRUCTURING

One year after patient care restructuring was implemented, marked differences have been noted on the unit. The patient population has changed with the addition of eight telemetry beds and patients who have undergone liver transplants. The new budget also has brought some changes in the staffing mix. RN FTEs have increased to support the higher acuity patients. LPN FTEs have decreased by attrition, and some FTEs have been converted to PCTs. PCT FTEs have increased dramatically to provide more basic care support to the RNs. PSA FTEs have not changed, but have been redistributed to accommodate all the early morning activity previously discussed. The revised staffing guidelines for direct care staff are listed in Table 21–3.

After 1 year of restructuring, it became apparent that a continuing education plan for the PCTs and PSAs needed to be formulated. Many changes had occurred and needed to be shared with all staff. Four-hour mandatory educational sessions were held for PCTs to update them on new changes pertinent to their roles. By sending a PCT representative from each unit, PCTs were brought up to date through the creation of a

Table 21–3 5 East Staffing Ratios (Including Telemetry), Fiscal Year 1993–94

RN 4.92
LPN 1.38
PCT 1.50
7.80 HPPD

Census	*7:00 A.M.*	*7:00 P.M.*	*Total Hours*	
			Budgeted	*Actual*
31	7 RN–2 LPN–3 PCT	6 RN–0 LPN–2 PCT	240	244
30	7–2–3	6–0–2	240	236
29	7–2–2	6–0–2	226	228
28	7–2–2	6–0–2	218	216
27	6–2–2	5–0–2	211	204
26	6–2–2	5–0–2	203	204
25 (budgeted standard)	6–2–2	5–0–2	195	192
24	5–2–2	5–0–2	187	192
23	6–2–2	4–0–2	179	180
22	5–2–2	4–0–2	172	168
21	5–2–2	4–0–1	164	168
20	5–1–2	4–0–1	156	156
19	4–1–2	4–0–1	148	144
18	4–1–2	4–0–1	140	132
17	4–1–1.5	3–0–1	133	132
16	4–1–1	3–0–1	125	120
15	3–1–1	3–0–1	117	120
14	3–1–1	3–0–1	109	108

Note: Monday through Friday the charge nurse is out of ratio on the day shift and takes three patients on the night shift. On weekends the charge nurse takes three patients on the day shift and five patients on the night shift. The night shift should always have a charge nurse with three patients and be able to admit two patients. Weekends have one fewer RN and a third PCT on the day shift. Staffing guidelines are based on five immediate care patients.

monthly meeting. The representative would share information in the unit staff meetings and place written information in the PCT communication book on the unit. Each PCT would read the book, sign in, and take copies of materials for his or her own file. This has proven to be effective, and a similar system is currently being created for PSAs' continuing education.

A full-day retreat for all staff categories was held to refine roles and revise patient assignment methods. Staff listened as the clinical director gave an opening talk regarding health care trends nationwide and their impact on hospital and unit finances. The need to improve the efficiency of care to maintain quality and to keep costs contained was discussed. The nurse manager held a discussion regarding upcoming changes in Joint Commission on Accreditation of Healthcare Organization mandates and Arizona State Board of Nursing rules and regulations. Assignment methods needed to be altered to reflect these upcoming changes. Several small group meetings, including both same-job and mixed-job categories, were planned. These group meetings looked at how to refine roles and revise assignment methods to meet new mandates during the coming year. At the retreat, the following decisions were made:

- Move the LPN to a role of assisting an RN rather than having a total patient care assignment.
- Provide more detailed assignments to PCTs.
- Return to an audiotaped report at shift change.
- Create several task forces to refine workflow among the PCTs, PSAs, and unit assistants.

These changes are currently being implemented. The retreat was received positively by staff members and provided the impetus to improve morale and to take the group governance concept to a higher level of functioning. Staff members expressed the need to have some type of retreat quarterly. They proposed fewer meetings for information sharing so that there might be more quality time for group interaction.

All the issues that arose during the first few months of implementation indicated a need to develop performance tools, audit forms, and mechanisms for the unit to work with other departments to monitor quality issues. The unit revised performance tools for the PCTs and PSAs that had been developed by one of the original restructured units. The unit nurse manager worked with environmental services to begin periodic inspections and involved the unit PSAs in planning corrective actions where necessary. The unit also worked closely with the cardiology department to correct issues related to the performance of 12-lead ECGs. An assistant nurse manager joined a committee to troubleshoot the issues around phlebotomies and provided one-on-one education to staff who were making errors. Phlebotomy sent data related to this issue so that monitoring could occur. Within 6 months, improvements were noticed.

PATIENT AND STAFF OUTCOMES AFTER PATIENT CARE RESTRUCTURING

Informal evaluations indicated that staff and patient satisfaction increased as a result of restructuring. The most notable change in staff satisfaction occurred after implementation of the PSA role. The staff appreciated the new members, who emptied linen and trash containers and were available to transport patients and perform dietary roles. The licensed staff also became aware of other job categories where people worked as hard and efficiently as they did. This cut down dramatically on idle complaining regarding busyness. The addition of the PCT role did not increase staff satisfaction, probably because the unit already had experience with nursing assistants. The new roles that the PCTs assumed were not previously done by nursing staff. Therefore, there was not a perception that adding PCTs decreased the workload for the licensed staff.

Patient satisfaction has not yet been officially surveyed on this unit. However, unofficial assessment indicates that patient satisfaction has increased. Patients report fewer delays in getting their call lights answered or their minor needs met. Elderly patients seem to be more secure knowing that the person who cleans their room is the same person who brings them food trays and transports them to other departments. The care being provided is more personalized for the patient.

ISSUES RELATED TO MANAGEMENT OF NONPROFESSIONALS

In the first few months after full implementation, many issues surfaced that seemed to relate to supervising a large group of nonprofessionals. Absenteeism was an immediate issue. Not adhering to the dress code was another area that required more frequent counseling, especially among the PSAs. With the PCTs, several issues related to working outside the scope of practice occurred within the first few months. First, the PCTs wanted to do more for the patient either because they were being asked by physicians who did not understand the new role and its limitations or because they wanted to be perceived as people with more training and abilities. Second, some of the licensed staff did not understand the limitations of the new role and were too quick to ask the PCTs to assist with tasks that were not within the job duties. The PCTs, wanting to be perceived as good helpers, would sometimes not say that they could not perform that type of assistance.

A corrective plan was put together in which the entire direct care staff met with the managers, reviewed the pertinent section of the Arizona State Board of Nursing rules and regulations, and then signed a statement verifying that the rules and regulations had been reviewed. All new staff members in direct care go through the same procedure at the time of hiring. Disciplinary action can then occur quickly if people do not work within their scope of practice. Another issue relating to the management of nonprofessional staff is turnover.

Issues related to poor performance resulted in termination of some persons the first year. Continually replacing people was difficult. All PSAs are now hired directly into the float pool. They receive their orientation there and start working on the units as fill-in staff. When a unit has a vacancy, the appropriate paperwork is sent to the float pool manager and a replacement is transferred from the float pool. This means that the replacement PSA is already trained and has worked on the units, and his or her work can be evaluated before the individual is accepted for transfer.

Another concern that arose was a lack of supervision for the PSAs by the charge nurses on the unit. The role had never existed under unit management before, and some of the charge nurses did not make a smooth transition into supervising the PSAs and paying attention to issues. Charge nurses had no previous experience with counseling. They had never paid any attention to how quickly or thoroughly a room was cleaned or to whether the trays were collected in a timely manner. From a manager's perspective, it was enlightening to discover a couple of months after implementation that nearly all the new people on the staff had no concept of the unit management structure or the chain of command. They did not understand that the charge nurse was their immediate supervisor on a day-to-day basis. The manager's time was taken up endlessly with new people asking for help with issues that should have gone to the charge nurse. After a few months and much frustration, the issue was a topic of discussion at a unit management meeting with the assistant nurse managers and nurse manager. During a staff meeting, we clarified the chain of command.

SPECIAL CONSIDERATIONS FOR 5 EAST

This unit had some special issues related to the implementation of patient care restructuring. Because 5 East had already introduced basic group governance concepts, the initial approach was to expect integration of the new roles into the group governance model. Over time, the management team realized that many PCTs and PSAs were not able to function at a level of group governance. We are now implementing a mixed model of group governance. We continue to have participation in group governance by the licensed staff and all other staff members who are interested and able to participate in a committee or handle a project. Out of 23 PSAs and PCTs, about 5 (22 percent) have the potential to become active members of a group governance model.

As stated earlier, the 5 East team had originally planned to implement both patient care restructuring and telemetry in the same year. This proved not to have been such a good plan. By the time telemetry was implemented in December, the staff were, in general, overwhelmed with the multiple changes. Resistance resulted, affecting staff morale to the extent that patient satisfaction survey results were significantly less positive.

Another issue that arose on 5 East was some unexpected resistance from the LPNs to the expanded duties of adding phlebotomy and ECGs. All LPNs had initially agreed to the proposed changes. When the training programs started for both phlebotomy and ECGs, negative talk began to occur. Once training was completed, resistance was noted among LPNs performing the new duties. Special meetings were held with the LPNs and the human resources trainer. The issue was resolved, but it recurred a couple of months later with a variety of new staff in the form of resistance to attending the telemetry training. One of the major premises of group governance is accepting accountability for one's actions and being responsible as an individual. These LPNs needed to be accountable for their actions. The resistance was discussed in staff meetings. LPNs were given memos with specific deadlines to complete the training. After the deadline, three people were terminated, and two were disciplined.

Another issue specific to 5 East was self-scheduling and the nonprofessional staff members. Because of the group governance model, the unit staff participated in self-scheduling and had been doing so for about 4 years. However, it quickly became apparent that the nonlicensed staff did not demonstrate the accountability/responsibility necessary to take part in the self-scheduling program. Currently, some PCTs can plan their schedules and take part in revision, but for the most part the committee schedules for the PCTs and PSAs. All these issues were time consuming and sometimes very frustrating to solve, but the entire team is more cohesive and more responsible having been through the experience.

LESSONS LEARNED

Many lessons were learned during the implementation of patient care restructuring on 5 East. The major lesson was that the managers of units to be restructured must be willing to restructure, and they must be supported by administration to put many other usual activities on hold for about 6 months. The project requires much time, energy, and expanses of a cleared calendar at times. The nurse manager needs to maintain certain aspects of the role, such as fiscal responsibility, routine staff contact, counseling, discipline, and interviewing/hiring for all the old vacated positions. On 5 East, the nurse manager learned this lesson by trial and error but received much support from the clinical director. Support was provided for the entire project in terms of time constraints by the vice president for nursing.

A second major lesson learned on 5 East was not to plan more than one major project in the same year. The unit had a cynical saying, when we realized that morale was down on the unit, resistance to change was increased, and staff were tired: "Too much change in '92 = poor morale in '93!" The experience of 5 East was considered when another unit, not yet restructured, was showing some resistance to the planning process. The decision was made by the administrative team to put things on hold and to move more slowly with that unit.

A third lesson learned was the need to create a supplemental float pool for the roles of PCT and PSA as the units were being restructured. With the second two units implementing restructuring, the other departments no longer had resources to help out a unit when there was a sick call.

In addition, it was learned that more communication and healthy communication skills are key to successful outcomes. Education about communication skills before a change is implemented may improve the ability to decrease resistance to change and negative feelings in a healthier and more professional manner.

Another lesson learned was a need for a commitment to spend both time and money for group meetings and task forces. The staff cannot practice communication skills, assist with interviewing staff, and so forth if they do not have time allotted for group meetings in addition to their direct care work. Many will not participate if they are not paid for the time they spend. It is important to provide time and money in the beginning. Once the staff gets some experience in group governance and learns that there is positive change in the concept for them, then it is possible to achieve effective staff participation.

Last but not least, we learned that looking for certain background experiences in the potential PCTs and PSAs would provide more skilled workers, decreased training expenses, and decreased turnover. PSAs who had some background housekeeping experience performed much better overall. PCTs with experience in the nursing assistant role also performed better and required less training time. One factor may be that housekeeping and the basic nursing assistant skills are the least enjoyed parts of the two new roles for some people.

CONCLUSION

The initial year of patient care restructuring on 5 East has been referred to by the nurse manager as a time of blood, sweat, and tears. However, the results, in terms of improved patient care and staff growth, have been tremendous, and a wish for the good old days will never arise after completion of this project.

CHAPTER

22

Postpartum and Newborn Nursery Case Study

Marty G. Enriquez

Chapter Objectives

1. To describe the postpartum and newborn nursery units, including staff mix, patient population, and delivery systems, before restructuring.
2. To describe the staffing plan and patient care assignments before and after restructuring for the postpartum and newborn nursery units.
3. To describe the specific skills list developed for the patient care technician for the postpartum and newborn nursery units.
4. To discuss the full-time equivalent allocations after restructuring for the postpartum and newborn nursery units.
5. To describe the barriers to implementation of restructured care in the postpartum and newborn nursery settings.
6. To discuss special considerations for postpartum and newborn nursery in restructuring.

Patient care restructuring (PCR) is a new and innovative approach to delivering the highest quality of care to obstetrical (OB) and neonatal patients. This approach aims to improve the quality of care and service to patients and to address labor shortages in various health care occupations.

This chapter discusses the process for restructuring patient care in the postpartum/antepartum and neonatal areas at University Medical Center (UMC). A description of the service areas involved is included. The chapter describes the introduction of the concept to the staff and physicians, their participation via committees and open forums, and issues that were barriers to implementation. Specific information about full-time equivalents (FTEs) before and after restructuring as well as staffing plans are also provided.

GENERAL SERVICE DESCRIPTION

The OB program at UMC is part of the department of women and children's services. The program consists of two inpatient units: labor and delivery and the postpartum unit, also known as 7 East. The medical management and direction for the program are provided by the faculty through the Department of Obstetrics and Gynecology of the University of Arizona College of Medicine. The newborn nursery (NBN) is also part of women and children's services but is under the medical management and direction of UMC's department of pediatrics. The NBN is included in this case study because from a nursing perspective the same nurse manager manages both 7 East and the NBN. This chapter discusses PCR on 7 East and the NBN. The PCR project in labor and delivery is discussed in Chapter 34.

The OB program at UMC provides tertiary care for high-risk OB patients. It is recognized and certified as a high-risk center by the Arizona Perinatal Trust. The center is one of two tertiary centers in the community. UMC is well known throughout Arizona for the provision of high-risk care. For the past 10 years UMC has successfully attempted to change its image and be recognized also as a low-risk maternity center. An image campaign has begun in the community to focus on the fact that UMC is a community hospital and that its low-risk care is just as excellent as its high-risk care. Although six of the seven local community hospitals have inpatient OB services, UMC has the highest volume and the largest market share of OB and newborn admissions and patient days. The primary providers are the attending physicians, who are members of University Physicians, Inc. (UPI); the OB residents; and the private OB physicians, who belong to one of two major health maintenance organizations (HMOs) that bring OB and pediatric patients to UMC.

As mentioned in previous chapters, the PCR project was developed and implemented to improve patient satisfaction. In addition, PCR was an attempt to develop multipurpose workers in response to anticipated shortages of a variety of health care occupations, including nursing. Although no shortages of staff existed on 7 East and the NBN, PCR was started in these areas to improve care and free nurses from the nonnursing tasks that are identified as time consuming. Because both 7 East and the NBN had successfully used nursing assistants (NAs), the patient care technician (PCT) role was viewed as an improvement because the PCTs would have skills in addition to their already present patient care skills as NAs.

As is evidenced with any major change, PCR raised many questions and issues. The move toward PCR came at a time when the number of deliveries had dropped and the volume on 7 East and in NBN had decreased. The combination of the change in health care delivery and the volume decrease resulted in anxiety about job security and in open resistance to change.

Introductory PCR meetings were held with all staff to discuss PCR, its purpose, and UMC's plans for implementation. At the time PCR began on 7 East and the NBN, the project had already been underway in pediatrics and in two general adult medical-surgical units for 1 year. Naturally there were many rumors concerning PCR elsewhere, and this contributed to the staff's concerns about a major change. Issues and concerns were addressed and discussed at staff meetings; communication bulletin boards and notebooks were also made available.

Once the informational meetings were held, 7 East and the NBN selected unit-specific steering committees. These committees included staff volunteers and were developed to finalize the roles, job descriptions, and skills lists of the PCTs and patient support attendants (PSAs) to meet the needs of the OB/antepartum patients on 7 East and the newborns in the NBN. Also, the unit-specific steering committees participated in the screening, interviewing, and final selection of PCTs and PSAs. Another important role of these committees was to serve as liaison between the unit staff and the PCR task force. Any and all issues and concerns raised by the staff were addressed with the PCR task force, and the steering committees played a key role in problem resolution. Many of the members of the steering committees were supportive of PCR and served as advocates for the project to their colleagues. The critical role that the unit-specific steering committees play cannot be overstated. Staff participation in directing this major change is key to the success of PCR.

UNIT DESCRIPTIONS AND ROLES BEFORE RESTRUCTURING

Postpartum Description and Roles

The Postpartum Unit (7 East) is a 29-bed inpatient unit that is used primarily for postpartum women (both low and high risk) but also provides care to high-risk antepartum patients. Five of the 29 beds are in private rooms, and the other 24 beds are in semiprivate rooms. The unit is located next to the NBN. The labor and delivery unit and the neonatal intensive care unit (NICU) are both located above 7 East and the NBN on the eighth floor. After patients deliver, they remain in labor and delivery for 1 to 4 hours (time depends on the recovery period if the patient delivered by Cesarean section or by vaginal delivery). After the recovery period, the patients are transferred to 7 East until discharge.

The volume on 7 East is driven by the deliveries projected for that fiscal year and is budgeted by patient days. Currently there are 3,672 deliveries per year, or 306 deliveries per month. This volume translates into a budget of 8,960 patient days, or an average daily census (ADC) of 24.5 patients, on 7 East. Of this daily volume, approximately 4 patients (17 percent) are high-risk antepartum patients, and the remaining 20 patients (83 percent) are postpartum patients. The antepartum population on 7 East generates about 1,460 patient days per year. The remaining 7,500 patient days are projected based on the number of cases of a particular diagnosis and their projected average length of stay (ALOS). For the volume of 3,672 deliveries per year, it is assumed that 81 percent of the deliveries will be vaginal and that 19 percent will be by Cesarean section. Of the total vaginal deliveries, 10 percent will have complications with an ALOS of 2 days, and the other 71 percent will have an ALOS of 1.5 days. Of the total Cesarean sections, 4 percent will have complications with an ALOS of 5.6 days, and 15 percent will be without complications with an ALOS of 3.9 days. The estimated ALOS multiplied by the projected number of cases then provides the patient days for the budget.

Aside from postpartum and antepartum patients, 7 East will occasionally have gynecologic (GYN) patients. The placement of GYN patients on 7 East occurs if the GYN unit (which is part of the adult health services area) is on triage status and needs to transfer its GYN patients off the unit. The physicians who manage the GYN patients are usually the same physicians who manage the postpartum and antepartum patients.

The high-risk antepartum patients are usually referred to the care of the perinatologists. Some private physicians may choose to follow their own patients, but again, if the patient is high risk, the perinatologist is likely to be involved. The postpartum patients either are followed by the attending physicians and OB residents via the UPI clinic or are the private patients of the various physicians with the different HMOs. Many of the high-risk antepartum or postpartum patients are also patients referred into UMC's OB program from throughout southern Arizona.

All the high-risk antepartum or postpartum patients who are referred into UMC are admitted directly into labor and delivery for assessment. Once they are stabilized, the antepartum patients are transferred to 7 East until they deliver. If a patient is considered high risk after the delivery, the physician may decide to keep the patient in labor and delivery until the patient can safely be transferred to 7 East. Although the 7 East nursing staff is trained and competent in the care of high-risk postpartum and antepartum patients, the majority of the care provided is low to moderate risk.

The 7 East nursing staff providing direct care to the 7 East patients before restructuring primarily consisted of registered nurses (RNs), licensed practical nurses (LPNs), and NAs. The NAs had been on 7 East for a long time and were highly regarded and trusted by the nursing staff. Three of the RN positions on this unit were utilized for unit clinical management, with a clinical nurse leader (CNL) overseeing each shift. Before restructuring, these CNLs were called assistant nurse managers (ANMs). As ANMs, the CNLs spent 90 percent of their time in clinical work and 10 percent on management tasks. The 10 percent of time not on the unit was spent on unit-specific projects, committee work, and performance evaluations of the staff. The role was recently changed, and currently the CNLs spend 100 percent of their time on the units in a clinical leadership role. In the absence of a CNL, a charge nurse is always designated to manage a particular shift.

The only additional personnel on 7 East reporting to nursing before restructuring were the unit assistants, who provided 24-hour clerical coverage. Other staff involved with patients were from a variety of ancillary departments and did not report to nursing. These staff included housekeepers, dietary aides, phlebotomists, transportation aides, materials management personnel, and therapists from respiratory, occupational therapy, and physical therapy.

NBN Description and Roles

The NBN is a 30-bassinet nursery for only normal, full-term newborns. If a newborn at birth requires special care and/or observation as a result of prenatal history, gestational age, or physical or physiological problems present at birth, that newborn is admitted to the NICU, not to the NBN. If the newborn is full term (by gestational age) and is stabilized after a transitional period in the NICU, then that newborn may be transferred to the NBN.

The newborns are admitted directly from labor and delivery. They initially spend some time with their mother, and sometimes eye treatment and cord care are administered in labor and delivery before transfer to the NBN. When the mother is transferred to 7 East after delivery and recovery, the infant is brought to the NBN. The newborn is admitted by an RN. It is then closely observed for a maximum period of 4 hours to monitor its transition from intrauterine to extrauterine life. Once the newborn successfully completes its transitional period, it is then bathed and fed and is reunited with its mother. For the most part, the infant remains in the NBN until discharge. Rooming in is encouraged; otherwise, the newborn is brought out to the mother on 7 East for feedings.

The volume in the NBN is driven by the projected deliveries and the type of delivery (i.e., Cesarean section with complication, Cesarean section without complication, vaginal delivery with complication, and vaginal delivery without complication). The ALOS for the newborn is the same as for the mother based on her type of delivery. It is assumed that 78 percent of all the births will be of healthy infants. The NBN is budgeted for 5,217 patient days or an ADC of 14.29 newborns per day. The physicians who care for the newborns in the NBN are the attending physicians and pediatric residents from UPI and the private pediatricians from the different HMOs.

The NBN staff providing care before restructuring were RNs and NAs. However, one part-time LPN filled an RN position and was part of the core NBN staff. The two NAs who worked in the NBN had been employed at UMC and in the NBN for 13 to 20 years. These NAs were given patient assignments and were highly regarded by the RN staff. Three of the RN positions on this unit were utilized for unit clinical management, with a CNL overseeing each shift. Before restructuring, these CNLs were called ANMs. As ANMs, the CNLs spent 90 percent of their time doing clinical work and 10 percent doing management tasks. The 10 percent of time not on the unit was spent on unit-specific projects, committee work, and performance evaluations. With the recent change of the ANM role to CNL, the CNLs spend 100 percent of their time on the unit in a clinical leadership role. In the absence of a CNL, a charge nurse is always designated who is responsible for managing a particular shift.

The only additional personnel in NBN reporting to nursing before restructuring were the unit assistants, who provided 24-hour clerical coverage. Other staff involved with the patients were from the various ancillary departments and did not report to nursing. These staff included housekeepers, phlebotomists, and materials management personnel.

PCT Skills List Specific to 7 East and the NBN

The generic PCT skills list that was originally developed at the start of PCR was modified by the unit-specific steering committees for 7 East and the NBN to meet the specific needs of the postpartum, antepartum, and newborn patients. Because both units had utilized NAs for many years, the staff had some working knowledge about what the PCTs could do. The information did not necessarily make the process any easier because the NAs were highly skilled and had been UMC employees for many years. Often the nurses in both units gave the NAs full assignments (except for medications and assessments). The staff had developed trusting relationships with the NAs over the years, and the new PCTs were not viewed in the same manner. Although the NAs were encouraged to apply for the available PCT roles, the two NAs in the NBN chose early retirement, and all the NAs on 7 East were selected to be PCTs.

Exhibit 22–1 illustrates the 7 East PCT skills list, and Exhibit 22–2 is an example of the NBN PCT skills list. The unit-specific skills lists for the PCTs were intended to maximize the use of the PCTs. The more skills the PCTs have, the more support they can provide the nursing staff. RNs can be freed to spend more time with their patients, doing what only nurses can do. The PCT can only be as helpful and supportive as the nurse allows. If the RN does not utilize the PCT for direct patient care, the RN will have to absorb the extra workload because the PCTs are part of the direct nursing hours per patient day (NHPPD). As the project progresses and as the RNs become more comfortable with the PCT role, the skills lists are being expanded to allow for better utilization of the PCT.

STAFFING PLANS BEFORE AND AFTER RESTRUCTURING

Before restructuring, two levels of care were identified on 7 East. These levels were identified by the type of patient: antepartum, vaginal delivery, or Cesarean section. Within each patient level were variations regarding the amount of nursing care the patients would need. For example, same-day Cesarean sections were considered higher acuity than Cesarean sections 1 day after surgery or even 2 days after surgery. Also, contracting, unstable antepartum patients were considered higher acuity than stable, routine antepartum patients.

The standard 7 East patient required the first level of care, a 1:5 RN-to-patient ratio; the second level of care was identified as a complex patient requiring 1:3 or 1:4 care. Complex patients included the following: a patient experiencing fetal demise, a diabetic patient on insulin, an antepartum patient on IV tocolytics, an antepartum patient with bleeding or preeclampsia, a postpartum patient with a wound infection requiring triple antibiotics with postpartum hemorrhage or with moderate to severe preeclampsia, and a psychotic patient who was felt to be a danger to her-

Exhibit 22–1 7 East PCT Skills List

Skill	*Instructed*	*Assisted*	*Alone*	*Competent*
I. OB Care				
Fundal checks				
Lochia check				
Perineal check				
Pad counts				
Breast binder				
Tea bags, breast shells				
Ice packs Breasts Perineum				
Breastfeeding basics				
Use of breast pump				
Pericare Ambulatory Bed rest				
EFM placement				
EFM, care of equipment				
Sitz bath				
Exam room Familiarize with supplies Assist MD with exams				
OT for antepartums VCR teaching tapes Cart for diversional activities				
Baby care basics				
Infant car seat				
Birth certificate				
Sterile dressing changes				
Patient ambulation Cesarean sections Early postpartums Activity restrictions, BRP				
Use of Epifoam, Tucks, Anusol, Dermaplast				

continues

Exhibit 22–1 continued

Skill	*Instructed*	*Assisted*	*Alone*	*Competent*
Use of eggcrate mattress				
II. Admit or Transfer Patient				
Obtain appropriate vital signs				
Set up room				
Call light within reach; emergency light				
Condition of admit form signed				
Visitation rules				
Patient/family oriented to room and unit				
Weighing new admit				
Belongings unpacked, labeled, stored in proper place				
III. Patient Discharge				
Necessary RN instructions completed				
Patient has received DC meds				
Patient has all personal belongings				
Baby discharged—green card on crib, gift packs				
IV. Vital Sign Specifics				
Parameters to report to nurse: Temperature over 38°C Pulse less than 60, more than 100 Respiratory rate less than 16, more than 24 Systolic blood pressure less than 60, more than 90				
Duramorph protocol, charting				
Doppler fetal heart tones				
V. General Unit Duties				
Use of telephone				
Tube system				
Kardex				

continues

Exhibit 22–1 continued

Skill	*Instructed*	*Assisted*	*Alone*	*Competent*
Assignment worksheet				
Answering lights, use of equipment				
Knowledge of emergency measures				
Maintains neatness of work area				
Breaks				
Chain of command				
VI. Familiarize with PSA Duties				
Clean rooms				
Linen removal				
Empty wastebaskets				
Maintain neatness of overbed tables				
Pass meal trays, pick up				
Transport patients				
Transport speciments, supplies				
Unit restocking				
VII. Familiarize with Unit Assistant Duties				
Transcribe orders to Kardex, medication record				
Order evening snacks				
Telenote to dietary for patient diet orders				
Take first report from labor and delivery				
Record information from labor and delivery patient board for charge nurse				
Report patient discharges, transfers, admissions (with times) to admitting				

Exhibit 22–2 Normal NBN PCT Skills List

Skill	*Instructed*	*Assisted*	*Alone*	*Competent*
1. Handwashing				
2. 3-minute scrub				
3. Holding a baby				
4. Diaper changes				
5. Umbilical cord care				
6. Bathing an infant				
7. Infant skin care				
8. Linen change (crib)				
9. Operation of radiant warmer				
10. Set up for admission to transition				
11. Pack for discharge				
12. Circumcision: set-up				
13. Circumcision: clean-up				
14. Circumcision: routine care				
15. Feeding a baby				
16. Bottle feeding				
17. Breastfeeding basics				
18. Heelstick labs/specific				
19. Heelstick Chemstrips				
20. Heelstick hematocrit				
21. Heelstick PKU				
22. Mock Code skills/newborn emergencies				
23. Set up for administration of oxygen				
24. Use of bulb syringe				
25. Emergency equipment check				
26. Placement of urine specimen bag				
27. Universal precautions				

continues

Exhibit 22–2 continued

Skill	*Instructed*	*Assisted*	*Alone*	*Competent*
28. Handling of syringes or sharps				
29. Disposal of syringes or sharps				
30. Vital signs				
31. Location of NICU call buttons				
32. Hospital orientation				
33. Basic unit assistant orientation (hospital and on unit)				
34. Basic breastfeeding instruction				
35. Charge sticker system				
36. Quality control: Chemstrips				
37. Recalibrate Chemstrip machine				
38. Change Chemstrip machine battery				
39. Clean Chemstrip machine				
40. Quality control: hematocrit				
41. Clean hematocrit machine				
42. Normal newborn variations				
43. Phototherapy: set-up				
44. Application of phototherapy mask				
45. Maintenance of neutral thermal environment (NTE)				
46. Security issues: abductions				
47. Location of laboratory				
48. Location of microbiology				
49. Location of blood bank				
50. Location of ECHO				
51. Location of radiology				

continues

Exhibit 22–2 continued

Skill	*Instructed*	*Assisted*	*Alone*	*Competent*
52. Location of 7 East				
53. Location of supply/materials				
54. Location of NICU				
55. Location of labor and delivery				
56. Location of other units				
57. Location of nursing administration				
58. Basic unit orientation				
59. Stocking (carts/cribs)				
60. Picture taking				
61. ECG				
62. Cross-train to 7 East				
63. Cross-train to NICU (when restructured)				
64. Cross-train to PSA role				

self. The staffing guidelines before restructuring on 7 East reflected an NHPPD of 4.48.

The NBN, before restructuring, identified its level of care. That level was a normal, full-term newborn requiring a 1:6 RN-to-patient ratio. Although all the healthy newborns were admitted into the NBN and required a transitional period of close observation for up to 4 hours, the 1:6 RN-to-patient ratio allowed a nurse to handle successfully the admission and transition of one to two newborns plus up to four newborns older than 4 hours of age. If a newborn required special feedings, special treatments and procedures, or frequent vital signs after 4 hours of age, these newborns were usually cared for in the NICU on an intermediate observation level of care. The staffing guidelines before restructuring in the NBN reflected a 4.46 direct NHPPD.

After restructuring, the levels of care for 7 East and the NBN remained the same. The PCR project began on these units at the end of November (the fiscal year starts in July of each year). The budgets for the first fiscal year were adjusted after the start of PCR because PCR began at the end of November. The direct NHPPDs for 7 East were increased to 5.22, and the

NHPPDs for the NBN were increased to 6.07. The increases were due to the addition of the PCTs to the direct care hours. Before the budget planning for the new fiscal year that was to begin 7 months after the initiation of PCR on 7 East and the NBN, some minor budgetary changes were made. The direct NHPPDs for 7 East after these changes were increased slightly to 5.47. The NBN direct NHPPD decreased slightly to 5.88 to reflect that the second PCT budgeted for the evening shift was not always necessary. Table 22–1 illustrates the total FTEs by job classification before and after restructuring for 7 East and the NBN.

The RN FTEs were decreased significantly after restructuring. These decreases were also affected by a decrease in volume, as mentioned previously. Before restructuring, the ADC on 7 East was 28.2 patients; after restructuring, the ADC dropped to 24.5. The ADC in the NBN before restructuring was 16.2 newborns; after restructuring it dropped to 14.2. Tables 22–2 and 22–3 illustrate the staffing guidelines for 7 East and the NBN after restructuring. There were no PSA positions budgeted in the NBN, but the 7 East PSAs also covered the NBN on each shift.

Table 22–1 Specific Unit Job Classifications and Budgeted FTEs

		Budgeted FTEs	
Unit	*Job Classification*	*Before Restructuring*	*After Restructuring*
7 East	RN	17.4	11.0
	ANM/CNL	3.0	3.0
	LPN	3.6	1.3
	PCT	0.0	8.4
	NA	3.2	0.0
	PSA	0.0	5.2
	Unit assistant	4.2	3.5
NBN	RN	11.8	5.2
	ANM/CNL	3.0	3.0
	PCT	0.0	7.7
	NA	1.7	0.0
	Unit assistant	4.2	3.5
	Nurse manager*	1.0	1.0

*The nurse manager position appears in the NBN budget even though the same nurse manager oversees 7 East and NBN.

Table 22–2 7 East Staffing Guidelines after Restructuring

	Required Staff									
	Days			*Evenings*		*Nights*			
Total Patients	*RN*	*LPN*	*PCT*	*RN*	*PCT*	*RN*	*LPN*	*PCT*	*Direct HPPD*
1–10	2	0	0	2	0	2	0	0	N/A
11	2	0	1	2	0.5	2	0	0	5.45
12	2	0	1	2	1	2	0	0	5.33
13	2	0	1	2	1	2	0	0.5	5.23
14	2	1	1	2	1	2	0	0.5	5.43
15	2	1	1	2	1	2	0	1	5.33
16	2	1	1	2	1.5	2	0	1	5.25
17	2	1	1	2	1.5	2	0	1	5.41
18	2	1	2	2	1	2	0	1	5.33
19	2	1	2	2	2	2	0	2	5.47
20	2	1	2	2	2	2	0	2	5.22
21	2	1	2	3	2	2	0	2	5.33
22	3	1	2	3	2	2	0	2	5.45
23	3	1	2	3	2	2	0	2	5.22
24	3	1	2	3	2	2	1	2	5.33
25*	3	1	2	4	2	2	1	2	5.44
26	3	1	2	4	2	2	1	2	5.23
27	4	1	2	4	2	2	1	2	5.33
28	4	1	2	5	2	2	1	2	5.42
29	4	1	2	5	2	2	1	2	5.24

PSA: days 2
evenings 1
nights 1 (1.0 FTE)

*Budgeted ADC: 24.5
Budgeted NHPPD: 5.47

BARRIERS TO IMPLEMENTATION/SPECIAL CONSIDERATIONS

The PCR project has been perceived as a radical change. When PCR was introduced to the staff, little published information was available about PCR, and few hospitals were restructuring their care delivery systems. For units such as 7 East and the NBN where there was not a perceived staffing shortage, PCR was a difficult concept to accept. Historically postpartum and newborn care are routine and status quo areas, and PCR was a major change. Ongoing education and support had to be provided to the staff as they struggled to accept this. The staff was encouraged to be part of the change, to direct it, and to control it whenever possible.

Table 22–3 NBN Staffing Guidelines after Restructuring

	Required Staff						
	Days		*Evenings*		*Nights*		
Total Patients	*RN*	*PCT*	*RN*	*PCT*	*RN*	*PCT*	*Direct HPPD*
1–12	2	0	2	0	2	0	N/A
13	2	1	2	1	2	1	5.54
14	2	1	2	1	2	1	5.14
15*	2	2	2	2	2	1	5.87
16	2	2	2	2	2	1	5.50
17	2	2	2	2	2	2	5.65
18	2	2	2	2	2	2	5.33
19	3	2	2	2	2	2	5.47
20	3	2	3	2	2	2	5.60
21	3	2	3	2	3	2	5.71
22	3	2	3	2	3	2	5.45
23	3	2	3	2	3	2	5.22
24	3	2	3	2	3	2	5.00
25	4	2	4	2	4	2	5.76
26	4	2	4	2	4	2	5.54
27	4	2	4	2	4	2	5.33
28	4	2	4	2	4	2	5.14
29	4	2	4	2	4	2	4.97
30	4	2	4	2	4	2	4.80
31	5	2	5	2	5	2	5.42
32	5	2	5	2	5	2	5.25
33	5	2	5	2	5	2	5.09
34	5	2	5	2	5	2	4.94
35	5	2	5	2	5	2	4.80
36	5	2	5	2	5	2	4.67

PSA: days 0

evenings 0

nights 0

*Budgeted ADC: 14.29

Budgeted NHPPD: 5.88

The physicians involved with the patients on 7 East and the NBN were, overall, supportive of PCR because from their perspective it would improve patient outcomes. Forums were made available to discuss issues and concerns, and the physicians were encouraged to be advocates of PCR for their patients.

Of interest is that, although both units had worked with NAs, the RNs raised concerns about their liability with PCTs. They asked for ongoing clarification about RN scope of practice and issues involving delegation and supervision. Special workshops were held to address those concerns.

The nurses actively participated in the planning of PCR. Many decisions were made by the unit-specific steering committees with input from the staff. Nevertheless, because this was a major change, staff were still resistant, thinking that PCR would go away (especially if it did not work).

The same staff mix issues that arose in pediatrics with the use of LPNs were issues for the NBN. Although the NBN did not have a budgeted LPN position, an LPN worked on the evening shift. The position was a problem because of the issues mentioned in Chapter 16 regarding LPNs not being allowed by the Arizona State Board of Nursing to perform pediatric phlebotomy. Because of the budgeted ADC in the NBN, there was also a frequent issue with only one RN and the LPN working the evening shift with a PCT. Because only the RN can supervise both the LPN and the PCT and because only the RN can do the admissions, this staffing pattern was problematic. As a result, the decision was made to change the staffing pattern to RNs and PCTs.

PCR CURRENT STATUS

Initial information from patients, physicians, and staff indicates that PCR is accomplishing its goal of improving patient outcomes. Overall, the staff perceive that PCR is working. Problems with initial increased turnover of PCTs and PSAs have not always allowed for a full complement of core staff. Efforts have increased for recruitment and retention, and turnover rates have decreased over the past 6 months.

CONCLUSION

The process for the planning and implementation of PCR in the postpartum/antepartum (7 East) and NBN areas has been discussed. This new approach to health care delivery is a major change and requires education, clarification, communication, and most definitely staff involvement. The chapter has reviewed the importance of initial informational meetings to identify the need for PCR and the importance of staff participation early in the process as well as ongoing. Specific FTE information before and after restructuring as well as information about PCT skills lists and unit staffing plans are also included.

Any consideration of future changes must include the staff. They need to be a part of the planning as well as the implementation. It is important to remember that the patient must continue to be the focus of any change if that change is to be successful. PCR works because its main goal is improvement of patient outcomes.

CHAPTER

23

Emergency Department

Stephanie Higie and Kelly Morgan

Chapter Objectives

1. To describe the emergency department's implementation of University Medical Center's model of patient care.
2. To describe the two volunteer roles and their planned impact on patient satisfaction.
3. To describe the staffing plan before and after restructuring.
4. To describe assignments before and after restructuring.
5. To describe special considerations in restructuring an emergency department.

The emergency department (ED) was the first outpatient unit to restructure its patient care delivery system based on the University Medical Center (UMC) model. In addition, the ED was the second special care area to restructure. The first special care unit to restructure was the telemetry inpatient unit. In October 1992, the patient care services director for the department of emergency services requested the patient care restructuring (PCR) task force to approve the restructuring process, and an implementation date was planned.

The decision to restructure the ED was based on several factors: the belief that restructuring would support the ED goal of increased customer satisfaction, increased managed care demands, and the availability and allotment of resources throughout the organization.

This chapter discusses the following:

- the forces driving the restructuring of patient care delivery systems in the ED setting
- the ED's UMC model
- the roles and responsibilities of the restructured care workers
- staffing plans and assignment strategies associated with restructuring
- barriers to the implementation of PCR
- special considerations related to ED restructuring

HISTORY

Restructured care and the use of paraprofessional staff had begun in the ED at UMC 5 years earlier. At that time, nursing assistants were hired to assist the nursing staff with minor tasks. The nursing assistants spent the majority of their shift performing unit secretary duties. In the subsequent 4 years, the use of nursing assistants progressed slowly. Two years before the formal restructuring of care, the ED technician's (EDT) role was developed, and additional full-time equivalent (FTE) hours were added to the ED budget. The EDT role was implemented to support the professional nursing staff in transportation of patients, stocking of patient care areas, and some of the routine technical tasks. Although in 1992 the EDT was a great improvement over the basic nursing assistant, the ED management team investigated the possibility of becoming a fully restructured unit based on the model developed at UMC.

A literature review found that little information was available about the restructuring of patient care in an ED setting. Most articles describing patient care delivery in the ED described primary care system with professional nursing staff. Those sources that noted the use of paraprofessional staff in the ED setting described the use of staff in the context of their prehospital roles of emergency medical technicians (EMTs) and/or paramedics.[1] One article described the use of specific volunteer roles to support patient care and customer satisfaction in the ED.[2]

PLANNING AND IMPLEMENTATION OVERVIEW

The restructuring process was planned in a manner resembling that in the other units. As the ED progressed through the restructuring process, likenesses were found between the ED and other units, including the need for time line development, unit-based steering committee involvement, and training of newly hired technical workers. However, many of the needs of the ED regarding the restructuring process differed from those of the inpatient units.

Throughout the process, unique issues were encountered that affected the restructuring program, such as the driving forces behind the restructuring, the need to improve customer satisfaction, and the number of different roles involved in patient care in the ED setting. These differences prompted the revisions of the ED version of the UMC model to facilitate better the needs of the department. In addition, several budgetary issues needed individual attention.

DRIVING FORCES

Customer Satisfaction

A strong impetus for the decision to implement restructuring in the ED was the need to focus on the goal of improved customer service. The customer groups include the following:

- patients and their families
- physicians (emergency medicine physicians, UMC-related physicians, and private physicians)
- residents
- medical students
- outside agencies (police, prehospital personnel, and community service agencies)

Customer groups also include ancillary services within the hospital, such as the blood bank, pathology lab, and radiology. An additional goal was to be able to meet the needs of each customer group in a user-friendly environment. This required an intense effort to change the culture in the ED from a traditional teaching hospital model to a private practice model.

The private practice model involved a shift toward individual attention for customer groups. For example, if a private practice plastic surgeon required an assistant while procedures were performed, it was important to meet that need. By adding a technical worker to the patient care delivery team, assistance was provided to the plastic surgeon while leaving the registered nurse (RN) free to complete more complex tasks.

Managed Care

A second driving force was the advent of managed care. Arizona has the second largest infiltration of managed care of any state in the union. The mandate of managed care is to provide high-quality care while controlling costs. The PCR model provided the ED a means to deliver high-quality care in a cost-effective manner.

The restructured model allows the lower-cost technical and support workers to perform tasks such as restocking supplies, transporting patients, cleaning rooms, and collecting lab specimens. The more cost-intensive RN is then able to perform tasks such as patient assessment, patient teaching, and medication administration. The restructured system is a more efficient and cost-effective method of care delivery that meets the managed care mandate.

THE ED RESTRUCTURING MODEL

The ED restructuring model includes all the components of the UMC model: patient care delivery, interdisciplinary team management, and shared values of excellence in patient care. However, the ED's focus on customer satisfaction and additional job roles operationalizes the model differently (Table 23–1).

Goals

The goals of PCR have been stated in previous chapters:

- to maintain and enhance the quality of patient care and customer service (customers include patients, their families, physicians, residents, medical students, and ancillary personnel)
- to utilize personnel more effectively in the delivery of patient care
- to achieve cost containment through reduction in the annual rise in the cost of patient care services
- to enhance and maintain the patient care providers' satisfaction with their job roles

Patient Care Practice Model

Seven distinct role classifications are identified in the ED patient care practice model: volunteer liaison, volunteer associate, ED admitting clerk

Table 23–1 ED Patient Care Practice Model

Job Title	*Roles and Responsibilities*
Volunteer liaison	Acts as a waiting room attendant, facilitates communication between those waiting and those in the treatment area.
Volunteer associate	Provides comfort measures, basic transportation, child care.
ED admitting clerk (EDAC)	Performs patient registration and fiscal information gathering, acts as a managed care liaison.
Patient support attendant (PSA)	Performs departmental cleaning, ordering and stocking of supplies, basic transportation.
Patient care technician (PCT)	Performs unit secretarial functions, nursing assistant functions, phlebotomy, ECGs, trauma scribe duties.
Professional nurse	Collaborates with attending and private physicians to manage patient care through professional practice and appropriate delegation.
Nurse manager	Manages staff, promotes professional development, ensures involvement with the continuous improvement process, ensures unit staffing, performs performance evaluations.

(EDAC), patient support attendant (PSA), patient care technician (PCT), professional nurse, and nurse manager. These roles encompass indirect as well as direct patient care duties.

The indirect patient care delivery roles include a volunteer liaison. This volunteer worker facilitates communication between the waiting area and the patient care delivery area of the ED. The volunteer associate focuses on patient care area support such as caring for patients' children during examinations and procedures, performing transportation duties, and serving refreshments. The EDACs are a finance-based group that performs patient registration, information acquisition, and managed care financial liaison duties. PSAs are the final group of nondirect patient care workers. These attendants focus on departmental cleaning, transportation, and materials management.

The direct patient care delivery role classifications include the PCT and the professional emergency nurse. The PCTs function at a technical level. They perform phlebotomies, ECGs, selected respiratory care, and selected physical therapy functions. In addition, they perform the unit secretarial functions, provide patient transportation, and perform nursing assistant functions. The professional emergency nurse works in collaboration with both attending and private physicians to manage the ED patient's care. He or she is responsible for all patient assessments and for the primary patient education functions.

Finally, the department manager is included in the patient care practice model. The manager is responsible for coordinating staff development, staff performance evaluations, continuous improvement, and quality control activities. The manager demonstrates fiscal responsibility by developing the department's wage and nonwage budget. The manager also monitors the department's fiscal status throughout the year, intervening as appropriate.

ED Interdisciplinary Team Management

The patient care practice model focuses on interdisciplinary team management, which includes five components: the departmental participative management council, the patient care council, the customer service review committee, the ED administrative council, and career development with advancement.

The first component of the ED patient care practice model, the departmental participative management council, includes the ED physicians and residents, the social worker, financial and registration representation, and ED staff. This group, which includes all members of the ED team, shares in the unit governance via committee involvement and participation in communication opportunities.

The second element of the model is the unit-based patient care council. This committee includes the nurse manager in addition to committee chairpersons from the ED continuous quality improvement team, the standards project team, and advanced trauma and medical nursing committees. The UMC risk management team is also represented on this committee. Decisions guiding unit-based practices are made in the ED patient care council.

The third component of ED interdisciplinary team management is the customer service review committee. This committee's membership includes selected ED attendings and residents, finance and registration representation, and ED staff. The customer service review committee reviews issues related to all facets of customer service in the ED.

The fourth component is the ED administrative council. This group includes the clinical medical director, the emergency services nursing director, the ED nurse manager, and the emergency services associate director for finance. This group is responsible for short- and long-term strategic planning.

The fifth and final element is career development and career advancement. This advancement is accomplished via promotion through the patient care services clinical ladder. Professional staff career development may have either a clinical or a managerial focus. Clinical development of the professional nurse's career may be guided by the clinical ladder program. The development and advancement opportunities in the ED correspond to those in other patient care units in the hospital.

The ED promotes the following shared values of excellence in patient care:

- a corporate culture of excellence with customer-focused quality and service
- a strong support for internal creativity and innovation
- internal and external recognition via peer review and an ongoing peer recognition process

ROLES AND RESPONSIBILITIES

Seven specific job classifications support restructured care delivery within the ED: paid and nonpaid workers, those with medical and financial training, and technical, licensed, and professional levels of patient care. Management is involved in staff development, human resources, and financial issues. The job categories include volunteer liaison, volunteer associate, EDAC, PSA, PCT, certified emergency nurse, charge nurse, and unit manager.

Volunteer Program

The ED-based unit steering committee recognized the need for a nonclinical worker whose function would be to assist with communication and to provide comfort measures. At times, the hectic pace of a busy ED prevents staff from attending to the patients' and families' basic needs. Two specific volunteer roles, the volunteer liaison and the volunteer associate roles, were developed to meet these needs. Detailed job descriptions outlining the scope and function of these ancillary workers were written. Duties for both roles involve non–patient care functions.

The volunteer liaison focuses on the needs of people, both patients and significant others in the waiting room, and acts as a communication liaison. The liaison function includes keeping patients informed about the length of the wait to be seen and assisting families to find a telephone or the cafeteria. In addition, the family liaison facilitates communication between patients receiving treatment and their caregivers and significant others during their wait.

The volunteer associate assignment focuses on traditional ED volunteer tasks. Their responsibilities include performing patient and specimen transportation, providing child care support, and promoting patient comfort utilizing measures such as offering a blanket or coffee.

Applicants for both volunteer roles are selected on their ability to communicate and provide compassionate customer service. Mature, adult volunteers with skills in communication and diplomacy are preferred, although several volunteers at UMC are students. A 24-hour orientation program is required before the volunteers begin work in the department. The orientation includes components of basic orientation to the function and structure of the department as well as communication techniques and customer service information. The goal of the volunteer program is to improve patient and family satisfaction.

EDAC

The EDAC is responsible for patient registration, information acquisition, departmental billing, and managed care liaison. The EDAC collaborates with the triage nurse to register and obtain authorization to treat each patient. An intensive 6-week training program is necessary in which the new member is teamed with the EDAC trainer. During training, the orientee receives didactic instruction, practical computer training on a test system, and clinical experiences.

PSA

The PSA also functions in the ED, where the primary responsibility is departmental cleaning. In addition, the PSA orders departmental supplies based on inventory needs, stocks patient rooms, and performs unmonitored patient transportation. Given the large volume of patients treated per day, the rapid turnover of patients, and cleaning related to trauma and other critical care needs, environmental services duties engulf the greatest proportion of the ED PSA shift.

PCT

PCTs fulfill several critical roles in the ED: unit secretarial functions, nursing assistant functions, and the various technical procedures, including phlebotomy, ECG, selected respiratory care procedures, and selected physical training. Functions of the PCT are limited to procedures within their scope of practice as defined by the division of patient care services, the Arizona State Board of Nursing, and licensure restrictions from other professional groups.

PCT training is coordinated by the PCR educator and consists of a 10-week course. The course includes didactic content, skills labs, and phlebotomy training and clinical experience. Unit-based on-the-job training is also included. At the completion of the course, newly hired PCTs are fully functional in the ED.

Professional Emergency Nurse

Employment in the ED is restricted to experienced RNs. The RNs are strongly encouraged to take the certified emergency nurse exam sponsored by the Emergency Nurses Association. This baseline certification is augmented with mandatory advanced cardiac life support and pediatric advanced life support certification. Trauma nurse core course certification is also recommended.

The ED RN works in collaboration with the attending and private physicians to manage emergent, urgent, and nonurgent care. Assignments for RNs rotate among triage, urgent care, trauma, and general care duties. All assignments have high customer service expectations.

Charge Nurse

The ED charge nurse is a certified emergency nurse who functions in a coordinating role on a rotating basis. Responsibilities include decision making about resource allotment, staffing and overtime approval, and facilitating teamwork among ED workers. The charge nurse directs the departmental activities in conjunction with the ED attending physician. He or she ensures appropriate patient placement, makes assignments, and acts as a contact person for prehospital and ancillary personnel. PSAs and PCTs report to the charge nurse. Professional staff collaborate with the charge nurse to coordinate assignments. The charge nurse reports directly to the nurse manager. The clinical supervisor acts as a resource for the charge nurse during weekend, evening, and night shifts.

Certified emergency nurses become eligible for the charge nurse role after 6 months of employment. The charge nurse training is based on departmental need and consists of 24 hours of duty with a preceptor. Charge nurses meet on a regular basis with the nurse manager to discuss role development and other issues as they arise.

Unit Manager

The ED manager is an RN who has demonstrated clinical competence in emergency nursing in addition to indirect patient care duties and responsibilities. With the advent of restructured care delivery and the related group governance focus, the manager's role has changed dramatically. The unit manager manages all staff, assumes responsibility for all operational aspects of the department, oversees the continuous quality improvement process, and manages the departmental budget. For example, with PCR the manager became responsible for many non–patient care activities, such as housekeeping and materials management. Finally, the number of staff reporting to the manager has increased with the addition of the PCT and PSA positions.

Another PCR-related change was implemented to support the development of shared governance. This change involved the assistant nurse manager (ANM) role. The ANM role was transitioned into a clinical nurse leader (CNL) role, in which staff development was the focus in lieu of managerial tasks. The immediate result of this transition was that the responsibility for staff performance evaluations and schedules belonged to the unit manager. The change from ANM to CNL created a mandate for increased staff involvement and accountability. New performance criteria, including customer service, team building, and delegation, were designed for the professional staff. Staff feedback was also initiated as part of the evaluation process.

STAFFING AND ASSIGNMENT STRATEGIES

Before and after Paraprofessional Introduction

Before the implementation of technician staff support, the staffing plans in the ED reflected fixed staffing patterns consisting of four to five professional nursing staff and one unit secretary per shift. Nurses were responsible for all functions related to patient care. Daily responsibilities for the RN included stocking the department's general supplies and linens as well as transporting patients to ancillary services and inpatient units.

The primary care staffing pattern became inadequate as the volume and acuity of the ED patients increased dramatically over a few short years. Professional nurses with ED experience were difficult to recruit. The turnover of nursing staff was high. The implementation of the EDT role assisted in decreasing the turnover rate of the nursing staff. Several additional methods were used in an attempt to maximize staffing and unit organization.

Creative (Staggered) Staffing

A review of volume statistics demonstrated consistent patterns in ED volume. In an attempt to provide maximum staffing while maintaining efficient staffing patterns, creative staffing was implemented. Creative, or staggered, staffing consisted of staff members working shifts that covered the peak hours between 11:00 A.M. and 2:00 A.M. Please refer to Table 23–2 for details of the staggered staffing pattern.

Patient Assignments

The patient assignment method was also reviewed. The department had historically used a zone method to assign patients to nurses. This method was discontinued in favor of an individualized assignment system. In an individualized assignment system, patients are assigned to a nurse based on acuity and the existing patient load for which the nurse is responsible. Although this method had the potential to complicate the role of the charge nurse, the general staff approved.

PCR-Related Changes

The transition into a restructured model of patient care delivery supported the changes already in progress related to ED staffing patterns and assignments. Creative staffing was applied to both the PCT and the PSA roles. The number of PCTs on duty increased between 12:00 noon and 12:00 midnight, and the number of PSAs on duty was increased between 2:00 P.M. and 2:00 A.M. The patient assignment system remained essentially the same.

BARRIERS TO IMPLEMENTATION

Patient Population

One of the distinct barriers to implementation of a restructured care delivery system in the ED is the diverse patient population treated in the ED. This diversity mandated special training for all levels of caregivers. The training involved special housekeeping procedures for the PSAs as well as special phlebotomy and computer training for the PCTs. The rapid turnover and variety of ED clientele also made it difficult for the newer ED team members to develop routines to assist in their acclimation to the department.

Table 23–2 ED Restructured Staffing Pattern

Day of Week	*Time*	*RN*	*PCT*	*PSA*	*Volunteer Liaison*	*Volunteer Associate*
Monday–Thursday	0700–0900	4	3	1	0	0
	0900–1200	5	3	1	0	0
	1200–1500	5	4	1	0	0
	1500–2300	6	4	2	1	1
	2300–0300	5	3	2	1	1
	0300–0700	5	3	1	0	0
Friday	0700–0900	4	3	1	0	0
	0900–1200	5	3	1	0	0
	1200–1500	6	4	1	1	0
	1500–2300	7	4	2	1	1
	2300–0300	6	3	2	1	1
	0300–0700	5	3	1	0	0
Saturday	0700–0900	5	3	1	0	0
	0900–1200	6	3	1	0	0
	1200–1500	6	4	1	1	1
	1500–2300	7	4	2	1	1
	2300–0300	7	3	2	1	1
	0300–0700	6	3	1	0	0
Sunday and holidays	0700–0900	5	3	1	0	0
	0900–1200	6	3	1	0	0
	1200–1500	7	4	1	1	1
	1500–2300	7	4	2	1	1
	2300–0300	6	3	2	1	1
	0300–0700	5	3	1	0	0

Acceptance of PCR

The plan to restructure the patient care delivery system in the ED met with mixed reviews. All the members of the ED interdisciplinary team were affected by the restructuring process. The physician ignored the plan until after implementation. The professional nursing staff was excited about having the additional support roles in the ED. They also verbalized perceptions of a loss of power and control associated with delegation of skills to other job classifications, however. Acceptance of the PCT role proved to be a complex process.

The implementation of the PCT role was one of the most challenging aspects of the restructuring. A paraprofessional technical caregiver had been employed before restructuring. The role was known as an EDT. The transitioning of the EDT to the PCT level involved more than was initially thought. Skill level and motivation in addition to the normal change process had to be examined during the transition phase.

The difference between the skill level of the EDT and the PCT was phlebotomy training. The steering committee believed that the transition would be simple. In fact, the additional training required for the EDT was quite complicated. Training was scheduled to accommodate ED staffing needs, FTE status of the employees, school schedules, and laboratory training restrictions. In addition, given the diverse population requiring phlebotomy in the ED, the training had to include pediatric didactic content and pediatric experience.

Motivation was lacking at times in that the EDT group did not perceive any advantage to becoming PCTs. They perceived a greater workload with fewer people and no additional pay to compensate for their skill enhancement.

Acceptance of the ED's restructuring program by ancillary staff was more easily achieved. The ancillary departments each had experience with the restructured inpatient units. The ancillary departments became a resource to support technical tasks. The support was appreciated by the ED staff and was supported by the ED PCR steering committee.

Scope of Practice

The scope of practice of the restructured care providers was an issue almost immediately upon the implementation of PCR in the ED. Before implementation, each member of the ED team was provided information about scope of practice. Even with the information, the various patient care provider roles were challenged in the ED as in other patient care areas.

The factors driving the scope of practice issues puzzled the restructuring team. The diversity of the patient population was one possible reason why the ED encountered the problems. The fast-paced, often critical care environment was listed as another possible cause. The previous experience of some of the care providers in the restructured roles also may have been a factor. Many PCTs had patient care experience before beginning their role at UMC. For example, the ED PCT staff included armed service medics, nursing students, EMTs, and paramedics.

Regardless of the forces driving the scope of practice issues, the PCR steering committee immediately addressed the problems that were experienced. Additional information and education related to the scope of practice were made available. Delegation issues were reviewed with each level of caregiver. Additional guidelines were drafted to define explicitly the

PCT scope of practice. Finally, a commitment was made among steering committee members to confront individual breaches of scope of practice in a manner defined by the organization. The approach ensured consistency throughout the facility.

SPECIAL CONSIDERATIONS

Budgetary

Budgetary issues affected the restructuring of the ED differently from previous units. The ED was restructured during the middle of a fiscal year. Restructuring was not planned for in the wage and nonwage portions of the budget for the year.

Each portion of the budget was affected. The wage budget changed to reflect the additional positions and FTEs added to the department. Calculation of the subsequent budget was an additional challenge given the lack of historical data about salary expenditures, overtime usage, and turnover rates.

The nonwage budget reflected an increase in unit-based revenue. This increase was due to the acquisition of procedure-based charges from other departments. The ability to charge for phlebotomy and ECGs was transferred to the ED. Given the large number of both procedures performed in the ED setting, this transfer made a large difference in the revenue in the fiscal year during which restructuring occurred as well as in planning for subsequent years.

Tracking Methods

The increased responsibility of the unit manager led to the implementation of several tracking mechanisms within the ED. These computer-based mechanisms were developed to assist with following direct and indirect wage utilization, skills and performance issues, and retention trends.

Direct and indirect wage utilization was tracked on an individual and unitwide level. The amount of time (FTE) required to cover unscheduled absences was tracked. The information was reported to the staff and used to determine the amount of prescheduled vacation time approved for all team members. In addition, education and teaching time was examined to ensure equitable utilization.

Given the various roles functioning in the department, tools to evaluate job performance objectively were required. These quality control tools were used to monitor PCT and PSA job expectations. They were developed for use on a random basis by either the manager on the on-duty charge nurse. The tools assist with the scope of practice–related development of each staff member. In addition, they are invaluable during the formal performance evaluation process.

Retention trends required a separate tracking method. The tracking was accomplished in collaboration with the human resources department. A report was issued from human resources listing each termination associated with the ED over the past 7 years. Reasons for termination were also listed. The manager developed a spreadsheet with the information that divided the terminations into job classification, year of termination, and reason for termination. The historical information was valuable in evaluating PCR-related turnover.

CONCLUSION

The ED was the first outpatient unit to restructure its patient care delivery system. The success of restructuring demonstrates that the PCR model is applicable in the emergency services setting. Restructuring supports the ED goal of increased customer satisfaction while meeting the demands of managed care. Finally, PCR in the ED enables changes to occur in resource allotment that may be mandated within health care organizations in the future.

NOTES

1. D.P. Sklar, et al. Emergency Department Technicians in a University-County Hospital: A 15-Year Experience, *Annals of Emergency Medicine* 18(1989): 401–405.
2. M.F. Johnson, et al. Emergency Department Volunteer Liaison Family Communication Program, *Journal of Emergency Nursing* 19(1993): 34–37.

PART

III

Quality Control and Operations

CHAPTER

24

The Laboratory in a Restructured Environment

Valerie J. Evans

Chapter Objectives

1. To identify the steps needed to establish a training program for teaching phlebotomy skills to nonlaboratory personnel.
2. To describe the operational strategies utilized in the process of decentralizing the laboratory's phlebotomy service.
3. To describe the quality assurance system needed to support and maintain the quality of phlebotomy practice within the restructured environment.

Phlebotomy services have traditionally been the responsibility of the clinical laboratory in hospital settings. Medical technologists, medical laboratory technicians, and laboratory phlebotomists are the usual personnel trained to perform the specialized venipuncture and skin puncture techniques used to obtain specimens for laboratory testing. This chapter describes the approach utilized by the pathology department at the University Medical Center for the decentralization of phlebotomy services in collaboration with patient care restructuring (PCR). Key to this process was the participation of laboratory personnel in the design of the training programs, operational systems, and quality assurance mechanisms needed to transfer, support, and maintain phlebotomy service in the restructured setting.

PREPARING LABORATORY STAFF FOR CHANGE

The concept of PCR was first viewed by the laboratory as a radical departure from traditional systems of patient care management. Many discussions were held with employees responsible for the management of phlebotomy services to develop an awareness of the concept of PCR and to solicit their input on its adaptation to current laboratory practices. Staff meetings regarding PCR were also held within individual laboratory sections to inform personnel and to involve them in determining PCR's potential impact on routine laboratory operations.

A major focus was the preparation of the phlebotomy staff for change. Operational strategies involving training and general phlebotomy services would be changing dramatically. The phlebotomy staff also needed to be prepared for the eventual downsizing they would undergo as the result of the transfer of services to nursing. Discussion sessions conducted by laboratory management and representatives from the human resources department were held with the phlebotomists to help alleviate immediate concerns about the future of their employment in the hospital. Handling this situation required a great deal of diplomacy, and gradually most staff members developed a comfort level with the process. All phlebotomists were encouraged to explore the possibility of becoming a patient care technician (PCT). However, only a few phlebotomists did initially apply for these positions. Because it was generally acknowledged that many would remain skeptical of the program until experience had been gained by the first pilot units, it was understandable that more of the phlebotomists did not seek to be hired into the program. Ongoing reassurance was given to the phlebotomists that their positions would not be eliminated in the form of a layoff. Gradually, as the staff focused their attention on the training aspects of this project, they worried less about these concerns. Despite participating in a program that would eventually result in the elimination of the majority of their positions as they presently existed, the phlebotomists helped develop and conduct an effective and successful training program. This resulted in an increase in employee self-esteem and a great deal of respect by the PCTs for the skills of their trainers.

EDUCATIONAL PLANS

PCT Training

Initial preparations to decentralize the laboratory's phlebotomy service involved an adjustment in our traditional operational processes as well as in our thought processes as we planned for implementation of PCR on the first nursing units. Because we had worked closely on the PCR task force, our input into the recommended criteria for selection of PCTs included educational background and general experience requirements. Laboratory personnel became the individuals responsible for providing phlebotomy training to the PCTs. It was recognized that the traditional approach utilized by the laboratory for training phlebotomists would not be effective for training PCTs, and a new training plan was developed. The chief differences in training involved the number of employees being trained at one time, the number of weeks of training, and the actual training system.

Class Size

Because four nursing units were involved in the piloting of PCR, a large number of PCTs were hired for the initial training class. Laboratory classes were divided into two sessions, and each averaged 12 to 15 PCTs. Training large numbers of students at one time seemed almost impossible considering the size of the laboratory's drawing station as well as the fact that normally training had been limited to two employees at any given time. To facilitate the increased numbers of students, it was decided to utilize the lead phlebotomist as the main PCT trainer, and four additional phlebotomists assisted with training. Each trainer would be responsible for precepting no more than three to four students simultaneously. Arrangements were made to provide a meeting room away from the laboratory to review procedures, conduct tests, practice phlebotomy technique, and so forth when the trainees were not involved with actual patient procedures. Removing the students from the laboratory for their classroom work was helpful in minimizing congestion in areas of major workflow and also provided a quiet place for the students to concentrate on the theoretical aspects of the phlebotomy process.

Training Timeframe

Employees hired to be phlebotomists in the laboratory usually received an orientation and training period of 6 weeks. Ideally, the desire was to train the PCTs in the same manner as laboratory phlebotomists. An initial recommendation to the task force was to require a 6-week training period as part of the PCT curriculum. However, because the training process was a separate period from actual work time, it became apparent that 6 weeks would be excessively long and would seriously affect training costs. A compromise was reached to require only 3 weeks of clinical phlebotomy training for PCTs, with 80 hours being dedicated to learning venipuncture and 40 hours for skin puncture skills. As more units were restructured, the specific phlebotomy needs of the unit were considered in determining the length of phlebotomy training. Currently, if the PCTs are going to be working on a unit with adults only, training time is set for 80 hours. If skin puncture skills are required because of a pediatric patient component, an additional 40 hours is added to the training. The challenge currently faced is how to continue providing the same level of training for new groups of PCTs as the laboratory staff is downsized.

Training Process

The laboratory developed an educational plan for training PCTs in phlebotomy skills. The plan was divided into three parts: an 8-hour classroom didactic session, a 3-week clinical practice session, and a 4-week on-the-job training period. The classroom didactic was used to provide trainees an initial exposure to the skills they would be expected to learn in their clinical phlebotomy training. The didactic was also used as a practice session in venipuncture and skin puncture techniques where the PCTs practiced on each other in a controlled environment. The following topics were presented in all classroom didactic sessions:

- basic medical terminology
- basic overview of the blood system
- specimen collection supplies
- test requirements
- the practice of universal precautions and other safety policies
- venipuncture and skin puncture procedures
- client relations
- quality assurance

The entire phlebotomy training plan was based upon three objectives that were designed to ensure that at the conclusion of training each student PCT would be able to accomplish the following:

- appropriately perform venipuncture and skin puncture techniques in accordance with hospital and departmental policies and procedures

- apply the practice of universal precautions and infection control policies for the safe handling of specimens, needles, and equipment and the proper disposal of biohazardous materials
- demonstrate good client relations with patients, family members, and all members of the health care team relating to the practice of phlebotomy

A phlebotomy skills list was established with the PCR education coordinator. The list included venipuncture and skin puncture techniques, transfusion specimen collection, blood culture specimen collection, genetic disease screen collection, and two-syringe technique for specialized coagulation testing. Collection of arterial specimens and line draws were not included within the scope of practice of the PCT. These restrictions were in keeping with the limitations of practice set for laboratory phlebotomists. The only major procedural limitation placed on the PCT groups was to restrict the performance of bleeding times to laboratory staff.

The PCTs are expected to report to the laboratory daily at 6:00 A.M. during training. This is the time of the largest scheduled blood draw workload. Morning phlebotomy assignments are distributed to the trainers, who escort their training group to assigned patient units. Each trainee performs required venipuncture or skin puncture collections under the watchful eye of the trainer. Only one trainee is allowed to perform a phlebotomy procedure at a time to prevent collection or patient identification errors. Gradually, as training progresses into the middle of the second week and depending on the individual abilities of each PCT, the trainees are sent on collection assignments without the trainer. The trainer still goes to the unit but circulates on the floor to provide answers to questions, to facilitate difficult draws, and to serve as a general resource person. By the third week of training, students are sent on their draw assignments alone. This is important in ensuring that each is capable of independently handling all aspects of his or her assignments. By the conclusion of training, it is expected that each PCT will have performed between 80 and 100 specimen collections. The number of collections varies depending upon how many students are training in the laboratory at one time. Intensive care and cancer treatment patients are restricted from being drawn by PCTs who are in training. All other nursing unit adult and pediatric patients as well as ambulatory patients seen on an outpatient basis in the laboratory are utilized for PCT phlebotomy training.

Training Evaluation

Midcycle in the training process, a progress evaluation is completed and discussed with each PCT. Exhibit 24–1 provides an example of the format

Exhibit 24–1 PCT Phlebotomy Midtraining Evaluation

DATE ______________________
NAME ______________________
TRAINING PERIOD ______________________

RATING SCALE	Strongly Agree				Strongly Disagree
A. Demonstrates good client relations with patients and staff (emphasis on teamwork).	5	4	3	2	1
B. Adheres to phlebotomy policies and procedures with special emphasis on safety.	5	4	3	2	1
C. Meets requirements with respect to number of patient draws performed.	5	4	3	2	1
Number of draws to date _____					
D. Demonstrates understanding of specimen collection requirements.	5	4	3	2	1
E. Demonstrates a low error rate.	5	4	3	2	1

COMMENTS: ______________________

EVALUATOR'S SIGNATURE ______________ DATE ______________

used for this review. These status reports are forwarded to the PCR education coordinator. If a PCT is having difficulty in any of the areas of evaluation, a conference is held with the educator to determine an appropriate course of action. One day before the conclusion of training, a written exam consisting of both multiple-choice and essay questions is completed to evaluate practical and theoretical knowledge. A passing grade of 65 percent is required. If a PCT scores between 65 percent and 70 percent, he or she is required to retake the exam. If a score of less than 65 percent is obtained, the PCR education coordinator is notified immediately, and a determination is made about the advancement of the individual in the program.

On the last day of training, a final review is conducted with the students, and this is recorded on the form shown in Exhibit 24–2. This form is used to document an evaluation of the PCT's skills and provides a record of the written exam score, the total number of phlebotomy draws performed, and any written commentary by the lead trainer or the trainee. Copies of the evaluations are forwarded to the PCR education coordinator to be placed in the employee's personnel file.

An on-the-job training period is assigned to all PCTs at the conclusion of their clinical training period. During this time, they are encouraged to practice their phlebotomy technique while developing their nursing assistant skills. To provide skills reinforcement, laboratory phlebotomists will circulate on newly restructured units at peak draw times to serve as resource individuals and to provide back-up support in difficult phlebotomy situations. Once the unit has been operational as a restructured area for 1 month, laboratory personnel no longer make rounds in this area. Nursing has developed a flowchart for handling situations in which the PCT is unable to obtain a specimen after two attempts. The laboratory responds only when a specific request is made by the patient or physician for lab support.

Nurse Education

Because assessment of PCT performance is now the responsibility of the registered nurse (RN) staff, a 3-hour session is given to all nurses on how to oversee and manage PCT phlebotomy skills. This presentation includes the following:

- an overview of the PCT's phlebotomy training process
- phlebotomy policies and procedures
- how to process physician orders for lab work
- quality assurance indicators for monitoring phlebotomy skills
- how to obtain phlebotomy supplies
- identification of laboratory resource personnel
- regulatory requirements pertinent to the practice of phlebotomy

After the first nursing units were restructured and the RNs became the back-up for specimen collection to the PCTs, it was realized that there was also a need to train RNs in basic phlebotomy practice. These sessions now

Exhibit 24–2 PCT Phlebotomy Training Final Evaluation

NAME ____________________ TECH # __________ DATE OF TRAINING ________

RATING	*0* *Unsatisfactory*	*1* *Needs Improvement*	*2* *Satisfactory*	*3* *Above Average*	SCORE
CLIENT RELATIONS AND COMMUNICATION SKILLS					
1. Demonstrates ability to establish rapport with patients; introduces and explains procedure to be done.					
2. Works cooperatively with others.					
3. Reacts positively to constructive criticism.					
4. Notifies supervisor in a timely manner of any problems.					
5. Seeks advice from trainer when unsure of procedures or policies.					
6. Displays a professional appearance.					
TECHNICAL SKILLS					
1. Demonstrates ability to locate suitable veins for venipuncture.					
2. Demonstrates dexterity when utilizing blood collection equipment.					
3. Demonstrates ability to take appropriate measures on difficult draws.					
4. Demonstrates ability properly to perform venipuncture and skin puncture techniques.					
CLERICAL PERFORMANCE					
1. Demonstrates ability to read and review physician orders such that tests are not missed and patients do not have to be redrawn.					
2. Maintains rigid accuracy in the identification of all patients. Follows transfusion specimen protocol in all cases.					
3. Demonstrates knowledge of specimen labeling procedures and applies this knowledge by accurately labeling all specimens.					
4. Demonstrates an understanding of specimen requirements by awareness of proper anticoagulation, special handling procedures, etc. as designated per each test in the laboratory handbook.					
5. Consistently applies the practice of universal precautions and other safety measures when performing phlebotomy procedures.					
6. Demonstrates knowledge of medical terminology as applicable to the practice of phlebotomy.					
				Total Evaluation Score	

continues

Exhibit 24–2 continued

Total draws performed in training ________		Attended didactic session ________	
Exam score ________	Attended lab safety tour ________		
Instructor's comments: ________________			
Instructor's signature: ________________		Date: ________	
Student's signature: ________________		Date: ________	
Coordinator/supervisor review: Initials: ________		Date: ________	
PCR educator's review: ________________		Date: ________	

include additional time to review the basics of venipuncture collection and to familiarize the RNs more closely with the different types and uses of blood collection equipment.

OPERATIONAL PLANS

Even though the laboratory will no longer have responsibility for inpatient phlebotomy once the entire hospital becomes restructured, it will still conduct a large outpatient phlebotomy service. Responsibility for the development of phlebotomy procedures, content revision and updates, and initial training of all individuals involved in performing phlebotomy will also remain with the laboratory. Therefore, decentralization of the laboratory phlebotomy service has necessitated the development of standardized systems that will ensure phlebotomy quality of practice throughout the institution.

Phlebotomy Manual

One of the first systems devised was the development of a phlebotomy manual and handbook for use on restructured patient units. Included in this manual are the following:

- specific phlebotomy procedures (e.g., venipuncture, skin puncture, bleeding time collection, transfusion specimen collection, and use of microtechniques for specimen collection)
- procedure for processing lab work ordered by physicians
- procedure for obtaining specimen collection supplies

- identification of laboratory resource personnel
- quality assurance standards for phlebotomy practice

PCTs receive specific training in each of the above procedures during their clinical training. RNs receive instruction during their seminar regarding how to manage phlebotomy. Additional meetings are held with the nurse managers to review all procedures and to ensure a smooth transition of practice. This manual is reviewed by the laboratory on an annual basis as required by regulatory standards. Throughout the year as procedural revisions occur and new procedures are developed, copies are sent to the nursing department for distribution to all restructured units.

Processing Physician Orders

One of the goals of restructuring is to reduce the amount of delay and turnaround time between specimen collection and receipt of specimens in the laboratory. Having personnel trained to perform phlebotomy working on each unit effectively eliminates much of the preanalytical time between receipt of physician orders in the laboratory, dispatch of a phlebotomist from the central lab, and specimen collection. It was clear in the initial stages of restructuring that the laboratory would have to alter its system of processing physician lab orders to facilitate specimen collection by the PCTs.

Routine orders for lab work are received in the laboratory on a continual basis via the pneumatic tube system. These orders are read and entered into the laboratory information system (LIS) in advance of the time of collection. The LIS assigns an internal accession number and generates collection labels for use at the time of collection. Worksheets are also generated that list the time of specimen draws by nursing unit. These are posted for the phlebotomists who circulate on the nursing units each hour from 6:00 A.M. until 8:00 P.M.

Recognizing that the PCTs had other responsibilities besides phlebotomy, the laboratory wanted to develop a system that would provide maximum flexibility for the units but would ensure that specimens were still received in a manner that would preserve the testing schedules already in place. Therefore, it was decided to request that all routine orders still be sent to the laboratory before specimen collection. The generation of specimen collection worksheets continued to organize the phlebotomy workload on an hourly basis for each patient unit.

Receiving routine blood work orders before specimen collection also provides for the generation of standardized specimen labels. The labels and worksheets also are printed with codes that describe the exact number and type of specimen collection tubes required for each test ordered. This coding system is helpful in minimizing collection errors. The labels and worksheets are generated on an hourly basis and distributed by a phlebotomist from the laboratory to each nursing unit. Routine specimens are picked up and delivered to the laboratory each hour by personnel from the transportation department. Stat orders are not sent to the laboratory in advance of drawing blood from patients. These are collected immediately by the PCT and sent to the laboratory by a patient service attendant (PSA).

Timed orders are processed in a different manner to ensure that they are always drawn as ordered. To ensure the timeliness of specimen collection, a system was developed by which unit assistant personnel remove the orders from the chart and complete a timed order pick-up form. These are posted on the unit and monitored for collection by the PCTs. The orders are then sent to the laboratory for entry into the LIS. In this manner, the PCTs can make sure that the specimens are collected at the correct time even if labels and a worksheet have not been returned to the unit for these specific draws.

Phlebotomy Supplies

With the transfer of specimen collection responsibilities to the nursing department also came the transfer of the billing charges for these procedures to each patient care unit's cost center. Specimen collection supply costs for everything but the collection tubes are now a unit-budgeted expense. The laboratory captures the costs for the specimen collection tubes in the test charges, and these items remain a laboratory-budgeted expense. Additionally, the laboratory maintains responsibility for ordering and supplying all collection tubes to the units. The PSAs are responsible for maintaining an appropriate volume of supplies by requisitioning them from the laboratory as needed using the form shown in Exhibit 24–3. Requests are completed, and the forms are sent to the laboratory. Supplies are distributed Monday through Friday between 8:00 A.M. and 6:00 P.M. within 72 hours of receipt of the request. The PSAs are also responsible for ensuring the rotation of stock so that no collection tubes are used past their expiration dates. Some special collection tubes are not distributed to the units at the time of specimen collection because of special handling requirements. These include plastic collection tubes for specialized coagulation testing and blood culture bottles.

Laboratory Resource Personnel

The identification of a group of laboratory resource personnel is also an important consideration in the restructuring process. Supervisory staff

Exhibit 24–3 Order Form for Laboratory Specimen Collection Supplies

This form is used to obtain the specimen collection supplies listed below ONLY. All other supplies are to be obtained through the department of materials management. *Orders will be filled within 72 hours after this form is received in pathology, Monday through Friday only.*

Date ______________________ Patient Care Unit______________________

Originator ______________________ Extension______________________

ITEM	*QUANTITY*	*COMMENTS*
VACUTAINERS		
10 mL SST RED 5 mL SST RED		
10 mL PLAIN RED 5 mL PLAIN RED		
7 mL NAVY		
7 mL GRAY 3 mL GRAY		
7 mL sodium heparin GREEN		
3 mL lithium heparin GREEN		
5 mL LIGHT BLUE (sodium citrate) 3 mL LIGHT BLUE 2 mL LIGHT BLUE		
5 mL PURPLE		
MICROTAINERS		
PLAIN PEACH		
RED SERUM SEPARATORS		
GREEN		
PLAIN RED		
PURPLE		
FAILURE TO DRAW SLIPS (FTDs)		
UNOPPETTE COLLECTION VIALS		

ORDER FILLED BY: ______________________ DATE ______ TIME ______

NOTIFIED FOR SUPPLY PICK-UP: ______________ DATE ______ TIME ______

SUPPLIES RECEIVED BY: __________________ DATE ______ TIME ______

SEND REQUESTS TO THE PATHOLOGY LABORATORY

members from the phlebotomy section of the laboratory, from all shifts each day of the week, have been identified to serve as resource individuals for PCT questions about phlebotomy skills. Medical data technicians have also been identified to field questions about processing lab work orders and test requirements. Laboratory management is responsible for working closely with the nurse managers on general operational issues and problems related to PCR. A list of phone numbers and beeper assignments is provided in the PCR phlebotomy procedure manual.

QUALITY ASSURANCE

Data Tracking

A mechanism to ensure the quality of phlebotomy practice on the nursing units was established upon implementation of the first pilot units. Monitoring was designated to be a joint responsibility of both the nursing service and the laboratory. The total number of draws performed by each PCT, the turnaround time from specimen collection to the receipt of the specimen in the laboratory, the number of unsuccessful draws, the number of improperly labeled specimens, the number of missed tests, misinterpreted orders, and specimen collection errors are tracked by the laboratory. Client relations and universal precautions monitoring is performed by nursing staff.

To capture data on individual PCT performance, the laboratory assigns a code number to each PCT. A unique set of numbers is assigned to each nursing unit (e.g., 1000 series for the emergency department, 4000 series for the fourth floor units, etc.). The PCTs are instructed to use this number to identify all specimen collection work they perform. This number is input into the LIS after specimens are received by the laboratory. The laboratory also assigns workload codes to the different types of specimen collection that reflect unit location. This procedure enables the laboratory to generate monthly statistical reports that identify the total number of phlebotomy collections by nursing unit and the total number of phlebotomy procedures performed by each PCT.

One problem that remains unresolved at this time is how to track the number of draws each nurse performs per month. More than 1,000 RNs are employed in staff positions, and the laboratory's LIS is not equipped to handle this large volume of specimen tracking transactions. The volume will be a future consideration as the hospital selects and implements an order entry computer package for processing physician orders for all ancillary services.

Quality Standards

The standards that have been established for each phlebotomy skill are listed in Table 24–1. Monitoring tools have been developed to provide feedback to charge nurses about phlebotomy performance. Some of these feedback systems are part of ongoing hospitalwide continuous improvement plans. The number of unsuccessful draws performed by a PCT is monitored through the use of a failure to draw (FTD) slip, an example of which is seen in Exhibit 24–4. These slips are filled out in duplicate. One copy is sent to the laboratory, and the second remains on the unit. Reasons

Table 24–1 Phlebotomy Quality Assurance

Skill	*Standards*	*Monitoring Tool*
Patient identification	Only draws patients who have arm bands. Always verifies patient identity via arm band. Always matches order, labels, and arm band patient information.	Daily reports from lab
Specimen collection	Always collects specimens in proper tubes. Always collects proper sample volume for required test.	Daily reports from lab
Transfusion specimen collection	Always follows banding policy. Always completes transfusion form correctly. Always labels specimen with correct transfusion labels.	Daily reports from lab
Reading physician orders	Draws all specimens for tests ordered. Collects all specimens in a timely manner per physician request.	Daily reports from lab
Phlebotomy technique	Makes no more than two attempts to collect sample. Maintains a low patient misdraw rate.	Monthly reports from lab
Specimen labeling	Always labels samples with correct patient information.	Daily reports from lab
Practice of universal precautions	Always wears gloves when performing phlebotomy. Follows safe needle handling practices. Disposes of biohazardous waste in appropriate manner.	Daily direct observation

Exhibit 24–4 FTD Form

Date ________ Location ______________________________ Time ________

Patient's name ____

Tests to be drawn ____

Specimen was not collected at this time because:

____ Patient was not in room.

____ Condition of the patient required assistance by a physician.

____ Patient refused to have blood drawn.

____ Phlebotomy attempt unsuccessful; another PCT or nurse needed to try.

____ Patient has A-line ____ Hickman ____ Heparin lock ____ Triple lumen ____

____ Patient has been discharged.

____ Patient is now deceased.

____ Patient has been transferred to another unit.

Signature of PCT ________________________ PCT I.D. No. ______________

NOTE: ONE COPY OF THIS FORM IS TO REMAIN ON THE NURSING UNIT WITH THE NAME OF THE NURSE NOTIFIED MARKED ON IT. SEND THE SECOND COPY TO PATHOLOGY.

PATHOLOGY'S USE ONLY:
Before slip is filed, the following must be completed:

1. Billing has been credited __________
2. Order status (recollection) ________________________________

____

____

for incomplete specimen collection include the following: The patient was not in the room, another procedure was occurring that delayed specimen collection, or the patient refused. The FTD allows a formal tracking of order status. Routine requisitions are preordered into the LIS, and billing for all test procedures occurs at this time. If collection is delayed significantly, the laboratory will credit the patient's account for the preordered test and reorder it when the specimen is finally received in the lab. This policy provides a control mechanism against unwarranted test billing.

Another use of the FTD is to allow tracking of unsuccessful phlebotomy performance. Experience with this monitoring has been that the PCTs were initially fearful of this tracking strategy and saw it as a punitive measure. In actuality, the use of FTDs provides for the identification of individuals who are having difficulty performing phlebotomy and allows an opportunity to schedule additional training to improve performance. FTDs are also used to indicate when the laboratory is being requested to assist on a difficult draw. As new units are restructured, the FTDs are monitored to identify the number of failed phlebotomies requiring repeat collection by laboratory staff. After the PCTs become more experienced with phlebotomy, the number of FTDs markedly declines, and laboratory support is no longer required.

All mislabeled and unlabeled specimens received by the laboratory are closely tracked on a daily basis. The details are communicated to the charge nurse immediately, and decisions about the recollection of the specimen are made. Forms documenting each incident are completed and reviewed by a laboratory manager and are forwarded to the appropriate nurse director. Unacceptable transfusion specimens collected, inadequate newborn genetic disease screen collections, and unacceptable specialized coagulation test specimens are also tracked by PCT code number. The total number of errors per unit per month is tallied. Each unacceptable specimen is followed up as it occurs.

All data are summarized monthly, and reports are issued from the laboratory to the PCR committee on quality control and operations for review and discussion. Exhibit 24–5 is an example of the format used for these reports. The committee meets on a biweekly basis for the first several months after a new unit is restructured. Quality control data are further discussed at monthly PCR task force meetings, where opportunities to improve are discussed and strategies for correction are considered.

In conjunction with this quality control strategy, a mechanism for effectively communicating changes in procedures and equipment has been defined. This forum allows PCTs an opportunity to direct their phlebotomy questions to laboratory experts. A monthly meeting is held at which PCT representatives from each restructured unit meet with the PCR education coordinator and resource personnel from other ancillary services to discuss a predetermined agenda. The agenda includes discussion of changes in policies or procedures, correction of specific problems observed by the ancillary services, and other related matters of general concern. PCT networking with the ancillary departments is important in maintaining communication flow among departments. When PCTs train in the laboratory, they develop a good working relationship with the phlebotomists and rely on them as resource individuals. These monthly meetings have maintained those relationships and have increased the sense of team involvement by laboratory staff members.

Exhibit 24–5 Department of Pathology PCR Phlebotomy Quality Assurance Report

MONTH ______________ YEAR ______________

Nursing Unit	Total Draws	Number of Draws Requiring Support by Lab	Number of Specimen Labeling Errors	Number of Rejected Genetic Disease Screen Collections	Number of Incorrectly Collected Samples Requiring Specialized Draw Techniques (e.g., Transfusion Specimens, Blood Cultures)	Average Turnaround Times for Stat Specimens (from Collection to Receipt in Lab)
Pediatric						
Adult						
Emergency Department						
Nursery						
Totals						

NOTES: ____

Number of Draws per PCT

PCT I.D. Code	Total Draws for Current Month

EFFECT OF PCR ON THE LABORATORY

Three principal effects were felt by the laboratory as the result of implementation of PCR. The first two, as previously discussed, were a shift in the revenue for phlebotomy services from the laboratory to nursing and a redefinition of laboratory operations involving the LIS, the processing of physician orders for lab work, and quality assurance monitoring. The third effect was a decrease in phlebotomy staffing.

A goal of the PCR task force has been to maintain budget neutrality with staffing. To do this, the number of laboratory full-time equivalents (FTEs) currently responsible for phlebotomy on a given unit, 24 hours a day and 7 days a week, must be determined. These FTEs are shifted from the laboratory's cost center to that of the nursing unit being restructured. The laboratory is committed to reducing staffing without layoffs, and FTEs have been successfully lost through attrition.

Many communication meetings have occurred with the laboratory staff to inform them of the restructuring process. Phlebotomists are encouraged to apply for PCT positions and to consider transferring to other open medical laboratory technician positions in the laboratory for which they are qualified.

Consideration of long-range PCR goals produced initial worries among the phlebotomists regarding future staffing reductions in the laboratory. At this time, with 10 nursing units having been restructured, some of the laboratory phlebotomists have successfully transitioned to the position of PCT, others have transferred to different positions within the laboratory, and some have chosen to take positions as phlebotomists outside the institution.

CONCLUSION

The collaboration among nursing, laboratory, and other ancillary support services has resulted in many benefits. Improved understanding, better use of resources, innovation and creativity, and a commitment to improving quality are among those recognized and felt by personnel involved on this project. What appeared to be an overwhelming challenge for the laboratory resulted in an increased sense of unity by the laboratory personnel involved.

The development of the laboratory's phlebotomy training program became a source of pride for all staff members involved. All phlebotomists who participated in PCT training as either lecturers or clinical trainers expressed that they experienced personal growth as the result of their redefined roles. Development of their training skills has enhanced personal self-esteem and has resulted in the establishment of a good sense of rapport with their PCT counterparts.

Laboratory staff members have transitioned their thought processes to allow for a more creative approach to the issues of restructuring. This collaborative effort has resulted in improved opportunities to appreciate the goals and services that each hospital department provides to support patient care. With the initial restructuring of the four pilot units, the laboratory realized that the approach taken to preserve the traditional systems of phlebotomy service had to be looked at from the eyes of nursing counterparts. Fear of losing control was an initial reaction that has since been discarded. The team's shared goals were achieved through the interactive development of norms and operating procedures. Efforts are continuing to support appropriate phlebotomy training and the development of needed operational systems as other nursing units restructure. Educational strategies are being tailored to accommodate the specific needs of individual units. Operational systems and quality assurance mechanisms are refined on an ongoing basis as lessons are learned about their effectiveness and clinical utility.

CHAPTER

25

Respiratory Care/ Electrocardiography/ Rehabilitation Services

Tim Brown, Carol Stumpf, Lora Pirzynski, and Betsy Lindsey

Chapter Objectives

1. To describe the quality control model in each clinical area in a restructured environment.
2. To describe and illustrate quality control monitors.
3. To include sample results of quality control monitoring.

The concept of patient-centered care affected the operation of the ancillary services of respiratory care, ECG, and rehabilitation services at University Medical Center (UMC) in various ways. Normally, in a change process such as this, literature reviews or site visits are always helpful in developing a plan of action. Unfortunately, without published documentation these ancillaries had to develop the concept of patient-centered care from its infancy.

By participating in the restructuring process, these three ancillaries were completing a business cycle. Each ancillary was developed as a subspecialty from nursing because the nursing staff was becoming too diverse. Over the years, the departments of respiratory care, cardiology, and rehabilitation services had become their own specialists, rivaling the nursing profession. Now it was time for the ancillaries to reevaluate their duties and concentrate on their specialty skills that were unique to each service.

Normally, in a change process many difficulties are anticipated that may or may not be justifiable. These three particular ancillaries were not accustomed to change, partially because of their evolution into the health care arena. Over time each ancillary has had to adapt to the changing environment. In the beginning, the ancillary was an extra pair of hands to assist in patient care. Then the ancillaries were viewed as major revenue generators, which helped offset non–revenue generating departments. With the advent of diagnostic-related groups, ancillary departments needed to develop appropriateness standards and cost-cutting measures and to justify their existence. Perhaps because of this history, the concept of patient-centered care was not viewed as negatively as one would think.

The remainder of the chapter describes each ancillary's operational and thought process from idea development to implementation. Each ancillary paid particular attention to ensuring that quality of patient care was maintained and closely monitored.

RESPIRATORY CARE

Operational Process

The respiratory care department at UMC is similar to most respiratory departments around the country. The UMC department provides a wide range of care, from simple oxygen administration and incentive spirometry to mechanical ventilation and aerotransport. The staff of 45 full-time equivalents (FTEs) made up of registered and certified practitioners manage all respiratory needs of the patients throughout the institution. Since 1987 the department has been instrumental in controlling inappropriate treatment requests with the use of a patient classification system that matches the patient's disease process with appropriate forms of therapy and corresponding frequencies of care. With the well-published shortages of respiratory practitioners nationally and the diversity of the department, the need to be everywhere at any time and to provide quality patient care in the face of dwindling hospital resources was having a negative effect on the staff by increasing the level of frustration. Performing routine therapy and being available to their patients was becoming increasingly difficult. The staff was finding that more and more of their time was being spent outside the critical care area treating non–intensive care unit (ICU) patients with routine respiratory modalities.

Impact and Reaction

In the initial discussions of patient-centered care, the respiratory care department was expected to play a major role in providing educational support and quality assurance. The plan was to transfer many modalities that were commonly given to non-ICU patients by respiratory care practitioners to a new member of the patient care team: the patient care technician (PCT). The therapies discussed were as follows: oxygen administration, aerosol therapy, incentive spirometry, metered-dose inhalers, and chest physiotherapy. The rationale behind selecting these treatment modalities was that the PCTs could be easily trained and the therapy would be given on non-ICU patients. Also, the respiratory care practitioner would continually evaluate the patients on a daily basis to ensure appropriateness of care and proper outcomes of therapy.

The director of the department had the opportunity to learn about the concept directly from the vice president of nursing several weeks before the assembly of the patient care restructuring task force. At the time, overall thoughts were that this concept was the direction in which the hospital needed to be heading if it was to remain competitive within the Tucson community. The issue was how to convince the management team of the respiratory care department and the staff. Was immediate buy-in correct? Was this the way to survive into the 21st century in health care, or was it selling out? After several discussions with peers at UMC and around the country, it was decided that the concept held merit and was the wave of the future.

The hierarchy of the respiratory care department includes a department manager, assistant manager, and shift supervisors all reporting to the director. The management team within the respiratory care department is young and aggressive and possesses a vast array of clinical and managerial talents. Initial meetings with the management team centered around the general concept and impact of patient-centered care and the specific direction of health care. The team listened and had concerns regarding the quality of patient care and the legality of having non–respiratory care practitioners performing the selected therapies. During the initial discussions of patient care restructuring, the Arizona Society for Respiratory Care had submitted a licensure bill to the state legislature. Because the bill had not been signed into law, the exact respiratory care support role of the PCT could not be clearly defined, and there were concerns about getting involved with a program that had no published data to support its efficacy. The management team accepted the idea of restructuring but wanted to pursue the idea of expanding the role of the respiratory care practitioner, not just creating another caregiver.

The department manager was asked to conduct a survey of other institutions that had restructured. A total of nine institutions were contacted, and all had a variety of plans. The plans could be separated into three categories: plans that assigned to a group of patients a respiratory care practitioner and a nurse who would manage the total patient care needs from admission to discharge, plans that created a super tech similar to the PCT but utilizing the respiratory care practitioner, and plans that paralleled UMC's. Most of the departments surveyed were only in the planning stages and were unsure whether the project would get off the ground. Also, because of the perceived confidentiality surrounding patient care restructuring, many hospitals were unwilling to share their ideas or state whether their programs were cost effective.

The management team became excited about the prospect of expanding the role of the respiratory care practitioner. Unfortunately, because of initial project intentions of restructuring the noncritical care units first, expanding the role of the practitioners was neither feasible nor budget neutral. Budget neutrality was a goal of the patient care restructuring task force. The management team within the respiratory care department had accepted the idea of restructuring and was willing to participate in the project. The team did decide to wait to explain the concept to the staff until clarification could be obtained about the status of the licensure bill.

Legal Issues

The Arizona legislation that was signed into law was the Respiratory Therapy Practice Act, which defines the scope of respiratory care and those licensed individuals who may administer this care. In essence, this bill restricts the delivery of respiratory care to specific specialty groups, in particular, respiratory care practitioners, physicians, and nurses. Because of the limiting nature of this licensure bill, the role of the PCT was changed to the following: performing incentive spirometry therapy only after the initial assessment and goal setting had been completed by the respiratory care practitioner or the nurse, and recording of pulse oximetry readings and setting the alarm limits.

Although the impact upon the respiratory care department was minimal, discussions were held with the staff to ensure its understanding of the project and the global impact of restructuring as it relates to both the health care environment and hospital personnel. The primary focus of the discussions held with the staff was the concept of future plans for the respiratory care department. With the assistance of the vice president of nursing, each medical director was met individually to explain the overall project. The medical directors of the department were informed of the wishes of the patient care restructuring task force. Because the change would not significantly affect the duties or the role of the respiratory care department, the medical directors were more interested in the entire concept. The medical directors each took a "wait and see" attitude; their acceptance would be predicated on the impact of restructuring on the quality of patient care.

FTE Determination

Now that the role of the PCT could be defined, the respiratory care department needed to adjust its FTEs to accomplish the transfer of duties. To determine the number of FTEs that would be transferred, the department utilized the cost accounting system that was established by the UMC finance department. This system determines the cost of procedures based on timeframes. These timeframes were originally determined by the American Association of Respiratory Care's *Uniform Reporting Manual.* Subsequently, the timeframes were adjusted to meet the uniqueness of UMC. The finance department was able to supply the total number of incentive spirometry treatments specific to each nursing unit. By utilizing these values, the number of FTEs transferred from respiratory care to the restructured unit project could be determined. Salary dollars also needed to be identified. This was accomplished by multiplying the number of transferred FTEs by the average hourly wage rate for the particular job code affected by the transfer.

Training

Once the FTEs had been identified, the task of training became the main concern for the respiratory care department and the patient care task force in general. The respiratory care department developed a didactic course concentrating not only on the application of incentive spirometry and pulse oximetry but also on simple oxygen administration devices and oxygen cylinders. The reason for expanding the didactic education to respiratory modalities other than just what the technicians were going to perform was to familiarize them with the practitioner's role in the patient environment and to get them accustomed to items seen on the patient care unit. The course work included basic anatomy and physiology of the respiratory system, basic assessment skills, and oxygen support. The PCTs were also taught specific safety requirements and the handling process for all the equipment. To assist the PCTs in the respiratory care skills, each PCT was assigned to a respiratory care practitioner for 1 week to demonstrate the clinical skills and to understand better the role of the respiratory care practitioner. The didactic and clinical education of the PCT was overseen and administered by the education coordinator in the respiratory care department. After the first few groups were trained, it was decided that the didactic education could be provided by the education personnel within the patient care restructuring department. Also, the clinical rotation was eliminated because it did not appear to be a value-added process necessary for the PCTs' training.

Quality Control

To document the quality of the PCT skills as they related to incentive spirometry, the respiratory care department developed monitors specific to patient outcomes. The department monitored all patients receiving incentive spirometry for the following: the ability of the PCT to perform and document the results of therapy, and whether the patient required additional respiratory care (e.g., bronchodilator therapy) because of inadequate use of the incentive spirometer. The treatment and documentation of the therapy were completed by randomly reviewing the documentation within the nursing flowsheets. The PCTs were expected to document volume achieved, frequency of use, breath sounds, and quality of cough on the nursing flowsheet or within the patient's chart. The department keeps a log of all patients receiving incentive spirometry to monitor whether the patient mode of therapy is increased to include more intensive pulmonary hygiene. If the patient was placed on additional therapy and the use of incentive spirometry was considered inadequate, then the PCT was not considered responsible for the patient's deterioration. The quality of care review after 1 year indicated that incentive spirometry therapy was a modality that the PCT could adequately administer. Because of the noninvasive application of pulse oximetry, no quality of care monitors were developed.

Summary

In retrospect, the effect of restructuring on the respiratory care department has been minimal because of the licensure bill. The benefits to the project will pay off in the next phase of ICU restructuring because the respiratory care practitioners understand the concept fully and are eager to go forward. If the process could be constructed differently, the only changes would be to solidify the task force's understanding of the licensure bill. At the time the task force did not fully understand the impact or strength of the Respiratory Care Practice Act.

ECG

Operational Process

At the time of restructuring, the current practice of performing ECGs was completed primarily by the ECG lab personnel, who are members of the diagnostic cardiology department. This department consists of several diagnostic laboratories: ECG, Holter analysis, exercise testing, echocardiography, and cardiac rehabilitation. The ECG lab personnel have a wide variety of backgrounds, not all necessarily related to health care. For the most part, the staff are college-age students with science backgrounds and are trained on the job to function as ECG technicians.

The art of performing ECGs has not changed much over the past few years, but the equipment has changed dramatically. The department utilizes computerized interpretive carts for obtaining ECGs. These carts not only produce the ECG tracings but also store them for transmission through the phone lines into a center management station. The practice of performing ECGs is as follows:

- The ECG staff makes rounds every morning to obtain the consults from each nursing unit.
- If these consult forms are properly completed, then the staff performs the ECG, leaving an uninterpreted copy on the unit.
- Once the rounds are completed, the staff transmits the ECGs to the central computer and prints a copy for the cardiologist to review. This interpretation is typed onto the ECG and returned to the patient's chart.
- The cardiologist uses the consult form to bill for both the hospital and the physician group.
- The consult form is the only piece of paperwork that is available to the cardiology staff for orders and billing.

Impact and Reaction

Over the years a small transition had been occurring with the ECG staff in the sense that they were not performing all the ECGs ordered. Nursing has always performed ECGs in emergency situations if the ECG staff has not been available. As a result of recent budgetary cuts in ECG staff, the respiratory care practitioners were performing the ECGs during evening and night hours. Because of these changes, the ECG staff was not surprised about the proposed changes with patient-centered care.

FTEs

The concept called for the PCT to perform all the ECGs on the noncritical care units. This would require a transfer of FTEs from both the ECG lab and the respiratory care department. Fortunately, the ECG department utilized a float pool of individuals who normally worked so infrequently that their positions were cut from the budget and transferred to the patient-centered care project. In determining the number of FTEs to be transferred, the same methodology used in the respiratory care department was employed with a slight modification. Because the ECG staff would still be required to perform the editing and storage of the tracings, only a portion of the timeframe was used to determine the FTEs. Also, the nursing units would be performing their own ECGs, so that adjustment in revenue needed to be made because nurses would be generating the charges.

The FTE reallocation was difficult because the ECG department did not keep statistics based on each nursing unit, only floor totals. The financial services department generated a report detailing the total number of ECG charges submitted by diagnostic cardiology per nursing unit. This number was much higher than the ECG lab predicted, and it raised concern of its accuracy. Because the department could not verify those numbers, the finance department's report was utilized.

Training

The didactic and clinical training for the ECG duties of the PCTs was performed by the ECG laboratory supervisor. The topics covered during the didactic session were as follows:

- proper lead placement
- use of the computerized carts
- paperwork, including both the consult form and the PCT billing sheet

This training was somewhat hampered because the nursing units were using a slightly different type of ECG machine than the main laboratory. The functionality of the machines was not different, but the nursing units' equipment printed out the 12-lead tracing different from the laboratory machine. The PCTs were required to tear the tracings and mount the strips for their floor copy. The machines within the lab and the central computer printed the ECGs on an 8 1/2 x 11 sheet of paper.

Clinically, the PCTs spent a week in the laboratory demonstrating their skills. If at the end of the week the PCTs could not perform ECGs to the supervisor's satisfaction, they were not approved to perform the task. The education coordinator for the patient-centered care project was informed of the lack of performance, and further didactic or clinical education was provided.

Quality Control

Initially, the quality control monitor for the successful transition of ECGs was the number of repeat ECG requests. A repeat request was generally required because of a poor tracing resulting from improper lead placement or inappropriate sampling rate on pediatric patients. In reviewing the quality control data, the number of repeats was minor and apparently not a problem. The ECGs that were required to be repeated were normally due to an agitated pediatric patient causing an uninterpretable tracing. These isolated situations were managed on a one-on-one basis with the PCT or the nursing manager by the ECG lab supervisor.

The quality control monitor was subsequently changed to what was perceived as a problem by the ECG lab: paperwork. Because the ECG staff was still performing the editing function, more and more of their time was being devoted to completing the patient consult form completely and searching for ECGs in the computer system that had been transmitted without any patient demographics (e.g., patient name or hospital identification number). With the reduction in personnel in the lab, the ECG technician did not have the time to complete the consults for the PCTs. Initially, these problems were managed on a one-on-one basis with the nurse managers. The nurse managers were informed that the patient care staff needed to complete the consult form, enter the patient demographics, and complete the nursing billing sheet to perform a complete ECG.

Exhibit 25–1 is a sample of the form used to monitor each nursing unit's progress in rectifying the problem. On a monthly basis at the quality review sessions for the patient care task force, the issue was discussed. The majority of the problems lay in the fact that patients were receiving multiple ECGs within minutes of each other. This frequent practice was occurring because the technician, practitioner, or nurse did not feel the previous tracing was of high quality, because the nursing staff was trying to document a cardiac event, or because some type of training was occurring. Be-

Exhibit 25–1 ECG Quality Assurance Form

		JUL	AUG	SEP	OCT	NOV	DEC	JAN	FEB	MAR	APR	MAY	JUN	TOTAL
ER	total ECGs								302	504	533	527	353	2219
	# complete								191	402	417	420	329	1759
	# incomplete								111	102	116	107	24	460
	poor quality													
	%								0.4	0.20	0.22	0.20	0.07	0.21
PACU	total ECGs									16	6	7	6	35
	# complete									14	5	6	5	30
	# incomplete									2	1	1	1	5
	poor quality													
	%									0.13	0.17	0.14	0.17	0.14
3rd floor	total ECGs									43	48	47	56	194
	# complete									23	32	30	22	107
	# incomplete									20	16	17	34	87
	poor quality													
	%									0.47	0.33	0.36	0.61	0.45
4th floor	total ECGs								36	93	54	86	80	349
	# complete								21	73	44	74	63	275
	# incomplete								15	20	10	12	17	74
	poor quality													
	%								0.4	0.22	0.19	0.14	0.21	0.21
5 east	total ECGs								18	129	109	117	62	435
	# complete								15	90	75	97	52	329
	# incomplete								3	39	34	20	10	106
	poor quality													
	%								0.2	0.30	0.31	0.17	0.16	0.24
6 east	total ECGs								370	531	340	570	329	2140
	# complete								320	471	307	532	285	1915
	# incomplete								50	60	33	38	44	225
	poor quality													
	%								0.1	0.11	0.10	0.07	0.13	0.11
7th floor	total ECGs									25	43	50	39	157
	# complete									17	34	35	28	114
	# incomplete									8	9	15	11	43
	poor quality													
	%									0.32	0.21	0.30	0.28	0.27
Am Surg	total ECGs								143	141	128	143	122	677
	# complete								143	134	128	143	122	670
	# incomplete								0	7	0	0	0	7
	poor quality													
	%								0	0.05	0.00	0.00	0.00	0.01

complete = ECG with appropriate paperwork and good-quality tracing
incomplete = ECG without appropriate paperwork
poor quality = ECG uninterpretable

cause the computerized carts automatically save all ECGs performed, the ECG department was receiving three to four ECGs per patient and retaining only one consult form. Unable to assume what the nursing unit was doing, the ECG staff would complete consults for the ECGs that were not completed by the nursing unit and then charge the patient for each ECG.

In addition to the individual meetings with the nurse managers and the task force to correct the problem, the PCTs were taught to delete any unwanted ECGs. The staff was further taught when documenting a cardiac event to complete the cardiology consult, especially if the documentation is needed in the patient's chart. The consult form is the only mechanism by which the cardiologist can interpret the ECG. All uninterpreted ECGs in patient charts are discarded by the medical record department. This situation has also affected the verification of billing ECGs. Because the computerized carts save the ECGs, the cardiology statistics were higher than those from the nursing units, which caused concerns on the physician side of the patient billing issue. However, the physicians had not lost any charges because the ECG staff was completing the consult forms.

Summary

Overall, the transition of ECG duties to PCTs was easy from the standpoint of their ability to obtain an adequate tracing. Paperwork was, and still is, the main problem.

In retrospect, the transition should not have been attempted until the ECG machines that were currently on the unit were replaced. Since the inception of the project, nursing units have all changed to equipment that prints out on an $8^1/_2$ x 11 sheet of paper. Also, because the ECG department did not keep records by nursing units but only as totals per floor, the actual transfer of FTEs may have been too high. This was based on the fact that the number of ECGs predicted by the nursing unit was far below the amount estimated by the ECG department and verified by reviewing the billing. The continual paperwork problem is still a mystery. To date, the nursing units have shown improvement but still submit, on the average, 20 percent of the ECGs without the proper cardiology paperwork.

REHABILITATION SERVICES

Operational Process

Rehabilitation services at UMC, including physical therapy (PT) and occupational therapy (OT), serve virtually every patient care area within the hospital. The trend has been for PT and OT to consult on inpatients to begin early mobility, enable patients to regain strength and independence, and facilitate discharge. Therapists, assistants, and technicians work together to carry out rehabilitation treatment plans in anticipation of the patient's discharge to home, a skilled nursing facility, or an inpatient rehabilitation facility.

With this in mind, rehabilitation services played an integral part in restructuring. Much effort was used to plan which tasks could be delegated to the PCTs and patient support attendants (PSAs). As will be discussed, legal implications were reviewed, which paved the way for choosing tasks appropriate for the PCT and PSA entry-level knowledge base. The theory was that, if PCTs were assisting higher level patients, rehabilitation staff would then have more time to focus on skilled tasks such as patient evaluation, treatment, and discharge planning.

Impact and Reaction

Just as the PCTs and PSAs had to be trained in their respective duties, so did the rehabilitation staff. Their immediate active participation was crucial to their buy-in of the program. Each staff member was inserviced on when appropriately to refer a patient to the new team member, thereby ensuring that adequate care was maintained for each patient. Specific rehabilitation policies were written and instituted to standardize the process. These standards included minimum guidelines that had to be met before referral. Protocol has been important to ensure similar results on each restructured unit.

Referral to the PCT was initially slow after all clinical and didactic training was complete, partly because of the therapist's hesitancy to delegate a task to an unfamiliar member of the team and partly because of ignorance of the new system. Currently, on any given unit of 30 patients, three to five PCT referrals are provided by rehabilitation on the day shift. Evening and weekend shift personnel are also provided with referrals to facilitate the patients' therapy.

Reaction by the rehabilitation staff has been overall positive. The level of confidence in the PCTs is directly related to the fact that each PCT was trained by internal rehabilitation staff. This reinforced that the PCT was well qualified to assist with the nonskilled tasks.

Legal Issues

The American Physical Therapy Association (APTA) and the American Occupational Therapy Association (AOTA) have distinct and separate guidelines governing each profession, as does each state's chapter. At UMC, care was taken to abide by the Arizona APTA and AOTA chapter bylaws and standards of practice.

As the patient care restructuring task force was establishing a plan for implementation at UMC, the Arizona Board of Occupational Therapy Examiners was working with the Arizona legislature on an OT licensure law. Like the situation with respiratory care, it was difficult to define the OT component of the PCT role until the bill was finalized. Development of the OT licensure bill was closely monitored to ensure compliance with the law. The permanent version of the licensure law states that the OT must be on the premises during any patient-related activity performed by unlicensed personnel and that the nature of the tasks shall be limited to duties that support treatment, such as transportation. Consequently, PCTs are trained by OTs. The level of care and the nature of the tasks, however, are nonskilled, rehabilitation related.

APTA guidelines on supervision of ancillary personnel require a ratio of one therapist to three technicians, aides, assistants, or students. This guideline set the state for the PCTs' scope of practice in relation to PT. The PCTs perform duties that facilitate the patients' therapy program. They do not perform PT, but may assist with ambulation, for example, to enhance the program. Because of this supervisory issue, all PT-related tasks delegated to the PCT are nonskilled and are directly supervised by nursing.

Another consideration was identifying the appropriate descriptors to use for charging. Because PCT tasks are nonskilled, OT- and PT-specific descriptors were not used. For example, a PCT cannot perform gait training but can perform assisted ambulation. The PCT charges are reflective of the differentiation.

With regard to PT practice, only therapists are allowed to initiate and progress treatment. Ancillary therapy personnel within PT carry out treatment plans or supervise activities performed by the patient under the supervision of a therapist. Similarly, on a lower level PCTs may only perform those rehabilitation-related, nonskilled activities for which they have been trained. Training, discussed in the next section, is only for those tasks considered nonskilled by the patient care restructuring committee.

Training

Staff PTs and OTs were chosen to provide the didactic portions of the PCT and PSA education. Instructors were chosen based on length of employment at UMC (i.e., those familiar with current inpatient operational processes) and length of experience as a clinical instructor for PT or OT interns (i.e., those with prior teaching experience). This was of greatest benefit because the therapists had direct insight as to exact types of patients with whom the new personnel would be in contact, thereby relaying the most appropriate and relevant information. This increased the confidence level of the rehabilitation staff in knowing specific scenarios and techniques to instruct.

Instructors were briefed about the particular tasks the PCTs and PSAs were legally and ethically able to accomplish. A syllabus to be used during lectures was developed, and prewritten lesson plans were formulated for each PCT (Exhibits 25–2 through 25–4). This was a helpful tool for PCTs to use as future reference.

For didactic training, two UMC therapists are assigned to each PCT class. PT provides 8 hours of classroom time, and OT provides approximately 4 hours. During this time, students listen to lectures, watch demonstrations, and have an opportunity to apply techniques to each other. Close supervision with feedback is apparent in every classroom. This orientation seems to benefit the students the most, allowing them to ask per-

Exhibit 25–2 PT-Related Activities Taught to PCTs

Hot pack/cold pack application	Transfer techniques
Supervised exercise	Body mechanics/safety in the workplace
Supervised ambulation	Wheelchair mobility, parts, and accessories
CPM monitoring	Patient safety with mobility

Exhibit 25–3 OT-Related Activities Taught to PCTs

Feeding/grooming assistance	Adaptive equipment awareness
Supervised exercise/activity	On-site/unit-specific training
Bed/chair positioning	Infant stress signals/readiness cues
Splint application/monitoring	Infant handling
CPM monitoring	

Exhibit 25–4 PT Instruction to PSAs

Wheelchair parts and accessories	Body mechanics/safety in the workplace
Wheelchair mobility	Patient safety with mobility

tinent questions, view set-ups, and practice tasks in a comfortable environment. A written examination at the end of the teaching session covers pertinent information and emphasizes quality of care.

For specialty units, such as orthopedics or pediatrics, classroom time is focused to instruct the PCT. For instance, a cardiac monitoring unit will probably never have the need for continuous passive motion (CPM) training, so that this is deleted from the curriculum. Additional time is provided for the students to focus on scenarios related to the patient types seen on their respective units.

Team Concept

The PCT is directly involved with assisting in rehabilitation-related duties as often as appropriate on the patient unit. Once the patient has an established rehabilitation program and is at the minimum level of dependence that is required according to rehabilitation's PCT utilization policy, the patient is referred to the PCT. Although the patient is not discharged from therapy, the PCT is responsible for supervising the patient with ambulation, exercise, and CPM usage when appropriate. Therapists continue to provide service to the patient as well as to monitor the PCT tasks, thus ensuring the proper follow-through and appropriate use of assistance.

Rehabilitation policies have been developed and implemented to ensure appropriate referrals on restructured units. This facilitates a standardized manner of referrals as well as consistency of PCT usage. As mentioned earlier, the rehabilitation staff had to be trained in this procedure, which was strictly enforced. As with any new departmental change, resistance was met. Some therapists were unwilling to refer to PCTs, and others overutilized the new system. Therapists provide a written list of PCT referrals for each shift that is appropriate (Exhibit 25–5).

Exhibit 25–5 PCT Referral Sheet

Patient Name	Room #	PCT Shift	Diagnosis	Tasks To Perform
Jones, J.	4523-1	Evening, 6/23/93	Left total knee arthroplasty	Supervise amb × 50 ft with walker. Apply CPM (preset 0–80) × 2 hours

Quality Control

As a unit was restructured, plans for continuous quality improvement needed to be revised. There were many questions. Some issues were deciding which indicators to monitor, who would do the monitoring, and how to establish interdepartmental communication.

Initially the established plan was somewhat informal, although it served the purpose. The plan was continually modified to be unit specific with respect to the unit being restructured. Phase I of restructuring included an orthopedic unit; hence indicators that were most appropriate were use of safety techniques during patient transfers and complete, timely documentation. For the medical-surgical units, the indicators focused on were documentation and PCT follow-through on a referral.

The data were to be collected quarterly by direct observation of a random sample of 20 PCT activities. The indicators would be changed when thresholds were being met for two consecutive quarters. Not long after the plan was instituted, it was realized that the quarterly timeframe was not adequate to keep pace with the changing needs of the program. The quarterly concept was replaced with daily observation of PCT activity. Choosing indicators to be monitored was not based on meeting the threshold for two consecutive quarters but rather on the frequency and importance of issues as they became apparent. This continually evolving plan was the only way to meet the needs of restructuring.

To accomplish the daily observation of PCT activity with time management and productivity in mind, each rehabilitation staff member was given a simple checklist to carry to document every PCT activity directly observed. At the end of each week, the checklists were submitted to the managers of rehabilitation, and new ones were started for the next week. The rehabilitation staff needed to be involved in quality control because it enhanced the team approach and the awareness of PCTs and PSAs being a part of that team (Exhibit 25–6).

Then there was the next question: How and to whom should the findings be reported? From the beginning, when restructuring was only an idea, rehabilitation was a player in the patient care restructuring task force and quality control committee (QCC). Rehabilitation's quality control report was communicated in QCC meetings and at times was also presented in the task force meetings. If issues could not wait until the next meeting, the respective nurse manager was contacted. Quality control could not be maintained without close and frequent interdepartmental communication.

The indicators were summarized by percentage compliance. Other restructuring-related issues were also included. Consequently, rehabilita-

Exhibit 25–6 Rehabilitation PCT Quality Control Checklist

Observed by: ________

For each PCT activity observed, check the appropriate column. Submit to manager on a weekly basis.

	Compliant	Non-Compliant
Referral follow-through		
Safe transfers		
Knowledge of total joint precautions		
Proper documentation		
Good communication between therapist and PCT		
Other		
Comments		

tion restructuring quality control is now a part of rehabilitation's continuous quality improvement plan as an interdepartmental indicator. The focus is PSA transport, monitoring rehabilitation staff, and PSAs' roles in the tasks assigned. Copies of the report are shared with the patient care restructuring QCC, restructured units, the quality and utilization management department, and a medical staff advisory board for rehabilitation. Again, as quality control issues become apparent and require action, the original, informal plan is still followed.

Another facet of continuous quality improvement is continuing education. Through the patient care restructuring education coordinator, a rehabilitation representative meets with PCT representatives from all restructured units to relay information to the other PCTs. So far, these meetings have been useful in updating participants on quality control issues.

Operational Issues

Operationally, the restructuring program has benefited patients in many new ways. For example, before patient care restructuring, patients referred to PT or OT would receive daily or twice-daily treatment. After restructuring, patients are assisted with their exercise or ambulation in the evening and on weekends in addition to their daily therapy sessions. By supplementing the formal therapy sessions, the goal of functional independence is more quickly achieved. In addition, with the creation of the PCT, therapists can now spend more quality time with patients, as the following case scenario demonstrates.

A total knee replacement patient at postoperative day 4 requires supervision only for progressing ambulation distance. However, the patient requires hands-on therapy for increasing knee range of motion, a goal that has been difficult to achieve. The PCT is able to continue the supervised ambulation on a twice-daily basis, thereby allowing the therapist to focus on specific techniques to increase the range of motion. Skilled therapy is necessary to increase range of motion after joint replacement. Skilled therapy is not required to increase walking distance once the patient demonstrates a safe and independent gait. A PCT assisting with the latter is more cost effective and allows more time for therapy staff to focus on reaching the other goals required for discharge.

Finally, with restructuring, patients not only have the same therapist throughout their hospital stay but also have the same PCT assisting them with ambulation and attending to special needs.

PSA Benefits

The role of the PSA has interacted well with the rehabilitation department. These employees transport the patient to and from rehabilitation. This has added to continuity of care in that the patient is being transported by a familiar unit-based staff member. Referral is simplified by informing the unit assistant of the need for transport, who in turn relays this directly to the PSA.

As alluded to previously, this aspect of patient care restructuring is currently included in rehabilitation's continuous quality improvement plan. Transports are tracked to ensure successful outcome. This was an initial focus because of patients arriving late to scheduled appointments. Tracking has significantly lowered the incidence of tardiness or no-shows.

As stated previously, the components of restructuring serve to complement the services offered by rehabilitation. It takes time to appreciate the benefits of the program because one tends to be consumed with the day-to-day operations. As with any new change, the restructuring project developed with peaks and valleys. As the program expanded, newly restructured units benefited from previous units' shortcomings.

As part of restructuring, the volume of procedures and revenue that was reduced from rehabilitation are now volume and revenue for the restructured unit performing the procedure. For example, rehabilitation's volume of hot pack application was reduced by 30 percent for inpatients. This volume was allocated to the orthopedic unit. Because the unit is now performing the procedure, the charge for that procedure needs to be generated by that patient care unit. In their training, PCTs were instructed how and when to charge a patient. It was stressed to them that they would only use the rehabilitation-related charges when a patient was referred to them by rehabilitation. For example, they could not use the bedside assistance charge when performing a nursing assistance task (which would not have been charged to the patient before restructuring). This was in support of the program's being budget neutral. As the program developed, the issue was not that the PCTs were charging inappropriately but that they were not charging at all. The charge system was new to the PCT, in addition to all other tasks. The percentage of duties that are chargeable (rehabilitation, ECG, and phlebotomy) is low in comparison to duties that are nonchargeable (nursing assistance). This low frequency may have been the reason why the charges were neglected. The tracking system that is now established utilizes a report generated by UMC's finance department. This report shows the volume of PCT charges generated on a given unit per month. The nurse manager compares the report to actual PCT referral forms generated during that month (see Exhibit 25–5).

Another issue that surfaced immediately after restructuring was the lack of follow-through on rehabilitation referrals to PCTs. With the diversity of tasks assigned, rehabilitation referrals were not considered priorities compared with phlebotomy, respiratory, or nursing-related tasks. Initially, the PCTs were responding to rehabilitation that they had no time to follow through. No time was not acceptable. Each incident had to be researched with the PCT, nurse manager, and therapist to address the time management issue. It was stressed that a patient's rehabilitation care was just as important as respiratory care, for example. Therefore, compliance on referrals was crucial. The importance of follow-through on rehabilitation referrals was reiterated in a PCT continuing education session. As a result, the incidence has decreased.

CONCLUSION

The transition to patient care restructuring was well received. Ancillary departments at UMC (respiratory care, ECG, and rehabilitation services) experienced a gradual, positive change. The ancillaries' understanding and acceptance of PCR were vital to its success.

Patient care restructuring aims to provide quality patient care while enhancing cost-effective delivery of health care. Cost-controlled strategies are ever present in rehabilitation, ECG, and respiratory care; hence PCR has complemented this objective. Respiratory, PT, and OT services now are able to focus on the complexities of therapies as opposed to the nonskilled tasks.

Stumbling blocks were found along the way, as with any change. This was expected; therefore, each ancillary department focused on problems as they occurred. The departments were proactive in the development and implementation of the program and as a result created a team atmosphere. This approach to restructuring or any type of change enhances and facilitates its success.

CHAPTER

26

Restructuring from the Ancillary Support Departments' Perspective

Pam Sapienza, Ken Gilbert, John C. Mahn, Alice Pollard, Katherine K. Duncan, Michael Lortie, and Joseph Maltos

Chapter Objectives

1. To describe, from the ancillary departments' perspective, the operational processes utilized to design and implement the patient support attendant role on the patient unit.
2. To describe the quality control models utilized to ensure the maintenance of multidisciplinary standards.

University Medical Center's (UMC's) patient care restructuring (PCR) project was driven by four key objectives: to maintain or enhance the quality of patient care, to utilize personnel effectively, to promote cost containment, and to maintain or promote job satisfaction of patient care providers. The intent was to simplify processes and to streamline the number of employees having contact with a patient during his or her hospital stay. The project entailed hospitalwide restructuring, not just a restructuring of the traditional nursing tasks. The tasks and resource pool needed to be large enough to create financial and operational economies of scale. It was with this guiding philosophy that the ancillary support departments and the nursing department redefined roles and responsibilities. The patient support attendant's (PSA's) new role included housekeeping tasks, traditional food service responsibilities, transportation functions, and involvement in the unit's necessary medical supplies.

From the beginning and throughout the entire process, the ancillary departments were actively involved. The process began with an initial subcommittee composed of representatives from nursing, environmental services, food and nutrition services, materials management, and transportation services. It was crucial to have director participation and support in the initial design phase. However, various levels within each of these areas were involved at different times. A key to the successful creation of a working team was the ongoing involvement of the ancillary departments from design through training, implementation, and monitoring.

This chapter describes the operational processes, from the ancillary departments' perspective, utilized to design and implement the PSA role on the patient unit and describes the quality control models utilized to ensure the maintenance of multidisciplinary standards.

THE NEW ROLE OF THE PSA

The job functions of the PSA include responsibilities previously tended to by the support department:

- cleaning patient rooms and restrooms daily
- cleaning patient rooms upon discharge
- cleaning nurses stations (including cleaning refrigerators, trash removal, carpet spotting, vacuuming, and mopping)
- removing and replacing draperies
- cleaning interior windows
- cleaning surfaces of air conditioning vents
- monitoring and replacing mattresses
- distributing patient menus and assisting with selection and collection
- delivering and retrieving trays
- documenting intake for analysis
- maintaining inventory and storage of bulk nourishment
- delivering nourishments
- maintaining inventory of supplies for the unit
- keying needed items into the centralized inventory control system
- picking up supplies from the dock
- delivering and placing supplies on the unit

- transporting patients
- delivering stat lab specimens
- picking up stat pharmacy prescriptions and supplies

Environmental services retained responsibilities more centralized in terms of institutional functionality:

- refinishing all floors
- cleaning all carpets
- cleaning up construction areas
- distributing cleaning supplies
- providing cleaning equipment and tools
- repairing and maintaining cleaning equipment
- removing trash from the building
- cleaning in emergency situations

Food and nutrition services retained responsibilities for functions occurring physically off the patient unit:

- checking patient units for last-minute diet orders that can be processed in the unit pantry
- validating accuracy of the diet order against the prepared trays
- ordering additional trays
- final preparation of the rethermalization cart
- initiating the rethermalization process
- delivering carts to the units
- delivering menus to the patient unit
- filling bulk nourishment inventory requests and delivering to the patient unit
- preparing, labeling, and delivering nutritional formulas
- maintaining unit pantry equipment

Materials management also retained responsibility for functions occurring in the ancillary department:

- receiving orders by computer at the off-site warehouse
- picking the needed supplies within the warehouse
- delivering supplies to the hospital dock

- checking the central control desk for needed back-up and stat supplies

Transportation services retained responsibility for the systematic runs and for patient transports not involving the inpatient units:

- conducting routine runs for lab specimens
- conducting routine runs for pharmacy and supply deliveries
- completing outpatient transports

After the job responsibilities were delineated, each ancillary department was asked to determine the associated work effort required to complete the tasks on each unit. Unlike direct patient care activities, for which volume and time information was available in the hospital's cost accounting system, the ancillary areas either had to utilize internal data systems or had to complete time studies. Although each area calculated full-time equivalents (FTEs) to be transferred differently, emphasis was placed on reliable and quantifiable data sources that would facilitate a fair redistribution of work hours. After the direct work hours were identified, a 10 percent relief factor was added to calculate the total number of FTEs to be transferred from the ancillary area to the patient unit.

The FTE transfer necessitated that the ancillary areas' budgets be reduced by the associated number of FTEs and dollars. The process did not dictate the transfer of people affected by these reductions to the new unit. All the new PSA roles were filled through a formal application and hiring process. In many instances, employees from the ancillary areas applied and were appointed to fill PSA positions. In many cases, fractions of FTEs were identified to be transferred. The ancillary departments reviewed the workflow of the remaining jobs and responsibilities and realigned personnel, assignments, and schedules where necessary. To date, the FTE reductions in the ancillary areas have been accomplished through attrition. In all phases, some of the new PSAs have been hired from the ancillary areas. Not all the needed reductions were accomplished by personnel transfers. In some circumstances, areas anticipated the start-up of another restructured unit and held recruitment so as not to fill vacancies as they occurred. The ancillary areas worked closely with human resources personnel to inform them of the number of positions to be reduced in each phase and to be informed of the number of their employees accepted into new PSA or patient care technician (PCT) roles.

Environmental services determined its contribution of FTEs by utilizing predetermined engineering standards currently in use by the department.

Staff hours were calculated based on space and cleaning requirements. Examples include the following:

100- to 150-ft^2 office = 1 work station	= 5 minutes
each additional workstation	= 2–3 minutes
patient room	= 15 minutes
patient restroom	= 5 minutes

The FTE calculations for environmental services displayed in Table 26–1 include direct labor requirements, a relief factor for 7 day per week assignments, a discharge load factor based on a historical average number of discharges per day, additional time for units requiring multiple trash rounds, and the predetermined 10 percent benefit relief factor. Of all the ancillary support departments participating in the restructuring project, environmental services had the greatest number of FTEs to be transferred. As discussed later, the sheer volume of personnel changes had a significant impact on the remaining department.

Food and nutrition services conducted studies to validate the estimated time for the tasks to be assigned to the PSA. Based on average census figures, a total number of hours per day per unit was determined. The FTEs per unit are displayed in Table 26–2.

Table 26–1 FTEs Transferred from Environmental Services to Restructured Units

Unit	*Description*	*Beds*	*Square Feet*	*FTEs*
3 East	Peds (child/adolescent)	24	5,546	1.63
3 West	Peds (infant/toddler)	18	4,946	1.57
4 East	Medical-surgical	31	5,890	1.65
4 West	Medical-surgical	31	6,268	1.61
5 East	Surgical	31	5,890	1.83
6 East	Telemetry	30	5,508	1.66
5 West	Medical-surgical ICU	16	3,822	1.58
6 West	Cardiovascular ICU	16	3,909	1.58
7 East	Obstetrics	29	5,652	2.29
7 West	Oncology	31	5,640	1.58
Neonatal intensive care unit (ICU)		33	8,128	2.10
Labor and delivery		13	12,572	8.40
Emergency department		17	5,030	4.20
Newborn nursery			2,977	0.63
			TOTAL FTEs:	32.31

Table 26–2 FTEs Transferred from Food and Nutrition Services to Patient units

Units	*FTEs*
3 East, 3 West (42 pediatric beds)	0.64
4 East, 4 West (62 medical-surgical beds)	0.97
5 East, 6 East (51 medical-surgical beds)	1.74
7 East, 7 West (29 obstetrical and 29 oncology beds)	0.86
TOTAL FTEs:	4.21

Note: Floor stock inventory responsibilities, 6 percent of time;
Tray delivery and retrieval, 63 percent of time;
Menu distribution, assistance, and retrieval responsibilities, 31 percent of time.

For tasks relating to supply acquisition, materials management based its calculations on observations and on the average number of supply items needed for each unit's inventory. In most instances, there were approximately 500 line items requiring about 45 minutes per unit per night, or 0.125 FTE.

Transportation services' computer system was utilized to extract historical data by unit to determine volume of transports and time required to complete. This information was converted to FTEs and is displayed in Table 26–3.

TRAINING REQUIREMENTS

The PSAs needed to be equipped with a diverse set of technical skills to perform their varied responsibilities. Based on the defined job role, each ancillary area identified the key skills to be taught during the training period.

Traditional housekeeping skills were taught through a combined 1-hour didactic session and 2 days of on-the-job training. Key concepts included disinfection, infection control, appropriate use of chemicals, proper use of equipment, and cleaning procedures.

A 1-day training session in the area of food and nutrition services focused on a tour of the kitchen and diet office, the ordering of bulk supplies, tray delivery and retrieval, calorie counts, snack delivery, and menu distribution and collection. The day was designed so that the PSA worked alongside the food and nutrition services host/hostess (and now alongside a fellow PSA because this food and nutrition services position has been eliminated). A short exam was administered at the end of the training day.

Table 26–3 FTEs Transferred from Transportation Services to Patient Units

Unit	*Average Hours/Day*	*Annual FTEs*
3 East	2.03	0.38
3 West	0.83	0.15
Pediatric ICU	1.98	0.37
4 East	5.04	0.95
4 West	4.65	0.87
5 East	5.78	1.08
5 West	5.35	1.00
6 East	4.43	0.84
6 West	3.97	0.74
7 East	2.90	0.54
7 West	3.89	0.73
Labor and delivery	1.42	0.26
Neonatal ICU	0.94	0.17
	TOTAL ANNUAL FTEs:	8.08

A 3-day training session was designed to meet the requirements of materials management. One day was spent in materials management, and two additional days were spent on the unit with a fellow PSA. Skill requirements included the following:

- data entry
- familiarization with medical-surgical products
- determination of par levels for the patient unit
- location of the unit-based inventory
- documentation requirements

Transportation skills were taught in a 1-day session. The essentials of body mechanics were taught by the physical therapy department. Oxygen use was taught by the respiratory therapy department. Each PSA received instruction in CPR from nursing education. Finally, the employees were instructed in the proper use of the transportation equipment. See Chapter 6 for more information about PSA training.

ORGANIZATIONAL IMPACT

The results of the PCR project to date are positive. Results are meeting and, for some parameters, exceeding expectations. However, the organizational change imposed upon the patient units, the ancillary support departments, and even areas of the hospital not directly affected by restructuring should not be overlooked. Other chapters address the team-building efforts that occurred to assist these new multidisciplinary teams to function effectively (e.g., Chapters 12, 14, and 27). Similar processes need to occur in each of the ancillary areas. Common themes are learning to deal with change, learning to deal with loss, and learning new ways to communicate. New systems need to replace the status quo.

Eleven units are restructured. Environmental services transferred 27 FTEs to the patient units. In addition to the housekeepers, four supervisor positions were eliminated. One day shift supervisor position was reduced after the first four patient units were restructured, and three supervisor positions (one from each shift) were reduced after a total of eight units were restructured. The department's workforce was reduced by one third. It has been particularly challenging to maintain the morale of the employees desiring to remain with the department in the same line of work.

A smaller, centralized workforce decreased the environmental services department's flexibility and response time to calls for emergency housekeeping services throughout the facility (e.g., overflowing drains or broken water pipes). Furthermore, the facility's emergency preparedness plan, which relied on the ready availability of a large pool of workers from the environmental service and transportation service areas, was altered to reflect the new location and access to workers in a disaster situation.

Many housekeepers took advantage of the restructuring project to broaden their job skills by accepting positions as PSAs and PCTs. However, this significant loss of trained workers placed a strain on the department forcing it to face the reassigned workload with a new and less experienced workforce. In addition, environmental services and nursing services now competed for the same qualified applicants.

The shift of personnel resources to the patient units was just as significant for transportation services. Before restructuring, the whole service equaled just over 22 FTEs to provide 24-hour coverage 7 days per week. After eight units were restructured, transport personnel were reduced by 25 percent.

The continual shift of resources out of this small pool eroded the economy of scale that allowed the service to transport patients and supplies efficiently throughout the building during peak activity times. Transportation standards that required routine transports to be accomplished within 30 minutes and stat transports within 15 minutes were still expected. Unmet goals were frustrating to employees and customers alike. Frequently, two transporters were not available to assist with more difficult transports (e.g., bed transports from the ICUs). Employee schedules were frequently shifted to attempt to meet service demands. One dispatch position was eliminated after six units were restructured. After eight units were restructured, the remaining service was merged with materials management, where similar dispatch and transport functions reside. A second dispatch position and a manager position were eliminated with the merger.

Three transportation models have been used in recent years at UMC. For years, transportation functioned as a decentralized and departmentally focused service. A centralized, hospitalwide system was created 2 years before restructuring of the first patient units. Now with PCR, a decentralized, patient unit service is evolving. A full transition, which addresses all the needs and issues of patients, patient units, and diagnostic areas, is still not complete.

For food and nutrition services, the decrease in the number of employees who had a direct interface with the patients presented quite a challenge. The host/hostess position previously had responsibility for menu distribution/collection and tray delivery/retrieval. These individuals were the department's link to the patient for information and were now replaced by the PSA. The change represented a loss of contact and a perceived loss of control in their delivery of service to the patients. A shift in mind set was required to accept their new role as a resource and support to the team of direct care providers rather than as direct participants. The diet technicians and registered dietitians had to broaden their focus to include the department's full scope of food services, not just nutrition services. Responsibilities shifted to provide the diet technician with more direct patient contact. The registered dietitians had to become visible and accessible to the PSAs to channel patient information from the patient care unit to the department. For materials management, the impact was negligible because of the fractional FTE affected.

OPERATIONAL LESSONS

The PSA role is evolving. This new worker and the patient units are learning to balance multiple demands and tasks in a whole new way. Each patient unit is encountering different concerns and hurdles. For the PSAs who transferred from one of the ancillary services, they are usually most comfortable with the skills that evolved from their previous position. This increased knowledge often translates into better service and fewer concerns.

Before restructuring, environmental services maintained a tightly controlled supply distribution system. Supply usage became more difficult to monitor in a decentralized, unit-based system. Problems with two particular products, cream cleanser and bowl cleaner, were noticed first (Figures 26–1 and 26–2). Normal inventory levels became insufficient, and monthly expense reports were increasing. After other variables such as patient volume were accounted for, discrepancies between restructured and nonrestructured units were monitored. A tracking mechanism was implemented. Quality control rounds began assessing product mixing ratios and chemical residues (e.g., a heavy chlorine smell and product residue would be indications of excessive use of bowl cleaner in the patient restrooms).

Regular feedback regarding cleaning, supply utilization, and environmental quality control rounds is provided to each patient unit. The unit manager and environmental services management collaborate on trends, possible causes, and possible solutions.

In the food service arena, menu distribution and collection has received the most attention. Concerns were identified within the first few weeks, and a series of corrective actions was implemented over several months with little success. As Table 26–4 illustrates, a number of patient menus

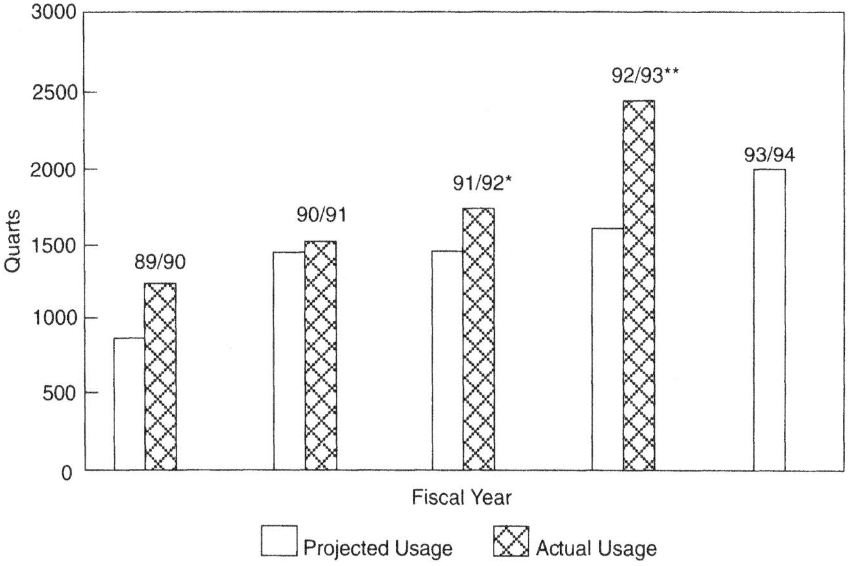

*Total of six restructured units during FY 1991–1992

**Total of nine restructured units during FY 1992–1993

Figure 26–1 Bowl cleaner purchases, projected and actual.

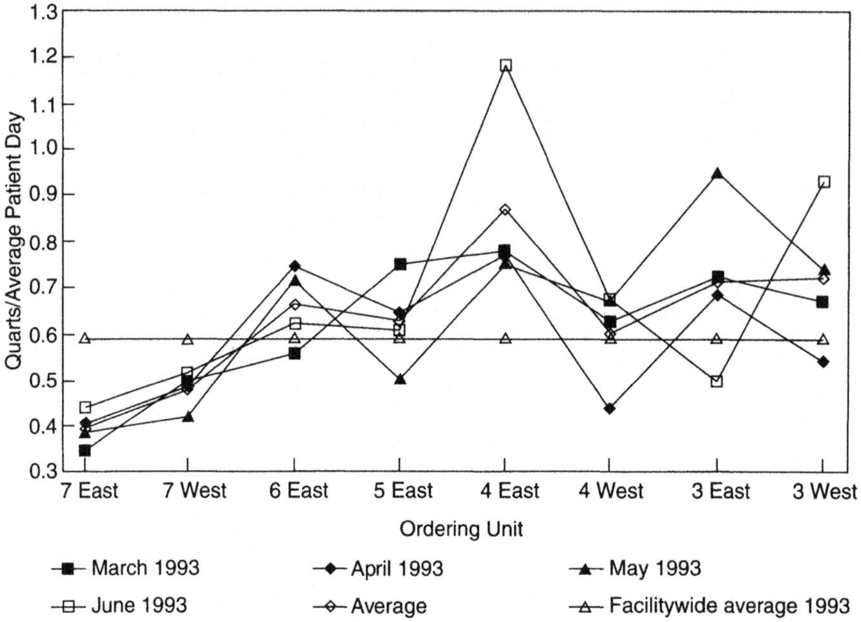

Figure 26–2 Bowl cleaner usage: Usage to census 3/1/93 to 6/30/93.

were not being returned to the food and nutrition services department for use in the routine tray assembly process.

Multiple factors contributed to the problem. The menu was a restaurant style format, requiring the patient to select from multiple options and to transcribe this information onto the daily menu sheet. Many patients re-

Table 26–4 Food and Nutrition Services PCR Quality Improvement Report, Menu Collection Data

	PSA Responsibility			*Diet Office Responsibility*	
Unit	*Oct 92*	*Nov 92*	*Dec 92*	*Feb 93*	*Mar 93*
3 East	64%	83%	Change	93%	96%
3 West	100%	95%	in	71%	75%
4 East	63%	43%	responsibility	95%	96%
4 West	89%	85%	for menu	95%	95%
5 East	58%	50%	distribution	93%	99%
6 East	66%	73%	and	93%	96%
7 East	55%	39%	retrieval	97%	98%
Average	71%	67%		90%	94%

quired some sort of assistance with the selection process because of the menu complexity as well as patient acuity, language limitations, and dexterity and mental status. The nutrition hosts/hostesses, who previously assisted the patients, had learned how to compensate for this through their familiarity with the task and with patients' preferences. The menu has subsequently been changed to a simplified format.

The PSA was required to juggle this responsibility with multiple others. If the task was delayed from a peak activity time to later in the evening, sometimes the change in personnel at shift time did not allow for a smooth transition in task responsibilities. If the PSA's background included working in the food and nutrition services department, fewer problems occurred. For other PSAs, insufficient knowledge of how their task contributed to the whole system and how to problem solve appropriately frustrated their efforts to do a good job. During the same time allotted to complete the menu selection process, multiple demands are placed on patients (e.g., scheduled procedures, nursing care, physician visits, and visitors). The best of intentions to check back with a patient are sidetracked by multiple priorities.

Formal patient satisfaction survey results did not indicate a decline in the patients' perception of service. However, staff frustrations and inefficiencies in the patient units and in the food and nutrition services department increased. Over the first 12 months of the restructuring project, several collaborative efforts were implemented in an attempt to improve the menu collection process. A formal procedure was written delineating parameters and responsibilities (Exhibit 26–1). Data collection occurred and was routinely discussed at the quality control task force meetings (see Table 26–4). Ultimately, a multidisciplinary group was formed to review the entire situation and to make recommendations.

Even though the majority of attention to date had focused on the menus, the group identified several additional issues:

- incomplete diet orders
- timeliness of transmittal of diet orders
- knowledge deficit of the tray delivery process
- multiple work priorities at high activity times
- trays not removed from patient rooms by scheduled times
- menus not distributed to patients after delivery to the patient unit
- limited time for PSAs to assist patients in menu selection
- critical diet information not communicated to nutrition services
- breakdown in accountability for the return of menus

Exhibit 26–1 PCR Procedure for Menu Distribution and Pick-up

1. The bulk of the menus will be sent to the third- and fourth-floor units at 2:00 P.M. along with a computerized list from nutrition services for the PSA to use as a checklist. The dietary assistant from nutrition services will check any names of patients whose menus have already been received in nutrition services for that day.
2. The dietary assistant will call the unit assistant to inform him or her that the menus have been sent up to the floors.
3. The unit assistant will inform the PSA to pick up the menus from the dumb waiter immediately.
4. Menus will be distributed to patients immediately, and the patients will be informed that the menus will be picked up at 6:30 P.M. or earlier if they are completed.
5. Menus will be returned to the food service clipboard after they are completed.
6. At 6:30 P.M., the PSA is to use the computer checklist with the menus to ensure that all menus have been picked up or are accounted for.
7. If any menus are outstanding, the PSA is to check with the patients and get any outstanding menus. Exceptions may be the following: the patient is too ill to fill out the menu, the patient is away at a procedure, the dietitian needs to consult with the patient, or the patient needs a Spanish interpreter. With any of these exceptions, the PSA is to write next to the name on the computer checklist the reason why a menu is not returned.
8. At 7:00 P.M. the PSA returns the menus that have been filled out along with the computer checklist to nutrition services on the dumb waiter using the intercom in the pantry area to request the dumb waiter.

The next step was flowcharting each of the critical processes needing to occur to ensure completed service to the patient. An example from the menu distribution and retrieval process is included in Figure 26–3. All the identified issues were grouped under important aspects of care and became four indicators of a quality improvement plan focusing on food services and nutritional care of the patient (Exhibit 26–2).

Through the problem-solving exercises, many unmet educational needs were identified that would facilitate the transition of the menu distribution and retrieval tasks. However, education alone would not solve the issues at hand. Additionally, the planned introduction of a 1-day turnaround menu selection process, which would shorten the time allowed for patients to complete the menu selection and would require that the return occur during the unit's peak activity time, only compounded the difficulties.

Food services was providing numerous duplicate menus and processing a significant number of late trays in an attempt to compensate for inadequate information and to meet patient requests. A series of unrelated

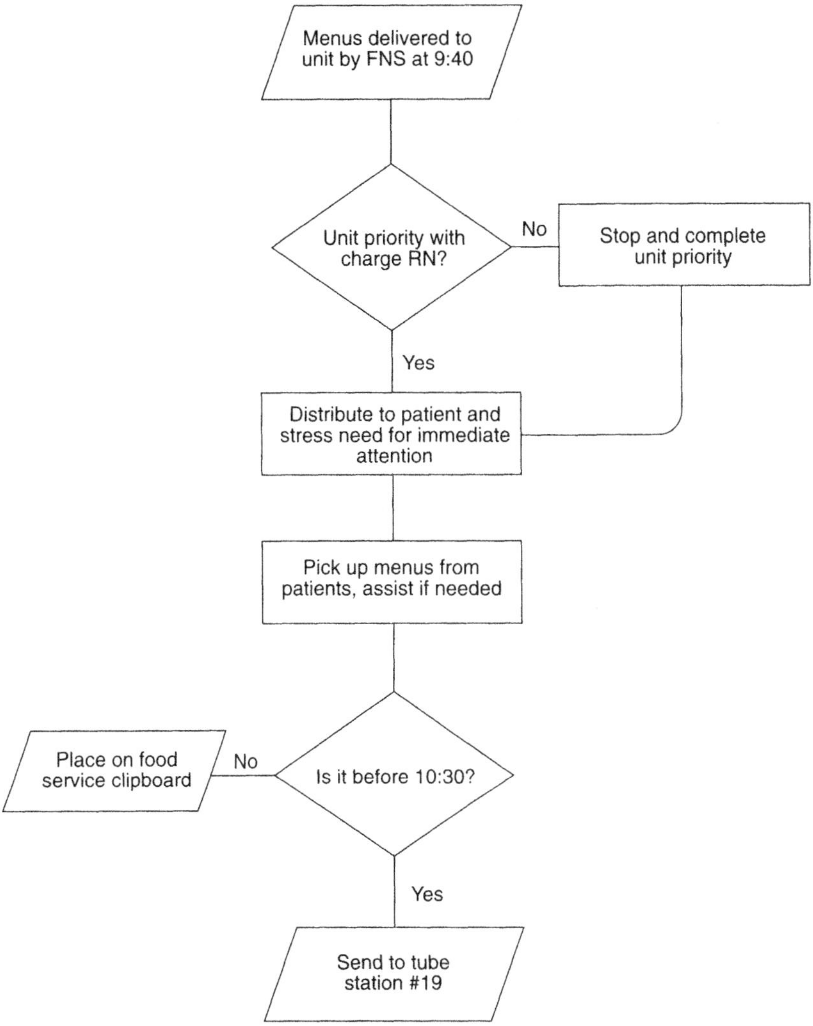

Figure 26–3 Menu distribution and collection

workflow changes in the food services department and the elimination of duplicate work efforts allowed the department to reabsorb responsibility for this task without requiring the transfer of one FTE or more back from the patient units. This recommendation was adopted and implemented 12 months into the restructuring project. As Table 26–4 shows, improvement

Exhibit 26–2 UMC Department of Food and Nutrition Services, PCR Quality Improvement Plan

IMPORTANT ASPECT OF CARE

The provision of optimal nutritional care and food service to the patient.

INDICATOR 1

Menus will be delivered to the patient, be available for a designated period of time to allow for selection, and then be collected and returned to nutrition services.

- *Indicator rationale*: The opportunity for patients to select their menu contributes to patient satisfaction. The successful distribution and collection of menus facilitates the delivery of the patient's selections and reduces the cost of replacement menus and trays when patients receive selections they did not order.
- *Threshold*: Ninety-five percent of menus delivered to patients will be returned to the nutrition service. The percentage of menus selected by patients will be tracked to establish a threshold.
- *Data collection:* Computer sheets for menu delivery/collection will be reviewed and data tabulated by nutrition services.

INDICATOR 2

Trays will be removed from the patient rooms and placed in the retrieval cart in a timely manner.

- *Indicator rationale:* The timely removal of trays from the patient room and the availability of the cart at designated times are necessary to avoid operational disruption for patient tray and support service (PTSS). Lack of availability of the cart increases the labor expense to return multiple times to the patient care unit, requires calls to the patient care unit to resolve the situation, and may delay the next scheduled tray line if adequate trays are not available.
- *Threshold*: Carts will be available within 15 minutes of the determined schedule. Delays in cart delivery for meal service will be communicated to the patient care unit and the cart retrieval schedule adjusted accordingly.
- *Data collection*: The manager of PTSS will monitor the log sheets documenting cart retrieval and will identify problem areas. Direct communication will occur with the nurse manager to identify solutions.

INDICATOR 3

Trays and snacks will be delivered to the patient within the established timeframe.

- *Indicator rationale:* Delay in the delivery of the tray to the patient results in a loss of serving temperature and necessitates the ordering of a replacement tray, resulting in increased labor cost and decreased patient satisfaction. Failure to provide snacks to the patient jeopardizes the provision of necessary calories and nutrients to the patient and increases the potential for a decline in nutritional status.

continues

Exhibit 26–2 continued

- *Threshold*: Tray delivery should be completed within 40 minutes of the arrival of the cart on the patient care unit. Snacks should be provided to the patient within 30 minutes of the designated time. Delivery of both meals and snacks should be appropriately documented.
- *Data collection:* Log sheets documenting delivery of meals and snacks will be monitored by the manager of PTSS, and results will be reported to the clinical dietitian and nurse manager of the patient care units where problems are identified.

INDICATOR 4

Diet orders containing complete and accurate information will be transmitted in a timely fashion to nutrition services.

- *Indicator rationale:* Completeness of the diet order as to the specificity of nutrient restriction avoids call-backs to the patient care unit to clarify the order. Timely transmission of the diet order maximizes the efficiency of providing nutrition support to the patient, reduces the increased labor cost of late trays, and contributes to increased patient satisfaction.
- *Threshold:* One hundred percent of diet orders will contain complete and accurate information and will be transmitted to nutrition services according to established procedures.
- *Data collection:* The number of incomplete diet orders requiring phone calls to clarify information and the frequency of delay in transmission of diet orders will be monitored by nutrition services.

has been achieved. Work continues toward the goal of 95 percent menu collection.

In the area of materials management, operational difficulties were initially encountered when a limited number of PSA FTEs were available. If a unit's PSA was unavailable for inventory activity, that unit ran low on supplies. A back-up system was eventually established that allowed the PSA from an adjacent patient unit to conduct inventories on multiple units if necessary.

In the early weeks of implementation, the patient units struggled with the volume and length of time consumed by patient transports. This was particularly the case for transports occurring during the peak activity times, primarily on the day shift. Adjustments in staffing levels allowed for two PSAs on most patient units during the day shift. This staffing change allowed one PSA to be primarily responsible for transportation, one PSA to be primarily responsible for housekeeping tasks, and a built-in relief factor to be available should work effort need to be temporarily doubled.

With the decentralization of the transportation functions, the equipment was also dispersed to the patient units. Before restructuring, if a transporter found a broken piece of transportation equipment, it was taken out of service and sent for repair. Initially, this programmatic function was not delineated in the functions, nor was it included in the PSA orientation and training. This identified need was later addressed.

QUALITY CONTROL MODELS

The development of the environmental quality control model began with the definition of cleaning standards that apply to all locations in the facility. Exhibit 26–3 includes standards developed for patient rooms and patient restrooms. These standards defined the basis for training efforts,

Exhibit 26–3 Housekeeping Standards

Patient Rooms:

A. Exhaust/intake vents—Outside surface dust free.

B. Ledges and horizontal surfaces—Free of dust and debris, finger marks, and soiling.

C. Walls and permanent wall fixtures—Free of stains and soiling without evidence of paint deterioration, gouges, or heavy marks. Fixtures are dust and soil free.

D. Furniture and bed surfaces:

1. All bed surfaces will be free of soil, stains, and dust. Bed will be made up (linen) in accordance with unit preference. Bedspreads will fully cover bed linen up until the time of patient admission. All bed nurse call, audio-video connections, and bed controls will be properly attached and tested for proper function. The bed will be placed in the proper location directly below the overbed (head) light fixture.
2. All room furniture including chairs, overbed table, and bedside cabinet will be soil, stain, and dust free and in proper working condition [drawer pulls intact, proper reclining function (reclining chair), overbed table adjustable]. Trash can is clean without rust, soil, or stains, and with a fresh liner.

E. Floor surfaces—Free of soil, stains, and dust. Baseboards will be free of dust, stains, and soil build-up. Particular attention should be paid to corners for signs of soil build-up. Whenever feasible, heavy furniture items will be placed on dollies for relocation. Dragging of units will cause excessive floor scraping.

F. Drapes/shower curtains—Soil and stain free, all seams intact, proper lengths for the application, all hooks and grommets properly attached, and all strings properly functioning.

continues

Exhibit 26–3 continued

Patient Restrooms:

A. Exhaust/intake vents—Outside surface dust free.

B. Ledges and horizontal surfaces—Free of dust and debris, finger marks, and soiling.

C. Walls and permanent wall fixtures—Free of stains and soiling without evidence of paint deterioration, gouges, or heavy marks. Fixtures are dust and soil free.

D. Sink—Free of soil/stains, free of calcium build-up at the bottom and sides of basin as well as the area surrounding faucets.

E. Shower—Walls free of soil/stains including soap/calcium build-up. No visible signs of green oxidation at faucets and shower head. Drain cover free of build-up and evidence of hair.

F. Toilets:

  1. Interior—Free of visible soil including area under the bowl rim. All interior areas free of calcium build-up.
  2. Exterior—Seat free of soil and stains. Surface under bowl free of stains, especially at rear wall mounting area.

G. All plumbing supply and drain lines free of dust, soil, and stains. No visible signs of green oxidation (brass oxide).

H. Accessories—Trash can clean without rust, soil, or stains and with a fresh liner. Towel and toilet tissue dispenser free of stains and rust. Soap and paper dispensers clean and filled. Shower curtain clean, hooks intact and operable.

I. Floor surfaces—Free of soil, stains, and dust. Baseboards will be free of dust, stains, and soil build-up. Particular attention should be paid to corners for signs of hair and soil build-up.

procedures, staffing needs, institutional expectations for cleanliness, and inspections.

Regular inspections are now performed on the patient units. A multidisciplinary team conducts these inspections. Participants vary but include a representative from the environmental services management, the unit's management, and sometimes a PSA. The purpose of the inspections is to provide an assessment based on objective criteria, to provide technical information and expertise in an informal educational setting to the unit personnel, and to provide a forum for collaborative problem solving.

During the initial inspection, the participants jointly record the survey results. The inspection form is illustrated in Exhibit 26–4. The data collection tool is designed to minimize documentation and time needed to complete. This allows time to be spent on inspecting multiple units within a short timeframe. A copy of the completed inspection is forwarded to each

Exhibit 26–4 Environmental Quality Control

Date: ____________________ Inspected by: ____________________________________

Patient Room Number:

Standard Item	*S*	*U*	*Comments*
Vents			
Horizontal Surfaces			
Walls/Fixtures			
Bed			
Furniture			
Floor			
Drapes/Shower Curtains			

Restroom Number:

Standard Item	*S*	*U*	*Comments*
Vents			
Horizontal Surfaces			
Walls/Fixtures			
Sink			
Shower			
Toilet			
Plumbing			
Accessories			
Floor			
Drapes/Shower Curtains			

Nurses Station:

Standard Item	*S*	*U*	*Comments*
Vents			
Horizontal Surfaces			
Walls/Fixtures			
Enclosure Panels			
Furniture			
Sink			
Floor			

inspector as well as the unit manager. A follow-up inspection occurs not more than 1 week later by the same inspection team. Results are again recorded and compared with the initial inspection. Repetitive deficiencies are noted, and corrective action is identified. This information is regularly reported to the quality control task force, an organizational component of the PCR project. Sample data to date indicate that quality is being maintained at an acceptable level. Areas of concern have included vent surfaces, toilet seats, high dusting, and access to rooms for floor refinishing.

The food and nutrition services quality improvement plan focuses on four areas: patient menus, patient meal trays, the timely delivery of meal trays and snacks, and diet orders (see Exhibit 26–2). Quality improvement to date has focused on the first two indicators. As discussed previously, the primary effort has been directed toward improving the number of menus collected and returned to food and nutrition services for use in tray assembly (Table 26–5). The next step will be to assess the number of menus actually reflecting patient selection. Subsequent efforts have been directed at minimizing delays in the retrieval of trays from the patient care units

Table 26–5 UMC Food and Nutrition Services, PCR Quality Improvement Report: Tray Retrieval Data, June 1993

Patient Care Unit	*Number of Delays**	*Total Delays (%)*	*Meal Delays (%)*
3 East	6	17	7
3 West	7	19	8
4 East	4	11	4
4 West	5	14	6
5 East	9	25	10
6 East	4	11	4
7 East	1	3	1
TOTAL	36		

*A delay is documented if tray retrieval carts are not available more than 15 minutes after scheduled time and food and nutrition services has returned twice to attempt pick-up.

Conclusions

1. On 57 percent of days, a delay occurred for at least one meal.
2. At 22 percent of all meals, there was at least one delay in the availability of the tray retrieval cart.
3. At 40 percent of meals where a delay occurred, more than one unit was delayed.

Action

1. Charge nurses were notified of problems as they occurred.
2. The nurse manager was notified of follow-up.

after meal service. Data are collected to document the frequency of delays (Table 26–5) and are reported at scheduled PCR quality control meetings. The occurrence of these delays affects operational efficiency for food and nutrition services and stresses the need for a collaborative working relationship with the patient care units. All instances of problems related to indicators 3 and 4 receive follow-up, but no ongoing data collection currently exists.

Quality control for materials management attempts to ensure that appropriate inventory levels are adhered to in each patient unit. The preferred method of supply distribution is a nightly bulk issue of supplies needed to bring the patient unit back up to a preestablished par level. This par level is set by the nurse manager of each unit in conjunction with materials management based on historical usage reports. The required quantity of each item is keyed into the mainframe inventory control system by each unit, resulting in an order being generated at the off-site warehouse for assembly and delivery during the night shift. The indicators monitored include the number of credits returned and the number of emergency phone orders to materials management. A credit means that too many items are ordered in the nightly bulk order. An emergency order means that not enough items are ordered in the nightly bulk order.

Tables 26–6 and 26–7 summarize sample data collected from the materials management computerized inventory control system on items issued. An acceptable limit for credits returned is up to 1 percent of total monthly issues to the unit. An acceptable limit for emergency issues is up to 5 percent of total monthly issues to the unit. Areas with credits or emergency orders outside the acceptable range need to collaborate with materials management to identify causes and solutions.

Since implementation, some of the restructured areas show an increase in their rate of credits and emergency issues. This is not unreasonable given the learning curve and has been experienced in materials management in the past when a new employee has started. The preliminary data have been shared with the nurse managers on the restructured units. A nursing/materials management corrective action plan has been developed to evaluate credits and emergency issues by line item. It is felt that these indicators can be brought into line in the near future and monitored quarterly for continued compliance.

Quality control measures in transportation have presented the most difficulty. Each unit functions independently, and data collection would be cumbersome and time consuming. Patient satisfaction results have indicated positive benefits. Anecdotal comments and situations, however, leave concerns regarding the consistent timeliness of transportation ser-

Table 26–6 Number of Items Ordered by Unit: Bulk (Warehouse) Issues vs. Emergency (Phone) Issues vs. Credits (Returns)*, April–June 1993

	April			May			June		
Non-PCR Units	*Bulk Issues (% Total Issues)*	*Emer. Issues (% Total Issues)*	*Credits (% Total Issues)*	*Bulk Issues (% Total Issues)*	*Emer. Issues (% Total Issues)*	*Credits (% Total Issues)*	*Bulk Issues (% Total Issues)*	*Emer. Issues (% Total Issues)*	*Credits (% Total Issues)*
3 ICU	8,399	788	147	6,908	545	24	5,657	215	28
	(91.4%)	(8.6%)	(1.6%)	(92.7%)	(7.3%)	(0.3%	(96.3%)	(3.7%)	(0.5%)
5 West	21,805	1,237	160	22,186	534	55	14,978	247	28
	(94.6%)	(5.4%)	(0.7%)	(97.6%)	(2.4%)	(0.2%)	(98.4%)	(1.6%)	(0.2%)
6 West	15,666	721	62	18,831	751	333	11,334	267	51
	(95.6%)	(4.4%)	(0.4%)	(96.2%)	(3.8%)	(1.7%)	(97.7%)	(2.3%)	(0.4%)
7 West	7,348	240	45	6,917	379	39	6,971	279	4
	(96.8%)	(3.2%)	(0.6%)	(94.8%)	(5.2%)	(0.5%)	(96.2%)	(3.8%)	(0.1%)
Neonatal ICU	22,146	287	281	18,057	367	124	15,684	253	95
	(98.7%)	(1.3%)	(1.3%)	(98.0%)	(2.0%)	(0.7%)	(8.4%)	(1.6%)	(0.6%)
Labor and delivery	23,389	413	94	21,569	441	65	20,996	715	116
	(98.3%)	(1.7%)	(0.4%)	(98.0%)	(2.0%)	(0.3%)	(96.7%)	(3.3%)	(0.5%)
Total Issues	98,753	3,686	789	94,468	3,017	640	75,620	1,976	322
(% Total Issues)	(96.4%)	(3.6%)	(0.8%)	(96.9%)	(3.1%)	(0.7%)	(97.5%)	(2.5%)	(0.4%)

continues

Table 26–6 continued

PCR Units	April			May			June		
	Bulk Issues (% Total Issues)	*Emer. Issues (% Total Issues)*	*Credits (% Total Issues)*	*Bulk Issues (% Total Issues)*	*Emer. Issues (% Total Issues)*	*Credits (% Total Issues)*	*Bulk Issues (% Total Issues)*	*Emer. Issues (% Total Issues)*	*Credits (% Total Issues)*
Emergency department	19,244 (83.9%)	3,693 (16.1%)	293 (1.3%)	18,484 (90.1%)	2,031 (9.9%)	258 (1.3%)	17,010 (87.1%)	2,517 (12.9%)	396 (2.0%)
3 East	5,493 (93.5%)	382 (6.5%)	262 (4.5%)	5,907 (91.7%)	538 (8.3%)	228 (3.5%)	4,177 (93.4%)	296 (6.6%)	661 (14.8%)
3 West	10,449 (95.5%)	489 (4.5%)	167 (1.5%)	8,655 (94.0%)	554 (6.0%)	112 (1.2%)	8,785 (94.1%)	550 (5.9%)	368 (3.9%)
4 East	6,696 (94.5%)	389 (5.5%)	144 (2.0%)	8,267 (93.6%)	568 (6.4%)	115 (1.3%)	5,125 (94.6%)	292 (5.4%)	122 (2.3%)
4 West	6,827 (92.6%)	549 (7.4%)	42 (0.6%)	7,680 (92.8%)	599 (7.2%)	77 (0.9%)	6,588 (92.9%)	506 (7.1%)	36 (0.5%)
5 East	11,013 (94.3%)	665 (5.7%)	103 (0.9%)	11,846 (93.3%)	846 (6.7%)	155 (1.2%)	10,649 (95.1%)	543 (4.9%)	222 (2.0%)
6 East	7,560 (90.8%)	769 (9.2%)	68 (0.8%)	8,717 (88.7%)	1,106 (11.3%)	172 (1.8%)	7,845 (92.2%)	668 (7.8%)	177 (2.1%)
7 East	4,630 (93.6%)	314 (6.4%)	35 (0.7%)	4,312 (94.6%)	245 (5.4%)	70 (1.5%)	4,019 (96.8%)	134 (3.2%)	15 (0.4%)
7 Newborn nursery	12,805 (99.4%)	75 (0.6%)	43 (0.3%)	9,498 (99.7%)	27 (0.3%)	2 (0.0%)	7,946 (99.4%)	46 (0.6%)	0 (0.0%)
Total Issues (% Total Issues)	84,717 (92.0%)	7,323 (8.0%)	1,157 (1.3%)	83,366 (92.8%)	6,514 (7.2%)	1,189 (1.3%)	72,144 (92.9%)	5,552 (7.1%)	1,997 (2.6%)

*All data gathered from computerized inventory control system.

Table 26–7 Total Number of Emergency Phone Calls (Placed to Materials Management for Missing Items) vs Total Number of Units Emergency Issued*, April–June 1993.

Non-PCR Units	*Number of Emergency Phone Calls*	*Number of Units Emer. Issued (% Total Issued)*
3 ICU	350	1,548 (6.5%)
5 West	462	2,018 (3.1%)
6 West	359	1,739 (3.5%)
7 West	388	898 (4.1%)
Neonatal ICU	154	907 (1.6%)
Labor and Delivery	318	1,569 (2.3%)
Total	2,031	8,679 (3.5%)

PCR Units	*Number of Emergency Phone Calls*	*Number of Units Emer. Issued (% Total Issued)*
Emergency Department	730	8,241 (13.0%)
3 East	282	1,216 (7.2%)
3 West	271	1,593 (5.5%)
4 East	499	1,249 (5.8%)
4 West	618	1,654 (7.3%)
5 East	585	2,052 (5.7%)
6 East	507	2,543 (9.4%)
7 East	247	693 (5.0%)
7 Newborn Nursery	31	148 (0.5%)
Total	3,770	19,389 (6.6%)

vices. It has been difficult to distinguish between perception and reality. A multidisciplinary task force is being established to assess the situation, establish standards, and set priorities.

FUTURE PLANS

UMC's PCR project is patient focused. This project brings the control of many services to the patient unit. This does not mean that the ancillary service departments can be eliminated. Future plans focus on how to solidify these new departmental roles as technical experts, resources, and members of the multidisciplinary teams.

Efforts continue to maintain and improve the quality control measures. Environmental services is an example. The department no longer controls the cleanliness and appearance of an area by controlling the process. It serves as a technical resource in the process. Institutional standards for all the facility continue to be written. Additional areas and standards are included into the model as they are developed.

Evaluation continues. Each of the ancillary areas struggles with how to communicate training needs and informational items efficiently to all the 53 PSAs now dispersed throughout the facility. Plans include monthly update sessions that will parallel the sessions initially started for the PCTs.

Transportation systems continue to present a dilemma. If the diagnostic ancillary services (e.g., laboratory and radiology) continue to be centralized, a combined centralized/decentralized approach to transportation may be necessary. Further study is necessary.

CONCLUSION

The new PSA role encompasses multidisciplinary tasks previously provided by the ancillary support departments. Staff hours required to complete these tasks were determined, and the resources and responsibility were transferred to the patient units.

Results of the project have been positive. The organizational and cultural changes that have been introduced cannot be minimized, however. Significant resource shifts were seen in the ancillary support departments, resulting in reorganization of various degrees. The project created job opportunities and career ladders for some employees who chose to transfer to the patient units. For other employees, the project meant the loss of a job function or the loss of a position that was no longer necessary. New systems had to be created within the departments as well as within the hospital. Numerous challenges were turned into opportunities to learn from our mistakes and to create better ways to do things.

The quality control models continue to be a major focus. The ancillary support departments' role is technical expert, resource to the patient units, and ongoing member of the multidisciplinary team. Quality control begins by defining expectations in terms of written standards. The patient unit and the ancillary departments regularly measure performance and report outcomes. Collaborative corrective action plans are developed. This process continues to evolve.

SUGGESTED READINGS

American Hospital Association. 1991. *Policy and procedure manual for environmental services.* Chicago, Ill.: American Hospital Association.

Anderson, H. 1993. Patient centered care changes focus of materials management. *Materials Management in Healthcare* 2:12–15.

Craig, K. 1992. Restructuring materials management functions: A method for prioritizing changes and reducing costs. *Hospital Materials Management Quarterly* 13:78–88.

Dershin, H., and M. Schaik. 1993. Quality improvement for a hospital patient transportation system. *Hospital and Health Services Administration* 38:111–119.

Hibbert, W. 1992. Housekeeping time standards justify staff levels. *Health Facilities Management* 6:62–69.

Hibbert, W. 1992. Why (housekeeping) time standards based on square footage won't always work for you. *Health Facilities Management* 6:64.

Kaiser, L. 1993. Managing in uncertain times. *Journal of Healthcare Materials Management* 11:22–23.

Puckett, R.P., and B.B. Miller. 1988. Food service manual for health care institutions. Chicago, Ill.: American Hospital Association.

Rose, J.C. 1984. *Handbook for health care food service management.* Gaithersburg, Md.: Aspen Publishers, Inc.

Scheyer, W.L. 1985. *Handbook of health care materials management.* Gaithersburg, Md.: Aspen Publishers, Inc.

Sullivan, N., and K. Frentzel. 1992. A patient transport pilot quality improvement team. *Quality Review Bulletin* 18:215–221.

CHAPTER

27

Support and Maintenance of Restructured Units and Departments

Mickey L. Parsons

Chapter Objectives

1. To describe the infrastructure integration necessary to support and maintain a restructured patient care unit and ancillary department.
2. To report on lessons learned, continuous improvement, and future plans.

No guide books are available about the organizational support and maintenance of a restructured unit and/or department. The staffs' previous work experience, educational background, and common sense in working within a new delivery system provide the sources with which to manage the new units and ancillary departments. The excitement of the major change and intense focus from the hospital decrease over time after a unit is restructured. Therefore, maintenance and continuous improvement must be ongoing in order to accomplish the full set of objectives. This chapter describes the infrastructure integration and refinement that must be addressed to support restructured units/departments and reports on lessons learned, continuous improvement, and future plans.

INFRASTRUCTURE INTEGRATION

A new delivery model that restructures the organizational departments, functions, and responsibilities necessitates that one determine how the units and departments will be supported. When more than one unit is involved, the support issue must be addressed from the beginning. The primary areas with which University Medical Center (UMC) has experience to date are integration into the human resources infrastructure, the nursing operational support infrastructure, the nursing educational support infrastructure, and quality assessment and improvement. Each area is described below.

Integration into the Human Resources Infrastructure

From the beginning, human resources was intimately involved with the restructuring plan. The hiring, selection, and training processes were planned by multidisciplinary teams. The employment manager and training manager were actively involved with all levels of staff as the employment and training processes were defined. Because of the design of the new delivery system, it was obvious that human resources needed to participate. The procedures to accomplish the employment activities were also well developed. As a result, the employment process quickly became a clearly defined support infrastructure. The training plan for building the team and managing the change process continues to evolve based upon employee needs and hospital experience with the new model. Programs to develop directors and managers have continued to be identified and planned cooperatively by the patient care restructuring (PCR) task force with the human resources professionals. For detailed information about the human resources involvement, please refer to Chapters 10 through 12.

Integration into the Nursing Operational Support Structure

At the onset, it was recognized that a support float pool would need to be created for the new workers. Initially a small pool was created, but the PCR task force underestimated the requirements. After a faulty start, the operational support staff, clinical supervisors, staffing clerks, and the staff in the float pool were educated about restructuring. The clinical supervisors were provided the information needed to fulfill their role of facilitating all workers on the units. The staffing clerks became responsible for assisting with replacement staffing for sick calls and vacancies for the patient support attendants (PSAs) and patient care technicians (PCTs). A moderate-size float pool of PSAs and PCTs was created. They report to the clinical supervisor, who manages the entire float pool of prescheduled staff, per diem staff, and on-call employees.

The second area of the operational integration of nursing was the PSA hiring process. The nurse managers found that it was extremely time consuming to interview many candidates for replacement positions. Long lapses of up to 6 weeks occurred between interviewing and actual role performance. After a new employee was hired, the PSA training program then had to be completed. The lapse between hiring and functioning in the role resulted in inadequate coverage for a total of 2 months.

Therefore, the nursing leadership group opted to try a hiring approach similar to that of the environmental services department. The new approach provides for PSA hiring to be centralized with the clinical supervisor of the float pool. All PSAs are hired directly into the float pool. When a unit vacancy occurs, the nurse manager notifies human resources and the float pool clinical supervisor. The position is posted, and any PSA in the float pool may apply. The PSA is immediately transferred to the unit after being selected, and no lapse in staffing coverage occurs. The position is advertised both inside the hospital and for outside applicants at the same time.

Nurse managers reported increased satisfaction with the new approach. Human resources personnel were satisfied with the system. Experience is needed to reveal the impact of the new hiring approach on PSAs.

Integration into the Nursing Educational Support Infrastructure

A PCR educational coordinator was hired early in the project and organizationally placed into the nursing staff development department. Initially the nursing staff development staff had little interaction and involvement with PCR. This occurred because some educators did not agree with the restructuring project and preferred to avoid it. Nevertheless, the educational needs of all staff members are now totally integrated into the responsibilities of all educators in the department. The educators have specific unit assignments in addition to their program teaching assignments. They complement the role of the PCR education coordinator.

Additionally, the patient care services division orientation for new employees was totally revised. The need to introduce new employees to PCR, the professional nursing role and expectations, continuous quality improvement, and issues of health care finance led to a total revision of the new employee orientation program. The program evaluation is not yet available, but initial staff feedback is quite positive.

The next two program areas are important responsibilities of the staff development department. They are assisting with the next phase of unit-based nursing case management program definition and staff education for all units and the further development of a management development program. Both areas require continued collaboration with multidisciplinary teams and direction by the PCR task force and steering committee.

Integration into Quality Assessment and Improvement

When UMC began to discuss PCR, the total quality management or continuous quality improvement movement was just beginning in the health care industry. The PCR effort was viewed as the initial continuous improvement hospitalwide effort. Since then, the hospitalwide clinical and service continuous quality improvement initiatives have been formally established. As each hospital department and unit has developed and implemented continuous improvement plans and multidisciplinary teams, the PCR issues are being integrated for consistent management of the entire hospital. Restructuring raised the issues and provided forums for staff members to learn process flow analysis and to apply analytical thinking. An example is the step-by-step process of phlebotomy for routine and emergency situations.

LESSONS LEARNED AND FUTURE PLANS

The management of the change process was the most important lesson learned in the support of restructured units and departments. A major administrative focus was on the actual kickoff date for implementing the first two roles of PSA and PCT and the new nursing case manager roles. In retrospect, it may have been wise also to have identified the kickoff day as the day the actual change was realized and the point in time when the transition began. A tremendous emphasis has been placed on learning and applying the concepts of change. However, the extensive time and energy required to plan and implement the actual restructuring change itself left the managers and unit staff leaders excited but exhausted. Perhaps the hospital managers and staff would have been able to anticipate the challenges of the change in the subsequent 18 months if they had been better prepared for the transition after the actual change, or the kickoff date. Change is indeed a continuous improvement process, and this approach is now followed.

The second important lesson learned was in the classical continuous improvement process area. Every effort was made to avoid paralysis by analysis and not to stall the change project at various points in the planning process. This administrative approach meant that detailed education of the staff in process flow analysis was not an early part of the project. Although it has not been detrimental to the implementation of the UMC model, ongoing support and continuous improvement conceivably could have been managed better if the analytical education had been provided earlier. Currently, interdisciplinary quality improvement efforts are the number 1 objective of the PCR task force utilizing process flow analysis.

The third important lesson learned was in the preparation of the registered nurses (RNs). Education was provided in communication, delegation, supervision (including licensure and legal issues), and case management. The PCR task force underestimated the magnitude of the needs in delegation and supervision. This has proven to be a critical area for support and maintenance of restructured units as well as for implementation. These concepts are now included in new RN orientation, and continuing approaches to these needs are being evaluated by the staff development department and nurse educators.

The fourth important lesson learned was in management development. The directors and managers were involved in the planning and implementation process from the inception of the idea. Because the PCR task force was the first major interdisciplinary forum when the project was initiated, a trial and error method was followed to identify the needs of the leadership. Experience indicates that it would have been helpful to have had more education on communication skills, conflict resolution, and negotiation skills and more education and practical skill building in the management of the people during the change process. Future educational endeavors are being explored for members of the hospital leadership group.

The final lesson learned was to be prepared for constant refinement of roles, systems changes with process analysis, and ongoing problem solving. Effective leaders recognize that the continuous improvement process is indeed ongoing and are encouraged rather than discouraged. Fortunately, employees in the health care industry are most often guided by a higher sense of purpose and truly desire to provide outstanding care and service and to improve continuously .

CONCLUSION

This chapter has provided early information about the support and maintenance of restructured units and departments based on 2.5 years of UMC experience. The need to integrate the support infrastructures of human resources, nursing operations, nursing educational support, and quality assessment and improvement is addressed. The most important lessons learned and future plans are outlined.

PART

IV

Evaluation

CHAPTER

28

Evaluation Plan

Carolyn L. Murdaugh

Chapter Objectives

1. To describe the rationale for systematically evaluating patient care restructuring efforts.
2. To describe the proposed evaluation model for patient care restructuring at University Medical Center.
3. To describe the timeframe for evaluating the results of implementing a patient care restructuring model.

Restructuring has been the magic word in business and industry since the mid-1980s and is fast becoming the buzz word in health care organizations. Restructuring in health care institutions means changing the basic structure of delivering services. Patient care restructuring (PCR) is more than a tune-up; it is a major overhaul, a new way of providing health services. A common statement in the health care literature is that work systems that continue to focus on the 19th century bureaucratic model of care delivery are considered impaired in the 1990s.

The purpose of this chapter is to describe briefly the rationale for evaluating PCR efforts. The proposed evaluation model for PCR ventures at

University Medical Center (UMC) is presented and discussed. The evaluation plan is an expansion of the differentiated group professional practice (DGPP) model (see Chapter 3) to evaluate the job dimensions of support staff (patient care technicians and patient support attendants) and physicians. In addition, the model was expanded to evaluate changes in the professional practice climate of the registered nurse (the author was instrumental in developing and implementing the DGPP model, so that expansion of the model was a logical progression). The evaluation timeframe is delineated, and issues related to evaluation of change in health care organization are highlighted. Evaluation results to date are presented in Chapters 29 through 32.

RATIONALE FOR EVALUATION PLAN

The factors that have contributed to the need to restructure the delivery of patient care have already been discussed. The nursing shortage is well documented. However, in spite of the severe shortage, registered nurses, the largest health care resource, continue to operate far below their potential. The final report on the nursing shortage of the Department of Health and Human Services stated that major restructuring of health care settings and organizations is necessary to create environments that will facilitate professional nursing practice. Rising health care costs are another major reason for recognizing the need for fundamental changes in the structure of care delivery. A third factor forcing restructuring of the health care delivery system is a focus on the delivery of quality services. High-quality care is considered necessary and appropriate care.

Restructuring traditional delivery systems means promoting the professional practice of nursing, in which the traditional role with its accompanying lack of control is exchanged for the new role of decision maker. Decision making is considered the basic ingredient of professional practice and a key to recruitment and retention of nurses in health care settings. Kantor's study of organizational behavior found that support, information access, and opportunity promoted risk taking, achievement orientation, and career aspiration.[1] The study found that persons without access to these resources were less committed to the organization, did not take initiative, and resisted change.

A major weakness in PCR efforts has been failure to evaluate systematically the results for all persons who are affected by the change. Until recently, evaluation efforts included only anecdotal information or small case studies. The usual response has been "we just know it works" without any data to substantiate the statement. Large scale evaluation efforts are necessary to assess the effects of changes in restructuring on the providers of care as well as the recipients of care in the new system. Nurse, support staff, and physician and patient outcomes, including satisfaction with care, quality of care, and costs of care, must be evaluated to assess the appropriateness and effectiveness of the restructuring efforts.

When an innovation, in this case PCR, has been adopted, the consequences or changes brought about as a result of the innovation must be evaluated.[2] Typically, however, change agents, or persons who implement restructuring models, usually overemphasize the implementation, assuming that the consequences will be positive. Second, consequences are often difficult to measure. Morbidity, mortality, and disability statistics have been the traditional consequences (measures) of the adequacy of patient care. However, these measures are not appropriate for assessing the changes brought about by PCR, and new approaches have had to be developed. The new evaluation approaches have expanded the traditional measures to include satisfaction with care, satisfaction with one's practice and organization, quality of care, and fiscal outcomes. These new consequences may be confounded with other simultaneous effects operating in the health care environment, making it difficult to untangle the cause and effect relationships. In spite of these difficulties, both process (ongoing) and product (outcome) evaluation can be accomplished. Evaluation models provide the plan that enables us to evaluate how effective we have been in accomplishing our goals for restructuring.

EVALUATION MODEL

The PCR evaluation model (Figure 28–1) depicts the influence of both professional practice climate and positive job dimensions on job satisfaction, which in turn influence the quality of care and the cost of care. Each of these concepts is briefly described to provide the justification for inclusion in the evaluation model. The operational or measurement level of the con-

Figure 28–1 PCR research evaluation model.

cepts, as shown in Figure 28–2, is also reviewed. Copies of the instruments to measure the concepts in the evaluation model are available from the authors of the particular scale. The instruments are listed in Table 28–1.

Professional Practice Climate

The environment in which care is delivered and the relationship between the caregiver and the organization have received little attention in the design of care delivery models. However, evidence continues to suggest that change in the organizational climate will increase job satisfaction and decrease turnover. Autonomy has frequently been cited as a major factor in overall job satisfaction of professional employees in hospitals.[3–5] A practice climate that promotes autonomy and shared values for excellence in patient care has been shown to increase job satisfaction, organizational commitment, and intent to stay with the organization.

Two strategies for improving organizational climate and employer well-being dominate organizational development theory and practice: the human process approach and the technostructure approach.[9] The human process approach focuses on changing dysfunctional behavior and practices and using interventions that include team building, intergroup interventions, and organizational diagnosis and feedback. The techno-

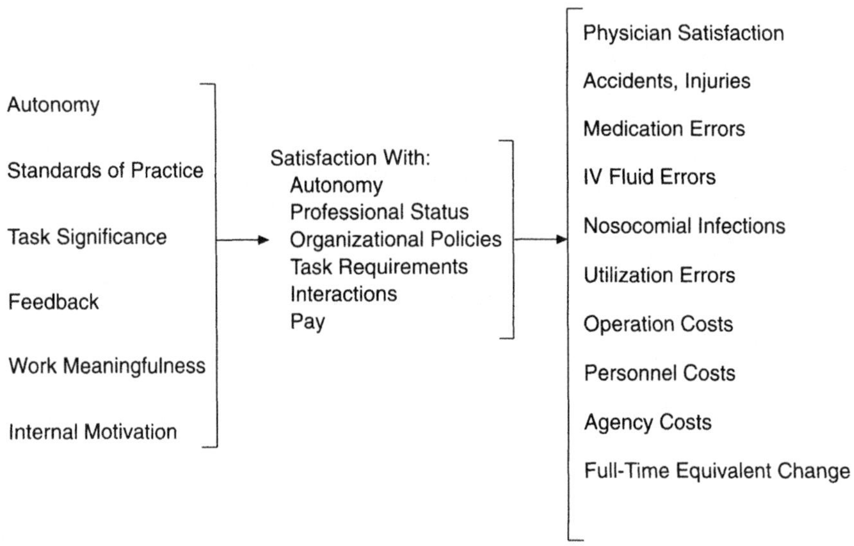

Figure 28–2 PCR operational model.

Table 28–1 Instruments To Measure Concepts in the Evaluation Model

Concepts	*Measures*
Professional practice climate	Professional Practice Climate Scale (PPCT)[6]
Positive job dimensions	Job Diagnostic Survey (JDS)[7]
Job satisfaction	Job Satisfaction Scale (JSS)[8]

structural approach assumes that motivation and behavior are influenced by job design and control, information, and reward systems. This approach focuses on structure change, work redesign, compensation systems, and new information technology. Both types of interventions, when accompanied by human skills, shared values, and culture changes, result in long-lasting organizational change. The UMC model of care restructuring included both approaches to build a professional practice climate. The human process approach was incorporated into the technostructure approach, in which the work redesign intervention included restructured roles, interdisciplinary team management, and the development of shared values of excellence in patient care.

Characteristics of the work environment that represent professional practice have been identified by the American Nurses Association. The major characteristics emphasize autonomy, or perceived independence or control over job performance; and standards of practice, or preestablished ideals for clinical and management practice that have been developed by experts and accepted by the profession.[10] Professional autonomy implies not only control over work but control over the standards regulating work. The extent to which employees provide input into their work environment determines the degree of autonomy experienced. Autonomy is operationalized in practice through participation in decision making in a shared governance structure. Standards of practice are generally accepted principles of both clinical and management practice.

The professional practice climate was assessed with Miller and Polentini's Professional Practice Climate Tool (PPCT).[6] The instrument was developed in the Measurement of Clinical and Educational Nursing Outcomes Project at the University of Maryland. The PPCT measures the work environment in which the dimensions of autonomy and standards of practice are perceived to be present. Nurses respond to what they believe is the ideal and what they perceive to be present in the organizational environment. The scale consists of 43 statements on a Likert type format. Two types of responses are elicited: "Importance to me" is rated on a 5-point scale ranging from unimportant (1) to extremely important (5), and "degree present in the department of nursing" is rated on a 5-point scale ranging from minimum (1) to maximum (5).

Content validity was established using a panel of experts who were asked to evaluate whether the statements interpreted the components of professional practice. Revisions were made based on the expert input. Eight factors have resulted from factor analysis in previous studies. The autonomy subscale contains three factors: individual decision making, administrative decision making, and collaboration and collegiality. The standards of practice subscale contains five factors: professional development, compensation, monitoring and evaluation, management strategies, and patient care.

Reliability assessment using Cronbach's α, indicated that the total scale and subscales are internally consistent. The total scale α has been reported to be .93. The subscale α reliability coefficients range from .58 to .86.

Work group functioning was also assessed as part of the professional practice climate. The work group is considered the people with whom the respondent usually works on a day-to-day basis, sharing the same or adjoining workplaces, and engaging in tasks that are similar or related. The work group is an important part of the individual's work environment and can have a strong influence on a member's job experiences and behavior. Work groups that promote open communication and discourage fragmentation promote a professional practice environment.

The Work Group Functioning Scale measures internal group processes and was used to evaluate the openness of communication and influence in the group and interpersonal friction or internal fragmentation of the group.[11] The Work Group Functioning Scale was developed as a component of the Michigan Organizational Assessment Questionnaire (MOAQ) to provide insight into the perceptions of members of an organization. The scale contains 10 statements on a Likert type format with responses ranging from disagree (7) to agree (1). Factor analysis supports two subscales: communication and fragmentation. The authors provide evidence for both theoretical and empirical validity of the MOAQ and its subscales.

Positive Job Dimensions

Job characteristics have been identified that promote high performance motivation and satisfaction with work.[13] These positive job dimensions include characteristics of the tasks performed as well as psychological states thought to be associated with the tasks. One job dimension is the degree to which the job is perceived to have a substantial impact on the lives of other people, or the significance of the task. When employees realize and understand the influence of their work on patient care outcomes, the work becomes more significant and satisfying. A second job dimension is feedback received from doing the work. Knowledge of the effects of one's work on patient care provides direct and clear information about the effectiveness of one's performance.

Another critical condition is that the person must experience the work as meaningful. In other words, the work must be seen as something that counts. Dimensions of the job that enable persons to use and test personal skills and abilities tend to be experienced as meaningful, regardless of whether the task is significant or trivial. Work meaningfulness is influenced by both skill variety and task identity. Skill variety focuses on the degree to which the job requires a variety of activities to carry out the work. The more skills involved, the more meaningful the work. Task identity focuses on the degree to which a job requires completion of a whole and identifiable piece of work with a visible outcome.

Last, positive job dimensions include internal motivation, or the degree to which one is self-motivated to perform effectively on the job. In other words, the person experiences positive internal feelings when performing effectively and negative internal feelings when doing poorly on the job. Persons who are internally motivated are more satisfied when their tasks are thought to result in positive patient outcomes.

Positive job dimensions were assessed with the Job Diagnostic Survey (JDS).[7] The instrument has been developed to measure the effect of job changes and assesses task significance, feedback, meaningfulness of the work, and internal motivation. The short form of the JDS, which was used to evaluate the results of implementing the UMC PCR model, consists of 53 statements on a Likert type format. The short form is recommended in longitudinal studies of work redesign because it can be administered repeatedly without excessive demands on the respondents.

The JDS has been administered to more than 1,500 persons working in more than 100 different jobs in 15 organizations. The scale has undergone three major revisions based on psychometric and substantive considerations. Subscale internal consistency reliability coefficients range from .50 to .88. The components of the JDS relate to each other and to external criterion variables as predicted by the theory on which the scale is based, which is evidence for beginning construct validity.

Job Satisfaction

Job satisfaction is the perceived enjoyment and fulfillment of activities performed for pay.[13] Two types of job satisfaction are suggested: organizational satisfaction and professional job satisfaction.[14] Organizational job satisfaction is concerned with one's positive or negative view of job-related factors or working conditions, such as interaction with colleagues, administrative style, and pay or other rewards. Professional job satisfaction relates to individuals' opinion of the quality of work. Research has substantiated that people leave employment situations when they are dissatisfied. In addition, people who are discontented in their jobs are less motivated to perform as effectively as persons who are satisfied. Job satisfaction and commitment are related. Persons who are satisfied in their jobs are committed to the organization and are willing to exert greater effort on behalf of the organization.[5]

Job satisfaction was assessed with the Index of Work Satisfaction (IWS).[8] The IWS measures satisfaction with six components of work satisfaction: pay, autonomy, task requirements, organizational policies, interactions, and professional status. The scale consists of 43 statements to which a person responds on a 7-point scale ranging from strongly disagree (1) to strongly agree (7). A total satisfaction score as well as subscale satisfaction scores can be calculated.

Since 1972, the IWS has undergone extensive empirical validation studies. Internal consistency reliability for the final revision of the total scale was reported to be .82, with subscale α coefficients ranging from .52 to .81. The scale has undergone factor analysis with indication of beginning construct validity.

Quality and Cost of Care

The critical issue in restructuring patient care delivery systems is the effectiveness of the new systems in terms of quality and cost outcomes. In lay terms, quality is defined as delivering what the consumer wants the first time and every time. Quality of care outcomes are the effects of care delivery on the health status of patients. Quality of care outcomes include the traditional indicators of morbidity, disability, and mortality as well as functional status, quality of life, degree of patient satisfaction with care, and, in the PCR model, degree of physician satisfaction with care.[15]

Quality of care was assessed by recording patient care complications, including admissions for complications of previous hospitalizations, hospital-incurred injuries, unplanned transfers, nursing variations, utilization variations, radiology variations, medication delivery errors, documentation variations, intravenous fluid delivery errors, and nosocomial infections. Quality of care outcomes and issues in quality of care measurement are discussed in detail in Chapter 33.

The cost of care relates to the actual costs of delivering patient care services. In the UMC PCR model, costs of care were the expense of delivering a new system of patient care. The cost outcomes include operational expenses and personnel expenditures. Costs are measurable outcomes that must be addressed to determine the cost–benefit ratio of implementing new delivery systems. See Chapter 30 for a discussion of evaluation of cost outcomes in the restructuring model.

Other Evaluation Parameters: Organizational Culture

Organizational culture is the mix of values, beliefs, meanings, and expectations that members of a particular organization or group hold in common and that they use as behavior and problem-solving guides. The key concept in culture is sharing; commonality is vital to culture formation. Culture serves several functions. It conveys a sense of identity of its members and enhances social system stability. Every organization has a culture composed of normative values and beliefs that holds the organization together.[16] Peters and Waterman stated that the dominance and coherence of culture proved to be essential qualities of excellent companies.[17]

Change always threatens a culture.[18] Change strips down the heroes and the daily rituals of work life, leaving employees confused, insecure, and often angry. Cultural change means changes in the behavior of the people in the organization: identifying of new heroes, telling different stories, and spending time differently. Culture can be developed and shaped to produce effective organizational outcomes, or specifically shared values that promote quality patient care. Therefore, an understanding of the culture of each unit to be restructured, including the shared beliefs and values, heroes, and rituals, is necessary before implementing change. The culture assessment also provides the restructuring team with valuable information about aspects of the culture that make persons on the unit more resistant to change or about aspects of the culture that must be addressed before implementing any change.

The Cultural Assessment Survey (CAS) was used to assess the existing culture on each patient care unit before restructuring. The CAS is based on the work of Deal and Kennedy and del Bueno and Freund.[18,19] Deal and Kennedy identify five elements that describe the organizational culture: environment, values, heroes, rites and rituals, and cultural network. The CAS evaluates environment, values, and heroes. The scale contains seven open-ended questions in which persons are asked to respond according to their own personal viewpoint. Subject responses are content analyzed to describe the organizational culture perceived by the unit staff. Content validity has been established by the authors of the questions. However, no other psychometric evaluation has been performed.

EVALUATION TIMEFRAME

A pretest/posttest longitudinal evaluation design was implemented in which information was obtained about each patient care unit 1 month before implementing restructuring efforts. Information was also collected at 6 months and 1 year after the initiation of PCR on each patient care unit during Phase I. The second data collection point was considered a formative or process evaluation, and the third (12-month) data collection point was a summative or final evaluation. Collection of patient and physician satisfaction data deviated slightly from the timeframe. Please see Chapters 29 and 32 for details of patient and physician satisfaction, respectively, and Chapter 5 for a description of the data collection process.

ISSUES RELATED TO THE EVALUATION OF CHANGE

The development and testing of evaluation models to measure the influence of changes in health care delivery services on outcomes raise several issues that have just begun to receive attention. The first issue is concerned with the inclusiveness of measures. This issue addresses the question: Are all relevant concepts included in the evaluation model? In other words, are any important concepts thought to be affected by restructuring omitted from the evaluation component? The greatest potential for this error rests with the evaluation of patient outcomes. Patient outcomes must be selected to reflect accurately the dimensions of care being affected by the new care delivery model.[20] Numerous types of outcomes may apply, and the definitions of outcomes vary across evaluation models.

A second issue, the lack of sensitivity or responsiveness of the measures, is a major issue in outcome evaluation research. There is no clear consensus about how best to measure outcomes or which tools are most accurate and valid. Reliability and validity issues must be addressed as carefully with subjective measures as with objective measures. A lack of significant findings must be interpreted in light of the amount of measurement error in the instruments operationalizing the concepts in the model.

The unit of analysis, the individual versus the nursing unit or the organization, is another major issue in evaluating change in organizations. Different levels of analysis require different methodological approaches, measurements, and timing. The issue is complex, and the reader is referred to Ferkatich and Verran for an in-depth discussion.[21]

The timing of measurements is the fourth issue to be taken into account when evaluating organizational change. Questions that need to be addressed include the following: What time period is needed to observe change? What are the critical time points? Multiple evaluation points may be necessary to capture the change. At least 1 year is needed to evaluate the results of implementing a new patient care model to avoid measuring the effects of the chaos of implementing change or the honeymoon phase immediately after implementation.

Last, the complexity of the health care system is a major issue in testing outcome evaluation models. Multiple uncontrollable factors contribute to patient and cost outcomes: organizational characteristics, patient characteristics, and health care provider characteristics. Many patients, the consumers of care, are not yet educated enough to create a demand for quality outcomes. In addition, a diverse, fragmented health care system means that no one provider has responsibility for monitoring or ensuring the quality of patient care. In spite of these issues, outcome evaluation models provide a blueprint with which to begin systematic evaluation of the effects of implementing new delivery systems of patient care.

CONCLUSION

This chapter has described the need to evaluate change efforts after restructuring the delivery of care in today's health care system. The evaluation model that has been implemented at UMC has been reviewed with a description of the rationale for including the various model concepts. In addition, the measures selected to evaluate the concepts have been reviewed. Last, issues of concern in evaluating organizational change have been examined. Evaluation models must be a component of all restructuring models, because the results will provide findings on which sound decisions can be made to improve the quality and decrease the cost of care.

NOTES

1. R.M. Kantor, *When Giants Learn to Dance* (New York, N.Y.: Simon & Schuster, 1990).
2. E.M. Rogers, *Diffusion of Innovations* (New York, N.Y.: Free Press, 1983).
3. L.S. Chan, et al., Determining Nursing Retention Strategies in a Large Public Teaching Hospital, *Quality Research Bulletin* 16 (1990):373–377.
4. J.C. McClosky, Two Requirements for Job Contentment: Autonomy and Social Integration, *Journal of Nursing Scholarship* 22 (1990):140–143.
5. G.U. Alpander, Relationship between Commitment to Hospital Goals and Job Satisfaction: A Case Study of a Hospital Department, *Quality Research Bulletin* 15 (1990):51–62.

6. M. Miller and A. Polentini, Professional practice climate (Unpublished Paper, Measurement of Clinical and Educational Nursing Outcomes Project, 1985).
7. J.R. Hackman and G.R. Oldham, *The Job Diagnostic Survey: An Instrument for the Diagnosis of Jobs and Evaluating Job Redesign Projects,* Technical Report No. 4 (Springfield, Va.: U.S. Department of Commerce, 1974).
8. P.L. Stamps and E.B. Piedmont, *Nurses and Work Satisfaction: An Index for Measurement* (Ann Arbor, Mich.: Health Administration Press Perspectives, 1986).
9. F. Friedlander and L.D. Brown, Organizational Development. *Annual Review of Psychology* 25 (1974):313–341.
10. M. Mantheny, Retention. What Satisfies Nurses Enough To Keep Them, *Nurse Managers Bookshelf* 1, no. 1 (1989):61–71.
11. C. Cammann, et al., "Assessing the Attitudes and Perceptions of Organizational Members," in *Assessing Organizational Change: A Guide to Methods, Measures and Approaches,* ed. S.E. Seashore, et al. (New York, N.Y.: Wiley, 1983).
12. J.R. Hackman and G.R. Oldham, *Work Redesign* (Reading, Mass.: Addison-Wesley, 1980).
13. D.B. Slavitt, et al., Nurse Satisfaction with Their Work Situation, *Nursing Research* 27 (1978):114–120.
14. A.S. Hinshaw, et al., Innovative Retention Strategies for Nursing Staff, *Journal of Nursing Administration* 17 (1987):8–16.
15. A. Donabedian, The Quality of Care: How Can It Be Assessed?, *Journal of the American Medical Association* 260 (1988):1,743–1,746.
16. D.J. del Bueno, An Organizational Checklist, *Journal of Nursing Administration* 17 (1987):30–33.
17. T.J. Peters and R.H. Waterman, *In Search of Excellence: Lessons from America's Best-Run Companies* (New York, N.Y.: Harper & Row, 1982).
18. T.E. Deal and A.A. Kennedy, *Corporate Cultures: The Rites and Rituals of Corporate Life* (Reading, Mass.: Addison-Wesley, 1982).
19. D.J. del Bueno and C.M. Freund, *Power and Politics in Nursing Administration: A Casebook* (Owings Mills, Md.: National Health Publishing, 1986).
20. C. Weisman, "Nursing Practice Models: Research on Patient Outcomes," in *Patient Outcome Research: Examining the Effectiveness of Nursing Practice,* NIH Publication No. 93-3411 (Bethesda, Md.: National Institutes of Health, 1992).
21. S. Ferkatich and J. Verran, "Analysis Issues in Outcomes Research," in *Patient Outcome Research: Examining the Effectiveness of Nursing Practice,* NIH Publication No. 93-3411 (Bethesda, Md.: National Institutes of Health, 1992).

CHAPTER

29

Patient Satisfaction

Denise Dillon Brice

Chapter Objectives

1. To describe the instrument and methodology used to evaluate patient satisfaction.
2. To report the results of patient satisfaction before and after restructuring.

Evaluation of patient satisfaction is of primary importance to health care providers, insurers, and patients. An institution's success or failure will be based upon three essential criteria for insurers to contract with health care providers: patient satisfaction, patient outcomes, and cost reduction. Therefore, care providers must focus on the needs of patients, not the needs of the system. According to Steiber and Krowinski, most patients are generally satisfied with their service experience but not equally satisfied with all aspects of care. They note that, "at its fundamental level, satisfaction is a positive evaluation of specific service dimensions based on patient expectations and provider performance."[1(p.23)] Providers of patient care services must recognize that the expectations of customers (patients) are very real. Meeting and exceeding customer expectations is a top agenda for today and the future.[1]

Whiteley reported the results of the Forum Corporation's research on business success. Findings revealed that "almost 70 percent of the identifiable reasons why customers left typical companies had nothing to do with the product."[2(p.9)] In their study of identifiable reasons for customers switching to a competitor, 15 percent switched because they found a better product from another company, and another 15 percent switched because they found a cheaper product. Twenty percent, however, switched because of lack of personal attention, and another 45 percent switched because service was rude and unhelpful.[2] If product quality is equated with technical quality in health care, this presents powerful information to health care leaders and providers.

Leebov documents the price health care providers and institutions pay for dissatisfied customers:

> On average, 96 percent of your unhappy customers don't complain to you. However, 90 percent of your unhappy customers will not choose your organization again. When customers are dissatisfied with service, they tell twenty relatives and friends. When customers are satisfied, they tell only five. That means you have to satisfy four times as many people as you disappoint just to stay even in terms of public image.[3(p.3)]

At University Medical Center (UMC), staff have been interested in these statistics and willing to expand their perspectives regarding service and quality of care. Historically, staff have thought of quality from a technical perspective. Leebov states emphatically, however, "The fact is, employee behavior toward customers is the most powerful marketing and customer satisfaction tool an organization has."[3(p.3)]

PATIENT SATISFACTION EVALUATION

Methodology

All patients from four units (two medical-surgical and two pediatrics, encompassing approximately 100 beds) were evaluated before and after restructuring. Inpatients from these units were surveyed about their satisfaction with various elements of their stay during three time periods: 9 months before restructuring, 4 months after restructuring, and 10 months after restructuring. All patients discharged during a 1-month time period were administered a telephone survey from 1 to 7 days after discharge. This format was chosen because, at UMC, mail surveys of patient satisfaction have historically had a 32 percent response rate. A telephone methodology was expected to produce a higher response rate. For adults, the questionnaire was administered to the patient. For pediatric patients, the parent or guardian of the child was surveyed. Three call-backs were conducted before the patient was considered unavailable. Response rates for the three surveys were approximately 50 percent (Table 29–1).

The survey instrument (see Appendix 29–A) was developed by the planning department. Domains assessed included cleanliness of facilities, food service, nursing care, medical care, and ancillary services. Indicators were chosen based upon their value in evaluating the effectiveness of patient care restructuring (PCR). For example, one of the goals of the patient support attendant (PSA) role was to assist the patient with feeding. A question was therefore constructed to evaluate the patient's satisfaction with assistance provided with meal service and/or feeding. Selected control variables were also included. For example, the patient was asked to evaluate the taste of the food, an indicator that should not be influenced by restructuring.

A 4-point Likert type response scale ranging from excellent to poor was chosen because of the telephone methodology. A longer response scale was thought to be too difficult for the patient to keep in mind. Assessment of scale reliability resulted in a Cronbach α of .95 for the baseline survey.

Data Collection and Analysis

The completed questionnaires were returned to the planning department for data entry and analysis. Comparison of change in mean scores over time was analyzed using analysis of variance (ANOVA) at $p \leq .05$.

FINDINGS

Table 29–2 presents mean scores, standard deviations, and significance levels for all indicators with a 4-point response scale before implementation, time 1 after implementation, and time 2 after implementation. The results are grouped by service area.

Table 29–1 Patient Satisfaction Survey Response Rates

Parameter	*Baseline*	*Time 1 after Discharge*	*Time 2 after Discharge*
Number of patients surveyed	358	338	261
Response rate (%)	60.0	52.6	45.4

Table 29–2 PCR Patient Satisfaction Evaluation: Mean Scores and Standard Deviations (SDs) by Question with Statistical Significance*

	Baseline	Time 1 after Discharge	Time 2 after Discharge	
Question	*Mean (SD)*	*Mean (SD)*	*Mean (SD)*	*p*
Facilities				
Cleanliness of room	3.41 (0.69)	3.42 (0.63)	3.50 (0.64)	.29
Cleanliness of bathroom	3.31 (0.73)	3.31 (0.70)	3.43 (0.70)	.11
Cleanliness of public areas	3.35 (0.64)	3.38 (0.64)	3.46 (0.64)	.13
Food services				
Timeliness of food delivery	3.12 (0.77)	3.10 (0.74)	3.22 (0.80)	.21
Courtesy of food server	3.32 (0.74)	3.41 (0.62)	3.48 (0.63)	.34
Temperature of hot foods	3.14 (0.78)	3.04 (0.78)	3.08 (0.89)	.32
Temperature of cold foods	3.18 (0.71)	3.19 (0.62)	3.13 (0.81)	.59
Assistance with feeding	2.84 (1.05)	3.22 (0.72)	3.30 (0.80)	.00
Taste of food	2.74 (0.90)	2.72 (0.83)	2.69 (0.95)	.79
Nursing care				
Courtesy of nurses	3.60 (0.65)	3.64 (0.57)	3.71 (0.51)	.08
Response to call button	3.29 (0.88)	3.35 (0.81)	3.42 (0.79)	.19
Availability of nurses	3.29 (0.81)	3.41 (0.75)	3.51 (0.71)	.00
Explanations of procedures	3.43 (0.68)	3.49 (0.64)	3.56 (0.64)	.07
Effort to make you feel comfortable	3.53 (0.68)	3.54 (0.62)	3.66 (0.57)	.02
Attention to your worries/concerns	3.45 (0.73)	3.48 (0.66)	3.62 (0.60)	.01
Explanation of care after discharge	3.44 (0.73)	3.46 (0.71)	3.63 (0.62)	.00
Clinical skills of the nurses	3.52 (0.64)	3.53 (0.57)	3.62 (0.61)	.11
Medical care				
Courtesy of physicians	3.62 (0.58)	3.67 (0.53)	3.65 (0.59)	.46
Availability of physicians	3.41 (0.78)	3.39 (0.71)	3.40 (0.76)	.93
Explanations of medical treatments	3.49 (0.71)	3.51 (0.66)	3.57 (0.66)	.35
Effort to make your feel comfortable	3.57 (0.61)	3.56 (0.54)	3.56 (0.69)	.97
Explanation of care after discharge	3.45 (0.72)	3.47 (0.63)	3.57 (0.64)	.10
Clinical skills of the physicians	3.67 (0.50)	3.66 (0.50)	3.69 (0.54)	.79
Ancillary services				
Courtesy of transportation staff	3.37 (0.73)	3.44 (0.56)	3.67 (0.59)	.00
Promptness of transportation staff	3.19 (0.81)	3.29 (0.71)	3.58 (0.69)	.00
Efficiency of technician who drew blood	3.43 (0.65)	3.28 (0.68)	3.33 (0.82)	.03
Coordination of scheduled tests	3.27 (0.74)	3.21 (0.70)	3.11 (0.88)	.07
Quality of physical therapy/occupational therapy care in department	3.33 (0.79)	3.48 (0.58)	3.49 (0.64)	.32
Quality of physical therapy/occupational therapy care in room		3.43 (0.69)	3.42 (0.66)	.91
Quality of respiratory therapy care in department	3.55 (0.58)	3.50 (0.54)	3.53 (0.61)	.86

continues

Table 29–2 continued

Question	Baseline Mean (SD)	Time 1 after Discharge Mean (SD)	Time 2 after Discharge Mean (SD)	p
Quality of respiratory therapy care in room		3.49 (0.52)	3.49 (0.62)	.94
Quality of radiology care in department	3.54 (0.54)	3.36 (0.63)	3.57 (0.62)	.00
Quality of radiology care in room		3.43 (0.54)	3.53 (0.57)	.70
Neatness of hospital personnel	3.52 (0.57)	3.44 (0.57)	3.56 (0.56)	.03
Confidence in hospital personnel	3.47 (0.64)	3.44 (0.60)	3.55 (0.61)	.10
Attention to worries from staff	3.41 (0.70)	3.43 (0.58)	3.54 (0.63)	.05
Caregivers worked as a team	3.41 (0.69)	3.39 (0.61)	3.54 (0.60)	.02
Overall satisfaction with care	3.49 (0.68)	3.50 (0.59)	3.62 (0.57)	.03

*$p \leq .05$ indicates statistically significant change by date of survey. Mean scores tabulated from a 4-point scale: 4, excellent; 1, poor.

Cleanliness

Cleanliness included the patient room, bathroom, and public areas. For cleanliness, the mean scores improved over time, but the improvement was not statistically significant. A summary score for cleanliness is presented graphically in Figure 29–1.

Food Services

Food services items relevant to PCR were related to timeliness, courtesy, and assistance. A significant increase in mean scores was noted for assistance with feeding. The mean score increased from a preimplementation level of 2.84 to 3.22 4 months after restructuring and to 3.30 10 months after restructuring. A summary score for timeliness of food delivery and courtesy of service is presented graphically in Figure 29–2; the score for assistance with feeding is presented in Figure 29–3.

Nursing Care

Nursing care items addressed care issues perceived as important by patients. Mean scores for all nursing indicators increased. Statistically significant increases were observed in the following four indicators: avail-

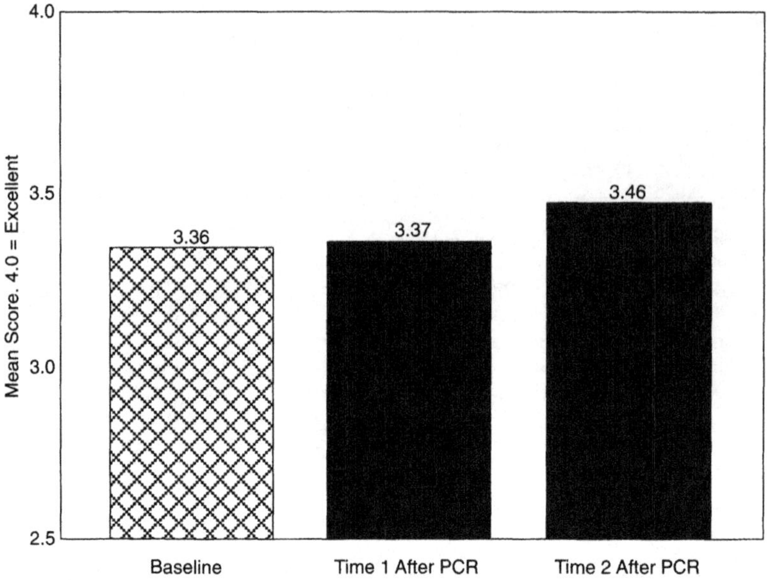

Figure 29–1 Cleanliness of facilities.

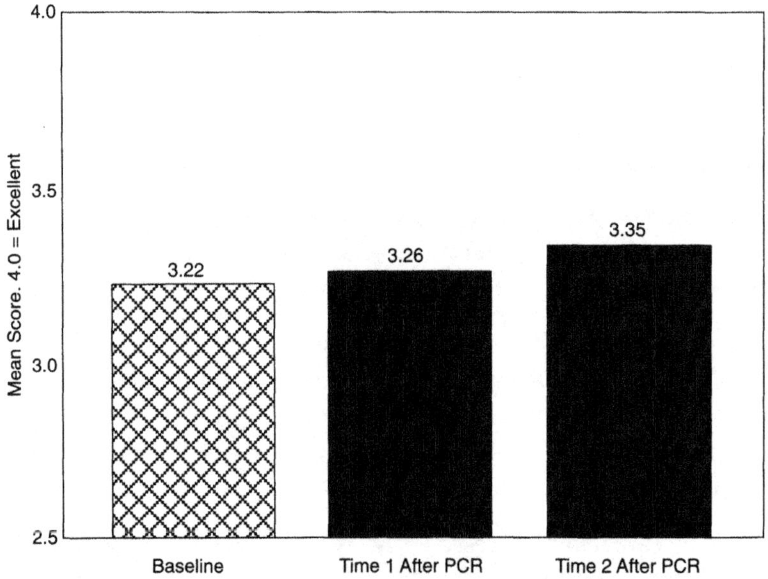

Figure 29–2 Timeliness of food delivery and courtesy of server.

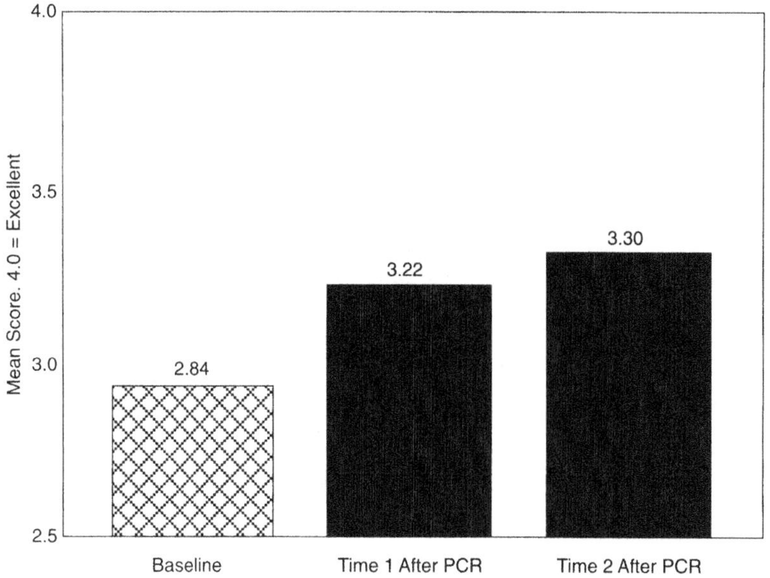

Figure 29–3 Assistance with feeding. *Note:* Increase in score is statistically significant by ANOVA at $p \leq .05$.

ability of nurses, effort to make you feel comfortable, attention to your worries and concerns, and explanation of care after discharge. All these indicators plus clinical skills of the nurses are presented in Figures 29–4 through 29–8.

Medical Care

Significant change was not found in any of the medical care indicators, although mean scores for explanations of medical treatments and explanation of care after discharge have steadily increased. A summary measure of patient satisfaction with medical care is presented as Figure 29–9.

Ancillary Services

Ancillary service indicators were relevant to the new patient care technician (PCT) role and changes in unit care delivery. Ancillary indicators that have shown significant improvement include courtesy and promptness of transportation staff, neatness of hospital personnel, attention to worries by

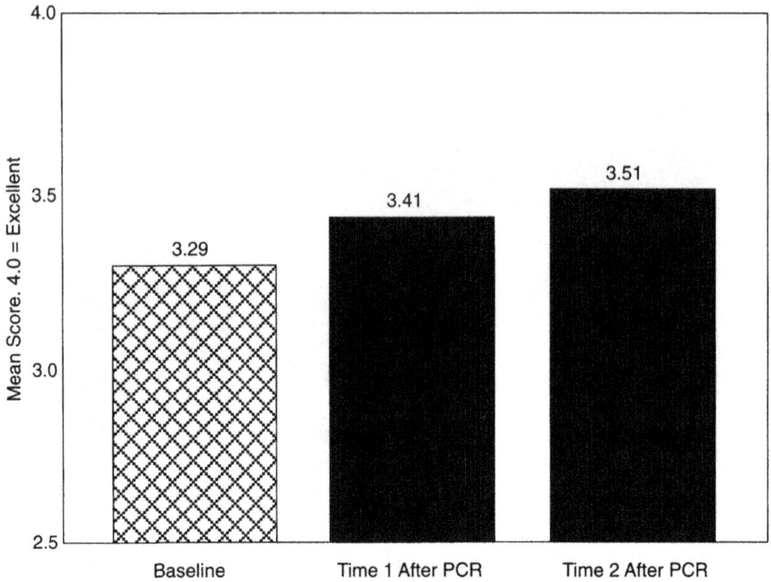

Figure 29–4 Availability of nurses. *Note:* Increase in score is statistically significant by ANOVA at $p \leq .05$.

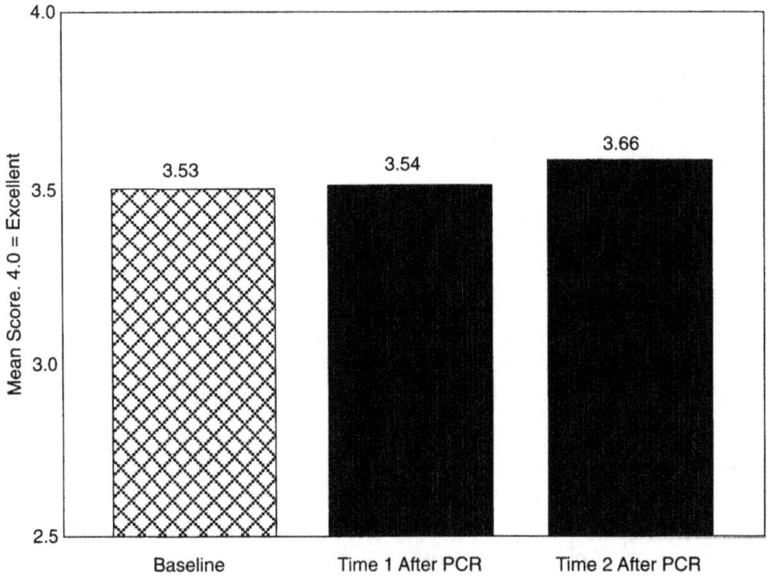

Figure 29–5 Effort to make the patient feel comfortable. *Note:* Increase in score is statistically significant by ANOVA at $p \leq .05$.

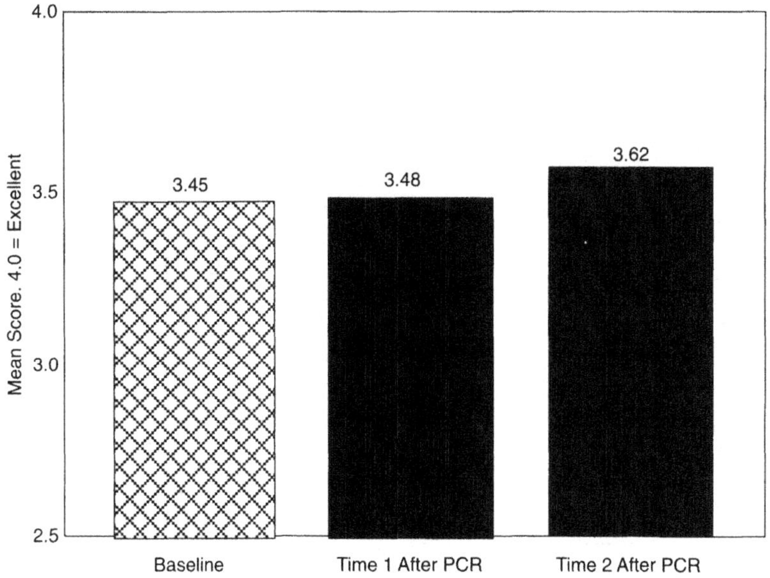

Figure 29–6 Attention to the patient's concerns. *Note:* Increase in score is statistically significant by ANOVA at $p \leq .05$.

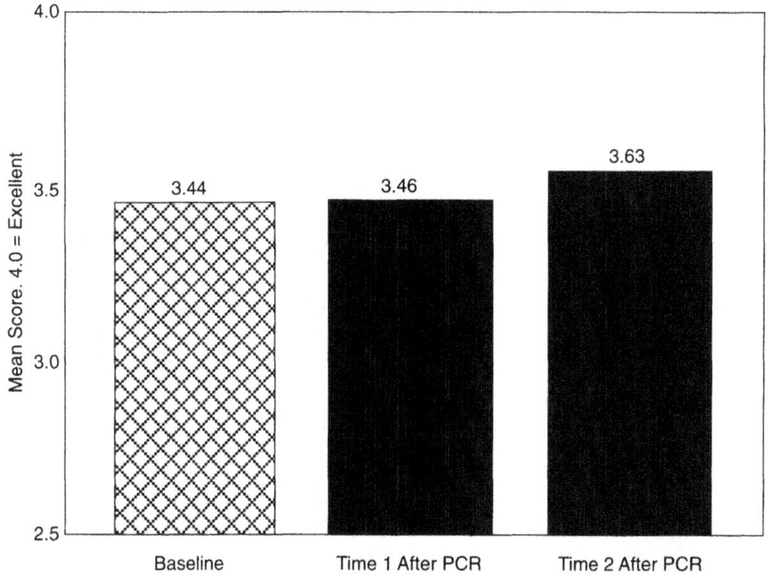

Figure 29–7 Explanation of care after discharge. *Note:* Increase in score is statistically significant by ANOVA at $p \leq 0.5$.

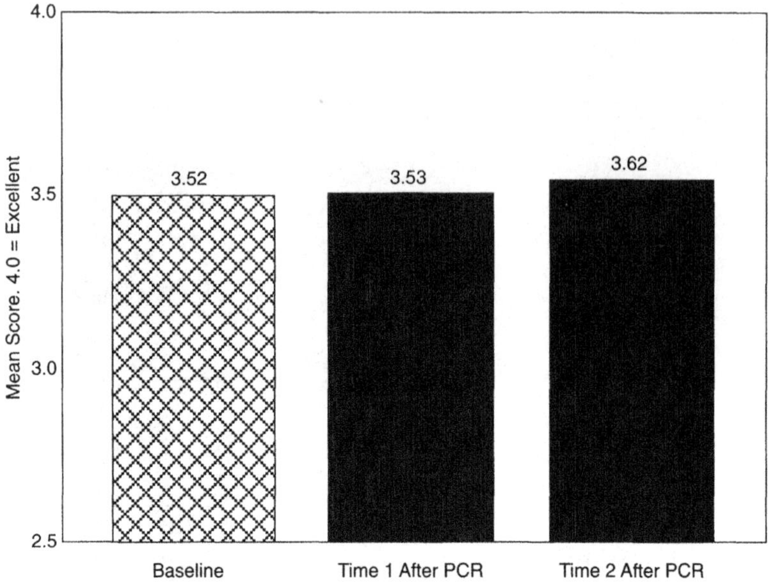

Figure 29–8 Clinical skills of the nurses.

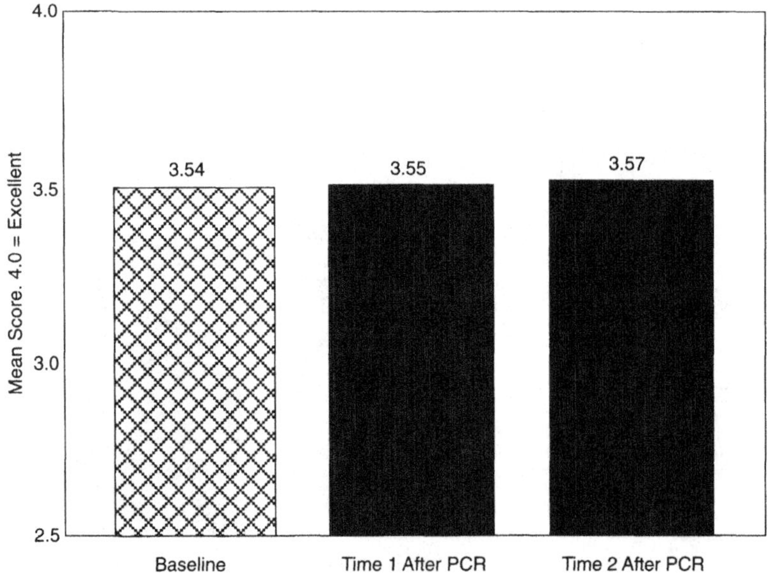

Figure 29–9 Patient satisfaction with medical care.

staff, caregivers working as a team, and overall satisfaction with care. These indicators are presented graphically as Figures 29–10 through 29–15. Mean scores decreased on two items: efficiency of technician who drew blood and coordination of scheduled tests. Postimplementation scores for both these indicators were below baseline scores. Scores for efficiency of the technician who drew blood decreased significantly (Figure 29–16).

DISCUSSION

Results of the patient satisfaction surveys provide evidence of the effects of PCR on patient satisfaction, both positively and negatively.

Cleanliness

Cleanliness of the patient care units has remained constant, indicating that the shifting of unit housekeeping responsibilities to the PSA role has not changed patient satisfaction with cleanliness. Mean scores fall into the good to excellent range.

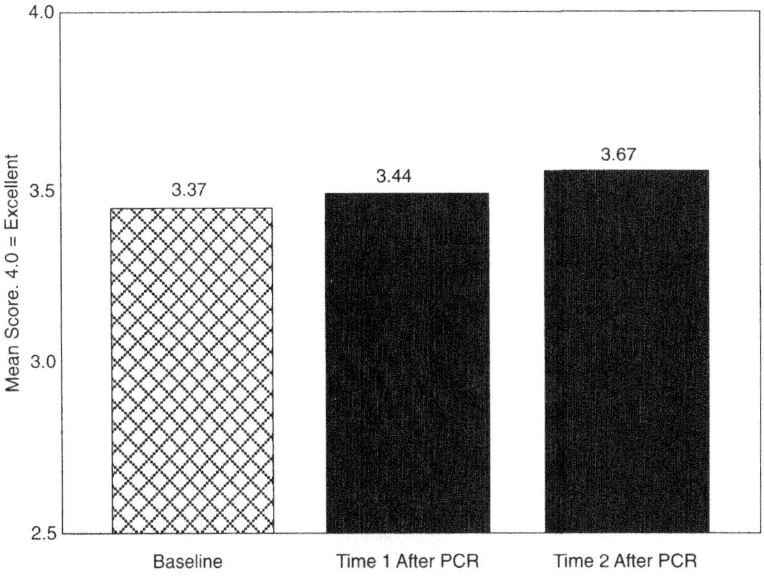

Figure 29–10 Courtesy of transportation staff. *Note:* Increase in score is statistically significant by ANOVA at $p \leq 0.5$.

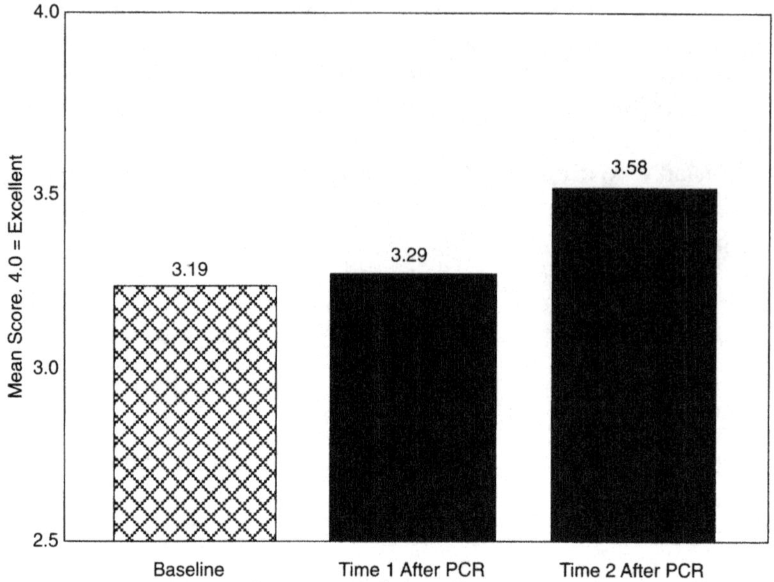

Figure 29–11 Promptness of transportation staff. *Note:* Increase in score is statistically significant by ANOVA at $p \leq 0.5$.

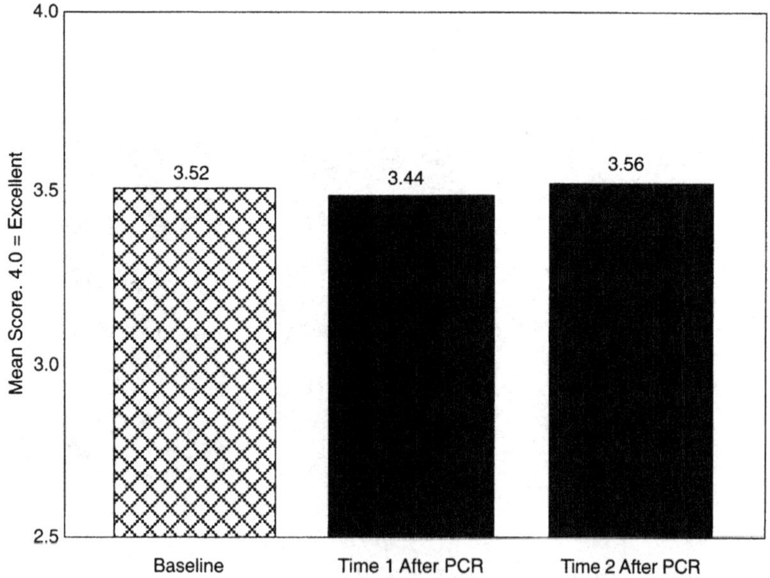

Figure 29–12 Neatness of hospital personnel.

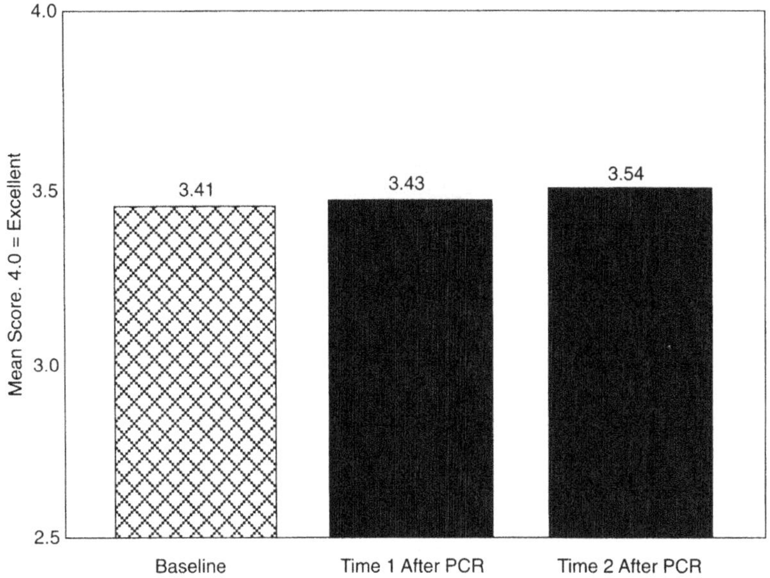

Figure 29–13 Attention to patient worries from staff. *Note:* Increase in score is statistically significant by ANOVA at $p \leq .05$.

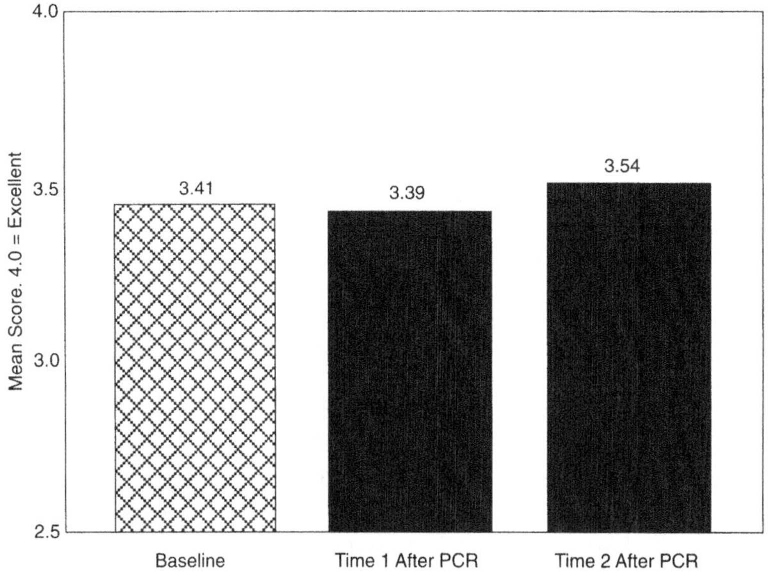

Figure 29–14 Caregivers working as a team. *Note:* Increase in score is statistically significant by ANOVA at $p \leq .05$.

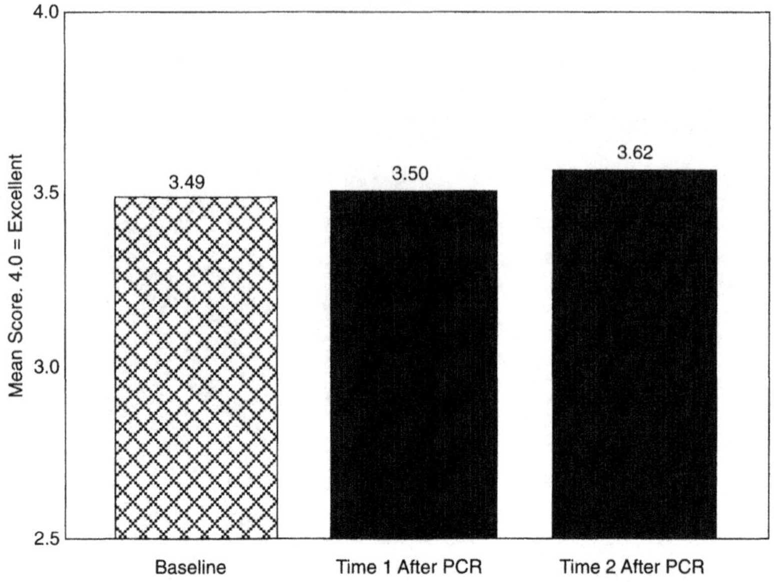

Figure 29–15 Overall satisfaction with care. *Note:* Increase in score is statistically significant by ANOVA at $p \leq .05$.

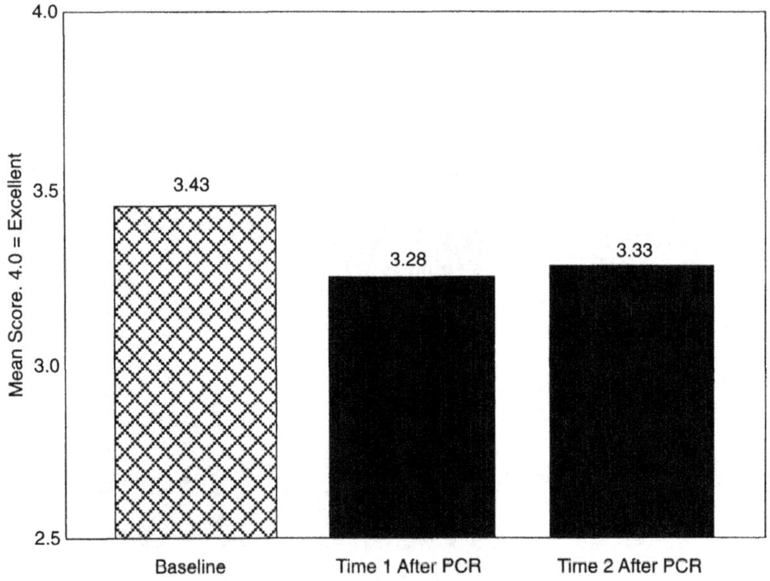

Figure 29–16 Efficiency of technician who drew blood. *Note:* Decrease in score is statistically significant by ANOVA at $p \leq .05$.

Food Services

Mean scores for food services indicate success of the PSA because satisfaction with assistance with feeding increased. Other indicators remain essentially unchanged. This was expected because changes were not made in patient care delivery for these indicators.

Nursing Care

Improvements in all nursing care indicators provide evidence for the dramatic change in the role of nursing in restructured units. The ability of the nurse to spend more time at the patient's bedside is evident with the increased scores on the availability of the nurse. A primary focus in restructuring the registered nurse role was to provide the infrastructure to support professional nursing practice. The significant increase in the mean scores for explanation of care after discharge supports this change. The positive increases in mean score for attention to your worries and concerns and effort to make you feel comfortable also support the change. The most significant improvements in patient satisfaction were observed for nursing care.

Medical Care

All indicators of medical care remain unchanged. Formal change was not made in the delivery of medical care through restructuring, so that no major changes occurred.

Ancillary Services

Changes in scores for ancillary services reflect where PCR has been successful and highlight areas in need of improvement. Courtesy and promptness of transportation staff have improved significantly, indicating that the shifting of transportation duties to the PSA role has improved patient satisfaction. In addition, improvement in attention paid to the patient from the staff and caregivers working as a team highlights the effectiveness of the nursing role as case manager. Two areas declined: efficiency of the technicians who drew blood and coordination of scheduled tests. Laboratory quality control indicated that a problem does not exist with technical phlebotomy ability of the PCTs. Patients today are familiar with a phlebotomist coming from the laboratory and may have perceived the PCT as a less qualified technician. Therefore, PCTs are now informing patients that they are also phlebotomists trained by the laboratory. Reasons for a decrease in satisfaction with coordination of tests are being explored.

CONCLUSION

Postimplementation scores at two time points are presented. Results from time 1, 4 months after implementation, indicate improvement in a few areas, most notably assistance with feeding and availability of the nurse. More significant improvements are demonstrated in the results at time 2, 10 months after implementation. The long-term changes indicate that patient care is improving with time as the staff become more comfortable and skilled in their new roles.

Many acute care hospitals in America are restructuring the patient care delivery process. Evaluation of customer satisfaction must be a primary criterion for measuring success. The patient satisfaction results of the first four units restructured at UMC demonstrate the benefits of restructuring care as well as potential areas for further operational change.

NOTES

1. S. Steiber and W. Krowinski, *Measuring and Managing Patient Satisfaction* (Chicago, Ill.: American Hospital Association, 1990).
2. R. Whiteley, *The Customer Driver Company, Moving from Talk to Action* (Reading, Mass.: Addison-Wesley, 1991).
3. W. Leebov, *Customer Service in Health Care* (Chicago, Ill.: American Hospital Association, 1990).

Appendix 29–A

Patient Satisfaction Survey

TIME INTERVIEW STARTED: _________ ENDED: _________ ATTEMPT: 1st 2nd 3rd
INTERVIEWER NAME: ______________________________ DATE: ________________
TELEPHONE NUMBER: ________________ TYPE OF PATIENT: Adult..1 Pediatric..2

(*INTERVIEWER:* IF ADULT PATIENT, *DO NOT INTERVIEW SPOUSE.* ONLY INTERVIEW PERSON WHOSE NAME IS ON THE LIST. IF PEDIATRIC PATIENT, ASK TO SPEAK WITH PARENT OR GUARDIAN WHO WAS *MOST CLOSELY INVOLVED* IN THE CHILD'S CARE AT UMC. *IF THE PATIENT HAS DIED, APOLOGIZE AND TERMINATE CALL, THEN NOTIFY YOUR SUPERVISOR IMMEDIATELY.)*

Hello. My name is ________________. I am calling from ________________, a Tucson-based public opinion company. We are calling on behalf of the University Medical Center and would like to speak with __________________ (name of patient) [or a parent or guardian of ____________________ (name of patient)] about their recent stay at UMC.

We are not selling anything, and all questions are strictly a matter of personal opinion. The purpose of this survey is to find out your level of satisfaction with services provided during your [your child's] recent stay at UMC. All your responses will be kept confidential.

1. Is this a convenient time to ask you some questions regarding your [your child's] recent stay at UMC? (*DO NOT READ)*
   Yes.......1 *(SKIP TO 0.2)*
   No..........2 *(ASK 0.1a)*

1a. When would be the most convenient time for me to call you back?

(*INTERVIEWER:* SCHEDULE TIME TO CALL BACK. IF *REFUSED,* THANK RESPONDENT FOR HIS/HER TIME. *TERMINATE* AND INDICATE INFORMATION ON REFUSAL SHEET.)

2. First, I'd like to ask you several questions regarding UMC facilities. Would you rate the following as excellent, good, fair, or poor.

	Excellent	Good	Fair	Poor	DK/NA
a. Cleanliness of your [your child's] room	1	2	3	4	5
b. Cleanliness of your [your child's] bathroom	1	2	3	4	5
c. Cleanliness of hospital public areas	1	2	3	4	5

3. Next, I'd like to ask you about disturbances during your [your child's] stay. Please let me know if you agree or disagree with the following statements. If you have no opinion, just let me know.

	Agree	Disagree	No Opinion
a. Respect was shown for your [your child's] privacy	1	2	3
b. There were too many disturbances by visitors to your [your child's] room	1	2	3
c. There were too many disturbances by hospital staff in your [your child's] room	1	2	3
d. The daytime noise level was too loud.	1	2	3
e. The nighttime noise level was too loud	1	2	3

4. Now I'd like to ask you some questions about food services. Please evaluate the following as either excellent, good, fair, or poor.

	Excellent	Good	Fair	Poor	DK/NA
a. The timeliness of food delivery	1	2	3	4	5
b. The courtesy of the food server	1	2	3	4	5
c. The temperature of hot foods	1	2	3	4	5
d. The temperature of cold foods	1	2	3	4	5
e. Assistance with feeding and/or reaching your [your child's] food, if necessary	1	2	3	4	5
f. The taste of the food	1	2	3	4	5

5. Now I'd like to ask about your [your child's] nursing care. Please let me know if you consider the following to have been excellent, good, fair, or poor.

	Excellent	Good	Fair	Poor	DK/NA
a. The courtesy of your [your child's] nurses	1	2	3	4	5
b. The nursing response to your [your child's] call button	1	2	3	4	5
c. The availability of the nurse when you [your child] needed him or her	1	2	3	4	5
d. The clarity of explanation of nursing treatments and procedures	1	2	3	4	5
e. The efforts of the nurses to make you [your child] feel comfortable	1	2	3	4	5
f. The attention paid you by nurses regarding your worries and concerns	1	2	3	4	5
g. The explanations by the nurses about how to care for yourself [your child] after discharge	1	2	3	4	5
h. The clinical skills of the nurses	1	2	3	4	5

6. Moving on, I now have some questions regarding your [your child's] medical care. Again, please let me know if you rate the following as excellent, good, fair, or poor.

	Excellent	Good	Fair	Poor	DK/NA
a. The courtesy of your [your child's] physicians	1	2	3	4	5
b. The availability of your [your child's] physicians	1	2	3	4	5
c. The clarity of explanations by physicians of medical treatments and procedures	1	2	3	4	5
d. The effort made by physicians to make you [your child] feel comfortable	1	2	3	4	5
e. The explanations by physicians about how to care for yourself [your child] after discharge	1	2	3	4	5
f. The clinical skills of the physician	1	2	3	4	5

6a. Can you recall the name of your attending physician? That is, the doctor who had primary responsibility for your care.

____

7. Next, I'd like to ask about other departments and services. Again, please evaluate the following as excellent, good, fair, or poor. If you did not use a particular service, just let me know.

	Excellent	Good	Fair	Poor	DK/NA
a. The courtesy of the transportation staff	1	2	3	4	5
b. The promptness of the transportation staff	1	2	3	4	5
c. The efficiency of technicians who drew blood	1	2	3	4	5
d. The coordination of scheduled tests	1	2	3	4	5
d1. Did you [your child] have to wait too long for tests to be performed?		Yes...1		No...2	
e. The quality of care received from physical therapy or occupational therapy in the department	1	2	3	4	5
e1. The quality of care received from physical therapy or occupational therapy in the room	1	2	3	4	5
f. The quality of care received from respiratory therapy in the department	1	2	3	4	5
f1. The quality of care received from respiratory therapy in the room	1	2	3	4	5
g. The quality of care received from radiology in the department	1	2	3	4	5
g1. The quality of care received from radiology in the room	1	2	3	4	5
h. The neatness of hospital personnel	1	2	3	4	5
i. Your confidence in hospital personnel	1	2	3	4	5
j. The attention paid to your worries and concerns by hospital personnel	1	2	3	4	5
k. The extent to which your [your child's] caregivers worked as a team	1	2	3	4	5
l. Your overall satisfaction with the care you [your child] received at UMC	1	2	3	4	5

8. Now I would like to ask you about your *expectations* of hospital care. Would you say that each of the following was better than you expected, the same as you expected, or worse than you expected.

	Better	Worse	Same
a. The quality of nursing care	1	2	3
b. The quality of medical care	1	2	3
c. The availability of staff to meet your [your child's] needs	1	2	3
d. The sensitivity of staff to your worries and concerns	1	2	3
e. Your overall satisfaction with the care you [your child] received	1	2	3

9. Is there anything else you would like to tell us about your [your child's] stay at UMC that is important to you?

____

____

10. In conclusion, if you [your child] needed hospitalization again, would you want to return to UMC? Yes...1 No...2

11. Finally, I have just a few more questions regarding yourself [your child].

    a. What is your [your child's] age? ______________

b. What is the ZIP code of your home address? ________________

c. How will your bill be paid? *(DO NOT READ)*

AHCCS ("Access")	1
Medicare	2
Blue Cross/Blue Shield	3
Intergroup	4
CIGNA	5
Self-pay	6
Commercial/indemnity insurance ________________ (Specify)	7
Other________________ (Specify)	8
Don't know/no answer/refused	9

(IF RESPONDENT HAS DIFFICULTY REMEMBERING HOW BILL WILL BE PAID, THEN READ ANSWERS TO JOG HIS OR HER MEMORY.)

Thank you for your time. The information you provided is valuable in guiding the future operation of the hospital.

(DO NOT ASK BUT RECORD FROM PHONE LIST)

UNIT	3 East	1
	4 West	2
	4 East	3
	4 West	4

(DO NOT ASK, BUT RECORD *SEX*)

Male	1
Female	2

CHAPTER

30

Financial Results

Lisa Sinclair Olson and Mickey L. Parsons

Chapter Objectives

1. To describe the training and management support expenses.
2. To describe the approach used to evaluate cost savings.
3. To describe actual and expected cost savings from six units.

As the health care industry enters an uncertain economic era, hospitals must continue to generate adequate net income to meet capital needs. Hedging against inflationary factors by increasing rates has become less effective over the past few years as a result of flat or declining reimbursement. Leaders in the industry are turning their talents to designing and implementing alternative operational models. The literature is full of articles touting the virtues of operational redesign with an obvious absence of information about the results. To date, University Medical Center (UMC) has restructured nine inpatient units, including more than 200 beds. The UMC model of patient care restructuring (PCR) has met the original goal to address cost containment by reducing the annual rise in cost of patient care services. The financial results of the program are presented in this chapter, including details of the methodology used to determine overall cost savings.

NEW ROLES

The PCR project created three new roles. All report to the nurse manager, who is a registered nurse (RN). RN case managers plan and coordinate care for a designated group of patients in conjunction with physicians and other health care professionals. Critical paths developed by all members of the health care team are utilized to manage the care process. Supervision of other members of the team may be provided by RN case managers.

Patient support attendants (PSAs) function as multipurpose support workers. They perform the responsibilities of housekeeping, dietary, transportation, and materials management on the unit as well as other related duties as assigned. Patient care technicians (PCTs) function as multipurpose technical workers. They perform nursing assistant functions, phlebotomies from the laboratory, ECGs from cardiology, selected physical therapy and occupational therapy skills, and selected respiratory therapy skills, all based upon state licensure laws.

TRAINING EXPENSE

Before the hospital realized any net savings from the restructuring process, approximately $420,000 was spent for training and other related costs. Table 30–1 illustrates the expense for years 1 and 2; training costs for year 3 are projected to be higher (approximately $478,000) because of the increased number of units undergoing restructuring, including two adult intensive care units. Before year 2, training and development costs consisted of clerical and administrative salary expenses of approximately $5,000 and nonwage expenses of about $8,000. The training costs for year 2 totaled about $408,000 for six units, including approximately 160 beds.

Table 30–1 Training Expenses (Dollars)

Expense Category	*Year 1*	*Year 2*	*Total*
Training	12,840	221,394	234,234
PCR Staff wage and nonwage	0	138,395	138,395
Team building	0	48,489	48,489
Total	12,840	408,278	421,118

MANAGEMENT SUPPORT EXPENSE

A specific department, called the PCR department, was established separate from the staff development department. The project manager of the program and an assistant occupy two of the three permanent full-time equivalents (FTEs) in the new department. They are responsible for program management, training, and tracking the data. The training manager position is currently in the staff development office, but the training manager works exclusively for the PCR program, and the applicable full-time hours, salary, and related expenses have been considered in the PCR financial analysis.

The increase in expenses from $13,000 to $408,000 in year 2 was due to the wages incurred during the training period for the PCTs and PSAs. As stated in previous chapters, Phase I of the restructuring process involved four units: two adult medical-surgical units and two pediatric medical-surgical units. The number of trainees depends upon the average daily census and the new staffing pattern ratios developed to include these new employees. Salaries and wages are charged to the PCR department to keep track during the training phase.

PCTs hired from outside earn a training wage that is increased $.50 per hour upon completion of training. The starting rate for the PSAs does not increase after training. Employees hired from within the hospital are paid the same rate they had been unless it is a lower pay grade, in which case their salary is raised to the standard applicable PCR rate. PCTs hired from within receive a 5 percent increase upon completion of training. Approximately 50 percent have been hired from within.

Phase II consisted of two intermediate care units, the postpartum unit, and the newborn nursery. Training costs associated with Phase II are included in the year 3 total training expenses.

PCTs are currently trained in 10 weeks. The training period for Phase I PCTs was 14 weeks. Over the past 2 years the training program has been streamlined. Today, some technicians are fast-tracked through the process in 6 weeks, depending upon prior education and experience. By the end of year 4, 75 percent of the patient care units will be restructured. At that point the budget for training costs will be reduced to the extent of coverage for replacement employees only.

Replacement costs are currently being evaluated. Retention levels have risen since Phase I. Current trainees sign an agreement with UMC to remain in their roles long enough to cover their training costs, or they are requested to reimburse the hospital for the difference if they change roles or resign. The training received is valuable because of the comprehensive nature of the program. The employees who complete the training are valuable not only to UMC but to other hospitals as well.

COST SAVINGS EVALUATION

Because restructuring of the patient care units rarely occurs right at year end, careful evaluation of the cost savings is critical. A formula has been developed to calculate the savings by adjusting the period before restructuring to current dollars.

Savings result from the change in the skill mix of the patient care unit. Table 30–2 details the change in the percentage of paid RN hours for the first six restructured units. As mentioned in Chapter 16, the percentage of hours that were RN hours changed by up to 28 percent. Skill mix percentage changes are developed from a payroll system report called the labor cost distribution (see Chapter 16). For the staff classes that represent RNs, total paid hours are compared for periods before and after restructuring. A total of 17 RN FTEs on four units were eliminated throughout Phase I. Coincidentally, overall FTEs were increased by 17.

The analysis of savings for each individual restructured unit begins by adjusting a period of data immediately before the unit restructuring has been implemented. Implementation begins immediately after training is completed. Table 30–3 summarizes the analysis for one of the adult medical-surgical units that was part of the Phase I restructuring process.

The first column of numbers contains the adjusted salary and wage dollars. In the case of 4 East, a medical-surgical patient care unit, the period that is adjusted was the 12 months ending June 30, year 1. Total salaries and wages and agency dollars are tied to the general ledger to ensure accuracy.

During the restructuring process, FTEs were transferred from the ancillary services, such as physical therapy and occupational therapy or the

Table 30–2 Percentage Change in Actual RN Skill Mix by Unit

Unit	*% RN FTEs before Restructuring*	*% RN FTEs after Restructuring*
3 East pediatrics	74	57
3 West pediatrics	75	47
4 East med-surg	74	47
4 West med-surg	57	44
5 East med-surg	56	45
6 East med-surg	61	43

Table 30–3 Patient Care Unit Analysis of Savings after Restructuring

Cost Category	*Year 1, Adjusted (12 Months before Restructuring)*	*Actual Year to Date, Year 2 (9.5 Months after Restructuring)*
4 East (medical-surgical unit)		
Salaries and wages	$968,189	$870,294
Team-building workshops	N/A	7,463*
Agency	117,229	100,986
Total 4 East salaries and wages	$1,085,418	$963,817
Ancillary		
Salaries and wages	$68,620	N/A
Total personnel services	$1,154,038	$963,817
Merit adjustment	$102,169	N/A
Market adjustment	73,638	N/A
Total adjusted salaries and wages	$1,329,845	$963,817
FTEs		
4 East	34.67	47.06
Ancillary	4.41	N/A
Total FTEs	39.08	47.06
Patient Days		
Adjusted salaries and wages per patient day	$158.43	$150.27
Additional (cost)/savings per day		$8.16
Percentage (cost)/savings per day		5.15%

*Reduced from direct care expenses.

laboratory, to the patient care unit in the amount that was required to cover the services for that unit. For example, if 10,000 venipunctures are taken on average on 4 East and 10 minutes is required to complete each venipuncture, then the patient care unit received 0.80 FTE from the laboratory. The ancillary salaries and wages are included in the adjusted column for year 1 as if the 0.80 FTE was actually working on the unit during that time period. The wage rates used are the average salary rates for the staff classes affected. In the case of venipuncture, the average rate of pay used would be for that of a phlebotomist.

Estimated merit increases are added to the salary and wage figures for the period of time necessary to adjust upward to the present day analysis. Merit adjustment for the patient care unit is based on the department average merit increase over the past year. From the end of the adjustment period to the present, there would have been approximately $102,169 additional dollars spent by the unit for merit increases.

Market adjustments are scheduled once annually and are set amounts based on the staff class. At UMC, a total increase of $1.25 per hour has been paid to all RNs since year 1. Total salaries and wages including agency, plus ancillary salaries and wages including merit, plus RN merit and market increases add up to the total adjusted salaries and wages for the patient care unit.

Table 30–3 also provides an example of the unit analysis of change in staffing. For example, on 4 East FTEs for year 1 were 34.67. The 34.67 added to those FTEs relinquished by the ancillary departments total the adjusted paid FTEs of 39.08 for 4 East. Patient days are the total patient days for year 1. Total adjusted salaries and wages per patient day are the key figures used to compare against the current actual figure.

Actual year-to-date figures were obtained from the labor cost distribution report, which is prepared on a pay period basis (every 2 weeks). Team-building workshop expenses incurred by the patient care unit were reversed and allocated to the training cost schedule. All staff now attend the 1-day workshop after implementation.

The analysis of 4 East resulted in a savings of $8.16 per day, or a 5.15 percent per day savings. Table 30–4 shows the actual operational cost savings and projected savings for all six restructured units. Before training costs, the actual operating savings are about $537,000 for year 3. Savings are projected to be close to $650,000 in year 4 based on budgeted patient

Table 30–4 Actual and Projected Savings after Restructuring

Cost Center Number	*Patient Care Unit*	*Year 3 Annualized Savings ($)*	*Year 4 Budgeted Savings ($)*
	Direct savings		
6117	Intermediate care unit 6 East	127,742	143,636
6122	Med-surg 4 East	66,111	66,210
6123	Med-surg 4 West	101,651	109,875
6124	Med-surg 5 East	135,655	149,835
	Total med-surg	431,160	469,556
6212	Pediatrics 3 East	68,776	70,898
6213	Pediatrics 3 West	(53,365)	(54,604)
	Total pediatrics	15,412	16,294
	Other savings		
	Unit management restructuring	N/A	73,985
	3 Housekeeping supervisor FTEs	79,723	83,709
	2 Transportation downgraded FTEs	11,190	11,750
	Total hospital savings	537,485	655,293

days. An operating savings of $650,000 demonstrates the impact of cost containment after the initial training costs for restructured units.

One unit, pediatrics (3 West), experienced a net increase in cost per patient day. The small unit was unable to take advantage of economies of scale when the average daily census decreased to fewer than 10 patients.

Other savings that resulted from PCR include a decrease in the partial indirect care position assistant nurse manager. The nurse manager for each patient care unit that has assistant nurse manager FTEs reduced those FTEs by 0.1 after restructuring. In addition, three housekeeping supervisor FTEs were eliminated, and two transportation positions were downgraded.

CONCLUSION

Implementation of the UMC model of PCR has met and exceeded our original goals. Personnel are utilized more effectively in the delivery of patient care. Successful rollout of an operational redesign prototype such as this demands the commitment of wide-ranging personnel resources—administrative, financial, and clinical. For hospitals to remain competitive within the health care industry, it is critical that new processes be developed and implemented that affirm or improve viability in the industry.

CHAPTER

31

Staff Satisfaction

Carolyn L. Murdaugh

Chapter Objectives

1. To describe the results of unit-based culture assessments.
2. To describe changes in the professional practice climate of registered nurses after restructuring.
3. To describe changes in job dimensions of support staff after restructuring.
4. To describe changes in job satisfaction after restructuring.

One of the primary objectives of restructuring at University Medical Center (UMC) was to maintain and enhance the satisfaction of all patient care providers in their job roles. The objective was addressed in that several components of the UMC patient care restructuring (PCR) model were believed to enhance the professional practice of registered nurses (RNs) and the positive dimension of the job for support staff. Specifically, the restructured case management role provided the nurse an opportunity to become an active decision maker in patient care, interdisciplinary team management contributed to the establishment of group governance and autonomy in practice, and the development of shared values of excellence in patient care strengthened organizational commitment by encouraging open communication and attention to standards of practice.

The objective was also addressed for support staff within the same component of the PCR model. The creation of two new roles provided an opportunity for development of technical skills and increased participation in tasks perceived to be significant in quality patient care. A career ladder contributed to a sense of empowerment among support staff because they were afforded opportunities to advance within the hospital setting.

This chapter reviews the results of PCR on the professional practice climate of RNs, job dimensions of nurses and support staff, and job satisfaction of RNs and support staff. Persons who completed the questionnaires are described, and the data collection procedure is reviewed. Results of the unit cultural assessments in Phase I are reviewed to provide examples of the types of information obtained and how the information was used in restructuring. The results are examined in relation to some of the limitations described in Chapter 28.

METHODOLOGY

The questionnaire booklet was submitted to the University of Arizona Institutional Review Board for Research on Human Subjects and was considered an exempt project. The purpose of the questionnaire was initially reviewed in staff meetings on the individual units, and all questions were addressed. All persons were informed that completion of the questionnaires was voluntary and that their decision not to participate would not affect their jobs in any way. They were also assured of confidentiality and anonymity because no names were placed on the questionnaires, only on the envelopes that were distributed on the units. Persons were tracked with code numbers on the questionnaires for longitudinal purposes. A master list of names and code numbers was kept in a locked file in the PCR office, and no one except persons directly involved in data collection, including the PCR program coordinator, had access to the list. Prior experience with data collection in hospital settings indicated that confidentiality of responses needed to be ensured to obtain honest responses to the questions.

Nurse managers and the PCR program coordinator played a major role in the distribution and completion of questionnaires. Staff were allowed to complete the booklets while on duty. The questionnaires were placed in brightly colored envelopes so that envelopes left unopened in mailboxes could be easily identified for follow-up. Envelopes were also provided for staff members to seal their completed questionnaires. Brightly colored boxes were located in a strategic place on the unit for depositing the completed questionnaires.

The PCR questionnaire booklet was professionally designed and printed. The booklet contained a disclaimer that introduced the staff member to the project and reviewed confidentiality issues and the right to refuse to complete the booklet (see Exhibit 31–1). Demographic data were obtained, including age, gender, marital status, education, employment, and licensure (Exhibit 31–2). The measures described in Chapter 28 followed, including the Cultural Assessment Survey, the Work Group Functioning Scale, the Index of Work Satisfaction, the Job Diagnostic Survey, and the Professional Practice Climate Tool (RNs only). Information about

Exhibit 31–1 Introduction for PCR Project Staff Questionnaire Booklet

The purpose of this project is to evaluate the implementation of an innovative approach to the delivery of patient care.

Participation involves completing the questionnaire packet. Although there may not be any direct benefits to you, there are no known risks. Approximately 30 to 45 minutes of your time is needed to complete the packet. A master list of names will be kept in the PCR office for follow-up purposes. No one else will have access to the list. In addition, findings will be reported in group form so that individuals cannot be identified.

You are being asked to voluntarily give your opinion on the statements. By completing them, you will be giving your consent to participate in the study. You may choose not to answer some or all of the questions, if you so desire. Whatever you decide, your job will not be affected in any way. You may ask questions at any time during the study.

Thank you for your assistance.

Keith Waterbrook
President
J. Verne Singleton
Senior Vice President
Greg Pivirotto
Senior Vice President
Mickey Parsons
Vice President
John Duval
Vice President
Pam Sapienza
Vice President

Exhibit 31–2 Staff Participant Profile Information

ID # ________________

1. What is your job title? ____

2. Where do you work? ____

3. Age: _____ years

4. Gender: _____ male _____ female

5. Marital status (check one:
   _____ single
   _____ married
   _____ separated
   _____ widowed

6. Years of education (circle years completed):

Grade/intermediate	1 2 3 4 5 6 7 8
High school	9 10 11 12
Training school/college	13 14 15 16 17 18 19 20 >20

7. Highest degree:
   _____ associate _____ none
   _____ bachelor's
   _____ master's
   _____ doctorate

8. Employment status: _____ employed in this hospital part time
   _____ employed in this hospital full time

9. Length of time employed in this hospital: _____ years _____ months

10. Length of time employed on this unit: _____ years _____ months

11. Shift most frequently worked (check one): _____ day
    _____ evening
    _____ night

12. Length of shift normally worked: _____ 8 hours
    _____ 10 hours
    _____ 12 hours
    _____ other

13. Current licensure: _____ RN _____ LPN _____ Physical Therapist
    _____ Resp. Tech. _____ (etc.) _____ other: specify______________ _____ none

continues

Exhibit 31–2 continued

14. Current certification: ____ CCRN ____ ANA ____ AORN ____ (etc.)
____ other: specify______________ ____ none

The following questions pertain to RNs only. If you are not an RN, skip to question 1, Unit Assessment.

15. Basic educational preparation in nursing (check one):
    ____ diploma
    ____ associate degree
    ____ baccalaureate
16. Year you completed basic education in nursing: ______________
17. Highest degree you completed (check one):
    ____ associate degree (nursing)
    ____ associate degree (not in nursing)
    ____ baccalaureate degree (nursing)
    ____ baccalaureate degree (not in nursing)
    ____ master's degree (nursing)
    ____ master's degree (not in nursing)
    ____ other (please specify) ______________
18. Year you completed highest education in nursing: ______________

the psychometric properties (reliability and validity) is reviewed in Chapter 28.

Sample

All personnel who were employed on a patient care unit before restructuring were asked to complete the PCR project questionnaire booklet. Before implementation of Phase I, all support staff members in other departments who spent time on the four pilot units were also asked to complete the questionnaire booklet because no patient care technicians (PCTs) or patient support attendants (PSAs) had yet been trained and hired. Inclusion of other staff members was justified on the basis that both PCTs and PSAs would be recruited from these other departments, which included food services (dietary assistants, dietary attendants, and nutrition hosts), environmental services (housekeepers I and II), respiratory services (respiratory care assistants), clinical pathology (senior phlebotomists and lead phlebotomists), physical therapy (rehabilitation technicians), transportation (transporters), and central service attendants. Dietary, housekeeping, central service, and transport responsibilities were consumed in the PSA role, and respiratory, phlebotomy, and rehabilitation responsibilities became part of the PCT role after restructuring. Nurses who were asked to complete the questionnaire booklet included assistant nurse managers, nurse managers, case managers, RNs, and licensed practical nurses.

Staff members who participated in Phase I are described in Tables 31–1 and 31–2. Nursing refers to nurses employed on the four pilot patient care units, clinical refers to staff members who were in roles similar to the PCT, and support refers to staff members who were in roles similar to the PSA. Most of the staff were women, as would be expected. More than one third of the support staff were men, however. Marital status was similar for the three groups. At least 50 percent in each group were married. A greater percentage of clinical and support staff were employed full time. The percentage of nurses working part time was consistent with rates in the western United States. Exactly half the nurses were baccalaureate prepared.

Ages were similar for the three groups. Length of time employed in the hospital as well as length of time employed on the unit/department were also similar for the three groups, although variations were noted within each group.

Table 31–1 Sample Characteristics: Basic Staff Description

Parameter	*Nursing**		*Clinical*		*Support*	
	n	*%*	*n*	*%*	*n*	*%*
Gender						
Female	78	91.8	17	77.3	52	62.7
Male	7	8.2	5	22.7	31	37.3
Marital status						
Single	35	41.7	8	36.4	34	41.4
Married	43	51.2	12	54.5	42	51.2
Separated	4	4.8	2	9.1	2	2.4
Divorced	2	2.4				
Employment						
Full time	59	68.6	20	90.9	65	78.3
Part time	27	31.4	2	9.1	18	21.7
Basic education						
Baccalaureate	39	50.0				
Associate	23	29.5	NA		NA	
Diploma	16	20.5				

*Four nursing units.

Table 31–2 Sample Characteristics: Age and Length of Service

	Nursing		*Clinical*		*Support*	
Parameter	*Mean*	*SD**	*Mean*	*SD*	*Mean*	*SD*
Age (years)	35.30	9.09	33.42	6.78	35.32	13.24
Length in hospital (months)	53.90	50.51	45.19	42.74	51.26	54.76
Length on unit (months)	43.03	39.03	42.90	41.83	35.54	43.82

*SD, standard deviation.

Response Rates

The response rates for baseline in Phase I for the first four patient care units (4 East, 4 West, 3 East, 3 West) ranged from a low of 69 percent for one patient care unit to 100 percent for one support service. A total of 297 booklets were distributed and 235 were returned, for an overall response rate of 79 percent. The results were disappointing at time 1 after implementation. A total of 321 booklets were distributed and 174 were returned, for an overall response rate of 54 percent. Response rates ranged from a low of 42 percent to a high of 80 percent. The response on the four patient care units dropped from 78 percent at baseline to 47 percent at time 1 after restructuring. Possible reasons for the low response rates after restructuring are discussed later in the chapter.

RESULTS

Culture Assessment

Culture Assessment Survey

Responses to the seven questions on the Culture Assessment Survey were transcribed exactly as worded by shift on each unit. The responses were then content analyzed as a total unit. Shift responses were explored separately, however, to assess differences in unit culture within the various shifts. The information was categorized as follows: the players (the type of person who fits in on the unit), how the players work together, unit values, changes desired, barriers to change, and miscellaneous information.

On all four units, persons who fit in were seen as competent team players. Competence and willingness to work as a team member were two dominant themes. The units differed on other themes. For example, a caring team player was emphasized on one of the pediatric units, whereas assertiveness was important on one of the adult medical units. Staff members on all four units perceived that they worked together as a team to meet patient care needs. The dominant value for all four units was the delivery of quality patient care. Teamwork, or working together as a cohesive unit, was also valued on the units.

Differences existed between the adult medical and pediatric units on desired changes. Both adult units indicated that working relations among the shifts were a concern. In addition, the adult units expressed a desire for increased professional practice: greater participation in decision making and elimination of nonprofessional tasks. The pediatrics staff focused on what they would not change. The overriding concern was a fear of change that was forthcoming with restructuring. The major barrier to change perceived by the staff on all four units was the lack of control or powerlessness in implementing change at the unit level. Overall, the staff voiced a desire for increased professional practice and a role in the decision-making process. Fear of change was only noted on the pediatric units.

The above baseline responses indicated that much time and energy would need to be invested in staff on the pediatric units if PCR was going to be successful. The culture assessment provided the pediatric director and the PCR project director with valuable information because the fear and lack of desire to change could be major stumbling blocks to restructuring on these two units. In contrast, the two adult medical units were interested in expanding their professional practice and eliminating technical tasks. They would be more responsive to change as long as they could visualize the benefits of the potential change for their practice.

Repeat cultural assessment of the four pilot units after restructuring indicated that the pediatric units were not happy with PCR. The overriding change desires on both units were to eliminate the PCT role and to return to primary nursing. The adult medical units both indicated a desire to improve the way in which staff members and shifts worked together. In other words, how people worked together as a team needed attention. This desired change was an outcome of restructuring as well because the assessments were completed when the staff was adjusting to new roles and learning delegation skills. These findings again provided helpful information about issues that needed attention during restructuring.

The above information was in all likelihood known by the nurse managers, patient care directors, and PCR administrator before they received the results. However, the assessments validated the strengths and weaknesses of the unit cultures in relation to the restructuring process. The documented information provided data on which to take appropriate action on the pilot units.

Baseline culture assessment continues to be obtained on each unit before restructuring, and the information is shared with the administrative staff. Assessment will also be obtained at times 1 and 2 after implementation on all other units.

Work Group Functioning Scale

The Work Group Functioning Scale, a second assessment of the unit culture, measured open communication in the group as well as interpersonal friction. An analysis of variance (ANOVA) was performed to assess any significant difference in scores between baseline and time 1 after implementation. No differences were noted for the nurses or support groups. A significant decrease in mean scores was observed in the clinical group (Table 31–3). The results must be interpreted with caution because of the differences in sample size and potential differences in personnel. However, the findings are not unexpected, because the PCTs were in a role unlike previous roles in the hospital and the PSA role was quite similar to environmental service and dietary roles. The PCT role was initially a threat to nursing because many saw the role as potentially taking responsibilities from nursing. For these reasons, the low score was not unexpected.

Table 31–3 Changes in Culture Assessment Scores between Baseline and Time 1: ANOVA

	Baseline		*Time 1*	
Group	*Mean*	*SD*	*Mean*	*SD*
Nurses				
$n = 88$	4.69	0.98		
$n = 57$			4.60	1.08
PCTs				
$n = 22$	4.49	1.14		
$n = 11$			3.65*	1.18
PSAs				
$n = 83$	4.06	1.03		
$n = 14$			4.22	1.04

*$p \leq .05$.

Professional Practice Climate

The professional practice climate was assessed with the Professional Practice Climate Tool. As previously stated, the scales assess what is perceived to be important to the nurses as well as what is perceived to be present in administration, specifically the nursing administration, designated as the department of nursing in Table 31–4. The autonomy subscales were individual decision making, administrative decision making, and collaboration and collegiality. The standards of practice subscales were professional development, compensation, monitoring and evaluation, management strategies, and patient care. A significant increase was noted in mean scores for the importance of management strategies between baseline and time 1 after restructuring. Significant increases in mean scores were also observed for the perceived presence of collaboration and collegiality, compensation, and monitoring and evaluation within nursing administration.

The changes in the professional practice climate indicate an increased involvement of administration, which is a reality because the PCR project director and program manager were both employed in nursing administration services. The positive perceptions of increased collaboration and collegiality reflect the increased participation of nurses in decision making for both patient care and management issues. The nurses also perceive a greater compensation for their educational and professional experience

Table 31–4 Change in Professional Practice Climate Scores between Baseline and Time 1: ANOVA

	Baseline (n=88)		*Time 1 (n=57)*	
Variable	*Mean*	*SD*	*Mean*	*SD*
Importance to Me: management strategies	3.97	0.75	4.17*	0.62
Present in department of nursing				
Collaboration/collegiality	3.11	0.78	3.33†	0.69
Compensation	2.77	0.89	3.25‡	0.88
Monitoring/evaluation	3.32	0.85	3.55§	0.71

* F test 2.78, $p = .10$.
† F test 2.69, $p = .10$.
‡ F test 9.84, $p = .00$.
§ F test 2.89, $p = .10$.

and competence by nursing administration. Creating new roles, such as case manager, and compensating for the increased responsibility and experience needed for the role is a reality. Last, the staff perceive a greater attention to the monitoring and evaluation of nursing practice issues by administration. The need to monitor nursing practice is also a reality with restructuring to ensure continued quality care during the change process.

Positive Job Dimensions

Changes in job dimensions were measured with the Job Diagnostic Survey. The scale was completed by nurses and the support staff. Results related to four subscales are described: task significance, feedback, meaningfulness of the work, and internal motivation (Table 31–5). Significant increases in mean scores were observed on all four subscales for nurses, indicating a perceived increased significance of the tasks performed, increased feedback, a greater meaningfulness of the work, and greater internal motivation. For the clinical staff (PCTs), a significant increase was noted in feedback. Scores increased for both task significance and meaningfulness of the work, but the increases were not statistically significant. For the support staff (PSAs), although scores increased for feedback, the change was not statistically significant. The scores for both the clinical and the support staff must be interpreted with caution for reasons outlined earlier in the chapter.

Positive changes in job dimension scores indicate that the nurses perceived benefits as a result of PCR. The PCR model facilitated professional practice, so that the increased scores were in the expected direction. It is surprising to find significant changes early in the process, indicating that changes in professional practice were rapidly taking place.

Job Satisfaction

Job satisfaction was evaluated with the Index of Work Satisfaction, which measured six dimensions of work satisfaction: pay, autonomy, task requirements, organizational policies, interactions, and professional status. None of the mean scores significantly changed for any of the three groups (nurses, clinical, or support) between baseline and time 1 after restructuring (Table 31–6). The short timeframe between measures was a possible factor. However, the nonsignificant findings were not expected as satisfaction was theorized possibly to decrease as a result of the turmoil of change on the units.

Stepwise regression analyses were performed to explore the predictors of job satisfaction at baseline and time 1 for nurses. The dependent vari-

Table 31–5 Changes in Job Diagnostic Survey Scores between Baseline and Time 1: ANOVA

	Task Significance				*Feedback*				*Work Meaningfulness*				*Internal Motivation*			
	Baseline		*Time 1*		*Baseline*		*Time 1*		*Baseline*		*Time 1*		*Baseline*		*Time 1*	
Group	*Mean*	*SD*	*Mean*	*SD*	*Mean*	*SD*	*Mean*	*SD*	*Mean*	*SD*	*Mean*	*SD*	*Mean*	*SD*	*Mean*	*SD*
Nurses	4.19	0.34	4.99*	0.40	3.84	0.39	4.11†	0.59	4.28	0.52	5.06§	0.56	4.71	0.44	5.14‖	0.60
PCTs	4.13	0.47	4.31	1.01	3.93	0.44	4.37‡	0.82	4.27	0.45	4.47	0.96	4.65	0.56	4.54	0.88
PSAs	3.77	0.68	3.71	0.65	3.82	0.60	3.99	0.99	4.27	0.61	4.32	0.69	4.46	0.72	4.44	0.94

* F test 163.68, $p = .00$.
† F test 10.43, $p = .00$.
‡ F test 4.01, $p = .05$.
§ F test 75.46, $p = .00$.
‖ F test 25.65, $p = .00$.

Table 31–6 Changes in Job Satisfaction Scores between Baseline and Time 1: ANOVA*

	Pay [Mean (SD)]		*Interaction [Mean (SD)]*		*Tasks [Mean (SD)]*	
Group	*Baseline*	*Time 1*	*Baseline*	*Time 1*	*Baseline*	*Time 1*
Nurses (*n* = 88, 57)	3.06 (1.34)	3.25 (1.18)	4.95 (0.08)	5.11 (1.00)	3.72 (0.93)	3.57 (1.04)
PCTs (*n* = 22, 11)	2.75 (1.19)	2.26 (0.87)	4.43 (0.96)	3.98 (1.21)	4.35 (1.10)	3.83 (1.24)
PSAs (*n* = 83, 14)	2.98 (1.25)	3.11 (1.19)	4.13 (1.24)	4.37 (1.42)	3.80 (1.00)	3.89 (1.04)
	Policies [Mean (SD)]		*Autonomy [Mean (SD)]*		*Status [Mean (SD)]*	
Group	*Baseline*	*Time 1*	*Baseline*	*Time 1*	*Baseline*	*Time 1*
Nurses (n = 88, 57)	4.24 (0.77)	4.22 (0.77)	5.04 (0.87)	4.88 (0.82)	5.62 (0.81)	5.62 (0.77)
PCTs (*n* = 22, 11)	4.21 (1.01)	3.85 (1.07)	5.07 (1.00)	4.46 (1.39)	5.06 (0.82)	5.52 (1.02)
PSAs (*n* = 83, 14)	4.16 (1.15)	4.20 (1.31)	4.11 (1.07)	4.11 (0.99)	4.82 (1.12)	4.49 (1.47)

*Not significant.

ables were pay, interactions, task requirements, organizational policies, autonomy, and professional status. Independent variables were work group functioning (culture), autonomy (individual decision making, administrative decision making, and collaboration and collegiality), standards of practice (professional development, nursing leadership, collaboration and collegiality, compensation, monitoring and evaluation, management strategies, and patient care), and positive job dimensions (task significance, feedback, meaningfulness of work, and internal motivation). The results are considered exploratory because of the small sample size (n=79 at baseline and n=54 for time 1 after restructuring) and the large number of independent variables, and must be interpreted as such.

Preliminary results indicate that the amount of explained variance increased after restructuring. For satisfaction with interactions, for example, the R^2 increased from .34 to .47 (Table 31–7). However, the predictor variables also changed. At baseline, open communication (culture) and internal motivation were predictors, but at time 1 internal motivation, feedback, and the perceived presence of collaboration and collegiality in administration were predictors of satisfaction with interaction. The amount of explained variance also increased over time for satisfaction with autonomy and professional status. The R^2 increased from .31 at baseline to .44 at time 1 for autonomy (Table 31–8). A culture of open communication was a predictor at both time points. However, feedback replaced the perceived presence of nursing leadership at time 1. The amount of explained variance increased from R^2 = .22 at baseline for professional status to R^2 = .51 at 6 months after restructuring. Only two of the predictors remained the same: general satisfaction and feedback. Feedback was a negative predictor at baseline, however, a finding that cannot be interpreted. Internal motivation and the perceived presence of attention to pa-

Table 31–7 Regression Analysis Comparing Baseline and Time 1 for Satisfaction with Interactions (Nurses)

	β (Order of Entry)	
Variable	*Baseline*	*Time 1*
Culture	.54 (1)	
Motivation	.26 (2)	.42 (1)
Feedback		.32 (2)
Collaboration/collegiality present		.31 (3)
R^2	.34	.47

Table 31–8 Regression Analysis Comparing Baseline and Time 1 for Satisfaction with Autonomy (Nurses)

	β (Order of Entry)	
Variable	*Baseline*	*Time 1*
Culture	.39 (1)	.33 (2)
Nursing leadership presence	.35 (2)	
Feedback		.54 (1)
R^2	.31	.44

tient care standards in nursing administration were predictors at time 1 after restructuring (Table 31–9). For pay, the amount of explained variance decreased over time. No significant predictors were observed for satisfaction with organization policies at baseline. At time 1, management strategies predicted satisfaction with organization policies, accounting for 20 percent of the variance.

DISCUSSION

Results indicate that implementing the UMC PCR model produced positive outcomes for the nursing and support staffs on the pilot units. Characteristics of a professional practice climate were perceived to be increasingly present after restructuring. Nurses were more internally motivated, perceived the work to be more meaningful and the tasks performed to be more significant, and reported greater feedback from the job. Such clear-cut changes were not as evident among the PCT and PSA personnel. However, results must be interpreted in view of the methodological issues

Table 31–9 Regression Analysis Comparing Baseline and Time 1 for Satisfaction with Professional Status (Nurses)

	β (Order of Entry)	
Variable	*Baseline*	*Time 1*
General satisfaction	.39 (1)	.27 (1)
Nursing leadership importance	.26 (2)	
Feedback	−.21 (3)	.31 (2)
Motivation		.28 (3)
Patient care presence		.22 (4)
R^2	.22	.51

in measuring baseline data when the two roles were not in existence. Job satisfaction did not increase, but it did not decrease during the early stages of PCR implementation, another positive finding.

The findings must be interpreted cautiously, as previously stated, because of the small sample size, especially at the second data collection point. The poor response rate has been examined by the PCR staff. The second data collection period occurred during a stressful, overwhelming period, when implementation efforts were occurring for all components of the model. The PCTs and PSAs had just completed their training and were adjusting to their new role. The PCR project staff admitted that data collection efforts were a low priority given other demands at that time. In addition, nurse managers were engrossed in unit changes and also neglected to provide the needed encouragement for staff members to complete the booklets. A detailed data collection strategy has since been outlined and implemented to ensure response rates of at least 75 percent at all data collection points on all units.

The timing of data collection efforts is another issue in addition to the response rates. The second data collection was planned to occur immediately after implementation of the PCR model on the pilot units. However, because of the newness of the project, the time schedule was slightly delayed. Therefore, data collection probably occurred during a period of chaos created by the ongoing changes. In spite of this limitation, positive indications of the change were evident. Data collection efforts have been more timely on other units based on lessons learned during the first phase of the project.

The issue of no comparison groups must also be addressed; no patient care units served as controls for the restructured units. However, baseline data collected immediately before restructuring efforts enabled each unit to serve as its own control. Although this does not justify the lack of comparison units, the longitudinal nature of the evaluation plan enables us to assess changes as a result of implementing and maintaining a new system of patient care delivery.

CONCLUSION

The staff satisfaction results have been presented and discussed for the four pilot patient care units in Phase 1 of the project. In spite of the methodological limitations in implementing the evaluation plan, the findings provide beginning evidence that PCR has positive effects on persons whose roles are changed by the process.

CHAPTER

32

Physician Satisfaction

Denise Dillon Brice

Chapter Objectives

1. To describe the instrument and methodology used to evaluate physician satisfaction.
2. To report the results of physician satisfaction before and after restructuring.

Physician satisfaction with nursing and the patient care delivery process is vital for the success of today's hospital. Physicians admit patients and influence the health care insurers in their choice of hospital contracts. Therefore, it is essential to evaluate the perceptions and opinions of physicians before and after patient care restructuring (PCR). Although at University Medical Center (UMC) no change was implemented in physician roles, a project goal was to maintain and enhance physician satisfaction.

METHODOLOGY

All active and associate medical staff members of UMC were surveyed to gain insight into their perceptions and opinions of the hospital. When PCR was implemented, the decision was made to use the results of that survey as a baseline measure of physician satisfaction. The same instrument was used after restructuring to survey all active and associate medical staff members.

The survey instrument was developed by the planning department based on interviews and focus groups with the medical staff. Areas addressed ranged from nursing and ancillary services to cleanliness of facilities and medical staff relations. The information obtained from the interviews and focus group was used to generate the survey items. A 6-point Likert type scale was constructed with responses ranging from very satisfied to very dissatisfied. In addition, the instrument contained open-ended questions to enable physicians to provide additional information.

This instrument was designed to assess physician satisfaction with most operational aspects of UMC. Much of the survey has no direct relevance to the implementation of PCR. However, physician satisfaction with the nursing services component of the instrument was considered a measure of physician satisfaction with PCR. Items 1a to 1e in Exhibit 32–1 describe the nursing services content.

A cover letter from the chief executive officer of UMC and a response postcard were contained in the first questionnaire packet mailed to physicians. The response postcard allowed responses to be monitored and physician anonymity to be protected. A second package was mailed 2 weeks later to nonresponding physicians. This package contained a reminder postcard, a duplicate survey form, and a duplicate response postcard. A third packet was mailed 2 weeks later to nonrespondents, including a second cover letter, duplicate survey, and response postcard. Response rates for the surveys were greater than 50 percent for both surveys (Table 32–1).

RESULTS

Survey results for the nursing questions by physician specialty are presented in Table 32–2. Results indicate that physician satisfaction with nursing services has remained unchanged since the implementation of PCR. Although some indicators have changed, none has changed significantly by analysis of variance (ANOVA) at $p \leq .05$. Results are presented in Figures 32–1 through 32–5.

Physicians were asked to indicate the unit to which they most frequently admitted patients. Mean scores for the same nursing questions by the restructured nursing units are presented in Table 32–3. As with physician specialty, results by nursing unit are not statistically significant. Results are presented graphically in Figures 32–6 through 32–10.

Exhibit 32–1 Physician Satisfaction Survey

Nursing Services	Dissatisfied Very	Dissatisfied Mostly	Dissatisfied Somewhat	Satisfied Somewhat	Satisfied Mostly	Satisfied Very	Not Applicable
1. Please indicate your level of satisfaction with nursing services provided at UMC:							
a. Availability of nursing staff for your assistance at rounds.	1	2	3	4	5	6	0
b. Accuracy of nursing staff in following your patient care orders.	1	2	3	4	5	6	0
c. Quality of nursing services.	1	2	3	4	5	6	0
d. Adequacy of unit assistants in providing help when asked.	1	2	3	4	5	6	0
e. Timeliness of nursing questions regarding changes in your patient's status.	1	2	3	4	5	6	0

2. What aspects of nursing care are working well on the nursing units?

____

____

3. What areas of nursing care would you like to see improved?

____

____

Table 32–1 Physician Satisfaction Survey Response Rates

Survey Time	*Number Mailed*	*Number Returned*	*Response Rate (%)*
Before implementation	293	202	69
After implementation	496	290	58

Table 32–2 Comparison of January/May 1991 (before) and September 1992 (after) Physician Satisfaction Surveys

	Family/ Community Medicine			*Internal Medicine*			*OB/GYN*			*Pediatrics*			*Surgery*			*Other (1)*			*All Specialties (2)*		
Survey Question	*Before*	*After*	*p*	*Before*	*After*	*p*	*Before*	*After*	*p*	*Before*	*After*	*p*	*Before*	*After*	*p*	*Before*	*After*	*p*	*Before*	*After*	*p*
NURSING																					
Availability of staff to assist at rounds	3.70	4.13	.47	3.71	3.66	.86	3.96	3.90	.87	4.52	4.55	.90	3.76	4.71	.89	4.33	4.65	.33	4.07	4.13	.66
Accuracy of staff in following patient care orders	4.00	3.71	.63	5.02	4.84	.35	4.70	4.33	.21	5.05	5.14	.52	4.76	4.69	.79	5.13	5.02	.62	4.90	4.84	.50
Quality of nursing services	4.36	4.22	.73	4.79	4.82	.88	4.79	4.71	.81	5.16	5.05	.51	4.95	4.63	.27	5.12	5.08	.83	4.94	4.87	.47
Adequacy of unit assistants providing help	4.33	4.25	.90	4.52	4.40	.63	4.39	4.52	.67	4.45	4.55	.64	4.86	4.57	.36	4.91	4.75	.57	4.55	4.55	.99
Timeliness of nursing questions regarding patient status	4.42	4.71	.38	4.70	4.69	.96	4.59	4.43	.53	4.91	4.77	.50	4.71	4.59	.70	5.09	5.04	.84	4.78	4.75	.75

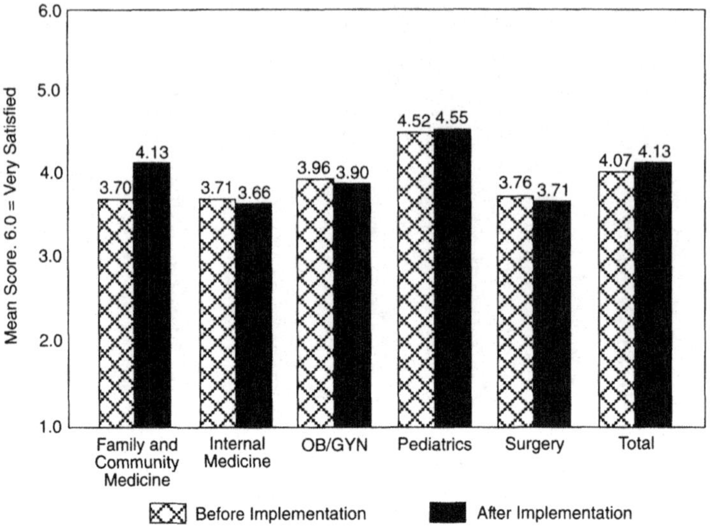

Figure 32–1 Availability of nursing staff to assist at rounds: by physician specialty. *Note:* Differences in mean score by date are not statistically significant by ANOVA at $p \leq .05$.

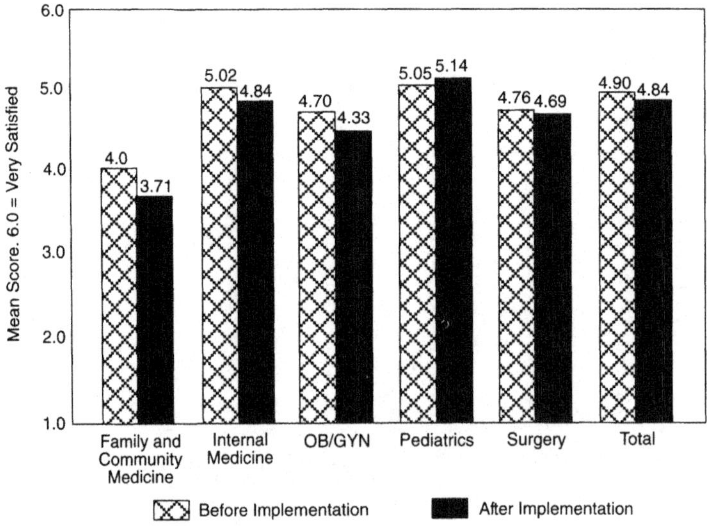

Figure 32–2 Accuracy of nursing staff in following patient orders: by physician specialty. *Note:* Differences in mean score by date are not statistically significant by ANOVA at $p \leq .05$.

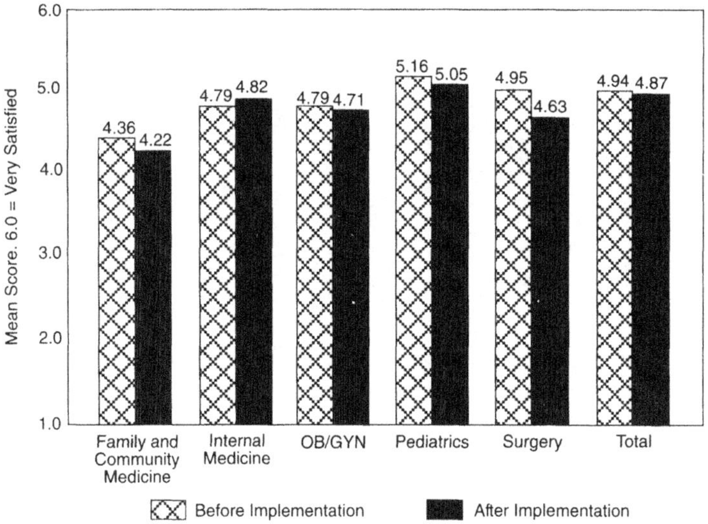

Figure 32–3 Quality of nursing services: by physician specialty. *Note:* Differences in mean score by date are not statistically significant by ANOVA at $p \leq .05$.

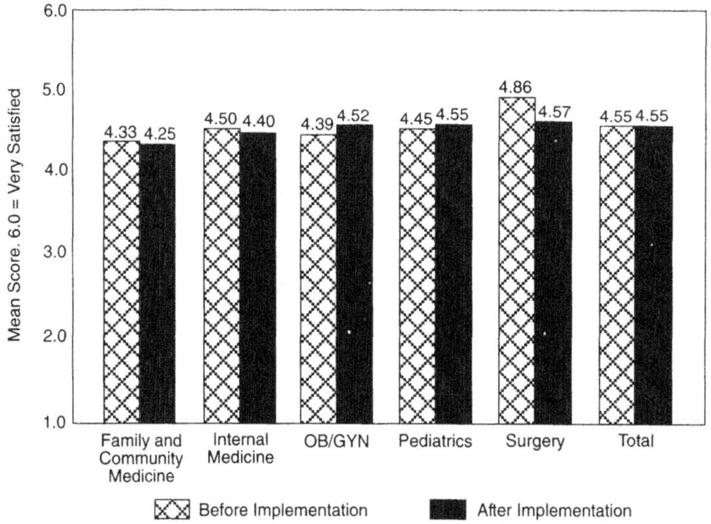

Figure 32–4 Adequacy of unit assistants providing help: by physician specialty. *Note:* Differences in mean score by date are not statistically significant by ANOVA at $p \leq .05$.

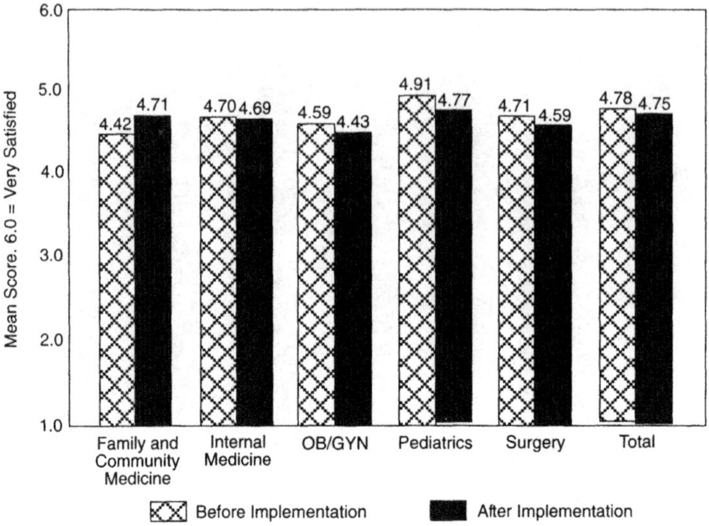

Figure 32–5 Timeliness of nursing questions about patient status: by physician specialty. *Note:* Differences in mean score by date are not statistically significant by ANOVA at $p \leq .05$.

Table 32–3 Comparison of January/May 1991 (before) and September 1992 (after) Physician Satisfaction Surveys: Analysis by Unit

	3 East, 3 West, 3 Intensive Care Unit, Neonatal Intensive Care Unit			*4 East*			*4 West*		
Survey Question	*Before*	*After*	*p*	*Before*	*After*	*p*	*Before*	*After*	*p*
NURSING									
Availability of staff to assist at rounds	4.38	4.40	.92	3.92	3.83	.84	4.21	4.10	.80
Accuracy of staff in following patient care orders	5.03	4.98	.74	4.69	4.58	.74	4.93	5.00	.81
Quality of nursing services	5.16	4.89	.12	4.73	4.91	.50	5.06	5.20	.53
Adequacy of unit assistants providing help	4.45	4.48	.87	4.47	4.42	.90	4.87	5.20	.32
Timeliness of nursing questions regarding patient status	4.89	4.57	.15	4.80	4.87	.73	4.94	5.16	.38

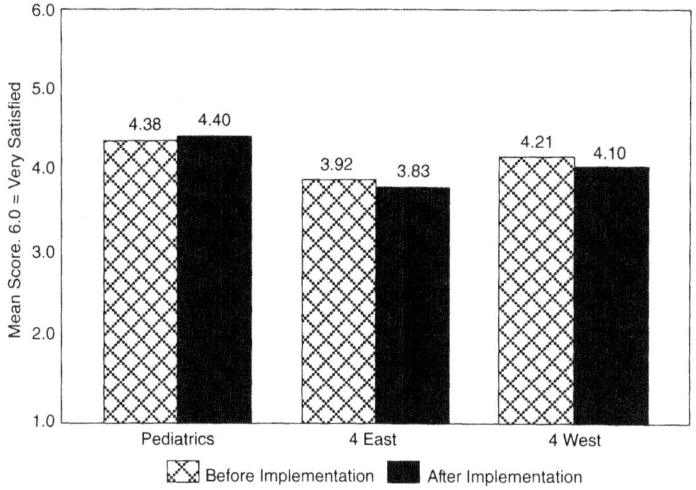

Figure 32–6 Availability of nursing staff to assist at rounds: by nursing unit. *Note:* Differences in mean score by date are not statistically significant by ANOVA at $p \leq .05$.

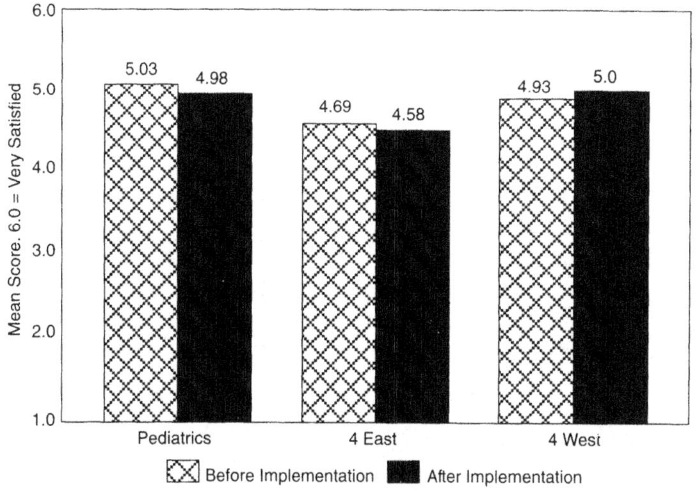

Figure 32–7 Accuracy of nursing staff in following patient orders: by nursing unit. *Note:* Differences in mean score by date are not statistically significant by ANOVA at $p \leq .05$.

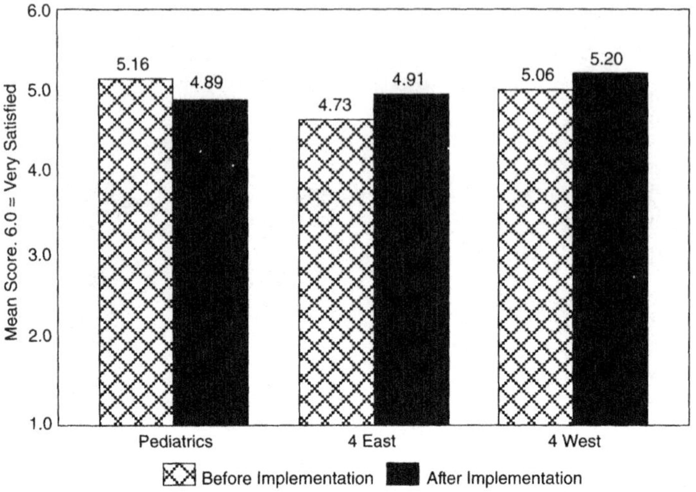

Figure 32–8 Quality of nursing services: by nursing unit. *Note:* Differences in mean score by date are not statistically significant by ANOVA at $p \leq .05$.

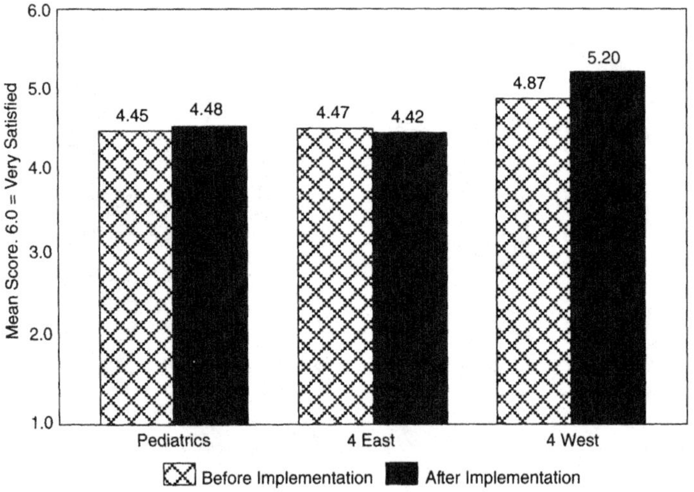

Figure 32–9 Adequacy of unit assistants providing help: by nursing unit. *Note:* Differences in mean score by date are not statistically significant by ANOVA at $p \leq .05$.

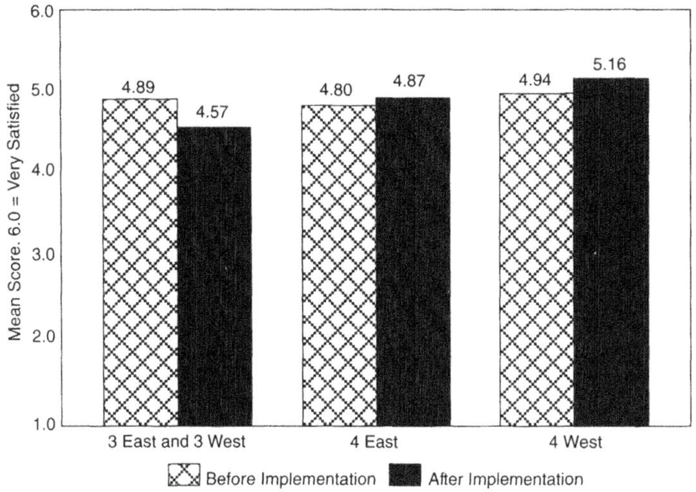

Figure 32–10 Timeliness of nursing questions about patient status: by nursing unit. *Note:* Differences in mean score by date are not statistically significant by ANOVA at $p \leq .05$.

DISCUSSION

The specific questions about nursing services were based on what physicians viewed as important in interviews and focus groups. Areas of importance included assistance at rounds, accuracy of following patient care orders, quality of services, assistance from the clerical staff (unit assistants), and timeliness of questions and communications about patient status. There are several possible interpretations for the nonsignificant changes. First, because change in physician satisfaction did not occur after restructuring, the turmoil of change did not result in lack of attention to physician concerns. Unit-based nursing case management was in the pilot stages during the postimplementation survey. It is hoped that the development and implementation of interdisciplinary protocols will have a positive effect on physician satisfaction over time. Second, nurses in private hospitals have known for years that facilitating physician practice and making it easier for the physician to get in and out of the hospital and to the office are essential. In teaching hospitals, nurses and faculty physicians have been buffered from this reality by residents. In today's health care economic climate, the inefficiencies and culture of the traditional teaching hospital are no longer accepted, and hospital care providers, including physicians, are challenged to change. No solace can be taken from the somewhat and mostly satisfied mean scores, and the results will be used to take this challenge.

CONCLUSION

Physician satisfaction with all elements of patient care delivery will continue to be a prime concern in today's health care delivery system. Physician satisfaction will continue to be monitored with results being incorporated into hospitalwide quality improvement programs.

CHAPTER

33

Quality of Care Outcomes

Carolyn L. Murdaugh

Chapter Objectives

1. To describe the importance of measuring quality of care outcomes.
2. To describe the type of information collected for quality of care outcomes.
3. To describe issues in measuring quality of care outcomes.

Quality of care was one of the two major end points in the evaluation model of patient care restructuring (PCR) at University Medical Center (UMC). Both quality and cost of care were considered two significant concepts to evaluate as a result of PCR. This chapter discusses the rationale for measuring quality of care outcomes. The types of outcomes for which measures were obtained are described, and the issues in outcome measurement are further elaborated. Because data analysis is in progress at the time of this writing, no results are presented.

WHY MEASURE QUALITY OF CARE OUTCOMES?

Three factors have led to the current emphasis on measuring the quality of care outcomes.[1] The first factor is the need for cost containment. Cost containment points to the need to evaluate the effectiveness of treatments and other types of interventions to enable the elimination of unnecessary expenditures. In addition, measurements of quality of care outcomes function as a monitoring system directed at preventing the deterioration of quality care in a cost-cutting environment. The second factor relates to the renewed competition in the health care industry. The proliferation of health maintenance organizations has resulted in vigorous competition for health care dollars. However, buyers of care desire to compare quality of care outcomes as well as costs. The third factor relates to the documented geographic differences in the use of various medical procedures, even when controlling for severity of illness. The differences raise questions about the unnecessary costs in high use areas and less than optimal care in underused areas. A focus on outcome measures will enable this issue to be resolved.

Until recently, quality of care has been considered too subjective to measure. Defining quality and quality health care has proven to be an immense task. In spite of the difficulty in defining quality, it is said to exist if the health status of the patient is positively altered. In recent years, the focus on outcomes to evaluate the health results of treatments for patients has resulted in the development and expansion of quality of care measures. Both caregivers and patients agree that the ideal measure of quality is the patient's quality of life.[2] Quality of life measures include evaluation of symptoms and patient distress, functional ability, cognitive status, anxiety, depression, ability to perform self-care activities, ability to return to work, and the like. However, these nontraditional measures have been considered too difficult to obtain, and more easily defined measures are used, such as mortality, morbidity, unnecessary hospital procedures, readmissions, and patient satisfaction with care.

Quality of care outcomes need to be evaluated for several reasons. For one, purchasers of health care can assess the outcomes of what has been purchased and make wiser decisions about future investments. Also, health care providers have the opportunity to evaluate the results of their care, enabling them to develop improved guidelines to provide higher-quality care to patients.

Groups that are interested in measuring quality include the federal government, health care providers, and patients.[3] The federal government's concept of quality consists of utilization criteria, such as number of visits or number of times a service is rendered. Health care providers are concerned with the clinical aspects of quality and focus on the delivery of technically correct care. Last, patient concerns focus on satisfaction and achievement of expected outcomes. Thus patient satisfaction with care is still considered a significant outcome measure of quality of care provided.

MEASURES OF QUALITY OF CARE

Traditional measures were used to document the quality of care outcomes in the PCR project at UMC, specifically morbidity and mortality information. Outcomes measured included patient care complications and hospital-incurred injuries; examples are burns, skin breakdown, falls or slips, medication delivery errors, intravenous fluid delivery errors, and nosocomial infections.

The information was obtained from three sources. Quality assurance (QA) data were used to record admissions for complications due to previous hospitalizations, unplanned transfers, nursing variations, utilization variations, unanticipated delays, delays in treatments, and so forth.[4] At UMC, 100 percent of inpatient charts were reviewed by master's prepared registered nurses (RNs) for deviations from established generic screens.[5] The data were considered accurate because they represented what was documented in the patient record. Interrater reliability was assessed among the 17 RNs employed in the department and was reported to be high.

The information about nosocomial infections was collected by an infection control RN using criteria developed by the directors of infection control and clinical pathology.[6] The information was obtained from several sources, including the emergency department log and the operating room log. In addition, daily unit rounds were conducted to obtain verbal reports of infections and to perform chart reviews. Last, culture reports from the pathology department were used to document the infections. Prior studies at UMC indicated that 96 to 100 percent of infections are documented before discharge. In general, reports are distributed to the infection control committee, where a plan of correction is proposed and communicated.

Incident reports were a third source of quality of care outcome measures. Incident report data were obtained from the risk management department. Incident reports were considered fairly accurate because only 1 percent of total incidence was thought not to be reported.[7] RNs received a 1-hour orientation to incidence reports early in their employment to stress that documentation does not result in punitive measures; however, disciplinary action may result from an incident report. The types of information obtained from these reports included burns, skin breakdowns, falls and slips, medication errors (omission, delay, dose/drug errors, or other), and intravenous fluid errors (omission, dose/drug error, delay, or other).

All the above information is currently collected by an RN who is employed in the PCR office. Because of the time needed for input of data in the above departments, the time lag for availability of data collection averages 3 months. Information was collected for each of the pilot units 3 months before restructuring and for 3 months at time 1 (6 months) after implementation. The 3 months of data will be averaged to obtain a quarterly perspective.

RESULTS

Analysis of the results of the above quality of care outcomes is currently in progress, so that final results are not reported. A major limitation of the data collection on the four pilot units in Phase I is the lack of change from month to month for each quarter. For all four units, there were almost no incidences of QA variations or documented incidents. Exceptions were noted for falls and slips, medication errors, and nosocomial infections, although the total numbers reported were quite small. The level of analysis will be the patient care unit, which will add another unit of measurement to the evaluation model.

Patient satisfaction was also measured as a quality of care outcome. The patient satisfaction results are reported in Chapter 29.

ISSUES IN MEASURING QUALITY OF CARE OUTCOMES

Issues that surfaced when change was evaluated at UMC are briefly reviewed in Chapter 28. Several of these issues need to be revisited because they are of concern in measuring outcomes. The first issue raises the question: Which outcome measures accurately reflect the changes in patient care delivery that have been implemented? Quality of care outcome measures are not lacking. What is lacking is a strategy to decide which outcomes are the most sensitive measures of the results of the intervention. The issue is complicated by the fact that no one health care provider, treatment, or intervention can be considered solely responsible for the outcome, whether positive or negative. Extraneous, often uncontrollable influences are operating to influence the outcomes in addition to the treatment or intervention. Also, no clear consensus has emerged on how best to measure outcomes or which instruments are most reliable and valid. Finally, the lack of baseline measures for the patient population makes it difficult, if not impossible, to assess the effects of the treatments or interventions. All these obstacles deserve more attention as we begin to examine outcomes in practice.

Quality of care outcomes are often measured and analyzed at the group level. For example, mortality reports the rate of deaths for a group of individuals. The use of group or aggregated data limits the types of techniques that can be used.[8] In addition, the sample size is reduced when the data are aggregated. These issues are currently being confronted with consultants as the data are being analyzed.

CONCLUSION

Attention to quality of care outcomes in patient care has refocused attention on the patient. As new patient care delivery models are implemented, the challenge becomes how to measure the effects of these models on patient outcomes. We first need to identify the outcomes that will be sensitive to such change, develop accurate and valid measures of the outcomes, identify appropriate timeframes to assess the change adequately, and revise our delivery systems based on the results.

NOTES

1. A.M. Epstein, The Outcome Movement—Will It Get Us Where We Want To Go?, *New England Journal of Medicine* 323 (1990):266–270.
2. R. Geigle and S.B. Jones, Outcome Measurement: A Report from the Front, *Inquiry* 27 (1990):7–14.
3. D.A. Peters, An Overview of Current Research Relating to Long-Term Outcomes, *Nursing and Health Care* 10 (1991):133–136.
4. B. Marks, Personal communication, 1993.
5. A. Whitaker and L. McCanless, Nursing Peer Review; Monitoring the Appropriateness and Outcome of Nursing Care, *Journal of Nursing Quality Assurance* 2 (1988):24–31.
6. A. Costello, Personal communication, 1993.
7. L. Saunders, Personal communication, 1993.
8. S. Ferkatich and J. Verran, "Analysis Issues in Outcomes Research," in *Patient Outcomes Research: Examining the Effectiveness of Nursing Practice*, NIH Publication No. 93-3411 (Bethesda, Md.: National Institutes of Health, 1992).

PART

V

The Next Generation

CHAPTER

34

Restructuring in Labor and Delivery: Case Study

Pat McGee

Chapter Objectives

1. To describe the labor and delivery unit, including staff mix, patient population, and delivery systems, before restructuring.
2. To describe the labor and delivery model of patient-centered care.
3. To describe the roles and responsibilities of the various job classifications in labor and delivery before and after restructuring.
4. To describe the staffing plan and patient care assignments before and after restructuring in labor and delivery.
5. To describe the specific skills list developed for the obstetrical technician and patient support attendant in labor and delivery.
6. To describe the barriers to implementation of restructured care in labor and delivery.
7. To discuss special considerations in restructuring for labor and delivery.

Restructuring labor and delivery (L&D) was a process requiring nursing staff and physician education, support, involvement, and feedback on a continual basis. Even though the L&D unit at University Medical Center

(UMC) is a high-risk center, the focus is a family-centered birth process. The patients are encouraged prenatally to develop a plan that will allow them to be in charge of their own birth. The goal is to provide comprehensive care while supporting and enhancing patients' wishes for the birth experience. Patient care restructuring (PCR) in L&D grew out of a need to have cross-trained staff to assist the licensed personnel in nonnursing duties, freeing the nurse to perform nursing tasks. Although the unit utilized obstetrical technicians (OBTs) for Cesarean sections and other surgical procedures, the skills list beyond these procedures was limited in assisting the nursing staff. PCR was planned to allow for more personnel to attend to the wishes and needs of our customers. In addition, PCR offers financial savings to the hospital by utilizing less expensive personnel to perform the nonnursing functions. PCR offers benefits to the patients, the nursing staff, and the physicians.

GENERAL SERVICE DESCRIPTION

The L&D unit at UMC is certified by the Arizona Perinatal Trust as a high-risk tertiary (level III) center. It is one of two tertiary centers in a community of 700,000 people. The primary source of patients who deliver are residents of Tucson or outlying communities. They either are seen through the University of Arizona College of Medicine outpatient OB clinic, which is managed by attending OB physicians employed through University Physicians, Inc. (a corporation of University of Arizona College of Medicine faculty) or are patients of private health maintenance organizations (HMOs) whose physicians admit to UMC. Approximately 60 percent of the OB patients at UMC are under managed care through one of three major HMOs that have contracts with UMC. The other source of patients is maternal high-risk transports from level I and level II hospitals throughout southern Arizona. The high-risk patients compose about 10 percent of the total deliveries at UMC and represent a combination of maternal transports as well as patients being followed prenatally by any of the physicians delivering at UMC. The College of Medicine employs four perinatologists, who provide high-risk consultation to the private physicians from the HMOs. Additionally, there are five staff neonatologists for the level III neonatal intensive care unit.

STAFF PARTICIPATION

PCR is a major change, and with it come anxieties and many questions. Staff education throughout the process plays a key role in control of rumors and uneasiness. It is critical that the staff be part of the planning process. A unit-based steering committee was formed for the development of PCR in L&D. This committee comprised staff members from all job classes and shifts and was valuable in developing the role of the patient care technician (PCT) and patient support attendant (PSA), answering questions and providing education and support to the restructuring project. A time line was developed months ahead of implementation to plot out deadlines for job descriptions; develop skills lists; design performance standards, staffing plans, and requirements; post positions; interview and select; hire and transfer; and, last but not least, train. The training program of 13 weeks for OBTs consisted of 3 weeks of didactic training, 2 weeks of phlebotomy training, 4 weeks in the operating room (OR), and 4 weeks in L&D. All surgical skills cannot be learned in 4 weeks, so that this portion will be ongoing with a goal that the skills list for all OB and gynecological (GYN) cases will be completed by 1 year. The training program for the PSA role is completed in 2 weeks and consists of both didactic and on-the-job training.

UNIT DESCRIPTION

The L&D unit at UMC has a projected volume of 3,672 births annually with an average of 10 deliveries per day. As with any other L&D unit, the census is not always predictable, and the number of deliveries and/or antepartum patients who are low or high risk can vary from day to day. The unit consists of a 6-bed outpatient evaluation center; 13 labor, delivery, and recovery rooms (LDRs); a 4-bed postanesthesia care unit (PACU) recovery room; and 2 OB ORs. Most patients are assessed in the evaluation center before being admitted to L&D. Patients who appear to be in active labor are evaluated directly in an LDR to save an uncomfortable transfer at a later time. Also contained within the unit is a GYN surgical suite with an annual volume of 600 cases.

Before restructuring, the L&D staffing per shift, based upon volume and acuity, included nine licensed personnel [seven to eight registered nurses (RNs) and one to two licensed practical nurses (LPNs)], one OBT, two unit assistants (UAs), and one runner. The PACU was staffed with two RNs and one UA/nursing assistant (NA), and the GYN OR was staffed with an RN and an OBT. The PACU is shared between L&D and the GYN OR for recovering both Cesarean sections and surgical cases. Plans are currently underway to remodel the unit to expand to 15 LDRs and a 6-bed PACU. The goal is to have a facility large enough to handle a maximum of 5,000 births per year.

ROLES AND RESPONSIBILITIES BEFORE AND AFTER RESTRUCTURING

As mentioned previously, before restructuring the staffing mix in L&D consisted of RNs, LPNs, and OBTs, who provided direct patient care; UAs, who provided clerical support; and runners, who provided general unit support. The following describes the roles of each job classification before and after restructuring.

- before restructuring
    1. *RN* —The role of the RN in L&D included total direct care of patients from low to high risk during pregnancy, ranging from early second trimester through delivery. Direct care included circulating for Cesarean sections and other OB surgical procedures. The RN was also responsible for the supervision of LPNs and OBTs.
    2. *LPN* —The role of the LPN in L&D included patient care for low-risk OB patients under the direct supervision of an RN. The LPN was also cross-trained as an OR technician.
    3. *OBT* —The OBT's primary responsibility was the OR. Responsibilities included keeping it in readiness for surgical procedures as well as being the scrub tech. The OBT utilized basic NA skills to assist the RN with patient care. An OBT was present for most deliveries to assist the physician as needed as well as to help with care of the newborn.
    4. *UA* —The role of the UA included organizing charts; ordering lab tests; answering telephones, intercoms, and patient call lights; paging; submitting patient charges; and basically keeping the unit organized. The role of the UA did not change with restructuring and is the only position not directly affected by restructuring.
    5. *Runner*—This position was developed to assist the department with auxiliary duties, including patient transportation, stocking of supplies, distribution of linen, and UA relief. This position was eliminated with restructuring.
- after restructuring
    1. *RN* —The duties and responsibilities of the RN with direct patient care do not change with restructuring. The change for the RNs is the type of assignment/patient mix and the supervision and delegation required as they work closely with the restructured role of the OBT.
    2. *LPN* —The role of the LPN remains basically the same. The LPN also will have the benefit of additional support from the OBT and

PSA, however. The LPN is also trained in phlebotomy, which has enhanced the previous role.

3. *OBT*—The role of the OBT is greatly intensified with restructuring. NA skills are added along with phlebotomy, limited respiratory therapy, and training in GYN surgery. Throughout the hospital this restructured position is called the PCT. Considering the addition of the OR skills, we have elected to continue to call this role the OBT.
4. *PSA*—The PSA role in L&D is quite diverse. The responsibilities include housekeeping, transportation duties, dietary aide, running to ancillary departments such as lab and pharmacy, and materials management tasks including daily inventory of floor stock and ordering and stocking of supplies in the general floor stock as well as in the patient rooms as vacated.

STAFFING PLANS BEFORE AND AFTER RESTRUCTURING

Staffing plans in any L&D unit need to be adjusted according to the types of patients, census, and acuity. The staff is cross-trained between L&D and GYN surgery, so that both areas are complemented and staff can assist where there is need. The nurse-to-patient ratios at UMC follow the established American College of Obstetricians and Gynecologists (ACOG) guidelines, with ratios ranging from 1:1 to 1:3. Considerations are given to the variety of patients (active labor, observation, antepartum, postpartum, etc.), acuity of the patient's condition, patient turnover, educational needs of patients and family members, birth plan presented, regional anesthesia, staff mix, and bereavement care.[1]

The figures listed in Table 34–1 for the RN category include one charge nurse and one nurse scheduled in the evaluation center. The OBT role before restructuring was primarily OR duties and limited assistance with patient care. The expanded role allows for greater assistance to the licensed personnel, thus increasing the overall number of staff members present to provide direct patient care. One OBT is assigned to be the pri-

Table 34–1 Daily Staffing Plan per Shift

Before Restructuring	*After Restructuring*
7–8 RNs	7 RNs
1–2 LPNs	1 LPN
1 OBT	4 OBTs
2 UAs	3 PSAs
1 Runner	2 UAs

mary scrub tech for the shift, and one is assigned to the evaluation center, leaving two OBTs to assist with admitted patients. Phlebotomy by OBTs is appreciated by patients because they already know the OBT as one of their caregivers. The PSA role has included the duties of the runner position. An example of efficient use of these new restructured roles is as follows: Upon completion of a venipuncture by an OBT, the PSA takes the specimen(s) to the lab, saving phone calls to the lab and time getting the specimen(s) to the lab for testing. This new staffing plan has improved staffing and added support to the RNs, giving them time to be nurses again.

The first change in job classification, illustrated in Table 34–2, is from assistant nurse manager (ANM) to clinical nurse leader (CNL). The focus of this change was to eliminate management responsibilities and to target clinical leadership. Management responsibilities previously performed by the ANMs are shared between the nurse manager and clerical staff. An administrative secretary was hired and is shared by L&D, postpartum, and newborn nursery. Although the UA position has not been altered, the reduction of full-time equivalents (FTEs) shown is due to eliminating the runner position and a UA/NA position utilized in the evaluation center. The OBT and PSA role increases reflect a contribution of FTEs from other departments, such as housekeeping, materials management, lab, and transportation.

OBT SKILLS LIST SPECIFIC TO L&D

The generic PCT skills list developed for UMC encompasses the following skills:

- phlebotomy
- general NA patient care skills
- selected respiratory care

Table 34–2 Total Budgeted FTEs by Job Classification

Before Restructuring	*After Restructuring*
NM—1.00	NM—1.0
ANM—4.00	CNL—4.0
RN—37.73	RN—25.4
LPN—5.60	LPN—4.2
OBT—4.75	OBT—16.8
UA—14.10	UA—8.4
	PSA—12.6
Subtotal: 67.18 FTEs	Grand total: 72.4 FTEs

- physical therapy
- occupational therapy
- 12-lead ECGs

Several areas originally developed for this role do not pertain to the L&D department, so that the OBT skills list (Exhibits 34–1 and 34–2) had to be redesigned to meet the needs of OB patients. The formation of the OBT role and the skills list was the most substantial change in restructuring L&D. The changes in this position enhance our present care delivery system by supporting the role of the nurse. The success of the OBT in L&D depends on appropriate utilization by the RN. It is the nurse's responsibility to assess maternal and fetal status, and this activity must never be delegated to an OBT. Proper utilization of the OBT frees nurses from nonnursing duties. The skills list needs to reflect the role accurately, and RNs must fully understand the scope of practice of the OBT. The role of a technician is defined by the American Nurses Association as "a skilled worker who has specialized training or education in a specific area, preferably with a technological interface. If the role provides direct care or supports the provision of direct care it should be under the supervision of a Registered Nurse."[2(p.8)] In development of the skills list, careful attention must be paid to observations. There is sometimes a fine line between observation and assessment, and this must be clearly defined so that no confusion exists for either the OBT or the RN.

PSA SKILLS LIST SPECIFIC TO L&D

The PSA role in L&D was developed by combining the hospitalwide skills list with the previous role of the runner in L&D (Exhibit 34–3). The PSA is utilized by all members of the health care team.

BARRIERS TO IMPLEMENTATION OF RESTRUCTURED CARE IN L&D

Acceptance of change is probably the biggest barrier to restructuring. Nursing staff members and physicians were offered the opportunity to assist with developing the program from the beginning. The unit-based steering committee was comprised of members interested in restructuring. This committee was invaluable in all their hard work and determination to generate job descriptions and skills lists that were functional and advantageous to L&D. Education and feedback were provided at monthly meetings for both nursing staff members and physician groups. Their in-

Exhibit 34–1 L&D OBT Skills List

SKILLS	INSTRUCTED	ASSISTED	ALONE	COMPETENT
1. Admission of Patient				
A. Orientation to Room/Routine				
B. Application of EFM/Doppler/Belts				
C. Documentation				
• Database (OBT role)				
• Admission Consents				
• Newborn Documentation				
• L&D Record				
• Flow Sheet				
• Social Service Consult				
2. Care of Laboring Patient				
A. Labor Support				
• Family Involvement				
• Birthing Techniques				
B. Comfort Measures				
• Universal Precautions				
• Pericare				
• Position Change				
• Oral Hygiene				
• Enemas				
• Diet				
• Voiding				
• LDR Cleanliness/Climate Control				
• Activity				
• Assist with Pushing/Squat Bar				
3. Assisting with Delivery				
A. Vaginal Delivery				
• Set-up of Instruments				
• Check Stabilet				
• Forceps Cart				
• Positioning for Delivery				

continues

Exhibit 34–1 continued

SKILLS	INSTRUCTED	ASSISTED	ALONE	COMPETENT
• Assist MD/RN/LPN				
4. Immediate Care of Newborn				
• Maintenance of NB Temperature				
• TPR				
• Footprints/Fingerprints				
• Identification Bands				
• Weighing Baby				
• Assist with Basic Breastfeeding/ Bonding				
• Security Issues				
• Transporting to NB Nursery				
• Appropriate Documentation				
5. Recovery Period				
A. Fundus				
B. Lochia				
C. Vital Signs				
D. Pericare				
E. Epis/Perineum Observation				
F. LDR Cleanliness/Climate Control				
G. Activity				
H. Transfer				
LABOR ROOM–SPECIFIC ASSISTANCE/ SET-UP				
1. Vaginal Exams				
2. Artificial Rupture of Membranes				
3. Intrauterine Pressure Catheter/Fetal Scalp Electrode (UPC/FSE)				
4. Amnio Infusions Equip Set-up				
5. Ph Scalp/Cord				
6. Pudendals/Paracervicals				
7. Emergency Equipment				

continues

Exhibit 34–1 continued

SKILLS	INSTRUCTED	ASSISTED	ALONE	COMPETENT
• Appropriate Emergency Notification				
• NICU Access				
• Stat Pages				
• Mock Code/Pregnant Woman				
OUTPATIENT ROOM				
1. Admission				
2. Phlebotomy/Chemstick Checks				
3. Procedures Assist/Set-up				
A. SVE				
B. Sterile Speculum				
C. Amniocentesis				
D. Versions				
E. Sonograms				
F. CST/NST				
G. Catheterization				
H. Specimens				
4. Assistance with Preterm Labor Care				
5. Assistance with Preeclamptic Patients				
6. Demonstrates Appropriate Reactions for Precipitous Delivery				
PACU				
1. Preparation of Appropriate Equipment				
2. Assist with Monitor Placement				
3. Computer/Log				
4. Transportation				
5. Inventory/Stock Supplies				
ASSIST WITH C/SECTION				
1. Preparation of Patient				

continues

Exhibit 34–1 continued

SKILLS	INSTRUCTED	ASSISTED	ALONE	COMPETENT
2. Assist RN with Pre/Post Op				
3. ORT Skills Specific (see attached Skills List)				
4. Abdominal Scrub				
SPECIFIC L&D PATIENT SKILLS				
1. Preterm				
2. Preeclamptic/Eclamptic				
3. Diabetic				
4. MVA/Trauma				
5. Previa/Abruption				
6. Other Duties as Assigned				
INVENTORY/FLOOR STOCK				
1. Carts				
2. Rooms				
3. Stabilets				
4. ORs				
5. Linens				
6. PACU				
7. Eval Room				
8. Med Room				
9. Autoclave				
ADDENDUM				
1. 1-Year Goals				
A. UA				
B. Gifts				
C. OR-10				

Exhibit 34–2 L&D OR Skills List

SKILL	INSTRUCTED	ASSISTED	ALONE	COMPETENT
1. Surgery				
A. Set-up equipment/materials				
• Aseptic				
• Sterile				
B. Scrub				
• 3-minute				
C. Gown/Glove				
• Self				
• MD/assistant				
D. Sterile technique				
• Principles				
• Boundaries of sterile field				
• How to unwrap a sterile package				
• How to hand off a specimen				
• How to add instr/suture to a sterile field				
E. Handling of sharps (needles, blades)				
F. Handling of instruments—how to pass				
G. Handling of fluids at the sterile field				
H. Appropriately prioritizes activities in surgery				
• Counts				
I. Ability to anticipate needs of surgeon				
J. Postsurgery				
• Dispose of materials in appropriate bags/containers				
K. Restock and set up OR for next case				
2. Obstetrical surgery procedures				
• D&C				
• Tubal ligation				
• C-section				
• C-section/hysterectomy				
• Gift procedure				

continues

Exhibit 34–2 continued

SKILL	INSTRUCTED	ASSISTED	ALONE	COMPETENT
• Cervical cerclage				
• Set-up for multiple births				
3. GYN surgical procedures				
• Total abd hyst				
• Radical abd hyst				
• Total abd hyst with MMK				
• Vaginal hyst				
• Total vag hyst				
• Laparoscopic-assisted total vag hyst				
• Anterior, posterior repair				
• Stamey procedure				
• Minilap for TL				
• Laparoscopy, diagnostic—chromotubation				
• Laparoscopy, tubal fulguration				
• Laparoscopy, fallopian ring band TL				
• Laparoscopy, Hulka clip TL				
• Laparoscopy/ectopic pregnancy				
• Laparoscopy/ovarian cystectomy				
• Laparoscopy/oophorectomy				
• Laparoscopy with KTP laser				
• Hysteroscopy, diagnostic				
• Hysteroscopy, rollerball endometrial ablation				
• Hysteroscopy, resection of myomas				
• D&C				
• Suction D&C				
• Leep loop cervical cone				
• Cold knife cervical cone				
• KTP laser cone				
• Exp lap, pelvic mass, washings				
• Infertility lap, tuboplasty				
• Chromotubation, hysterosalpingogram, D&C, or lap				
• Laparoscopy with gift procedure				
4. Forceps cart				

Exhibit 34–3 PSA Skills Check-off List, L&D

SKILL	SUCCESSFULLY DEMONSTRATED	OBSERVER'S SIGNATURE & DATE	COMMENT
I. DIETARY			
Floor stock			
• Inventories taken and forwarded to food services within designated time guidelines			
• Inventories are accurate			
• Outdated items are removed			
• Food rotation follows FIFO rule			
• Refrigerator temperature documented twice daily			
II. GENERAL			
Demonstrates working knowledge of the following:			
• Hand-washing techniques			
• Universal precautions			
• General abbreviations			
• CPR			
III. HOUSEKEEPING			
• Linen change—unoccupied bed			
• Soiled linen collection and proper disposition			
• Complete cleaning of room using eight-step cleaning procedure			
• Proper handling and disposal of trash			
• Weekly cleaning of unit microwave			
• Weekly cleaning of NM and secretary offices			
• Monthly cleaning and defrosting of refrigerator			
• Chemical use/dilution			
IV. TRANSPORTATION			
• Proper body mechanics with patient transfers			
• Wheelchair transfer/transports			
• Stretcher transfer/transports			

continues

Exhibit 34–3 continued

SKILL	SUCCESSFULLY DEMONSTRATED	OBSERVER'S SIGNATURE & DATE	COMMENT
• Introduce yourself to the patient and explain where you will be taking him/her			
• Check patient's name band to ensure that the proper patient is being transported			
• Notify appropriate staff of the patient's departure from the nursing unit or department			
• Secure proper transport equipment and obtain assistance if necessary to transport patient (e.g., lock brakes on transport equipment)			
• While transporting patient, make sure all IV/O_2 lines are free and clear of wheelchair or stretcher wheels			
• Notify appropriate staff of patient's arrival			
• Assist in taking patient off transport equipment if necessary			
• Identify proper pick-up/drop-off points for diagnostic departments (i.e., radiology, echo lab, ECG, cath lab, etc.)			
• Identify proper pick-up point for pharmaceuticals			
• Obtain signatures on appropriate pharmaceuticals			
• Identify proper pick-up points for materials management supplies			
• Identify proper drop-off points for lab specimens			
• Identify proper methods for exchanging O_2 regulators			
• Proper storage areas for O_2 tanks (never in alcoves or floors)			
V. MATERIALS MANAGEMENT			
Adequately performs the following tasks:			

continues

Exhibit 34–3 continued

SKILL	SUCCESSFULLY DEMONSTRATED	OBSERVER'S SIGNATURE & DATE	COMMENT
• Charge system			
• Inventory-specified supplies by item number and par level			
• Proficiently enter cart list into computer and print at the warehouse for pulling			
• Receive carts of supplies that were ordered and deliver to appropriate area			
• Pick up CS supply list, pull, and deliver to area			
• Pick up credits from area and fill out appropriate form; send back credits to materials management warehouse			
• Weekly Saturday and Sunday floor inventory			
• Stock OR substerile area, C lockers, and stabilization nursery			
• PACU and OR-10 inventory by staff, pick-up by PSAs			
• Stock patient rooms and LDR carts, pass linen			

put was taken back to the committee, evaluated, and incorporated as appropriate. Because the committee consisted of staff members from all shifts and job classifications, it was able to answer questions and offer and receive suggestions. Implementation of new roles also allows the opportunity for employees within the hospital to be promoted. Teaching new skills to employees from the unit (e.g., UAs) has been gratifying to the staff.

Anxieties and concerns were expressed by physicians throughout the restructuring process. Will there be enough nurses? Who will be monitoring the fetal heart rate tracings? Will the technicians be taking care of my patients, or will I still have a nurse? These issues raised and concerns voiced about professional staff indirectly addressed medical-legal issues as well.

The scope of practice for the OBT must be clearly defined by skills list and job description. The RN needs to recognize clearly the OBTs' limitations and work within their scope of practice. The role in supervision and delegation needs to be clear to the RN. Delegation is clearly defined as the transfer of responsibility for the performance of an activity from one person to another while retaining accountability for the outcome. The RN uses professional judgment in determining appropriate activities to delegate. Any nursing intervention requiring independent skill or judgment cannot be delegated.[2] It is imperative to keep in mind that the objective of restructuring is to give the professional nurse increased opportunity or time to provide nursing care for patients. Staff mix varies with types of patients, census, and acuity. Appropriate assignments are essential on a restructured unit. ACOG guidelines are followed for the nurse-to-patient ratio, with OBTs assisting the RN or LPN.

CONCLUSION

At the beginning of restructuring, when the committee met the first few times, the project appeared monumental. As the ideas flowed, enthusiasm was generated, and it became apparent that everything would fall into place. Being organized in the plan of action is essential to timely decision making and progress. The formation of a time line was beneficial in keeping the committee on track and meeting goals. Education of staff members and physicians throughout the process as well as accepting feedback and suggestions assisted the process of accepting change. As applications were accepted and the interviewing process began, the reality hit that the restructuring project was really going to happen. Once the training process started, the enthusiasm of the committee was transferred to the entire nursing staff by their involvement in teaching the new OBTs. This also was the time to look again at the skills list to determine whether the vision was realistic and to make changes as appropriate.

Education and training for the OBTs will be ongoing. The training period of 13 weeks allows for basic OR skills, and time is scheduled for continuation of learning OR skills. Education for the nursing staff continues in delegation and supervision, communication skills, and team building. The opportunity to discuss and evaluate progress is presented at monthly meetings with nursing staff and physician groups. Change is ongoing, and with the restructuring of L&D and the interface with GYN, surgery and PACU adjustments are made as needed. The biggest challenge in restructuring is acceptance of change and overcoming resistance to change. The key to a successful restructuring project is staff involvement, education, and acceptance of feedback.

NOTES

1. American Academy of Pediatrics and American College of Obstetricians and Gynecologists, *Guidelines for Perinatal Care,* 2d ed. (Washington, D.C.: American Academy of Pediatrics and American College of Obstetricians and Gynecologists, 1988), 43.
2. American Nurses Association, Position Statement on Registered Nurse Utilization of Unlicensed Assistive Personnel, *American Nurse* (February 1993): 8.

CHAPTER

35

Future Opportunities within Professional Ancillary Services

John F. Duval

Chapter Objectives

1. To outline key issues that must be considered in restructuring ancillary services.
2. To suggest potential strategies for achieving a patient-focused system for delivery of ancillary services in a cost-effective manner.

The University Medical Center (UMC) model for restructuring patient care delivery systems has provided a structure and a process for implementing patient-focused services at UMC. As discussed extensively in earlier chapters, the key element in this model is the redefinition of roles and responsibilities of care providers to create a minimally disruptive flow of services to the patient. Patient care services, both professional and support, have traditionally been functionally oriented, meaning that the management, standards, and assessment of quality/performance were focused on the services themselves rather than on their impact on the care delivery process. This functional orientation has led to a number of positive results over time. A strong professional orientation within specialties and generally highly efficient operations (when measured as independent units) are principal among these outcomes. The difficulty with the functional structure arises from the need for the overall care process to be integrated (cross-functional) to be maximally efficient. Although many support departments have operated well over time, efficiencies have been lost because of poor coordination with other departments and patient care units. Thus the structure of the historical care process at UMC (and most other hospitals) has led to many of the issues that frustrate patients and staff members, decrease efficiency and effectiveness, and increase delivery system costs.

The UMC model was designed to address these issues. At the heart of the model is the decentralization of many support services to patient care units. By placing these services under the control of patient care units, redefining staff roles, and cross-training staff for multiple tasks, many of the long-standing service issues that have frustrated the care process have been resolved. Restructured services include housekeeping, dietary service, supply management, phlebotomy, ECG, and elements of respiratory and physical therapy. Extensive monitoring of both operational and cost efficacy is being conducted, and favorable results are being documented. Given the successes to date, the question of what additional services need to be restructured must be addressed. Large ancillary services such as laboratory and radiology remain highly centralized operations and are potentially good candidates for restructuring to patient care units. The goal is to provide a more patient-focused array of services through distributing diagnostic technologies to the units as close to the bedside as reasonably achievable.

The goal of moving diagnostic services to the bedside, however, is much more complex than with the services restructured to date. In addition to all the job redesign and training issues, the restructuring of diagnostic services will be driven much more by technology, licensing laws, extensive regulatory requirements, capital intensity, information management needs, and operating costs. A number of these issues are explored.

TECHNOLOGY

The future potential for restructuring diagnostic services lies in the evolution of point-of-service technologies. These technologies enable services to be provided at the point of transaction, in this case the bedside. Traditionally, equipment-intensive ancillary services such as laboratory or radiology have largely relied on centralized operations to concentrate sufficient volume on their equipment to achieve operational efficiency. These equipment assets were usually large and poorly adaptable to distributed or mobile applications. Hence, when distributed services were established, they were generally clustered in satellite facilities. The down side was that patients would frequently still require transport for services. The explosion in microelectronics holds the promise that an increasing number of diagnostic devices will be available for portable bedside applications. These point-of-service devices will allow more and more services to be brought to patients, thus minimizing the disruption in patient care unit workflow resulting from patients being off the unit and inconvenience to the care receiver. Other examples of enabling technologies are modern and highly capable pneumatic tube systems that allow the efficiencies of centralized operations to continue to be realized while providing a rapid, safe, and dependable means of transporting clinical material.

Within the laboratory arena, portable and accurate on-line blood gas machines, whole blood chemistry analyzers, and hematology and coagulation devices are making point-of-care testing increasingly feasible. The emergence of these devices has been rapid; so rapid in fact that regulatory and accrediting agencies have been challenged to learn how to control their use. The operating costs associated with these devices remain relatively high, but in theory costs should begin to fall as these devices come into more general use.

Another area of point-of-care technology development is on-line physiologic monitors. These devices are evolving at a tremendous rate, constantly increasing both the number and the sophistication of patient care parameters monitored. As these devices continue to evolve and as their accuracy and reliability improve, one can expect a corresponding decline in the demand for laboratory tests. At UMC this phenomenon was demonstrated by a dramatic decline in arterial blood gas test volume after implementation of continuous oxygen saturation monitoring via the use of pulse oximetry. Although the capital versus personnel/training costs of such approaches must be closely monitored, one clear advantage is that the use of monitors carries a significantly lower regulatory overhead than definitive laboratory testing.

Within the imaging arena, numerous hospitals have attempted to achieve point-of-care radiology services through the use of satellite imaging suites placed on patient care units. Although these approaches have probably been successful from the patient's perspective, the units are often quite inefficient because of low utilization. A possible solution lies in the use of computed radiography (CR) and portable X-ray equipment. In the patient-centered care model there are two elements of radiology services that are material to the flow of services: actually taking the film and distributing the interpreted result in a timely manner. Both are critical, but taking the radiograph is often most disruptive to the patient, particularly when it requires transportation. The two primary reasons why departments of radiology around the country bring patients to their main service areas are economies of scale/convenience within department operations and the inferiority of portable images. With the shift to patient-centered services, the first issue is of a somewhat lower priority relative to overall delivery system efficiencies. Recent improvements to portable images through use of CR have now created a solution to the second problem.

CR is an emerging technology that has been the focus of significant research efforts at UMC over the last 10 years. At the core of this technology is the use of reusable imaging plates in cassettes instead of X-ray film. The imaging plates are exposed by portable or fixed X-ray equipment in the same way as film, but the image is held electronically on the imaging plates until read (digitized) by a laser scanner. Once the image is digitized, a powerful computer transforms this information into the final radiograph, automatically correcting for technique differences, overexposure or underexposure, and other parameters, thus providing a consistent, high-quality product ready for professional interpretation. These CRs may be interpreted in the electronic format or copied onto X-ray film.

The consistency of CR image quality has led radiologists to conclude that enhanced portable service is now a feasible approach to patient-centered care. However, the costs of this technology are material. Individual CR units cost approximately $200,000 plus the cost of fiberoptic networks and digital display stations. Thus the high costs render this approach only feasible if CR units are distributed to a limited number of high-volume areas of the hospital.

The technologies surrounding the actual taking of diagnostic radiographs have not changed materially for many years. However, image processing, transmission, interpretation, and report generation have been greatly aided by computer technologies. Computer image enhancement, picture archiving and communications systems, digital transcription, and clinical information systems are all making the feasibility of distributed imaging services (either fixed or portable) more feasible and, it is hoped, in the future less cost prohibitive.

REGULATORY CLIMATE

A key issue in future developments for patient care restructuring is designing a strategy to manage the diverse and at times restrictive regulatory environment.

As the UMC model has been implemented, issues related to licensure laws governing the scope of practice for a number of allied health professions were closely monitored. Although these affected the scope of activities available for restructuring, the impact of these laws was manageable. As more restructuring is moved into the diagnostic service arena, however, the impact of regulation becomes much more significant. State and federal regulation of the provision of health services is an increasingly frequent occurrence. An example is found in the implementation of the Clinical Laboratory Amendments of 1988. At the core of these regulations is the laudable goal of ensuring the availability of quality laboratory services. In achieving this goal, however, many restrictive requirements were established that essentially limited provision of lab services to individuals with certain levels of professional training and supervision, irrespective of the type of technology employed or its ease of use. Thus in restructuring the appropriate use of cross-trained, lesser skilled individuals, a regulatory overhead was created that has a significant impact on both the economics as well as the management of decentralized/restructured laboratory services. Furthermore, these regulations established extensive proficiency testing and quality assurance requirements that at best are difficult to comply with in a restructured environment.

The current regulatory climate requires that well-considered strategies be developed if restructured ancillary services are to be pursued. After a thorough assessment of these issues, UMC has elected to pursue a combined strategy involving the use of enhanced monitoring systems and the employment of improved distribution technologies, digital image networking, and CR. Through the use of these tools, it is believed that the essence of the intent of restructuring these services into a patient-focused model can be preserved while the benefits that centrally managed operations bring in meeting regulatory compliance goals are enjoyed.

COSTS

To date, the UMC model has been implemented in an essentially cost-neutral fashion. In pursuing a restructured approach to diagnostics, however, this is far more difficult to achieve. The issue largely relates to the balancing act among code-mandated staff levels employed, their efficiency in a satellite/point-of-care setting, and the extent to which a point-of-care approach results in duplication of facilities and equipment. Hospitals that maintain limited outpatient and/or referral business may find it more feasible to distribute services to patient care units because the major demand is from these areas. In facilities such as UMC, the large outpatient and referral activity mandates staffing and equipment levels that result in the unit-based operations being truly incremental costs to the delivery system. Based on the efficiency and needs of the unit, however, these costs may be justified.

The point in emphasizing system cost issues is not to identify them as a barrier but rather to identify key elements that must be considered before distributing diagnostic services to patient care units. In UMC's study of these issues, the full continuum of costs remains a definite concern.

CONCLUSION

Patient care restructuring has been implemented at UMC with significant success. The redefinition of roles, duties, and management responsibility has provided a solid platform upon which to build a patient-centered care philosophy of practice. The restructuring of support and some unit-based ancillary services has worked well with minimum disruption to the organization. When entertaining the restructuring of the major ancillary services, though, a number of issues arise. Staff training and utilization, technology, information systems, licensure laws, other regulatory requirements, and their incremental costs to the delivery system must all be considered. The evolution of enabling technologies such as CR, on-line physiologic monitors, and sophisticated pneumatic transport systems is providing potentially lower-cost alternatives to more traditional approaches to patient-focused care (e.g., satellite laboratories and radiology suites). Furthermore, these alternatives appear to be more easily integrated into the inpatient delivery process and carry a lower regulatory overhead.

CHAPTER

36

The Future: Where Do We Go from Here?

Mickey L. Parsons

Chapter Objectives

1. To discuss key issues in critical care restructuring and suggest potential approaches.
2. To describe other potential changes in the patient care delivery process.
3. To discuss possible integration of holistic concepts into the UMC model of care.

The implementation of the University Medical Center (UMC) model of patient-centered care represents the infancy stage of development in work redesign. The driving forces for change and the strategic necessity that mandates change require hospitals to meet the needs of their customers. An institution's success or failure in the future will be based upon patient satisfaction, patient outcomes, and cost, the three essential criteria for insurers to contract with health care providers. For providers in the state of Arizona, the future is today, which reflects the aggressiveness with which UMC has approached the timetable for implementation. However, the need for continued studies and pilot projects is ongoing. If we simply listen to the voices of our internal and external customers, opportunities for further restructuring will be discovered. Many other possibilities exist for continuing to decrease the compartmentalization of the entire patient care delivery system. The preceding chapter on opportunities for further restructuring within professional laboratory and radiology services provides excellent examples of alternative approaches to patient-centered care. This chapter discusses additional opportunities in critical care and other functional services. Finally, the potential for integration of holistic care components into the UMC model is discussed.

CRITICAL CARE OPPORTUNITIES

Restructuring the adult, pediatric, and neonatal critical care units provides opportunities for development and enhancement of the basic UMC model. The special considerations and patient needs make critical care practice a unique area. The most fundamental difference in the intensive care unit (ICU) is the role of the respiratory therapist, which is due to special needs of patients, including ventilator management. The respiratory therapy function is another example of a centralized department resulting in compartmentalized care. In the neonatal and pediatric ICUs, respiratory therapists are already major team members by virtue of the nature and frequency of patient needs and the teamwork already established among the nurses, therapists, and physicians. Discussions are beginning about the possibility of creating a high-level, professional respiratory therapy clinician role that would be a regular member of the critical care staff. The roles of patient support attendant, patient care technician, and unit secretary are under evaluation by critical care unit-based steering committees. Many critical care units have 24-hour secretary coverage. The implementation of a comprehensive patient care information system may result in role changes in clerical support. It is anticipated that the adult critical care unit steering committees will identify a restructuring model within the year and that those for the neonatal and pediatric units will do so within the following year. The planning phases are too new to predict any outcome.

OTHER OPPORTUNITIES

The goal of restructuring is to reduce the fragmentation of services throughout the health care facility to enhance the quality of patient care and service. Recently, another classic example came to the leadership's attention. Patients are instructed in the physician's office to obtain financial clearance and complete diagnostic tests before ambulatory surgery. The patient is instructed to go first to the physician's financial office for clearance, then to the hospital's financial office for more paperwork, and finally to ambulatory surgery for more paperwork, preoperative anesthesia work-up, ECG, and laboratory tests. Ironically, ambulatory surgery staff members were the first to request to decentralize to a unit secretary position, cross-training for the completion of ECGs and phlebotomy. The financial information decentralization, both from the physician's office and from the hospital, was missing. However, the first pilot of financial information decentralization is being discussed.

The second area that will bring more opportunities for restructuring of roles will be the implementation of a comprehensive patient care information system encompassing order entry, results reporting, database management, and patient care documentation. The high cost of documentation in terms of staff time has been identified as a major area requiring revision. At UMC the issue will be addressed via systems analysis in planning for the information system. These endeavors make further opportunities for changes more plausible in the medical record function and design of the unit secretary role.

Additionally, a new wing is under construction at UMC and will be occupied shortly. The facility design will provide for decentralized charting stations outside patient rooms and for adjacent medical supplies. The entire system becomes patient centered with the patient care information system terminals and hand-held charting devices for direct caregivers. The roles are restructured, the facility supports the decentralized functions at the bedside, and the information system supports all clinicians who utilize the terminals at the charting stations outside each patient's door and at any other point of service.

INTEGRATION OF HOLISTIC CARE CONCEPTS

The public sees hospitals as cold, stark, and frightening. Fears of medical diagnoses and treatment are normal reactions for patients. However, the cold and stark environment can be transformed into a more humane and caring one. The stimulus for the integration of holistic care concepts is patients and staff members. The need to create a more caring system for patients and staff members has never been greater. Technology continues to expand at record speed; the pace of life and work toward the end of the 20th century is steadfast and in a state of constant change, leaving consumers and caregivers also in a state of constant change. Consumers and caregivers struggle to find ways to cope successfully with the pace and to fulfill both personal and work obligations. Some facilities have introduced holistic concepts such as recreational therapy, humor, massage therapy, music therapy, guided imagery, and visualization to facilitate patients in their quest for wholeness in body, mind, and spirit. The role of the hospital chaplain is also more integrated into the entire process of care as new approaches are added to enhance the well-being of all staff members and patients. These national changes indicate future possibilities for enhanced service and care.

CONCLUSION

This chapter addresses the need to continue to restructure services to improve care to patients. Challenging the traditional hospital bureaucracy, which represents compartmentalized care, is the best avenue to improve service. Possibilities in critical care restructuring and other functional areas are discussed. The need for health care leadership to expand the possible realms of service into holistic care concepts is also addressed. It is essential that hospitals evaluate and refine current restructuring efforts and continue to pilot new ways to deliver care.

Index

G

H

I

M

P

Q

9 780834 209831

Printed in Dunstable, United Kingdom

77472001R00368